The Founding of the Red Trade Union International

Historical Materialism Book Series

VOLUME 334

The titles published in this series are listed at *brill.com/hm*

The Founding of the Red Trade Union International

Proceedings and Resolutions of the First Congress, 1921

Edited by

Mike Taber

BRILL

LEIDEN | BOSTON

The Library of Congress Cataloging-in-Publication Data is available online at https://catalog.loc.gov
LC record available at https://lccn.loc.gov/2024038122

Typeface for the Latin, Greek, and Cyrillic scripts: "Brill". See and download: brill.com/brill-typeface.

ISSN 1570-1522
ISBN 978-90-04-71285-0 (hardback)
ISBN 978-90-04-71286-7 (e-book)
DOI 10.1163/9789004712867

This book is printed on acid-free paper and produced in a sustainable manner.

Contents

Editorial Introduction

> Workers all over the world! The First International Congress of Revolutionary Labour Unions, gathered on the bit of the globe that was wrenched by the Russian proletariat from the hands of capital, in the name of the millions of those crippled and murdered in the criminal war, in the name of the sufferings that the working class has gone through under the dictatorship of capital, in the name of the victims of bourgeois terror, in the name of your defeats suffered under the leadership of the yellow traitors, in the name of the future victories under the revolutionary banner of the Red Labour Union International, and lastly in the name of the Russian working class, steadfastly keeping up all alone, for the fourth year, the red flag over the land of the soviets and waiting for help from its comrades beyond its frontiers – we are calling upon you to join our ranks. We call you to the last and decisive battle.

∵

The words above are the conclusion of the 'Manifesto to the Workers of the World' issued by the 1921 congress in Moscow that founded the Red International of Labour Unions (RILU), commonly known as the Profintern.[1] That congress set out to build a world movement of trade unions that could draw tens of millions of working people into the struggle to overthrow capitalism and usher in the rule of the proletariat, working closely with the Communist International (Comintern).

In its first years, the Red Trade Union International was a movement with millions of members and supporters in virtually every corner of the world, and with genuine weight and importance in the international class struggle. It was

1 The word 'Profintern' is a contraction taken from the RILU's Russian name: Krasnyi internatsional profsoyuzov.

At the RILU First Congress and immediately afterward, its name was rendered inconsistently in English, including 'Red Trade Union International', 'Red Labour Union International', 'Red International of Trade Unions', and other variants; the Russian term 'Profintern' was also used. In the present volume, we have tried to maintain the rendering used in the English translation of the proceedings and resolutions at the time.

 | DOI:10.1163/9789004712867_003

also by far the largest independent auxiliary organisation of the Communist International, and as such sheds important light on the Comintern and the world Communist movement as a whole during this period. For these and other reasons, the RILU deserves to be studied in detail.

Despite its obvious importance, however, the Red International of Labour Unions has not fared well in historical accounts, receiving underappreciation and negative assessments almost universally.

In Geoffrey Swain's view, the RILU 'will never be more than a footnote in the history of the labour movement – it never amounted to much.'[2] Robert Service dismisses the RILU and other Comintern auxiliary organisations by saying that they 'made little impact'.[3] E.H. Carr, the noted historian of the early Soviet Union, states that the creation of the RILU 'was a step taken in a moment of hot-headed enthusiasm' that 'had unexpected and fatal consequences'.[4] Albert Resis, author of a serious study of the RILU, speaks of its 'hopeless mission'.[5] For their part, Kevin McDermott and Jeremy Agnew downplay the RILU's role as a *trade union* body, and state that 'the Profintern became little more than an adjunct of the Comintern'.[6]

Most left-wing and socialist historical treatments also give the Profintern a less than stellar rating. In his book on the Comintern, Duncan Hallas writes that 'it is questionable whether the formation of the Red International was a useful operation.'[7] Pierre Broué's authoritative history of the Communist International roundly characterises the RILU as a 'failure'.[8] Tony Cliff and Donny Gluckstein go a step further, terming it an 'embarrassing failure'.[9] To a large extent, these assessments reflect actual problems and contradictions faced by the RILU that marked the years of its existence.

One exception to the almost exclusively negative balance sheet of this organisation is Reiner Tosstorff's history of the Red International of Labour Unions. This work, widely seen as the definitive account, gives a balanced and

---

2 Swain 1987, p. 73. Revealing the bias guiding his conclusion, Swain also asserts, without presenting a shred of evidence, 'As every student of *What is to be done?* knows, Lenin did not think much of the trade unions' (p. 58). Such an assessment is contradicted by Lenin's whole corpus of writings.

3 Service 2007, p. 114.

4 Carr 1953, p. 208.

5 Resis 1964, p. 346.

6 McDermott and Agnew 1997, p. 34.

7 Hallas 2008, p. 81.

8 Broué 1997, p. 235.

9 Cliff and Gluckstein 1986, p. 55.

rounded assessment of the Profintern's strengths and weaknesses, and outlines the various stages of its evolution.[10]

The present volume, based on the proceedings and resolutions of the Red Trade Union International's 1921 founding congress, will help enable readers to make their own evaluation of this important international movement at its birth.

At the same time, this book presents yet another dimension of the Communist International as a whole. It is part of a multi-volume series on the Comintern under Lenin, letting this world organisation speak for itself.[11]

The early Communist International was a living mass movement, with tens of millions of members and sympathisers around the world. The Profintern was one of a number of its auxiliary organisations that came into being in the Comintern's early years, each having its own unique history, characteristics, and leadership, and with an important degree of autonomy and independent initiative. Taken together, these auxiliaries' sphere of influence reached far beyond that of the Comintern's national sections. Recording the history of these formations therefore helps round out our view of the early Communist International.[12]

1 Background

The First International, which existed from 1864 to 1876 and whose central leaders were Karl Marx and Frederick Engels, consisted primarily of workers'

10 Tosstorff 2016 (Haymarket paperback edition 2017).

11 The volumes in the series containing Comintern congress proceedings are: *Founding the Communist International: Proceedings and Documents of the First Congress, March 1919*; *Workers of the World and Oppressed Peoples, Unite! Proceedings and Documents of the Second Congress, 1920* (in two volumes); *To the Masses: Proceedings of the Third Congress of the Communist International, 1921*; and *Toward the United Front: Proceedings of the Fourth Congress of the Communist International, 1922*. Additional volumes include *Lenin's Struggle for a Revolutionary International: Documents 1907–1916, The Preparatory Years*; *The German Revolution and the Debate on Soviet Power: Documents 1918–1919, Preparing the Founding Congress*; *To See the Dawn: Baku, 1920 – First Congress of the Peoples of the East*; *The Communist Movement at a Crossroads: Plenums of the Communist International's Executive Committee, 1922–1923*; and *The Communist Women's Movement 1920–1922*. All volumes were edited by John Riddell with the exception of the last two, which were edited respectively by Mike Taber and by Mike Taber and Daria Dyakonova. See the bibliography for publication details.

12 Among the other important Comintern auxiliary organisations were the Communist Youth International, the Communist Women's Movement, Red Sports, the cooperative movement, International Red Aid, International Workers' Relief, and the Peasants International.

societies and relatively small trade unions in Europe and North America, as working-class political parties had not yet emerged on a significant scale. Formally known as the International Workingmen's Association, the First International recognised the central importance of trade unions in the class struggle.

A resolution adopted by the First International in 1866, and drafted by Marx, stated that 'If the Trades' Unions are required for the guerilla fights between capital and labour, they are still more important as *organised agencies for superseding the very system of wages labour and capital rule.* … [T]hey must now learn to act deliberately as organising centres of the working class in the broad interest of its *complete emancipation*.'[13]

This world movement became known in particular for organising concrete acts of international solidarity to strike struggles in various countries, including raising funds to help sustain workers in battle. By doing so, it helped initiate the tradition of modern international working-class solidarity. As Marx put it in 1872, 'Let us bear in mind this fundamental principle of the International: solidarity! It is by establishing this life-giving principle on a reliable base among all the workers in all countries that we shall achieve the great aim which we pursue.'[14]

The history of the First International is important for another reason: it was the scene of a decisive struggle between Marxists and anarchists led by Mikhail Bakunin. That fight led to a split in the working-class movement throughout the world. While the Marxist wing went on to form social-democratic workers' parties and mass trade unions in a number of places, the Bakunin-led forces also left their mark in the form of anarchist and anarcho-syndicalist currents in different countries.

By the time the Second International was founded in 1889, working-class and socialist parties were emerging and gaining strength. Simultaneously there was a significant growth of trade unions, along with the emergence of national union federations. Working-class parties and trade unions were both member organisations of the Second International.

The creation in 1901 of the International Secretariat of Trade Union Centres – renamed International Federation of Trade Unions (IFTU) in 1913 – on the initiative of the German trade unions marked a new stage, as unions and parties increasingly were recognised as distinct and independent entities. The IFTU included within it a left wing represented by the French General Confederation of Labour (CGT), which called for action by the international federation

13 Marx, 'Trades' Unions: Their Past, Present and Future' in *MECW*, 20, pp. 191–2, emphasis in original.

14 Karl Marx, 'On the Hague Congress', in *MECW*, 23, p. 256.

around political issues such as militarism and other international questions.

Under its German leadership, backed by unions in Britain and other countries, this first trade-union International was primarily an instrument to provide information, and did not aim to organise trade-union action on a world scale. But it did help deepen the dichotomy between unions and parties within the Second International.

A 1907 resolution adopted by the Second International on 'The Relations between Trade Unions and Socialist Parties' stated:

> The unions and the party have therefore an equally important task to perform in the struggle for proletarian emancipation. Each of the two organizations has its distinct domain, defined by its nature and within whose borders it should enjoy independent control of its line of action. But there is an ever-widening domain in the proletarian struggle of the classes in which they can only reap advantages by concerted action and by cooperation between the party and trade unions.[15]

The strongest unions – particularly those in Germany and Britain – were generally part of the reformist right wing of the Second International. These forces, whose perspective was largely limited to fighting for obtainable improvements within the capitalist system, adopted the principle of 'trade union neutrality' – the idea that on a day-to-day level, unions should steer clear of politics and broader social questions, focusing almost entirely on everyday issues such as wages and working conditions and generally leaving politics to political parties. That perspective included an increasing tendency toward class collaboration and identification with the national interests of the employing class in one's own country.

The full consequences of such an outlook were revealed in 1914.

World War I and Russian Revolution

World War I tore a hole through the world trade-union movement, as it did through socialist political parties on a global scale. The main union federations in Germany, France, Britain, and elsewhere lined up in support of the capitalist governments of their own countries, and declared for a 'sacred union' or 'civil peace' involving all classes in support of the war effort.[16] The trade-union International formed in 1901 fell apart, as did the Second International.

---

15 Taber (ed.) 2021, p. 106.

16 *Union sacrée* in French; *Burgfrieden* in German.

Opposition to this perspective, however, soon emerged within both parties and unions. At Zimmerwald, Switzerland, in 1915, a conference of socialists and syndicalists rejected support to the war effort. An effort began to rebuild the international working-class movement.

As the war dragged on, workers increasingly showed their dissatisfaction with the burden imposed on them by the war, and acts of resistance began to multiply. But workers received no support from their union leaderships. As a result, a legitimate hatred for these officials arose among class-conscious workers, and many were attracted by calls to turn their backs on the old unions and to instead build entirely new revolutionary labour organisations.

Despite the union officials' refusal to act, however, important workers' actions nevertheless did break out. Strike waves occurred in 1917–18 in Germany, Austria, Britain, France, and other belligerent countries. A growing sense of militancy was palpable.

That sentiment was given a major boost by the victorious Russian Revolution of 1917, which inspired rebellious workers throughout the world with its vision of working-class power and opposition to the war. Millions of workers everywhere hoped to emulate the example of their Russian sisters and brothers.

The end of the war in November 1918 brought about a new situation. Revolutionary upsurges and big class battles broke out in country after country in Europe. Within the nations oppressed by colonialism and imperialism in Asia, Africa, and Latin America, rebellion against the colonial yoke was also the order of the day.

In this context, workers streamed into the trade unions, seeing them as their first line of defence to protect their basic interests. Statistics tell the story eloquently, as reported to the RILU founding congress: before the war there were 9.5 million members of trade unions around the world; immediately after the war this figure ballooned to 40 million.

As union strength grew, calls were made for effective international trade-union action. Beginning in the fall of 1917, Russian unions led the way in calling for a revival of the trade-union International, to be built on a militant class-struggle basis. Specifically, they called for a world trade-union conference to take place in Moscow in early 1918. Given the blockade of Soviet Russia that was imposed by the imperialist powers, however, such a meeting could not occur.

Amsterdam International

Meanwhile, the very same social democrats and trade-union officials who had lined up behind their respective governments' war efforts in 1914–18 now sought to create their own organisational pole. With the goal of heading off the unfolding revolutionary upsurge, they sought to quickly re-establish international connections.

On a political level, the Second International was reconstituted in February 1919. On a union level, the International Federation of Trade Unions was also re-established, holding its founding congress in July–August 1919 in Amsterdam, which became its seat – leading it to become known as the Amsterdam International. The IFTU's leaders continued to advance the perspective of tying workers' interests to those of the capitalist rulers. In particular, they gave enthusiastic support to the Versailles Peace Treaty and to the new League of Nations along with its creation, the International Labour Organization (ILO), also known as the International Labour Bureau.

The Amsterdam International saw itself, in the words of Albert Resis, as 'an international pressure group designed to keep the ILO and the League of Nations on a democratic path'. A resolution of the refounded IFTU's First Congress in 1920 stated that 'if the working classes want to prevent the League of Nations from becoming the center of reaction and oppression, they will have to organize internationally and attain in this way such power as to become an effective organ to control the League of Nations'.[17]

Linked to the Amsterdam International were also a number of trade federations organised by industry, known formally as international trade secretariats. These were independent and parallel bodies that predated the IFTU, but after the latter's formation they were incorporated into it.

Revolutionary Syndicalism

In addition to the Amsterdam International and its affiliated unions, there was another significant force in the world trade-union movement at the time: syndicalism.

Many of the adherents of this movement traced their lineage to anarchist Mikhail Bakunin. Anarchists played an important part within the syndicalist movement, although anarchist groups often existed as parallel structures that had conflicted relationships with syndicalism. The anarcho-syndicalists' strongest contingents were in southern Europe, primarily Spain, France, and Italy. But syndicalist unions also developed in many other European countries, as well as North and South America.

17 Quoted in Resis 1964, p. 106, which cites 'Report of the Proceedings of the International Trade Union Congress Held in Concertgebouw Amsterdam, July 28–August 2, 1919', Supplement II to *The International Trade Union Movement* (July 1921), p. 53.

While there were numerous currents within syndicalism, the most influential organised force was undoubtedly the French. Its perspective was codified in the Amiens Charter adopted by the General Confederation of Labour (CGT) in France in 1906.[18] That document became a model for many revolutionary syndicalists around the world, embodying some important principles:

– Recognition of the class struggle, and of the irreconcilability of labour and capital.

> The congress [of Amiens] views this declaration as a recognition of the class struggle, which brings workers, in the economic framework, into strong opposition to all forms of exploitation and oppression, whether of a material or moral nature, that is employed by the capitalist class against the working class.

– Rejection of politics, and a determination to keep politics out of the unions.

> [T]he congress assures to all union members the right to take part, outside the union framework, in any form of struggle that corresponds to their philosophic or political conceptions, reserving only the right to ask, in return, that they not introduce within the union the opinions that they profess on the outside.

– Recognition of unions as the primary revolutionary instrument both to overthrow capitalism and to rebuild society.

> In its daily work for specific demands, the trade-union movement strives to coordinate the workers' efforts to improve their well-being by achieving immediate gains, such as reducing working time, increasing wages, and so forth. These efforts, however, are only one side of the trade-union movement's aims. It is preparing for full emancipation through a general strike and an uprising, as its main weapon. It considers that the trade unions, which today are instruments of resistance, will in the future be organisations for production and distribution and the foundations for social reorganisation.

– Recognition of the need for direct action by the working class.

18 For the text of the Amiens Charter, see the Appendix, p. 673.

> [T]he congress declares that, in order to achieve the maximum success, the trade-union movement must carry out action directly against the employers.

Interestingly, while the CGT was seen by many as the model syndicalist organisation, in one area it was at variance with virtually all other syndicalist currents in the world: it rejected the perspective of splitting from established unions and establishing separate syndicalist ones. That difference was registered by the CGT's decision not to participate in the world syndicalist congress of 1913, which had been called with the aim of forming a separate syndicalist International in opposition to the International Federation of Trade Unions. The CGT, on the contrary, remained a member of the IFTU, although it existed within it as an isolated left-wing minority. The 1913 syndicalist congress revealed the wide diversity of syndicalist organisations and views. After a heated debate on a number of questions, the gathering was unable to agree on the basis for a syndicalist International, and could decide only to form an information bureau.[19]

During World War I, the syndicalist movement experienced the same divisions and splits as did other parts of the workers' movement. The majority of the CGT leadership in France, for example, joined the 'sacred union' backing the French war effort. For their part, anti-war syndicalists participated in the Zimmerwald movement, which was opposed to the chauvinist course of the pro-war socialist and syndicalist leaders.

Toward a Red Trade Union International

The Red International of Labour Unions, as it developed, was not part of a grand master plan of the Communist International's leaders. The Bolshevik leadership had no preconceived idea of an organisationally independent trade-union International. The creation of the Profintern and the form that it took were largely the results of conjunctural factors.

As indicated above, left-wing unions of all stripes were drawn to the Communist movement and the example of the Russian Revolution. On the one hand, this included important forces within trade-union federations that had been affiliated to the International Federation of Trade Unions before the war.

---

19 The First International Syndicalist Congress was held in London from 27 September to 2 October 1913. The congress was unable to agree on the formation of a new International, but it did create the International Syndicalist Information Bureau as a vehicle of exchange and solidarity. For a detailed account of the congress proceedings, see Westergard-Thorpe 1979, pp. 68–99.

Also included were various syndicalist unions that had been outside the IFTU.

After the Communist International was founded in March 1919, two of the early affiliates were large and influential syndicalist organisations: the National Confederation of Labour (CNT) of Spain and the Italian Syndicalist Union (USI). All over the world, syndicalists were attracted to the new movement, to varying degrees. In addition, some large national union federations were also drawn to the Comintern, such as the General Confederation of Labour (CGL) of Italy and the Norwegian Confederation of Trade Unions.

The Communist International's leaders originally anticipated the creation of a trade-union department of the Comintern. A resolution of the Second World Congress in the summer of 1920 stated: 'Trade unions that uphold communism and that are united internationally under the Communist International's leadership constitute a trade union section of the Communist International.'[20]

Toward that end, a number of conferences and informal meetings were held involving trade-union forces that came to Moscow in June and July 1920, with the goal of creating a new international trade-union organisation. Participants included members of a British labour delegation, central leaders of the Italian CGL, and various syndicalist representatives. Most of the syndicalists strongly objected to having the new trade-union body be formally affiliated to the Comintern, declaring they would not participate if that were the case.

Out of these preliminary conferences and informal discussions, a proclamation was issued on 15 July 1920 signed by representatives from the trade-union movement of seven countries, calling for the creation of a Red Trade Union International and setting up an International Trade Union Council that would work toward this end together with the Communist International – although the exact relationship between the two Internationals was not specified.[21]

The new movement attracted the attention of syndicalists around the world. A December 1920 conference in Berlin, representing some of the most important syndicalist organisations in the United States, Germany, Czechoslovakia, Argentina, France, Holland, Sweden, and England decided to participate in the RILU founding congress, while expressing their differences with the Comintern's point of view.

The Moscow-based council called for unions around the world to disaffiliate from the Amsterdam International and align themselves instead with the new

20 From point 14 of the Comintern's Statutes. In Riddell (ed.) 1991, *2WC*, pp. 698–9.

21 For the text of this call, see pp. 65–66.

revolutionary trade-union centre. To that end, it sought to popularise the call of 'Moscow vs. Amsterdam'.

As more and more unionists were attracted to the embryonic revolutionary centre, Amsterdam grasped the threat and began to expel left-wing union militants who favoured the revolutionary trade-union International.

Referring to Moscow's 'declaration of war', a resolution adopted by the Amsterdam International's London Congress in 1920 declared that it 'forbids any obedience on their part to any resolutions from outside bodies to support their particular movements in the Trade Union International'.[22] The IFTU leadership followed this up with a May 1921 decision that 'it shall not be permissible for the trade-union organizations to be affiliated to two trade-union internationals at the same time.'[23] In the words of Amsterdam leader Edo Fimmen, 'In May 1921 the International Federation of Trade Unions took steps to uphold the unity of trade union action by deciding that any organisation affiliating with the Moscow International would automatically exclude itself from the International Federation of Trade Unions.'[24]

A wave of expulsions soon followed, carried out in a particularly aggressive manner by the General German Trade Union Federation (ADGB), arbitrarily throwing out individuals and entire local unions. The top leadership of the CGT in France began to do the same, leading by the end of 1921 to a split down the middle between the reformist-led CGT and what became a new confederation: the Unitary CGT (CGTU) led by revolutionary syndicalists, which affiliated to the RILU in 1922.

A commonly held view is that 'in forming the Profintern, the Communists had decided to split the international trade-union movement'.[25] That view is not entirely accurate. Regardless of how one interprets what eventually happened, by calling for unions to disaffiliate from the Amsterdam umbrella and align themselves instead with the Red Trade Union International, the RILU's partisans did not intend to deliberately provoke trade-union splits or to create 'dual unions'. The Profintern in its early years strongly opposed most such splits and tried to position itself as a champion of trade-union unity. It refused to turn its back even on unions that had expelled them, fighting instead for their readmission.

---

22 *First Special International Trade Union Congress: London November 22–27, 1920* (Geneva: International Labour Office, 1921), pp. 23–4.

23 Quoted in Resis 1964, p. 108.

24 Fimmen 1922, p. 12.

25 Resis 1964, p. 69.

Solomon Lozovsky

The central leader of the Red International of Labour Unions throughout its entire existence was Solomon A. Lozovsky. A look at the biography of this figure is therefore essential for understanding the Profintern's history.

Solomon Abramovich Dridzo, who used the pseudonym 'Lozovsky', joined the Bolsheviks in 1904. Between 1908 and 1911 he was a 'Bolshevik conciliator' who sought to heal the split between Bolsheviks and Mensheviks, after which he abandoned activity in the Russian revolutionary movement. Living in exile in Paris 1908–17, Lozovsky was active in the French labour movement and the CGT. During this time, he was outside Bolshevik ranks, although he was involved in the Committee for the Resumption of International Relations, working with left-wing forces within the French workers' movement and other Russian exiles.

Returning to Russia in 1917, Lozovsky joined the Bolsheviks, and became a prominent trade-union leader. But weeks after the October Revolution, he issued a public letter calling for a coalition socialist government and attacking the early moves of the Bolshevik leadership. For this he was expelled from the party, and was readmitted only in December 1919.

With such a chequered history, Lozovsky was not the early choice to lead the Profintern. Mikhail Tomsky, head of the Russian trade-union federation, was originally slated by the Russian Communist Party (RCP) leadership to head the RILU as its general secretary. A few months before the scheduled international congress, however, Tomsky was relieved of his position in the Russian trade-union federation owing to differences with the RCP leadership, and he was sent away from Moscow.[26] Tomsky was thus unavailable to attend the founding RILU congress, and was replaced by Lozovsky.

Writing in 1928, Leon Trotsky stated that Lozovsky's appointment was regarded as 'temporary', adding: 'In the Political Bureau, when we found ourselves faced with this fact, we all – Lenin first of all – shook our heads; we consoled ourselves by saying that he [Lozovsky] would have to be replaced at the first opportunity.'[27]

Assuming the accuracy of Trotsky's recollection, it nevertheless must be acknowledged that with Lozovsky's organisational efficiency, knowledge of languages, and familiarity with the European labour movement, Solomon Lozovsky quickly was able to make himself indispensable to the Profintern and its leadership. He was never replaced.

---

26 For two accounts of Tomsky's dismissal, see Tosstorff 2016, pp. 302–3; Wynn 2022, pp. 172–73.

27 Leon Trotsky, 'Who Is Leading the Comintern Today?' in Trotsky 1981, pp. 197–8.

Moreover, Lozovsky became an early and consistent supporter of Joseph Stalin during the latter's rise to power within the Russian Communist Party. This fact, however, did not save him from ultimately becoming one of Stalin's victims; he was arrested in 1949 and executed in 1952. To his credit, Lozovsky courageously defended himself and his co-defendants at their secret frame-up trial, unmasking the absurdity of the charges.[28]

II RILU Founding Congress

Attendance

The founding congress of the Red International of Labour Unions that opened on 3 July 1921 was an impressive gathering, attended by 380 delegates from 41 countries.

Communist forces were in the majority at the congress. In some countries Communists led their countries' trade-union federations, as was the case in Russia, Bulgaria, Ukraine, Azerbaijan, Armenia, Georgia, and elsewhere. For other countries with mass Communist parties, such as Germany and Czechoslovakia, the Communists constituted powerful minorities within their countries' union movement, and they had begun the work of creating Communist 'nuclei' within them. In places with small CPs, Communists had less influence within the trade-union movement, but nevertheless still maintained an important presence.

Syndicalist forces were strongly represented at the congress. The two most important contingents were the CNT delegation from Spain and delegates from the Revolutionary Syndicalist Committees (CSR) in France – the *minoritaires*, who in several months would be expelled from the CGT and create their own federation of roughly the same size. Other important syndicalist forces present at the congress were the Italian Syndicalist Union (USI), the Industrial Workers of the World (IWW) in the United States, One Big Union (OBU) in Canada, a number of German independent syndicalist unions, and unions in the Netherlands, Sweden, and Latin America.

Two national union federations affiliated to the Amsterdam International also attended the congress: the Norwegian Confederation of Trade Unions, represented by official delegates, and the General Confederation of Labour from Italy, which sent two observers.

---

28 For the text of Lozovsky's courtroom speech, as well as background on the case, see Rubenstein and Naumov 2001.

A number of countries had divided delegations.

The German delegation majority consisted of members of local unions and Communist nuclei within the main, reformist-controlled trade-union federation in Germany. A minority of the delegation was made up of representatives from various syndicalist unions such as the Free Workers' Union [FAUD], the General Workers' Union (AAU), the Gelsenkirchen Free Workers' Union, the Seamen's Union, and the Union of Hand and Brain Workers.

The French delegation consisted of members of the CSR, but they were divided on their approach to the Communist International: some wished for close collaboration with the Comintern, while others took a stance of open opposition. In addition, a small left-wing organisation that had split from the CGT was present.

The Italian delegation was divided between the Communist minority within the General Confederation of Labour (CGL) and members of two syndicalist unions: the Italian Syndicalist Union (USI), and the Italian Railroad Workers' Union (SFI). In addition, there were official observers from the CGL, who were there for 'information purposes only'.

The US and Canadian delegation consisted primarily of Communist Party members active in local unions. The Industrial Workers of the World also sent an official delegation, which put itself in opposition to all major decisions at the congress. But several supporters of the pro-Communist minority within the IWW were also present. In addition, attending from the United States was William Z. Foster, a prominent labour leader who had been involved in important union struggles and was not yet a member of the Communist Party. The Canadian delegation consisted of two members of rival factions within, or that came out of, the syndicalist-oriented One Big Union, which was similar to the IWW.

Among the delegates to the congress were several well-known figures in the world trade-union movement who had originated in the syndicalist movement. The most prominent such individuals were William D. ('Big Bill') Haywood from the United States and Tom Mann from Britain.[29]

All told, the founding congress of the Red International of Labour Unions constituted a significant trade-union power, with a breadth of forces reflecting different currents of thought within the world trade-union movement. Given this composition, the congress was the scene of a lively debate on a number of questions with the syndicalist forces. It should be noted that none of the syndicalists were afraid to deliver sharply dissenting views at times, and all delegates at the congress received a hearing.

29 For information on Haywood and Mann, see the glossary.

Credentials Debate

The first point of contention at the congress was on delegate credentials and the allocation of votes. This question was an early subject of controversy, with a debate that took up almost an entire session.

The syndicalists at the congress were upset at the relatively small number of votes allocated to them. As a result, the Spanish syndicalist leader Hilario Arlandis accused the congress of creating a 'fictitious majority'.[30]

There may well have been legitimate grounds for the syndicalists' assertion that Communist trade-union forces were overrepresented in the allocation of votes in several places. But at the same time, with the exception of France, Spain, and several other countries, syndicalist currents constituted a distinct minority within the trade-union movements of their countries. Moreover, some syndicalist membership claims were clearly exaggerated. For example, the delegate from the IWW demanded that he receive almost all of the thirteen votes given to the US delegation, despite the declining size of the IWW and the inclusion of delegates representing small but significant forces within the American Federation of Labor. In the end, the IWW received three of the thirteen votes.

Comintern-RILU Relations

An important debate occurred on the question of the Red Trade Union International's relationship to the Communist International.

Alfred Rosmer gave the first two main reports at the congress. Rosmer, who had originally been a leader of the French syndicalists, started by reporting on the work of the International Trade Union Council (ITUC), and then gave the report on the RILU's relationship with the Comintern. Calling for close ties between the two Internationals in this latter report, Rosmer urged the organisationally independent Profintern to accept the Comintern's political leadership. But that perspective was sharply opposed by a number of syndicalists. Rosmer explained this opposition:

> [A]mong many comrades there is a lot of mistrust and fear that the Communist International, if one establishes permanent and direct links between these two organisations, will immediately take a preponderant role and interfere with the trade-union International in its activity. But I think that is a completely illusory fear. The trade-union International

30 See p. 172.

> that we are going to create here will be such a strong organisation, it will have a field of action so wide and so special, that I believe one cannot even think that it could be only an instrument of the Communist International. …
>
> By asserting that close and permanent ties are necessary between the two Internationals, we will by no means imply that we desire to subordinate the trade-union International to the Communist International. It means only that we desire to organise our forces on a serious and solid basis.[31]

Disagreeing with Rosmer, French syndicalist Henri Sirolle asserted:

> The necessity of our independence from the Communist International arises from higher motives than we are usually credited with. We consider the interests of the revolution ahead of the interests of the party. Revolution is the action of the masses and not of the party. Therefore the interests of the revolution cannot be subjected to the interests of a party, but entrusted to the revolutionists of the world.[32]

Albert Lemoine echoed this view, stating that 'the French delegation declares that it cannot accept any representation whatever of the political International within the trade-union International'.

For his part, Spanish syndicalist Hilario Arlandis asserted that 'we are ready to enter into the closest relations with the Communist International. But in return, we insist upon relations on the basis of equality'. He insisted that 'we must use all our forces to defend our independence and not permit our organisation to be subordinate to any political party'.

Grigorii Tsyperovich, a leader of the trade unions in Soviet Russia, replied to the syndicalists:

> Comrade Arlandis recommends caution and distrust of the Third International. While he speaks of mutual agreement, he also recommends caution and the 'preservation of independence'. He considers the Red Trade Union International to be in opposition to the Communist International, as if the latter does not defend working-class interests.[33]

31 See pp. 184, 190.

32 See p. 256.

33 See p. 199.

At the end of the discussion, it was decided that each International, while organisationally independent, would have representation on the executive body of the other. It was also decided that there would be an 'organic link' between the two Internationals. That expression, however, would be the source of ongoing objections and friction, and would come up again for debate at the Profintern's Second Congress the following year.

The Amiens Charter

In the discussion on RILU-Comintern relations, the ideas of revolutionary syndicalism itself became the subject of debate. Andreu Nin from the CNT of Spain summarised these ideas:

> Revolutionary syndicalism is a doctrine with sound foundations, with a very precise and determined aim. Marxist and Proudhonist at the same time, it takes from the fundamental principles of scientific socialism the class struggle, which considers the union as its most living expression, and adopts from Proudhon and from anarchism the spirit of criticism, federalism, and opposition to the state. Revolutionary syndicalism considers itself to be the most powerful instrument of the direct struggle against the bourgeoisie, and as the only force capable of building up on new foundations the communist society of tomorrow.[34]

Much debate at the RILU congress centred on the Amiens Charter. The debate over the character of this document extended into the discussion on other agenda items. In Lozovsky's words:

> We must propose to our French comrades to work out a new programme instead of their charter. The Amiens Charter was good for a certain period, but now it has lost its significance. It is dead, and let it rest in peace. We want a new programme to answer the requirements of the present day, in which the forms, means, and methods of struggle needed at present would find their echo and reflection. This should be the duty imposed by the congress upon our French comrades.[35]

In his report, Rosmer presented a somewhat different perspective, going out of his way to stress commonalities between Communists and revolutionary syn-

---

34 See p. 396.

35 See pp. 136–7.

dicalists, emphasising the strong points of the Amiens Charter and criticising unjust attacks he felt were being made against the syndicalists, stating that 'we must not exaggerate the weak points in the Amiens Charter':

> The Amiens Charter is a document of great importance. To understand its significance, one must not read its text alone, but consider the very history of the French syndicalist movement, especially at the moment of its inception, why and how this document was accepted. It was at a time when syndicalism firmly established itself in France. It contained different elements: some coming from the anarchists, some from different socialist parties, and others coming from nowhere – the pure syndicalists. All these diverse elements were united by the ideal they aimed at: the suppression of the wages system. They did not care so much to define a new theory, but to establish a correct method of action. In this they succeeded.[36]

One key area of debate involved the relationship of politics to economics.

As Albert Lemoine put it: 'The originality of revolutionary syndicalism in France is that it intends to emancipate the working class from the tutelage – whether disguised or not – of all those who proclaim the supremacy of politics over economics.'[37]

George Williams, delegate of the Industrial Workers of the World from the US, shared this conception:

> [T]he IWW stands and says that since the workers are robbed of their production in the factories, the revolution should be purely economic. It should not be and cannot be a political revolution, because the state is subordinated to the economic power. … The position of the IWW toward the Communist International is that the revolution, once it takes place, must be of a purely economic character.[38]

Lozovsky responded to these claims:

> The syndicalists suffer from their usual malady of not understanding what is politics and what is economics. This is the fundamental trouble with all

---

36 See p. 180.

37 See p. 229.

38 See p. 232.

of them in different countries. They consider as politics the parliamentary struggle, parliamentary negotiations, and nothing else; while mass action is economics. …

Ask any bourgeois whether they are carrying on any discussion of this kind, whether they bother themselves with such questions, and he will look at you as upon a madman. And he will be right, because the bourgeoisie is fully conscious of its class interests. Any bourgeois organisation that in its aims and methods supports the bourgeois order is welcomed by the capitalists. In their struggle against the proletariat, the capitalists refuse to recognise metaphysical or abstract theories, because they find no difference between politics and economics.[39]

Class-Struggle Unionism

One of the central agenda points at the congress was on trade-union tasks and tactics, kicked off with a report by Lozovsky.[40] The resolution adopted on the subject included a programme of action.[41] Among this programme's central precepts were:

Opposition to class collaboration, the idea that workers and bosses share common interests. At the time, numerous class-collaborationist schemes were being put forward by the Amsterdam International and the trade-union bureaucracy, whether it be 'socialisation' or 'business collaboration'. These schemes had a common aim, the resolution stated:

> To divert the attention of the workers from their immediate revolutionary task and to awaken in them petty-bourgeois aspirations, the capitalists and reformists are bringing forward the idea of profit sharing, i.e., to return to the workers an insignificant part of the surplus value produced by them. This plan of corrupting the workers should be met with severe and merciless criticism. Not 'profit-sharing', but 'doing away with capitalist profit' – this is the slogan of the revolutionary trade unions.

Direct action. In his report, Lozovsky explained:

> The programme of action now presented to this congress is based on the principle of direct action. Direct action is action against the rule of the bourgeoisie, against the exploiters, and against the capitalist system in

39 See pp. 208, 209.

40 For Lozovsky's report, see pp. 129–49.

41 For the Programme of Action, see pp. 619–24.

> general. It may be manifested in different forms and methods, beginning with a strike and ending with armed insurrection, seizure of factories, etc. These slogans for direct action should especially be spread widely in all countries, because they express the organisational, political, economic, and practical aspects of our struggle.

Industrial organisation. At the time, most unions around the world were structured on a craft basis, with each factory and workshop usually containing a number of different unions. This type of organisation, the resolution asserted, diluted workers' strength and weakened their capacity for collective action. 'The slogan of organisation that we believe should be put in the foreground', Lozovsky stated in his report, 'is the transformation of craft and trade unionism into industrial unionism.' As the resolution stated:

> The last years of the struggle have shown with particular vividness the weakness of strictly craft organisations to meet the situation. The fact that workers in the same enterprise belong to different craft unions weakens their struggle. It is necessary – and this should be the starting point of an implacable struggle – to pass from purely craft unions to industrial organisations. 'All workers employed in the same enterprise should be in the same union' – this is the militant slogan in the field of workers' organisation. The fusion into a single union in a revolutionary way should be put directly before the members of the union in the factories and enterprises, as well as before local and regional bodies, and national congresses.

Most points in the RILU programme of action were advocated by Communists and syndicalists alike. This discussion and resolution therefore helped convince a section of the syndicalists of the need for close collaboration between the two.

Transform Existing Unions or Build New Ones?

One of the main subjects of debate at the congress was how to approach existing bureaucratised unions: whether to fight to transform them, or to leave them and instead build expressly revolutionary unions.

On this question, most syndicalist forces advocated breaking from the old unions entirely. In the words of Andreu Nin, 'we must carry on the fight against Amsterdam not inside the old unions, but outside'.

The German syndicalists, for their part, referred to the old trade unions as 'counterrevolutionary' and put forward the slogans 'Out of the unions!' and 'Smash the old unions!' As Arthur Bartels explained:

> Once we recognise that the proletariat must take the offensive, and that the old methods are holding back the attack on capital, it is necessary for the proletariat to adapt to the new conditions of struggle. It must completely change its tactics and methods of struggle, which were fine for defence, but not for the attack. The proletariat must create a true attack apparatus. … Owing to this fact, we say to the workers: 'Out of the trade unions – your place is in the factory committees'.[42]

Delegate Emil Gieseler, representing the syndicalist German seamen's union, stated that 'to follow the slogan of returning to the old trade unions would be equivalent to suicide for any revolutionary movement'.[43]

Speaking about the German syndicalists, the Polish delegate Gliński (Stefan Królikowski) pointed to a curious coincidence:

> The representatives of the counterrevolution came to the conclusion that all Communists must be thrown out of the trade unions. And here comrades, supposed revolutionists, say the same thing: 'Out of the trade unions!' There is a danger for the revolution here.[44]

Georgi Dimitrov from Bulgaria spoke of the same danger: '[N]ow, when the Amsterdam leaders themselves have put forward the question of expelling the revolutionary elements from the trade unions, an appeal to withdraw from them would simply be a crime toward the emancipatory task of the proletariat'.[45]

Lozovsky echoed this view:

> In fact this slogan, at the present juncture, is not only dangerous but counterrevolutionary. Just think of it. We come to the workers and tell them to smash their unions, when we know that it has taken the working class dozens of years to build them, and those unions have proved to be beneficial to the working class. The workers and the union are strongly linked together. Workers consider the union as their home, and when we come to them and say, 'smash the union', we meet with the obstinate resistance of the masses. The masses are unwilling to destroy the unions they have built.[46]

42 See pp. 360, 365.
43 See p. 239.
44 See p. 381.
45 See p. 417.
46 See p. 138.

These syndicalists, Lozovsky asserted, think that 'the bureaucracy is unconquerable. But if you think this way, then how do you expect to overthrow capitalism?' The RILU leader laid out the goal of transforming the unions, of 'conquering' them:

> [O]ur task is not to destroy the unions, but to conquer the masses in the unions. What does it mean to conquer the masses? Does it imply that we are to take possession of their treasury or premises? No, to conquer the workers means that we are to gain control over the minds of the proletariat, over its feelings and conscience, and to make it understand the class struggle. … Our task does not consist in pulling the best elements out of the unions, and building separate organisations with them. On the contrary, we should stay in the unions and see that the militant elements with the most revolutionary and selfless spirit work inside of these unions.[47]

Throughout the congress the German syndicalists in particular repeatedly raised objections to this perspective.

Approach to Amsterdam and Union Expulsions

The question of conquering the unions and building Communist nuclei within them was closely connected to the RILU's stance toward the Amsterdam International and its expulsions of revolutionary opposition forces. That question was a theme of Lozovsky's organisation report. The discussion and debate revolved primarily around three points.

The first of these was to establish as RILU policy that dual affiliation to the Red International and to Amsterdam was impermissible. That question was most sharply posed in relation to the Italian General Confederation of Labour (CGL). Although the CGL had been one of the original signers of the call for the creation of the Red Trade Union International, it remained affiliated to Amsterdam, and had in fact strengthened its ties with the IFTU. The CGL sent two representatives to the RILU congress, but they were there for 'information purposes only'.

There was universal condemnation of the CGL stance by all sides at the congress, both Communists and syndicalists. The policy prohibiting dual affiliation was therefore adopted unanimously.

The second question taken up concerned the Amsterdam International's policy of expelling Communists. Should Communists accept these expulsions

---

47 See pp. 106, 138.

and form their own unions? Or should they fight against them and instead seek readmittance? That question was addressed by Lozovsky in his organisation report:

> Comrades, if you're expelled – organise yourselves! It's not just the Communists who were expelled. When the Communists are expelled, they still have their own organisation they belong to. But when 4,000 metalworkers were expelled in Halle, not all of them were Communists; they were just revolutionary workers. They will not all enter the party and will consequently remain unorganised. You risk losing several thousand workers. For the sake of what will you lose them? To this they answer: 'If we organise them, we shall play into the hands of the splitters.'[48]

After a long discussion and mutual compromise, a conclusion was reached that Lozovsky summarised:

> [T]he main organisational problem for Germany consists in getting the expelled workers together and connecting them with an organisation that works within the unions and leads them to the conquest of the unions under the slogans: 'Down with the splitters!', 'Down with the trade-union bureaucracy that expels revolutionary workers from the unions!'.[49]

Upholding trade-union unity, the RILU sought to show that it was Amsterdam, not Moscow, that was weakening the power of the working class through its splitting policy.

The third question involved the international trade federations that were affiliated to Amsterdam. These federations, too, had begun to expel Communists from their ranks. What to do about this? Should Communists form their own separate international federations?

The decision arrived at was not to do so, but instead to form what were called 'international propaganda committees' for each industry. As Lozovsky explained:

> [W]e have to consider whether we are now to create red international federations of transport, textile, and metalworkers, etc. – yes or no? I believe that to create such federations at the present time would be premature. It

48 See p. 446.

49 See p. 502.

> might suffice for us to create ten or fifteen international propaganda committees among the textile, transport, wood, metalworkers, etc., and begin propaganda in the respective unions in various countries in order to win them to our cause. Only when we have secured sufficient forces and selected a definite quantity of organisations can we develop these propaganda committees into larger and more important groupings and turn them into something more.[50]

Workers' Control and Factory Committees

An important agenda point at the congress was that of workers' control and factory committees.

The issue of workers' control was a particularly important question at the time. The term here refers to the perspective of workers keeping close tabs on the operations of the factories under their capitalist owners – through oversight, monitoring, and supervision – and through a process of struggle increasingly taking charge of these operations.

Grigori Tsyperovich's report to the RILU Congress on this question gave a clear and concrete description of this process, pointing out how it could help lead to the political rule of the working class. This very phenomenon, he stated, had been widespread in Russia in the months following the February 1917 revolution, and it also occurred in a number of European countries during the post-war upsurge. Referring to the dynamic of this process, he stated:

> [W]orkers' control inevitably acquires political forms and turns into a struggle for the conquest of the state apparatus. This is why in its last stage it turns into a social struggle for the dictatorship of the proletariat. … In carrying out workers' control, it is necessary to remember that while it in itself is unable to resolve the fundamental question of the expropriation of the means of production, it is nevertheless an excellent preparatory school for the final battle to capture the means of production, i.e., for the dictatorship of the proletariat.[51]

Alongside the workers' control report, Fritz Heckert presented a companion report on factory committees. Such committees, open to all workers in a factory, were especially important in the context where multiple unions existed in

---

50 See pp. 448–9.

51 See p. 288.

most workplaces, as was the case in the majority of countries at the time. The demand for factory committees was thus tied to the perspective of building unions constructed along industrial lines.

Tying factory committees to the issue of workers' control, Heckert stated, 'The creation of factory committees is the expression of the will of workers to have a voice in matters concerning the factory, workshops, and industry in general, and to limit the employers' absolute power over production.'[52]

The significance of factory committees was summarised by Lozovsky:

> We must pose to all unions the task of changing the basis of their system, replacing the system of guilds and delegates with factory committees and shop stewards. Once based on the organisation of factory committees, the struggle will be inspired by and conducted within the factory. These workers will be drawn into the struggle and won over. This system will afford an opportunity to the revolutionary minority – who so far are only a minority in all countries – to organise the millions of workers, thus making this system a starting point for revolutionary mass action.[53]

RILU Organisational Structure

Considerable attention was paid at the congress to preparing statutes for the Red Trade Union International. The RILU statutes ultimately adopted went over all aspects of the organisation's structure, including its leadership committees, membership, finances, and so on.

Five conditions for admission were presented, which were expressly put forward as 'ultimatums': (1) recognition of the class struggle and carrying it out in practice; (2) recognition of the dictatorship of the proletariat; (3) prohibition of dual affiliation with Amsterdam; (4) unity in action by RILU affiliates within a country; (5) international discipline.

With regard to this last point, which was largely modelled on the Comintern, Lozovsky stated:

> It is inadmissible for us to adopt a decision today and then tomorrow each organisation would begin to act in whatever way it chooses, every way other than the way adopted by the congress. The congress establishes international proletarian discipline and considers its decisions binding and obligatory: whoever disagrees with these decisions, finds them inad-

52 See p. 292.
53 See p. 148.

> equate, etc., can carry on discussions within the respective organisations in a friendly, fraternal, comradely way, up to the next congress, but unity of action should not be violated. Submitting to the decisions of the congress should be obligatory.[54]

Nevertheless, the requirement that affiliated unions implement all congress decisions without exception on pain of expulsion proved to be problematic for the Red International of Labour Unions.

As outlined by the Comintern, democratic centralism was intended for voluntary political parties in which membership was based on agreement with a particular political perspective. But it was not necessarily appropriate for a *trade union*, which by definition sought to organise all workers within a given industry, and as such encompassed workers of different political persuasions and levels of consciousness. Establishing such a norm for the Red Trade Union International must also have seemed at variance with union members' right to decide their own union's policies. Moreover, it gave ammunition to the leaders of the Amsterdam International who claimed RILU was not a real organisation, but only a front for the Comintern.

In actual practice, however, international democratic centralism in the early world Communist movement was not implemented in as draconian fashion as is sometimes suggested. In Lenin's time, the early Comintern leadership generally dispensed advice rather than issuing edicts.[55]

Other Reports and Discussions

A number of other items were discussed at the RILU congress, along with corresponding resolutions adopted:

- Unemployment. The resolution on this question pointed to the fact that unemployment could not be ended under capitalism. It nevertheless stressed the need for working-class struggle on the question, and went over how unions could best fight against this scourge.[56]
- Women in industry and the trade unions. A resolution was adopted following a report by Hertha Sturm and discussion by Rosa Bloch and Clara Zetkin. The Sturm report and the resolution laid out the importance of women's role in the work force and in the unions. Workers were urged to fight for equal pay for equal work; against discriminatory layoffs for women, for strengthening

54 See p. 451.

55 For a discussion of centralism in the early Comintern, see Taber (ed.) 2018, pp. 32–5.

56 For the resolution on unemployment, see pp. 658–60.

women's participation in the unions and their leadership, and seeing women as comrades in struggle, not as competitors of male workers.[57]

- War victims and veterans. With tens of millions of workers having participated in World War I, and with millions of them disabled as a result, large organisations of war veterans and victims had sprung up throughout Europe. Many of these groups had governmental sponsorship or were linked to social-democratic groups. The Communist movement participated in this movement, and built its own 'International Union of War Victims'. The report on this movement given to the RILU congress recognised the need for close collaboration by unions with it.[58]
- The white terror. Reports and resolutions were adopted on the wave of counterrevolutionary repression that emerged after the war as a way to prevent the spread of the revolutionary movement. The Red International called attention in particular to the bourgeoisie's creation of paramilitary forces increasingly deployed against the organised working-class movement, and the importance of organising workers' self-defence guards.[59]
- International solidarity. Several resolutions calling for international workers' solidarity were adopted, notably for workers in struggle in Britain and Spain.[60]
- A manifesto to workers of the world reviewed the international situation and the capitalist offensive that was then taking place. It called on workers to leave Amsterdam and affiliate to the Red Trade Union International.[61]
- A report on anarchists in Russia was given to the congress by Nikolai Bukharin on behalf of the Russian Communist Party Central Committee.[62] Two weeks earlier, a number of jailed Russian anarchists had begun a hunger strike to protest their imprisonment. The French syndicalist delegation was involved in behind-the-scenes negotiations on this question with the Soviet leadership, including Lenin himself. Also involved in these discussions were exiled US anarchists Emma Goldman and Alexander Berkman.

For some of the syndicalist delegates in attendance, this issue was as important as any other matter discussed at the congress. In light of this fact, it was decided

57 For the report and resolution on women in industry and unions, see pp. 462–71 and 656–7.

58 For the report and resolution on war veterans and victims, see pp. 489–94 and 661.

59 For the resolution on the white terror, see pp. 664–8.

60 For the resolutions on solidarity with workers in Britain and Spain, see pp. 669–70 and 671.

61 For the manifesto adopted by the congress, see pp. 597–600. A draft manifesto read out in session 3 can be found on pp. 82–93.

62 See pp. 518–21.

to give a report to the RILU congress on the Russian anarchists. Bukharin's report, however, was seen as a provocation by many of the syndicalists, as he attempted to link all Russian anarchists to the armed struggle against Soviet power being led by a Ukrainian partisan leader, the anarchist Nestor Makhno. Such a linkage was angrily rejected by the syndicalists, and the report led to tumult that almost broke up the congress. The floor was given to Henri Sirolle, who heatedly responded to Bukharin.[63] Given this clear danger to the congress's unity, it was decided to let the matter rest and move the agenda.

With regard to the anarchists' hunger strike, negotiations continued in the days following Bukharin's report, leading to an end to the hunger strike and to the anarchists' release and eventual departure from the country.

Balance Sheet of Congress

Considerable ambiguity surrounded the founding of the Red International of Labour Unions. Was the new formation to be organisationally independent of the Comintern or a department within it? Was it directed at winning forces from within the main trade unions affiliated to the International Federation of Trade Unions? Was its axis meant to be an alliance with the syndicalist movement? None of these questions have simple or straightforward answers.

In drawing a balance sheet of the first Profintern congress, its strengths and weaknesses should both be examined.

Its strong points included:

- Raising the banner of industrial and class-struggle unionism, rejecting class collaboration and business unionism. The congress presented an alternative, revolutionary vision as to what unions should be, having the ultimate goal of overthrowing the capitalist system and establishing workers' rule.
- Putting the RILU on the map, showing that it had real strength and appeal. In doing so, the Red International became a pole of attraction to left-wing unionists internationally, with powerful support in union federations in France, Italy, Germany, Czechoslovakia, and elsewhere.
- Drawing closer a section of the syndicalists, most importantly those in France, as well as a number of important forces and individuals in other countries from that movement.

As far as the congress's weak points:

- The sharpness of the attacks on the Amsterdam International, and the either/or alternative of Moscow vs. Amsterdam, gave a handle to those national union leaders looking for reasons to remain in Amsterdam. For

63 For Sirolle's reply to Bukharin on the Russian anarchists, see pp. 522–5.

the Amsterdam leaders themselves, it provided justification for their persecution and expulsion of left-wing unionists. It became harder to mount a defence of the expelled unionists among other trade-union members and leaders who might not agree with the Communists, but who opposed the undemocratic measures used against them. Using more defensive formulations might have helped enlist a broader array of union forces to oppose Amsterdam's split moves.

– While some important syndicalist forces were drawn closer to the Communist movement, others were alienated from it. This was inevitable to some extent, given the nature of some of the groups involved, but one is left to wonder whether with a little more tact and less stridency, a greater number of the syndicalists could have been drawn closer rather than driven away.

Ian Birchall puts the responsibility for much of this stridency on Grigorii Zinoviev, the main day-to-day leader of the Communist International, involved in the initial discussions with international trade-union leaders and syndicalists who had come to Russia:

> Zinoviev thought it enough to denounce reformist leaders, believing workers would be convinced by having their leaders insulted. Thus an 'appeal' to the IFTU began: 'You are the chief bulwark of capitalism, now living out its last days – you are the watchdogs of capital, barking furiously at all those who approach your master's lair.'[64]

But as the proceedings of the First RILU Congress show, Lozovsky too was the source of much of this stridency toward the syndicalists and other opposition forces. Based on Lozovsky's chequered political past mentioned earlier, many Communists probably did not fully trust him. For this reason, Lozovsky seemed to go out of his way at all times to prove his Leninist mettle, apparently seeking to present himself as the 'best Bolshevik', with little tolerance for disagreements. Similar phenomena have been seen all too frequently in the history of the revolutionary movement.

In any case, Lozovsky's strident attitude, and his resistance to making tactful compromises with the syndicalists – if only in matters of language – did not help the process of winning over more syndicalists to RILU affiliation. Along these lines, Tosstorff refers to the original idea of having Mikhail Tomsky be the central leader of the RILU, and suggests: 'One can only speculate as to what

---

64 Birchall 2020.

other effects his [Tomsky's] presence might have had, perhaps in creating a different atmosphere more favourable to cooperation between syndicalists and communists.'[65]

Despite its weaknesses, the founding RILU congress nevertheless established a strong basis for the new trade-union International, with clear potential for growth. The adoption of the united-front perspective at the end of 1921 gave a boost to the RILU's prospects and began to show what was possible.

III RILU Development and Evolution

Once the new organisation was founded, with a sizable apparatus and leadership structure, the Red International's existence took on a life of its own.

Following the RILU founding congress most of the main syndicalist organisations distanced themselves from the Profintern. This included the CNT in Spain, the USI in Italy, the IWW in the US, and the FAUD and AAU in Germany. Many of these forces participated in founding the anarcho-syndicalist International Workers' Association in December 1922.

In addition, a few of the national confederations that had at one point considered affiliation to the Red International decided against it, at least for the time being, such as the CGL in Italy and the labour confederation in Norway. Many union leaders were deterred from affiliating by the Amsterdam International's expulsion threat against any organisation adhering to the Profintern.[66]

All told, the RILU's prospects dimmed in the first months following the founding congress.

Adoption of United-Front Perspective

On 1 January 1922 the executive committees of the Red International of Labour Unions and the Communist International issued a joint appeal, 'For the United Front of the Proletariat' addressed to 'Working men and women of all countries'.

Stating that 'the capitalists of all countries are uniting for an attack on the working class', the call urged workers to:

---

65 Tosstorff 2016, p. 391.

66 A few important syndicalist organisations remained and were drawn closer to the RILU, such as the French CSR, which soon became the CGTU, a wing of the German syndicalists, and some important individuals such as Andreu Nin.

> [J]oin forces for the struggle for a bare existence, for the struggle for a bit of bread and for peace. Join your forces in a battle front, unite as a proletarian class against the class of the exploiters and pillagers of the world. Tear down the walls which have been built up between you, take your place in its ranks – whether Communist, Social Democrat, Anarchist or Syndicalist – for the battle against the misery of the hour.[67]

The adoption of the united-front policy led to an improvement in the RILU's prospects. Calling for common action by all working-class organisations to defend workers' basic interests against the capitalist offensive resonated in proletarian layers that had remained aloof from earlier Communist and RILU pronouncements. Workers increasingly responded to these calls, which corresponded to the real needs of the moment.

Over the course of 1922 and 1923, this policy began to bear fruit. Given working-class sentiment overwhelmingly in favour of joint action, the united-front policy also began to create fissures in the Amsterdam International, with the emergence of what was perceived as a left wing favouring at least limited collaboration with the Russian trade unions in particular.

In December 1922 the Amsterdam International helped organise a World Peace Congress in The Hague. The Russian trade unions sent a delegation, and the organisers felt compelled to let Lozovsky speak and present the views of the Red Trade Union International.

In May 1923 conferences were held between Russian trade unions and the Amsterdam International metalworkers' and transport workers' trade federations. Among other things, these conferences discussed the openings for united-front action against war, reaction, and fascism.

Developments such as these began to show the potential of the united-front policy for the Red Trade Union International, and led to a brightening of its prospects.

RILU Second Congress

The impact of the united-front policy could be seen at the Second RILU Congress, held 19 November–2 December 1922 and attended by 213 delegates. Much of the congress was dominated by discussion on the impact of the united-front campaign. In country after country, delegates reported progress made.[68]

---

67 *International Press Correspondence*, 6 January 1922.

68 For more on the Second Congress, see Tosstorff 2016, pp. 572–603. Its proceedings were published in *II. Kongress Krasnogo Internatsionala Profsoiuzov v Moskve. 19 noiabria–2 dekabria 1922 goda*, Moscow/Petrograd, 1923.

Substantial discussion took place once again at the Second Congress on the relationship of the RILU to the Comintern. In order to secure the affiliation of the CGTU in France, the congress decided to drop the 'organic connection' formulation decided by the First Congress.[69] Based on this decision, the CGTU formally affiliated to the Profintern, giving a substantial boost to its authority.

One agenda point at the Second RILU Congress is worth noting: its discussion on the trade-union movement in the colonial and semicolonial world. Delegates came to the congress from Japan, China, Latin America, and elsewhere. and there was a report on the agenda about the labour movement in these countries, which described the growth of trade unions, and escalating workers' struggles in India, the Dutch Indies (Indonesia), China, Korea, Turkey, Egypt, and other countries.[70]

There was also considerable discussion on consolidating RILU's organisational structure, along with the question of the International Propaganda Committees.

Comintern's Degeneration

The new opportunities for the RILU did not last long, however, as Profintern prospects declined quickly and sharply due to developments within the Communist International.

Following the death of Lenin in early 1924 and the march toward Soviet Russia's Stalinist degeneration, the Profintern was continually undermined by various zigzags and flip-flops in Comintern policy. Among these:

(a) The years 1924–7 saw several contradictory policies. On the one hand, the Comintern moved away from the united front as originally conceived in 1921–2. Adopting the perspective of the 'united front from below', it rejected efforts to address leaders of other mass workers' organisations. In the case of the Amsterdam International, which was coming under pressure as a result of the Comintern and RILU united-front efforts, the IFTU leaders were let off the hook.

Alongside this seemingly ultraleft course, however, was a growing tendency to adapt to the Amsterdam trade-union bureaucracy. The original 'Moscow vs. Amsterdam' stance was replaced by repeated public calls for unity between the

69 See 'Resolution on Relations between the Red International of Labour Unions and the Communist International' on pp. 602–3. For a summary of the RILU Second Congress discussion on this question, see Tosstorff 2016, pp. 582–7.

70 See *II. Kongress Krasnogo Internatsionala Profsoiuzov*, pp. 257–62 for the report to the

Red Trade Union International and the IFTU.[71] Along this road, views advocating the RILU's unilateral liquidation began to grow within the world Communist movement.

(b) Beginning in 1928 the Comintern adopted its 'third period' perspective that called for Communists and left-wing militants to leave the main unions and build their own 'red unions'. This disastrous ultraleft period lasted for five years. That move in essence sealed the RILU's death as a significant force in the trade-union movement.[72]

(c) In 1934–5 the Comintern shifted toward a 'popular front' perspective of building alliances with liberal bourgeois forces such as Franklin D. Roosevelt in the United States, supposedly to combat the fascist threat. The existence of the RILU was an obvious impediment to this policy, which led to its final dissolution in 1937, although the organisation had in fact been moribund for years before that.

IV Assessment and Legacy

What historical assessment should be made of the Red International of Labour Unions? That question is not easy to answer.

At the Communist International's Fifth Congress in 1924, Grigorii Zinoviev made a revealing comment:

> The Red Trade Union International was founded at a moment when it looked as though we could break through the enemy's front by a head-on attack and quickly win over the trade unions. ... We believed we were going to win over the majority of the workers very quickly. ... All the

---

Second RILU Congress on this question. For a description of RILU progress and work in the other countries of the colonial East, see Tosstorff 2016, pp. 677–8, 733–9.

71 The call for trade-union unity was a theme of the RILU's Third Congress in 1924. See Tosstorff 2016, pp. 687–702.

72 The creation of the Profintern in 1921 is often conflated with the Comintern's post-1928 position on this question, as if from the beginning the Profintern advocated the creation of dual, 'red' unions to be split off from existing trade unions. The Red Trade Union International of 1920–1, however, *did not* call for the creation of separate revolutionary unions, and in fact vigorously opposed such a course. It stood instead for trade-union unity, and for participation in existing unions, with the perspective of transforming them into revolutionary class-struggle instruments. In 1928, during the Stalinist 'third period' turn, however, the Comintern and RILU reversed this position and indeed called for the creation of 'red unions'.

> problems, all the tactical difficulties of the Communist International during these five years are rooted in the fact that developments were much slower than we expected.[73]

In citing the RILU's founding, Zinoviev was referring to the first moves in 1920 to create a red trade-union International. These discussions were held at the time of the Communist International's Second Congress, with Zinoviev's close involvement. At the Second Congress the perspective of a short-term revolutionary victory dominated most Communists' thinking.

But by the time RILU held its founding congress the following year, the world situation had changed significantly. The Third Comintern Congress that met at the same time as the RILU founding congress recognised this shift and pointed to the need for an adjustment in tempo and strategy. It adopted a turn toward what became the united-front perspective.

The RILU that was created in 1921, however, still largely operated in the framework of a year earlier. The turn toward a united-front perspective that had marked the Comintern's Third Congress was not projected at the RILU gathering. The absence of that perspective put the Profintern at a distinct disadvantage, imposing a handicap at birth that it struggled to overcome.[74]

As referred to earlier, for a brief period in 1922–3 – after the RILU had begun implementing the united-front approach – signs appeared that the Red International of Labour Unions was gaining traction within the world labour movement. That potential, however, was largely short-circuited by developments within the international Communist movement. Given that period's brevity, it is difficult to accurately assess what the real possibilities might have been.

Regardless, the RILU did have two noteworthy successes to its credit:

First, drawing in a layer of organised syndicalist forces. Most importantly, the Profintern obtained the affiliation of the French CGTU, along with that of other prominent syndicalists around the world, such as Andreu Nin in Spain. In this sense, the Profintern significantly expanded the reach of the world Communist movement.

Second, the RILU achieved important trade-union successes in the colonial and semicolonial world, where federations affiliated to the RILU often became

73 From remarks by Zinoviev at the Communist International's Fifth Congress. In Communist International 1924, pp. 911–12.

74 On the RILU's difficulties with the united-front issue, see Fowkes 2017.
For his part, Resis stated that 'though the Comintern had succeeded in forming an international "united revolutionary front" of political leaders, the Profintern had failed to form a similar front of trade-union leaders'. In Resis 1964, p. 229.

the dominant labour force. The growth of RILU influence in these countries contrasted sharply with the Amsterdam International, which made few efforts in this direction and had little influence outside Europe and North America. As an illustration, the London Congress of the IFTU in 1920 had not a single delegate from the colonial and semicolonial world.

By contrast, Communists in China helped spearhead the establishment in 1925 of the All-China Federation of Trade Unions, which affiliated to the RILU. Growing to almost three million members by 1927, this federation was crushed with the defeat of the Chinese revolution that year.[75]

Related to its orientation toward peoples oppressed by imperialism was the Profintern's attention to Black workers, illustrated by its 1928 creation of the International Trade Union Committee of Negro Workers, which sought to organise Black workers in the United States and South Africa, as well as Britain, France, and their colonies.[76]

Legacy

As stated earlier, the decision to form the Red International of Labour Unions was largely conjunctural in nature, as was the concrete form it took. Despite this origin, however, the Red International of Labour Unions left behind an important legacy of international working-class action.

Its call for opposition to the capitalist offensive, to imperialist war, and to right-wing and fascist reaction, as well as its appeal to solidarity with the Russian Revolution still bear study. Likewise, its examination of the issues of workers' control, factory committees, and other questions remains of value. In particular, the fight for trade unions to adopt a class-struggle perspective, and break from business unionism and class-collaborationism, continues to be an urgent need.

While from an organisational standpoint, the Red Trade Union International cannot be presented as a model for future attempts at international working-class action, it does provide important experiences that new generations can learn from.

Today, a century after the events recounted in this book, working people again face an escalating offensive against their most basic interests and conditions of life, along with the threat of war and growing rightist forces. The concept of militant international trade-union action remains as compelling as it was a hundred years ago.

---

75 See Pringsheim 1965.

76 See 'Pan-Africanism and Communism: An Interview with Hakim Adi' at https://johnriddell.com/2021/04/19/pan-africanism-and-communism-an-interview-with-hakim-adi/

Challenges facing working people and their unions on a world level are, if anything, even more closely interconnected. As the phenomenon of capitalist economic globalisation develops, so too is there a need for a globalisation of the working-class struggle. In this context the example and lessons of the Red Trade Union International deserve serious attention.

Additionally, the Red International of Labour Unions remains an important part of the legacy of the Communist International under Lenin. Understanding the RILU's relationship to the world Communist movement as a whole gives us a better appreciation of the power and potential of that living mass movement, whose lessons continue to be of relevance to those fighting for revolutionary social change in the world.

Mike Taber
October 2022

About this Edition

The proceedings of the 1921 founding congress of the Red International of Labour Unions were taken down by stenographers and published quickly in a series of sixteen bulletins in German, French, Russian, and English.[1] These bulletins were prepared presumably for use by the delegates themselves, as well as by leaderships of Communist parties and red trade unions in the various countries, and did not receive broad circulation. The Russian bulletins were subsequently assembled together and published as a book.[2] No other editions of the congress proceedings were ever published, although the resolutions adopted by the congress did come out in various languages and were circulated widely. The overwhelming majority of the present book therefore appears in English for the first time since its original publication in bulletin format a century ago.

For this volume, we have used the English versions as an initial basis in preparing the manuscript, but have heavily edited these in close comparison with the German, French, and Russian versions.[3] Transcripts of interventions by English speakers, however, have been only minimally edited. Inconsistencies between the various languages have been noted.

One major item was missing from the English, German, and French versions: the report on the world economic crisis by Eugen Varga in session 4, which appeared as a supplement to Russian bulletin no. 4. For this volume, we have therefore translated it from the Russian.

A task requiring substantial work was identifying the delegates. For this, files contained in the Comintern archives – housed at the Russian State Archive of Social and Political History (RGASPI) – were utilised.[4] While the identity of some delegates still remains a mystery, we have successfully identified the vast majority of them.

1 The Russian version contained a seventeenth bulletin, which consisted of the proceedings of meetings of the International Propaganda Committees – groups organised by trade – that took place during the course of the RILU congress. Those proceedings have not been included in the present volume.

2 *1-yi mezhdunarodnogo kongressa revoliutsionnykh, professional'nykh i proizodstvennykh soiuzov. Stenograficheskii otchet*, Moscow, 1921.

3 A full set of the English, French, and Russian bulletins were obtained. We were only able to obtain bulletins 1–7 of the German, however.

4 Material from the Profintern First Congress can be found in RGASPI fond 534. Delegate credentials are found in opis 4 of that fond, and delegate profiles and questionnaires are found in opis numbers 5–10.

 | DOI:10.1163/9789004712867_004

Related to the identity question is that of inconsistent spellings of names from one language to the next, and from one bulletin to the next. To correct inconsistencies, we have worked diligently to systematise these spellings.

The RGASPI archives were also used to obtain various unpublished documents produced by participants at the RILU congress. These were utilised both in the Appendix to this volume as well as in annotation.

This volume would not have been possible without the collaboration and assistance of a number of people. Three who helped at every stage of the project deserve special mention: Reiner Tosstorff, author of the definitive history of the Red Trade Union International, provided advice and suggestions from the beginning, reviewed the entire manuscript, and was always available for consultation. Bob Schwarz helped track down and obtain copies of the original bulletins, and then worked tirelessly at researching names and events for the glossary and footnotes. John Riddell, long-time general editor of the Comintern publishing project, gave important guidance and advice. All three of these individuals read the manuscript and provided valuable insights, corrections, and suggestions.

Daria Dyakonova obtained many hundreds of pages of documents from RGASPI in Moscow.

Sonja Franeta translated Eugen Varga's report on the world economic crisis from Russian.

Helping to obtain and copy the original bulletins in the four languages were David Broder, Maria Grazia Meriggi, Stéphanie Prezioso, and Lyndon White.

Linda Loew, Geoff Mirelowitz, Delpfine Welch, and Jeff White retyped the original English-language bulletins.

Providing answers to research questions for the footnotes and glossary were Barbara Allen, Jon Bekken, Jeannie Cardilini, Kristen Chinery at Wayne State University Walter P. Reuther Library, Tobias Crabus at the Saxon State Archives, Cristina Diac, Jean-Numa Ducange, Daniel Gaido, Mark R. Hatlie, Norman LaPorte, Ralf Hoffrogge, Stuart Macintyre, Will Mawhood, Scot McCullough at the Wisconsin Historical Society, Nienell Melkasze at the National Parliamentary Library of Georgia, Nils Meyer of the Deutsche Digitale Bibliothek, Uwe Müller of the Chemnitz City Archives, Tomáš Patzelt of the National Library of the Czech Republic, Michel Pigenet, Gražina Rinkevičienė of the National Library of Lithuania, the National Library of Latvia, Philip Ruff, Tauno Saarela, John Sexton, Simon Sheppard of the People's History Museum in Manchester, Marco Swiniartzki, Ellen van Veen of the International Institute of Social History, Sarah Christine Wefel of the Friedrich-Ebert-Stiftung, Lyndon White, Lüko Willms, and Kenyon W. Zimmer.

Other help on the project was given by Tom Alter, John Beadle, Peter Cole, Clifford Conner, Russel Durst, Jonah McAllister Erickson, Joe Evica, Pedro Gellert, Paul LeBlanc, Ben Lewis, Johan Pries, and Nancy Rosenstock.

Jeff White copy-edited the manuscript, as he has done with numerous other Comintern volumes.

Finally, Sebastian Budgen and Danny Hayward from the Historical Materialism Book Series deserve thanks for their encouragement and assistance throughout the entire preparation of this project.

Abbreviations

2WC	Second Congress of the Communist International proceedings
3WC	Third Congress of the Communist International proceedings
AAU	General Workers' Union
ADGB	General German Trade Union Federation
AFL / A.F. of L.	American Federation of Labor
CGL	General Confederation of Labour (Italy)
CGT	General Confederation of Labour (France)
CGTU	Unitary General Confederation of Labour (France)
CNT	National Confederation of Labour (Spain)
CSR	Revolutionary Syndicalist Committees (France)
CTM	Confederation of Workers of the World (France)
FAUD	Free Workers' Union of Germany
FORAC	Argentine Regional Workers' Federation-Communist
IFTU	International Federation of Trade Unions
ILO	International Labour Office
ITUC	International Trade Union Council
IWW	Industrial Workers of the World
KAPD	Communist Workers' Party of Germany
KPD	Communist Party of Germany
LCW	V.I. Lenin, Collected Works
MECW	Karl Marx and Frederick Engels, Collected Works
NAS	National Labour Secretariat (Netherlands)
OBU	One Big Union (Canada)
PSI	Italian Socialist Party
RCP	Russian Communist Party
RGASPI	Russian State Archive of Social and Political History
RILU	Red International of Labour Unions
RSFSR	Russian Soviet Federative Socialist Republic
RTUI	Red Trade Union International
SPD	Social-Democratic Party of Germany
UGT	General Union of Workers (Spain)
USI	Italian Syndicalist Union
USPD	Independent Social-Democratic Party of Germany
VKPD	United Communist Party of Germany
WIIU	Workers' International Industrial Union (USA)

 | DOI:10.1163/9789004712867_002

Proceedings of the RILU First Congress

SESSION 1. 3 JULY 1921, EVENING

Opening Session; Greetings

(*The session is opened at 8:00 p.m. Comrade Lozovsky in the chair.*)

Solomon Lozovsky: Allow me, comrades, in the name of the International Council to open the First Congress of the revolutionary unions of the world, uniting about 17 million workers in all countries organised in trade unions.

Our organisation, comrades, is still a young one. Eleven months ago the first International Council of Trade Unions was formed. It was created on the initiative of the All-Russian Central Council of Trade Unions, which disagreed entirely with the policy of the union leaders of other countries.[1] This group of revolutionary unions eleven months ago created the first nucleus, which is growing so rapidly that at the present moment there is not a single country in the world – from the nearby Western European countries down to distant Australia and New Zealand – in which workers are not only friendly to our cause, but are our fervent adherents: workers standing on our platform and leading a similar struggle in their own countries.

We see our organisation come forward as a rival competing with the Amsterdam International, which sprang up after the war in February 1919 and adopted its statutes in July 1919, and which united at that moment some 23–4 million members.[2]

We may say that these eleven months of our existence have plainly shown the vitality of the revolutionary ideas that are the basis of the Russian trade-union movement. These eleven months have proved that, with the development of the revolutionary movement in all countries and the sharpening of the class struggle, with the tremendous conflicts that arise in one country after another, the trade-union movement is widening its area of struggle and shaping itself into a revolutionary class movement.

---

1 The International Council of Trade and Industrial Unions was founded on the eve of the Comintern's Second Congress in July 1920. The process of its formation is reviewed in a report by Alfred Rosmer on pp. 60–67.

2 The 'Amsterdam International' was the commonly used name for the social-democratic-led International Federation of Trade Unions (IFTU), headquartered in Amsterdam. Formed before the war, it was reconstituted in 1919, holding its formal constituent congress in Amsterdam 28 July to 2 August 1919.

 | DOI:10.1163/9789004712867_005

We rely upon this revolutionary movement of the masses. Although this movement has not yet found its full expression and is not yet sufficiently developed, it still poses the issue sharply in a proletarian way – as for instance the miners of Britain did when they entered into battle with the entire bourgeois state. This ever-sharpening class struggle, these conflicts, the fact that the bourgeoisie is passing to the offensive – all these facts combined are the surest guarantee of the growth of our organisation, while the Amsterdam International, relying upon old theories such as class collaboration and seeking peaceful solutions of the conflict, is losing ground from day to day. In opposition to this Amsterdam International, we open our First Congress, in which we lay the foundation for a new international trade-union federation.

Our congress is a constituent one. It should indicate general outlines, develop tactics, direct the struggle, and give our activity a unified expression on the basis of our experience. It should collect from everywhere all the lessons that the revolutionary working-class struggle of many years has given us. Our congress should express these lessons in clear and definite principles, so that the revolutionary proletariat of all countries is guided by this collective experience. Our congress has a historical significance internationally, because it occurs during the transitional period from one epoch to another.

Although at the present time we are better organised than the Amsterdam International, we still have enormous difficulties to overcome. Out of the 40 million organised workers all over the world, we count in our ranks some 16–17 million. The others are partially with the Amsterdam International, while the rest have not yet attained enough understanding of the problems of the working class to join us. The misfortune of the working class is not the small number of organised workers – 40 million proletarians – but the absence of a spirit of class struggle and a will to overthrow capitalism. There is little solidarity among these 40 million proletarians; there is no unity among them. They are not sufficiently inspired by the desire to fight in order to lead the working class to victory.

Moreover, the workers' organisations and the trade unions are poorly united and contain many of our class enemies. Therein lies the great advantage of the bourgeoisie. Look around and you'll see what a solid and united front the bourgeoisie presents; how they advance against the working class in a compact phalanx. Take for instance France, Germany, Britain, and you'll see that all the elements of the bourgeoisie form a united bloc against the working class. Not only is the entire working class not united, but even in the midst of our organisations, even in our own house, we have enemies. Therein lies the strength of the bourgeoisie. It rules the working class not only through the medium of police and bayonets, not only by the militia and the army, but also by spiritual enslavement.

The teachers of this spiritual enslavement, the disseminators of bourgeois ideas among the working class, are the oldest and most prominent leaders of the labour movement. Knowing our tactics, living in the midst of the labour organisations, among our own ranks, they demoralise and disorganise the working class. The bourgeoisie and their hirelings present a united front, while the disagreements and disorganisation of the workers increases still further the power of the enemy. The labour organisations that wish to see their aims achieved must start by cleansing their ranks of traitors. Only when this is done, and when the ranks are compactly united, can labour move to a battle against capitalism.

I feel certain that in face of the great social conflict taking place, after the tremendous strikes, with millions of workers being thrown onto the street, this congress will serve as a guide for the labour movement of the entire world. We see tremendous outbursts in every country, and the time is not far off – and it depends on our activity to bring it nearer – when those separate outbursts will be transformed into a social revolution that will ultimately destroy the entire capitalist system.

Long live the revolutionary proletarian movement of the world!

Long live the world revolution of the proletariat! (*Applause*)

Lozovsky: Comrades, before we decide to grant the floor to the comrades on the speakers' list to greet us at the opening, it is necessary to elect a Presidium. The delegates recommend the following:

The International Council of Trade and Industrial Unions proposes that the Presidium consist of eleven members. To this effect, the council proposes to designate the representatives of the countries. (*The motion is accepted.*)

The Council proposes that the following countries be represented on the Presidium: America, Canada, Germany, Switzerland, Britain, Australia, South Africa, France, Belgium, Poland, Spain, the Balkan states, Russia, Ukraine, the Far Eastern Republic, Czechoslovakia, and Italy. (*The motion is accepted.*)

Comrade Lozovsky reads the list of members for the Presidium: (1) Lozovsky – Russia; (2) Rykov – Russia; (3) Knight – America, Canada; (4) Heckert – Germany, Austria, Hungary, Switzerland; (5) Tom Mann – Britain, Australia, South Africa; (6) Rosmer – France, Belgium; (7) Maciejewski – Poland; (8) Nin – Spain; (9) Pavlović – Balkan states; (10) Hampel – Czechslovakia; (11) …[3] – Italy.

We are to vote. Any objections? None.

3 Left blank in the original.

On the advice of the delegations, the following secretaries are recommended: (1) Schmidt, Kasparson, Denisov – Russian; (2) Maier, Düwell, Callam – German; (3) Godonnèche, Heuchel, Lemoine – French; (4) Howie, Pollitt, Williams[4] – English.

Editors: (1) Tsyperovich – Russian; (2) Melcher – German; (3) Godonnèche – French; (4) Ballister – English.

Credentials Commission:[5] Sergeyev, Reinstein – Russia; Watkins – Britain; Béla Szántó – Hungary; Gorbanov – Balkan states; Leval – Spain; Labonne – France.

Greetings to Congress

Wilhelm Koenen (Germany): In the name of the revolutionary proletariat,[6] I greet the congress of the Red International of Trade and Industrial Unions. With deep satisfaction and great enthusiasm, the congress of the Communist International heard the fact that our trade-union International is already 17 million strong. It is with pride that we welcome this movement of workers, who have joined with us in the great army and are ready to fight for the liberation of the proletariat. This inspiring number, even had it been a trifle smaller, is vivid proof that the Communist International is part and parcel of the council of the Red Trade and Industrial Unions. This council is the work of true revolutionary fighters. The remarkable number [of members] is striking evidence of the falsity of the claim that we're trying to provoke a split among the indifferent masses. These millions of workers have sent their delegates to the capital of the first proletarian republic in Moscow to discuss the methods and tactics that will bring unity and action.

We cannot allow ourselves to be neutral. The proletariat of all countries must lead a united class struggle; otherwise the bourgeoisie will take the opportunity of strengthening its position. We must learn to develop the class struggle in all parts of the world. We must attract and select those fighters who are in complete accord with the teaching of Marx, Engels, and Liebknecht.

It was necessary to come out against the treacherous Amsterdam International, which turned yellow, and we must continue this fight energetically. The

4 From the German, French, and Russian texts. The English lists only 'Ballister' here.

5 The list of the composition of the Credentials Commission is found only in the German text.

6 Koenen was presenting greetings from the Third Congress of the Communist International, which was meeting at the same time.

leaders of this yellow International have shaken hands with capitalism.[7] They have fooled the workers, taking bribes from capitalism. Before the war this was done on a small scale. Currently, thanks to the help of the Geneva Bureau, it is everywhere increasing.[8]

The Amsterdam International has become the centre of the typically yellow trade-union organisations. Their leaders are agents of the bourgeoisie, its servants and bloodhounds, oppressors of the proletariat. They are bribed with positions in the government, and are utilised to beat down those workers who are fighting for their freedom. To fight against such rascals and chase them away is not a split; rather, it is our first and holiest duty toward the emancipation of the entire working class. Within the Red International we unite all those who are against passivity enslaving the workers, those who are anxious to fight and are not satisfied with mere talk about fighting. The Council of the Red International aims to overcome the last bastion of capital. The capitalist class rests upon the yellow International. This is the last rampart of capitalism. The bourgeoisie long ago would have been overthrown but for those traitors. We must therefore, with the help of the Red International, organise the workers for our final inevitable victory. The Red International is convinced that we are bound to win if we have the masses on our side.

But we can hope for victory only when the Red International works in harmony with the Comintern. International capital knows the power of our unity. An example of this is shown by a telegram from Berlin that I read today. A meeting took place in Berlin of the chief of the German secret political police, Weissmann, with the heads of the political police in Britain, Switzerland, and France. They decided to persecute Communists and syndicalists; they know the danger that is threatening them, and they have joined hands. Therefore, we too are uniting all our forces to go beyond national borders for the overthrow of capitalism!

Terror is raging in all countries. In Finland, in Germany, and in Spain tens of thousands of our best fighters have been killed. We must therefore insist on the greatest international solidarity. It is important to note that the meeting in Berlin of the heads of the political police has one aim in view: to wipe

7 The word 'yellow' was a term of abuse for pro-capitalist and pro-employer forces in the workers' movement. The use of that colour to signify 'scab' began in France, where the pro-employer trade unions, first organised in 1899, took as their insignia a yellow acorn and a bush with yellow flowers.

8 A reference to the International Labour Organization, founded in 1919 as an agency of the League of Nations concerned with labour conditions, with an International Labour Office in Geneva. It is now a United Nations agency.

out the leaders of the proletariat in every country, so as to leave the great masses leaderless. We must therefore unite politically, economically, and militarily.

The world congress of the Communist International is waiting for the revolutionary fighters to recognise the necessity of political action. It is our duty to help one another at all times, and nobody has a right to stand on the sidelines. Political neutrality may become a great danger for the proletariat in the future. We must be organised economically and politically, in order to be able to forge ahead.

Some of our delegates here might say that the congress has nothing new to offer; it can only tell us the experiences of the past. This is of prime importance. We must share our experiences as revolutionary organisations; we must take advantage of the experience of other countries to find common tactics and clearly defined methods.

The trade unions are bound to come over to us. Such is the point of view of the Bureau of the Third World Congress, and of the Executive Committee of the Red Trade Unions.

Comrade Zinoviev correctly stated in his speech today that even in Russia the trade unions, notwithstanding all the efforts made to break their unity, have remained a solid organisation.[9] The important thing to note is that the political and economic elements work side by side. Trade-union unity does not mean sending representatives from one group to another; it means unity in struggle and applying uniform methods. We recognise as a necessity the unity of isolated centres, based on a common struggle.

If we organise ourselves on such a basis, we shall reach our goal – the dictatorship of the proletariat through the power of the soviets. Only on such grounds can we expect mutual understanding. The dictatorship of the proletariat and soviet power constitute precisely the central idea under which we shall conquer.

Our problem consists first in how to organise all the revolutionary elements in one body; and secondly, how to forge the best fighting weapons. The congress has seen that our Russian comrades have solved these questions. Our Russian comrades have sacrificed not tens but hundreds of thousands of lives on the altar of the world revolution.

And if today we contrast the insignificance of the work done in other countries, we must not forget that even this work is of historical value, thanks to the

9 A reference to Zinoviev's report to the Comintern's Third Congress earlier that day on the relationship of the Red International of Labour Unions to the Communist International. See Riddell (ed.) 2015, *3WC*, pp. 599–613.

Russian proletariat and its sacrifices. It has given us its blood to lead a victorious struggle for the world revolution against the bourgeoisie, against the assault on the proletariat by world capitalism. (*Vigorous applause*)

Tom Mann (Britain): Comrades: This being the first time that I've had the honour of being present at a gathering of this kind in this country, I desire that my first word shall be just to express my most sincere admiration and rejoicing at the stupendous work the Russian comrades have carried through, and to the glorious example they have set to the rest of the workers of the world. I have the honour to speak not for the British Isles only, but also America and South Africa and Australasia. I desire therefore to say that as a student of the world movement, as one who knows a little of America, most of us I think will know that there the same forces are being manifested against the workers that the older countries are familiar with.

Our comrades in America are seeking to organise their fellows and are subjected to a degree of ferocity from their government almost unprecedented. Many hundreds of them are now languishing in prison; others have literally been done to death for no alleged crime other than that of endeavouring to educate and organise the workers. Among those who have been subjected to the harshest treatment are some who are in this congress tonight, and included in these is Comrade William D. Haywood, a glorious and stalwart old comrade whom we are glad to see here, I am quite sure.[10] They have immense resources there. They are declared to be democratic by a very large percentage of workmen in other countries, but the plutocracy dominates there in every part.

In the still younger countries of Australia and New Zealand and South Africa, there also plutocracy dominates the government and there also the plutocrats are using all the forces at their disposal to destroy the working-class advance.

In South Africa they are endeavouring to educate the workers, men who are facing this situation and accepting the greatest sacrifices. They are confronted there, too, with the violence of the government. Deportation and imprisonment have been given to many of them. There are delegates here from South

10 William 'Big Bill' Haywood was a founding leader of the Industrial Workers of the World (IWW). Convicted and sentenced to twenty years' imprisonment in 1918 as part of a mass trial of IWW members, Haywood had been out on bail since July 1919 as his case was being appealed. Faced with the likelihood of returning to prison, Haywood jumped bail and went to the Soviet Union, arriving in April 1921. Among his fellow defendants in the same trial were Leo Laukki (Tiura) and George Andreytchine, who also jumped bail and attended the RILU congress.

Africa and from Australia, and these, with the Americans and with the Britishers, unite in one common aspiration for the overthrow of the capitalist system that we are suffering under.

Speaking for the British Isles, I regret very much that there is not a larger delegation from that country. We all do. But it must not be supposed that no work is being done there of a revolutionary character. The work of organisation has received and is receiving attention. Not merely the organisation of the workers industrially, but also the educational work is being carried on systematically to encourage the workers to take their eyes entirely away from relying upon the capitalist institutions. A considerable and growing percentage have already declared definitely, with full knowledge of what they are declaring, in favour of the entire overthrow of the capitalist system and the undertaking, on the part of themselves as workers, of the entire organisation, management, and in every direction complete control of production and industry. This they have declared to be their objective. They are working for it, and I am sure they will achieve it.

It is permissible for me briefly to refer to England. There are seven and a half millions organised in the trade unions of Great Britain. Amongst these are many reactionaries, as is the case in all countries – at least in most. But amongst them also is a very considerable percentage, not yet equal to dominating the unions, but a rapidly growing percentage of class-conscious workers aiming at and working for the overthrow of capitalism and the bringing of a true communist condition into society.

As one of those who has had the privilege for a number of years of endeavouring to organise, endeavouring to educate, and endeavouring to inspire my fellow workers, I rejoice that before I take my departure I have had the privilege of being present in a country that has dared to achieve and has accomplished so much, that deserves our thanks, our admiration, and our imitation.

I can assure you all, whether you doubt it or not, it is the case that the big unions in the country to which I refer – for instance the union of which I am a member, known as the Amalgamated Engineering Union – there is a rapidly growing section of truly class-conscious workers prepared to face any risk, to pay any sacrifice, who know that they have a great work to achieve to affect the vast mass. That vast mass is nevertheless being affected.

But you are aware undoubtedly that we are very respectable people in England, and there is an immense amount of rotten hypocrisy there. We are fully conscious of it. We are ashamed of it. We wish it were not so. Nevertheless, that it is hypocrisy is understood by a good 20 per cent of the workers. We see through it clearly. We are ashamed and disgusted with it. We regret exceedingly that so many of the members of the trade unions who have organised well numerically and are able to make a good stand on certain lines still kowtow to the authorities, still work hand in glove with the plutocracy, still look upon and seek to worship at the shrine of Parliament, hoping to get honours from the government. That they should be so is of course pitiful, but all peoples must travel stage by stage, and the British people are travelling. You will not be without us in the future, I can assure you, as one who knows the movement intimately and knows almost every section with a degree of intimacy I am sure you would count satisfactory. I solemnly declare to you that you may rely upon the rapid growth of the red trade-union principle there. It is working in all organisations and will switch all the big unions from their reliance upon the orthodox position they now occupy. This I am sure will be the case.

I am glad to be here, and in the name of the comrades who sent me and of the many others who would have gladly been responsible for sending more, I congratulate the revolutionary work that is being done here and those who are doing it. We will imitate it and endeavour to be equal to you in a very short time.

Let one reference be made to the miners. A million miners, organised to 100 per cent, confronted with the government and the whole of the plutocracy, fought with a degree of solidarity that was wonderful against immense powers against them. I am glad, and I am sure many of you are glad, that this million men remained solid to the end and continued the fight for thirteen long weeks, and that at the finish they were entirely solid and agreed as to what was the proper course and attitude. Had we had more solidarity, had the transport workers, after having promised, been equal to the occasion, there is no knowing how far we might have carried the situation.[11] It is only waiting, however, until more educational work is done, until more advanced methods are proceeded with. These are going on, and the result will be not merely solidarity on the part of the rank and file at the time, but achieving its true aim.

While we have had a million miners out, we are now confronted with another struggle in industry, in engineering and shipbuilding, where there are at

11 A reference to the 1921 British miners' strike. The struggle began when coal owners locked out miners following expiration of a temporary wage agreement on 31 March. Some 1.2 million miners turned the lockout into a strike to protest the owners' planned wage cuts and extended working hours. Authorities responded by declaring a state of emergency, moving police and the army into the coalfields. Leaders of the transport and rail workers' unions promised solidarity strike action. But in a move widely seen as a betrayal, on 15 April ('Black Friday') the leader of these unions called off the scheduled solidarity strike, leaving the miners in the lurch. The strike lasted until 29 June.

See the appeal, 'To the Workers of the United Kingdom' on pp. 669–70.

least a million and a half men directly affected.[12] These are now to be fought by the government and the employing classes. I believe this congress will send them its good will and encourage them to go on with their fight, and the result will be an exhibition of solidarity on an unprecedented scale.

I thank the comrades who are here from the various countries, and from Russia in particular. I express again my pleasure at being here to participate in some small way in the proceedings, and I rejoice again that we can meet here, where the world revolution has begun, and from which its progress will go on to the worldwide revolution which we hope for, aim for, and aspire to.

Henri Sirolle (France): Comrades, the French delegation is bringing to the congress opening the fraternal greetings of the revolutionary working class of our country. Comrades, this first constituent congress of the united trade-union International is of considerable historical importance. The French delegation, true to the principles of French syndicalism, its original features, traditions, conceptions, and the aims it pursues, asks all the members of this congress to show the necessary tolerance during our debates.

If we really seek to give the trade-union International its importance, broaden its activity, and grant it the opportunity to widen its scope, one must understand that today, at a time when all the capitalist countries are going through a sharp economic crisis, the working masses – the producers of wealth – close ranks and organise themselves instinctively into international units that build the natural basis of life in every country. The powerful development of union organisations destroys one by one, day after day, the narrow framework of craft unionism and enters more and more into the social field.

It is essential that our trade-union International be guided by these principles and aims in order to create an organisation that can allow the working masses of all countries to obtain a real life, and so that the world revolution leads to the worker, as producer of all riches, being the forebear and pioneer of the ideals of the future society.

The French delegation, in conformity with the mandates it has and the syndicalist spirit guiding it, will defend such a viewpoint at this congress, which will meet objections from a large number of countries.

The French delegation believes that syndicalism, thanks to the forms of its organisation and its administrative machinery and owing to its structure based on the territorial principle, is qualified – immediately if necessary, by means

12 In March 1921 British employers made clear their intentions to cut wages of workers in the engineering and shipbuilding industry, together with wholesale attacks on working conditions. This offensive ultimately led to the engineering lockout of March–June 1922.

of industrial federations and local unions – to establish proletarian rule in our country, where union organisation would direct the destiny of the country, and enable it to direct all its forces for further development.

The view that we intend to develop, which we will attempt to obtain approval of, must be understood in the broadest sense if we really wish to realise a united front in our struggle against the capitalist classes, to carry out that unity on the trade-union level, if we wish to have our trade-union International be independent and autonomous, free from any outside influences. But the life of the Red Trade Union International must be real. Here at the opening of the congress we are willing to thoroughly discuss the question. For this it is essential that each national movement and each delegation spell out its position and ideology.

If we are anxious that the working masses should realise unlimited power, if we desire to impress upon the workers the revolutionary significance of the industrial process, we must build our Red Labour International on a solid foundation. In order to add strength and power to our work, we would ask the delegates of the congress to realise that a true united front of the workers of the world will be reached not by empty words and phrases, but through hard, diligent labour in the field of work and production – in a word, in the heart of the Red Labour International.

Lozovsky: The floor is given to Comrade Rykov on behalf of the All-Russian Trade Union Council and other trade-union organisations of the countries federated with Russia.

Alexei Rykov (Russia): Comrades, I have the honour to greet the First International Congress of Red Trade Unions. This greeting is especially dear to us Russian trade unionists at the present moment, when the international labour movement is entering the revolutionary arena. Thanks to the revolutionary traditions of our working class and our programme and tactics, we have succeeded in overthrowing capitalist rule. I must tell you, however, that we can reap the benefit of our victory and bring the Russian Revolution to a conclusion only when the workers of the entire world come to our aid.

The problem of the Russian trade-union movement differs in a certain degree from the movements in Western Europe and America. We at present are more occupied with the problems of economic and industrial reorganisation. Only to a small extent can we compare our fight to yours, since ours is to protect the workers against the restoration of bourgeois power. On this field we have met with gigantic difficulties. The main reason for our failure in the past, and which might also affect us in the future, is the small number of workers in Russia compared to the other classes. The number is too small to be able to attain the highest possible results in the industrial field and to realise the final victory of our programme.

The other obstacle has been the international blockade of Soviet Russia and the long-drawn-out civil war.

We were glad to receive the help extended us by the workers and trade-union movement in our defence against the combined might of capital of the entire world, but such help is not quite sufficient for the task that is before us. I have already pointed out the goal and aims of the Russian movement. Our goal is the international revolution. We consider the October Revolution as the introduction to the world revolution. We are convinced that the only guarantee against our foes would be an international revolution on the widest possible scale. It is up to us to help organise the revolutionary workers in Western Europe and America. I again repeat that our success depends upon the revolutionary forces of the West. The revolution that started here must not stop until it reaches Paris and London.

You will notice that at the present moment capital, not only in Russia but throughout the entire world, stands united against the divided and disorganised working class. This has been and still is the weak point in the international revolutionary movement. By looking at the labour movement of the world, we cannot see a single nation or country, scarcely a single city, where strikes and clashes between employers and employees have not recently occurred and are still going on. While groups, factions, and individual nations keep on fighting, capital is united and delivers blow after blow against the millions of members of the working-class army.

This congress is of great importance, for unless the working class is firmly organised, united, and well-disciplined, defeats similar to those sustained by our British comrades are unavoidable. The unheard-of heroism of over a million striking coal miners in Britain for a period of three months has been entirely ignored by the rest of the workers of Britain. Such narrowness and self-interest is the cursed result of the capitalist era. Without a bitter fight against this narrow horizon, against this idea of class collaboration, against Amsterdam, we cannot hope for a final, decisive victory. The most important problem at present is international unity and solidarity. We have a League of Nations that is an international organisation of capital. Affiliated with it is the Amsterdam International. So here we have a working class that is being attacked by an enemy well organised internationally, while our forces are divided into separate national groups. The most important work of this congress is forming a power to oppose the yellow International, fully equipped for revolutionary action.

Max Hausding (Germany): I am directed to greet the First Congress of the Red International of Trade Unions on behalf of the workers of Germany, Austria, and Switzerland.

The workers of the world are watching this First Congress of the Red International with the keenest interest.

In receiving the invitation of the Russian comrades to attend the congress, we were glad to learn that you have succeeded in overcoming the difficulties that were in the way of arranging the present congress. We appreciate the task of the Russian comrades and offer our hearty thanks.

This congress is quite different from previous international congresses, as we have now not only trade-union officials here, but also rank-and-file members who are directly connected with the shops and factories, and who are therefore in a position to decide what forms of organisations are to be founded and what tactics are to be employed in this final struggle with capitalism.

The Red International of Trade Unions has issued an appeal to the leaders of the conservative trade unions of the Amsterdam International, but the yellow leaders have declined to attend the First Congress, for they fear the judgement of the working class that this congress would issue. They have also forbidden their members from being delegates to this congress, under threat of expulsion. Still, they have not succeeded in preventing the workers from sending their representatives to Moscow. The miserable role these 'revolutionary leaders' have played during the period of the war and the revolution is quite clear to everyone. The number of workers who are renouncing their counterrevolutionary trade-union bureaucrats grows day by day in order to unite with us under the banner of the Red International of Trade Unions.

If the German workers' revolution is not making as much progress and is not going at the speed we wish it to, the explanation can only be that the crisis of German capitalism is not so much a catastrophic one as a prolonged one. The slow process of decay of the capitalist order, the closing of factories and reducing the workday multiplies day by day the number of unemployed workers, who fall victim to the capitalist disorder; their number is now in the millions. The bourgeois lieutenants have so far succeeded in holding the workers back from the revolutionary struggle. But even those working who are not on the front lines with us are clamouring for the fulfilment of the promises made. Our problem was – and still remains for the future – to convince the workers that they cannot better their conditions under capitalist rule, and that they must fight to overthrow the old order.

This sort of work has not been unsuccessful. We may say that we have on our side three million – one-third of all the organised proletariat of the old unions.

The work ahead of us is complicated and hard. Our victory will be the more triumphant.

We, the opponents of Amsterdam in Germany, are not welded together in a single organised body; some problems of tactics still divide us. This congress must find a basis to form a solid front in order to defeat our common enemy, and it will be found.

We are fully convinced that the trade unions alone are not able to defeat world capitalism. In order to do so, we must all get together, hand in hand, shoulder to shoulder, together with the Communists.

If the congress will find the basis to unite all trade unions into one solid front, then we may be fully convinced that the trade unions, in conjunction with the Third International and the Communists, will defeat capitalism and world imperialism.

Our objective is to overthrow the old system of society and to create the new order of communist society. (*Applause*)

Lozovsky: Comrades, the greetings are ended. A motion is made to accept the agenda, the rules and procedure of the congress, election of the Credentials Commission, and to discuss a few other questions that confront us.

The agenda is as follows:

1. The report of the International Council of the Red Trade and Industrial Unions, by Comrade Rosmer.
2. The world economic crisis; problems and policies of the trade unions, by Comrades Bukharin and Lozovsky.
3. Trade unions and parties; the Red International of Labour Unions and the Communist International, by Comrades Zinoviev and Rosmer.
4. Trade unions and factory committees, by Comrade Heckert.
5. Trade unions and workers' control over production, by Tsyperovich.
6. Unemployment, by Comrade Bell.
7. The international trade and industrial affiliations (the reporter is not indicated).
8. The organisation question, by Comrade Lozovsky.
9. Elections.

(*The agenda is approved.*)

Hilario Arlandis (Spain): Comrades, for the last two years the Spanish proletariat has suffered terribly under the boot of capitalist and militarist reaction. For the last two years it has suffered torture, deportation, and imprisonment. Hundreds and thousands of our militants have been killed in the factories, cafes, on the streets, and as they were leaving prison. These crimes are being systematically committed by the government through its representatives: the white guards, the police, and militia. We do not enjoy freedom of assembly; our press is suspended; freedom of opinion no longer exists; we cannot develop our activities. Such are the conditions under which we are greeting the Russian Revolution in the name of the Spanish proletariat.

In affirming our solidarity with the Russian and world revolution, we are not just repeating words of sympathy for Russia; rather, we are taking part in revolutionary action. Although the working people in Spain are being jailed, although we are being killed, still we are continuing our fight against the state and capitalism. It will comfort those who are dying for the movement to know that the general staff of world revolutionary unionism, gathered here in Moscow at its First Congress, is calling on them to continue their struggle for the final victory over capitalism.

(*An Appeal to the Spanish Proletariat is then read signed by the congress Presidium: Lozovsky, Rykov, Heckert, Knight, Mann, Nin, Hampel, Pavlović, and Maciejewski. For the text of this appeal, see page 671.*)

Lozovsky: Is anyone opposed to the appeal that was read out? No. Approved.

Comrades, the working class is suffering not only in Spain, but also in all other bourgeois countries. The workers in Hungary, as well as in Latvia, are pursued with particular cruelty. We are also aware of the current events in Italy. There is no bourgeois country at all in which the blood of the proletariat is not being spilled. I therefore think it will be useful, comrades, if we decide to instruct the Presidium to make a call to all countries on behalf of our congress, in addition to issuing a protest about the victims of this bourgeois terror.[13] (*Applause*).

I suggest not only drafting a call against white terror, but instructing the bureau to issue a manifesto on behalf of the unions to workers around the world, calling for the unconditional struggle against international world imperialism.

Now comrades, on the further work of the congress, we propose that tomorrow morning the Credentials Commission meet and finish its work.

The day after tomorrow at 10:30 a.m., the second session of the congress will take place, starting with reports of the trade-union council. The meeting will take place in the Blue Room.

(*Adjourned at 12:30 a.m.*)

13 For the text of the appeal against white terror, see pp. 664–8.

Congress Organisation; Work of International Council

(*The session is opened at 8:00 p.m. Comrade Lozovsky presiding.*)

Lozovsky: Before we take up the agenda for the session, I am instructed by the Presidium to make the following motion regarding the formation of commissions. We have three commissions: on the questions of organisation, on tactics, and on workers' control. The Presidium moves that commissions be organised as follows: countries having 16 votes – four members; countries having 12 votes – three members; countries having 8 votes – two members; countries having 4 votes – one member.

Comrades should hand over to the Presidium a list of each group, beginning tomorrow morning, when the commissions will start working. Is there any objection to the motion of the Presidium? No objections.

Comrade Lemoine will now speak on a point of order.

Albert Lemoine (France): A number of delegates of this congress consider the personnel of the Presidium as not entirely correct. Those who want to protest are not present.

Lozovsky: Owing to the absence of these delegates, I move that this be tabled.

I will take up the next question we have to decide upon. Our congress, as the first of its kind, consists of representatives of entire organisations, of minority representatives [within unions and federations], and of those representing separate groups in the labour movement of different countries. Therefore, this congress cannot be considered as having a sound basis for normal representation. Wherever all the national unions are represented, it is easier to form a basis for representation. Here we have certain countries that are fully represented; others have only a representation of 1/10, others 1/50 – we have thus many different representations.

On this account it is difficult to come up with a normal representation and to fix the basis of voting. The council decided before the opening of the congress to instruct a committee of six members to work out a representation plan. The system of representation has already been discussed.

 | DOI:10.1163/9789004712867_006

(*After a very brief discussion, the following formula on distribution of votes was accepted.*)

1. All countries are to be divided into four groups, corresponding to the size and importance of the country and of the trade-union movement in it.
2. Each country of the first group obtains 16 votes; the second group has 12 votes; the third group has 8 votes; the fourth group has 4 votes.
3. If there is more than one trade-union organisation in a given country, the total number of votes of the country must be divided among them, based on the mutual agreement of the delegates from each organisation.
4. In case they fail to come to an amicable agreement, the votes are to be divided among the different contending organisations by the Credentials Commission, in accordance with the size and importance of each organisation.
5. In the event an organisation is not satisfied with the decision of the Credentials Commission, it may, within two days after the decision is rendered, present, through the general secretary of the RTUI, a written appeal to the latter's executive bureau. The decision of the bureau is to be final and binding.
6. The delegations to the congress of the Third, Communist International from countries that have no delegates or fraternal delegates to the congress of the RTUI may select from their midst a representative to the congress of the RTUI as a fraternal delegate.
7. The countries are to be grouped as follows:

Group 1 – 16 votes each: Germany, France, Britain, Russia, United States, Italy, Spain, Poland and Eastern Galicia, Czechoslovakia.

Group 2 – 12 votes each: Austria, Hungary, Bulgaria, Yugoslavia, Ukraine, Norway, Australia, Argentina.

Group 3 – 8 votes each: Belgium, Holland, Switzerland, Romania, Ireland, Canada, Mexico, Greece, Sweden, Denmark, Finland, Far Eastern Republic, Azerbaijan.

Group 4 – 4 votes each: all other countries.

The arrangement into four groups is agreed upon without discussion.

Béla Szántó (Hungary), on the question of supplementary votes, speaks in favour of such votes. We must plainly say that in the distribution of votes it is necessary to give Russia a greater preponderance than, say, to Britain, where the number of adherents of the Red International of Trade Unions is quite insignificant.

Joseph Tommasi (France) argues against, due to the difficulty of establishing the exact number of organised workers represented by each delegation.

Ivan Perepechko (Russia) proposes not to go into detailed discussion on this question at the present time, but to make every effort so that at future congresses the principle of proportional representation is obligatory. (*The motion of the Russian delegation is carried.*)

Arthur Bartels (Germany) and **Albert Lemoine** (France), seconded by the British delegation, propose the following amendment to point 5 of the plan: 'In cases where no agreement could be reached by the delegations of the different countries as to the distribution of votes between the representatives of different organisations, the final decision upon the point under debate is to be given by the congress and not by its Presidium.'

(*The amendment is carried without discussion. No other objections or amendments being offered, the motion of the committee with the Bartels-Lemoine amendment is carried.*)

Lozovsky: The floor is given to Comrade Rosmer for his report on the activity of the Provisional International Council of Trade and Industrial Unions.

Work of the Provisional International Council

Alfred Rosmer: Comrades! It is today exactly one year since, on these same premises – only in the large hall, where we met last Sunday – Comrade Lozovsky announced to the workers of Moscow the creation of the International Council of Red Trade Unions. The endeavour might have appeared a rather bold one. The declaration that was the first foundation of the council may seemingly not have had a sufficient basis, since none of the big countries were represented, except for Russia and Italy. What I mean is that none of them could present the formal affiliation of their labour organisations. I must add, however, that our comrade [Ángel] Pestaña came here in order to participate in the work of the Second Congress of the Communist International, and that the organisation he represented [the CNT of Spain] joined the Third International even before there was any question of creating either a trade-union section of the Communist International or a trade-union International. Comrade Pestaña can legitimately be considered, under the circumstances, as the representative of his organisation.

In spite of everything, the list of signatures may have appeared small, but all who participated in the preparatory work shared the conviction that in a short time, as soon as the information from Russia reached other Western nations, the appeal would be immediately responded to, and that the number of organisations that affiliated to the International Council of Trade Unions would be significant enough to constitute the nucleus of an International of revolutionary trade unions.

Before considering the nature of the work performed during the last year by the provisional council that was elected here, I should like to recall the conditions under which it was formed, how it originated, and where the idea of an International of Red Trade Unions came from. It does not date by any means, as one might believe, from the Second Congress of the Communist International. The idea sprang from within the trade unions themselves. Already on the long-ago date of 28 June 1917, under Kerensky's regime, the Third Conference of Russian Trade Unions recognised the need to form an international organisation of trade unions.[1]

Several months later, this idea was taken up at the First Congress of Russian Trade Unions, which crystallised the rather vague notions formulated at the earlier conference of trade unions, and whose resolution upon the tasks of trade unions during the period of the dictatorship of the proletariat reads as follows:

> The Russian trade-union movement cannot carry out its tasks without getting in close touch with the international trade-union movement. The congress deems it its duty to cooperate in the revival of the international trade-union movement, and to raise the question of the calling of an international congress of trade unions as an immediate question. In order to indicate the first steps to be taken in this direction, the congress decides to convene an international congress of trade unions in Petrograd on 5 February 1918.[2]

Our Russian comrades showed the same spirit of enterprise and audacity under these circumstances as they did in many other circumstances. On 5 February 1918 the imperialist war was still raging, the working masses and soldiers were still too intoxicated with war chauvinism, and could not even think of responding in their countries to the idea of organising a trade-union Interna-

---

1 The Third Russian Trade Union Conference was held in Petrograd 3–11 July 1917 (20–28 June in the old-style calendar).

2 The First All-Russian Congress of Trade Unions met in Petrograd 20–27 January 1918 (7–14 January old style). The text of the resolution it adopted set the date for the international conference as 15 (not 5) February; that conference never took place.

tional and taking part in the congress. The idea naturally slumbered for long months, and our Russian comrades were outdistanced by the leaders of the old trade unions, who were able to reconstruct the former pre-war trade-union International.[3] Yet even prior to the above enterprise, they went to Washington where, in contact with the League of Nations, they organised an International Labour Bureau, which had been stipulated by the Versailles Treaty.[4] All these old-time leaders of the old trade unions, who had disgraced themselves during the war, got the organisation of a trade-union International under way before the revolutionists were able to do the same.

Not only did they have the opportunity to do this, but they carried it out in a double form: the International Labour Bureau and later the International Federation of Trade Unions. These are in fact twin organisations, though naturally of different compositions. But the personnel is the same, and consists of the same delegates found at both the Washington Conference and at Geneva.[5] We fight them again in the Amsterdam International Federation. Not only are these organisations identically constituted, but the same policy and spirit guides them and determines the actions of both organisations.

The ideas that had germinated within the Russian labour organisations could not be converted into action immediately, but our Russian comrades never thought of abandoning their plans. They even sought, at a moment when postal communications between Russia and Western Europe were almost completely interrupted, to avail themselves of every opportunity to inform us of their plans and goals, and at last succeeded in reaching France. We were able to publicise these ideas to some extent, and naturally they met with a favourable response. Yet even then there was a long delay before the idea of an International of Revolutionary Trade Unions – for which Comrade Lozovsky worked tenaciously – could even begin to be realised.

Even though communications were difficult, a favourable opportunity presented itself last June, when it just so happened that two delegations were

3 A conference of social-democratic trade-union leaders took place 5–9 February 1919 in Bern, Switzerland. The meeting was a forerunner of what became the Amsterdam International; it occurred alongside the better-known Bern conference of social-democratic parties that reconstituted the Second International.

4 A reference to the 29 October–29 November 1919 Washington Conference of the International Labour Organisation, which was set up by the League of Nations. Attended by government representatives and leaders of the Amsterdam International, the meeting formulated draft conventions on the eight-hour day, unemployment, employment of women and children, and workers' safety. The Amsterdam leaders hailed the conference as a victory for organised labour.

5 Geneva was the seat of the International Labour Office.

present at the same time: the British labour delegation and one from Italy. In terms of composition, the revolutionary elements constituted a very small minority of these delegations. The Italians in those days were considered to be in the vanguard of the Socialist parties in the West, but their delegation was composed in such a way that the truly revolutionary elements were in a small minority. As for the rest of them, through the interviews and articles they contributed to bourgeois magazines and in the books that were published, one could see that the delegation contained a great number of counterrevolutionaries. As for the British delegation, we were not surprised, as we knew full well that official Labour circles were in large part composed of pure-and-simple trade unionists, i.e., narrow-minded people moving within strictly trade-union boundaries.

Russia opened its doors wide to these delegations. The Bolsheviks had been accused of not showing Soviet Russia in its true aspect, and they answered the accusation by granting the two missions free travel in Russia, although it was well known that most of them would not leave Soviet Russia with the intention of singing the praises of either the Bolsheviks or Soviet Russia.

But the British delegation contained two men – Purcell and Robert Williams – who, prior to the war, belonged to the better part of British trade unionism. The Russian comrades therefore availed themselves of the presence of these two in order to invite them to a joint session with members of the Italian mission.

At a first meeting, convened in Moscow on 16 June at the initiative of the Third International, we met the two members just mentioned, Purcell and Williams. Williams was secretary of the Transport Workers' Federation, although he was there in a personal capacity. Purcell participated in the meeting on the same basis. For Italy, D'Aragona and Bianchi represented the CGL; Colombino came from the Federation of Metal Workers and Dugoni from the Federation of Agricultural Workers. As for Russia, from the trade-union federation there were Lozovsky, Tomsky, Tsyperovich, and Schmidt; also Comrade Zinoviev, the president of the Third International's Executive Committee. The initiative for the meeting came from the Executive Committee of the Communist International.[6]

The theses on the trade-union question taken up at the Second Congress [of the Comintern] discussed the creation of a trade-union International. This explains why the initiative to create the International of Red Trade Unions did not come from the Russian trade unions but rather from the Communist

6 For the minutes of the 16 June 1920 meeting, see the Appendix, pp. 674–8.

International's Executive Committee. Advantage was taken of the presence in Moscow of the representatives of the working class in order to meet and discuss with them the question of the International of Red Trade Unions. At this 16 June meeting – at which British, Italians, and Russians had the opportunity to exchange views regarding the constitution of the Red International, as well as its aims and purposes, its composition and tasks – Comrade Zinoviev made an initial proposal that was discussed; some parts of it were accepted, while others were rejected. Finally the following motion by Comrade Williams was adopted:

> The present private conference of the revolutionary leaders of the militant trade-union movement of Great Britain, Russia, and Italy, recognising that the existing trade-union International is incapable of directing and controlling the class struggle and crushing the international bourgeoisie through the dictatorship of the proletariat, resolves to convene a more complete and representative conference of revolutionary trade unions for the establishment of a true trade-union International free from any connection whatsoever with the capitalistic League of Nations and with the so-called leaders of the labour movement who have acted the part of social patriots and chauvinists during the World War, and continue to maintain the same policy up till the present time.

That was the resolution that ended the first important meeting held with regard to the creation of the trade-union International.

The British comrades who attended the conference were obliged to leave Russia almost immediately; the Italians stayed in Moscow and, notwithstanding Williams's and Purcell's departure, the negotiations proceeded. Other delegates had by this time arrived. Williams and Purcell had left a large number of mandates permitting them to use their signatures for an appeal and a call to a congress. There were at that time other British comrades, representatives of the Shop Stewards' and Workers' Committees. There was a representative of the German syndicalists and members of the American and Australian IWW. In short, it was thus possible to discuss with representatives from all organised tendencies the question of creating a Red Trade Union International.

Many meetings were held and we had heated discussions, but I do not think it necessary to go into details, because the same discussion will be renewed here at this congress on an even larger scale.

During those conferences we could not reach complete agreement with all the participants, but seven of the comrades sat down together and issued and signed the declaration of principles, thus constituting the International Council of Red Trade and Industrial Unions. Here is the text:

> Whereas the conditions of proletarians in all countries resulting from the imperialist war demand with every day a clearer and more energetic class struggle to put a definitive end to capitalist exploitation and to establish a communist system;
>
> Whereas such a struggle must be conducted on an international scale through the very closest unity of all workers, united not by individual craft but by industry;
>
> Whereas so-called social reforms – for example, reduction of the working day, an increase in wages, regulating the conditions of labour, and so on – may under certain circumstances alleviate the class struggle but are in themselves unable to resolve the social question;
>
> Whereas during the dark years of the war, in most countries that took part in it, most of the unions that had supported neutralism (non-political unions) became servants of imperialist capitalism, playing a fateful role in delaying the final liberation of the working people;
>
> Whereas the primary responsibility of the working class is to gather all organised union forces into a powerful revolutionary class association, which, working side by side with the political organisation of the international communist proletariat and in close connection with it, would be able to develop all its forces for the final victory of the socialist revolution, for the establishment of the world republic of soviets;
>
> Whereas the ruling classes use all their forces and take every measure to suffocate the liberation movement of the exploited;
>
> Whereas to the dictatorship of the bourgeoisie it is necessary to counterpose the dictatorship of the proletariat, as a decisive transitional instrument that alone is capable of suppressing the resistance of the exploiters and ensuring and consolidating the achievements of proletarian power;
>
> Whereas the Amsterdam International Federation of Trade Unions is incapable in its programme and its tactics of achieving the triumph of these principles and ensuring the victory of the proletarian masses in all countries;
>
> The undersigned representatives of trade unions of Russia, Italy, Spain, France, Bulgaria, Serbia, and Georgia, convened by the Executive Committee of the Third International, resolve:
>
> 1. To condemn the policy of withdrawing the advanced revolutionary forces from the existing unions. These forces must, on the contrary,

take every measure to expel the opportunists from the unions. The opportunists have collaborated and are collaborating even now with the bourgeoisie by accepting the imperialist war. They continue to serve the interests of capitalist imperialism by participating in the deceitful activity of the League of Nations;

2. To conduct methodical communist propaganda inside these unions around the world, creating in every organisation Communist and revolutionary cells for propaganda and to affirm our programme;
3. To create a committee of action and organise an international struggle for the transformation of the trade-union movement along these lines. This committee functions as an *International Council of Trade and Industrial Unions*, working in accord with the Executive Committee of the Third International under conditions to be determined by congresses. All trade and industrial workers' organisations that join the council must be represented in it. One representative of the International Council of Trade Unions must be included on the Executive Committee of the Third International, and vice versa.

S. Lozovsky, All-Russian Council of Trade Unions
L. D'Aragona, Italian General Confederation of Labour
A. Pestaña, Spanish National Confederation of Labour
N. Shablin, Central Trade Unions of Bulgaria
A. Rosmer, Revolutionary Syndicalist Minority of France
Mikadze, Communist Minority of Georgian Trade Unions
Milkić, for General Labour Confederation of Yugoslavia

I have described the condition under which the text of the declaration was adopted. I have also stated that at the time there were other comrades in Moscow, who, for different reasons, did not want to sign the manifesto – some because the declaration was entirely unsatisfactory to them, others because they had some criticism on one point or another. It was stipulated, however, that the text would in no way be binding upon the organisations that agreed to participate in the First International Trade Union Congress. In other words, it was clearly specified that the comrades who constituted the first council considered their most essential task to be preparation and convocation of the congress, whose sole purpose would be the definitive creation of the trade-union International. But it was also considered useful to outline the essential principles on which agreement could be reached by all the revolutionary trade unionists who are against Amsterdam. But opposition to Amsterdam, while important, is not enough for the creation of a trade-union International. The basic principles of the Red Trade Union International were presented in the theses.

Initially the declaration was signed by seven comrades. All the comrades present in Moscow gave their support to the council, even those who were the most intransigent, for instance the German syndicalist [Augustin] Souchy, who at that time gave his adherence to the International Trade Union Council and helped prepare the appeal to the workers of Germany.

The first task of the council consisted in informing the workers of the Western nations of the creation of the International Trade Union Council. Special appeals were issued to the workers of each country. Having done this, the council proceeded with the systematic organisation of its work.

It had a double role. On one hand it had to inform Russian workers about the international workers' movement. On the other hand, it had to establish connections between the International Council and the trade unions of all countries in Europe and America, with the purpose of preparing for the international congress.

For the purpose of informing the Russian workers, the council established different work sections, which regularly gathered the most important items of the international working-class movement and published them in a monthly bulletin.

For the information of the comrades of other countries we issued pamphlets and a journal, the fifth issue of which is now appearing in Russia,[7] but we had no means as yet to publish rapidly in other languages. We had many difficulties in publishing the review, and the five issues that appeared did not reach the proper destinations.

But we had still another means to make known the existence of the International Trade Union Council: directly engaging in the struggle against the Amsterdam International and its followers. Last September a delegation left Russia for Britain, seeking to return the visit made by the British labour leaders who had come to Soviet Russia. But the government of Lloyd George, which had consented to the admission of the Russian delegation, refused them permission to enter Britain while they were en route. Being refused admission to Britain, they headed to Germany, which pretends to be a free country. Germany let them in, and Comrade Lozovsky, who was in the delegation, immediately proceeded with active propaganda.

7 The journal referred to was *Mezhdunarodnoe Rabochee Dvizhenie* (International Workers' Movement).

In Scandinavia a pamphlet had already been published about the formation of the International Council of Red Trade Unions, and, once in Germany, they had the possibility to publish pamphlets and call meetings. They got in direct contact with the German workers, mainly in Berlin, and the attack on the Amsterdam Federation at the Halle Congress brought a strong reaction.[8] The old trade unions during and after the war grew tremendously. Not only the members of the old party – the Majority Socialists [SPD] – protested with indignation. But even the more advanced elements – the Independents [USPD], who succeeded in dislodging the majority leaders in some unions – also protested with vehemence against the intrusion of the Russian comrades in their trade-union politics. At the Halle Congress Comrade Lozovsky raised a storm of protest by his attack on the Amsterdam International, and the extreme right wing of the Independents even went so far as to make it impossible for him to finish his speech.[9]

At the close of the Russian mission in Germany, a deep impression had been left on the labour movement. The Russian comrades did their best there to agitate by speech and in writing, which the comrades made full use of, and the debate continued everywhere. Later on, the propaganda was systematically organised, but then the struggle started; a breach was made. Since then revolutionary ideas have entered the old trade unions, which up to the present day are still a pillar of Social Democracy and its successive German governments, coloured with different political shadings.

On the work being accomplished in foreign countries, the delegates will receive a special report prepared by the service of the International Council of Trade Unions, where they will find complete information.

Fernand Loriot (France): Will you allow me one word? It seems to me that the report has some shortcomings. Rosmer spoke of the activity of the Rus-

---

8 The Halle Congress of the Independent Social-Democratic Party of Germany (USPD) was held 12–17 October 1920. At the congress, the majority voted to join the Comintern and fuse with KPD, resulting in formation of United Communist Party of Germany (VKPD). The minority split off and retained the USPD name. Lozovsky attended and spoke at the congress, together with Zinoviev, for the Comintern Executive Committee.

9 Following Lozovsky's speech at the Halle USPD congress, there was 'a temporary adjournment in order to ascertain whether Lozovsky had "insulted" the German trade union movement', followed by a series of personal declarations. See Lewis and Lih 2011, p. 31; and Tosstorff 2016, p. 190.

Lozovsky's speech was published in German as *Moskau oder Amsterdam? Rede des Genossen A. Losowsky/Moskau, gehalten auf dem Parteitag der USPD in Halle, Oktober 1920* (Leipzig: Frankes Verlag, 1920).

sian delegation in the old trade unions. Did not the delegation meet with any opposition outside the unions, in other working-class organisations? And if so, what did it consist of?

Lozovsky: I'll answer this question after the report of Comrade Rosmer.

Rosmer (*continues*): I must state that the tolerance of the German government very soon reached its climax, and finally, after the Halle Congress, Comrade Lozovsky was deported.

Concerning the propaganda activities in different countries, I must dwell briefly on the methods applied in the struggle against the old trade unions. In countries like France, Spain, and Italy, the bureau of the council had no need to undertake special efforts, as in Spain the National Confederation of Labour [CNT] was in favour of us. The other existing organisation, the General Union of Workers [UGT], is completely controlled by opportunist socialists and is seeing its importance constantly diminishing.

In Italy there exist two labour organisations: the CGL and the Italian Syndicalist Union [USI], composed of syndicalists. Both organisations adhere to the Third International. What is the current position of the CGL? That cannot be answered precisely. It seems that the leaders of the CGL are voluntarily equivocating. They have one foot in Moscow and one foot in Amsterdam. They are in Moscow because D'Aragona himself signed the declaration in favour of Moscow, but the CGL of Italy has stayed with Amsterdam. It remained there, and recently they accepted a subsidy of 50,000 lire from the Amsterdam Federation, which is not at all an indication of willingness to leave it.[10]

I would have dwelled even longer on the position of the Italian CGL had we not been informed of the arrival soon of two of its representatives to the congress. I think it would be better to wait for their presence, and then discuss their attitude in detail. While they are here, we will ask them and see whether it will be possible to get a clear answer from them. We will then know which way they intend to go.

In France the work in the old unions was conducted along the lines of the methods laid down by the Communist International and later by the declaration I read earlier, undoubtedly with one big difference, in that the then-existing syndicalist nuclei were not in any way contented with the Socialist Party. There was a special need to assist the work going on in France. This work

10 A donation of fifty thousand lire was given by the Amsterdam International to the CGL in April 1921, under the guise of helping its struggle against Fascist reaction.

gradually developed with prospects of rapid success, and we would like to let the French comrades continue their work.

In Germany and Britain, on the contrary, the struggle was much more difficult, because the trade unions there are solid and resistant organisations much more difficult to penetrate than the French unions. They are very old, with a long existence. This is especially true for the British trade unions, which are at the same time mutual-aid societies. It is very hard to displace them. Our work in that country was consequently the most difficult, and we have made great propaganda efforts there.

In Germany the work was begun by Lozovsky and his comrades, and systematically continued by the bureau that was created. It was this bureau that conducted the work in favour of the Red Trade Union International and directed the fight against Amsterdam and the leaders of the old unions.[11] Although the leaders considered their organisation solid enough, they were nevertheless alarmed by the size of the movement started against them, and immediately proceeded to expel the Communist leaders before the minorities could obtain sufficient strength. They were afraid of the contagion of the French example, although the conditions in each country are somewhat different.

In Britain we also conducted our propaganda under similar conditions. We established a bureau there directed by Comrade Murphy.[12] The results of the Bureau's work were excellent and immediately visible. In Britain an important evolution could be observed in the old trade unions. It was in Britain during and after the war that we saw the largest strikes, which, despite the fact that their objectives were narrowly craft-oriented, quickly went straight to the heart of capitalist society. So the situation was very favourable for our work in support of the International Council of Trade Unions. It is very hard to state precisely at this time which are the elements we can count on, what their exact number is, but we can say that they represent an important force within the old trade-union movement.

It is interesting to emphasise the attitude observed by the leaders of the trade unions in which the movement in favour of Moscow has manifested itself vigorously. Our comrade Tom Mann, who recently arrived here, has given

11 The RILU Central European Bureau based in Berlin was set up in January 1921. It issued a weekly information journal, *Die Rote Gewerkschafts-Internationale*, with a print run of 100,000 copies. This journal was to become the publication of the RILU executive committee (originally titled *Mezhdunarodnoe Rabochee Dvizhenie*; its name was later changed to *Rotes Gewerkschafts-Bulletin*).

12 The RILU bureau in Britain was organised at the end of 1920, chaired by Jack Murphy and including Robert Williams, Albert Purcell, Emile Burns, G. Kaye, and V. Williams.

us information about this. The powerful association of machinists [Amalgamated Society of Engineers], of which he is the secretary, is strongly attracted to Moscow. Very often the central office received resolutions from local branches urging an immediate rupture with Amsterdam and affiliation with Moscow. But the central office shelved the resolutions and buried them in the archives.

Two months ago our British comrades called a conference, where all the organisations expressed themselves for Moscow. At that conference 150 local delegates of the machinists union were present. If we consider that a section sends one delegate comprising 300 members, and that 150 locals presented a membership of 45,000, we will get an idea of the force represented by their conference of a single labour organisation, categorically expressing itself in favour of Moscow. We asked our comrade Tom Mann what is the attitude of the members of the executive committees of those different locals, and almost all of them are animated with the spirit of the old trade unionism. When the question of affiliation with the Moscow International came up for discussion, they did not take any part in it. This was the answer to his question; they waited. They do not know yet whether they should engage in an offensive, as was done in Germany. They vacillated. Undoubtedly they hope that the movement will never be strong enough to swing the entire organisation and force them from Amsterdam to Moscow. They hope that this manifestation will not be followed by any action, and so they remain neutral. Such is the stand of the British trade-union leaders, who are completely opposed to the propaganda of Moscow; it is a stand apparently of passive resistance.

Concerning other branches of industry, Comrade Tom Mann told us that among the miners of Wales and Scotland the movement is growing with extreme rapidity. In other mining centres, for instance in Yorkshire and Lancashire, the movement is developing gradually, although in a somewhat slower manner. In the Transport Federation, of which Robert Williams is one of the secretaries, the big majority of the membership is animated with a revolutionary spirit, but the leadership of their federation is still in the hands of an executive committee that is composed not only of leaders animated by 'trade unionism' [in English], but leaders who during the war were the faithful servants of the bourgeoisie. For example, Havelock Wilson, Sexton, and Ben Tillett, whose role during the war is well known. These are members of the executive committee.

To give you an idea of the approximate forces that we have grouped around the International Council of Trade Unions, I am going to read you a list of organisations that have voted for affiliation with Moscow and their respective membership. Of course these figures are approximate. In the case of Germany or Britain, we are compelled to calculate the followers of the Moscow International more or less arbitrarily. We have not got here all the organisations adhering to Moscow in every country. Some of them are minorities in organisations still affiliated with Amsterdam; sometimes there are majorities that are demanding to break with Amsterdam and go over to Moscow.

We have first of all 6.5 million members in Russia. In Germany we have the revolutionary minorities, which existed long ago within the old trade unions and comprise about two million. Now we have there two entire organisations, one consisting mostly of miners. The Gelsenkirchen Free Workers' Union numbering 148,000[13] members, and the General Workers' Union [AAU] with 120,000[14] members. In Austria the revolutionary minority in the trade unions is about 20,000;[15] in France, 500,000; in Switzerland, 90,000; in Czechoslovakia, 290,000.[16] I should state that the 290,000 figure is not an approximate figure, but is the real number of adherents to the Red Trade Union International. In fact the number of trade unionists who are partisans of Moscow is far greater – 1 million, but the other 700,000 belong to unions whose leaders are opportunists and avoid posing the question directly and who try to delay the convening of conferences or congresses, because they have no doubt of the decisions that would quickly be made.

In Poland we have 70,000[17] members; Turkey 50,000; Romania 90,000; Greece 50,000; Bulgaria 45,000.[18] Almost all the labour organisations of Yugoslavia have affiliated with us – 200,000 members.

Belgium in this list is credited with a membership of 60,000, but I do not know what this figure is based on, since the struggle in Belgium has only just begun. The Belgian trade unions form a part of the Belgian Workers' Party, which includes not only political groups, but labour unions and cooperatives as well. This fact will complicate and make even more difficult the fight within the Belgian trade unions. At the same time, comrades carry on a campaign in favour of having the union disaffiliate from the Belgian Workers' Party. Should this campaign be successful, the situation of course becomes much clearer. We would then have political organisations at one end and labour organisations at the other. But the chances of this campaign being rapidly successful are small.

13 This is per the English and German texts; the Russian and French versions say 140,000.

14 This is per the English, German, and Russian texts; the French version says 12,000.

15 This is per the English and French texts; the German and Russian versions say 25,000.

16 This is per the French text; the English version says 230,000; the German version says 520,000; the Russian version says 490,000.

17 This is per the French and English texts; the German version says 250,000; the Russian version says 25,000.

18 This is per the English and French texts; the German version says 50,000; the Russian version says 55,000.

The leaders of the party have a tight hold on it. During the very recent split we saw the left wing of the party carry out a split with a very significant following of party members.[19]

In Italy we have 3 million; Spain, 800,000; Portugal, 50,000; Sweden, 50,000; Norway, 199,000;[20] Britain, 400,000; Finland, 60,000; Latvia, Lithuania, and the Near and Far East combined, 300,000; United States, 450,000; Mexico, 129,000; Argentina, 214,000; and Australia and New Zealand, 60,000.

This list, which will be given in the report soon to be printed, needs some correction, and the comrades arriving here from different countries will help us to state the exact figures. This will also help to present a clearer picture of the current situation.

Nevertheless, these figures are of great value in showing us to what a great extent the working masses of all countries gravitate to the Red International in Moscow. It is their class instincts that guide them. They will understand the present situation, and realise that they cannot rely on the old trade unions, whose leaders are incapable of defending them. These masses flock to us almost spontaneously, without any propaganda on our part.

For this reason the task before us, the task of creating the Red Trade Union International, on the one hand, is easy; on the other hand, it's difficult. The easy part is that the masses see the current economic situation, making things favourable for us.

During the period immediately following the war, one could see a period of prosperity developing in the Entente countries. In France we know that the economic situation that existed in the first months after the end of the war was relatively favourable; there was no unemployment, prices were approximately the same as before the war. At the same time, family income was increasing. There was the possibility of life as it had been before the war. Workers were fatigued and were not receptive to revolutionary propaganda. The bourgeoisie continued its wartime policy and its ruinous financial measures, since these guaranteed keeping a lid on revolutionary explosions that might have been provoked by the masses' discontent.

But of course this prosperity was completely artificial, and at the end of 1920 it was replaced by an economic crisis. This crisis is perhaps not equally acute in all countries; it can fluctuate in this or that direction, with alternating periods

19 In August 1920 the Belgian Socialist Youth split from the Belgian Workers' Party and formed a Communist group. A second split of Communist forces occurred in May 1921. With encouragement from the Comintern, the two groups fused in September 1921.

20 This is per the English and German texts; the Russian version says 145,000; not in the French.

of ups and downs. But we know that this crisis will inevitably characterise the economic situation, insofar as it is based on the contradictions of capitalism. For this reason, we can regard the situation as being favourable for us.

But we should not overestimate the immediate impact of economic conditions. We also need to take into account the forces of the bourgeoisie with which we have to contend in order to precisely determine the situation.

First of all, we are facing the leaders of the old trade unions, who will never willingly give up their positions. The case of France shows how hard it is at present to replace the old trade-union leaders. Were it otherwise, it would be quite a simple matter to steer the trade-union movement in the right direction by obtaining a majority of the union.

But we know that matters are not so simple, as it is quite evident that the reformists now at the helm mislead the workers and employ all the means at their command to not lose their positions. At the last congress of railroad workers, the majority declared in favour of the revolutionary currents, but the old leaders manoeuvred to keep their positions.[21] By outwardly conforming to the demands of the moment, they are frequently successful in maintaining influence over the masses. We have now in France two trade-union federations.[22] Under normal conditions we would no doubt have with us the revolutionary organisation of the railway workers. We knew, however, that the leaders would not relinquish the field to us under any circumstances.

The idea of class collaboration is so deeply rooted in the minds of the leaders of the trade unions that it has led them not only to participate in bourgeois organisations, but has also led them to lay aside class principles. Such is the case with Amsterdam. The leaders of the Amsterdam International boast of the millions of workers whom they represent. They have in view the official number of all the unions nominally belonging to them, knowing full well that the majority of these members are affiliated [to the Amsterdam International] simply because they are members of organisations adhering to it. We also know that union members are losing faith in their leaders more and more. We must nevertheless admit that the Amsterdam International remains a power against which we must fight, mainly for this one reason: it pretends

21 At the June 1921 Congress of the French Railroad Federation, revolutionary unionists won a narrow majority. But the defeated conservative officials, backed by French courts, used a technicality in French trade-union law to seize the national union offices and other assets. The revolutionary leadership was forced to set up their own offices in a new building, which after the split in the CGT became the headquarters of the CGTU.

22 A reference to the General Confederation of Labour (CGT) majority and the *minoritaires* of the Revolutionary Syndicalist Committee (CSR), which was in the process of being expelled from the CGT and would form the Unitary CGT (CGTU) within a few months.

to be something other than what it really is. The bourgeoisie, on the other hand, finds it beneficial to consolidate all the trade-union organisations with large memberships and a certain weight that are willing to collaborate with it.

But the bourgeoisie is not satisfied with that alone; it is preparing, through extralegal means, to stop us from advancing too much. The bourgeoisie no longer considers legal repression sufficient. They do not limit themselves to governmental pressure. They have the white guards at their command under different names in different countries: the Somatenes in Spain, the Fascists in Italy, the Civic League in France, and others.[23]

I have already said that in this area the bourgeoisie is ahead of us. We allowed them to get the upper hand, thinking that our old methods were sufficient. But the weapons of the past that we thought were formidable are insufficient, as is the case with the general strike. We must find means to organise a defence against the bourgeois white guards. The existence of white guards is in itself proof of a revolutionary situation. The fact that the bourgeoisie is compelled to depart from its own legality in itself shows that the capitalist system has been deeply shaken.

The bourgeoisie has lost confidence in its own legality. This is why our immediate task is to establish special tactics corresponding to the present period. All over the world the bourgeoisie is engaged in an offensive against the working class. After the post-war period of fictitious prosperity, the bourgeoisie thought of balancing the budget and putting its finances in order. For this it had no alternative other than to squeeze more out of the working class. This accounts for its campaign against the eight-hour working day, and for cutting wages.

The bourgeoisie has thrown itself against the working masses, with the idea that high wages were the reason for the excessive cost of living and unemployment. We have found ourselves disarmed against this offensive on the part of the bourgeoisie. We engaged in partial struggles in which we were defeated in advance. In most cases, the workers' organisations simply acknowledged the proposed wage cuts, and the Amsterdam leaders, instead of steering the working class toward resistance, on the contrary took great pains to persuade them that this was normal, fair, and necessary.

23 The Somatén was an armed paramilitary group in Spain organised primarily by large landowners, with the goal of defending 'civilisation and order'.

The Civic League in France was founded in November 1917, led by Hubert Bourgin, to support the war effort and oppose anti-militarist efforts. It worked to oppose strikes and formed a private militia called the Civic Guard.

Even on this ground, however, we might have waged a successful fight, a struggle that could have had considerable consequences for the capitalist system itself.

Since the end of the war, the British Miners Federation set forth a number of demands. Taking note of government promises, the British comrades' resolution demanded conditions of life better than those before the war. They thus established a principle of great importance around which all the toiling masses could rally. Had a true trade-union International existed at that moment, it would have made this a point of departure for its programme of action.

The British miners formulated other demands that have lessons for our struggle against the bourgeoisie. They demanded the nationalisation or socialisation of the mines. They might have believed for a moment that the nationalisation of mines could be obtained without revolutionary struggle. The government appointed a commission, which, after long debates and interesting investigation of the working conditions in the mines and the profits obtained by the big mining companies, finally adopted a scheme of socialisation. But the government, which had agreed in advance to adopt the decision taken by the commission it had appointed, retracted its promise.[24] The British workers then addressed themselves to other workers' organisations – first to the Triple Alliance,[25] then to all workers' organisations. They were promised the full assistance of all the workers, resorting to all means, including a general strike, in order to compel the government to keep its promises and to compel the companies to give in. But the 'labour leaders', as soon as they realised that the government was resolved not to capitulate, resorted to their usual policy; they succeeded in having the final decisions postponed, gaining time and finally crippling the impulse of the British proletariat. Now nobody talks any longer about the nationalisation of mines.

Many projects of socialisation have been put forward over the years, but there was nothing revolutionary about them. What characterised the miners was that the issue of workers' control was playing a considerable part from the

---

24 In September 1919 the British miners' union secured the near-unanimous backing of the Trades Union Congress for a mass campaign around nationalisation of the coal mines. To avert the threat of coal miners' strikes and industrial unrest, the government formed the Sankey Commission (named after its president, John Sankey). The commission's findings endorsing the principle of nationalisation were rejected by the government.

25 The Triple Alliance was an agreement for joint action between the mine, railway, and transport workers' unions, dating from 1915. The alliance broke down in April 1921 when the rail and transport union leaderships rejected strike action in support of the national coal miners' strike against wage reductions.

For the British miners' strike, see p. 51, n. 11.

very outset and promised to rapidly become dominant. This accounts for the fact that the government opposed it squarely.

The British miners found themselves defeated, and the second great battle engaged in by them in opposition to the wage cuts also resulted in a relative defeat. The Triple Alliance they had relied upon had failed to support them, and international workers' solidarity reached them only weakly.

When we set our rules and tactics of struggle, we must bear in mind the reconciliation among the bourgeoisie of all the countries, including those that had been enemies [in the war]. The Anglo-Saxon and German bourgeoisies have already begun to collaborate; the former understood quite well that as long as Germany remained in a difficult economic position, it would constitute a dangerous revolutionary place.

Not only have we recently witnessed that the Anglo-Saxon and German bourgeoisies could work hand in hand; we have seen the meeting of two ministers, Loucheur and Rathenau – both of them symbolic individuals – who are great exploiters and war profiteers. And we've seen that it is perfectly possible for the French and German bourgeoisie to make peace on the backs of the workers of both countries. This is a fact that we must draw particular attention to.

The question of strategy and tactics is first on the agenda. We will have to define our methods of action and of penetrating the old unions. We have comrades in Germany, America, and other countries who advocate leaving the old trade unions, but the big majority of the organisations present at this congress oppose that point of view.

The French example would be very useful in this discussion. We shall also profit from the experience of Comrade Tom Mann, who already before the war was engaged in a revolutionary struggle within the British trade unions and obtained valuable and encouraging results. A similar point of view will be developed by the comrades from America, who show that even Gompers's trade unions are not absolutely impregnable strongholds, as they were long believed to be.

We will have many more problems to solve; we will have to compare information, examining and discussing the various methods of struggle that we all have been employing. We will be able to draw from these discussions the most profitable lessons. Especially valuable will be those lessons drawn from the Russian Revolution, which we shall be able to study.

We shall be able to accomplish our main task under the most favourable conditions. The proletariat of the world is anxiously awaiting the results of the work of this congress. It entertains great hopes, and it really would be a great disappointment if we failed to unite and create an organisation capable of leading the struggle, to rally together the revolutionary workers' organisations, with all their different characteristics and diversity.

Trade unions have developed in their respective countries under entirely different conditions and during different epochs. In some countries they are extremely weak, while in others they are very old, with old traditions. We must find a way to unite within our trade-union International all genuinely revolutionary trade-union organisations and to adopt a programme that can throw them into the struggle. So that a mighty international organisation comes out of this congress capable of defending the working class against all the trade-union leaders who betray them, and against the bourgeoisie that crushes and oppresses them. (*Applause*)

Lozovsky: We will now hear a brief report from the Credentials Commission.

Boris Reinstein: The commission is unable, as yet, to submit to the congress the ultimate results of its activity. On the one hand, not all the delegates have arrived; on the other, not all of the questions discussed have received their solution. The preliminary data is as follows:

There are 310 delegates present at the current congress representing 37 countries; 269 of them have a decisive vote, 30 have consultative votes, and 11 are guests. The different countries are represented as follows:

Azerbaijan: 1 decisive vote. Britain: 7 decisive, 4 consultative, 1 guest. Austria: 10 decisive, 2 consultative, 1 guest. Australia: 3 decisive. Abkhazia: 1 decisive. Armenia: 2 decisive. Bulgaria: 13 decisive. Hungary: 3 decisive. Holland: 7 decisive. Georgia: 4 decisive. Germany: 60 decisive, 7 consultative, 7 guests. Denmark: 2 decisive. Far Eastern Republic: 3 decisive. Spain: 5 decisive. Italy: 1 decisive and more delegates are to arrive. Canada: 1 decisive, 1 consultative. Korea: 1 decisive. Latvia: 5 decisive. Luxembourg: 4 decisive. Mexico: 1 decisive. Lithuania: 1 decisive. Poland: 9 decisive. Palestine: 2 decisive. Russia: 58 decisive, 1 consultative. United States of America: 6 decisive, 8 consultative. Turkey: 1 decisive. Ukraine: 2 decisive, 1 consultative. France: 12 decisive. Finland: 12 decisive. Czechoslovakia: 2 decisive. Switzerland: 11 decisive, 5 consultative. Estonia: 3 decisive. Yugoslavia: 10 decisive. South Africa: 1 consultative, 1 guest. Greece: 1 consultative. Romania: 5 decisive.

In addition, the Norwegian delegation is expected at any time, to the amount of 10 comrades.

The above figures of the delegates will not have any influence on the voting, as, according to the decision taken by the congress, the voting will be carried out for each country separately within the fixed number of votes allotted to it, for example, 16, 12, 8, and 4, irrespective of the number of delegates present.

Lozovsky then moved the rules of procedure:

1. The plenary sessions, with the exception of special cases, will be held from 11:00 a.m. to 4:00 p.m.
2. One hour's time will be granted to the first reporter and thirty minutes for a summary speech.
3. Thirty minutes are granted to the co-reporter.
4. On points of procedure, two minutes will be granted only once.
5. Each delegate is allowed to speak only twice on any of the questions debated: fifteen minutes for the first time and five minutes for the second time.
6. The respective delegations select their own speakers. In special cases separate speakers are given the floor with the permission of the Presidium.
7. The question as to the method of voting – whether by paper ballot or orally by the corresponding delegations – is to be decided by the Presidium.
8. All motions, even if they relate to the agenda, should be submitted to the Presidium in writing.

Victor Labonne (France) proposes that in cases of especially important questions the vote should be taken by countries and by a roll call, as the number of delegates does not correspond to the actual relationship between the tendencies in the trade-union movement in different countries. (*The amendment of Comrade Labonne, seconded by Lozovsky, is declared carried.*)

Albert Lemoine (France) considers that, at the first constituent congress, on such an important question as the relationship with the Third International, the time allotted to the speakers should not be limited, because it would be impossible to argue with speakers who are given one and a half hours to present and defend their point of view, while the other representatives have no more than ten minutes to expound their point of view.

Lozovsky is opposed to Lemoine's proposal to give unlimited time to the speakers, because the congress would last two months. By giving to each group the right to put forward a co-reporter, the different tendencies are fully guaranteed the ability to express and defend their point of view.

Henri Sirolle (France) argues against Comrade Lozovsky, stating that the right of choosing a co-reporter does not settle the question, because even within the delegation it is not always possible to agree upon a reporter. He moves to extend the time of each speaker to 30 minutes, without limiting the number of speakers.

Fritz Heckert (Germany) moves to limit the time to 15 minutes.

One of the members of the German General Workers' Union moves to allow each delegation to choose its own reporter, with one hour for the report and a quarter of an hour for a summary speech.

A member of the German Seamen's Union proposes that the syndicalists communicate with each other and designate a common speaker, regardless of the delegation they belong to.

Arlandis (Spain) supports the motion of Sirolle not to close the list of speakers and not to limit the time, at least for the first few sessions.

Lozovsky: I have four motions on the floor: (1) in favour of unlimited discussion; (2) to limit the time of each speaker to 30 minutes; (3) to limit the time of each speaker to 15 minutes; (4) to limit the time of each speaker to 10 minutes.

The motion for limiting the time to 15 minutes is carried by a majority.

The rules of procedure as amended are put to a vote and carried.

Lozovsky: The floor is granted to Comrade Rosmer for a special statement.

Rosmer: We read in *La Vie ouvrière* of 24 June the following communication:

On Saturday 18 June Comrades Evelio Boal, Antonio Oriel, and José Domínguez Rodríguez, who had been arrested on 1 March and were kept in prison without any reason, were released at 1:00 a.m.

While on their way home they were assassinated by 'unknown killers'.

Boal was general secretary of the National Confederation of Labour of Spain, Oriel was its treasurer, and Rodríguez one of its best fighters.

There is no doubt whatever that the murderers were paid for by the military governor of Catalonia, Martínez Anida.

Lozovsky asks the congress to honour the memory of the victims by all rising.

Gaston Leval (France) says that to the list of victims should be added the name of Comrade Arlandis, one of the most determined fighters of the Spanish proletariat and brother of the delegate here present.[26]

---

26 Hilario Arlandis had just been informed of his brother's death in Valencia at the hands of right-wing forces.

Lozovsky: I call on Comrade Nin to read a communication.

Nin reports to the congress that our comrade Borghi, an Italian trade unionist who participated in the organisation of the Red Trade Union International last year, is currently in prison.[27] The congress must express its sympathy with him.

Sirolle proposes not to discuss this question today, and to send greetings tomorrow to all the victims of the white terror on behalf of the congress.

Lozovsky: Comrades, we honour the memory of those who have fallen in the fight for our cause. It is certain that the members of the congress keep in their memory the names of these victims, as they do all the victims of the bourgeois regime.

Next on the agenda is the adoption of the manifesto to the workers of the world in the name of the congress. Comrade Murphy has the floor.

Jack Murphy (Britain) proposes that the text of the manifesto be distributed through the secretaries of the four groups for the purpose of information and reading in the groups, so as to be in a position to throw the subject open for discussion after the report of Comrade Rosmer.

Lozovsky declares that the Presidium is in agreement with Murphy's proposal. (*Murphy's proposal is adopted.*)

(*The session is closed at 11:40 p.m.*)

---

27 Armando Borghi was in prison between October 1920 and July 1921.

Manifesto; Debate on International Council Report

(*The session is opened at 11:00 a.m. Comrade Lozovsky in the chair.*)

Lozovsky: I declare the session opened. We shall presently take up for discussion the report presented yesterday by Comrade Rosmer on behalf of the Council of Trade and Industrial Unions. Before doing this we shall read the manifesto, the text of which was worked out the day before yesterday, printed in four languages, and distributed.

(*The manifesto is read out in Russian, English, French, and German.*)

The International Congress of Revolutionary Trade and Industrial Unions to the Workers of the World

The war has ended, but humanity continues in the grip of its convulsions. The promised good fortune and peace have not come. The conquerors, as well as the conquered, feel more and more the great sacrifices that have been exacted by the years of carnage. Immediately after the close of the war, when the unparalleled butchery had ceased, it seemed to many naïve people, and even to some of the toilers, as though a definite change had taken place and that humanity had again entered upon a peaceful road of development. At least the bourgeoisie and its hired agents talked in this way about it; they shouted loudly, and with their noise and oratory they tried to smother the discontent that had accumulated within the working class. At the same time, those who spoke in the name of the working masses, leaders of the socialist parties and trade unions of the Entente, shouted 'Hosannah' to the conquering butchers, aiming to join in with them at the well-spread table of the conquerors. Especially zealous in this direction were the leaders of the trade unions, Messrs. Jouhaux, Gompers, Appleton, and others who walked around the League of Nations, which was in a state of formation, and, with the devotion of servants, looked into the eyes of Lloyd George, Clemenceau, and Wilson.

'Democracy' was victorious, German imperialism was thrown off its pedestal. Like a pack of rapacious animals, the bourgeoisie of the Entente has thrown itself upon the German people. All that was said about right, justice, and perpetual peace proved, as might have been expected, to be mere lies and

 | DOI:10.1163/9789004712867_007

hypocrisy. The toiling masses of Germany, Austria, and Hungary at once felt the pressure of the iron heel. The more the results of the war took effect, the more eagerly did they throw themselves upon the toiling masses of the conquered countries. The watchword advanced by the bourgeoisie and supported by the leaders of the trade unions, regardless of the insolvency of the conquered, was 'the conquered should pay for everything'.

The war has not in fact been ended. Here and there it breaks out with new force. The allies of yesterday are already sharpening their knives against each other. Japan, with the evident sympathy of Britain, is arming against America. America, appearing as though it does not wish to interfere in European affairs, engages herself more vigorously in the fight for world power. The time has irrevocably passed when Britain was master of the world market. The exchange value of the British pound sterling at present is fluctuating and declining, and is yielding its place on the market to its powerful rival, the dollar. The dollar is now ruler of the world. Britain is passing into second place, while powerful US capitalism has moved into first.

However, Britain is still strong enough to hold France the 'conqueror' tenaciously in its hands. Britain, with its coal, industries, and economic policy, dictates the conditions of France, throwing the bourgeoisie there into a state of fury by the single thought of losing the Russian loans and possible bankruptcy. The French petty bourgeoisie, with great madness and sadism, throws itself upon and fastens its teeth into the body of the German people to avenge itself for all the humiliations and defeats in the international diplomatic game.

'Germany must pay for everything'. But Germany cannot pay, because its national economy has been considerably exhausted by the war. The pressure put upon the German people exceeds the national wealth of the country. The German bourgeoisie, being just as guilty in the imperialist war as the other countries, does not want to pay in any way at all – it prefers to have the German working class pay for it. The German working class, misled by the Social Democrats and trade-union leaders for many years, has followed the road of national unity, remaining on this road even after the revolution of 1918. The mass of workers still find themselves hypnotised by the bourgeoisie.

Poverty, unemployment, hunger, and devastation, which like a hurricane have swept over Germany, did not however stir up sufficiently the giant of the country – the proletariat. Now and then separate groups rise up, fight, and perish in the struggle because the trade-union bureaucracy, availing itself of the full force of the machinery of the allies, directs its actions against these uprisings to repel the offensive against capitalism and the bourgeois state. At the same time that the trade unions of Germany enthusiastically protect the bourgeois order, they speak more and more of socialisation and big reforms.[1] The aim of this talk is simply to fool the great mass of the German workers. Everything thus remains as it is.

The bourgeoisie, which accumulated billions, holds them fast and does not allow them to slip out of its hands. While Allied imperialism is putting pressure upon Germany, the bourgeoisie, which for years called for unity, turns to its outside enemies and, pointing to the workers of Germany, says, 'These are the ones who are the cause of our inability to pay'.

All this nevertheless does not interfere in the least with the leaders of the trade unions continuing their policy of class collaboration in their country. On the contrary, this collaboration becomes more cynical and impudent. Together with the bourgeoisie, the leaders are in a united front against the revolutionary struggle of the workers whenever the latter engage in open struggle with their class enemies.

So unemployment grows, factories are shut down, and by the hundreds of thousands the workers are thrown onto the street. The bourgeoisie, seeing its approaching end and trying to delay it, is organising and arming itself. Reaction raises its head, seeing the working class insufficiently organised and politically divided.

The situation is not much better in the victorious countries.

France is suffering chronic financial derangement. The country of creditors and moneylenders, the country of bankers and owners of wealth, is unable to cope with this catastrophic situation in any way. France does not issue any loans; on the contrary, she has to resort to them herself. She does not dictate the conditions of the world market, which are under the influence of the rich countries, and she therefore seeks quick relief. The hope that Germany would pay for everything is daily losing ground. The most backward shopkeeper of France is beginning to doubt the ability of the Germans to pay. The masses are losing their confidence in tomorrow. Industry is undergoing a crisis. The number of unemployed is rising.

Side by side with this growing struggle, the General Confederation of Labour continues to exist. It retains its name, but has entirely lost its class-struggle

---

1 At the time various social-democratic socialisation schemes were being put forward that avoided posing the question of overturning capitalist rule and confiscating the bourgeoisie's property. For example, a resolution on the question passed by the Amsterdam International's 1920 London Congress stated: 'This Congress therefore demands, in the interests of society, the socialisation of land and other means of production … [in] all branches of production which in the estimation of the proletariat of every country are realisable. … The right of the workers to co-determination in regulation of production and enterprise must be assured.'

character. As in Germany, the leadership of the trade-union movement fears the revolution above all.

The growing crisis here also finds the working class insufficiently organised; one part of the unionised workers marches with the bourgeoisie against the other part, thus delaying the birth of the new order.

In Britain the situation is growing worse from day to day. Industrial prosperity, which followed immediately at the close of the war, has been replaced by a deep depression. Great social conflicts are raging in that country. Unemployment is growing. Strike follows strike; lockout follows lockout. Even the old trade unions, led by lackeys of the bourgeoisie, are now forced desperately to repulse its attack. The miners' strike, the approaching lockout of hundreds of thousands of textile workers, millions of unemployed – this is what we see in Britain.

What do the trade unions do for these millions thrown into the street? What do they propose? How do they expect to fight, to smash the antiworker policy of the ruling class? Do not ask, for you will receive no reply from the old trade-union leaders. They hide themselves in shells and wait for the next crisis. Then they become enraged at the insolence of their 'exploiters', and organise opposition in their particular branch of industry.

They lack the class consciousness to understand that the miners' struggle is the struggle of the entire working class, of all the trade unions of Britain. They even lack the ability to understand elementary knowledge about the class struggle. While the bourgeoisie is attacking the unions individually, a handful of the leaders talk about social peace and betray the working class in the struggle. Unfortunately, a large number of proletarians still have confidence in these traitorous leaders.

In America the same situation exists. Five million workers are unemployed. War profits have ceased; factory after factory is being shut down and workers thrown out into the street. 'Your work is no longer needed. You may go.' The safes are full of money. 'Democracy' is celebrating its victory and is beginning to introduce open shops, i.e., employing non-union workers. Those who were supposed to sound the alarm – what are they doing about the misery inflicted upon the working class? The leaders of the trade unions do nothing. They consider it inevitable, like the ocean tide. And, like obedient serfs, they kiss the hands of their masters.

The American Federation of Labor, to do something, convened an emergency conference of its Executive Council at the end of February 1921, attended by representatives of 109 federations. At this meeting an appeal was issued to the nation, complaining of the fact that 'the trade-union movement is being attacked by the shameless dictators of industry, and defenders of "European fanaticism".[2] Gompers and his aides contend that if either side gains the upper hand our generation will have to go into mourning for liberty and equality. In order to maintain all the principles as laid down by the American Constitution, the appeal calls for the right of organisation, boycotts, collective bargaining, taking action against strikebreaking agencies, restriction of immigration, etc. This is all the pitiful bureaucracies can think of, seeing that they consider the victory of the social revolution as the victory of 'European fanaticism', and as a great misfortune.

The lieutenants of the bourgeoisie must be ejected from the ranks of the working class. Woe to a working class that tolerates these servants of capital within its unions.

The Offensive of the Bourgeoisie against the Working Class

At a time when the leaders of the trade unions – some by premeditation and others by stupidity and blindness – are trying to avoid the demands of life and divert the approaching storm, the bourgeoisie, understanding the true state of affairs, persistently and methodically prepares itself to meet the social resistance. It follows very attentively what is going on within the working class.

At the close of the war the bourgeoisie was rather prudent in its attitude toward the union movement, fearing that moves by the likes of Gompers, Jouhaux, and Appleton would result in the threat of action by the trade-union masses before the bourgeoisie would have a chance to organise itself. The discontent of the working masses forced the bourgeoisie to be on its guard. In many countries it was obliged to make concessions, such as the eight-hour day, etc. The bourgeoisie soon convinced itself that the tamed union leaders were efficiently doing the job for it. Despite appearances, these leaders' aim was to confuse the workers, disorganise them, and kill their belief in their own strength.

The bourgeoisie recognises its good servants. But as the economic depression started and the weight of the crisis fell upon small and large countries alike, the bourgeoisie began to launch an offensive without regard to the moderation of its leaders.

The policy of reduction of wages swept like a hurricane through Europe and America. In Britain, France, Germany, Italy, America, Sweden, Norway, Switzerland, Czechoslovakia, and everywhere else the bourgeoisie marches in a united

2 The American Federation of Labor's emergency conference of 23–24 February 1921 was organised to protest an antilabour bill pending in the US Congress. The final declaration issued by this conference stated, 'Converging upon labor from the extreme right is autocratic reaction, while from the opposite extreme is the insidious propaganda of radical European fanaticism.'

front against the working masses. Wage reductions, poor working conditions, the tendency to set back the progress of the working class by decades, lockout after lockout – all this takes place in small and large countries alike. Millions of workers are thrown into the street and suffer the economic offensive of the bourgeoisie.

What do the trade unions do in the face of this unheard-of pressure? What is the Amsterdam International – which is supposed to solidify the struggle of the workers of all countries – doing now? What all those who propagate 'social peace' and class collaboration do is to urge calm and tranquillity, promising workers victory without bloodshed, civil war, or terrorism. These gentlemen continue to visit the drawing rooms of government officials, appealing to the sentiments and good sense of the ruling class, stressing the disadvantages of class conflict.

The Amsterdam International is supposed to be at the head of all the discontented masses, to be the focus upon which the revolutionary workers of all countries should be centred, to organise and coordinate the struggle. The Amsterdam International, in the person of its representatives, dances around the greatest social conflagration in the history of humanity and occupies itself with sorcery. This organisation, which styles itself a workers' organisation of the masses for the overthrow of capitalism or for the uprising of the exhausted and subject people, merely appeals to the workers to be moderate and practise good sense.

The leaders of these organisations, individually and collectively, have occupied themselves with the 'equitable' application of the Versailles Treaty. While the French patriots Jouhaux, Dumoulin, and Merrheim express verbal sympathy with the German workers, they elaborate methods to rebuild French capitalism at the expense of the German people. They also wish to show to the big and petty bourgeoisie that the workers are at least as concerned with the welfare of the homeland. At the same time, as lackeys, they conduct themselves in the same manner as the 'saviours' in other countries. As if accidently, the trade-union International and the living corpses of the Two-and-a-Half International[3] meet simultaneously in Amsterdam to discuss the problems of reparations and reconstruction of the devastated provinces.

3 The term 'Two-and-a-Half International' referred to the centrist International Working Union of Socialist Parties, or Vienna Union, founded at a congress in Vienna, 22–27 February 1921. It was established in opposition to both the reformist Second International and the Communist Third International. The Two-and-a-Half International fused with the Second International in May 1923.

Amsterdam Supports the Bourgeoisie

How do these venerable gentlemen of Amsterdam think to reconstruct the dislocated national economy? How do they expect to fill the abyss that has been formed in the world economy as a result of this war? Who is going to pay? Oh, they have found the solution: the vanquished should pay!

True, they are not as rapacious as the representatives of the bourgeois government; they demand much less. They want the German working people to pay whatever they can. They are liberal and understand the condition of the conquered people. These gentlemen overlook one small thing: it is impossible to reconstruct the world economy merely by levying taxes on the German workers. It would be like trying to drain the ocean with one's hand.

The bourgeoisie of all countries should pay and it can pay. It must pay and it will pay, whether the leaders of the trade-union movement of Europe and America want it to or not. The bourgeoisie must be expropriated and be swept off the earth as a class. That is the only way historically to pull humanity out of the swamp.

The indebtedness of all countries is an incontestable fact. Hundreds of billions in debt lie as a burden upon the shoulders of the German, French, British, and other nations. Who will pay for all this? If payment of these debts were to be possible, who would profit from these riches? Millions of toilers would be paying for it, while tens of thousands of capitalists – who prior to the war already possessed great wealth and expanded their riches during the struggle – would profit by it. They will operate with these hundreds of billions and will keep in their tenacious hands tens of millions of human beings. A pleasant prospect for the proletariat! Only people belonging to the ruling class or imbued with the spirit of exploitation and slavery are unable to see these monstrous contradictions in which modern humanity is struggling.

Look at any capitalist country. Take its social life; go into the streets of the big cities, the workers' quarters of Paris, London, Milan, Barcelona, and Berlin, and you will see the growth of poverty. You will find a huge growth of prostitution. Women workers are driven by the unmerciful weight of hunger and destitution to the streets. And while the wives and daughters of working people are increasing the ranks of prostitutes, children die of starvation. At the same time that workers by the millions pace the streets owing to unemployment, there is unheard-of dissipation and debauchery among capitalist robbers who have been fattened by this war.

The leaders of the trade unions, instead of preaching to the hungry workers the idea of class antagonism and class war, spread ideas of social peace, moderation, and propriety toward the principles of private ownership. These lackeys of the bourgeoisie, who possess a petty-bourgeois spirit even though they are of working-class origin, have a very limited intellectual horizon. The whole wisdom of life for these people consists only in questions of how to stay afloat through critical times and, as quickly as possible, restore social peace and class harmony.

Amsterdam Fears Revolution

The followers of the Amsterdam International fear revolution; they want no bloodshed. The first issue of the organ of the Amsterdam International[4] stated that they do not wish to add new victims of the revolution to the bloody sacrifices that were enormous during the war. When in the interests of the bourgeoisie, tens of millions of workers' lives were laid down on the fields of Europe, and the whole world was transformed into a cemetery for the glory of the golden calf, these gentlemen did not come out with speeches against the slaughter. At that time they had other sermons in their bag. They were calling for a 'holy alliance'. They appealed for firmness in the battles at the front, and called on the workers to smash their enemies, to smash the heads of workers on the other side of the battlefield. They were not against bloodshed then! Their hands are stained with the blood of tens of millions of people.

By the close of the war, the bourgeoisie had finished its work and implanted chauvinist ideas into the minds and heads of the broad masses. Then, when humanity was driven into a position from which it can extradite itself only by rising up against its class enemy – and there is no other way for the working class to save itself – these lackeys of the bourgeoisie come and say, 'We are opposed to bloodshed; we don't wish to produce any new corpses'. What terrible hypocrisy! What an insult to the millions of workers who fell in the capitalist war! These are the hypocritical priests of the trade-union movement. They lie, just as the ministers lie, when they preach on the one hand the gospel of 'love each other', and on the other hand bestow blessings in the name of Jesus Christ on fratricidal war.

Upon what do the leaders of the Amsterdam International base their hopes when they appeal to the working class not to rise up against its oppressors? By what means and powers do they expect to rid themselves of the pressure of the capitalists? Oh, they foster great hopes! Their vision is directed toward the International Labour Bureau of the League of Nations, which is supposed to settle these conflicts. By what means did the League of Nations charm the heroes of Amsterdam? They were simply tempted by the thought that this bureau,

4 The International Federation of Trade Union's journal in English was *The International Trade Union Movement*, whose first issue was in March 1921. Editions were also published in French and German.

as the foremost socialist and union gathering, is the greatest expression of international solidarity. What can be more soothing and touching than the unity of the representatives of the working class, the capitalists, and the government? True, the unequal representation of the workers in this grand institution does cause great discontent on the part of Amsterdam. They would like equality, but they don't lose hope of gaining this equality and making the International Labour Bureau a tool of the international working class, as Oudegeest thinks.

Dictatorship of the Proletariat the Only Alternative

The working class cannot take such a stand. The history of humanity cannot point to a single conquest that did not involve a hard struggle and great sacrifices. The working class, in the long years of its struggle, gained absolutely nothing – not even the smallest accomplishment – without heroic sacrifices.

The period of peaceful struggle caused the working class no less harm than did the time of bloody confrontation. The so-called 'peaceful workings' alone take hundreds of thousands of victims of horrible exploitation. If the working class should hesitate over the forcible overthrow of capitalism, if it fears to raise its hand against the existing order simply because it does not wish to add to the sacrifices already demanded by the bourgeoisie, it will remain in the same state of perpetual slavery, not worthy of liberation. But no, this hypocritical morality of the priest is refuted by the development of the social struggle. While the treacherous leaders of the trade unions are preaching Christian submissiveness to the workers, the bourgeoisie at the same time is doing its work. It creates its own organisations, leaving it to imbeciles and scoundrels who come from the working class to preach to the workers an aversion to revolutionary class struggle.

Workers! Toilers! It is time to put an end to this continuous lie. It is almost three years since the war ended and two years since the Amsterdam Federation of Trade Unions came into existence. From day to day we are told of social peace and class collaboration. Through the many pages of the bourgeois press, as well as from the representatives of labour organisations of the Amsterdam International and the International Labour Bureau of the League of Nations, appeals are made every day to peace and tranquillity. Is this merely an accidental coincidence? Is it really possible that this collaboration between the League of Nations, the International Labour Bureau, and the most significant trade unions of the different countries is purely accidental? Is it possible that the bourgeoisie, which was unable throughout the war to hold the working class in its hands both morally and materially, has suddenly grown so stupid that it creates institutions for the benefit of the working class? It is sufficient to pose these questions in order to get a clear answer.

The international bourgeoisie, feeling its end approaching, is persistently trying to catch hold of anything that will help to obstruct the development of any attack by the working class. One of the best methods of disorganising the ranks of the working class is to draw them into collaboration with the bourgeoisie and transform workers' organisations into tools of bourgeois policy, thus transforming them into a force opposed to revolution. The bourgeoisie has certainly succeeded in that. The leaders of the Amsterdam Federation; of the French CGT; of the General German Trade Union Federation; of the majority of the British unions; Jouhaux, Dumoulin, Merrheim, Wissell, Grassmann, Oudegeest, Fimmens, Thomas – they are sabotaging the social revolution on a national and international scale. These kinds of enemies within the organisation are by far the most dangerous of class enemies. Being inside our organisation, in our very midst, knowing our weaknesses and the peculiarities of the working-class movement, they therefore know best how to disorganise it, and to nip in the bud any effort of the workers. For that reason, they are held in high esteem by the bourgeoisie, which is fully capable of appreciating its friends and enemies. The bourgeoisie does not waste praise upon anybody. It knows what it wants. If the Amsterdam Federation finds itself in special favour with the most conspicuous imperialist robbers, it clearly deserves such favour.

We, the representatives of the revolutionary trade unions of the world gathered here at the first constituent congress in Moscow to lay the foundation for a real international revolutionary brotherhood, we turn to all the workers' organisations as well as to the individual workers and ask them how long will the working class tolerate the exploitation of man by man? Will the workers of advanced countries, who bear the record of many years of struggle, continue to follow the treacherous leaders of the working class, thereby strengthening the rule of the exploiters? How long will you keep on transforming the trade unions, their millions of members, into tools for the suppression of the revolution instead of a tool for the overthrow of the bourgeois order? Just look around and see the stirring of struggle all over the world. The impudence of the bourgeoisie is proportional and equal to your docility and your confidence in the old leaders who fear and do not wish to struggle. If the bourgeoisie at the present time dares to be aggressive and throw millions of workers into the street, it is because the working class feels itself inferior and imagines that the bourgeoisie is invincible.

You continue to look up to the bourgeoisie. Many of you consider the established division of labour quite natural, the rule of one class and the subjugation of the other. Arise from your knees, and the bourgeoisie will not appear so strong to you as before! Remember, if bourgeois society is able to pass without punishment for the world butchery; if the exploiters of each country are able to survive the economic crisis that has shaken Europe, should the working class not arise and take into its hands the fate of humanity and take advantage of the crisis to smash its class enemy – then the rule of the bourgeoisie will continue for a long time.

It is therefore necessary in each country to concentrate all revolutionary energy, to create one solid front of all the revolutionary trade unions and Communist parties that are against Amsterdam and are for the social revolution and proletarian dictatorship. It is imperative to organise and put up a counterforce of organised workers against the organisation of the black hundreds. It is also necessary to form special units and battalions to teach the bourgeoisie not to use scabs and bands of terrorists. The white guards and fascists cannot be overcome merely by complaints and appeals to justice, but with an armed hand. Blow should be answered by blow, attack by counterattack. Class antagonism and discontent is rampant in all countries. Trade unions one after another are moving away from the old position and are going in for militant preparedness. The struggle promises to be a very hard and prolonged one indeed. Only by great intensive will, maximum concentration of power, and close coordination of trade unions with the Communist Party, is it possible to resist the attack and defeat the bourgeoisie.

Revolutionary workers of all countries: To action! Close ranks! Rid yourselves of all those who come to you and preach social peace and class collaboration. Show no pity to these renegades; they are the emissaries of the enemy. Do not surrender to pessimism if you suffer defeats. Do not give an inch to the old trade-union leaders. The trade unions shall belong to those who will be followed by the vast mass of the working class.

The capture of the trade unions is therefore the immediate task of the working class. The delegates of the trade unions who have gathered from all parts of the world are thoroughly convinced that the social revolution is knocking at the door of all capitalist countries. Let all the trade-union leaders maintain that the working class is not ready for socialism. It is an old bourgeois song, which the workers of the world hear as soon as they want to engage in real action. Throw these gentlemen out of your ranks, and you will prove to them by this action that you are ready.

Workers of all countries! From the country where the social revolution is already into its fourth year; from the country where the proletariat in great misery and suffering has fought and is continuing the fight against world capitalism; from the country of the vanguard of the proletariat, we the organisers and creators of the general staff of the international trade-union movement that, in fraternal collaboration with the Communist International, will fight against world capitalism; from this country, we send to all the exploited and oppressed masses our fraternal greetings and a call to relentless struggle against our class enemies.

Greetings to all the exploited and oppressed the world over. Raise high the banner soiled by the hands of treacherous leaders. Raise high the standard and inscribe in glaring letters:

> Workers of the world, unite!
> Death to world capitalism!
> Long live the international congress of the revolutionary trade unions!
> Long live the world proletarian revolution!
> Long live the dictatorship of the proletariat!
> Long live the international social republic!
> Long live communism!

Lozovsky: Comrades, we agreed yesterday to begin the session at 11:00 o'clock. Today we started at 11:00 o'clock sharp, although the manifesto had to be read in a half-empty hall. We shall conform to this rule in all subsequent sessions, even if only one-fourth of those the hall can accommodate are present. Delegates, please take note!

Now we are going to discuss the manifesto. Comrade Murphy will speak on this question.

Jack Murphy (Britain): I move to refer the manifesto back to the commission made up of representatives of different delegations, as it does not at all answer its purpose. The manifesto should give a graphic account of the economic and political situation confronting the trade-union movement in various countries and trace its problems and tactics. But this is just what the manifesto failed to do. This document is from beginning to end a mere tirade, an impassioned attack hurled against our enemy, but contains no positive facts. The manifesto should be drawn up and worded in a calm, dignified tone. It should first contain matter firmly establishing the basis of our position, and then wind up with a confident and calm appeal calling upon the organised proletariat of various countries to come under our banner.

Lozovsky: Comrade Labonne has the floor.

Victor Labonne (France): On behalf of a part of the French delegation, I support the motion of the British delegation to the effect that the manifesto be referred back to the commission for redrafting, since in the first place it is too long; and it is really more of a report than an appeal.

Lozovsky: Comrade Williams has the floor.

George Williams (USA, IWW): I quite agree with Comrade Murphy's proposition. I am also of the opinion that this manifesto is only a long tirade of general phrases on capitalism. Nearly all countries are absolutely tired of such a kind of literature, and for a nickel you can buy such pamphlets anywhere. A manifesto in the name of a congress such as this one should indeed be a real creative effort, and should also make clear the methods and tactics of the struggle. I shall even go further than Comrade Murphy, and will say that such a manifesto ought to be issued after the congress and not at its beginning. Here at this congress there are two fighting currents, two directions, and two tendencies, and their mutual relations were not yet made clear. If a manifesto should be issued in the name of the congress now, one would wonder whether it would be the right expression even of the dominating tendency of this congress. The proposed manifesto cannot be considered as a manifesto of the congress so long as the mutual relations of the prevailing tendencies are not known yet. Therefore, the manifesto should be issued after the congress and not at its beginning.

Lozovsky: Comrade Bartels, from the Free Workers' Union of Germany, has the floor.

Arthur Bartels (Germany, Gelsenkirchen Free Workers' Union): I also think that this draft should be referred back to the committee for correction. In my opinion, there are some concessions to nationalism in it that are near to the heart of the German bourgeoisie. It might serve as water to the mill of German patriots of the government type unless these passages are thrown out or amended. Besides, mention is made too often about the organisation of a revolutionary headquarters, and so on. There is too much revolutionary terminology instead of concrete points concerning tactics and the programme of labour organisations. It is about time we discontinue using such terminology.

I agree with the previous comrades that this manifesto should include a criticism of the modern international labour movement and point out its further aims and problems. This could only be decided upon after the congress has taken a positive stand on all questions involved. Then we can proceed with the draft. I am in favour of the motion made by Comrade Williams that this manifesto should be considered at the close of the congress and not at its beginning. Meanwhile I move to refer it to the commission for redrafting. It is certainly too long.

Grigorii Tsyperovich (Russia): Allow me to say that the opponents of the manifesto are not correct, because it is only an appeal. What the comrades from Spain, France, Murphy, and Bartels are looking for would only be a mere collection of our resolutions with an introduction on behalf of the council; this will be done as soon as the congress is over. But it is impossible to present in an appeal all the history, tactics, and programme of our movement. Our task is to attract the attention of the workers of all countries to this congress, to show them that our intention is to solve the pressing problems of the moment, and to keep up the interest of the large masses so that our congress should not pass unnoticed. We will act very wisely if we issue our appeal at the beginning of the congress.

At present a series of congresses and conferences are expected abroad, among others the Lille Congress.[5] The spirit of our congress needs to be reflected at Lille, and not merely its tactics. Where the former is concerned, I agree that the appeal should be shortened, but that can be easily done by an editing commission.

Now about 'phrases' contained in it, let me tell you that if we wish to express our wrath we must use the language that conveys our feeling, and use words that create an atmosphere of indignation, of hatred, toward our foes. In this respect our language is very correct; it is not a language of phrases but of revolutionary action. In our resolutions and reports we will use a dignified, accurate language. Just now we have heard the report of our Spanish comrades of the atrocities committed on the working masses. We know the brutalities of the white terror, and therefore we must use language burning with indignation and hatred, the language of the worker when he speaks about his class enemies.

Now it was said that this kind of literature is already known to everyone. Such can be said only of the leaders and those most active in the trade-union movement. For the simple worker, however, who can barely afford even the nickel for this literature that was mentioned here, it is of great value.

For the sake of style, it might be advisable to give this manifesto either to a commission or to the Presidium, to shorten it and to correct it in some places,

5 A congress of the French CGT was scheduled in Lille later in the month. It was held 25–30 July 1921 and was the scene of a heated struggle between the left and right. The right wing carried the majority by a vote of 1,556 to 1,348, with 46 abstentions. Within a year the confederation was to split virtually down the middle.

but I insist that the spirit of the appeal should not be altered. Its tone should be fiery and impassioned, first of all, and secondly, it should be issued at the beginning of the congress.

Arlandis (Spain): We insist that the manifesto is much too long; too long to be read by the workers of Europe. The congress must appoint a commission of three or five members to prepare concisely and forcefully a manifesto containing the substance of the report.

Lozovsky: The list of speakers is closed, but I have a motion to close the debate and to proceed to concrete proposals. Any objections? No. The proposal is adopted.

It is moved to accept the manifesto as a basis and to return it to the Presidium for final editing. Any objections to the motion to return it to the Presidium? Hearing none, it is accepted. Now the question is whether we will issue it within the next twenty-four hours or at the close of the congress. I have two motions: one to appoint a special commission, the other to turn the manifesto for final editing to the Presidium.

Williams (USA): I want to know who proposed to revise the appeal?

Lozovsky: That proposal is mine. The floor is given to Comrade Murphy.

Murphy (Britain): I would like to have an answer to my question whether this manifesto aims to be a simple appeal to the workers of the world without any indications as to the principles and tactics agreed upon by the congress, or a summary of the ideas and tactical methods that the congress will approve. If it is to be a simple appeal, I then have no objection to its being referred back for final shaping to the Presidium. If not, I will insist upon the election of a special commission.

Lozovsky: The manifesto being already approved as a basis, the question raised by Murphy automatically drops. I will now put to a vote the motion whether the draft is to be referred to a commission or to the Presidium.

It is resolved by a majority of votes to refer the draft of the manifesto to the Presidium.[6]

6 For the text of the manifesto that was eventually issued at the conclusion of the congress, see pp. 597–600.

Debate on Rosmer Report

Albert Király (Hungary): Comrades, only part of Comrade Rosmer's report has been translated for us. It is clear to us, however, that this report deals only with the preliminary work of the International Council. For that reason there can be no question of a detailed criticism here. It must be said, however, that the authors of this report were the first to declare war on the powerful Amsterdam Federation. We must place this work in historical context, and we must agree that it was only preparatory work. The real work starts today.

I take note of this report, but the Red Trade Union International is powerful enough to dispense with inaccurate data. For example, we are not yet in a position to state that the number of Hungarian workers adhering to the Red Trade Union International is in line with the figure given by the reporter. Regardless, the leaders of the revolutionary movement in Hungary are imprisoned, which is one of the things that makes propaganda work in Hungary more difficult than elsewhere. The figures given by the report should be published only after a careful check. This is why I propose not to publish the report as it has been presented to us. We are fighting obstinately against the Mensheviks, and we must be careful not to give them any grounds for charging us with exaggeration.

Comrades, let us accept Comrade Rosmer's report. The bureau has accomplished enormous work. But I repeat: this is preparatory work. In the future, we will have to carry out a truly revolutionary activity, for which the congress must give directives.

Lozovsky: With regard to the figures mentioned by the comrade, they were given us by the representatives of various countries, and if they are exaggerated the blame is to be laid on the representatives who supplied the information. We request all the comrades to give us exact information and figures, in order to enable us to proceed immediately to the corresponding corrections. Better to let the figures be smaller rather than exaggerated. It is necessary that accurate figures be given on the authority of each organisation.

Jack Murphy (Britain): The report of Comrade Rosmer includes very valuable material, but it says nearly nothing about the tactics on which the work of the council was based. It does not mention the frictions that existed between them and other countries, for instance, with Italy, which joined the Amsterdam International as well. The report does not show what effect the letter addressed to the Italian Confederation of Labour has produced.[7] The Italian Confederation

7 Lozovsky's open letter to the CGL, dated 23 October 1920 and written on behalf of Russian

was requested in that letter to withdraw from the Amsterdam International. Further, the report does not inform us of the extent of success the revolutionary labour organisations arrived at in different parts of the world during the last year, or what was the attitude of the workers toward the Provisional Council. The report does not tell us of the nature of the difficulties we met on our way. Such information would be of great value to the congress.

The report also says nothing about the literature produced by the International Council. Did our literature at least reach the working masses abroad? The report does not record the result of our manifesto issued to the Western workers and signed by the Red Labour International and the Communist International.[8] I for one must say that contrary to our expectations it did not shake the great masses of workers. The report also fails to relate the internal contradictions that exist in the council itself.

In the council, particularly in the English groups, there were industrial workers and trade unionists, in other words a right and left wing. Furthermore, the existing contradictions, without doubt, will keep on growing. Therefore, it would be beneficial to us to study them and their methods. Let Comrade Rosmer correct the gaps in his report so that the congress may derive the full benefit of last year's experience.

Arthur Bartels (Germany, Gelsenkirchen Free Workers' Union): Comrades, we have various comments to make about Comrade Rosmer's report. We were unable to follow him as closely as we would have liked, and therefore we're glad that the report has also been submitted in writing.

The translation, if it was correct, was performed very quietly, so it was very difficult for us to follow. We nevertheless noted that Comrade Rosmer issued opinions about tactics in Germany that did not belong there, and which anticipate the discussion still to come. We are opposed to the fact that a one-sided atmosphere has already been set here in the congress.

The references made to the attempts to conquer the trade unions in Britain and Germany are not entirely true. I note that Comrade Tom Mann recently

---

unions, was published in *Avanti*, 25 November 1920, under the title 'I Sindicati russi e la Confederazione Generale del Lavoro d'Italia: Lettera aperta alla Confederazione Generale del Lavoro italiana'. That same issue of *Avanti* also published the CGL leadership's reply, 'La risposta del Consiglio Direttivo Confederale'.

8 The referred-to August 1920 manifesto, signed jointly by the RILU and Comintern, was published in issue no. 13 of *Die Kommunistische Internationale*. It appeared in English in *Communist International* no. 13, under the title 'The Third International to the Trade Unions of the World'.

said that the movement in Britain is still so weak that we cannot draw any conclusions from it.

In Germany comrades have been building nuclei in the counterrevolutionary unions, following the tactic adopted by the VKPD [United Communist Party of Germany] Zentrale.[9] The German comrades who have done this work would have had a larger number of organised workers on their side had a different tactic been used.

The influence of the VKPD in the unions is extremely small. I only point out that wherever a revolutionary mood within the trade unions was noticeable, the individual comrades and local groups who had been won to the revolutionary cause were thrown out of the trade unions, and unions that declared in favour of joining the Red Trade Union International were expelled. (*Interjection: 'So this influence does exist.'*) If this is the result of their influence, then I can assert that nuclei lead to splits. (*Laughter*)

A Hungarian comrade has already pointed out that the report's figure for the number of organised workers in Hungary is incorrect. I also claim that the figures given by the German comrades are likewise incorrect. (*Protests from German comrades*) Calm down, you can take the floor later.

We say that the figures given for Germany of two or two and a half million are wrong. The number of union members standing on a revolutionary platform must never be overstated. We have our own statistics, which are contrary to the one given by the reporter. The congress cannot rely on false statistics; these only hurt ourselves.

Missing from Comrade Rosmer's report was an explanation of the activity in the individual countries, particularly of the German bureau.[10] We must submit the activity of this bureau to severe criticism. The bureau did not display sufficient activity in trying to unite all the revolutionary organisations. I should note that the bureau was only in direct contact with the VKPD Zentrale, while only a loose connection was sought with the Gelsenkirchen Free Workers' Union, and only to defend its political point of view. It did not make contact with other revolutionary organisations in Germany, such as the Agricultural Workers' Union, the Hand and Brain Workers' Union, etc. In the disputes between the Free [syndicalist] Unions and the National Trade Union Office [of the VKPD], it always took the side of the latter. These are the conclusions we draw from Comrade Rosmer's report. The report did not mention the concrete activity of the bureau, which was nil. I can cite only the bureau's activity during the

9 The Zentrale was the Central Bureau of the German Communist Party, a subcommittee of its Central Committee.

10 For the Central European Bureau based in Berlin, see p. 70, n. 11.

British miners' strike (*Exclamations: 'Very good.'*) I have nothing else to add to that.

Comrades, the report also contains interesting points on the manner in which the Presidium established relations with the delegations present here at the congress. We will talk about that when we discuss the Credentials Commission's report.

Finally, with regard to Comrade Lozovsky, who is alleged in the report to have made a breakthrough in Germany. We have to say something without diminishing the merits of Comrade Lozovsky, who has dealt blows in the struggle against the trade-union bureaucracy. But the fight against the German trade-union bureaucracy did not start with Comrade Lozovsky a year ago. It began much earlier, during the war.

Franz Reichmann (Switzerland): Dear comrades: This is really the first time that the International Council of Red Trade Unions is in a position to hand in a report covering, with a few exceptions, almost the entire continent. When we heard this report, we recalled the fact that just a year ago, a rump international congress took place and it was composed of a total of seven organisations.[11] But at this present congress, dozens of countries are represented. That fact, more than any phrases, shows that the idea of the revolutionary class struggle is making progress.

Although there are shortcomings in this report, which we may have to criticise, we should not lose sight that the main idea – that is, to stay inside the trade unions and conquer them – has gained tremendous strength. (*Shouts: 'Very good'.*) I believe, comrades, that this idea runs like a red thread all throughout Comrade Rosmer's report. Moreover, when we keep in mind the enormous difficulties of communication with the different countries, we must acknowledge the great work accomplished by the International Council of Red Trade Unions.

It is not so easy to gauge correctly the exact membership of each particular country, especially when we keep in mind that reports can be frequently obtained only through illegal channels. I know by experience that it is impossible to maintain regular relations with Switzerland. The same situation holds true in other countries. For that reason, there is no way to obtain exact figures. One can simply state, without exaggeration, that the declared membership of the Red International of Labour Unions is constantly increasing.

11 An apparent reference to the 15 July 1920 meeting of seven organisations that formed the International Trade Union Council.

At this point I should like to take up the figures presented here with reference to the Swiss trade unions. We learn from Comrade Rosmer's report that, as estimated by the union statisticians, the total Swiss trade-union membership in favour of the Red Trade Union International totals 130,000. There are two independent union federations, representing two different tendencies. One of these sides with Amsterdam; the other is with Moscow. Syndicalist organisations of the French, Spanish, or even the German type are non-existent in Switzerland. I want to have this fact formally established, so that Comrade Rosmer's report may not lead to false conclusions.

I wish to add that the organisation whose delegates represent Switzerland at this congress has approximately 90,000 members, that is, about one-third of the total number of workers organised in the Swiss trade unions. We know that we are dealing with small numbers, since Switzerland has a population of only 3 million. Of this number about 250,000 are workers organised in the Swiss Trade Union Federation. Of these, 90,000 are represented at this congress; this is as near the correct figure as the Swiss delegates were able to ascertain. I should like to emphasise in this connection the fact that no one should imagine that 90,000 Communists are represented; this would be a false inference. We, who here represent the Swiss trade unions, carry on with these unions a very hard fight against the Amsterdam International. But so far, none of these organisations have joined the Red Trade Union International.

Comrades, you must understand that the revolutionary activity of the Swiss comrades is all the more difficult given that most of them belong to smaller federations. The large federations of Swiss trade unions, such as those of the railway workers and metalworkers – which together represent almost half the total number of organised workers and have a membership of 120,000 – have, with the exception of a few sections, come out solidly against Moscow and against anything coming from Russia. The leaders at the helm of these federations aim their heaviest artillery against the idea of the Red International. Just at present there is a fierce struggle raging in all the federations on the issue of whether to affiliate with the Red Trade Union International or to remain within the Amsterdam International. We shall speak more about this when we take up the question of tactics. My time is limited and I must confine myself to dealing with essentials.

In our view, the principal task before the Red Trade Union International after its foundation stone has been laid must be to consolidate all parts of our organisation. It is not advisable to shout loudly that 16 million workers were represented in Moscow. I agree with Comrade Lozovsky that we should take care not to furnish the trade-union bureaucracy with any doubtful statistics by which it could demagogically attack us. We have no ground for overestimating our strength, as we know quite well that we are fighting for a revolutionary idea, which is continually gaining headway and is not at all, as our opponents would have it, dying off.

We should, therefore, like to move the following:

1. That the Credentials Commission give us a clear-cut and exact statement showing how many members and organisations are really represented, and which ones are actually championing the revolutionary class struggle against the Amsterdam International and for organised affiliation to Moscow.
2. That the same commission should hand in an exact statement showing the number of organisations and their membership upon whom this congress of the Moscow International can count even today, showing the number of those who have already affiliated and those who have as yet not done so.

We further move that the commission on this report, which had to depend on the material that the Council of the Red Trade Union International obtained from figures supplied by individuals – the council had to be glad to get any reports from anyone – should carefully sift through and supplement this material. The strange picture we have before us can apparently be explained only by the character of the material from individual sources. I believe the moment has come when this sort of thing must stop. I believe every single country is now in a position to supply this congress, through its own delegation, with an accurate picture of its own situation. In the future this must be done semi-annually or quarterly, according to the decision the congress may take in each case.

The International Council or the Executive Bureau must get accurate reports. Only such reports can have any decisive and objective value. If each country entrusts its own representatives with the task of carrying out this work, we will get a clear picture based in reality of the strength and the resources of the Red Trade Union International.

Erich Melcher (Germany): I think I'm voicing the opinion of the majority of the German delegation when I say that we in Germany felt the greatest joy at the stand taken by the International Trade Union Council that we should work within the unions and not leave them. Since we in Germany took this stand and worked along these lines within the trade unions, we have left no stone unturned to consolidate all the revolutionary councils of the German workers into one unified front. If our success was not as great as we had wished, and the results obtained fell short of what we had expected, the only ones to blame are those who declare on all occasions that they are the simon-pure 'revolutionists' and, at the same time, fail to act in accordance with the stand taken by the Third International and submit to the conditions imposed by the Second Congress of the International. These are the same strange revolutionists who paid just as little attention to the decisions of the International Trade Union Council. I believe the German delegates know that I refer to the Gelsenkirchen Free Workers' Union, who even today only keep on fault-finding and advancing all sorts of carping objections in connection with our work on the report of the ITUC. Nor have they accomplished anything in Germany beyond this carping criticism.

I have proof of all I've said. We trade unionists strive to unite in a single front the revolutionary forces of Germany, as we know that our work can be successful only through solidarity. But all our efforts in this direction were thwarted by the machinations of the Gelsenkirchen Free Workers' Union and others, organisations that share its view and carry out their work apart from the marching army of labour and without giving any thought to its organisations. Instead of striving to reach our common goal and fight the capitalist foe by means of concerted action, we in Germany had to waste time and energy in wrangling with the adherents of the above unions, who ought to be our allies, over the tactics to be employed in fighting the Amsterdam International. On this account, the real work against Amsterdam was relegated to the background, and the success that could have been attained was not realised.

I do not want to speak about the origin of the Free Workers' Unions [*freie Unionen*]. The United Communist Party of Germany has always been confronted with the fact that these organisations were here. We would have advanced much farther in our fight against the reactionary Amsterdam International, if we had not been a house divided against itself. These internal dissensions were an obstacle in the way of any proper and successful fight against the trade-union bureaucracy in Germany.

When we, as Communists and adherents of the Red Trade Union International, declared that we would not leave the trade unions, but on the contrary stick to those organisations where the working masses still remain, we know that we chose a more successful way than those who preach the doctrine of 'smashing the unions'. We must act as a leader within these organisations, and show the workers that the trade unions must be transformed. The demand that the revolutionary masses break away from the reactionary leaders should be aimed not at the beginning, but at the end of our struggle.

Bartels, who preceded me, criticised the Berlin bureau of the ITUC for failing to accomplish its tasks. I shall not go into these questions any further, because this will be done by the comrades from the Berlin bureau who had to take up this question with the Free Workers' Unions. Bartels then attacked the Berlin bureau for failing to establish connections with the revolutionary organisations standing on the platform of the Red Trade Union International. As a matter of fact, the Berlin bureau tried by every means in its power to do this. If, in spite of this, no concerted and fruitful action was possible, the blame rests solely with the unions that, disregarding the decisions of the Provisional Trade Union Council, stuck to the slogan of 'Out of the trade unions', and thus rendered any comradely cooperation impossible.

Bartels next referred to the unions existing in Germany, also the Free Agricultural Workers' Union. This organisation, as with the other unions listed by Bartels, was formed against the will of the [VKPD] National Trade Union Office and the Berlin bureau. The Berlin representatives of the Provisional Council were, at the formation of all these unions, always confronted with an accomplished fact. We must shed a little more light on the above Free Agricultural Workers' Union referred to by Bartels as one of the revolutionary organisations. This alliance, through its representatives, approached the government with the request to be admitted to the Association for Collective Bargaining with Employers. That is, they have done, or wanted to do, just the opposite of what separates us from the Amsterdam people. We are much obliged for such 'revolutionaries'.

Bartels: This is your cell tactics.

Melcher (*continues*): We are quite willing to believe that this statement of fact is quite unpleasant to you, but it must once and for all be stated in what company the Free Workers' Union finds itself in. Your objection is the best proof of the inglorious ties binding you to such confusions.

Other outrageous things can be found in the practice of the Gelsenkirchen Union. At one of its district council conventions it passed a resolution to hold fast to the slogan of 'Smash the trade unions'. This resolution was passed for the express purpose of putting the First Congress of the Red Trade Union International face to face with a fait accompli. We protested against such an attitude. We declared that – in opposition to Bartels, who laid special stress upon the consistent and revolutionary attitude of his friends – our position on this point was entirely different. It is neither consistent nor revolutionary for a minority to want to precipitate such an action for the sake of confronting a world congress with a fait accompli. It is far more necessary that we utilise the experience of the delegates of the different countries at this congress as a basis to firmly lay down our future tactics, the tactics that must then be binding on all real revolutionaries and that must guide us in striving for our common goal.

In this direction the Provisional Council of the Red Trade Union International deserves praise for the service it has rendered the movement by bringing together at this congress representatives of the revolutionary workers of various countries. This work involved very great difficulties that had to be overcome. Let us utilise this congress by firmly laying down the guidelines that will lead the workers of all countries against the Amsterdam trade-union bureaucracy. If we consider all the resolutions adopted as binding on us, we shall be in a position to defeat the counterrevolution in all countries, and especially in Germany, by unchaining the working masses from counterrevolution's best support, that is, from the Amsterdam trade-union bureaucracy. In this way we will take a big step toward our goal: the social revolution.

Lozovsky: Comrades, the report presented here has been subjected to quite severe criticism from different angles. Its defects have been pointed out to be manifold. Comrade Murphy stated that nothing has been said of the conditions existing in different countries, or of the differences within the council itself. According to other criticisms, some of the most important and more practical questions that should have been included in the report have been omitted. Let us begin with the omissions.

How do matters stand in Italy? When we concluded our agreement with Italy, which was signed by the Italian Confederation of Labour, we intentionally did not demand that it break away from the Amsterdam International. Why did we not present such an ultimatum to the Italian confederation? Comrades, this was because we had just started to organise ourselves. We were well aware of the difficulties of drawing into our ranks a large organisation. I wish to remind you of the fact that many Socialist parties joined the Third International without having severed their relations with the Second. If the change was difficult for the political parties, all the more difficult and slow would be the transition from the old policies to the new among the large and amorphous working masses. We purposely did not press this issue very strongly, in order to give workers the time to see for themselves that dual affiliation was not possible.

After the Russian trade-union delegation arrived in Berlin, we then raised the question fully in our open letter to the General Confederation of Labour. Is it possible simultaneously to be in two organisations? Is it possible to have two passports – one for Moscow and the other for Amsterdam? We have not as yet received any reply from the Italian Confederation of Labour, which is still affiliated to two organisations, and of its two passports it has not a single one on hand. This congress will have to give its decision to the Italian confederation, that it will have to choose either one or the other organisation. But at the initial period of the existence of the ITUC, our policy was a correct one. It was necessary that the masses have the time and possibility to direct their attention to these facts and to win them over to our side. It was also necessary to take by their necks the representatives of the Confederation of Labour and compel them to obey the will of the masses.

As to Germany, the situation is more complicated, and the passionate debate between the German comrades, which we witnessed, are the echoes of the painful process that the German movement is now passing through. If each revolutionary action results in a failure, it is on account of the lack of unity. It was with particular acuteness that the question was raised in Germany about the revolutionary minorities within the trade unions. It is asked: What was the course taken by the ITUC with regard to this question over eleven months? We used to say, and continue to do so, 'Stick to the old unions'. If we want to clean a house, it is incongruous to pour petrol on it and burn it down. In fact, the slogan calling for the destruction of the trade unions is a counterrevolutionary slogan. We must explain and bring home to the masses everything that is going on, because our task is not to destroy the unions, but to conquer the masses in the unions. What does it mean to conquer the masses? Does it imply that we are to take possession of their treasury or premises? No, to conquer the workers means that we are to gain control over the minds of the proletariat, over its feelings and conscience, and to make it understand the class struggle.

When we see people without experience in the struggle but with a revolutionary temperament, with insufficient ideas but with ardent hearts and hot temperaments, we used to tell them: Take care when you come to a turn, so that you don't break your neck during the revolution. I am well acquainted with the situation in Germany, I was a witness there to the internal struggle. One hundred thousand workers gathered and declared, 'We have rallied the most revolutionary workers!' We asked them: 'Where are the remaining ten million?' Where are they? By wresting the most revolutionary elements from the trade unions, you remove the soul of the workers, you take out the cement, and the house will fall to pieces. Those who say, 'Out of the unions!' do not believe in revolution, for the revolution will be achieved by the masses, not by isolated workers, even if they are good ones.

Now we shall pass over to the remarks made by Comrade Murphy. To the inquiries regarding the way the Western European movement responded to the activity of the council, I would answer this way: The Western European and American labour movement clearly shows its attitude by your presence here. The numerous representatives of thirty-seven countries assembled in this hall testify to the enormous amount of work achieved by the council. The council was the centre to which the revolutionary movement and the class-conscious workers gravitated. We need no better testimony. Of course, our connection with most of these countries was not close enough, but you, what were you doing in your countries? Comrade Murphy says, 'The ITUC published literature, but it did not reach us.' To which we might answer: 'Why did you not translate our publications, why did you not distribute them, why were you unable to do so?' Comrades, if it is anyone's fault, the responsibility must be shared evenly. It is evident that you did not accomplish the work that was possible to do.

Let us go farther. The question of internal frictions in the International Council of Trade Unions was raised. Yes, comrades, there are frictions. It would have been unwise and foolish to ignore them. But what do they consist of? For the first time in the history of the working-class movement, we see new and powerful trade-union organisations coming out of the revolution and standing up to the old organisations. Among everyone present in this hall there are no disagreements about this; all are opponents of Amsterdam and are partisans of the social revolution. The disagreements are these: How best to get rid of the Amsterdam International? How to bring nearer the social revolution? Which tactics are best suited for the purpose of organising the workers around our slogans? These are the differences. The disagreements are not in the council, but in life itself. Each country has its objective conditions, old ones, inherited from the past, that created a specific psychology, a specific turn of mind, traditions of life different from other countries – all this together causes the new ideas to be applied differently in different countries. A different conception of the aims and problems causes the disagreements to be sharply revealed here.

The task of our congress is not to smooth over these disagreements, not to obscure them, as is done by the Amsterdam International, which says, 'Come over to me all you oppressed, all you sufferers, and you will find shelter within the International Labour Bureau of the League of Nations.' We are not permeated with such an evangelical love for everyone. We say that only those who are anxious for the dictatorship of the proletariat and the social revolution can be with us. We will do everything necessary to determine who shall be admitted into the ranks of the fighters for the revolution. We will say: Here is the decision of the majority, which stands until the next congress, when a different majority will give us something new. This is how we understand internal disagreements and misunderstandings, which are unavoidable in any living body. Workers live and fight in different conditions; they understand differently the problems before them. They are differently educated; their economic and social relations are different. All this reflects itself in the workers' organisations, and on the workers' psychology. Workers in different countries conceive differently the same slogans and the same idea. These differences must be overcome. We can achieve this only by formulating our line straightforwardly, without obscuring the differences, by helping in a fraternal way those of us who need help and support, not by inventing new slogans. It is by following a common line of conduct. There is no other way.

If delegates say at the close of our congress: The resolutions are indeed good, but for some countries new slogans are needed such as, 'Out of the unions!' and so on, this will only weaken our proletarian front. Under such conditions we will be beaten in each country, individually and collectively.

Comrades, out of all the discussions we can clearly see that the international council has not done even a hundredth part of what it ought to do, but you comrades in each country have not done even a thousandth of your task. We ought to grasp the bourgeoisie by the neck and step on its chest. We are all equally guilty. I hope that out of this congress will come a strong, solid organisation that will mend the gaps, and that at the next congress we will give a substantial report about greater success than we have had in the past. (*Applause*)

Lozovsky: Comrade Mann has the floor.

Tom Mann (Britain): Comrades: Some of the criticisms offered to the report of Brother Rosmer are no doubt well merited.

That which I think is the chief one is its inordinate length. I think it could well be reduced considerably, and one of the little items that might be eliminated perhaps is that reference to myself. I feel it necessary to make a brief reference to that which was stated here by Comrade Bartels of the Trade Workers' Union [Gelsenkirchen Free Workers' Union] of Germany. He made some reference there to the strength, the relative or alleged strength of the revolutionary movement in Britain and to something that he said I had said. I do not know when that statement was made as to the alleged strength of the movement. I am sure he is desirous of being correct, he and his comrades. Those of you who heard me make the statement at the opening meeting of this congress remember perhaps that I then said, definitely and clearly, that the estimates of the strength of the revolutionary movement in Britain – that is, of the organised workers, could be correctly put down at 20 per cent. There was no half-and-half business about it. I have taken great pains to try and understand the exact strength of the movement. Not represented here, no, only a small portion of it is represented here, because that would mean a million and a half of the seven million men. How then is it estimated?

I will give one instance. In one of the old unions known as the Amalgamated Society of Engineers a year or two ago, there was an election where one candidate stood for a revolutionary programme, stating quite definitely that the discussions in regard to the Spartacists of Germany and the principles they stood for we also stood for, and that he also stood for the Bolshevik attitude and also for the syndicalist attitude in all main essentials, and that was said in his address. I was the particular person, so I know what I am talking about. Nevertheless, in that union, considered to be one of the most reactionary, or at any rate one of the most respectable, steady-going, recognising orthodox institutions, still the vote was very largely preponderant in favour of the revolutionary candidate who was returned. There is only one explanation for it, and that explanation is this: the revolutionary principles had been accepted by so considerable a percentage of the rank and file that they therefore decided that vote. There was a considerable number who did not vote, of course, who must always be allowed for.

Again, I am well familiar with all portions of the British Isles and have been for a long time. I know the various sections at work there, and the revolutionary forces are known under different headings in different areas. In South Wales for instance, the miners work under the head of the unofficial movement, and there they are carrying on a systematic educational and revolutionary propaganda. They have done so for a period of years and they have done it very effectively. In other parts it is known as the Workers' Committees.[12] In Scotland they have carried on a systematic and intensive educational organising and revolutionary campaign. But it is known and the work is being done.

Just recently, immediately prior to taking the boat to come to this congress, I was addressing a series of meetings of the miners in Northumberland and Durham counties. At every meeting – and I held five in succession – I talked definitely about the Red Trade Union and the desirability of separating from Amsterdam and focusing attention upon the revolutionary movement of the world, and I urged them to use their influence with their executives to pursue a propaganda favourable to the revolutionary attitude. At every one of these meetings a vote was taken, and in every case the vote was unanimously in favour. I mention these as an indication of the growth of the movement as being not accidental nor spasmodic, but as being a systematic one being carried on by a very considerable number of capable advocates. I therefore know that I am correct in saying that 20 per cent of the total of the organised workers of the United Kingdom are definitely and strongly out for a full-fledged revolution aiming for the overthrow of the capitalist system and the establishing of genuine communism.

Reference has been made time and again to tactics, as to whether we should be inside the unions or not. Comrade Barker has also referred to this. He took a

12 The National Shop Stewards' and Workers' Committee Movement emerged in Britain in the course of militant struggles during World War I.

different attitude from the one that my experience teaches me is the right one for the country to which I belong. I am not here to advise other countries, but in the country in which I have had considerable experience, I say that the result of that experience is beyond all question to tell me and those who wish to work along the lines we are discussing, who wish the revolution, that it would be exceedingly unwise to leave the old unions. I am perfectly sure of it.

That is so far as such human faculties as I have could admit of my drawing conclusions. What could have happened had the miners begun five years ago or earlier to pursue a policy opposite in character, and to have endeavoured to build up a revolutionary organisation drawing members or aiming at drawing members from the existing miners' federation? It is permissible to try and estimate. I have endeavoured to try and estimate, and have myself every time come back to this. Knowing the situation well enough, I am perfectly sure that the result would have been not to have thrown the whole movement on a revolutionary basis aiming at a revolutionary objective, but what would have happened would have been to draw 10 per cent or 15 per cent or more from the old union and thus solidify the old unions by the hostility that would have been displayed, and they would have been reactionary with the aid of all the bourgeois forces that would have given them assistance. Every capitalist paper would have helped. There would have been six or seven editions every day of the half-penny papers pumped to every man amongst us, every group amongst us, every revolutionary section amongst us, and it would have made our task much greater.

To my mind it is preposterous in Britain – I say nothing of Germany, France, or other countries, but in Britain I know the way to proceed, and I say we have had up to now and for a good number of years – and we have not always been on the orthodox side either – this experience, and I put it to the young men: it is a serious mistake to build up a lot of smaller organisations, with a view to drawing members from the older ones. How about our members of the Amalgamated Engineering Union, 450,000 strong? Why should they be advised to leave that union possessing buildings and the funds of the organisation to which they have contributed? When all that is required is the requisite revolutionary fervour pumped into the members in the first instance and into all parts and ramifications of the organisation. That is what is called for, and that is what is forthcoming.

I therefore stand definitely in favour, and I believe every member in our group will stand definitely in favour of working inside the unions, confident, not hopeless, confident that, in a comparatively short time, we shall switch them every one from their present position and make it far too hot for the old reactionary officials to remain there in their present positions endeavouring to keep the pot boiling in their particular way. It is getting too hot for them now. It will be hotter still, and they will clear out by and by, and all the power will be in the hands of the revolutionary forces. Therefore I stand by this and defend that attitude.

Lozovsky: Comrade Gliński has the floor.

Gliński [Stefan Królikowski] (Poland): I consider it my first duty to declare in the name of our delegation that we fully agree with the tactical lines followed up to the present moment by the International Council of Red Trade Unions. Not only do we agree with it theoretically, but we consider that during the last year the development of the trade-union movement and practical experience have shown that the course taken was the right one, particularly with regard to Poland. The correctness of this policy is quite evident.

Up to the spring of 1919 we had special Communist unions. There were also parallel unions in the same branches of industry, which were known under the name of 'neutral' unions and developed under the guidance of the Polish Socialist Party – a party corresponding to the Mensheviks in Russia and the Scheidemannites in Germany [the SPD]. It was in the spring of 1919 that we decided to merge those two types of unions on the following conditions:

First, considering that we are living in an epoch of social revolution, we are firmly convinced that the political development of our country, the class contradictions and struggles between the exploiting classes and the exploited, will undoubtedly bring the working masses to the Communist Party, because everyday experience will bring home to the workers that only the Communists are qualified to serve as their real guides and leaders in their actual struggles with capitalism, pointing out the shortest way to victory. This is the first point. We are convinced, further, that the working masses organised in trade unions are actually the elements who will fight for the social revolution, for the dictatorship of the proletariat, and will thus take up our positions by the natural development of things.

But, besides, there is another consideration: we know that the Amsterdam leaders and the Polish Socialist Party are not only traitors to the historical mission of the working classes, but also traitors to the interests of the workers in their everyday struggle. We knew that they were bound to ignore the urgent needs of the working class in its everyday struggle, and did ignore them. Therefore, the differences between ourselves and the Polish Socialist Party will become clear and will, in the long run, open the eyes of every worker. Thus we need not fear that by this merging of the unions we should, at first, allow them to take the whole trade-union movement into their hands, for we know full well that we will succeed in beating them out of their positions in the course of daily struggle.

We created accordingly within all the branches of the trade-union organisations, corresponding Communist units that we designated by the name of 'Communist fractions', and commenced so successful a struggle that we now include 40 per cent of the whole mass of the organised workers. I believe, comrades, and I am fully convinced of this, that in the further struggle complete victory will be on our side.

I intended to bring these instances to the attention of those comrades who are issuing to the masses the slogan, 'Communists, leave the trade unions!' Comrades, this is used in our country by the most hot-headed, staunch counter-revolutionists; it is the order of the day with them. They are struggling against the Communists precisely by means of expulsion from the trade unions.

It is quite possible, of course, that with the trend of events, they might split the trade-union movement, but then it is they, and not us, who will have done it. They will split the unions, because they realise that should the unions contribute to the unity of the trade-union movement, these would infallibly fall into the hands of the Communists. Yet the matter is by no means so simple. It is possible to exclude hundreds and thousands of workers, but if there were to exist in some countries a movement embracing millions of them, the matter becomes more complicated. I don't mean that they would not bring about a split, but I mean to say that our policy in the future ought to develop along these indicated lines.

These tactics have brought good results, and we have full grounds to believe, and even to feel convinced, that in the near future the trade-union movement will belong to the Communists and develop under the guidance of the Red International of Trade Unions.

Lozovsky: I have received a proposal to close the debate. I too think that the debate need not be continued and that a commission of seven should be elected to work out the final resolution.

Leval (Spain) (*from his seat*): I propose that the report be printed and distributed, after which the commission will be able to propose its resolution based on the report.

Lozovsky: Are there any objections to the organisation of a commission? No. I propose to include in this commission one representative each from France, Russia, Spain, Germany, Poland, USA, and Britain.

One of the delegates (*from his seat*): I propose to include one representative from the Balkan states.

Lozovsky: Are there any objections to the inclusion of a representative from the Balkan states? No. Carried. The delegations should transmit to the Presidium the names of the members whom they will elect on the commission.

Before closing the session, I must announce that the Organisation and Control commissions will sit tomorrow, 7 July, at 11:00 a.m. The plenary session of the congress will take place on 8 July, at 11:00 a.m.

(*The session is declared closed at 4:15 p.m.*)

SESSION 4. 8 JULY 1921, MORNING–AFTERNOON

World Economic Crisis; Trade Union Tasks and Tactics

(*The session is opened at 11:00 a.m. Comrade Lozovsky in the chair.*)[1]

Lozovsky: The Presidium proposes the following agenda: We shall start today with Comrade Varga's report on the world economic crisis in the German, French, and English languages in the Hall of Columns. Simultaneously a report on the tasks and tactics of labour unions will be presented in the Russian language in the Blue Hall. Tomorrow we shall have the reports on the relations between the Third, Communist International and the Red International of Labour Unions.

Viktor Drewnitzky (Germany, General Workers' Union): Comrades, I am against the motion of Comrade Lozovsky. I find it impossible to accept such a motion. If we are to discuss these two important problems – the world economic crisis and the tactics of the labour unions – simultaneously, the result will be fruitless. We did not come here with the intention of summarily expediting matters. Every question on the congress agenda should be thoroughly and clearly discussed and resolved. We cannot return home empty-handed; we must come back to our organisations with plain answers and a full report of our activities.

Lozovsky: Comrade Drewnitzky misunderstood me, which explains his protest. My proposal simply falls in with what our comrade just said. In order to save time I moved that while Comrade Varga reads his report in German, a Russian comrade will, at the same time, read the second report in Russian, thereby leaving us ample time after the report is translated for discussion and deliberation.

Disch (Germany), on a point of order, notes that there are enough members present and that we could proceed with the agenda. (*The proposal was adopted.*)

1 The French and Russian editions state that Lozovsky was in the chair; the English and German versions say that Andreev was chairing.

 | DOI:10.1163/9789004712867_008

Lozovsky asks to move the agenda, which is carried.

Session in the Hall of Columns

Report on the World Economic Crisis[2]

Eugen Varga: Comrades! The world economy has been gripped by an economic crisis completely unprecedented in size and intensity. Those gathered for this congress have been so closely connected because of their daily activities regarding the fate of the broad proletarian masses that it may even seem unnecessary to dwell on the essence and peculiarities of this crisis. Every participant in the labour movement of each country constantly encounters the direct and indirect manifestations of this crisis during the current fierce mass struggle to simply survive, in the crudest and truest sense of the word.

Here at the congress we will deal not so much with a description of the symptoms of this crisis as with an attempt to resolve the following question: Is the present crisis just one of those periods of economic depression that have accompanied the capitalist development of society from its inception, or is it a phenomenon of a new and different order? After all, we know that periods of crises and economic prosperity, the ebb and flow of economic life, are unalterable companions of the capitalist mode of production. We must ask ourselves whether the present epoch, characterised by our contemporaries as something we have not seen before, indicates the final irreparable collapse of capitalism, or, on the other hand, whether it is a phenomenon like the crises or periods of economic depression that we have known since the beginning of capitalist times. As I said, I think it superfluous to present here a detailed description, documented with figures, of the phenomenon we are considering. To answer the main question I have formulated above, it will be enough to outline several basic concepts.

So let us ask ourselves what are the characteristic features of the present crisis, those unique to it? First of all, let us note its absolute character from the point of view of geographical distribution. With just a glance at any British or other economic journal, there is no doubt that crises prevail in all corners and ends of the globe, in various forms and with different degrees of intensity, not only in Central Europe but in America and even distant Australia and the southern hemisphere. Moreover, as I affirmed only yesterday, those parts of

2 The report by Varga on the world economic crisis was printed in the Russian-language version of the congress proceedings, but appears in none of the other ones. There was no discussion on Varga's presentation, and it was accepted as an informational report.

the capitalist world were also drawn into the process of the capitalist world economy, showing symptoms of a serious disorder of the entire economic organism.

Along with its territorial scope, the second point that we must take into account is the unprecedented duration and severity of the crisis, which has been hanging on for over a year already. It is usually customary to consider the level of market prices as an indicator of the state of affairs, because as a general rule a good market situation is accompanied by an increase in prices. Turning to this case, we state that in the bigger capitalist countries – for example in America – the highest point of commodity prices was reached in March of last year, after which their rapid and continuous drop began, from which we can conclude that the crisis there has been going on for a year and a quarter. The truth is that at the beginning of this year there were signs of improvement in some places, but we nevertheless plainly assert that the situation has not changed for the better.

I do not want to say, like some comrades, that the crisis we are experiencing is the final crisis, in the sense that an improved conjuncture is no longer possible within capitalist relations. Such a statement would seem premature and insufficiently substantiated. On the contrary, one foresees a significant likelihood that capitalism is destined for better days. Nevertheless, the exceptional acuteness and protracted nature of the crisis are striking evidence of the special significance of this phenomenon. This leads me to the conviction that the period of decline that the capitalist economy is now experiencing on a global scale will never simply end without a trace. On the contrary, an intense crisis will take on a chronic character, and will be interrupted only from time to time by a short and weak upsurge in economic growth.

The external manifestations of the crisis in question are partly the same as those familiar to us from the history of capitalism. On the face of it, there is a huge mass of goods waiting in vain for sale, a catastrophic fall in prices, and other phenomena of the same order. Let me cite just one statistic related to Britain. In the monthly price reference ('Index') of the British *Economist* we find that in March the average price, derived from the market prices of a certain number of goods particularly important to the national economy, has fallen from 380 to 223, equivalent to the pre-war price level of 100. Many of you are undoubtedly aware that prices for many goods such as cotton, rubber, and some food items are now much lower than before the war. In particular, the price of cotton fell over the past year to one-quarter of its previous level.

Not less but rather more important in our eyes is another phenomenon. I refer to the colossal unemployment that is closely related to the crisis. I believe that in this case there is no need for me to cite the numerical data related to this question, for every representative of the labour movement of our day is extremely and fully aware of it. I will just say that in Britain there are currently over two million unemployed, not counting the workers in the coal industry. Since 1 April of this year, there are workers standing outside the plants in lockouts, not counting those workers who work only a few days a week because of a corresponding reduction in production. The total figure of unemployed is much more than four million. In America in this respect the situation is similar to that of Britain. The situation is somewhat better in France and Germany. Perhaps, in characterising the state of affairs, the percentage is more indicative of the number of unemployed in Britain, and precisely those who receive official benefits in relation to the total number of workers. This percentage was 4 per cent in November 1920, 7 per cent in January 1921, 10 per cent in March, and 22 per cent in May. Such figures have been completely unknown in previous economic history. And this monstrous unemployment is not an accident. We cannot but regard it as a result of a planned outflow of capital, which in recent years, during and after the war, has been extremely concentrated.

Capital strives to shift to the maximum the entire burden of the last war onto the shoulders of the workers. During previous crises, capitalists have always tried to throw all the stock of unbought domestic goods onto the world market, not just at half price, but literally for a pittance. At the present time we must tell of the existence of a new tactic by capital. Concentrated capital, especially in the field of heavy industry, follows the path of maintaining prices at the previous level and throwing workers out into the street. We must note that entrepreneurs have not just established a policy in connection with the experience of the world crisis, but they also have the desire, in reducing production, to gradually eliminate the surplus of goods that do not find buyers.

We must also indicate that without a doubt the capitalists are preparing a broadly planned offensive against the workers in order to lower the final wage-level surplus achieved during the war. From what has been said, it follows that the present crisis should be regarded differently from all previous ones. If before we had crises within capitalism, so to speak, now the phenomenon under consideration is a crisis of world capitalism as a whole, an all-encompassing crisis that affects simultaneously the world economic organism. This development may soon directly threaten the further existence of a system that has exhausted all its vital possibilities.

Let us try to get a little closer to the deeper causes of the present crisis. For this, it is necessary to consider the historical perspective, and dwell on some of the main points of the capitalist world economy before, during, and after the war.

When considering the world economy in its normal state, so to speak, we find the following: Western Europe as a whole occupies a specific place in the economy of the world. Britain, France, Belgium, Germany, Italy, and so on highlight the industrial part of the capitalist world. In their totality, these countries, with a population of approximately 300 million, are the industrial workshop of the world. All other countries supply them with raw materials that are processed in manufacturing, which thereafter spread throughout the ends of the globe.

At the same time, these countries possess the overwhelming part of the world's maritime tonnage, and simultaneously extract extremely large profits from the capital they have invested in all other countries. Britain, France, Germany, and so on have invested up to 200 billion gold marks in Eastern Europe and in Russia in particular, as well as in non-European countries. Interest from foreign capital again has been returned in the form of imported goods to Western Europe.

On these foundations a fairly stable equilibrium of the capitalist world was built before the war. There were periods of crises, but each time crises were eliminated by opening new sales markets and expanding the demand for goods of European manufacture, by drawing in new countries and enlarging the sphere of the capitalist economy, and finally by the fact that, through technical improvements, costs of production of goods were reduced.

Thus, economic depression was followed each time by a new upsurge in economic life, which lasted three, five, six, or eight years, depending on how cheap it was to produce goods and at the same time sell them without remaindering.

Another essential element of this stable balance was the relationship between labour and capital in Western European countries. A characteristic fact in these countries – which I have called the 'industrial workshops of the world' – and which were of particular importance in the course of the development of the world revolution during the half century from 1850 to 1905 – was that the position of wageworkers was steadily improving, albeit at a slow pace. I know that in trade-union circles, there are many comrades who argue that the real standard of living of the proletariat did not improve at all during this time. Let me just refer, however, to the simple fact that consumption of the most important food items – bread, meat, sugar, coffee, tea, cocoa, and so on – has shown a completely indisputable, steady, and very sharp rise. It goes without saying that this increased consumption of food items cannot be explained only by the fact that the capitalists themselves have absorbed the significant increase of bread, meat, and so on; fifty years ago they had already consumed a greater amount of these products than was good for their digestion. It is clear that the established statistical average increase in consumption per capita should be attributed to the proletariat, given the large percentage that the proletariat constitutes of the total population of Western Europe.

This steady, albeit slow, improvement in the living conditions of industrial workers and their obtaining a share in social life should undoubtedly be considered to be a result of trade unions during this period. Activists in the trade-union movement had the right and the opportunity to say to the workers: 'Thanks to the trade unions, you, comrade workers, have achieved an improvement in your material situation! You deserve this!'

Another reason for the stability of capitalism was the belief – or rather the superstition held by the broad masses of workers – in the stability of the capitalist system. Comrades, if we mentally turn to those agitational methods that have always been used by socialist parties both before the war and to this day, then we will be able to put the whole meaning of their content into the following formula: 'Improve the position of the working class within the capitalist system by organising and applying all legal means.' True, the Socialist Party and the trade unions before the war also sometimes talked about revolution, as it was considered good form. But in judging the extent to which they believed what they said, and the extent that they could be preaching a truly revolutionary transformation of society, it is enough to remember that even in our time social democrats and the yellow heroes of the trade-union movement portray the possibility of social upheaval as something very distant and by no means realistic.

Their activism has been limited to the struggle for wages, and the leaders of the trade-union movement have taken into account the business considerations and arguments of entrepreneurs concerning the possibility and profitability of production, provided workers' earnings were increased. They were not very interested in what the workers wanted when resolving the issue of wages. And having allowed themselves to be convinced by the capitalists that increases in workers' earnings in a given situation would harm the normal profit and reduce it, they have often refused to encroach on the entrepreneur's surplus value and have told the workers, 'In this state of affairs, nothing can be done, and you need to be reconciled to your previous pay.' This ideology of trade unionists and social democrats comes from the idea that sometime in the future the social revolution will be realised in a parliamentary way, that in all fairness it is necessary to provide the entrepreneur with an average capitalist profit, and to fight only if it is possible to raise wages from the capitalist's point of view. Despite the abundance of revolutionary phrases, this ideology strengthens the psychological prerequisites among the broad masses of the proletariat for the further existence of the capitalist system.

The ideological trend described above received a particularly concentrated expression in two ways: firstly, in the field of theory in the reforms of Eduard Bernstein, who transformed it completely into a consistent system.[3]

Secondly, in practice, pure trade unionism, which has its most distinct presence in the Amsterdam Federation, is only quantitatively different from the British trade unions and the pliable trade unions of the Germanic zone.

As I have described, the World War has severely tested the most economically and socially balanced countries of the capitalist world. If we approach the significance of the World War from this point of view, then we come to the following line of reasoning: on the eve of the war the capitalist world economy was disintegrating into separate national economies – British, German, French, Russian, and so on – and reached the limits of the available capacity of the world market under capitalist conditions. Given this state of affairs, the question of dominance in the world market of one or another Greater European state or one of the alliances formed in Europe, and ousting all competitors from the world market, could not be resolved in any other way than by force of arms.

Let us ask ourselves, comrades: What are the economic and social results of the World War? In order to answer this question, being realistic moreover about context, we must divide the world economy into territorial components. First of all, we must single out Eastern and Central Europe, which covers those countries most shaken by the war in terms of economic and social relations. This includes Russia, Poland, Germany, the countries that were part of the former Austro-Hungarian Empire, and the Balkans. What impact did the World War have on these countries?

This impact can be reduced to the following: all the material apparatus of industry, the entire means of production and means of communication, homes, and buildings were destroyed. Under normal capitalist conditions, the material apparatus of production must increase from year to year. In contrast, during the war, there was a significant reduction, which went in two directions: on the one hand, new means of production were not created, and on the other hand, available production resources – steam locomotives, factory equipment,

3 In 1896–8 Eduard Bernstein, a prominent member of the Social-Democratic Party of Germany (SPD), openly rejected Marxism's revolutionary goals and put forward the view that capitalism's contradictions were abating and that it was possible to secure more and more reforms for working people without revolutionary struggle. These positions, codified in his book *Evolutionary Socialism*, were labelled 'revisionism', and became the subject of an intense debate in the world socialist movement. Bernstein's views were formally rejected by congresses of the SPD and the Second International.

plants, power stations, railway repair shops, and so on – declined due to disuse and could no longer satisfy their purpose.

We see the same thing if we turn to the most important means of producing wealth from the land. Due to predatory, primitive, and irrational use, productivity in this area continuously fell during and after the war. Let me cite just one figure, which is very well known to the German comrades. The productivity of German agriculture, or pre-war productivity, has by now decreased by more than one-third. Simultaneously with this phenomenon, there was a sharp reduction in the field of processing.

The third point to consider is the destruction of human labour power. Colossal losses of workers in the prime of their lives, caused by war, poor nutrition, and illness, all led to an extreme decrease in the available amount of workers' labour.

It is clear that with a reduction in production, consumption inevitably decreases too. Hence, it just as inevitably follows that the standard of living of the broad masses should have dropped catastrophically. The situation benefitted only speculators and large landowners. Only they were able to benefit from it for themselves. The remaining 90 per cent of the population – and, primarily, the broad masses of hired workers – were forcibly reduced to the lowest degree of the already low standard of living that was normal for them before the war.

Let us turn to the Entente countries on the European continent. It is important to state that they have had the same process of development, although with slight differences. During and after the war these states enjoyed the support of wealthy Britain and the United States of America. To the degree that these states could draw on substantial industrial investment outside Europe before and during the war, they suffered less from this situation than the states of Central and Eastern Europe.

On to Britain. It must be said that Britain satisfactorily withstood the military pressures. Nevertheless, if we analyse British agriculture without bias, we cannot conclude that this country is unchanged from the one that existed before the war. During the period of the war, Britain was transformed from a world creditor into a debtor, owing heavily to the creditor.

Above all, the poorest country, Russia, suffered the most. If we depict the curve of economic decline, we can go upward from Russia to Poland, Austria-Hungary, Germany, France, and, lastly, Britain, where the national economy came to be preserved relatively better.

We will move on to considering the economy of the other hemispheres, America and Japan. These are the countries in which capitalism reached its highest development and that, during the whole time military operations were underway, were in a state of economic neutrality, energetically using all possibilities for enrichment at the expense of Europe's battles. Unsurprisingly, under these conditions, America's production increased extraordinarily during the five years of the war – the opposite of Europe, where as we saw production in general declined. From this follows that the chief differences between the economies of Europe and America at present determine the significance of the current world crisis. It is enough to cite as an example some particularly important data. In America in 1913, 514 million tons of coal were mined; in 1920, 600 million tons. In 1913, 248 million tons of kerosene versus 442 million tons in 1920. Production of automobiles: 900,000 in 1914 versus 2,350,000 in 1920. With these figures, one can characterise as gigantic the development of production in America. It is not in vain that a certain published representative of American banking circles once said that during the war each machine worked non-stop twenty-four hours a day and that there were no unoccupied workers in the whole of America. Indeed the gigantic orders for military material in the broadest sense of the word gave Entente support to American industry. What was said about America can be said in a somewhat weakened form about Japan at the time.

A third group of countries and territories, made up of young colonial states – Australia, Canada, South Africa – find themselves in a distinctive situation. These countries experienced a significant economic transformation during the war. Prior to the war, capitalism's equilibrium in these countries depended on the massive export of raw materials to Western Europe. Here they were worked up into finished products for export overseas. During the war, however, as I explained earlier, Western Europe was not able to produce for external markets – firstly because the means were lacking to export sufficient tonnage, and secondly because the means of production were fully absorbed in the manufacture of military materials. How did this group of countries accumulate enormous masses of raw materials, and at the same time begin to feel an acute shortage of manufactured industrial products? It seems unnatural that as a result of this phenomenon, a great contradiction was revealed between the unusual lowering of the cost of raw materials and the resulting difficulty in keeping up with the prices of manufactured products. It is curious to note that in all the countries of the third group we are considering, developments proceeded in a similar way. This is the reason for the phenomenon of the current economic crisis spreading to the ends of the world, even to Chile in South America and to Southern Australia. Here we see a picture of the changes in the world economy as a result of the war.

In summary, we will note two main facts: On the one hand, in Europe, the war resulted in the destruction of means of production, the depletion of the soil, and the destruction of manpower – all this leading to a catastrophic underproduction. On the other hand, there was a colossal development of the productive forces in America, and the emergence of new industry in the colonised countries.

Let us go further. After the war, it seemed at first glance that a period of economic growth had begun, which we, for our part, would more correctly call a period of deceptive minimal prosperity, or a period of speculative growth. We only need to look closely at the economic development of Europe from November 1918 to March 1920, in order to reveal its internal contradictions: the scale of transactions and operations versus the production of goods. The creation of real values during this time hardly developed in a positive direction, and the economic life of Europe, despite the deceptive semblance of well-being, not only did not show signs of recovery, but on the contrary continued to go further and further along the path of disintegration. Understandably, the negative development of the European economy in the countryside was especially clearly emphasised by the fact that the currency of all European countries – Germany, France, Italy, Britain, during this time – was continuously falling in comparison with America's currency. For example, taking the British pound sterling, which stood at parity with the dollar at the end of the 1918 war, at the present time, compared to the dollar, it has already lost one-fourth of its value. In addition, as an even more graphic expression of this, we must state in relation to the French and German currencies that the dollar used to be equal to 4 German marks; now it is 60 marks.

During this time huge profits were obtained by businessmen and speculators all over Europe. The poorer the country and the more grievous the suffering of the broad masses of the population caused by the consequences of the war, the greater were the profits realised by the speculators. Of course, there could be no question during this period that a revival of the economy was needed. The current crisis is a particular indicator that the economic growth we are considering was not a reality. Prosperity was an illusion.

If we think about all this, then immediately we see that the causes of the present economic crisis in the world economy were deeply rooted. It ceased to function as a separate integral body. On one side were those parts of the capitalist world that now suffer from chronic underproduction of all that is needed. This includes Russia, Germany, Poland, Austria, Hungary, the Balkans, and to a lesser extent, Italy, Spain, Belgium, and France, with a combined population of about 400 million, making up half of the capitalist world. On the other side were America, Japan, and the industrial relations that came about in the colonised countries during the war. In contrast, after the war and the economic shifts caused by it, we have all the external prerequisites for a large and expanded form of production.

In this way the whole economic situation today fits the following simple formula: in Europe, not enough goods are produced to support its population; in America, much more is produced than the population can use. One could perhaps recommend to America that it cede its surplus production to Europe. Europe could say, 'Give me what you have in abundance. I'll buy everything.' But in a capitalist economy, of course, this is not done. So what will be the price for Europe to meet an unlimited need of products and goods? For a long time they tried to get out of the situation by paying with paper money, but this led to the fact that at present, for example, the Austrian crown and the Polish mark have only 1 per cent of their previous purchasing power. Paper money can only be a means of payment in the external market when there is something to buy inside the country that issues it. Under present conditions, however, it is economically impossible for the reason already stated above: European countries do not have anything that could serve as means of exchange with America.

Comrades, there is another way to get out of the difficulty. Some measures have already been taken. These consist of the fact that Britain and America provide the impoverished countries with credit for a time, so that they can provide a certain amount of goods as payment for the corresponding loan interest. This could be a way out of the situation, but as you know, credit is willingly provided only to the rich. Poor proletarians are usually not given any, because they are not able to provide sufficient guarantees for the return of the amount borrowed. This rule of thumb is applied both in the private life of the individual household and on a global scale. Capitalists willingly lend to rich countries, but by no means to poor ones. They are willing to give loans to those countries where the capitalist system is firmly in place. On the contrary, to those countries where they hesitate one way or another, they are very reluctant to issue a loan. Now, in view of the fact that the capitalism of all European countries, especially after the war, is in many respects buckling, the reluctance of American capital to give goods generously on credit to European states is quite understandable. In one of the American newspapers, it was said that 'the Europeans have lost our trust because they are constantly making revolutions'.

So the internal contradictions currently boil down to the fact that, on the one hand, 400 million people live in conditions of absolute underproduction of goods from the standpoint of consumption, and on the other hand, the 300 million population of America, Britain, Japan, and a number of other countries bear the consequences of a relative overproduction of goods not being sold on the world market.

Now the question arises as to how to get out of this situation. You know, comrades, that the capitalists, the trade-union officials, and the Second and

Two-and-a-Half Internationals all believe that they know the appropriate solutions. Their question is, 'How to get out of this situation?' It's very simple: 'We need to put Europe on its feet again. But in order to make Europe rich again and create at least partly bearable living conditions, we must renew the weight of the production apparatus, set up all the railways and factories, put factories in full swing, get the mines in order, cover the soil with fertiliser, and improve cattle breeding.' In what ways can all this be achieved? Marxist teaching gives them a ready-made answer: 'You workers know that all value is created by the labour of workers. Therefore, you have to produce more. But you must not only produce more. You and the capitalists must consume less, so that the broad masses of working people will produce more new values, that consumption will be reduced to a minimum, and that the flow of new capital into production will increase. Only under these conditions will it be possible to create a new production apparatus so that in ten to twenty years you will be able to live decently.'

The capitalists, on their part, also resort to their own methods. They demand the lengthening of the working day and systematically reduce wages. The living wage of the working class in Europe has already decreased by one-third if not one-half compared to the pre-war period. Thus, the means of emerging from the current crisis proposed by capitalists and their henchmen are good only for the capitalists themselves.

Theoretically, of course, the possibility is that in this way, in thirty to forty years, the equilibrium of the capitalist system could be restored. To do this, first of all, it is necessary to assume that the workers will want to patiently participate in such an experiment. If we artificially exclude from the picture the revolutionary factor – meaning working-class opposition to strengthening capitalist rule – we repeat the absurd assumptions made by socialist-traitors, that the proletariat will completely reconcile itself with the capitalists' desire to impose their own interests. Then the economic development path depicted above might perhaps be possible. For we know that social upheavals do not happen automatically without the struggle of the working class. This course of events, however – is it possible? What would happen in the event of a reconciliation of workers and other prospects? It seems obvious that two generations of proletarians would be doomed to a pitiful existence, and that only the third generation would have some improvement in the situation. Meanwhile, we can definitely state that the broad masses of European workers – not only the most advanced communist leaders – are not inclined to sacrifice two generations of proletarians in order to restore the capitalist system in all its glory. A struggle is going on against attempts to restore the social equilibrium of the capitalist system, along with the shifts in consciousness of the masses produced by the war and its aftermath. At the same time, during the war the workers learned to use weapons necessitated by the struggle.

New solutions, which are inevitable during the collapse of capitalism, must, however, be much more revolutionary than simple modest improvements in living conditions. If someone lived well before and then living conditions deteriorated sharply, that alone can be a significant revolutionising factor. In addition, the Russian Revolution, as a real fact, transformed the abstract concept of social revolution – which social-democratic theory dealt with as something vague, abstract, and distant – into something imminent, tangible, and comprehensible in its full dimensions. The proletariat is now convinced by real-life experience, and not just theory, that it is not only possible for workers to become the masters of their own destiny but that workers are able to take political power into their own hands. This significant revolutionary factor would prevent European capitalism from using the only means of strengthening its position at the expense of the proletariat. There can be no dispute here.

There is no need to report on the need for Communist action. The British workers who are waging a fierce struggle are most definitely reluctant to help British capitalism get firmly on its feet once again at the expense of the proletariat. If we add to this the availability of the revolutionary worker to be part of the vanguard – the red trade unions and the Communist parties – clearly capitalism is not destined to return [as before].

The equilibrium of the capitalist system is shaken so much not only by the forces acting from the bottom up, not only by the ever-increasing pressure of the proletariat on the bourgeoisie, but also by internal contradictions and collisions that tear apart the ruling classes. The capitalist countries, in essence, have not yet emerged from the state of war. Every day the impossibility of implementing the Versailles Treaty is becoming increasingly evident, as is the sharp collision of the divergent aspirations of capitalists of the different countries participating in the robbery of the vanquished. Various governments resort more and more to import bans and try to squeeze their neighbours and competitors, thereby exacerbating the general economic chaos. In connection with these circumstances, there is a paralysis of monetary circulation on a global scale; the gold currency standard that was generally accepted has vanished. In a word, everything in the world is in flux.

The ruling class itself is split into separate groups, especially in Western and Central Europe. The class of property owners is distinctly divided between the peasantry and the urban bourgeoisie. And what about Bulgaria, Hungary, Poland, Bavaria, and Tyrol? We see that the proletariat there is opposed not by a united body of property owners, but by bourgeois groups pursuing diverse interests. True, Christianity is in solidarity with the entire bourgeoisie so that it takes a direct part in the struggle against the proletariat in defence of the 'sanctity of private property'. But on the other hand, the peasants do not have the slightest desire to sacrifice their immediate interests for the sake of restoring capitalism. The slogan 'dictatorship of the peasantry' has become fashionable among the peasants of Western Europe. This phenomenon takes on stronger and stronger organisational forms, and ultimately has led to the creation of the Green International.[4]

Before drawing final conclusions from what has been said, it is necessary to add a few more strokes to the picture I painted. All bourgeois newspapers and reports have not stopped blaming the proletariat for its unwillingness to work. Armed clashes have not ceased, again destroying production as soon as it begins to improve. The people groan and languish under the terrifying, incalculable burden of debt left behind by the World War (in Germany alone, about 300 billion worth of gold; France's debt is about 6,000 francs per capita; in Britain the sum is 174 pounds sterling per capita, and so on). Obviously, under these conditions, the only salvation for European countries is the dictatorship of the proletariat.

We might ask ourselves: Is it not possible for the relatively healthy parts of the capitalist world – above all, America – to completely break off economic ties with ailing Europe and organise their economies in isolation? However, it is precisely the severe crisis that now grips America that indicates the impossibility of implementing such a plan, because a particularly afflicted part of the capitalist world that numbers 400 million people are consumers of overseas raw materials and products of overseas industry. It is clear that it is not practical to simply throw Europe overboard and establish a new extra-European capitalist equilibrium. Theoretically, perhaps such a problem is solvable at some point, but not at this given time in a practical way. To do without the European market, it would be necessary to find new buyers for the goods produced. These could be found in China or India, but such countries must first be drawn into capitalist circulation to be of serious importance to American exports. Development in this direction, however, is proceeding at a very slow pace; it takes several generations. It is hoped that the growth of a revolutionary breakthrough for American workers will go much faster than the process of drawing these little-affected countries into the sphere of capitalist relations: India, China, Asia Minor, and so on.

4 The Green International (formally the International Agrarian Bureau) was founded in 1921 by bourgeois agrarian parties in Bulgaria, Czechoslovakia, Croatia, and Poland, with offices in Prague.

Consequently, the state of affairs at the present time is such that the way out of this crisis for the whole world would be possible only at the cost of sacrificing the vital interests of the working class, and at the cost of returning the proletarian masses to that terrible material and spiritual order that would have been normal for them in the early period of capitalism before the beginning of the trade-union movement. This way out, however, has now absolutely been ruled out, and is impossible. Rather, a new world war can be expected to break out if the revolutionary movement does not develop rapidly enough. Because large countries – America, Britain, Japan – do not have sufficient markets for the sale of goods, and they resort to force of arms to resolve issues of monopoly dominance in the world market. This must inevitably occur unless, of course, the onset of the proletarian revolution outstrips the course of events depicted here and saves humanity from a repetition of the horrors of a world war.

Let us turn to resolving the question of what should be the tasks of the trade unions at this stage of the disintegration of the capitalist world. Under the capitalist system of society, trade unions ultimately set themselves the task of ensuring that, in the process of distributing the goods produced, the worker will receive as much as possible. Under the conditions of a capitalist economy, strictly speaking, the problems of distribution were discussed.

In the present epoch in which the capitalist system is being shaken, the task of the trade unions is different. Their task is to organise the revolutionary struggle of the masses and precisely those who are not directly under the influence of the Communist Party against the ruling classes. Some theorists mistakenly say that the red trade unions should completely abandon the previous methods, and concentrate all their efforts solely on the immediate preparation of the revolution, neglecting the issue of wages and in general all the issues that arise in a capitalist economy. It should not be, after all, that the proletariat consists only of convinced Communists. On the whole, the worker still has no access to this consciousness under capitalism, because there is no way to really improve his life during the existence of a capitalist system.

Hence it follows that the trade unions must maintain the closest connection with the masses on the basis of participation in their daily struggle for wages. The unions must carry out this struggle and strive to expand and deepen it. In the struggle, it will be clearly revealed that satisfying the demands of the working class – increasing wages and improving living conditions – is objectively impossible during the stages of the collapse of European capitalism that we are experiencing. It is objectively impossible precisely because the very apparatus of production resulted in this objective clash between the demands of the working masses and the impossibility for the capitalists of meeting them, given that private ownership of the means of production is preserved.

In order to meet these demands, every conflict, every movement among the trade unions must sooner or later deepen and take the form of a revolutionary class struggle. This will happen, of course, only on condition that traitors will not be at the head of trade unions. In Britain, where the capitalists used to be able to make concessions, they can no longer give in, because they have become vulnerable. They do not know to what extent they are threatened with losses due to the competition of foreign capital. Therefore, if the trade unions wage a struggle and conduct it energetically, toward clearly set goals and by revolutionary methods, then the struggle even for purely union interests will inevitably spill over into a class struggle, whether we like it or not.

It is precisely this situation that provides our revolutionary will with objective starting points and points of reference. Since we are clearly aware of this, we cannot allow the tactics of the trade unions to take the wrong path.

Session in the Blue Hall

Report on Trade-Union Tasks and Tactics

Lozovsky: Comrades, the question of the tasks and tactics of trade unions is an extremely complicated one even when a single country is taken into consideration, let alone when it concerns the labour movement of all countries. What then should be our point of departure that would bring us to a decision as to what should be the aims and tactics of the period we are passing through? The point of departure in deciding on tactics is the irrefutable fact that we are living in an epoch of capitalist decay, a fact that arouses no dissension, at least in the mind of the left wing of the international labour movement. It is true that should we take the right wing of the labour and socialist movement we will find that they are convinced there is no sign of capitalist decay, and that in general the alleviation of humanity from its present ills, brought on by the war, is possible only through the complete restoration of the capitalist economy, which is where, according to them, we are heading. Thus the starting point for the revolutionary labour movement is the disintegration of capitalism.

It is therefore from the angle of inevitable capitalist breakdown that we must look for the line of action to be taken by the trade-union movement. It is also to be remembered that this collapse is far from having the same character in the different countries. Let us take, for instance, Czechoslovakia, France, Britain, and America. We see at once that the symptoms of collapse are identical, but the latter combine, in each case, in an entirely different manner. In some countries capital is still strong and powerful, while in others we already feel its disintegration, and we can say that the final collapse is only a matter of the near future. Owing to these circumstances, it is extremely difficult to formulate the tactics of the trade-union movement.

Another consideration should also be borne in mind, complicating the determination of the tasks and tactics of the trade-union movement on an international scale. This is the spirit of solidarity of the bourgeoisie created by the war and by the revolution. We must admit that the bourgeoisie is better organised and has profited to a greater degree from the lessons of the Russian Revolution than the proletariat. The creation of white guard organisations by the bourgeoisie, thus preparing the youth to fight and slaughter the leaders of the revolutionary movement, makes it quite evident that the bourgeoisie is using all its energies to fight the proletariat in an organised manner, and to completely smash the revolutionary struggle of the proletariat. If we consider the tasks pursued by the trade unions during the period of development of society, we see that it consisted in organising and maintaining the masses to improve working conditions, and not for the advancement of the revolutionary struggle. Unity and organisation of the masses is undoubtedly the practical slogan for trade unions all over the world at the present time. But then, what do we organise them for, what are the slogans, for what purpose? How shall we approach these problems in each country, and what would we suggest to each organisation as ways and means for the fight that is before them?

To trace this line we shall have to review briefly the events of this short but quite stormy period. Before the war we had three fundamental types of trade-union movements: the Anglo-Saxon, the Franco-Spanish, and the German-Austrian. Each one of these three types had its own tactics, ideology, programme, and peculiarities, reflecting the social, economic, and the purely economic relations in each country belonging to one of the above groups.

The Anglo-Saxon group was outspokenly anti-socialist in its tendencies. If we take a look even at the very recent pre-war period, we find that the British and American trade unions took their bearings from the viewpoint of the everyday economic struggle. They drew a dividing line between economics and politics, holding that economics is one thing and politics quite another. Economic action was their daily humdrum, fully absorbing all their attention. Their chief characteristic is their narrow guild spirit and a distrust of unskilled workers, with a host of similar 'trademarks' stamping them with the character of traditional 'trade unionism' [*in English*], as recorded in the history of the movement. 'Trade unionism', in general, may be characterised as the ideology of the labour aristocracy – the ideology that formed the most exclusive distinction of the Anglo-American labour movement before the war.

The Franco-Spanish labour movement grew up in a different social environment and bore the traits of anarcho-syndicalism, which placed it in direct opposition to Anglo-American trade unionism. The characteristic [of Franco-Spanish unionism] is the struggle against capitalism, against the state, and against parliamentarism. The essential idea is that revolutionary unions are the only bodies capable of making the revolution and building the new society. No other organisation is capable, in their view.

The same basic tendencies in French revolutionary syndicalism have penetrated organisations in other countries as well, such as Italy, America, and so on. In these countries however, the above tendencies are not the dominant ones in the labour movement, as the syndicalist organisations in these countries are only a small minority, whereas in Spain and France this trend is predominant and determines the character of the entire labour movement. This syndicalist movement suffers from utopianism and has misconceptions as to what are the mutual relations of economics and politics. But these negative traits notwithstanding, revolutionary syndicalism in many countries shows also a genuine revolutionary class sentiment, such as the importance of the struggle against capitalism, with direct action as the best means to this end, and so on. In that respect, this tendency stands far above the labour movement in other countries.

The third type of trade union is the German-Austrian. This type developed under the influence of social democracy, which for decades has been nursing this movement with its social-reformist ideas. As a result, these unions swallowed and digested the purest ideology of social-democratic reformism, preaching the gradual transition from capitalism to socialism without bloodshed or fighting. In actual practice this led them to the recognition that it was necessary to bring about such conditions under which capital and labour would face one another on equal terms, would have equal rights. They have thus advanced the notorious theory that capital and labour have the same rights, and that the present capitalist state and the capitalist system are here to stay.

In this respect the social-democratic reformists fully agree with [British] 'trade unionism' – both movements make the daily incidents of the workers' struggle the basis of all their practical work. As to the final aims of the working class, reformism as well as 'trade unionism' looked upon them as upon a remote future, many centuries in the future. They were solely concerned with questions of today, such as wages, working conditions, and collective agreements; in short, with the questions workers are interested in here and now, independently of the tasks before them in the future.

The German-Austrian trade-union movement did not address the problem of achieving socialism; it believed in the possibility of reaching this new system by gradual transition, by slow and gradual development, believing that in the long run capitalism would die a natural death.

It is curious that these three currents, expressing clearly the main tendencies within the world trade-union movement, approached the state, socialism, and the practical problems and concrete tasks before the workers in entirely different ways. Fighting among themselves before the war within the boundaries of each country, as we stated above, all three currents joined hands during the war owing to the predominance of entirely national interests over class ones. War appeared as a type of conciliator equalising these currents, and we find the same ideology prevailing in the trade-union movement of all countries. Revolutionary syndicalism in France, German-Austrian professional organisations (so-called pure unions), and British 'trade unionism' all came to resemble each other like peas in a pod.

War was the highest expression of the internal crisis that the labour movement passed through. It disclosed the degree of influence exercised by the bourgeoisie upon the working class. I believe that among those present here there is not a single person to be found who before the war would have believed that the working class and its organisations might be linked so closely with capitalist society. Not a single theoretician or practical activist in the trade-union movement – without excluding the most radical among our theoreticians (like Kautsky during the brightest period of his activities) – had realised how close was the connection between capitalism and the working-class movement. This connection manifested itself with tremendous force only during the war. This is a fact to be seriously understood and taken account of. But the matter concerns not only the well-known connection of the leaders of the trade-union movement with the bourgeoisie, their betrayal, and so on.

At any rate, there is now no doubt of the fact that bourgeois society exercised an enormous influence and control over the consciousness, feelings, and education – upon all the factors of the inner life of the worker. There is no doubt whatever that at a moment when national states were in peril, national feelings prevailed over class consciousness. It was only in the course of the war that we watched the workers' feelings and consciousness slowly clearing away the patriotic fog. But when at present many millions among the proletarian class stick to old bourgeois prejudices, it may be observed without exaggeration that if the war lasted four years, if it took from the working class and humanity at large so many victims and its costs were so dear, a great deal of the responsibility rests upon the trade unions and their leaders. In their respective native countries they were the real bulwark and foundation of the machinery of militarist policy.

Let us look at the Italian Confederation of Labour, let us take the German labour unions; these mass organisations and their leaders not only supported the war morally, but also materially, with all their vast union apparatuses and their very ideology. All this has resulted in friction and quarrels that have not ceased up to the present. This fateful legacy of the war, during which the trade unions served as tools for imperialist policies, could only be gradually (although not painlessly) overcome after the war. Looking back on this period, we must note that in all countries there was a growth of the trade-union movement. In the history of the working class, there has never been such a large influx of workers into the mass organisations as in the past three years.

You are aware that the trade-union movement is comparatively young; it began to develop side by side with the development of capitalism. The organisation of the oldest trade union dates back to 1760. This influx into the unions is explained by the fact that the workers were hurled by war out of their usual path of life. After the war they were faced with the growth of unemployment and worsening social conflicts, clearly feeling their individual helplessness. Driven by the consciousness of the broad masses of workers, they turned to the workers' organisations in search of answers to all those complicated problems that were agitating them.

The rapid growth of the workers' union organisation can be judged from the following figures. Before the war the number of organised workers of the world was about 9.5 million; at present it has already reached 40 million. The most characteristic feature about the growth of the trade unions is the fact that it does not confine itself to European countries, but is also noticed in the countries of the Far East, in Japan, China, and so on. There is not one country where the workers do not amalgamate and form their own unions, and where they do not seek close contact with the international trade-union movement. In some countries the development of the trade-union movement expanded enormously, without any exaggeration. The number of organised workers in Germany, at present, amounts to 13 million, which comprises about 65 per cent of the total number of workers and employees of Germany.

In turning to other countries, there is the French union movement. It would be correct to say that the abyss into which the unions of France have fallen is much deeper than in Britain or America, because Gompers and his followers have remained the same as before. The General Confederation of Labour [CGT] of France adhered to the slogan of opposition to the state and militarism, but in the period following the war, as well as during it, the treason of the leaders of the trade-union movement called forth protests within the Confederation of Labour itself. An opposition was formed, which organised the Revolutionary Syndicalist Committees [CSR] and united the dissenters against the reactionary policies. But this opposition was not one single unit, it contained three currents: (1) syndicalist-anarchists; (2) pure syndicalists; and (3) syndicalist-communists.

The connecting link between the three is the Amiens Charter, which they all recognise and which defines the whole basis of their work.[5] One can say that the slogan of the opposition group can be summed up as 'Back to the Amiens Charter'.

What does this Amiens Charter consist of? In 1906 at the congress of trade unions in Amiens, a resolution was passed that had been presented by the revolutionary minority. It declared that the trade-union movement in France is autonomous and independent of the various political parties and groupings. Members of the unions are prohibited from introducing their political convictions inside the union, and can only propagate them outside of it. With regard to parties, the charter contains a passage stating that the French trade-union movement stands in no relation whatever to any other organisation or philosophical school. This is the whole meaning and character of the Amiens Charter. The slogan 'Back to the Amiens Charter' under the present conditions is undoubtedly an extremely reactionary one, first of all on account of its being applied to all categories and leaders of trade unions, whatever be their main tendencies. All resolutions start with a reference to those adopted at the Amiens Congress. This alone might suggest to our comrades in France that there is something wrong with that charter.

Another question has to be posed: Does the Amiens Charter give, after all, an exhaustive answer to all questions demanding solution at the present moment? Between 1906 and 1921 many important events took place. Did we not have a World War, a social revolution, the bankruptcy of capitalism, etc.? The whole world is shaking; only the Amiens Charter remains unchanged. Against this conception of trade-union problems, a resolute struggle must be commenced, for this conception conceals a great danger. Indeed, what is the real nature of the slogan of autonomy and independence, which is the foundation of the French trade-union movement? If we look at the resolution adopted by the minority at the Amiens Congress or peruse the latest declaration of the French revolutionary syndicalists, we shall become convinced that they are inspired by the same idea.

French syndicalism is autonomous and independent. These two terms run like a thread through all the activities of the French Confederation of Labour. What does this independence and autonomy consist of? Autonomy with relation to what? Independence from whom? What is the essence of this? The essence consists in the fact that the whole course taken with regard to the

5 Adopted by the CGT in 1906, the Amiens Charter became the programmatic platform of revolutionary syndicalism. For the text of it, see the Appendix, p. 673.

leadership of the proletariat is defined, on the whole, by a distrust of political parties, which is characteristic of syndicalism. According to the syndicalist explanation, the party does not represent the proletariat with regard to its goals and tasks; workers' organisations are production associations, whereas from a class point of view, the party is a 'conglomerate'. As a result, revolutionary goals can be achieved only by trade unions, and they alone will be able to create a new ideology. Although this tendency has already become, in its essentials, a dead letter, there are nevertheless many 'living syndicalists' who are guided by it.

This theory of autonomous and independent trade unions must receive the sharpest condemnation by our congress. What shall we reject? When they talk about the independence of trade unions from the bourgeois state, we fully subscribe to that. But we protest energetically when the question is about independence in relation to the Communist Party. Indeed, both the Communist Party and the syndicalists claim they are heading to communism. There we have two parallel lines that, according to the laws of geometry, are never to meet. But how can they fail to meet when they both are heading to communism? If they follow the same direction they are bound to cross; there is no room for parallelism in this case, as there is no 'independence' of the trade-union movement from communism.

If the syndicalists really aspire to achieve communism, it is absurd to justify such independence of the trade unions. During a meeting with the representatives of the French organisations, I told the French syndicalists: Let us grant that syndicalism and communism are two parallel lines. Should we not build a bridge between them? In response, they professed to have nothing against such a bridge. But when I asked, 'Is it to be an iron one?' They said no, 'crossbeams will suffice for the purpose'. I asked them, 'Are not such bridges liable to collapse when you walk across them?' They answered, 'Perhaps, but we nevertheless do not want to have an iron bridge, because it would be binding on us.' This attitude of distrust toward communism and political parties undoubtedly has its origin in an erroneous conception of class interests and the balance of power in modern society.

To conclude, the peculiarity of syndicalist organisations consists in their ascribing too great an importance to the parliamentary kitchen and to the idle talk of the deputies, whereas politics is in its essence concentrated economics and the necessary class struggle. Class struggle is a political struggle. Not everybody clearly realises this fact. When at another meeting of the Executive Committee I put the question to a syndicalist comrade whether the struggle of British miners was an economic or political struggle, they were at a loss to answer me. It is exactly the same thing with [the IWW in] America. Our comrades fail to realise that by fighting against the capitalist system they are in fact fighting on a political level. Politics is generalised class struggle, by means of which the working class is opposed to the whole bourgeois state, to all its institutions. This should be applied to France, likewise, so if the game of the Amiens Charter had continued it might have led to most dangerous results.

As I mentioned earlier, in the French trade-union opposition are three currents: anarcho-revolutionary, syndicalist, and communist. The anarchists declare themselves against politics because politics is for them something akin to an apocalyptic beast sent by nature or by the almighty for the destruction of the 'humble man'. Therefore they write the word 'politics' in capital letters and refuse to have anything to do with it. An unwillingness and incapacity to understand the fundamental tasks of communism lies at the bottom of this opposition. Of course, for the organisations that are clear about these tasks and accept the dictatorship of the proletariat as a basis of their actions, this question is not so easy to settle at first glance. But inasmuch as the anarchists are adhering to the theory of 'independence', their association with the majority of the General Confederation of Labour should be quite possible. On the basis of the Amiens Charter, they are capable of showing their hostility to the Communists. Do they not declare, 'We have nothing in common with Communists; we want to be independent'?

At the Comintern congress I quoted an instance of two hostile groups that united on the basis of an old policy: In Brunswick [in Germany] the government was formed of two Independents [USPD members] and three Scheidemannites [SPD members]. When the question was raised about the course to be taken by the new government, they demanded that the new government should adopt the platform of the Erfurt Programme, written in 1891. I am afraid that the Amiens Charter will play a similar role as the Erfurt Programme played in Brunswick.[6]

Only one conclusion is to be drawn from all this. We must propose to our French comrades to work out a new programme instead of their charter. The Amiens Charter was good for a certain period, but now it has lost its significance. It is dead, and let it rest in peace. We want a new programme to answer the requirements of the present day, in which the forms, means,

6 The Erfurt Programme, adopted by the SPD in 1891, was viewed as a model for parties of the Second International. For the text, see: https://www.marxists.org/history/international/social-democracy/1891/erfurt-program.htm.

Lozovsky's remarks on this at the Comintern Third Congress can be found in Riddell (ed.) 2015, *3WC*, p. 724.

and methods of struggle needed at present would find their echo and reflection. This should be the duty imposed by the congress upon our French comrades.

Let us pass to Germany. Here the situation is much more complicated than in France, because the French trade-union movement was never as strong and as organised as in Germany. In Germany there exist the old trade unions with their old trade-union bureaucracy. The unions constitute an enormous machinery embracing tremendous numbers of workers. There are 10 million in the free trade unions.[7] There 2 million in the Christian-Catholic unions,[8] etc. In total there are 13 million organised workers. Of the 10 million in the free trade unions, 250,000 among them have left the federation and formed a small organisation, charging that the old unions are 'counterrevolutionary machines' that should be destroyed. No revolution in Germany is possible, they claim, without the destruction of these old unions. The ideology of the destruction of old trade unions is characteristic of the German left Communist Party.[9]

What is the real nature of this slogan to destroy the trade unions? What does it imply? If we read through all the voluminous literature written on this subject (I'm unable to quote it, because it would have required too many hours), it will be easy to establish that the very gist of this literature amounts to the following: The old unions are counterrevolutionary organisations. They suppressed the revolution. They took part in all the repression. They did everything in order to suppress the revolutionary movement. There is no possibility of conquering these unions because the trade-union bureaucracy is strongly entrenched in them, is too powerful. Therefore it is necessary to remove from them all the revolutionary elements and build up a separate organisation, which should consist of revolutionaries alone, which will gradually win over the masses, and through the new unions lead them to revolution.

But this declaration itself is theoretically unsound, in that the trade unions are considered hopeless and are condemned to always remain counterrevolu-

7 'Free trade unions' (*freie Gewerkschaften*) was a commonly used term referring to the Social-Democratic-led union federation (after 1919 the ADGB). The term was meant to distinguish these from yellow unions controlled by the bosses and Catholic unions tied to the Church. They are not to be confused with the '*freie Unionen*' – the syndicalist unions such as the Free Workers' Union (FAU), the General Workers' Union (AAU), and the Gelsenkirchen Free Workers' Union.

8 A reference to unions affiliated to the International Federation of Christian Trade Unions, organisations that existed in a number of countries and embraced the class-peace teachings of the Catholic Church hierarchy.

9 A reference to the Communist Workers' Party of Germany (KAPD).

tionary. It is unsound because, whether revolutionary or not, the trade unions are a reflection of the working class. Because if one actually says that 10 million workers will always remain counterrevolutionary, it's the same thing as saying that a revolution in Germany is not possible. If it is impossible to conquer those 10 million workers, it's superfluous to talk about unions at all. But if one admits the possibility of a revolution in Germany, it means that the working class in its entirety is marching to the revolution. Because who else will make the revolution? The bureaucracy, the 100,000 officials? The revolution can be made without the 100,000 officials, but it can never be made without the workers.

In fact this slogan, at the present juncture, is not only dangerous but counterrevolutionary. Just think of it. We come to the workers and tell them to smash their unions, when we know that it has taken the working class dozens of years to build them, and those unions have proved to be beneficial to the working class. The workers and the union are strongly linked together. Workers consider the union as their home, and when we come to them and say, 'smash the union', we meet with the obstinate resistance of the masses. The masses are unwilling to destroy the unions they have built.

Our task does not consist in pulling the best elements out of the unions, and building separate organisations with them. On the contrary, we should stay in the unions and see that the militant elements with the most revolutionary and selfless spirit work inside of these unions. It is only these elements who will guide the consciousness and the yearnings of the masses, who will lead and direct the unions. The more the revolution develops in Germany, the more the working masses are drawn into the revolutionary struggle, the more does the theory of 'smashing the old unions' become dangerous for the revolutionary movement of Germany. Life itself has proved the slogan to be wrong and senseless; its fallacy is proven.

Our French comrades of the General Confederation of Labour – the revolutionary syndicalists – have firmly declared their intention not to leave it, and now they have almost half the organisation with them. Even in Germany at the present time about two million members of the old unions have rallied to our point of view. A whole series of district conferences, of district unions and local branches, expressed themselves against Amsterdam, against the policies of their central bodies and for the necessity of affiliation to Moscow. These facts, picked out of everyday life, prove that within these old organisations we are gaining the masses to our side. The abstraction, the lifelessness and senselessness of the theory of 'smashing the unions' is thus categorically proven. Organisations resting upon this slogan are condemned to isolation and will end up by presenting perhaps a very interesting association, but definitely an antiquated one. Even our comrades of the IWW of America will not bring about the revolution unless this small organisation has the working masses with them.

This situation in Germany is complicated by the fact that the trade-union bureaucracy is not disposed to wait until the revolutionary communists conquer the unions. They immediately begin to expel the revolutionary unions from the federations. We thus observe a very curious fact: ardent revolutionaries and the trade-union officialdom are both saying the same thing: 'Revolutionary communists – out of the unions!'. The mere coincidence of this fact proves that some of our comrades advocating leaving the unions may have ardent emotions, but to our sorrow, are nonetheless hot-headed. This slogan is absolutely wrong; the union bureaucracy is expelling the revolutionaries precisely because they bring revolutionary ferment inside the organisation; they energetically reject the corporate spirit.

At the present moment about 50,000 workers – which include the Chemnitz and Stuttgart branches of the construction unions and others – have already been expelled. This is the beginning of the campaign organised by the Amsterdam International to expel the revolutionary workers from the unions. This campaign must be opposed with all our means. We must say that precisely because they expel us, we must not leave the unions; otherwise we are playing into their hands. By expelling 50,000 workers they expel the best part of the unions, but most of the revolutionary workers remain. In Germany after the expulsions one and a half million [revolutionary] workers still remain there; they have not been expelled. In six months; there will be three million and these will be even harder to expel. And when we have five million we will kick out the reformists. Because we do not share the belief that the union must remain united for all time. We do not approach the question from the viewpoint of religious fetishism: it goes against the Marxist-Communist grain. We approach it from the practical standpoint of conformity with our goal. We say, 'Just as the slogan of unity cannot always be good and obligatory, so too a split cannot always be our slogan'. In each country – in accordance with the prevailing conditions – we can be for or against a split. In Germany, particularly now, it makes no sense to split away or leave the unions, as that would mean playing into the hands of the trade-union bureaucracy.

We must dwell briefly upon three more countries: Britain, America, and Italy. The development of the trade-union movement in Britain in recent years is undoubtedly quite interesting. At the present time it can be said without exaggeration that the British trade-union movement has made the greatest step forward, compared with the pre-war situation, of any country in the West. Before the war British trade unions were essentially and deeply reformist. They were entirely linked with the bourgeois state. Its characteristic features were corporatism and a guild spirit. All the specific traditional features of British trade unionism are in the process of disappearing at the present time, amidst the storm of strikes and conflicts not seen in any other country.

Nowhere did we see such a tremendous strike struggle as in Britain; not a single country ever had a strike of 1.2 million coal miners lasting for fourteen weeks.[10] The British workers have gone through such a struggle. We can say with assurance that the labour movement of Britain has made a tremendous step forward, not only in comparison with what it was before the war, but even in comparison with the French and German trade-union movement. This comparison is relative and not absolute, because we have to take into account what the trade-union movement in each country was in the past.

In the years 1916 and 1917 shop committees made their appearance in Britain; these have grown quite rapidly and on a large scale.[11] Afterwards they began to dwindle down and they have little influence at present. But on the other hand, the old organisations notice an enormous change in the psychology and attitude of the workers. We must not think that the British masses have suddenly turned toward the Third International, that they have become Communists, and so on. The British workers are practical. They are capable – at least many of them – of waging a strike for three months without even realising the harm they are inflicting on the bourgeois class. This is a peculiarity of the British mentality that you have to understand. The present struggle is thus not a conscious fight against capitalism and bourgeois rule, but simply a sign of the approaching crisis in Britain, a sign that foretells the direction that British workers will take.

The negative aspects of the British labour movement, particularly among our partisans, is the fact that their actions take place outside the unions; opposition groups do not form and grow inside the unions, but outside them. Such an approach, such tactics are incorrect. You cannot create a true revolutionary mass movement, united in purpose and tactics, upon such grounds. In this instance the task of the revolutionary elements in Britain – already quite numerous – is to become an organic part of the unions.

10 For the British coal miners' strike, see p. 51, n. 11.

11 The Shop Stewards' movement developed in Scotland and England in 1915, primarily in the shipyards and engineering (machine shop) industry. In 1916 the National Shop Stewards' and Workers' Committee Movement was formed, whose goal was 'the organisation of the workers upon a class basis to prosecute the interests of the working class until the triumph of the workers is assured'. In 1917 the movement hailed the October Revolution in Russia. In January 1920 a national conference, representing 72,000 workers, voted to affiliate to the Communist International. See Klugman 1968, p. 23.

Tom Mann, in his speech at the opening of the congress, and during the discussion on the report of the [International] Council of Trade Unions stated that in the Engineering Union nearly 20 per cent of the workers have broken with their old ideology. If there are 20 per cent among the Engineers, this alone is a colossal power. Still Comrade Tom Mann failed to state that these 20 per cent are unorganised; they are not grouped together organisationally.

It is up to our British comrades to start creating and developing these cells and nuclei inside the unions. Though the field is ripe for it, nothing has been accomplished so far. During the coal strike I asked the comrades, 'What did you do then, you representatives of the Communist, revolutionary cells, to take advantage of this situation to intensify your propaganda work? What did you do to spread our ideas among the broad masses? What did you do to win the strikers over to us?' The British coal miners went out on strike not in the interests of the Third International, but against a reduction in wages and for better rates in the coal mines working part time. However, this struggle has taken such a wide scope and became so sharp that it developed into a conflict between the strikers on one side and the government and society on the other. This fight should have been utilised as proof positive of the inevitability of the class struggle against the capitalist system. The strike has not been well utilised in this respect. I would say still more: the strike was very weakly used, which shows the unpreparedness of our comrades for building a mass movement capable of carrying out a social revolution.

As for America, the conditions of the labour movement in that country are quite interesting and very characteristic. America, which suffered little from the war, is essentially the world's creditor. America is at the economic helm of the world. The American labour movement has experienced of late the same rapid growth as in other countries. In comparison to the British, the movement is more 'prudent'. At the head stands a gang, pure and simple. It is sufficient to take to heart the history of Gompers and Company, with their theories and practices, to convince ourselves that these people are not only anticommunist but that their deeds are out of harmony even with the elementary needs of the trade-union struggle.

For Gompers and Company even the Amsterdam International is too revolutionary and too subversive. Gompers, in the name of the Executive Committee of the AFL, has sent a letter to the Amsterdam International that essentially stated, 'We sever our connections with the Amsterdam International on account of the following three reasons: first, with your help, such a valuable member as Appleton has lost his seat as president of the Amsterdam Federation and had to be replaced;[12] second, in your First of May appeal you pro-

12 William A. Appleton, secretary of the British General Federation of Trade Unions and

claimed the socialist slogan that we cannot accept; third, you undermine the foundation of all governments, America included – this is also unacceptable.'

On receipt of this statement, the Amsterdam International replied as follows: Yes, Appleton had to be replaced, but only because the way he spoke at the Portsmouth Congress aroused the intense indignation of all the workers. As one of the workers who took part in the congress put it, 'No self-respecting worker will sit down at the same table with a man voicing such views.'[13] Consequently Appleton is no longer chairman of the Amsterdam International. It is not because the Amsterdam people are too revolutionary, but because the English workers did not want him. As to your accusation about socialism and the revolutionary spirit, we are struck by your lack of understanding of our May Day Appeal. Does it speak of 'socialism'? No, it says that socialisation and socialism are different things. You, Gompers, are you not a partisan of socialisation? As to socialism, we are for the same brand as you are in keeping aloof from any political organisation.

A delegate (*from his seat*): Why then do you accept the AFL delegates who are here?

Lozovsky (*continues*): I shall directly explain why it is we admit not Gompers or his friends, of course, but workers. The letter I read characterises very well Gompers's organisation, as it does the Amsterdam International. In view of such revolting 'labour politics', we can perfectly understand the state of mind and feeling that gave rise to a growing tendency within the American labour movement to smash this organisation and create a new one, etc. Fifteen years ago, the IWW was created, which adopted a class-struggle programme.[14]

---

closely linked to right-wing US labour leader Samuel Gompers, was elected president of the International Federation of Trade Unions (Amsterdam International) in July 1920. Facing growing criticism within the Amsterdam International and the Trades Union Congress in Britain, Appleton resigned as IFTU president in November 1920. He was replaced by J.H. Thomas.

13 Appleton was sharply denounced at the annual meeting of the Trades Union Congress of Britain, held 6–11 September 1920 in Portsmouth. Describing the attitude of that congress, IFTU secretary Jan Oudegeest wrote that 'one of the delegates observed that no self-respecting English worker would sit with [Appleton] at the same table on account of his undemocratic and reactionary conceptions … Mr. Appleton then chose the wisest course by handing in his resignation as president of our international in view of the opposition in his own country.'

14 A reference to the 27 June–8 July 1905 convention in Chicago that founded the Industrial Workers of the World (IWW). Its proceedings can be found on Marxists Internet Archive at: https://www.marxists.org/history/usa/unions/iww/1905/convention/index.htm.

America has now three types of organisations: Gompers's AFL, the IWW (politically neutral), and the One Big Union.[15] Generally, when a union in any of the English-speaking countries is called 'Big', one should say that it is most probably a small one. Independent organisations are not necessarily revolutionary as compared with Gompers's organisation. Different tendencies exist among them; some are in full harmony with Gompers. The IWW has for fifteen years carried on an energetic struggle and is atrociously persecuted by the government of capitalist America. But it is a very small organisation, mainly composed of unskilled labourers. The IWW certainly cannot, for the present, become the central organisation to embrace American workers. The reason is, apart from its numerical weakness, that this organisation is somewhat vague as regards its ideological outlook. Even within this organisation we find different tendencies, such as anarchists, partisans of the dictatorship of the proletariat, and opponents of it. There are also different methods and tactics of struggle.

A comrade just asked why we admitted representatives of the American organisation. I believe that we should take workers where they are and as they are. Since there are workers in the AFL we should not wait until they come to us, but we must go to them. It is our task to conquer one by one the unions dominated by Gompers's ideology. We accept representatives from each local group and organisation leading the class struggle. We are convinced that by such means hundreds of organisations will be conquered by us, and Gompers's clique will finally be thrown out.

It would be the most serious error if we would not receive revolutionary workers simply because they are still affiliated to the old organisations. More than half the members of the IWW are at the same time members of the AFL, because without a membership card in the AFL it is difficult to obtain employment in many enterprises. Besides, it is necessary to be a member of a union to be close to the masses, to conquer them, to win them to our ideas, and to throw out those who are corrupting the workers' movement.

Italy is the last country I want to refer to. In Italy there are three types of organisations: the Italian Confederation of Labour grouping more than two million workers, two independent unions, and the Italian Syndicalist Union [USI]. The Italian proletariat is undoubtedly revolutionary, and its experience of the last years has demonstrated that reformism does not find an echo among the working masses.

---

15 One Big Union was a militant union formed in Western Canada in 1919, with a membership that reached 40,000–70,000 by the end of the year; its claimed membership in 1921 was 13,000.

The General Confederation of Labour [CGL] is currently playing a double game: it is partly affiliated with the Red Trade Union International, while at the same time it submits to the orders of Amsterdam. Recently one sees that the relations between the General Confederation of Labour and the Amsterdam International have become even closer.

In April the CGL sent a letter to the Amsterdam International concerning the pogroms committed by the Fascists, and of the difficult position of the workers in Italy. The Amsterdam International sent a letter of condolence and 50,000 lire, expressing assurance of its belief in the victory of the proletariat and sending aid to the Italian workers from the workers of all countries. The Italian Confederation of Labour replied with an even more touching message. *Avanti*, the central organ of the Italian Socialist Party, became sentimental and declared that it will not reproach anymore the leaders of the Amsterdam International for past errors.[16] This curious trait proves that the Italian Socialist Party, which ideologically guides the General Confederation of Labour, took a big step to the right as soon as it parted company with the Communists.

The independent unions are to be distinguished from the American independent unions in that they are in fact communist. The Railway Union and Transport Workers' Union, embracing together more than 600,000 workers, share a revolutionary point of view and are not affiliated to the General Confederation of Labour, as they consider themselves syndicalists. The Italian Syndicalist Union was formed during the war on the basis of the French revolutionary syndicalist platform. Its ideology differs from that of the two above-mentioned unions, and therefore it rejects the idea of fusion with them.

What should our task in Italy be? It consists of rallying these three organisations, and in this way winning a majority of the revolutionary proletariat. The resolution adopted at Livorno and the spirit of the working-class masses are guarantees of this.[17] The leaders of the CGL state that they will rally to us if the right to preserve the agreement with the Italian Socialist Party is granted. When they arrive (they are on their way), we will hear them out.

It must be stated before their arrival that they had already attempted to postpone our congress for two months, proposing by a letter of 25 May signed by D'Aragona to organise this congress in Stockholm or Reval [Tallinn]. In that

16 A reference to the 11 May 1921 issue of *Avanti*, which contained a front-page article on the Amsterdam International's donation of 50,000 lire. The title of the article was 'International Solidarity'.

17 The Fifth Congress of the General Confederation of Labour (CGL) was held in Livorno from 26 February to 3 March 1921, a month after the Italian Socialist Party's congress in the same city. For the text of the resolution referred to, see pp. 604–5.

letter they indicate that transferring the congress to Stockholm or Reval would facilitate the communication of the delegates with their countries, and it would also secure the control and validation of credentials. That was a masked hint that in Russia it will be impossible to oversee and validate the credentials. How would overseeing and validating be more assured there? Why would the bourgeois government of Sweden grant more possibilities for overseeing and validating credentials?

The political meaning of this manoeuvre is plain: should such a congress be convened, the Russians would not be allowed to attend it, and this would, of course, be a gain for them because we have something to say about their past. On the other side, by making such a suggestion, they are perfectly aware that no government would be so foolish as to allow such a congress to take place in its country. Why? Would the bourgeois Estonian or Swedish governments allow a congress of 300 'brigands', as they call them, to convene in their countries?

We answered then that we cannot postpone the congress, as the delegates have already started to arrive. Our second answer was the appeal to the Italian workers, in the name of the delegates present here, that we are generally against all diplomacy within the ranks of the workers, and if you have something against us, then say it out loud without equivocation.[18] There is no need to walk in and use sophisticated diplomatic methods.

Summing up, I will not emphasise the ideology of 'independence'. I have already done so by characterising the point of view of the French syndicalists, the IWW, and other purely syndicalist groups. Still it will be necessary to indicate the groupings existing within the ranks of the 'independents'.

A part of the syndicalist groups are against the Moscow International on account of its connections with the Communist International. They are intending to create their own purely syndicalist International. Such groups are prevalent amongst the Swedish and German syndicalists. They refused to participate in the Moscow Congress; such was the decision of the international syndicalist conference in Berlin.[19] These groups have remained in the minority. The other

18 An open appeal to Italian workers – to members of the CGL and all other unions – was issued by a number of RILU congress delegates in response to the CGL's proposal to move the congress to Stockholm or Reval. It was published in the 25 June 1921, issue of *Moscow* (no. 25), the multilingual organ of the Third Congress of the Communist International.

19 An international syndicalist conference was held in Berlin 16–21 December 1920. Organisations with voting rights were the Free Workers' Union of Germany (FAUD), the Revolutionary Syndicalist Committee (CSR) of France, the National Labour Secretariat (NAS) of the Netherlands, the Central Organisation of the Workers of Sweden (SAC), the IWW of the US, the Syndicalist Union in Czechoslovakia, the Federación Obrera Regional Argentina (FORA), and the National Shop Stewards' and Workers' Committee Movement of Britain.

syndicalists, the French and Spanish, declared in favour of fusion with all the other revolutionary unions on the condition of complete independence. They believe that the political International and the trade-union International have to be entirely independent.

The Berlin conference of the syndicalists adopted six points. The six points, which I do not intend to read here,[20] deal with the question of independence; they were also approved by the last convention of the IWW. Generally speaking, the syndicalists understand rather oddly the creation of the International. They pass resolutions to affiliate to the Red International of Labour Unions on the condition that it adopts their point of view. But the International is based on the agreement of different revolutionary groups.

For example, the Spanish syndicalists deal with the question quite differently. Here is what they say: 'We are disciples of Bakunin, but the war and the revolution taught us a number of things, and we have adopted the communist platform.' On this basis reconciliation would be possible. We can respond, 'Wait another year or two, when the capitalists will also show you which is better: the bourgeois regime or the dictatorship of the proletariat.'

I will make only a short reference as to the formation and character of the Amsterdam International, as my report is long enough already. Besides, the history of the Amsterdam International's creation, its programme and tactics, are quite known by every one of us.

The Amsterdam International was founded in Bern in February 1919 and fully took shape in July 1919 in Amsterdam, adopting a number of resolutions about socialisation, etc. In November 1920 in London, it threw in its lot with the Washington Conference of 1919, consisting of governments and labour representatives.[21] The Amsterdam International is linked with the International Labour Bureau. In its May Day appeal, the Amsterdam International declared in favour of socialisation,[22] but the definitive decision on this issue was put to the Washington Conference.

In characterising the ideology and policy of the Amsterdam International, we cannot help citing one of the most stupid and shameless documents, which I found in the last issue of this International's organ. You know that a reign of terror is currently raging in Spain, and our comrades are being daily murdered

The conference, which claimed to represent around a million workers, voted to participate in the RILU founding congress.

20 For the text of the six points, see p. 207.

21 The London Congress of the Amsterdam International was held 22–27 November 1920. For the Washington Conference of the ILO, see p. 62, n. 4.

22 For socialisation schemes, see p. 84, n. 1.

there in plain daylight. It is already estimated that hundreds have been killed on the streets by hired gangs. Lately a new system of assassination has been adopted: the revolutionary workers are being killed upon their release from prison, which usually takes place in the middle of the night. Such a case happened a few days ago with the secretary of the Spanish Confederation of Labour.[23] The released prisoners while walking through the streets on their way home are followed and killed. The most medieval methods are used in Spain; the system of assassination of workers is also widely practised in Europe and America.

The Amsterdam International addressed a letter to the president of the Spanish Council of Ministers, which read, 'Your Excellency, Article 13 of the Versailles Treaty – which your representative, the Marquess of Ezo signed – solemnly declares the freedom of labour organisations. We do not find this to be the case in Spain at the present time, but we trust that the government of Spain will not retract its promise given in the solemn document' – the Versailles Treaty. This reference to the 'solemn' article of the Versailles Treaty, promising grace and freedom to the working class, is a most striking fact not because of its naïveté, but because of its sheer stupidity and its entirely bourgeois psychology. The Versailles peace is only looked upon with great favour by all the manifest enemies of the working class; no one else regards the Versailles Treaty to be of any importance, especially the act guaranteeing freedom of organisation to workers.[24]

What practical conclusions should we make for all countries on the basis of the facts I've cited? What are to be the tactics of the trade unions? Here we suggest to the congress to adopt in the resolution on the tasks and tactics of trade unions a special section on 'methods and means of struggle', in which we indicate our line of conduct in the struggle and methods of approaching conflicts and how to solve them. It outlines, at the same time, how to make use in our work of the smallest social contradictions within each country, to make it clear to the most hot-headed revolutionary elements that the revolution cannot be provoked whenever one wants, but that they have to patiently prepare for it.

---

23 A reference to the murder of Evelio Boal. See p. 80.

24 The Versailles Peace Treaty was signed 28 June 1919 between the Entente powers and Germany. Among its many provisions, the Treaty transferred 10 per cent of Germany's territory to France, Belgium, Denmark, and Poland, and established that Germany would pay reparations to the Entente powers, later established at $33 billion US dollars ($548 billion in 2022 dollars). It also restricted Germany's military and provided for occupation of German territory west of the Rhine by Entente armies for fifteen years, beginning in 1920.

Part XIII of the treaty reproduced the constitution of the International Labour Organization, whose preamble stated that 'conditions of labour exist involving such injustice,

These are questions of education of the masses, questions of organisation, of practical tasks. They are closely connected with systematic revolutionary work, and demand great revolutionary temperament and ever more revolutionary cool-headedness. This must be underlined, for there are comrades in many countries who imagine that a social revolution can be made whenever one wants, that all one needs to do is proclaim a general strike and the hour of revolution will arrive. This is an exaggeration of one's own strength and an underestimation of the strength of the enemy.

The programme of action now presented to this congress is based on the principle of direct action. Direct action is action against the rule of the bourgeoisie, against the exploiters, and against the capitalist system in general. It may be manifested in different forms and methods, beginning with a strike and ending with armed insurrection, seizure of factories, etc. These slogans for direct action should especially be spread widely in all countries, because they express the organisational, political, economic, and practical aspects of our struggle.

The slogan of organisation that we believe should be put in the foreground is the transformation of craft and trade unionism into industrial unionism. We must pose to all unions the task of changing the basis of their system, replacing the system of guilds and delegates with factory committees and shop stewards. Once based on the organisation of factory committees, the struggle will be inspired by and conducted within the factory. These workers will be drawn into the struggle and won over. This system will afford an opportunity to the revolutionary minority – who so far are only a minority in all countries – to organise the millions of workers, thus making this system a starting point for revolutionary mass action.

Further, the practical slogan for all countries at the present moment is the question of workers' control. This slogan should be raised by the congress and passed from factory to factory, in order to put concretely before the workers the question of workers' control as the one that will protect workers from ever-increasing unemployment, affording them an opportunity to extend their sphere of influence in the enterprise. In short, workers' control is a method and form, one that increases our influence and rallies the workers to our side. Therefore, it should undoubtedly be one of our battle slogans.

---

hardship, and privation to large numbers of people as to produce unrest so great that the peace and harmony of the world are imperilled' and that 'the failure of any nation to adopt humane conditions of labour is an obstacle in the way of other nations which desire to improve the conditions in their own countries'.

I will not enumerate the rest of the slogans advanced in our programme of action. You will read them in the theses that will be printed and distributed to all delegates.

So we have outlined our general plan of action, and suggested a number of slogans and methods coming out of our collective experience. On the other hand, we have adopted general tactics suited to the peculiarities of the individual countries.

The task of the trade-union International is to lay down these guidelines and to continually learn lessons based on our own experience and the experiences of workers in other countries. Only on the basis of collective experience and constant exchange of revolutionary opinions and learning from each other will the revolutionary organisations of all countries be able to overcome internal friction and sectional quarrels within the labour movement. This will also render it possible to overcome the existing evolutionary and reformist prejudices alike, and will be able to find the proper line of action that will lead the workers of the world to final victory.

These, in general terms, are our ideas and the main lines that define the tactics and aims of the trade unions presented by this international congress. (*Applause*)

Plenary Session

(*Session opened at 1:40 p.m.*)

Lozovsky: The discussions on the report on tactics will take place after the report has been published in foreign languages. The report of Comrade Varga has been translated into French and English. There is no need to translate it into Russian, as it was published among the materials of the Third Congress of the Communist International, and the Russian delegates have had the opportunity to acquaint themselves with it. I propose to accept the report of Comrade Varga as an informational report. Are there any objections? The proposal is adopted.

(*A motion by the French delegation proposes to hear from the Credentials Commission.*)

Lozovsky: The floor is granted to Comrade Reinstein.

Reinstein: The work of the Credentials Commission is not yet finished; not all the data has been gathered. Within the commission itself there are some issues of dispute that still need to be worked out. It will be necessary to postpone the report of the Credentials Commission until its work is finished.

Lozovsky: I propose to ask the commission to finish its work and submit its report to the congress tomorrow at 11:00 a.m.

Murphy (Britain): As the discussions on the report on tactics are adjourned until the reports are published, and as the report on unemployment and the role of women in the trade-union movement are placed on tomorrow's agenda, I propose to begin discussion on the question of the relations of the Red Trade Union International with the Communist International.

Lozovsky: The question concerning the relations with the Communist International is so big that the discussion will not be finished at this session. Tonight, in view of the statements made by a whole series of delegations about their attending the session of the Communist International's congress, the plenary session of the congress will not be held.

The Presidium proposes to take up the question about relations with the Communist International for discussion tomorrow, after the report of the Credentials Commission. Comrades Rosmer and Tom Mann are the designated reporters.

Williams (USA): I request of the Presidium that the report be submitted to the congress in foreign languages; otherwise the delegates will find it difficult to get their bearings.

Lozovsky: The Presidium is doing everything possible to have the documents published in foreign languages, but the lack of compositors knowing foreign languages greatly impedes the publication of these documents.

The French delegation brought in the question of whether the Presidium had finished editing the appeal to the workers of the world, and how the work of the commission on the report is progressing. The editing of the manifesto will be finished today. The commission will set to work after the publication of Comrade Rosmer's report.

Since there are no more questions, the session is adjourned.

(*The session adjourned at 2:30 p.m.*)

SESSION 5. 9 JULY 1921, MORNING–AFTERNOON

Credentials; RILU-Comintern Relations

(*Session opens at 11:00 a.m. Lozovsky in the chair.*)

Lozovsky: Comrade Reinstein has the floor for the preliminary report on the activity of the Credentials Commission.

Report of Credentials Commission

Boris Reinstein: We are not yet prepared, and we do not consider it advisable, to give today a complete report on the activities of the Credentials Commission, because late arrivals of new delegates make this impossible. Thus today we will give you only a partial report. The Credentials Commission was occupied all day yesterday until midnight with the examination of three cases:

First, we had to decide upon the Canadian delegation composed of two delegates of the One Big Union. One of them, representing a small faction of the organisation, was subjected to an attack by the other. These are the usual factional quarrels. The two factions together represent about 30,000 members. The question is whether they shall both have a decisive vote at the congress.

The second case was about the division of votes among the German delegates: an argument was raised by the representatives of the [VKPD] National Trade Union Office on one side and on the other side, the representatives of the Free Workers' Unions, the Agricultural Workers' Union, the Union of Hand and Brain Workers, and the Seamen's Union. The issue did not involve participation in the work of the congress itself; it was only a question of the distribution of votes within the German delegation.

The third question was the distribution of votes among the American delegation, in view of the declaration of Comrade Williams, delegate of the Industrial Workers of the World.

The examination of these questions took up yesterday's full day by the Credentials Commission. We intended to ask the congress that we be permitted to deliver a report at the end of the session, because Comrade Szántó, the chair of the commission who ought to report, could not attend the session.

As to the dispute of the Canadians, the question was whether a decisive or consultative vote should be given to Cascaden, the representative of the

 | DOI:10.1163/9789004712867_009

organisation of lumber workers, who declares himself to be the only real representative of the faction of the organisation known under the name One Big Union.

The case is as follows: Comrade Cascaden arrived in Moscow and presented his credentials. For unknown reasons, he refused to give us any information on the attitude of his organisation on the fundamental principles of the International Council of Trade Unions. In particular, he declined to give us information of the attitude of his organisation with regard to the question of the dictatorship of the proletariat. When the Credentials Commission, before taking the decision as to his right to a vote, again interviewed him on this, it became clear that he was the representative of the anarchist element of the One Big Union organisation, and that he was inclined to consider the dictatorship of the proletariat in the way many other anarchists do, i.e., as a new form of state oppression. Finally he told us that he would give his explanation on this question only at the congress itself.

As a result, the Credentials Committee decided to give Comrade Cascaden a consultative vote only.

Some comrades of the Spanish and French delegations demanded then that the comrade be given a decisive vote. For his part he handed in a statement in which he acknowledged the dictatorship of the proletariat as a provisional measure, but only as a dictatorship carried out by a trade-union and not by a political organisation. (*Voices in the hall: 'This means a dictatorship with reservations.'*)

We likewise examined the protest of Comrade Knight, the representative of another faction of their One Big Union. He objected to Comrade Cascaden being given a decisive vote. The Credentials Commission finally decided to give Comrade Cascaden a decisive vote.

On the American dispute, here is a summary: Comrade Williams, the delegate of the IWW, asserts that his organisation is the only one in America that is seriously determined to take part in creating a revolutionary trade-union International. In his view, all the other American delegates present at the congress, with the exception of Crosby, in spite of the revolutionary spirit animating them, are representatives of sections of the American Federation of Labor, and therefore cannot be considered revolutionary elements. Comrade Williams maintains that he is the only representative of revolutionary American trade unions. He protested against giving a consultative vote: (1) to Comrade Wells, delegate of the Seattle, Washington, Central Labor Council, which unites 500,000 organised revolutionary workers; (2) to a representative [Batt] of the Central Labor Council of Detroit, one of the largest industrial centres of America; this organisation encompasses 600,000 organised revolutionary workers;

(3) to a representative [Browder] of the Kansas miners local and of the New York Federated Labor Council; (4) to a representative [Bloor] of the three locals of the International Association of Machinists.

The American bureau of the provisional International Council of Trade Unions has issued a circular with copies of resolutions against the yellow Amsterdam International.[1] These resolutions were based on the principles of the class struggle, of replacing the bourgeois state with the dictatorship of the proletariat, and for affiliation with the Red Trade Union International. The comrades against whom Comrade Williams has protested were elected by their organisations as partisans of the principles of these resolutions. But these organisations have not withdrawn from the American Federation of Labor.

Besides these delegates, there is another delegate, Comrade Crosby. He represents several revolutionary and independent trade unions, which were either expelled or have withdrawn from the American Federation of Labor. Therefore, the organisations Comrade Crosby represents are affiliated to neither the American Federation of Labor nor the IWW.

Comrade Williams, on behalf of the IWW, demanded that a decisive vote not be granted to representatives of organisations affiliated with the American Federation of Labor. He was willing to grant 3 votes to Comrade Crosby as a representative of independent unions, but he absolutely demands that the other 13 votes of the United States should be given to the IWW. On the other hand, the comrades against whom Williams protested, proposed to give 3 decisive votes to the IWW representative, 3 votes to the representative of the independent unions, 3 votes to the representative of the Kansas Miners Union local and of the New York Federated Labor Council, 2 votes to the representatives of the Seattle and Detroit Central Labor Councils respectively, and 1 vote to the representatives of the three locals of the Machinists union.

It must be noted here that it is impossible to establish the exact membership of the IWW after sixteen years of existence. According to Williams, it has a total membership of 70,000 to 100,000; but according to the figures presented at the Communist International congress and the itemised statement of the receipts of the central treasury of this organisation, it has a membership of 15,000 to 16,000.

The Credentials Commission discussed the question and came to the conclusion that the motion made by the comrades against whom Williams protested should be carried: 3 decisive votes given to each of the five American

1 The American bureau of the International Council of Trade and Industrial Unions was formed in January 1921. See Tosstorff 2016, pp. 318–19.

delegates and 1 vote to the delegate of the three local sections of the Machinists Union. We consider this decision to be a fair one.

As to the German question in dispute, the German delegates are, no doubt, well informed as to the facts and merits of the case. Comrade Malzahn maintains, on behalf of the National Trade Union Office formed by the United Communist Party of Germany, which has pronounced in favour of Moscow, that out of the total of 9 million organised workers belonging to the large and so-called free German trade unions [the ADGB], 2.2 million side with the Communists.

On the other hand Comrade Bartels maintains, on behalf of a number of independent German trade unions, that, perhaps the National Trade Union Office really has the above number of adherents among the general mass organised in the free trade unions of Germany, but they cannot be relied upon as a revolutionary factor. The representatives of the independent opposition unions maintain that the so-called oppositional elements within the big mass unions are guided by the reactionary bureaucracy of their unions, which are affiliated to Amsterdam. They have not been up to the task during the revolutionary battles that have taken place. That is why, according to Comrade Bartels, the representatives of the Central Trade Union Committee, representing the opposition elements in the mass trade unions, should only be given 6 decisive votes. The other 10 German votes, in his view, should be distributed as follows: 3 decisive votes to the Gelsenkirchen Free Workers' Union, 3 votes to the General Workers' Union, 2 votes to the German syndicalists, including the small number of German Seamen, 1 vote to the Agricultural Workers' Union, and 1 vote to the Union of Hand and Brain Workers.

The Credentials Commission heard and discussed the arguments of the representatives of both sides concerned and finally decided that it would be fairer and in the interests of our Red Trade Union International to grant 11 votes to the representatives of the National Trade Union Office, which directs the activities within the mass trade unions of Germany, and distribute the remaining 5 votes to the representatives of the independent trade unions.

This is all that the Credentials Commission has to say for the moment.

Lozovsky: In connection with the report of Comrade Reinstein, we have before us three disputed questions to act upon. I suggest that we divide these questions as follows: (1) distribution of votes among the German delegation; (2) distribution of votes among the American delegation; (3) the declaration of the Canadian delegation.

I further propose that in each question the floor be granted to two speakers – one for the proposal of the Credentials Commission, the other against. Even in this manner, we will have six speakers and eighteen translations. The loss of time on such unimportant questions is more than enough. Apart from this, I move that the report of Comrade Reinstein be accepted as read, and that the Credentials Commission be instructed to prepare a detailed report indicating exact figures, etc., at the end of the congress.

Arlandis (Spain) (*from his seat*): I move that the Credentials Commission add to its report actual figures as to the number of members in the contending organisations, and the number of votes allotted to them. We do not know anything about it. We therefore are not in a position to discuss these questions.

Lozovsky: It is with great difficulty that we translate into four languages, and our French comrades do not help us at all.

Even at the congresses held abroad there is always a delay in the printing of important matter. It is much more difficult for us here, having a lack of typesetters of foreign languages. In any case, this demand cannot be met, for purely material reasons. Were we to wait until everything was printed, we would not be able to take a decision on the report of the Credentials Commission.

Victor Godonnèche (France) (*from his seat*): This question was not made by the French but by the Spanish comrades.

Ballister [Robert Minor] (USA) (*from his seat*): A point of correction. The English translation has been made incorrectly. The English translation given to us was that the commission is in favour of giving 11 votes to delegates here representing Communist nuclei in the old trade unions. The Central Trade Union Office [in Germany] does not represent Communist nuclei, but rather the oppositional minority within the old unions.

Lozovsky: The report has been given; there is nothing more to be said about it.

Arlandis: That explanation does not satisfy me.

Lozovsky: What is your proposal?

Arlandis: That the Credentials Commission give an account of what it has done.

Rosmer: The report has just been presented.

Arlandis: But no one understands anything about it.

Lozovsky: I ask whether or not we want to move on to the discussion of this question. If necessary, we might consider this question at the end of the congress.

Godonnèche (*from his seat*): There is another question. That of the French delegation: the question of Boisson. There is a representative here of a minority that is not included in the General Confederation of Labour: the Confederation of Workers of the World [CTM] (Marseilles organisation), who received a mandate for a decisive vote.

Lozovsky: I thought that Boisson had only a consultative vote. He cannot have a decisive vote, nor has he any right to it.

On the agenda is the question of distribution of votes of the German delegation. Comrade Bartels has the floor.

Bartels (*from his seat*): On what question?

Lozovsky: On the question of distribution of votes.

(*Comrade Disch asked for the floor to discuss the agenda, but since Comrade Bartels had already begun his speech, it was not granted.*)

Arthur Bartels (Germany, Gelsenkirchen Free Workers' Union): The question that will now be decided is of decisive importance for the whole congress. It is natural that we, who suffer from the present arrangement, are emphatically against the distribution of votes practised until now. The decision made on this question, which carries great weight with us in particular, has consequences on the well-being of the entire labour movement in the future. We cannot afford to have the labour unions put into a narrow channel, which may cripple developments and become detrimental to the growth of the revolution. Therefore, I speak against the distribution of decisive votes adopted by the commission. We must take notice that the Russian as well as the German delegation each consists of sixty delegates, while other countries in many instances have an insignificant number of delegates.

Lozovsky: I protest against this statement. The countries mentioned have no more than 16 votes each. The other large countries have just as many votes. I would ask you to talk to the point, without demagogic reproaches. (*Voices of approval are heard.*)

Bartels (*continues*): Yes, each country is entitled to 16 votes; hence the delegations represented here are to be given that number. This is not demagogy. Comrade Lozovsky's words against me might be construed that he is insisting upon the predominance of certain views at this congress. (*Voices of approval and of protest*) This congress is a reflection of the world proletariat, consisting of all sorts of different organisations; it aims to put the labour movement on a solid foundation. These organisations are welded together according to the decisions of respective national branches of the workers' movement. Still their opinions cannot be successfully voiced here, that is, they are given the right to present their views, but cannot influence decisions. (*Voices of approval and disapproval*) It should be noted that truly revolutionary organisations have their voices stifled. (*Energetic protests*)

I will speak now upon the following question: We have brought many statements to the Presidium. In our country and in others it is customary to have such statements issued for everyone's information. Meanwhile three days have passed and none of the delegations have been informed of our statements. (*Voices from the hall: 'That is false.'*) In that case, why does not Comrade Lozovsky read these statements?

I now call attention to the decisions of the Credentials Commission. I will not mention the decisions on the American delegation; it belongs to Comrade Williams to do this.

Let us consider the question of the distribution of votes among the German delegation. As is known, the situation in Germany is as follows: In some of the district and local organisations, in a series of central organisations – as for instance, the construction industry and the metalworkers – there are very revolutionary groups who vote 'For Moscow'. But this was only done where revolutionary elements dominated. In the others, this question was not even posed.

The representatives of the National Trade Union Office state that in some of the local organisations Moscow prevailed; in others – Amsterdam. From this they make a bold conclusion and maintain that they are indisputably entitled to represent those organisations here. But if we have it this way, why should we not state the same thing about Hamburg, for instance, where our union numerically surpasses the old miners' unions. I must point out that if our unions stand by the banner of Moscow, it is not for the sake of illusions. Illusions present a great danger for the revolution (*Shouts in the hall: 'Correct.'*) I am extremely pleased that you approve. (*Shout from the seats: 'You labour under illusions.'*) No, we don't give ourselves up to illusions. Concerning the present congress, we decidedly dispute the reasons given by the National Trade Union Office. We deny them, whatever be the sources the representatives would draw them from. We state that there exist in Germany five organised trade-union organisations, which we represent and which are undoubtedly revolutionary organisations. As opposed to this, separate nuclei in old trade unions that declared in favour of Moscow should not be considered as integral organisations. It behooves the National Trade Union Office to represent only those nuclei. However, the nuclei, by not breaking off from these unions of which they constitute a part, support reaction and lead to the repression of the proletariat.

If all these circumstances would be taken into consideration by the Credentials Commission, then the decision would be quite different. Let me emphasise that five votes granted to us, delegates of fully formed organisations, and eleven to the other members of the German delegation representing only separate nuclei that are not in a position to influence the revolutionary actions of the proletariat, cannot be considered other than violence against the real revolutionary forces of Germany. (*Laughter on the side of the Central Trade Office representatives; protests*) And still we have always been, and I hope will remain, the most reliable partisans of 'Moscow'. Of course, when the information reaches our workers at home how we were received and treated, possibly the sympathies toward Moscow will cool off.

Richard Müller (Germany): The German delegation entirely shares the point of view of the Credentials Commission on the question of the Canadian dispute. The delegation assumes a similar attitude in the American controversy. As to the protests by Comrade Bartels, on behalf of four unions, against an irregular distribution of votes within the German delegation, we find them groundless. We likewise resolutely oppose the efforts by Comrade Bartels to create for himself a favourable impression among the delegates at the congress by falsely depicting the real state of things. We refute with indignation his statement that 60 German and 60 Russian votes are dominating the congress. This is contrary to reality in that the German and Russian delegations each possess only 16 votes, irrespective of the number of delegates present. We therefore join in the protest expressed on this occasion by Comrade Lozovsky, and deem that this way of conducting the debate should be inadmissible.

The attempt of Comrade Bartels to appeal to the feelings of the delegates of this congress appears to be a rather questionable method of argumentation and entirely out of place. How are we to understand otherwise his reference to blood shed by his comrades? We question very seriously the correctness of this statement. We cannot allow ourselves to be seduced by the illusory facts that he lays at the foundation of his inferences. We cannot take any decision on the basis of his conclusions.

Bartels questions the number of adherents of the oppositions within the German trade unions, of whom we are the representatives. It cannot be denied us, however, that we availed ourselves of any opportunity to place in the forefront at every meeting and conference the question 'for' or 'against' Moscow, and the members who declared themselves at these conferences in favour of Moscow clearly expressed by this their revolutionary will. In his view, however, the revolutionary will of the workers is manifested clearly only when they are in possession of a membership card in the Free Gelsenkirchen Union. (*Bartels, from his seat: 'Yes indeed.'*)

A tenacious struggle is being waged in Germany against Amsterdam. This struggle inside the ranks of nine million members of trade unions is led by the Communists. On the other hand, this Free Union of Gelsenkirchen fails to exercise any perceptible influence on the German trade-union movement. The 300,000 members of which the Free Unions [*freie Unionen*] are composed – by their own count – are of no importance whatsoever in comparison to the nine million members in the central union confederation. Bartels states that he represents five distinct organisations that have adopted the programme of Moscow. He fears that they are being forcibly suppressed. Let us try once more to consider these organisations in the name of which Comrade Bartels speaks. At any rate we distrust very much the figures given for the members comprising the AAU [General Workers' Union] and FAUD [Free Workers' Union of Germany]. We know very well that the relative value of these organisations in Germany is very small.

Let us pass on to the Free Association of Agricultural Workers. What can be said about this organisation? It is known that it had declared itself for a collaboration with capital, for the so-called *Arbeitsgemeinschaft*,[2] which shows that this organisation is far from sharing the principles of the Red International of Trade Unions.

The Union of Hand and Brain Workers is generally not known to anybody outside Berlin. Its members have never yet showed a willingness to fight for our aims.

On the other hand, we can always determine the number of partisans of the United Communist Party of Germany. Here is a list of those militants who recognise the slogan of 'For Moscow':

2 *Arbeitsgemeinschaft* (or more precisely, *Zentralarbeitsgemeinschaft*) was a body created 15 November 1918 through an agreement between German employer associations and the free trade union and Christian trade-union federations. The term was also used more broadly to refer to the policy of class collaboration between trade unions and capital in order to achieve economic reconstruction.

Agricultural workers – 150,000 members
Miners – 150,000 members
Bricklayers and Builders – 300,000 members
Metalworkers – 500,000
Woodworkers – 120,000 members
Transport and Communication workers – 275,000 members[3]
Printing – 120,000 members[4]
Garment – 75,000 members[5]
Food workers – 90,000 members

Factory workers – 160,000 members.[6]

This incomplete data proves that the opposition to the Amsterdam International is uniting a great quantity of members. It may be roughly estimated that one-third of the organised workers are partisans of Moscow.

I ask whether there is any ground for complaint at the decision of the Credentials Commission under such circumstances. We consider the decision to be just and well founded.

Lozovsky: A group of comrades whom we have expected have just arrived from Norway. My hearty greetings to you, comrades. I beg you to take your seats among the other delegates.

We now pass to the vote. There are two proposals on the question of the German delegation.

The Credentials Commission suggests to distribute the votes as follows: 11 votes to the revolutionary minority working within the old trade unions, 2 votes to the Free Union of Gelsenkirchen, 2 votes to the General Workers' Union, 1 vote to the syndicalists. The representative of the Free Union of Gelsenkirchen moves a different scheme of vote distribution: 6 votes to the minority within the old trade unions, 3 votes to the Free Union of Gelsenkirchen, 3 votes to the General Workers' Union, 2 votes to the syndicalists, 1 vote to the Free Agricultural Workers' Union, 1 vote to the Hand and Brain Workers' Union.

Labonne (*from his seat*): I'd like to know before voting whether Comrade Cascaden of Canada was given a decisive vote, according to the decision of the Credentials Commission.

---

3 This is per the German, Russian, and English versions; the French text says 260,000.
4 This is per the German, Russian, and French versions; the English text says 300,000.
5 This is per the English text; the Russian version says 35,000; not in German.
6 This is per the French and Russian texts; the English version says 50,000; not in German.

Lozovsky: Yes. But he will have to refrain from voting when the question of Canada is on the agenda.

Let us pass to the vote. The entire German delegation is not voting. So will the other delegations refrain when the questions concerning them are dealt with. I shall call on the countries in alphabetical order, and will ask who is for and who is against the motion of the Credentials Commission.

I begin to put it to the delegates: Azerbaijan for. Britain for. Armenia for. Bulgaria for. Hungary for. Holland for. Russia for. Denmark for. Far Eastern Republic for. Spain against. Canada: the votes are divided. Latvia for. United States of America: 13 for and 3 against. Finland for. Ukraine for. France: 7 for and 4 against. Czechoslovakia for. Switzerland for. Yugoslavia for. Argentina against. Greece for. Romania for.

(*After the vote is taken, the following statement of the Dutch delegation was received by the Presidium*: 'On account of some misunderstanding, the Dutch delegation voted in favour of the decision of the Credentials Commission. In reality it intended to support the motion of the Free Union of Gelsenkirchen. We ask to make this correction in the stenographic report.')

The motion of the Credentials Commission has thus been accepted. Now comes the question of the American delegation. Comrade Williams has the floor.

George Williams (USA, IWW): The American delegation is very clear and it has stated its objections to some of the American delegates to this convention, on the grounds that their credentials were fraternal, and after going into the Credentials Commission and gaining access to the credentials, we found they are all fraternal delegates. They are sent here as what you might call observers with no power to take part in the proceedings, and no organisations to report back to on the question of affiliation. We found that one of the delegates had no credentials at all. He is sitting at the floor with three votes and no record of any credentials in the hands of the Credentials Commission. But the main point is that the credentials they have specifically state that they are fraternal.

In answer to this, one of the delegates says that the organisations that he represents cannot endanger their position in the A.F. of L.,[7] and explains, mind you, that they are credentials representing a minority of the A.F. of L. willing

7 In 1921 English speakers generally pronounced the abbreviation for the American Federation of Labor as 'A.F. of L.' Given the fact that such a spoken rendering is no longer commonly used, 'AFL' appears throughout this volume in translated text. But when the abbreviation is used by a delegate speaking English, we have maintained the rendering that appears in the English-language version of the congress proceedings produced at the time.

to consolidate with the Red Trade Union International. His excuse is that this organisation that he comes to represent does not want to jeopardise its position. That is a fine statement for a so-called minority! The fact of the matter is that they do not represent anybody but themselves, that all their credentials were issued by one man in New York, and that they came here to stuff the labour delegation and incite a vote against the IWW of America. Of course, it is natural and easy for people to come here and claim representation of mythical minorities. There are all kinds of minorities in the United States, people who are fighting the A.F. of L. machine. What is to hinder anybody from claiming that he represents a hypothetical mass of the A.F. of L. movement?

Now the question of credentials in this convention is about the most important thing that is before us. If whole blocks of delegates from any country can be seated on the assumption that they represent a minority in the labour movement, then what is to hinder the A.F. of L. from stuffing this convention with all the delegates they can send over? There is no way of stopping this, because all their credentials come from the same individual in New York.

There is another danger about this proposition. The practice of stuffing delegations with so-called nuclei in labour organisations is a game that can be played both ways. For instance, if it comes down to a fight, the issue becomes one of seeing who can send the most delegates in his particular delegation, and it will develop right in this congress, being that there will be enough delegates to fill up all the hotels in Moscow. Because the IWW can pick out each local in its organisation and send a delegate, and the others can do the same next year until there is an unending battle about who can send the most delegates, and then it depends upon who can gain the most information about how many the others are sending. And then instead of getting down to business, we will have to think about the people who are struggling to control the delegations.

That is going to happen, because the tendency here now – I have heard it discussed – is that 'next year there will be more and more delegates' to this or that particular organisation. That is the American style of attacking the A.F. of L., and it can work both ways.

There is one delegate here [Wells] who claims to represent a minority in Seattle. Just a few words about that minority. The particular minority that he represents is right now under the charge of using their position to create corporations such as real estate, moving picture corporations, private banks, and other things for their own material aims. It has been proved that the editor of the so-called progressive *Union Record* has made something like $50,000 or $60,000 out of a real estate project. Others are connected with private banks and moving picture theatres, and these people come here to represent them in a revolutionary congress of red trade unions. They say they are going back to organise minorities and fight like that. The fact is, when he goes back he will have nothing to say and nobody to report to, and nobody will ever know he came back or that he was ever here. I predict he will be afraid to make a report on the representations of the Red Trade Union International. What is he going to tell them in Seattle about the dictatorship of the proletariat? Is he going to put it to a vote? It is not even going to come up on the floor.

These delegates who have been sitting here with thirteen votes out of sixteen are going to be compelled to produce the goods when they go back to America, and I am going to attend to that job. I am going to see to it that their promises are fulfilled, every promise they make, and I know they cannot do it and they know it. The decision of the Credentials Commission is a good one from that angle. It is going to make these people show their hands and show them out in the open, and when the next congress comes there is going to be a question about what they have done in America.

I did not expect any other decision from the Credentials Commission than what they brought. I accuse Comrade Reinstein of being unfair both in his translation and in his information, and about the others I do not know anything, and I am surprised that they did not give me the one vote and the rest fifteen, from their standpoint.

One delegate here [Browder] claims to represent the Workers' Council of New York City. On examination of the credentials, there was another without credentials on the record, but only a statement from the Red Labor Bureau of New York City. I have inquired and they have admitted that perhaps he does not represent the Workers' Council of New York. I am sure he does not, because he doesn't know the name of the secretary or where they meet. I want to say something from the standpoint of what they claim they are going to do, that the Workers' Council of New York was organised by the IWW members. The president and secretary are both IWWs, and here a man steps in from Kansas City and does not even know where the headquarters are and comes here claiming to represent that organisation. Now when a man enters in that state of mind, it shows they are not sincere in their mission here. It shows they have some underlying motive in claiming to represent an organisation they do not represent. And when a man comes in here with that attitude and gains a majority in the delegation, then I say there is some trouble brewing for the Red Trade Union International and they are placing obstacles in the road of the progress of real industrial unionism.

Another delegate [Bloor], a woman, claims to represent three Machinists unions. The Denver local that she says she represents is something like two thousand miles from the other, and besides, I would like to know when a woman started working in machine shops in America. I would like to know that. I would like to know if she ever worked in a machine shop in America.

Comrade Billings's [Batt's] credentials state emphatically that they are fraternal. He doesn't deny it. This particular Detroit Federation of Labor was afraid to put anything else on his credentials. There are bitter haters of the IWW among certain elements in America. That hatred rises out of this, that the IWW as a labour organisation has always been a poor field for theoreticians and pie card artists. They know it.

I do not include Fellow Worker Crosby in any statement I made.

Flynn[8] (USA): It is with some considerable regret that I find it necessary to take the floor and speak for sustaining this just and proper division of votes among the American delegation. If there is any objection that could be given with propriety in the decision we have arrived at in the American delegation, that objection would be that we have been too liberal with the IWW in the distribution of votes. We have given them votes entirely out of proportion to their importance in the American labour movement. And before proceeding directly to the argument on this question, there are a few certain things I wish to call

8 The identity of 'Flynn' here has not been definitively established. 'Flynn' was the pseudonym used at the Second Comintern Congress in 1920 by Edward Lindgren. The evidence suggests, however, that Lindgren did not go to Moscow in 1921, as he was arrested in New York on 30 April. Moreover, had he nevertheless made it to Russia, Lindgren – a member of the Central Committee of the US Communist Party – would almost certainly have been a delegate to the Third Comintern Congress held at the same time as the RILU congress. But neither the names 'Lindgren' nor 'Flynn' appear in any of the numerous lists of delegates to the Third Congress found in the Comintern archives (RGASPI 490/1/182).

Based on Flynn's remarks to the congress – here in session 5 and subsequently in sessions 13 and 17 – the speaker appears to have been one of the four US voting delegates with credentials from AFL-affiliated unions – Dennis Batt, Earl Browder, Ella Reeve Bloor, or Hulet Wells.

The minutes of the Organisation Commission (pp. 535–9 of this volume) suggest an answer to the riddle. In several cases the German and French versions of the proceedings include speeches attributed to Flynn; in the English and Russian versions, however, these very same speeches are credited to Batt. Based on these conflicting attributions, it seems possible that 'Flynn' may be a reference to Batt, who also used the pseudonym Billings.

Moreover, a report written by Batt on the RILU congress published in *The Proletarian* of December 1921 argues along exactly the same lines as Flynn's remarks to the congress. This supposition is reinforced further by the speech given by Flynn in session 13. During his remarks there, Flynn refers several times to members of the US Communist Party as 'they' and not 'we'. At this time Batt was a member of the Proletarian Party, having split from the CP in 1920.

your attention to in the attitude of the delegates from the Industrial Workers of the World. I might say parenthetically that he reminds me somewhat of a drowning man. He grabs at one straw, and when he finds it is only a straw he lets loose and grabs another.

In our caucus that took up this matter, Comrade Williams of the IWW did not protest our right to step into this convention with decisive powers, but made us an offer to give us one vote apiece, taking the other 11 votes for himself. He was first willing to make this kind of a division, but when the matter appears before the Credentials Commission in the shape of an appeal, it takes on an entirely different character, and not only does he want to give us one vote, but he wants to take away all power. Further, I wish to call your attention to the fact that there are only certain delegates that he protests against. He religiously and carefully excludes Comrade Crosby, and that has important bearings upon the issues at stake. We who are under protest here this afternoon represent a section of the gigantic mass organisation of America. The one who is under no protest, the one against whom Comrade Williams does not protest, is like himself a representative of dualism, of the splitting of the American labour movement.

Now it seems to me that the first thing we have to consider in dealing with this question is the relative membership of the organisations. We have to consider their quantitative strength. We have to figure them quantitatively, and quantitatively the representative of the Industrial Workers of the World can have no argument at all. The minutes of his own convention, the records there show that the Industrial Workers of the World have a membership of 15,674. He claims these figures are incorrect. On what grounds? He came before the Credentials Commission last night and said these figures were not correct because such gigantic organisations as the lumber workers and others were excluded. And why? Because they had not paid dues for a year. Some fine organisation that must be. But the fact of the matter is that several quotations in the report show that the balance sheet of the [Lumber] Workers Industrial Union shows a membership of only about five thousand.

On the other hand, the delegates who are protested against here represent the strongest unions in the American Federation of Labor. Comrade Wells, who represents the Seattle Federation of Labor, was elected at an open meeting. That fact was attested, and resolutions were adopted endorsing the dictatorship of the proletariat and accepting the call of the Red Trade Union International. This is a matter of public knowledge. As to the history of that organisation – that speaks for itself. Anyone who knows anything about the general strike in Seattle, their general attitude on Russia, about what they did on the docks there, on the question of shipping munitions to Kolchak,[9] knows very well what the attitude of the Seattle Federation of Labor is, and will back the 50,000 members of the Seattle Federation of Labor against the 15,674 of the IWW any day in the week when it comes to supporting the dictatorship of the proletariat and other revolutionary ideas. In all, in the American Federation of Labor sections that are represented here, we have about 260,000 members. That question is not challenged. But the thing that bothers these people is the quality of our credentials and the quality of our membership. Now, you mark right well that the representative of the IWW does not claim to have any more power for himself than to go back and report; that the IWW does not come forward in endorsing the programme that will probably come out of the Red Trade Union International. They have no conception of the revolution and they never will, and they never can without completely disrupting their organisation to accept the idea.

As for the validity of the credentials: the American bureau of the Red Trade Union International anticipated the decisions of this convention to such an extent that they said that this convention was going on record against dual unionism, against splitting away. They were of the opinion that, like sensible revolutionists, we were going to take the attitude that we must stay within. Therefore, our credentials were couched in such language as to protect us against the bureaucracy of the American Federation of Labor.

In reality this is not a question of membership. This is not a question of the validity of credentials. Any of you who have sat in this convention knows what the issue is here. We have on the one hand Simon-purists, those people who want to withdraw from the mass unions, who want to get off by themselves with a pure Marxian union organisation. On the other hand, we have those who realise that the success of the revolution is dependent on getting control of these organisations. That is the fight. It is a question of principle, not a question of membership or credentials but a question of the principle of working within the big mass organisations of the working class.

We have the same thing in France, in Germany, and in America, the same principle. Are you going to recognise those groups in the mass unions as having the decisive power, or are you going to hand the vote of the Red Trade Union International in America to the IWW? That is the question, and if you want

9 The Seattle general strike took place 6–11 February 1919, when members of 101 unions affiliated to the AFL, along with IWW members, joined 35,000 shipyard workers already on strike.

Sympathy with Soviet Russia was particularly strong among workers in Seattle at the time. In the fall of 1919 longshoremen refused to load arms being sent to the counterrevolutionary white armies.

an International made up of these purists, going to withdraw themselves into little sections – and if you want that kind of convention made up of the IWW in America and others in France, Germany, and if you want that kind of International, you will vote to upset the report of the chairman. But if you want an International made up of the masses of the workers that really represent the workers, you are going to vote to sustain the Credentials Commission.

Lozovsky: We will pass to the vote. We have the following proposals. The Credentials Commission proposes to distribute the votes as follows: 1 decisive vote to Comrade Emmons [Bloor], delegate of the International Association of Machinists; 3 votes to Comrade Crosby [Cosgrove], delegate of the Amalgamated Society of Metalworkers, the Amalgamated Union of Food Workers, the Boot and Shoe Workers, and the minority committee of the Tailors Union; 3 votes to Comrade Wells, delegate of the Central Workers Council of Seattle; 3 votes to Comrade Williams, delegate of the Industrial Workers of the World; 3 votes to Comrade Batt, delegate of the Detroit Labor Federation; and 3 votes to Comrade Dixon [Browder], the miners' delegate.

Comrade Williams, representative of the IWW, proposes to give 3 decisive votes to Comrade Crosby and the other 13 to the representatives of the IWW, considering that the rest of the delegates have no right to obtain any decisive vote at all.

I will now proceed to the vote, using the same method as last time.

Arlandis (*from his seat*): I ask for the floor.

Lozovsky: It was decided that there would be two speakers, one for and one against. I cannot give you the floor.

So the vote:

Austria for. Australia for. Azerbaijan for. Britain for. Armenia for. Bulgaria for. Hungary for. Holland for. Georgia for. Germany: 11 for and 5 against. Denmark for. Far Eastern Republic for. Spain against. Canada: 1 for and 1 against. Latvia for. Luxembourg for. Poland for. Russia for. Ukraine for. Finland against. France for. Czechoslovakia for. Switzerland for. Yugoslavia for. Estonia for. South Africa for. Argentina against. Greece for. Romania for.

The decision of the Credentials Commission is ratified.

We have to take up two more questions; I hope the discussion on them will not take long. The floor is granted to Comrade Godonnèche.

Victor Godonnèche (France): We object to the decisive vote granted by the Credentials Commission to the representative of a small organisation bearing the high-sounding name of 'Confederation of Workers of the World' [Confédération des travailleurs du monde, CTM].

Following the Orléans Congress – the *minoritaires*' constitutive congress – we granted a consultative vote to the representatives of that organisation, which at the present time exists only in an embryonic form. We asked its members – which were very few in number then, and which have not grown much since – we asked them to bow to discipline in face of the decisions of the organised minority. A few of these elements did so and entered the Revolutionary Syndicalist Committees (CSR). Only a tiny part remained outside this organisation, declaring their intention to remain apart from the CGT. We believe that a lack of discipline is what weakens the revolutionary minorities in all countries.

It is easy to assemble a few comrades and form an organisation. Here in Moscow there are two comrades who belong to the Chapellerie organisation. If it is decided to grant a decisive voice to the CTM – which has at most a thousand members – a decisive vote should also be given to the minority of the Chapellerie organisation, with its 45 members.

We absolutely oppose giving a decisive vote to the representatives of the CTM. There is no ground whatever to grant a vote to this small group – a minority within the minority. If we do so, we will be encouraging the creation of new minorities that will arise in the course of the next year. The French delegation moves that a consultative vote only be given to Comrade Boisson.

Lozovsky: Comrade Boisson is granted the floor.

Louis Boisson (France, CTM): Comrades, the question posed by Comrade Godonnèche has been badly put, and I will tell you why.

Comrades, we note in the present labour movement in France three tendencies. The first is in favour of the yellow Amsterdam International; the second comprises the so-called *minoritaires* of the CGT, which is represented here by the revolutionary syndicalists; and finally the third, represented by the workers in whose name I speak and who are organised outside the CGT, as they were unwilling to pay membership dues to support an organisation that in its majority still remains yellow, and actions for which they were by no means inclined to bear any responsibility.

After the betrayal of the revolutionary movement in France of 21 July 1919, and after the betrayal of the May 1920 strikes,[10] our comrades separated from the CGT – and you should note that during this period the CGT had more than

10 A twenty-four-hour strike was scheduled for 21 July 1919 by the top leadership of the CGT, with support from the French Socialist Party, in conjunction with the Italian CGL,

2 million members, while today in 1921 it has only 600,000. You see from this, comrades, the danger of grouping all these forces in the same organisation in the interests of revolutionary unity.

As to the *minoritaires* [the CSR], we refused to adhere to it, on the grounds that its constitution is not sufficiently homogenous, and we cannot vouch for its revolutionary character. Besides, its attitude toward the Red International and the Communist International is not definite enough, whereas our organisation was the first in France to answer immediately the appeal of the International Council of Trade Unions.

Our refusal to merge with the *minoritaires* therefore bears a conditional character. We are ready to agree to a fusion if the representatives of the revolutionary syndicalist minority will state their unconditional affiliation to the Red International.

We have come here to the world trade-union congress with a spirit of impartiality to create revolutionary unity. At the same time, we want the comrades of the CSR to tell us what their position will be after the Lille Congress. Will these comrades declare that if the *majoritaires* of the CGT obtain a majority at the congress, they will split from it and join the revolutionary organisation? If so, then there will be no reason for us to remain outside this unity. If we refuse, it is so as not to make reformist propaganda, not to be activists for Jouhaux and Merrheim, and not to poison opinion.

Now, fellow delegates, you are troubled by this situation that the Credentials Commission has granted a decisive vote to the organisation that I represent. However, I do not want to challenge the *minoritaire* comrades of the CSRs having 15 votes, but I claim that our organisation should have a decisive vote in the congress.

One of the French delegates (*from his seat*): You did not mention how many members you count.

Boisson (*continues*): Comrades, I am asked a question and I will gladly answer it. We are asked, how many members we have. Well, here are the figures. In

to protest imperialist intervention in the Russian civil war. The day before the scheduled action, however, the CGT leadership cancelled it, in face of threats from French prime minister Georges Clemenceau.

A one-day general strike in France on 1 May 1920 opened a broad strike movement of CGT unions led by the railroad workers, eventually involving nearly 1.5 million workers. In face of severe repression, the railroad strike ended in defeat when the CGT leadership voted to call off the strike on 21 May. Following the strike some 22,000 workers lost their jobs.

Marseilles, the CTM organisation has more than a thousand members, while the CSR organisation has only a hundred. And we have several organisations here because, comrades, we are a legally constituted body, while the CSR is only represented within the CGT.

Lozovsky: Comrades, we have heard the representatives of both sides. Let us put it to a vote, which will be taken in the usual order, similar to the previous times.

The following delegates vote for the decision of the Credentials Commission, i.e., granting Comrade Boisson a decisive vote: the entire votes in Austria, Azerbaijan, Britain, Belgium, Holland, Georgia, Germany, Denmark, Canada, Latvia, Lithuania, Luxembourg, Russia, Ukraine, Finland, Czechoslovakia, Estonia, Yugoslavia, Romania, 6 votes of the Spanish delegation, and 3 of the American.

Against the motion of the Credentials Commission: Australia, Bulgaria, Far Eastern Republic, Poland, Argentina, 10 votes of the Spanish delegation, and 13 of the American. The Armenian delegation abstained from voting.

After the vote the following statements were sent in to the Presidium:

1. 'The Russian delegation voted for the motion of the French delegation against the granting of a decisive vote to the representative of the Confederation of Workers of the World of Marseilles, and wishes to amend the previous vote, which was due to a misunderstanding.' Signed by the delegations of Russia and Ukraine.
2. 'The Armenian delegation states that it refrained from voting in view of the absurdity of the motion, although it was against the decision of the Credentials Commission.' Signed by the secretary of the Armenian delegation.
3. 'The Azerbaijani and Georgian delegations declare that in view of the absurdity of the motion of the Credentials Commission, we voted for the admission of the representative of the Marseilles Trade Union with a decisive vote. After the explanation of the French delegation, we withdraw our votes and join them in favour of granting the Marseille delegate a consultative vote.'

Lozovsky: We now take up the last point of the report on the Credentials Commission: that of the Canadian comrades.

Reinstein: The question is dropped, as we succeeded in reaching an agreement between the parties concerned. The Credentials Commission will, upon formulation of the agreement, submit it to the congress.

Lozovsky: All questions relating to the Credentials Commission are thus exhausted. Allow me to announce a ten-minute break, after which we shall receive the report of Comrade Rosmer.

Arlandis: (*from his seat*): The Presidium is in possession of a statement signed by me on behalf of the Spanish, French, German, Canadian, and South American comrades.

Lozovsky: Comrade Arlandis is given the floor for his declaration.

Arlandis (Spain): Comrades, some delegates have found it necessary to move a resolution on the report of the Credentials Commission. The Spanish delegation is entrusted to develop this resolution, and defend it at this congress. I will read it. (*Reads.*)[11] This resolution was signed by the whole Spanish delegation and by the French delegation.

Louise Heuchel (France): I protest. You have no right to include the French delegation. If the French delegation has signed this resolution, it then has no right to dispute the granting of a decisive vote to Boisson.

One of the delegates: Some members of the French delegation were not consulted on this resolution. (*Murmur in the hall*)

Arlandis: Of the French delegation Comrades Boisson, Tommasi, Gaye, and both comrades Lemoine have signed this resolution.

One of the delegates: But the question at issue is about the French delegation as a whole.

Arlandis: This statement was also signed by Comrade Williams of the IWW, Comrade Cascaden of Canada, and by all the representatives of the three German organisations: the Gelsenkirchen Union, the union affiliated to the German Communist Workers' Party [the AAU], and the syndicalist unions at this congress.

I will now speak on the substance of the matter.

The Spanish delegation believes that the present congress in Moscow is a constituent congress of all revolutionary labour organisations – especially of

---

11 The text of this resolution is not found in the published proceedings.

those organisations that have from the very beginning of the Russian Revolution and, to a certain extent before it, fought the reformist policy of the Amsterdam International. We think the long history of the European and American trade-union movement indicates that there are organised forces that must be reckoned with, especially at the constituent congress of the Red International. We think of the history of the proletariat in Spain, which during all these years was true to its revolutionary viewpoint. We think of the history of the French proletariat, whose principles were always based on the independence of the trade-union movement and the fight against all political parties, and which strived toward a working-class view of the economic struggle. We think of the history of the American proletariat, in which the IWW has always supported the very same ideas and tactics as put forward by the revolutionary proletariat of Europe. We think of the revolutionary minority in Holland and other countries, which represent a powerful force. I speak from the syndicalist point of view.

We think that all these elements should be granted a sufficient number of votes to make their influence effective. In Germany we have to add three distinct organisations, which broke from Amsterdam and now have against the latter a strong body of 400,000 members.

We believed that all this would be taken into consideration by the constituent congress of Red Trade Unions. But our expectations were disappointed. We find that a decision was already made here in advance to create a majority, which we may call a fictitious majority. A feeling thus exists that there is an effort to suppress all the true revolutionary tendencies of international syndicalism, and give our trade-union International directives that a part of the Western European proletariat will not accept, despite the decisions of this congress.

On the other hand, present here are representatives from countries in which there are no revolutionary syndicalist organisations at all, or with little influence. And all these organisations were given decisive votes. In those countries with decisive votes – such as America, Germany, and Czechoslovakia, where the trade-union centres are not yet in favour of the Moscow International and still remain partisans of the Amsterdam International and where only a small number of nuclei adhere to Moscow, these nuclei – which are unable even to give the number of members they represent – claim to represent a majority of votes. It is said that the German nuclei embrace two million members. We have no means whatsoever of verifying this statement. In Czechoslovakia these nuclei are given the same 16 decisive votes as are given to the large organisations of France and Spain.

It is therefore our opinion that the first place should not belong to these nuclei, which, as Comrade Williams pointed out, can easily present themselves with doubtful millions of votes, but to those organisations that by their past, by their tactics, and by their everyday struggle represent a true revolutionary force from a trade-union standpoint.

We declare that countries such as Azerbaijan, Bukhara, Palestine, India, represented here – and about whose trade-union movement we are unable to judge – should not be given a decisive vote. The Western proletariat, which according to Marxist theory, represented for many years past a revolutionary force, should be able to define the orientation to be adopted by the organisations affiliated to the trade-union International. That is why those who signed this declaration protest against a decisive vote being given to the above countries prior to their having supplied data on the character and power of their organisations, data that would have made us accept their first demands.

(*Comrade Lozovsky passes the chair to Comrade Rykov.*)

Lozovsky: The speech of Comrade Arlandis deserves a sharp reply. It is important, when one addresses a congress like this, to be careful and weigh every word one has to say. Listening to Comrade Arlandis, one gets the impression as if the workers of the Latin countries alone are the true revolutionists, and that they exclusively are working toward the social revolution. He even left Russia off his list, and I dare say they have done something toward the revolution. Had we followed the advice of Comrade Arlandis, the international organisation that this congress intends to create would have become not an International of trade unions, but merely a small organisation of small groups. We on our part are aiming to unite all the revolutionary forces in all the unions.

There is nothing substantially important in the motion made by Comrade Arlandis, considering that the discussion was fully developed in the Credentials Commission, which is a body elected by the congress. The main feature is not the motion, but rather the speech itself, which had a most unpleasant tone. Comrade Arlandis charges us with the falsification of a majority. Such unfounded accusations should not be put forward lightly. As to the taunts about Khiva, Bukhara, and Palestine, etc., he is trying to break down open doors, as we have already a motion to refer the question mentioned above to the Credentials Commission, which has to report on the state of the movement in these countries, and distribute the votes accordingly.

(*Comrade Rykov turns the chair back over to Comrade Lozovsky.*)

Lozovsky: We shall now vote on the motion presented by Comrade Arlandis.

Joseph Tommasi (France) (*from his seat*): I wish to state that I signed the statement presented by Comrade Arlandis when the question of distribution of votes was not yet on the agenda. I then had in view solely the discussion on the question of the principle of distribution of votes. I disagree with Arlandis's speech.

Lemoine (France): I signed with the expectation that the comrades, when questioned, would come to the podium and explain the situation in their countries.

Lozovsky: Comrades, the motion made by Comrade Arlandis is that the delegates of Bukhara, Khiva, Turkey, Korea, Palestine, and India should immediately report to the congress on the union movement in their respective countries, so that we may be guided in the decision as to the number of votes they are entitled to. I move the following proposal: These questions should be brought before the Credentials Commission and reported to the congress, after which the final vote shall be taken. The representatives of Bukhara, Khiva, Turkey, Korea, Palestine, and India are not to vote on this motion. I proceed to the vote.

Who is in favour of the motion made by Comrade Arlandis? Austria against. Australia against. Britain against. Bulgaria against. Hungary against. Holland against. Georgia against. Germany: 11 against, 5 in favour. Denmark against. Far Eastern Republic against. Latvia against. Spain in favour. Canada: 1 against, 1 in favour. Luxembourg in favour. Mexico in favour. Poland against. Russia against. United States: 11 against, 3 in favour. Ukraine against. France: 5 in favour, 5 against. Finland against. Argentina in favour. Romania against.

The motion of Comrade Arlandis is therefore rejected.

We will now take up the report of Comrade Rosmer on the question of relations between the Red International of Trade Unions and the Third, Communist International.

Report on RILU-Comintern Relations

Alfred Rosmer:[12] Comrades, at the time the Third International was being organised and was making its appeal to every revolutionary organisation of the

12 As Rosmer subsequently related, 'On the agenda we had fixed for the Congress, the question of the relations between the two Internationals had been given an important position. Zinoviev was due to give the report, and I was to give an associated report. Although we

world, it addressed itself not only to political parties but to labour organisations as well. It seemed, therefore, from the very beginning that the new International had no intention of limiting its action, as the Second International had done, to political parties alone, but aimed to include all the parties and revolutionary labour organisations.

The Third International received almost instantly the adherence of numerous labour organisations. I will mention only the Italian Syndicalist Union [USI], the General Council of which voted its adherence to the Third International in June 1919. This vote was unanimously confirmed afterwards by the congress of the entire organisation at Parma in December 1919.[13] The other labour organisation that joined the Third International was the National Confederation of Labour [CNT] of Spain, adopting this decision also unanimously at its Madrid Congress in December 1919.[14]

At that time it was recognised by all that the Third International, which was going to revive the traditions of the First International, would include parties as well as labour organisations.[15]

The Second International broke this tradition, and it is interesting to note that the change was caused by the political parties. The socialist, reformist, and opportunist parties put so many objectionable clauses in the conditions of admission that they excluded all labour organisations.[16]

After the Second Congress of the Communist International, the question was posed somewhat differently. The two labour organisations connected with the Third International, as well as some other organisations, sent their deleg-

would not have differed in our main conclusions, we would have approached the question in different ways. ... At the last minute we had to change our plans. Zinoviev ... failed to understand developments in syndicalist circles. Only just before the Congress did he notice that there wasn't much affection for him there; rightly or wrongly the syndicalists didn't like him. As a result he decided to abandon his report and to withdraw from the Congress. Lozovsky communicated this decision to me, saying: "Instead of two reports there will be one only, yours".' In Rosmer 1971, p. 136.

13 The Third Congress of the USI was held in Parma, Italy, 20–22 December 1919.

14 The CNT's Madrid Congress was held 10–18 December 1919. For an account of the debate on the Comintern that took place there, see Meaker 1974, pp. 243–8.

15 The First International was formed in 1864, at a time when workers' political parties had not yet come into existence to any significant degree. It was formed largely by workers' societies and trade unions, as well as veterans of the Communist League such as Marx and Engels, who helped provide it leadership.

16 Rosmer's statement is not completely accurate. Social-democratic-led trade unions were indeed entitled to representation in the Second International in the years before 1914, as part of national delegations. The syndicalist CGT, however, did not participate in the French delegations.

ates to the Second Congress. Pestaña participated in the work of the congress. Borghi came after the congress was over. But when the congress placed on its agenda and carried a resolution on the question of creating a trade-union International,[17] it became clear that there must be two Internationals – the Communist International and the trade-union International.

I've related these facts to remind you that on the part of the syndicalist organisations there was no objection to including in one International both organisations – the political and the economic. The Italian and Spanish confederations had voted their affiliations unanimously. In other countries many labour organisations expressed themselves in favour of the Third International, and at the congress of the Third International, at its Executive Committee, there was willingness to accept the labour organisations. Only two members of the Executive Committee were opposed to the admission of labour organisations. These were Serrati and Levi, and both of them are now out of the Communist International.

In one of the theses submitted to the congress and adopted by it, we can read the following:

> [T]he Second Congress of the Third International considers it possible and desirable that those … organizations that have not yet officially affiliated to the Communist International should do so immediately. For in the present instance, particularly as regards the Industrial Workers of the World in America and Australia, as well as the Shop Stewards' committees in Britain, we are dealing with a profoundly proletarian and mass movement, which in all essentials actually stands by the basic principles of the Communist International.[18]

Thus the Communist International – through its Executive Committee first, and the congress subsequently – was prepared to accept not only labour organisations agreeing to its entire programme, but also those of them accepting the fundamental principles only.

The question to be decided by us today is thus not so much a theoretical matter as one of practical organisation. But a practical question that touches

17 In point 14 of the statutes approved by the Second Comintern Congress, it states, 'Trade unions that uphold communism and that are united internationally under the Communist International's leadership constitute a trade union section of the Communist International.' See Riddell 1991, *2WC*, pp. 698–9.

18 From point 18 of the Second Congress 'Theses on the Basic Tasks of the Communist International'. See Riddell 1991, *2WC*, p. 762.

on many other problems, for instance the relationship between trade unions and political parties.

The preliminary discussion of this question that took place simultaneously in conferences of delegates and in the congress commission revealed a whole series of gradations on this subject starting with the Russian point of view – clear and simple, unreservedly accepting the complete and formal collaboration with the Third International – and finishing with the viewpoint opposing any ties with the International, accepting only temporary collaboration in exceptionally serious circumstances and only for specific action. We also could see in the course of this discussion that in many countries the hostility of the labour organisations toward political parties remains, even now, very acute, and that there is a preconceived notion even against the new Communist parties. From these discussions we were able to learn how little the form and aims of the syndicalist organisations were known; how enormous and tendentious were the interpretations on these points. Outside of Russia, unfounded rumours were spread containing formulas of 'subordination of the trade unions to the political parties', aiming to maintain the unfriendly attitude of some elements in the labour organisations that were more or less disposed to accept collaboration with political parties, but were now absolutely opposed to the conception of the Russian comrades concerning the relations between the party and the trade unions. It became clearly evident that the activity, the form of the labour organisations in France and in other countries, were not well known and were very often misinterpreted.

The discussion at the Third Congress of the Communist International threw some light on this question, and I hope with the aid of some quotations to define the standpoint of the Russian comrades and show their conception of trade unions. The Second International considered the political parties as dominant, that they have the task of guiding all politics, of tracing the lines of conduct and general action of the proletariat, that trade unions have a secondary position and are limited to corporative interests.[19]

---

19 Rosmer's summary of the Second International's adopted stance is not completely accurate. A resolution of its 1907 congress on 'The Relations between Trade Unions and Socialist Parties' states, 'If the activity of the Socialist Party is exercised more especially in the domain of the political struggle of the proletariat, that of the unions displays itself in the domain of the economic struggle of the workers. The unions and the party have therefore an equally important task to perform in the struggle for proletarian emancipation. Each of the two organizations has its distinct domain, defined by its nature and within whose borders it should enjoy independent control of its line of action. But there is an ever-widening domain in the proletarian struggle of the classes in which they can only reap advantages by concerted action by cooperation between the party and trade unions.'

But this was not the conception of our Russian comrades. In one of the pre-war writings of Comrade Zinoviev we find the following definition of trade unions: 'The trade union is an organisation of the workers of the same industry' – note: of the entire industry, and not of a single trade – 'which assumes the direction of economic life and steadily participates, in harmony with the political party, in the struggle for the complete emancipation of the working class, for the abolition of the wages system, and the establishment of equality of rights in all spheres of life'.[20]

You can see that this conception is altogether opposed to the conception of the Second International.

I am in a position to add to this text a resolution of the Russian trade unions themselves, adopted at the congress following the October Revolution in Petrograd at the beginning of 1918:[21]

> The October Revolution, which wrested power from the hands of the bourgeoisie and gave it to the class of workers and peasants, has created new conditions of action for the labour organisations as a whole, and particularly for the trade unions. The trade unions, as class organisations, must be constructed on the industrial principle and must devote themselves to the task of organising production, of creating organs of supply, of increasing the production of the country, and of taking an active part in the organisation of workers' control and the control and distribution of labour power.

This resolution adopted by the congress was introduced by a representative of the Communist Party. Nevertheless, a difference of opinion still remained, despite the common ideas of the Bolsheviks and syndicalists. This difference is as follows: The party is the brains, the soul of the working class. By saying this I do not intend to say that the party must rule over the unions, no. The party must be very attentive to them, while they must constitute the starting point for the realisation of communism. There cannot be second-class comrades; no insolence between militants can be tolerated. The syndicalists are as good communists as

---

The resolution says nothing about political parties being dominant. See Taber (ed.) 2021, p. 106.

The concrete relationship between parties and unions within the Second International nevertheless differed from country to country.

20 Presumably this quotation is taken from Zinoviev's articles in *Pravda* in 1913, which were assembled as a pamphlet titled *The Workers' Party and the Trade Unions* and published by the Petrograd Soviet in 1918.

21 For the First All-Russian Congress of Trade Unions in January 1918, see p. 61, n. 2.

we are, but we must reject what is called 'equality of contracting parties'. This theory is incorrect; it is a heritage of the corrupted, perfidious, and outlived Second International. 'You will occupy yourself with political questions, and we will take the economic ones. You will stay out of our noses, and we will stay out of yours.' No! We must eliminate this kind of theory from the consciousness of the advanced workers.

I will cite another example, to specify the respective conceptions of the Bolsheviks and syndicalists. After discussing and criticising the syndicalist theory, Comrade Zinoviev very clearly indicated what, in his opinion, is good in syndicalism and what must be rejected. Here is what he said:

> We have been separated from the syndicalists. But we say that something very healthy is contained in their left wing, which, having cured itself of the gangrene of opportunism, may become the cells of a new socialist order. The idea is right; one time it was a new idea and we were in solidarity with the syndicalists on this point.

I think this is sufficient to show how the conception of our Russian comrades on the question of relations between the party and the unions has been distorted. You can see from these quotations that our Russian comrades never sustained the idea of subordinating the unions to the party.

To understand clearly their conception, we must consider what the Russian Communist Party really is. By grouping into its ranks all the revolutionary elements, it was always different, both by its doctrines and its action, from the Communist parties of other countries. Its members were always in the front ranks of the proletarian struggle; they penetrated every labour organisation. Naturally, they exercised a very great influence on these organisations, but it was their legitimate right, since every political tendency fights for hegemony in the unions. This is legitimate and conceivable, but unfortunately many neo-communists have contributed very much to creating a misunderstanding with regard to the relationship between syndicalists and Communists. Not long ago a secretary of an important Communist federation in France declared that the unions will have to submit to the party. It is obvious that by using such language, we will never reach an agreement. But we must admit that the Russian comrades never used such language or thought in this way.

The quotation from Comrade Zinoviev that I read a moment ago shows that he knows what syndicalism is in general, and particularly French syndicalism, which he accepts at least partially. Nevertheless, we could see by his speech of last Sunday at the congress of the Communist International that he was not always correct in his characterisation of French syndicalism. This was clear, for instance, when he criticised the Amiens Charter, stating that he did not see in it anything other than a profession of faith in neutrality.[22]

The Amiens Charter is a document of great importance. To understand its significance, one must not read its text alone, but consider the very history of the French syndicalist movement, especially at the moment of its inception, why and how this document was accepted. It was at a time when syndicalism firmly established itself in France. It contained different elements: some coming from the anarchists, some from different socialist parties, and others coming from nowhere – the pure syndicalists. All these diverse elements were united by the ideal they aimed at: the suppression of the wages system. They did not care so much to define a new theory, but to establish a correct method of action. In this they succeeded.

Owing to this fact, could one maintain that the General Confederation of Labour was neutral? That the CGT was ever neutral? No, it would be a big mistake to pretend that this neutrality had any place in the Amiens Charter. The CGT never intended to limit its activity to the corporative organisation only; it intervened in many if not all political questions; and not once but many times. If the CGT refused to deal with politics, it was because it condemned absolutely the politics of the French Socialist Party, because it had its own politics. The truth is that the CGT before the war was a genuine political party, but a party of a special and original kind.

When the charter was being discussed at the Amiens Congress, there were two currents vying for the leadership of French syndicalism: on one side the Socialist Party, which wanted to reserve politics for themselves, expressed the views of the Second International, and insisted upon the French trade unions keeping strictly to their corporative activities. And on the other side, elements representing a certain organisational force, but corresponding to a certain extent to British trade unionism. The latter were mostly represented by the printers' organisation (Fédération du Livre). The revolutionary syndicalists, thus found themselves between two groupings. The cooperative group, occupying itself with questions of wages, hours, etc., and the Socialist group, which spoke thus: 'You too are revolutionary, but the Socialist Party will bring about the revolution, and not the CGT; the CGT must cease to make any revolutionary propaganda.'

It was against these elements that the Amiens Charter was directed; this is why it is very hard to understand it from a distance. But if you study the French

---

22 For Zinoviev's comments on the Amiens Charter in his report to the Third Comintern Congress on trade unions, see Riddell (ed.) 2015, *3WC*, pp. 606–11. For the text of the Amiens Charter, see Appendix, p. 673.

syndicalist movement from 1900 up to the eve of the war, you will immediately be convinced that the claimed neutralism never existed.

To finish with the question, I will cite but one example, concerning an event that did not involve the working class only: the bloody repression of winegrowers in the South of France, mainly small and large owners.[23] The CGT published a manifesto that cost its leaders a court trial.

I remind you of these facts to show how little grounds there are to reproach the CGT for 'neutralism'. But recent documents show us how syndicalists today understand and interpret the Amiens Charter. One was written very recently by our Comrade Monmousseau, who says: 'The revolutionary syndicalist International is the continuation of the Amiens Charter, the same as the social revolution is the prolongation of the class struggle.'

Consequently, we must not exaggerate the weak points in the Amiens Charter, even if it contains a neutralist expression. It must not be said that, at the present time, it is a source of impotence, of hesitation, or of wavering. We see, on the contrary, that the syndicalists most closely linked to the present movement give this Amiens Charter an interpretation that shows they are not paralysed by this text of 1906.

However, it may seem that French trade unionists in particular have not taken sufficient advantage of the lessons of the war and the Russian Revolution and the consequences they must draw from it. But if we can rightly estimate that this essential, urgent revision work is progressing too slowly, that there is still too much confusion in the minds of a large number of French trade-union comrades, it is also fair to stress the importance of efforts that have already been made in this direction. For example, we find this declaration in the motion submitted by the revolutionary minority to the Federal Congress in Orleans a year ago:[24]

> Far from violating the Amiens Charter by joining the Moscow trade-union International, the congress declares that it is the clearest duty of the CGT

---

23 The winegrowers' revolt of March–June 1907 involved all classes of society within the wine-producing regions of southern France. Occurring in the context of a depression in the wine industry, the protesters demanded government controls on the production and marketing of wine. The revolt was marked by numerous mass demonstrations by up to half a million people throughout the region, and municipal operations in these areas were paralysed. The government in Paris sent troops to the region, and battles with the population occurred in which demonstrators were shot and killed. While the syndicalists of the CGT embraced the movement, the Socialist Party had reservations about it, due to the protests' multiclass character.

24 A reference to the CGT congress held in Orléans, 27 September–2 October 1920.

> to do so. Today the CGT has to go to Moscow, just as in 1915 it had to go to Zimmerwald.[25] There is but one International of revolution – the Third International, that of Moscow. Remaining faithful to the revolutionary spirit, the CGT must adhere to it and declare itself ready to collaborate with the political body that will act in a revolutionary way, in deeds and not just in words, nevertheless retaining complete autonomy in matters of economic activity.

There you have it, a statement that shows that the French comrades, profiting from the war and the Russian Revolution, have no intention of staying where they were in 1906. At this very moment the discussion is continuing in France on the most delicate and difficult question to resolve, that of the relations between the parties and the unions. The text I have just read marks a break with the old tradition.

The old tradition of syndicalism was very clear. We did not even conceive of any possibility of working with the old socialist parties. Not only was there no possibility of joint work, but there was always great hostility between the CGT and the Socialist Party, a hostility based on profound reasons, on the very methods of the two organisations. The party was reformist and the CGT was revolutionary. Therefore collaboration between these two organisations did not even arise.

Today, we find ourselves in different circumstances and situations. The formal pre-war opposition between the CGT and the parties has disappeared, and the revolutionary minority now declares that it wants to collaborate with the truly revolutionary parties. But even before this official collaboration, so to speak, of two organisations, there has been since the war a partial collaboration in different committees that were formed, first, to fight against the war, and then in favour of the Third International and the Russian Revolution.[26] Comrades who belonged to antagonistic organisations met for the first time in these committees. There were members of the Socialist Party, trade unionists, and anarchists too; they worked long enough together that one could

25 A reference to an international conference of socialists opposed to the social-patriotic position of the leading parties of the Second International during World War I. The conference in Zimmerwald, Switzerland, took place 5–8 September 1915. French syndicalist participants at the Zimmerwald Conference were Alphonse Merrheim and Albert Bourderon.

26 In January 1916 a number of prominent socialists and syndicalists in France came together to form the Committee for the Resumption of International Relations to oppose the pro-war stance of the leaderships of the SP and CGT. In May 1919 the work of this committee found continuation in the Committee for the Third International.

even imagine that a real party could have come out of these meetings born of the war and later of the creation of the Third International. But things have turned out differently. The former Socialist Party has become a Communist Party.

It is interesting to recall in this connection what Comrade Loriot said to the Executive Committee of the Communist International. He said: We believed at the time of the Tours Congress that many syndicalists were ready to come to our organisation, but we answer today that instead there has been a setback. This is a serious and significant fact. Why the decline? Quite simply because it turned out that the party was not yet a Communist Party and that it did not differ enough from the old Socialist Party.[27]

So the question of the relations between political parties and unions remains a serious question, difficult to raise again, and it does not arise in the same way everywhere. It is certain that we will gain nothing from trying to rush this reconciliation. Only cordial discussions between syndicalists and Communists can be effective, jointly examining the great problems of the present time.

Last year at the Second Congress of the Third International, the same question about the role of the Communist Party was discussed at some length. And our comrade [Jack] Tanner, who represented the Shop Stewards of Britain and who had in broad outline the same conception of workers' action as the French syndicalists, formulated in an intervention his objections to the role attributed to the Communist Party. To justify his objections, he expressed his conception of workers' organisations and the organisation of the revolutionary struggle: 'We want to group the most ardent and the most perceptive fraction of the proletariat, to make it an angry minority, because they alone will be able to lead and guide the mass'. When Comrade Tanner had finished speaking Comrade Lenin spoke and replied: The way you defined your concept of revolutionary action is also ours, only to this minority we give another name: we call it the Communist Party.[28]

---

27 Loriot's remarks were given to an expanded meeting of the Comintern Executive Committee on the eve of the Third Congress. A stenographic text of his speech can be found in Comintern archives, RGASPI 495/1/37.

The Tours Congress of the French Socialist Party (25–30 December 1920) voted by a 75 per cent majority to affiliate to the Communist International, giving birth to the French Communist Party.

28 In Tanner's remarks to the Comintern's Second Congress he stated that members of the Shop Stewards' movement 'are partisans of revolution … [who] have never ceased believing or propagating the principles of communism … But by our activities among industrial workers, we have done much more to put them into practice than most of the political parties.' Lenin's response was that 'if Comrade Tanner says that he is opposed to parties,

In Britain, moreover, things happened more easily than in France because there was no old socialist party that was bulky and made the task difficult. There was a small party in Britain – the British Socialist Party, two other political organisations, and the Shop Stewards' Committees. At first glance, however, merging these various elements into a single party seemed impossible.

Nevertheless we have seen that in a few months the work has been done and we have in Britain a unified Communist Party. The president of this Communist Party is a well-known activist of the Shop Stewards, Comrade MacManus. And Jack Tanner, who had appeared here at the Second Congress of the Communist International, expressing in a very clear and vigorous manner his reservations with regard to any political party, is also a member. So I believe that even on this point, which is the most difficult to cross, that is to say, related to the point of the Communist parties and the unions, we can hope that collaboration can be achieved fairly quickly.

But I repeat that in order to achieve this collaboration, so that there are no more lost efforts in the struggle between the good elements of the party and the union elements, it is essential that the parties understand their role and the role of the unions, and that they never dream of rushing the union members into making declarations, unionists who still rebel against the creation of Communist parties.

Regarding the relationship between the two Internationals, the question seems much simpler to me. Here we no longer find ourselves in the presence of a state of affairs that has existed for a long time, and that has created situations that cannot disappear overnight. We are in the presence of two organisations that no one would dream of denying that they are revolutionary organisations. The only point we have to discuss is that of the form we will give to the relations that must be established between these two organisations.

However, among many comrades there is a lot of mistrust and fear that the Communist International, if one establishes permanent and direct links between these two organisations, will immediately take a preponderant role and interfere with the trade-union International in its activity. But I think that is a completely illusory fear. The trade-union International that we are going to create here will be such a strong organisation, it will have a field of action so wide and so special, that I believe one cannot even think that it could be only an instrument of the Communist International. From the

---

but at the same time is in favor of a minority that represents the best organized and most revolutionary workers showing the way to the entire proletariat, then I say that there is really no difference between us'. In Riddell 1991, *2WC*, pp. 160, 168.

point of view of the principle itself, one cannot object to a more or less close union between the two Internationals.

I would like to remind you that the Italian Syndicalist Union and the National Confederation of Labour of Spain immediately accepted the call put out by the Third International the day after it was issued. The idea of being in the same organisation with political parties did not scare them. Therefore, it is no longer a question of today. The question could have arisen at the time of this appeal from the Third International. If back then we were hostile to any collaboration of political parties and unions, then not a single organisation would have responded to the call of the Third International.

But a big campaign has since been waged by leaders of the Amsterdam International against the trade-union International. At first they pretended to regard it as 'negligible quantity', and afterwards, when they realised that however weak it may have appeared at the beginning, it would develop rapidly, they adopted another attitude. In order to hinder the creation of the trade-union International, they immediately said: There will never be a trade-union International in Moscow; this will only be a dependency on the Communist International. This is the biggest argument they have found in directing propaganda against the trade-union International.

I believe that we must not allow ourselves to be stopped by critics of this kind. It is possible that this argument affects some workers, that it worries them. But we must answer it, and it's very easy to do so. It's easy to show that if there is indeed a trade-union International dependent on political organisations, it is none other than the Amsterdam International Federation. Its leaders conceal their reports from any political organisation; they want to be able to pretend that they remain a purely trade-union organisation. But we know this is a completely unacceptable claim. Not only do we know the relations of the leaders of this International with men like Albert Thomas, Renaudel, with socialists in Belgium like de Brouckère and many others, but there is a fact that by itself speaks volumes enough to demonstrate that the Second International, the Amsterdam International, and the Two-and-a-Half International are all one and the same thing.

Two months ago, the representatives of these three organisations met on the same date, as if by chance, in Amsterdam, to discuss the same subject. All of them tried to pretend it was just a chance encounter. But no one was fooled. And it is not for fear of being accused – in particular by them – of collaborating with political organisations that we should hesitate to establish the form of relations between the trade-union International and the Communist International that seems best to us. We must ignore their hypocrisy and their sham.

I received yesterday a draft resolution that the Communist Workers' Party of Germany [KAPD] proposes to submit to the Communist congress and which relates to the question before us. (*He reads the resolution.*)[29] We know that our comrades in the Communist Workers' Party of Germany do not fully accept the programme of the Communist International. But they have a point of view on this question that corresponds fairly exactly to that of our comrades in the Russian trade unions.

At the same time as I was reading this proposal by the comrades of the KAPD, I saw in *L'Humanité* an article by Comrade Verdier, entitled 'Syndicalism Must Be Free'.[30] Verdier declares himself for the absolute independence not only of the French unions vis-à-vis the French Communist Party, but also for the independence of the trade-union International vis-à-vis the Communist International. And I had seen a few days earlier the text of a resolution, presumably written by Verdier himself, at a meeting of a hundred workers on 10 June held in Roubaix.

> Workers of all organisations assembled, 800 strong, at the Velghe Hall on Friday, 10 June.
>
> After hearing that the CGT, standing in no relation whatever to any political school, unites all the workers conscious of the struggle for the abolition of the wages system and bosses;
>
> Whereas the reformist leaders of the CGT violated the Amiens Charter by the 'sacred union' during the war[31] and class collaboration since the armistice;
>
> Whereas the transformation of society is possible only by means of the proletarian revolution, already realised by our Russian brothers;
>
> Whereas reformist methods amount only to patching up capitalist society, and that the Amsterdam International is only an organ of class collaboration, by its close connections with the League of Nations;
>
> Be it resolved that they assign to syndicalism, which has regained its revolutionary spirit, the role of attacking the bourgeoisie on the economic field without let-up, leaving to political parties the task of organising and training the masses for the purpose of conquering political power.

---

29 For the text of the KAPD resolution on the trade-union question, see Appendix, pp. 679–83.

30 Verdier's article, titled 'Le syndicalisme doit rester libre', appeared in the 27 June 1921 issue of *L'Humanité*.

31 The term 'sacred union' (*l'union sacrée*) is a reference to the class-collaborationist policy of the majority of the French SP and CGT during World War I.

For my part, I find the attitude of Comrade Verdier entirely incomprehensible. He is a member of the French Communist Party. Prior to the Tours Congress he signed the theses drafted by the Committee of the Third International corresponding to the decisions of the Second Congress of the Communist International. And he assumes a position on the question of relations between Communist parties and unions that is neither syndicalist nor communist. He states that syndicalism should act in the field of economics, whereas the party should do so in the field of politics.

I say that this is not pure syndicalism. One may desire to keep precisely to the old platform of revolutionary syndicalism, but one should not speak of the division between unions and political parties.

The old CGT had a system that allowed simultaneously for the struggle to overthrow the old bourgeois society and for the realisation of communist society. This point of view can be defended today too, but I find it inadmissible that a man like Verdier, who claims to be an orthodox syndicalist and is a member of the Communist Party, should formulate a conception rejected by all revolutionaries but shared by the Second International.

The differences between the Russian and French comrades over the conception of the role of the unions are rather deep. The discussion that has started in the French press underlines the difference in viewpoints, but it also indicates the points in common.

In one of the most recent issues of *La Vie ouvrière* reproducing the main decisions of the last congress of the Russian trade unions, a short note is attached that shows the actual feelings of our French comrades. 'In no. 2 of *Moscow* we find an interview with Comrade Dridzo-Lozovsky that we wish to reproduce in order to allow the discussion to proceed in the clearest possible manner. He develops his point of view. We agree on many points; on others, not always. There is nothing surprising in this; neither is it an insurmountable obstacle.'[32]

I believe that the disagreements that exist between one side and the other are by no means insurmountable obstacles to determining the relations to be established between the two Internationals. If we decide here to establish the permanent links that are to exist between the Communist International and the trade-union International, we shall only be following the policy of the French syndicalists in 1915, at the time of the Zimmerwald Conference. There too were almost exclusively political parties, with only a few syndic-

32 Issue number 2 of *Moscow*, dated 26 May 1921, contained an interview with Lozovsky titled 'Tasks of the Forthcoming International Red Trade Unions'.

alist organisations; nevertheless it is a page of which the French syndicalists are proud. If they are proud of having participated in Zimmerwald, I do not see any reason why they should be unwilling to meet today for the purpose of preparing the daily work with representatives of the Communist International.

The motion for mutual representation in both executive committees establishes, in my opinion, only normal ties. I find it extraordinary that French revolutionists should be so hostile to it. If mutual representation were sufficient to prevent the trade-union International from living its own life, it would mean that this International is a mere phantom. But if it lives its own life, if it is really an International, then the relations between the representatives of the Communist International and those of the trade-union International will be simple. One cannot imagine the Communist International ever imposing its line of action on the trade-union International. Such fears only prove a lack of confidence in the force of the trade-union International. And I think that it would be sufficient to bring home to the workers in France and other countries alike that we want to distinguish between the Communist International and the trade-union International, and that a subordination to Moscow should not be feared.

The question is posed everywhere in a similar way. Even if the trade-union International were to remain entirely free and independent, this would not prevent our adversaries from asserting that the trade-union International is dependent on the Communist International and Moscow. Nobody can prevent the same thing being repeated tomorrow in the press of the Amsterdam leaders and in the capitalist press alike.

Everywhere the question remains the same: Amsterdam or Moscow? And it will never be put otherwise. It is an established fact that there are two large groups; on the one hand, the Second International, the Amsterdam International, and the Two-and-a-Half International; on the other hand, the Communist Party and the Red International of Labour Unions.

It may be added that there is now even a certain experience of the relations that we propose to establish between the Communist International and the International of Trade Unions. We have worked a year under these conditions. Although the International of Trade Unions is as yet a weak organisation, it never had to struggle against the encroachments of the Communist International.

The Council of the International of Trade Unions has worked out its methods and its organising work in complete freedom. Joint sittings were held, resulting in appeals issued by both organisations. And yet there is a danger we must combat, and not an illusory one, but rather a living reality.

The bourgeoisie has well realised the support it can gain in the trade-union organisations. At a moment when the political parties were pushed toward Moscow by the masses inside of them, the leaders of the future Socialist parties fell back at once to the trade-union organisations.

We have typical instances of this in France. Availing themselves of any opportunity, the capitalists arm the trade unions against the revolutionary parties, seeking to paralyse their revolutionary action and confining them to purely corporative actions. But when the bourgeoisie utilises the unions, when it asserts the hostility of the unions against political parties, when it raises them against political parties, when it raises antagonism between them, we must not be their dupes. And we would be such if, for fear of words, we are afraid to state clearly what we intend to do.

I came across a quotation in an issue of *Moscow* one of these days, which is very characteristic. It concerns Mussolini, the chief of the Fascists in Italy, the great partisan of the independence of unions. He writes in *Il Popolo d'Italia*:

> Bolshevism has outlived itself. The Italy of 1921 is very different from that of 1916. The Socialist Party is on the eve of a new split over the question of coalition. The Confederation of Labour will thus be able to break its chains and become independent. That will be a great step toward the formation of a labour party, which would reduce to a minimum the importance of the Socialist political party.[33]

Here you have a true partisan of trade-union neutrality. But I do not believe that there will be any among the revolutionists who would be ready to follow Mussolini and his Fascists. The formal recognition of the ties between the two Internationals would have a very precise meaning and would show that the working class organises its forces in a systematic way.

It may be acknowledged that in all countries the working class has committed many mistakes in the field of organisation. The bourgeoisie is better prepared for the fight; it has everywhere formed a solid bloc. Even in Britain, where political traditions are full of life, where the Liberal and Conservative parties never thought to unite until the present time, they have realised since the war that this is not a time to fight among themselves, and they formed their coalition to resist all attacks. The French bourgeoisie has also formed its national bloc. In Belgium the bloc is even broader, having socialists with ministerial portfolios.

---

33 Rosmer is paraphrasing a quote from Mussolini printed in the 8 July issue of *Moscow* (no. 36) in the front-page 'Telegraphic News' section.

In such circumstances we should not be afraid to state that we intend to form groups of revolutionary elements that are in the party and the trade unions alike. By asserting that close and permanent ties are necessary between the two Internationals, we will by no means imply that we desire to subordinate the trade-union International to the Communist International. It means only that we desire to organise our forces on a serious and solid basis.

That is why we should declare ourselves openly in favour of permanent contact between both Internationals, and we must do so frankly.

(*The session is suspended at 7:00 p.m.*)

SESSION 6. 9 JULY 1921, EVENING

RILU-Comintern Relations (continued)

(*The session is opened at 8:00p.m. Comrade Nin in the chair.*)

Andreu Nin: The question on the agenda is that of the relations between the Communist International and the Red International of Trade Unions. Comrade Tom Mann will now speak as co-reporter upon the above question.

Tom Mann (Britain): Comrade Rosmer having, I think, covered the situation so exhaustively it will require very little from me. At the same time, having accepted the responsibility of acting as co-reporter, I desire to make some comments upon the principal items now under review. The first question I deal with is – why bother about an International? Of course, the reply to that is that capitalist industry is already essentially international in character. And the workers having to cope with the capitalist controllers of industry find it increasingly necessary that they also shall be able to take concerted action along international lines.

Almost any workman of intelligence in any industrial country, say in England – workmen in Birmingham, Sheffield, Manchester, or any similar city – working with an engineering firm, knowing the directorate of that firm, and knowing as he can get to know, the relationships of that directorate to other directorates in that same country and in other countries, will find that from the board of directors in the establishment where he is working there are those who are appointed to sit upon other directorates dealing with one or another phase of the industry in an earlier or later stage of development. So the employers in the engineering industry, we find, are also the controllers of the producers of the metal; they are also directly financially connected with the iron ore mines; some in England, others in Spain, and others in other countries. They are also connected with shipping firms and are responsible for the carrying of the raw material from Spain and elsewhere. They are also responsible for carrying the finished articles after they have passed through the various firms. They are also connected with the requisite financial concern. And so we find an inner circle controlling not in one country only, but all working for the control of industry in other countries, which enables them to exhibit solidarity on an international scale in a manner never previously known in the world. There are other reasons, but this one fact will bc a sufficient reason as to why international action on the part of the workers is essential.

 | DOI:10.1163/9789004712867_010

Speaking of England – and it would apply largely to others – the workers in that country have heard of the International and many of them have had a more or less loose connection with organisations that have been identified with what has been called the International. No need to deal here with sectional international organisations such as the miners, transport workers, railroad men, dockers, but to deal with the more ambitious, which covered perhaps a third at one time or another of the organisations of workers of Britain that were related with the International that we now refer to as the Amsterdam International. One requires to know beforehand what is the outlook and objective of that Amsterdam International.

Knowing those who have been the principal active agents in connection therewith, knowing the source from which they are drawn, I can claim intimately that the personnel of that Amsterdam International would have no outlook whatever beyond that of the plutocracy only. They do not seek any drastic change in the basis of society. They aim at nothing higher, worthier, or nobler than that of occasional adjustment of wages and perhaps working hours of the workmen connected with the organisations they are identified with. The explanation of that is found mainly in the unions themselves, because for the most part the unions themselves have not had any further aim than that of adjusting the difficulties that arise under the capitalist system to make it possible for the capitalist system to continue to operate as such by relieving the difficulties of their members, which would otherwise be very serious. Therefore, the unions themselves have no other outlook beyond that of easing, as it were, and lubricating the wheels of the capitalist system, so that when men are thrown out of employment, the union seeks to provide in some measure for their welfare, so that the good capitalist, when he requires them again, should have them handed back to him in fit condition to make more profits for him. When men, through losing strength from perhaps overwork, are laid low by sickness, the capitalists could not be expected, under the orthodox system, to make any payment to them when they are incapable of operating the wheels of production. The unions therefore do something to enable these men, disabled in the capitalist system, to become once more qualified and hold them in reserve, ready to hand them over to the capitalist when he is good enough to call for their services once more.

The unions also endeavour to make some provision for old age, which has not been made by other agencies. I am not condemning this, but pointing out the fact that unions that have no wider or higher outlook and could not expect to have a very much better International than that which has been meeting under the auspices we know of. The unions themselves, the members, the rank and file, and the officers have subscribed to the continuance of the capitalist system in the hope that they would be able to have good trade and relatively good wages, and perhaps get the hours of labour reduced occasionally, and a comparatively good time, and they have had no other outlook. Of course, I am not intending to say that that governs the whole movement, but it is an explanation as to why there has been such an unsatisfactory International as that now being referred to.

Amsterdam stands therefore for nothing in the way of real change from the capitalist system. We have all been compelled to be familiar with the views they advocate, the objectives they aim at, as the only ones to be achieved. They believe that capitalism will remain for a very long time to come. Of course, in contradiction to that we now have the Communist International and the Red Trade Union International, and here the outlook is not on palliatives, but it fits with the aims, aspirations, and objectives of the revolutionaries of the past twenty-five years.

Among those who endeavour to contribute something towards bringing about the changes for that better revolutionary direction, I have had opportunities of mixing up with many trade unionists of other countries, and I prefer to continue to speak of the country that I belong to. I am confident that the arguments I shall venture to address to you will fit with the requirements of other countries also, at least according to my judgement.

It is necessary briefly to deal with the trade unions of Britain, their relations to the Labour Party, some members of whom declare that they wish to see a change of system. But experience has taught us that they rely upon the state machine to bring this about. They seek to achieve a change in society by means of the state, by means of Parliament. They do not rely upon their unions and do not try to make use of their unions to achieve economic or other changes. They make use of their unions incidentally and accidentally, and when it comes to talking upon anything of a definite character, and which is calculated to bring about an actual change in the economic basis of society for the common welfare of humanity, then the Labour Party relies exclusively upon parliamentary changes.

Years ago I found it necessary to break away from the advocacy of such a policy. I have not been in sympathy with all the work of the labour parties for the purpose of using parliaments as a means of achieving changes. I learned long ago to put aside the idea of relying upon the state machine. As regards the country I am speaking of, England, I know full well that during the whole of the more than six hundred years of the existence of Parliament, those who exercised influence on Parliament never once, not on one single occasion, ever introduced a measure into Parliament the object of which would be to enable the workers to attain economic freedom. Never once in the whole history of

Parliament, over a period of six centuries. During recent years they have exhibited a determination to prevent the successful development of working-class organisations that aim at achieving our economic emancipation from capitalism. It will be understood that what I am saying is literally correct in the country I am speaking of, and as far as I know, it is true of parliaments everywhere.

I became a syndicalist, and I was in close sympathy with the work of our French comrades. I recognised the wisdom and saw the necessity for similar actions in Britain when the French were working through the General Confederation of Labour. And during a considerable number of years, I did my utmost to win men from relying upon the parliamentary institution, declaring that more than 95 per cent of their troubles were economic in character, and that economic difficulties would be best solved by economic agencies. I therefore urged the wisdom of direct action and of shop organisation, and to get others to understand the wisdom of shop organisations on a scale that would result in transferring power from the union executives to the shops on a considerable scale. The Labour Party thinks that the capitalists have succeeded in obtaining the position they occupy by first exercising political power. In the early stages of the machine industry, having obtained control of industry, and thereby control of the men and women who created the wealth of industry, that economic fact gave them political power, which also enabled them to advance their interests in certain other directions.

Because of that misunderstanding on the part of workmen, the wrongfulness of that view, a very large percentage of men in the labour movement still rely upon Parliament to bring about changes for the better. While I have been a non-parliamentarian, and have fought against being identified with parliamentary institutions, there was warrant for it. No difficulty was so great in the whole of my experience as [that] of an organiser; no difficulty has confronted me in forty years of experience so great and so formidable as that of the average workingman who is obsessed with the idea of respecting and almost adoring parliamentary institutions.

To teach them to rely upon themselves was not only permissible but an absolute necessity. I am among those who have tried to learn and gain additional experience. I have not hesitated to change my viewpoint when I considered the necessity arose as the result of a different experience. What I was opposed to was relying upon the parliamentary institutions to bring about changes in working-class conditions, and the solving of the labour problem. I declared and still declare it cannot; none of the institutions that we have been familiar with as the governing bodies of the countries can serve such a purpose. It may be altogether different when one comes to consider the vastly changed situation.

Most people will admit the outlook upon life, the outlook upon society, must of necessity be different now than it was before the war. The relationships – economic, political, social – all require readjustment, and the outlook of the workers may also require readjustment. I know of nothing in connection with parliamentary institutions to command my respect, and certainly nothing to command my blessing. If I had reason to believe that the Communist International, and the advice and the instructions to be given, or decisions to be arrived at in connection with the Communist International, would call for action of a parliamentary character, that would mean that the workers must look to Parliament for the achievement of changes, I shall count it my duty, in my present state of mind, to have nothing whatever to do with it.

I take the position that nothing in the nature of political activity is ever to be understood as being favourable to work for the realisation of betterment of economic conditions through parliamentary institutions. This is what I have said myself many times when I have been questioned on the platform, 'Are you opposed to parliamentary action altogether?' I have said yes, with an exception – it may be worthwhile to give attention to Parliament with the object of going there in the hope of breaking it up. I have said and say so now: to break up the capitalist state is a necessity, not only that it may be done, but absolutely must be done. I understand it is the determination of the Red Trade Union International at all times to labour in that direction. That being so, then I can see the wisdom and the desirability of relationships between the two. It is one thing to give advice on tactics twenty years or more before you can get anything of a revolutionary character. It is quite another thing when we have passed through a World War including the stupendous event of the Russian Revolution, with the prospect of revolution in several other countries in a short time.

Taking that into consideration, I find myself in agreement with the proposal that there shall be a direct relationship between the Red Trade Union International and the Communist International; and that each should retain complete freedom of action in the interchange of opinion and advice with a view to obtaining the best advantage that is obtainable by collective action. Thinking that this is correct, I endorse it. And I am among those who can see that in a very short time in several countries, notwithstanding the fewness of the numbers represented here today from such countries, not only will we have a larger percentage, but I believe that I can forecast enough to declare that the United Kingdom will be well represented at future congresses and that inside of two years the old trade-union factions, those who have in the past been such hindrances, will find that they are in such uncomfortable conditions that they will not be able to contain themselves there; they will gladly make their clearance and the places will be cleared of hindrances of that character. And the intelligent, determined young man, mentally at any rate, will find that the course for action and the economic pressure will be there impelling and compelling action.

What are these men of the older type doing? I know them well, many of them; and I know that their outlook is such that they will readily, right gladly, in the event of an industrial dispute in the unions with which they are connected in dispute between the rank and file and the employing class; they will readily enter into conversational relationships with the employers, which generally result more or less in assurances that their influence will be used to checkmate any determined action on the part of the rank and file in trying to enforce better conditions. So that when a confrontation is brought about already without knowledge by the rank and file, there is an understanding between the officials – I am speaking of officials of the employers' side – resulting too frequently in disaster for the workers. We have seen this not just in one country alone, but in others also. Certainly in England we have witnessed prominent trade unionists who have rendered such valiant service to the cause of labour that they have been invited to Buckingham Palace, the residence of the king. The king himself has received that person. A special decoration has been presented. They have received the blessings therefore of the authorities. What revolutionary work is going to be attempted by such people requires no description. For some of them are invited to become privy councillors, so that the head of the state may confer with reliable persons who, by the acceptance of such posts, swear allegiance to the present order of society. For such men to be accepted and to be active in work in the trade-union movement only shows that the rank and file are not sufficiently class-conscious to understand in which direction their real interests lie.

But I venture to declare that there is no cause for despair; notwithstanding what may be thought by some who are speaking of the small number of those who are directly and definitely associated with the Red International. Just allow for this. How many months have transpired since the workers knew of the Red International? Only a few months, and before that happened the forces had been already shaping for a period of years. They cannot switch off in a month in a large percentage, but they may switch off in a year; it requires time – not too long a time, but a reasonable time is required. But the men are there; the men are developing the requisite class consciousness; the right outlook is there. Of all these things I am perfectly sure. There are men there who require no compelling to respond to the right ideals. They naturally respond to the ideal, the very proletarian blood responds to the idea, their hearts, souls, and spirit respond to the ideal. The work will be done, and it will be done on a large scale; I refer to

England particularly. I prefer that my remarks should apply to other countries also; natural modesty forbids me from attempting to deal with other countries, as experts from other countries are here.

With these remarks I have covered the case supplementing what Comrade Rosmer said so well and said so effectively.

Hilario Arlandis: On behalf of the Spanish delegation, I must state that we were instructed to defend the independence of the Red Trade Union International. By doing so we defend not our interests, our traits and characteristics, our national organisation, but rather the interests of the trade-union movement all over the world. The organic independence of our Red Trade Union International is the most necessary clause of the trade-union programme.

We understand very well that the Russian proletariat, which accomplished the great revolution marching under the banners of the Third International, is a very important part of the world working class. We realise this fact. This is the reason why we join Moscow and not Amsterdam. We clearly realise that the great Russian Revolution is the forge of the world revolution, and for this reason, despite our strict and implacable stand for the complete independence of the union organisations from every political party, we are ready to enter into the closest relations with the Communist International. But in return, we insist upon relations on the basis of equality and that the Communist International shall act, in regard to the Red Trade Union International, like an 'older brother'. The union movement must be organically independent – this contention is not a haphazard idea; it is the fruit of a half-century of experience.

The working class of the whole world was for many years fooled by the petty bourgeoisie and was a plaything in the hands of various political parties now finding their expression in the Second International. Members of these parties, disguised as revolutionaries, penetrated into working-class organisations, but in reality they were only petty bourgeois.

The great crisis of 1914 could occur only because the working class was unable to resist the bourgeoisie, only because the petty bourgeoisie remained at the head of the political parties. Today the Communist International is without doubt revolutionary. But where is the assurance that it will not abandon the revolutionary way, that it will not become opportunistic and renounce its task – the emancipation of the working class? Comrades, be careful. We are organising the new Red Trade Union International. Remember that it is nothing other than the organisation of the working class, and that the working class alone will destroy the capitalist order and build the new socialist system. Therefore, we must use all our forces to defend our independence and not permit our organisation to be subordinate to any political party.

In the conclusion of his speech, Comrade Arlandis said that his speech was simply a declaration of principles, but that on the whole the Spanish delegation agrees with the reports presented by Comrades Rosmer and Tom Mann. His delegation is fully in sympathy with the necessity of establishing connections with the Communist International.

Chair: The floor is given to Comrade Tsyperovich.

Grigorii Tsyperovich (Russia): Comrades, I find it necessary to make a few remarks in regard to Comrade Tom Mann's speech. I think that he struck the right note; still he did not characterise clearly enough the existing relationship between politics and economics under capitalism. The subject involved in his speech depends greatly upon our interpretation of this question. He did not go sufficiently into the international unity of trusts, syndicates, etc., which does not exist solely in the domain of production. This is not precise. We know that mutual relations among the various economic and political organisations take place in each country and on an international scale. This occurred before and during the war among the belligerent countries, and remains true today. If we are to cite as an example the steel trust or some other one, we would find that they also have an employment bureau for this particular branch of industry, that they are in close contact with parliament. We see that they have political organs such as the police, as well as ideological ones in religion and science. All of these converge in one iron fist to fight the working class, with the aim of crushing the dictatorship of the proletariat.

In light of this united action against the working class, we end up with the following conclusion: we will always be beaten unless we base our work on the same principle: complete national and international unity among the masses on the largest scale. That is the prior condition for a solution to this question.

Have we stabilised these close ties yet? We can say that we have them only in view, but the fact that this congress was convened proves the necessity of coordinating our activities and concentrating the energies of our separate and disunited trade unions. But at the same time, there is as yet no close connection between our striving for unity on a world scale and the already realised efforts of uniting our political parties.

This is the chief question that leads me to the speech of Comrade Arlandis. His ideas were greatly confused, leading him to draw many wrong conclusions that go against the viewpoint of our Russian comrades. Comrade Arlandis began by expressing formulas such as 'Beware! Defend your organisations!' He then went on to characterise political parties, pointing out that we had no guarantee that even the Communist International might not one fine morning be transformed into a yellow International. Such introductory remarks hardly agree with the sentiments Comrade Arlandis said inspired him.

Why does he fear that the Third International may not realise the hopes we now entertain? He referred to the past of the political parties that have reconciled themselves to the bourgeoisie and, swayed by their own leaders, betrayed the entire working-class movement.

He forgets at the same time that the same things also happened in the trade-union movement. During the war its leaders betrayed it and marshalled its ranks in the service of imperialism. It is not a question of blaming the political movement or the trade-union movement: the workers' movement as a whole has passed through a critical period, which the Third International is facing now. He also forgets the present-day circumstances, which are no longer those of the war. The class struggle has reached such a degree of sharpness that it would be impossible for the Third International to be defeated. He has not taken into consideration the report on the world economic crisis made by Comrade Varga. The conditions of the present struggle were left by Comrade Arlandis entirely unnoticeable, and therefore we have the old syndicalist phrases about political leaders, political parties, and so on.

At a time when the bourgeoisie has understood quite well the necessity of gathering all its political and economic forces in a single fist, to deliver one blow after another upon the divided working class, Comrade Arlandis recommends caution and distrust of the Third International. While he speaks of mutual agreement, he also recommends caution and the 'preservation of independence'. He considers the Red Trade Union International to be in opposition to the Communist International, as if the latter does not defend working-class interests. In reality, the workers in the Communist International are the very same as the workers who are in the trade-union movement. The only difference is that the Communist International is uniting the most conscious and determined forces in times of the decisive battle we are now facing. Comrade Arlandis has himself protested against the white terror in Spain and America. If at such a time he is going to discuss whether shock troops and the bulk of the regular army are necessary, and whether they should be ready to meet any attack – then such arguments are rather dangerous.

That is why I believe the Russian point of view to be the most correct, as it considers the Communist Party and the trade unions as a united military army that deploys its forces according to which the most responsible and the most self-sacrificing detachments of the Communist Party ought to fill the front ranks.

That is why the leadership must belong to the Communist International, which will naturally play the most responsible combat role. If the trade unions feel themselves strong enough to engage in combat, let them try. The unification of the trade unions lags behind that of the Communist parties, however, in spite of the latter's smaller size. Why is this? Because the trade-union organisations embrace larger masses of workers, but are unable to take advantage of the political moment. There is no question whatever of hegemony or submission, but of the elaboration of a single plan of struggle with a full utilisation and distribution of forces. That is why Comrade Arlandis's slogans: 'Beware!' and 'Fight for independence!' should be directed against the bourgeoisie.

He should say: Unite and defend the interests of the working classes not against the Communist Party, but against the dictatorship of the bourgeoisie. Cast aside all doubts in your ranks and victory will be assured. Otherwise we will be defeated and 'independence' from the Communist International would be transformed into dependence on capital.

Chair: Comrade Gliński will speak now.

Gliński [Stefan Królikowski] (Poland): Comrades, the question we are debating now has a very great significance. It consists of determining the position of the labour movement in regard to the political problems set before the working class. This question on the agenda challenges the syndicalist organisations to come out and clearly state what their position is now with regard to the political struggle, because in the past their stand was negative. At present the situation has changed altogether; new problems have arisen before the working class, and the syndicalists must tell us how they intend to solve them.

The question of relations between the Red Trade Union International and the Communist International is a question of the relations of the labour organisations to the political struggle of the working class. Comrades, there is a twofold difference between the red trade-union organisations of Moscow and the trade-union organisations of Amsterdam. The first consists of the trade unions' position on the political problems of the working class. The second involves the relations of everyday struggle for everyday interests. Where the latter is concerned, we Communists fully agree with the syndicalists. But the big question is whether they will follow us in our struggle for political aims.

Comrades, if the Red Trade Union International is striving to overthrow the capitalist power, if it intends to establish a soviet state ruled by the workers and peasants through the dictatorship of the proletariat, then its aims are the same as the Executive Committee of the Communist International. The syndicalists tell us that they too are against the dictatorship of capital, that they too are for the dictatorship of the working class, that they are striving for the destruction of the existing class, that they are striving for the destruction of the capitalist state. But at the same time they cannot cast aside their old political prejudices. And now, when the political struggle is being directed by the Executive Committee of the Communist International, they hesitate to bring the political struggle into the unions under their guidance.

We take this very much into account because we are convinced that the syndicalists are our brothers, with similar aims and problems, but they have not as yet overcome the influence and consequences of the political situation, which prevented them in the past from acquiring the correct views on the political struggle. Those past prejudices hinder them now in taking a clear and definite stand. The comrade from Spain warned us against political parties, insisted upon the independence of the Red Trade Union International from the Executive Committee of the Communist International, and in conclusion expressed his complete agreement with Comrade Rosmer and Tom Mann.

Our task is to convince the syndicalist comrades that only the Communist organisation of the workers of the world will accomplish the social and economic revolution they so ardently desire. They must be convinced that this social and economic revolution will not be brought about as long as the political government and power is not wrested from the hands of the bourgeoisie and given over to the working class, and that the working class, with the help of the dictatorship of the proletariat, will effect the social and economic revolution. The comrades of France and Spain should know that for all of us the struggle for political power is only a means to our common goal.

Chair: Comrade Schoenbeck has the floor.

Willi Schoenbeck (Germany): Comrades, we are assembled here with the strong determination and a firm will to affirm our unity for a common struggle against capitalism. This being our starting point, there is no doubt whatever that we shall succeed in finding common ground on all questions of tactics and methods for joint action by both the Red International of Trade Unions and the Communist International.

We consider it as an irrefutable truth that political and economic struggle cannot be waged separately; that, on the contrary, the one is always merging into the other. If so, we cannot fail to draw the necessary conclusion that the political parties of the proletariat and the trade unions must lead a common struggle, uniting their efforts.

Our comrades of the Free Unions [*freie Unionen*] and the syndicalist organisations, whose revolutionary spirit and determination to struggle we fully appreciate, will have to acknowledge upon reflection that the great struggle of the proletariat for its emancipation is undoubtedly beyond their power. An active participation of the masses themselves organised in trade unions, and even perhaps the active support of the unorganised part of it, would be necessary in order to be victorious in that struggle.

We must ask ourselves whether a struggle on a strictly economic level would bring us to the realisation of our aims.

An active participation of the political parties of the proletariat is indispensable in the struggle for emancipation. We quite understand the distrustful attitude of the syndicalists toward political parties. This lack of confidence is not entirely groundless, for the political struggle was sufficiently discredited in their eyes by social-democratic and opportunist leaders. On the other hand, the syndicalists cannot fail to see that the bourgeoisie, when opposing the economic struggle of the proletariat, uses in that struggle all possible means, frequently availing itself of its political power in order to suppress the proletariat and resist its economic struggle.

It must not be believed that we look upon the workers professing syndicalist views or upon the members of the independent unions as our enemies. We believe them to be our brothers with whom we wage and wish to wage a common struggle. But we are hostile to the syndicalist leaders, especially in Germany, where these leaders allowed themselves, during the recent revolutionary epoch, to slander in a most disgraceful manner our Russian brothers, suffering under the weight of their heroic struggle. We resolutely oppose these leaders. But as to syndicalist workers, we are determined to win them to our side. Our most urgent task should be to end their distrust toward political parties, at any rate to the only consistent party in the proletarian struggle. Naturally, this is not to be attained if we do so in the manner of Comrade Arlandis who, by his way of action, has only increased this distrust. We must demand from them that they clearly realise the nature and demands of the epoch we are passing through.

A Communist Party like the one to which our Russian comrades belong, which has succeeded in Russia in sending the capitalists to the devil and carrying out the dreams of the dictatorship of the proletariat, and now leads its heroic struggle for the construction of the communist system – such a party should be above distrust and should deserve universal acknowledgment.

The United Communist Party of Germany has also proved that it is ready for a decisive struggle, and that it does not tolerate any reformist elements in its ranks. We do not know of another case where a party succeeded in freeing itself of all reformist traits in such a short space of time. This fact, as well as the enormous sacrifices that the German Communist Party has offered on the altar of the revolution, is sufficient to guarantee against its sinking into the reformist swamp. Should Comrade Arlandis and all other comrades win the confidence of the great masses of workers on the side of the Communist parties and of the

Communist International, we shall then have enough strength to successfully continue the struggle and find the correct way to combat the enemy.

It is self-evident, therefore, that there must be a close relationship between the Communist International and the Red International of Labour Unions. This does not mean blind submission to the Communist International. It means a complete and harmonious combination and mobilisation of all forces for the same end. The numerically smaller Communist International composed of the class-conscious workers and Communists will be the vanguard of the numerically more powerful labour army of the Red International of Trade Unions.

If we consider the question from this angle, there is no doubt that the comrades at this congress will find a common ground for future action and a way to settle our differences. The two united organisations will thus be able to enter the world arena and lead the proletariat to final victory.

Lozovsky: Comrade Korolev has the floor.

E.A. Korolev (Russia): Comrades, I have a great deal to say on the subject raised by the syndicalists and discussed by comrades from Germany, Poland, and Russia.

It is up to the First Congress of the trade-union International to declare that the position taken by the syndicalists with regard to the Communist International is unacceptable to us and would hold us back from the forward movement of the social revolution. We must here and now tell our comrades, the syndicalists, that we did not gather here for the purpose of shaking up the old rags of syndicalism. We are not here to discuss the old, worn-out ideas of syndicalism, which had their logical and natural explanation long ago, during the epoch of capitalism when there was no war, when capitalism had not yet outlived its usefulness.

When Comrade Arlandis says that we must be independent of the Communist International and of any political party because they all – including the Communist parties – inevitably lead to the recognition of the bourgeoisie and to reconciliation with petty-bourgeois tactics, then he entirely forgets that petty-bourgeois tactics and collaboration with the bourgeoisie have been practised not only by social patriots or by the supporters of the Amsterdam International, but also by those who were involved in the revolutionary struggle.

The idea of class collaboration was also defended by the syndicalists, comrades-in-arms of Comrade Arlandis. Comrade Arlandis has forgotten the position that was taken by Citizen Hervé. When the World War broke out, Hervé, as he expressed himself, landed in his own country, as up to the present he was in the clouds of socialism and other utopias of all kinds. The war showed him his native country, his fatherland.[1] Besides defending his country, he also shouted, 'Long live Nicholas II!' What position was taken up by the syndicalist Jouhaux, and what is his position now? You must not forget your own history. Therefore, the question of where it leads and where we find the petty-bourgeois current, has already been answered by the history of the war and by the events after the war. We see that real revolutionary syndicalism is on the revolutionary communist path.

The vanguard of syndicalism realised through the struggle that it is impossible to separate the economic struggle from the political struggle, that economics and politics are two sides of the same thing, and that every act in the economic struggle leads to politics. And when the syndicalists and the American IWW prevent the transport of ammunition to Kolchak, then they are engaged in politics. But it was done separately and in an unorganised manner. If we stand for the overthrow of the bourgeoisie in an organised way, then we must absolutely recognise the organisation of a political party, which is the expression of the conscious experience and conscious struggle of the working class.

When the syndicalist comrades speak of autonomy and independence, they have in mind some abstract system of government. The Polish comrade was right in asking the question: You are talking about the independence of your syndicalist organisations in a bourgeois state. The bourgeois governments have often deceived the working class over decades to induce you to arrive at the opinion you hold. But when the proletariat gets at the helm of the state and assumes its dictatorship, will you still keep on defending your independence from the state? If in the sphere of education, you now stand for school autonomy and for handing it over to the revolutionary syndicalist organisations, will you do the same under the proletarian dictatorship? No, you will not do that.

And we must say very plainly on the question of neutrality of the revolutionary trade unions toward the Communist International that if the word 'revolutionary' is not just a figure of speech, they must unfailingly and inevitably recognise not only the theoretical, but also the practical matter of the leadership on the part of the vanguard of the working class as represented by its Communist Party and the Third International.

Lozovsky: A statement has been received, signed by seven delegates: 'Since the preliminary conference of the delegates decided not to take up the question of the relations between the trade unions and the Communist International

1 Gustave Hervé was a prominent French Socialist Party member who was known for extreme expressions of radicalism before World War I. After the war began in 1914, he became an equally extreme social patriot.

until the question has been decided at the congress of the Communist International, we protest against taking up the question at the present session, and declare that we will not take part in the discussion until we know the resolution of the Communist International on this question.'

Chair: Comrade Lozovsky has the floor.

Lozovsky: Comrades, this statement, both in form and in substance, will not stand up to criticism. No discussions at private meetings of delegates can in any way bind the congress, and the reference to the above private conference is, at best, a mere childish argument. Again, the comrades who stand for independence, who fear that someone may bind them to something, and at the same time are afraid to discuss the questions of the interrelations without it first being taken up at a private conference, take a position which, from the political viewpoint, is absolutely undefinable. It seems to me that the above comrades, in issuing such a declaration, have nothing to say on the essentials of the question as a whole, and it is a mere pretext for a protest that is really unworthy of being submitted to the congress.

Chair: The session is adjourned until 11:00 a.m. tomorrow.

RILU-Comintern Relations (continued)

(*Session opens at 11:10 a.m. Comrade Nin in the chair.*)

Nin: The discussion on the reports of Comrades Rosmer and Tom Mann is to be continued. Comrade Lozovsky will now speak.

Lozovsky: Comrades, the question of the relationship between the two Internationals is undoubtedly the most burning issue on our agenda. This is substantiated by the fact that many of the delegates on the way to the congress had very determined intentions to create conditions that will render impossible the joint work of both Internationals. We can easily judge that this is so by the large amount of literature upon this question that was issued on the eve of the congress. Many of the comrades had so specialised themselves on autonomy and independence that the more they wrote on this subject, the less it was possible to understand what they wanted to say!

I want to draw your attention, comrades, to an opinion expressed at the end of December 1920 by the syndicalists of a number of countries. A conference of syndicalists was held in Berlin from 16 to 21 December 1920.[1] Two distinct tendencies fought at this conference. One of these was represented by the German and Swedish syndicalists. These syndicalists were so anxious for independence that they refused to come to Moscow for this international congress. By independence they understand approaching the Communists only so they can stab them in the back. But the majority of the syndicalists there did not and could not agree to this proposition, and it was finally voted down. Nevertheless, the spirit prevailing at that congress – keeping as far away as possible from the Communists and from this diabolical thing – found its expression in the six points adopted by that conference. It may be worthwhile to note that the representative of the IWW at that conference[2] told me when I first met him that the last convention of the IWW decided to keep to the six points in regard to the relations between the two Internationals. These six points have thus become the six commandments of the syndicalist creed. I will read you these six points.

1 For the December 1920 Berlin Conference, see p. 145, n. 19.

2 A reference to George Hardy.

 | DOI:10.1163/9789004712867_011

1. The revolutionary trade-union International unreservedly stands on the platform of revolutionary class struggle and proletarian power.

'Power' from the lips of the syndicalists is something quite new; they never talked about it before, and the very word 'power' was always spelled with a capital letter and was considered a devilish invention of no interest to the proletariat. I will move on to the next points.

2. The revolutionary trade-union International strives towards the abolition and destruction of the economic, political, and spiritual domination of the capitalist system and state. It strives to establish a free communist commonwealth.
3. The conference is of the opinion that the working class can overthrow the political and spiritual oppression of capitalism only through the maximum use of economic methods of struggle, to be applied through the revolutionary action of the working class for the attainment of this aim.
4. The revolutionary trade-union International considers that the restoration and regulation of production and distribution is the task of the economic organisations in each country.
5. The revolutionary trade-union International is absolutely independent of any political party. In cases when the revolutionary trade-union International is ready for action, and when this action meets with the approval of political parties or other organisations, or vice versa, such action could be carried out in conjunction with these parties or organisations.
6. The conference urges the revolutionary trade-union organisations to attend the congress of the Red Trade Unions in Moscow (1 May 1921[3]) convened by the provisional Council of Red Trade Unions in order to create there a solid revolutionary trade-union International.

The ideological change on the part of the syndicalists is fully reflected in this resolution, like in a drop of water. The change is undoubtedly for the better, but on the other hand the old phantoms still hold the syndicalists in their grip. Thus, when we read in the first paragraph of the power of the workers, of proletarian power, we must have a definite and clear understanding of this power. In

3 The congress did not actually begin until 3 July.

the resolution it is nothing but a hollow phrase. Were a definite meaning given to this word, it would then express the necessity of a social revolution, of the conquest of power, and so on. This is precisely what we always argued about with the syndicalists. But the syndicalists reveal their spirit in paragraph 3, where they speak about the destruction of capitalism being possible through the economic struggle only.

The syndicalists suffer from their usual malady of not understanding what is politics and what is economics. This is the fundamental trouble with all of them in different countries. They consider as politics the parliamentary struggle, parliamentary negotiations, and nothing else; while mass action is economics. But why a mass demonstration protesting against [military] mobilisation in some country is considered an economic action cannot be explained by a single living syndicalist. Because it is quite clear to everyone that actions carried out through appeals, agitation, and campaigns – for example against the occupation of the Ruhr Basin,[4] etc. – these are political acts. They all concern the working class as a whole, in which the proletariat as a class stands opposed to the state and capitalism. Politics can be considered as the active opposition of one class against the other. Every working-class movement embracing large masses, and pitting them against the other class in the struggle, is a political movement.

Had it only been a terminological difference, there would have been no necessity of arguing with the comrades. But unfortunately, it is not only a question of terminology. There is a difference in conception of the tasks of the working class, of the methods of struggle to lead us to the same aims.

In the fourth paragraph we again see that the management of industry will be in the hands of the economic organisations of each country, i.e., the trade unions. But the clashing paragraph (to use a Russian expression) is the fifth one, where the absolute independence and autonomy from any political party is solemnly proclaimed. Yet later it is followed by a paragraph that is altogether comical, which says that if we want to organise a demonstration, and alongside us there is a neighbour called a 'political party', and this neighbour has the same intentions as we have, then such a joint action is possible. But I will ask you: How do you know the intentions of your political neighbour? If they are known to you, why not settle the basis of this joint action not just at the

4 The French army, with 130,000 troops, occupied the Rhineland cities of Düsseldorf, Duisburg, and Ruhrort on 8 March 1921, after Germany failed to meet an ultimatum on reparations payments. They withdrew in September. In January 1923, a larger invasion and occupation of the Ruhr was undertaken.

moment of action but during the process preparatory to the struggle? The mere way of expressing this paragraph shows that they do not understand the most elementary truths of the class struggle.

Let us take, for instance, France – the classic country of democracy in which this 'democracy' is now wildly raging. At the present time we have reaction that can be compared only to events after the Commune.[5] After the suppression of the revolutionary movement, France lived through a period of 'moral order'. It is now passing through similar conditions: ultra-criminal laws are being passed condemning people to five-year jail terms or hard labour for the slightest propaganda against militarism, laws concerning unions and parties, and in general relating to methods for fighting the proletariat. How could we organise the resistance of the workers were we to follow the opinion expressed by the syndicalists? It would be absolutely impossible, because it would split the forces of the proletariat by parallel, uncoordinated actions; we would not be in a position to deal a concerted blow in a single place. The thought that when we go into action and another organisation also intends to act, that this is enough to coordinate one's actions – this is childish and naïve. Such a policy is absolutely incorrect; it keeps us back from our aim; it hinders the class struggle.

It is evident that the syndicalists still possess many prejudices, which neither the war nor the revolution could make them forget. What other cataclysms do you need, if even the war and the revolution did not cure you of these prejudices? What other events do you want in order to make you take the right course? I think that life itself, in the nearest future, will cure these comrades of their last prejudices, and that in the everyday clash with the bourgeoisie they will clearly see that the bourgeoisie is a thousand times cleverer than their theoreticians.

Ask any bourgeois whether they are carrying on any discussion of this kind, whether they bother themselves with such questions, and he will look at you as upon a madman. And he will be right, because the bourgeoisie is fully conscious of its class interests. Any bourgeois organisation that in its aims and methods supports the bourgeois order is welcomed by the capitalists. In their struggle against the proletariat, the capitalists refuse to recognise metaphysical or abstract theories, because they find no difference between politics and economics.

---

5 The Paris Commune of March–May 1871 was the first effort to establish a revolutionary workers' government. Following the Commune's suppression, the French president, Adolphe Thiers (1871–3), presided over the counterrevolutionary terror in which more than 10,000 working people of Paris were executed, as well as 38,000 arrested, and 7,000 deported to penal colonies.

Now here are two more instances as to how irrationally our comrades approach the question of the relationship between the Communist International and the Red Trade Union International. I have before me the resolution of the Revolutionary Syndicalist Committees [CSR] published in *L'Humanité* of 21 May. There is a paragraph in this resolution that says, 'The Revolutionary Syndicalist Committees unreservedly proclaim the full autonomy and independence of revolutionary French syndicalism.' And further the declaration discusses the establishment of relations with the Communist Party. This is what it says: 'The Revolutionary Syndicalist Committees do not reject any eventual support that the revolutionary political parties may give, owing to the weight and authority that they possess at the present time, as well as the marked influence of different philosophical groups striving to bring humanity to a more perfect ideology.' What is all this? Always the same syndicalist prejudices, always counterposing politics to economics, thus breaking up the working-class organisations into two parts and rendering them powerless under the blows of the bourgeoisie.

In *L'Humanité* of 27 June, I also find the curious article of Comrade Verdier under the title 'Syndicalism Must Be Free'. But how is this freedom to be understood? If one is talking of freedom, it's clear that the danger comes from conquering imperialist powers. The power in question, based on the content of this article, is on the one hand 'the Communist International', and on the other, the 'Communist Party'. What have been the criminal and imperialist tendencies of these powers? Simply the desire to permeate working-class organisations with the communist spirit, so as to make them real working-class organisations. These are the imperialistic crimes of those organisations from the point of view of the syndicalists.

Comrade Verdier is stating that the French delegation has received an imperative mandate as follows:

1. To insist that the congress of the trade-union International shall stay independent of the Communist International.
2. That the congress should recognise the full autonomy and independence of the trade-union movement in each country, and particularly that it endorse the autonomistic principles and form of organisation of French syndicalism, whose forms and principles are the starting point of the social revolution.
3. That the clause on the relations between the two Internationals drawn up by the respective executive committees should be struck out from the draft of the statutes.

The last paragraph of this imperative mandate is as follows: 'No matter what the decisions of the congress may be, the French delegation cannot endorse them, but taking note of them, it should communicate them to the central committee, which will place the question before all the organisations. A special congress will decide the question of their acceptance or rejection.'

If such a mandate was given – and the fact that I know of it proves that it was – then it is the most absurd mandate I ever heard of. It's one of two things: If you send a delegation with full powers, you cannot say 'whatever the decisions will be, dear comrades, don't endorse them!' Or else you consider your delegation insufficiently mature, and don't think its members are capable of estimating events. It is really impossible to tell the delegation of eleven members you have sent here: 'Don't sign anything, but refer it back to us no matter what decisions may be arrived at there.' It is not only a lack of trust of the congress, but also a lack of trust of the delegates who were sent here, with the hidden thought and fear that, coming into contact with other comrades, seeing what is going on here, they might agree to logical decisions not necessarily coinciding with the specifically French principle of 'independence'.

I will proceed further. The syndicalists very often refer to the necessity to preserve the freedom of the trade-union movement in each country. I do not understand this position; neither do I understand the way it is approached. We understand very well the psychology of the French comrades and the difference of social conditions in each country. We understand the historic development of this psychology. We know all this fully, as a doctor understands a disease. But because we know the disease, we are not at all inclined to proclaim it a normal phenomenon of the working-class movement. We consider it an annoying survival of the past, because if we look over the working class in its entirety, then this revolutionary energy must find its forms of organisation. Our ideal must be the building up of a united International, comprising the entire field of activities in the sphere of political, trade union, and cooperative movements of the working class, so as to concentrate all the revolutionary energies of the working class in order to fight the solid, strongly united, and tightly welded class-conscious phalanx of the bourgeoisie. That is our ideal. Naturally, there are many gradations and transitional forms. There may be a different development in each country, but in principle it will be the same all over.

The fundamental error of our comrades consists in their unwillingness to see that the Communist International is the worst enemy of the capitalist system. This error shows that they have not learned anything the past ten years. It is sufficient to take a look around at the social situation, to see the tremendous influence of the Communist International. Comrades, it is time to cast away the absurd theory of independence vis-à-vis communism. Remember that the bourgeois press is writing about it; they are unanimously praising this theory. Those comrades who do not understand this are acting as a brake on the social revolution, and not as a factor of progress.

Chair: Comrade Szántó will speak next.

Béla Szántó (Hungary): The speech delivered by Comrade Arlandis yesterday proves that the revolution has not taught him anything, and that the role of the trade unions at the present time is incomprehensible to him. According to his reasoning it becomes clear that the aims of the trade unions, in his opinion, are the same as before the war. I think that on this basis he may shake hands with the representatives of Amsterdam.

During the epoch when the capitalist system of production was in flourishing condition and dominant, the aims of the trade unions were: increasing wages, reducing the working day, and other social and political demands. At that time trade-union tactics were purely defensive. They had to defend the working class from the excessive exploitation of capitalism. It was natural then for trade unions to be independent of political parties and not submit to their leadership. In the actual conditions prevailing at the time, it was possible to separate and divide the political from the economic fronts and get along without the guidance of the party. Hence in those countries in which there was no personal contact between the leaders of the parties and the trade unions, the trade-union movement was to a certain extent independent.

Now, however, as a result of the revolution, we have entered a new epoch, and the conditions of work have greatly changed. The revolutionary epoch now poses tasks before the trade unions different from what they were in the capitalist epoch before the war. Now the question is not about a defensive position within the framework of the capitalist system, but about an offensive against capitalism itself. It is no longer a question of increasing wages or reducing working hours or partial improvements of the conditions of labour. Now the trade unions are passing from the defensive to the offensive in order to be in position for the decisive attack on capitalism.

The question of knowing whether the trade unions are ready for this, whether current conditions are favourable, is not posed at the present moment. Our task is limited to mobilising the unions, making them recognise the necessity of action. We know that even the economic action that the trade unions carry out is at the same time political action. I put the question that arises point blank: What methods will our syndicalist comrades apply with a view of carrying on the fight against unemployment without the help of a political party? The struggle against unemployment is undoubtedly one of the main tasks of the trade unions, but it is also one of the main tasks of the Communist Party. Is it not clear that the trade unions and the Communist Party should lead this struggle together?

The experience of the German workers' movement in its fight for an increase of wages, and the recent tremendous miners' lockout in Britain has already taught us that the struggle bears a completely political character. If the syndicalist comrades will, as before, absolutely refuse to cooperate with the political parties, this will then disorganise the revolution.

The syndicalists have learned nothing from the revolution. They think that the old methods such as sabotage, passive resistance, and general strikes may be used, but we must say openly that all these methods have lost their revolutionary character today. Sabotage, passive resistance, and general strikes are only blunt weapons of struggle and are insufficient.

The weapons of the working class must be perfected. Once the syndicalist comrades become convinced that armed insurrection has become essential to proletarian action, then they will not be able to reject the principle of the Communist Party leading the revolutionary movement in the different countries.

The Communist Party must not adapt to those backward conceptions and submit to those old methods of struggle. On the contrary, it has to fight the old methods within the workers' movement, and to attract the masses and lead them to revolutionary action. It is therefore necessary to follow tactics we have adopted previously, because they serve the revolution.

When the syndicalists say that the proletariat has been betrayed by the Communist parties, then we challenge this statement without any hesitation. We say: The social democrats have betrayed you, not the Communists. The Communist parties have never betrayed and will never betray the workers. The Communist Party has taken the leadership of the revolutionary movement; it will never abandon its post.

There can be no mechanical submission of the trade unions to the Communist parties; that is the wrong way of posing the question. The main thing is to carry out revolutionary action within the trade unions, to strive to conquer the sympathy of the organised masses and to use our influence over them. Consequently, the order of the day is not the mechanical submission of the trade unions to the Communist Party, but for the ideas of the Communist Party to penetrate into the mass of the proletariat. And if this is clear, then the question seems to be solved.

The Communists will continue their previous tactics. They will try to conquer and to revolutionise the trade unions. And when we will have won them all over as a result of this inevitable process, we will take the lead in the trade unions and subject them to our influence. Then close relations between the

Communist parties and the trade unions will be naturally established. The Red International of Trade Unions will then naturally recognise the ideological supremacy of the Communist International.

Today we may still discuss the question of the relations between the two Internationals, but the chief subject of tomorrow will be how intensively and how well the Communists carry out their work within the trade unions. We strive for one International, and to achieve this the proletariat of the world, being united under the revolutionary banners of the social revolution, should recognise as their only leader – the Communist International. Strictly speaking, it is only a formal matter whether we recognise our organisation as a fully independent one, or whether we call the Red International of Trade Unions only a section of the Communist International. All this depends entirely upon the relationship of forces within the trade unions.

Today we clearly cannot declare the Red International of Trade Unions to be a section of the Communist International. But we do not want to deceive the proletariat and will therefore openly say: The unions must be permeated with the spirit of the revolutionary struggle; they must submit to the guidance of the Communist parties; they must recognise the ideological influence of the Communist International.

Chair: Comrade Bergmann has the floor.

Bergmann [Ludwig Meyer] (Germany, General Workers' Union): The conclusions drawn by the different speakers with reference to Comrade Arlandis's speech indicate either that they do not understand syndicalism or they refuse to understand it. Consider the speech made by the last speaker, Comrade Béla Szántó, who said that the revolution has not taught Comrade Arlandis anything. The syndicalists of all countries ought to protest emphatically against such a statement. It is precisely the Spanish proletariat, in its long struggle, which has proved that it is actually revolutionary in practice and does not stand for Amsterdam.

Some speakers, including Comrade Lozovsky, have found it necessary to speak even against those syndicalist views that are not represented here, as is the case with the German syndicalists. Comrade Lozovsky indicated that a resolution was proposed at the Berlin Conference that rejects the principle of any political organisation on a national or an international scale. This resolution was, in any case, rejected, and I cannot understand why such a method of fighting syndicalists was adopted here when it is our duty to come to an understanding. Not one syndicalist who spoke here has ever rejected the principle of a political organisation, both national and international. The syndicalists are only against those political organisations that have, by their past actions, shown that they are nothing else but political organisations of the pre-revolutionary epoch. We too do not recognise these political organisations.

As Comrade Rosmer stated, we are recommending for adoption the fundamental theses presented to the congress of the Communist International by the Communist Workers' Party [KAPD]. I need to make clear that these theses do not form a single whole; they are only a part of the theses that were presented by us to the congress of the Communist International.[6]

To those who say that the comrades of the General Workers' Union consider a political organisation as an unnecessary evil, we answer: read our fundamental theses and our programme. The aims of the Communist parties and of the Communist International were indicated in the theses presented by us. If these aims should be realised by the Communist Party, then we must and will be able to carry on the fight together with them in a dialectical process. If the Communist Party gains the confidence of the masses thanks to the clarity of its slogans, if it always advances with the workers during the fight, then the Communist Party – without any resolutions – would be able to lead the proletarian masses. Otherwise, these political organisations will not lead the proletariat either on a national or international scale. (*Voice: 'That means that we all have to join the Communist Workers' Party.'*) Well, and you, comrades of the United Communist Party, are you going to state that you have confidence in your leaders?

The latest events in Germany have proved that the proletariat is not carrying out the fight for the ten clauses of the programme of the trade unions, but rather for the overthrow of capitalism and the bourgeois government.[7] The slogans of the fight were thus not for some particular demands but for victory over the ruling class. In the theses presented by us to the Communist International, we indicate that the main problem of the Communist Party before the conquest of political power, and at moments when the proletarian revolution is wavering, is that of holding firmly and unmistakeably onto the only accurate compass – communism. The Communist Party must invariably and without any hesitation, under all circumstances, indicate to the proletariat the aims and the methods of struggle, not only in words but in deeds.

---

6 For the KAPD resolution on trade unions, see the Appendix, pp. 679–83.

7 A reference to the March Action of 1921, which was an attempt by the leadership of the Communist Party of Germany, with support from some within the Comintern leadership, to turn a defensive proletarian battle into a general strike and spark a revolutionary uprising through the efforts of a determined minority. The action failed and the German proletariat and Communist movement suffered a major defeat. The adventurist thrust of the action was criticised by the Comintern's Third Congress.

The Communist Party, prior to the conquest of power, must in all questions of political struggle draw a definite line between reform and revolution. It must brand each reformist action as an attempt to prolong the existence of the capitalist system of exploitation, as a betrayal of the revolution and the interests of the working class. Just as it is impossible to reconcile the interests of the exploiters with those of the exploited, or to shape a political agreement between reformists and revolutionists, so social-democratic reformism, under whatever mask it may hide itself, is at present a great brake on the revolution and the last hope of the bourgeoisie. Therefore, the Communist Party must turn away from every manifestation of reformism and opportunism in its programme, in its tactics, in its press, in its actions. It must not increase its membership before it is assured of the stability of the Communist nucleus.

The working class, in the course of the revolution, is inevitably subject to hesitations. The revolution is a dialectical process, not only as a whole but in certain phases. The Communist Party, as an organisation of the most class-conscious elements of the working class, must be able to lead the masses despite their hesitations. Owing to the fact that its slogans are clear to everyone, that in the struggle it is the vanguard of the masses, that its words are in harmony with its deeds, and that its predictions are being materialised, the Communist Party speedily helps to overcome all the hesitations of the masses. Thus the Communist Party, by its actions, should develop the class consciousness of the proletariat even at the cost of what may seem temporary, superficial divergence from the masses. Only by such means can the Communist Party, during the revolution, gain the confidence of the masses and carry out on a large scale the necessary revolutionary educational work.

Inasmuch as the Communists wish to lead the proletariat, they must always be in the very midst of the workers; they should take an active part in their struggle, approaching them with clear slogans. They should impress on them that amelioration of the conditions under which they live is impossible. They should be told that the solution will come only through the overthrow of the bourgeoisie, and that victory will be achieved by the unity of the revolutionary forces of the working class. Thus it becomes clear why we, as Communists, reject reformist methods in parliament, as it does not develop class consciousness but only weakens it.

The attitude of the United Communist Party of Germany toward the union struggle and trade-union organisations is illogical. From an organisational point of view, its members are combined in the Amsterdam organisation – that is, an international counterrevolutionary organisation – yet they claim that they are fighting shoulder to shoulder with the Red International. Neither in political nor union matters have they proved that they can be trusted with the leadership of the masses during the struggle. The masses cannot have any confidence in leaders who are wavering in their views.

The proletariat can recognise only those leaders who in all circumstances are capable of acting without hesitation, with a clear understanding of their aims. If you are unable to understand this truth, you have not learned the lessons of the history of revolution. It is necessary that the Communist Party not take any actions that create confusion as to its aims, and that by its actions it should prove that it is really capable of leading the masses. Such a Communist leadership that clearly understands its aims will be accepted by the syndicalists on the national as well as the international domain.

We must try to persuade the syndicalist comrades that the union of all revolutionary forces of the proletariat is at present more important than at any other period. Only unity and the general struggle of all revolutionary organisations will bring us victory over the ruling class.

Chair: Comrade Boisson has the floor.

Louis Boisson (France, CTM): The debates of today are being conducted around two points: (1) the independence of syndicalism from political parties; and (2) the relations between the Communist International and the trade-union International. Some of the speakers were in favour of independence, others against.

The question is whether revolutionary syndicalism has a doctrine, a method, and an organisation of its own. This is the point to discuss. To move in a vicious circle is not to solve the problem. Why is syndicalism not a political organisation in the usual sense of the word? Because the neutrality of syndicalism with relation to political parties implies more than a distrust of electoral or parliamentary methods. If this were not so, it eventually would mean a temporary position that would be subject to revision. In reality, this neutrality conveys the idea that syndicalism has developed on a quite different level from political parties, and that the political and trade-union struggles are carried on in two different fields: first, that of the liberation of work; and, secondly, that of 'workerism', which is communism.

Why does the Amiens Charter excite such passionate debate at this congress? Born in 1906, it is still alive in 1921. I shall try to dissect it in the clearest and shortest way.

We workers say that even after the revolution, the state – whether socialist or not – will always remain a centralised and dominating force, to which the workers, anxious to maintain their liberty, must counterpose their autonomous organisations. United in close ranks, they will always have to make supreme efforts as producers in order to resist the claims of a bureaucracy.

What is a trade union? A group formed on the basis of a community of interests. This allows it to have a programme without ambiguity, a definite line of conduct, methodical action and work under the leadership of competent individuals. It is this – and not the number of its adherents – that is the secret of its strength.

What is the basis of a political party? A clash and confusion of interests. It mixes systematically in the same party workers, employers, intellectuals, tradesmen, producers, and rentiers. It is therefore incapable of following a definite line of action and maintains itself by falsehoods and ambiguities.

What are the methods of the revolutionary syndicalists? The direct action of the proletariat taking possession of the means of production, having dispossessed the bourgeoisie of its privileges.

Workers possess the means of production and distribution; they assume the management of these through their trade unions; they are the source of nourishment in social life. They find themselves within the citadel they are to capture. If they want to, they may, upon a preliminary agreement with their organised comrades, free themselves at a single stroke from the yoke of capitalism.

The question of the peasants is not posed in the same way in France as in Russia, on account of industrial development. That is why the embryo of the cooperative movement now developing in the countryside will facilitate the mutual relations of the peasants and city dwellers.

The trade-union movement has become fully recognised throughout the country in spite of the restrictive laws and persecution by the government. Everywhere local sections have amalgamated into federations that then united into one confederation of labour and formed initial international links.

The proletarian movement all over the world has certain features in common, which strike the observer much more than particular traits in each separate country. Owing to this organisation of the class struggle, capitalism every day sees its foundation sapped by forces developing within it and preparing its complete collapse.

Everybody has spoken about the spirit animating the debate on the Amiens Charter. It has been said that both *majoritaires* and *minoritaires* have made it their platform. That is true, with the difference that some make use of it in order to distract from their dealings; others do so in order to organise expropriating violence. Comrade Lozovsky, we are partisans of a revision of the Amiens Charter, but we want to maintain its fundamental points, because it is always up to date. It says: syndicalism, the direct emanation of the organised forces of the workers, proclaims again that syndicalist ideas will be realised only with the total transformation of society.

Born of the class struggle, the Amiens Charter fully expresses the situation facing the proletariat, drawing inspiration for its action and its aims in the defence of trade-union interests and full development of the rights of labour. The workers' organisation repeats that its chief aim is to abolish the wages system and ownership. It acknowledges the class struggle as a fact from which all conclusions should be drawn. This struggle, which will end only with the suppression of all classes, of all economic and social privileges, must result in a new organisation of the collective body. Equal participation of all in the rights and obligations that the necessary intercourse of men gave birth to – such are the initial principles on the basis of which the workers' movement intends to establish a new social system. It will realise this system in conformity with its own conceptions and with the organ that it will create, the essential character of which should be to direct the collective economy, productive forces, and establish control over them. Labour – creator of all wealth, the element that commands all social activity – tends to be everything, for all other fractions of society are no more than subordinates or parasites to it.

Thus without any ambiguity syndicalism has from its origin declared itself to be, in its present-day character and its permanent ideals, a revolutionary force.

When the syndicalists published the Amiens Charter in 1906, the two great events that are now constantly before our eyes did not exist: firstly, the cursed war, and secondly, the Russian Revolution.

The revolution thunders all over Europe like an erupting volcano. The insecurity of the bourgeoisie manifests itself everywhere. All this combined induces us to open our eyes and renounce dogmatism. We must elaborate a new charter, introducing into it the point about the seizure of power by the trade unions; the local union would organise the commune; the regional union would organise the region; the national union would organise the nation.

How shall we pass from one system to another? How shall we compel the parasites and the counterrevolutionary forces to respect the conquests of the revolution? By establishing the dictatorship of the workers, exercised and controlled by the trade unions; that is, by arming the conscious workers in all branches of trade and industry.

We are partisans of a federalist decentralisation, which means that all orders, all impulses, energies, and stimuli are to come from below. Those who are at the top will only have to follow the instructions coming from below, to register them, to undertake their execution and development, up to the moment when the working masses would become the masters of their destinies.

Why does the left-wing proletariat keep its eyes riveted upon Russia? Because of its political party? No, for that had existed before the war. The proletariat beholds the rays of this big lighthouse because it is the lighthouse of the revolution all over the world, and because only the revolution in all countries will liberate the peoples from slavery. We shall always stand by the Russian Revolution, even with its errors and mistakes. We have loved and defended it since 1917, and will propagate its characteristic principles among the masses who are fighting for it. We are always in full harmony and in close connection with the party of the revolution, because we work for the same thing.

We are not afraid of relations with the International, but of creating a new bureaucracy all over Europe. We realise the difficulties of propaganda and of administration of the new order of things. We know that if we are not up to our task, we will be in disarray. It is not the republic that forms the citizens, but the citizens who create the republic. If we come to an agreement that each International should be independent in its own autonomous field of action and meeting only when necessary, we will be able to work with tact, for the simple reason that each International will oversee the other, and that each would be jealous of the progress of the other.

Comrades, at this congress we have a role to fill before the future generations. The working-class maxim that 'the emancipation of the workers will be carried out by the workers themselves' stands in opposition to parliamentary politics, which is the art of governing over the people.[8]

The report of Comrade Rosmer is somewhat vague in this sense. He says that either you are with us or against us. This means that opposition is not to be permitted, either from the right or from the left. That all oppositions are the same. Comrade Rosmer, you are mistaken; the rightist elements, as, for instance, Mussolini, whom you quoted, claim independence, as we do. We believe that there is a slight difference between the elements showing flexibility with regard to the bourgeoisie and the left elements that use violence in order to expropriate it. Your building is not very solid, and you are afraid of the rush forward.

In ancient Rome, when the slaves revolted, there existed neither communist parties nor revolutionary syndicalists; there were merely rebels against oppression. Who will lead the revolution? Will it be the political party or the revolutionary trade unions? The latter commit an error when they trail behind a political party, whichever it may be. Take for instance the two revolutions of Kerensky and Lenin. On this basis syndicalism should keep within its permanent framework, independent of all parties, and work in a revolutionary way

8 In the Provisional Rules of the International Workingmen's Association (the First International) drafted by Karl Marx in 1864, it states at the very beginning, 'The emancipation of the working classes must be conquered by the working classes themselves.' See *MECW*, 20, p. 14. That same basic idea appears in numerous other places in the writings of Marx and Engels.

on all occasions presenting themselves. United in insurrectionary action, independent in the period that follows, it would establish its planned basis of society and realise its social programme.

Comrade Lozovsky, yes, we have two false democracies, two distinct classes of exploiters and exploited. This situation is the result of three revolutions, which had been political revolutions and therefore negative ones.

Jack Murphy (Britain): The discussion up till now has revealed a fairly general support of the proposition for cooperation between the two Internationals. But the discussion has also revealed a considerable amount of differences between the various sections of the industrial movement as to their views concerning the relationship of the Internationals and action – and also the relations of the political parties and the industrial organisations in action. There appears to be a considerable amount of opposition to the political parties based upon three things: (1) There is the claim that the industrial movement has closer contact with the masses than political parties. (2) It is based upon the fear of the political reformists. (3) It is based upon the danger that is contemplated with regard to the growth of bureaucracy inside the international movement both before the revolution and after.

Now with regard to the first argument. Contact with the masses alone is not an actual test for us. It is a very important point; but the real test is contact with the masses and close and correct interpretation of the needs of the masses in their march towards their revolutionary goal. If we apply the test of action with the masses, then we would have a controversy between ourselves and the reformists, who also claimed that they had closer contact to express the consciousness of the masses in their own way. Well, we distinguish between the question of contact and the question of consciousness, and we say that the real test is not so much the contact – though that is very important – but contact plus correct interpretation of the needs of the working class as it proceeds with the revolutionary struggle.

Now, turning to the next point, we have the fears of the political reformists. These fears that we could become political reformists are based upon the experience of the betrayals by politicians. Especially do we find this fairly strong in countries where the political movement has only lately developed, and where the industrial movement has preceded the political movement by many years. But I want to remind all those who have these fears that the betrayal of the workers is not confined to members of political parties, even reformist political parties, or the trade-union leaders. Those who belong to the industrial movement are equally guilty with the politicians on this question of betrayal of the masses.

But what is the origin of this betrayal in reality? Is it not because the fallacy propagated deliberately by the capitalist class – the fallacy of the separation of the economic and political issues – has been taken up by those absorbed by them until it has become part of their political philosophy, and therefore they have been incapable of measuring the real needs of the workers in this economic and political struggle. For, mark you, the time has arrived now when there should be no debate on the question of separation. Economic and political issues cannot be separated. Anyone witnessing the struggle of the working class in every country today can see quite clearly that the revolutionary movement grows to the degree in which the industrial movement has developed in country after country, involving everywhere larger masses of workers, which has inevitably brought them [together] when an action to challenge the state was organised.

Take England, take Italy, take France, take America, take any country you like, and immediately the industrial organisation or any revolutionary organisation of any dimension go into action immediately when they come up against the challenge of the state. It cannot be avoided, and all the time we can see that it comes irrespective of whether the spark has come from some particular well-recognised political interests, or whether it has come even from what we call economic interests.

Call it what you like. Take for example the rise in wages. If you recognise that the fight to obtain this is all a question of the masses' active forces, then it must definitely be recognised that it is a manifestation of the political class struggle. We can see quite clearly that any attempt now to make this demarcation line between economics and politics is simply a betrayal of the workers themselves. There can be no demarcation line between economic issues and political issues. All of them are involved now in bringing on this mighty struggle between the classes; all of them are getting more and more into the struggle.

Now then, recognising this fact, let us come down to a clear recognition of our position in the industrial movement. Compare it with the political parties and let us see exactly what is the difference. When we say political party, we immediately recognise a group of people who have come together for a definite political objective. With regard to the industrial organisation, however, we see that they are being mobilised with a conscious political aim, but are mobilised on the strength of individual economic grievances: lowness of wages, bad industrial conditions, and so forth. All these flock into organisations that we call industrial organisations, and that is a big distinction between them and the political party.

Trade unions are organisations of the working class that are slowly preparing for the decisive struggle, raising the political consciousness of the masses united by the economic struggle. The fight within the unions for influence should not scare anyone. It's not just the reformists who are fighting for influence there; the revolutionary forces are fighting to do the same. And if at present the reformist majority has more influence than the revolutionary minority in the leadership of the unions and runs them, this serves as an even greater argument for the revolutionary minority to enter the old unions and establish our unity of action there.

Now, when a political movement has gone through the process of struggle and has passed through the flames of revolution in one country – out of that revolution a new International has sprung up. That International is the Communist International, and all the revolutionary forces should rally to it. There is one purpose before us, namely, the mobilisation of all the working-class forces that we can gather together for one objective, that is, for the overthrow of the capitalist state and the triumph of the proletariat – that is the immediate goal. And then, we are confident, the problems will solve themselves in the process of the struggle, as we proceed to consolidate our position and march to victory.

Franz Grölig (Germany, General Workers' Union): Comrades, we have digressed a long way from our theses proper, which deal with the relations between the Red Trade Union International and the Communist International.

We of the General Workers' Union who are also members of the Communist Workers' Party of Germany [KAPD] are convinced partisans of the necessity of having political parties in the struggle of the workers against capitalism. Our point of view is clearly expressed in *Die Proletarier* (June 1921, p. 16) as follows:

> The Red Trade Union International fights all parties of a parliamentarian character. It stands for the firm consolidation of all the most advanced revolutionary proletarians of every country in one independent political organisation, purely proletarian and communistic in character, and for the firm welding of this organisation with the political organisation of the Communist International, whose aims are identical with that of the Red Trade Union International and whose fighting methods are determined by the same fundamental situation.[9]

We should not be surprised that maudlin sentimentality has prejudiced the proletariat against political parties, especially when we consider that their lead-

9 Taken from the KAPD theses, 'Richtlinien zur Roten Gewerkschaftsinternationale' (Guidelines for the Red Trade Union International).

ers were instrumental in betraying the workers in their struggle against the bourgeoisie. Such things have contributed to the fact that the workers of all countries – and especially Germany – who really were good revolutionists – left the 'kaiser's unions' and passed into the ranks of the syndicalists.

We syndicalists of Germany took the most active part in the fighting. I know local groups, such as the one in Bremen, that always had their men in the various battles. In spite of this, we must draw a line between the syndicalist and the communist conceptions, and say that there can be only one alternative: either syndicalists or communists. However, we shall have, to a considerable extent, to take account of the fact that the French and Spanish syndicalists are of a different character and play a different part in the international proletarian movement than is the case with the German syndicalists. The Spanish comrades, especially, show that they are not pacifists trailing in tow of the petty bourgeoisie and fighting against the proletariat.

And now to the point. Comrade Radek found it necessary at the Communist Congress to severely criticise Comrade Gorter,[10] but it was precisely Comrade Gorter who already before the war spoke of something that even workers who received their training in capitalist primary schools could understand. I refer here to his book on historical materialism, from which even indifferent workers may learn that political organisations are necessary for the struggle of the proletariat against capitalism.[11]

After the party and the unions in Germany clashed, we felt it necessary to do something that would help clarify the whole matter at issue. Comrade Gorter, in his pamphlet *The Class-Struggle Organisation of the Proletariat*, makes it very clear that political parties are indispensable in the proletarian struggle. We read this on page 16:

> Firstly, almost all proletarians need small urgent reforms and measures for protecting and improving their standard of living. Their misery is so great that they will always, even during the revolution, demand and fight for such reforms. To obtain this, they will at times give up the revolution itself. They will also use their unions for this purpose. The unions and their organised membership are in danger of becoming infected with opportunistic reformism, and thus sabotaging the revolution in order to obtain small improvements and the illusions of power and thus increase their membership from among unreliable elements.

10 Radek's remarks on Herman Gorter at the Comintern Third Congress can be found in Riddell (ed.) 2015, *3WC*, pp. 412–15.

11 Gorter's book *Historical Materialism* can be found online at Marxists Internet Archive.

> There is no doubt that many union members, including many anarchists and syndicalists, do not recognise the Communist Party because it puts the revolution above reform.
>
> In the second place, there is a great danger of the unions falling victim to individualism. Individuals, such as union leaders, will, whether from ignorance or selfish motives, etc., put their own interests or their personalities above the revolution. The same thing may happen to a whole factory area or district. Thus revolutionary unity may vanish. This is already seen in many parts of the trade-union movement.

On the same page Comrade Gorter writes, 'There is a third danger, utopianism'. I want to say right here that the comrades who think that we should stay in the unions should not consider themselves immune against this danger. (*Continues reading*)

> Owing to inadequate knowledge of things as they really are, this part of the proletariat within the unions overestimates its strength. Important industrial unions, such as the railwaymen, transport workers, or miners, fancy that they alone can bring about the revolution, which in Western Europe and North America can be accomplished only by the entire proletariat.
>
> Finally – and this is the strongest reason why industrial and craft organisations are not sufficient – considerable sections of the proletariat lack adequate knowledge. Their theoretical training and the amount of information at their command is quite inadequate to get a clear and firm mental grasp of economics and politics. They are poorly informed on the important developments, both national and international, on economic and political questions, their interplay and their influence on the revolution. For this reason they fail to act at the right moment. They act when they should not act, and they fail to act when they ought to. They will frequently commit blunders.

On page 19 Comrade Gorter says:

> The industrial organisation supplies its members with the most general theoretical information on the revolution, such as the essential nature and significance of workers' councils (soviets) and the dictatorship of the proletariat. The party, on the other hand, is made up of those proletarians whose knowledge is deeper and more extensive.

> The industrial organisation can train the proletarian masses to become heroic and class-conscious fighters for the revolution precisely because they are industrial, not craft unions. The party brings together in its ranks the most clear-headed and therefore the most courageous elite – the vanguard of the proletariat.[12]

And so, comrades, such being the case, we must at once recognise the necessity of the political organisation. I believe I have logically established the principle that we must have the political organisations jointly with the economic organisations. I also think that I have clearly sketched Gorter's ways of thinking and logic. I leave it to your own judgement to decide how far I have succeeded in showing that Comrade Radek was wrong in his severe remarks against Comrade Gorter at the Communist congress.

The question is: Does the Third International show the right direction for all countries? We greatly honour and respect our tactics in regard to Russia, but we greatly doubt whether the same tactics would be applicable for Western Europe. Our comrades of the KAPD and the Dutch left-Marxists are convinced that in Western Europe the proletariat cannot triumph with leadership politics, but only with the help of methods that make the working class politically and organisationally self-sufficient. One must not do it like the comrades of the VKPD.

I will put forth only one question: Do you recognise the economic difference between Western Europe and Russia? (*Shouts: 'We do.'*) If such is the case, if differences do exist, it is very clear then that different circumstances dictate different methods. If you refuse to recognise this, you are not Marxists but utopians. (*Protest and laughter*) You do not know anymore what your desires are. (*Protest*) Yes, comrades, you ought to get clear on those things. Think a little more, and you will come to the same conclusion. This is the basic problem – I take into consideration the differences in circumstances here and there – for the KAPD, also for the other organisations to decide upon.

From this point of view, we must consider all the circumstances and act accordingly. The Spanish comrade has provoked a debate on account of his tactless warning, 'Be careful of those comrades who enter parliament'. The whole of Germany knows the 'parliamentary swamp flower', Dr. Paul Levi. He shall serve as a living example for the labour movement. Therefore, comrades, be careful,

---

12 Herman Gorter, *Die Klassenkampf-Organisation des Proletariats*, Berlin: KAPD, 1921. An English-language translation, under the title *The Organisation of the Proletariat's Class Struggle*, can be found online at the Marxists Internet Archive.

do not let yourselves commit betrayal! Had the Spanish comrade not spoken on this subject, there would not have been any debate, and everybody would have spoken more to the point.

Comrade Tom Mann stated in his speech yesterday that in his early days he was a syndicalist, and that he has now changed his views. He claims that it is necessary at present to join the unions, revolutionise them, and win them over. In this regard, I wish to express my sorrow that Comrade Tom Mann was not first old and then young. As this is a physical and natural impossibility, we had better stop talking about it. I wish to state that we, before the war, were already in favour of industrial organisations and their unification. This question was not then of such great importance as it is today.

Albert Lemoine (France): Comrades, dealing with the question of the relations between the trade-union International and the Communist International, it is necessary to be clear and positive and not resort to tricks. In the interests of both of these organisations, we should not carry back home from this congress any ambiguous resolution.

My aim is to ask you, Communists within the unions who constitute the majority of this congress, to tell us bluntly if you intend to avail yourselves of the militant revolutionary trade unionists in order to conquer the central trade-union confederations and afterwards, with the mighty moral and material support of both Moscow Internationals, wage a ruthless war on them, looking upon them as counterrevolutionary organisations.

As an opponent of subordination – whether disguised or not – and based on my credentials and as a member of the French delegation (and I would not have come to Moscow with any other credentials), I believe myself entitled to say that we, the French syndicalists, are strong enough to defend ourselves and not allow ourselves to be easily absorbed in France. We shall deeply regret having wasted our time in party strife, by which our class adversaries will doubtless benefit.

If I speak here this way, it is because I consider it necessary to quote something on the independence of the trade-union movement in relation to the Communist Party said by a man who counts for something in the revolutionary movement of the world: Comrade Lenin.

In his pamphlet 'The Party Crisis' (Petrograd, 1921), Comrade Lenin states:

> We must combat the ideological discord and the *unsound* elements of the opposition who talk themselves into repudiating all 'militarisation of industry', and not only the 'appointments method', which has been the prevailing one up to now, but all 'appointments', that is, in the last analysis,

> repudiating the *Party's* leading role in relation to the non-Party masses. We must combat the syndicalist deviation, which will kill the Party unless it is entirely cured of it.[13]

Further he writes:

> A syndicalist and anarchist deviation has been definitely revealed in our Party in the past few months. It calls for the most resolute measures of ideological struggle and also for purging the Party and restoring its health …
>
> Hence the views of the Workers' Opposition and of like-minded elements are not only wrong in theory, but are an expression of petty-bourgeois and anarchist wavering in practice, and actually weaken the consistency of the leading line of the Communist Party and help the class enemies of the proletarian revolution.
>
> In view of all this, the Congress of the R.C.P., emphatically rejecting the said ideas, as being expressive of a syndicalist and anarchist deviation, deems it necessary:
>
> First, to wage an unswerving and systematic struggle against these ideas … [14]

Now, we call this a clear and frank speech: Pay attention! I shall present, with as much frankness as I can command, my own point of view, that of a French revolutionary syndicalist, and tell you why I cannot accept the submission of syndicalism to the Communist Party, even at the risk of being called a fool.

To us from France, it will mean, in the very long run, renewing the old quarrels in our parliamentary history, our violent internal struggles within the trade unions, where particularly politicians and revolutionary syndicalists were in conflict since the formation of the First International (London, 1865 [1864]). This was the case even after Amiens (1906), although the struggle was conducted with more flexibility and skill, especially in the organisations partly or wholly dependent on the state, such as railroads, post office, mines, etc. The consequence of such political interference was that revolutionary syndicalist activity was considerably weakened. It did not achieve in the field of realisa-

13 Lenin, 'The Party Crisis', in *LCW*, 32, p. 53.

14 Lenin, 'Preliminary Draft Resolution of the Tenth Congress of the R.C.P. on the Syndicalist and Anarchist Deviation in Our Party', in *LCW*, 32, pp. 245–8.

tion as much as it was entitled to. Only a small number of genuine revolutionary organisations benefited by the improvement of conditions obtained by a hard struggle.

The originality of revolutionary syndicalism in France is that it intends to emancipate the working class from the tutelage – whether disguised or not – of all those who proclaim the supremacy of politics over economics. For we cannot admit that the bourgeoisie or petty-bourgeois intellectuals should presume to do all the thinking for the working class and have full control over their minds. Besides, we must not forget that in epochs of revolutionary upheaval, separate individualities, moved by this desire of playing a conspicuous part in the revolution for which the people have shed their blood, may not always be inspired by fair and sincere motives.

Much more than is generally believed, the workers, in spite of the obstacles put in their way by capitalist society, seek to acquire a superior mind by studying the works of the great masters of human thought, whom they honour. But if workers are entitled to and must utilise the services of bourgeois or petty-bourgeois intellectuals, they must not allow the latter to use them as a springboard or an object for investigation, even if they be of the highest moral integrity.

Within the Red Trade Union International, French revolutionary syndicalism does not contest the right of the proletariat in some countries that have not had the experience of parliamentarism or capitalist concentration, that do not possess class movements or economic struggles leading to a spirit of resistance by the working class – we do not contest their right to accept suggestions and directives of the Communist Party of their country should they deem it necessary.

It could not be any other way in Russia, which lacked parliamentary experience and well-established trade-union organisations. We fully understand that the honest and courageous elite of revolutionary workers, knowing full well the propitious moment, through working-class violence (and maintained by the dictatorship of the party) have replaced the former autocratic system with the system of Communist state politics, which will have to be replaced in turn by a communist economic system.

In France itself, with strong commercial and industrial development, we shall not be able to pass directly to the communist economic system. National and international capitalism has reached a maximum state of development of human exploitation.

After dispossessing the owners of the social riches, the working class, by means of its economic class organisations, will expropriate capital and take into its hands the direction over production, endeavouring to remove and suppress, as rapidly as possible, all that was bad and irrational in the management of production. It will at the same time utilise the main industries of the country, which have already attained the maximum of capitalist concentration, such as railway companies, banks, factories, marine transport, post office, refineries, flour mills, textiles, metallurgy, and so on.

French syndicalism intends to utilise as much as possible the technical forces that the country possesses. For the moment it cannot refuse the assistance of non-union technical specialists who would submit to the control of the producers, liberated from the oppression of capitalism and its lackey the government, and who would participate in a disinterested way in the construction of the new system. Technical specialists could fill responsible posts in the various branches of industry, under the direct control of the proletariat.

Revolutionary syndicalism affirms again its workers' charter, which stands apart from any political school of thought. It works toward the total disappearance of the wages system and boss control. It intends to establish, by its own means, by the direct participation of the people in the rational organisation of the social economy, the proletarian government of tomorrow. In achieving the above tasks, it inevitably accomplishes a political act, as it will have to forcibly assume economic and moral responsibility for the nation's forces and of its relations with the world.

To deny this right to syndicalism would imply that the French proletariat, organised in trade unions, has not reached the degree of maturity and development necessary to be fully invested with the proletarian power, and that only a political party and its elite will have to steer the working class toward emancipation.

We might fear, in this case, that a new centralised state would be established under a new label exercising the power by means of the dictatorship of a party elite and of a new aristocratic bureaucracy that, in principle, should work to allow the working class to attain the maturity of intelligence in all fields of human activity.

We are entitled and duty-bound to be on our guard lest the political party, which holds this whole machinery of the new state and exercises full control over the minds of the working class should at any moment compel the working class to give up the possibility of reaching its complete emancipation. We have the right to say that this cream of the aristocracy of the party will be forced to defend itself against the working class using, for this purpose, all its state machinery. French revolutionary syndicalism will not accept such subordination and cannot consent to being guided by political parties, absorbing the whole of the social hierarchy, making it not possible to conquer the great masses.

We energetically state our sincere desire to work for and devote all our forces to the realisation of a world revolution, as generalised as possible. We fully realise the urgency of supporting the Russian Revolution not merely in words but by the concentrated and violent action of the toiling classes. We are aware that by abandoning the Russian Revolution to its fate, to starvation and exhaustion, we would be diminishing our own possibilities for a long time of bringing about a revolution, the possibilities of which are very great in some of the countries adhering to the Red Trade Union International. The imperialist war has plunged world capitalism into difficulties that it will be unable to overcome through a lasting period of social peace and the support of the treacherous leaders who are still under its influence.

Regarding the mandate we have, the French delegation declares that it cannot accept any representation whatever of the political International within the trade-union International.

Nevertheless, in compliance with the will expressed by the revolutionary syndicalists to collaborate with all organisations that are revolutionary not just in words but in deeds, and in the primary interests of the international movement, we declare ourselves ready to find the proper ways for establishing effective connections with the political International, on condition that we preserve our autonomy.

We do not refuse, by any means, to build a bridge. The French delegation has unanimously adopted my motion indicating under what conditions this bridge should be built between the two organisations. This statement is now in the possession of the Organisation Commission. We are quite willing to come to an agreement. It is for you to decide, bearing in mind our deep interest in the Red International of Labour Unions.

Nin: Comrade Williams has the floor.

George Williams (USA, IWW): The question of the relationship with the Third International, according to the different reasons advanced by the speakers, resolves itself finally into the question of the nature and the course that the revolution should take. Comrade Lozovsky, indicating the reasons why there should be a connection between the Comintern and the Red International, claims that the Comintern is the most important of the two bodies, that is to say, that the political current of the revolution is more important than the economic one. Therefore, it is necessary to discuss the nature and the course that the revolution should take.

Now, what is revolution and what are its aims? I think everybody will agree that the principal aim of revolution and the reason we want a revolution is to emancipate the workers from the capitalist system, a system that, as Marx pointed out, robs the workers of the full product of their toil. On those grounds, the IWW stands and says that since the workers are robbed of their production in the factories, the revolution should be purely economic. It should not be and cannot be a political revolution, because the state is subordinated to the economic power – at least that is the position in America. I think that it is the position everywhere. The Communist International, on the other hands, wants a political revolution, that is, they want to give to the workers part of the fruit of their toil in the end. We state, with regard to the transition period, that no revolution is complete unless economic development reaches the point where the workers get the full product of their toil.

Now then, the question arises as to who is going to be the leader of such a revolution. The position of the IWW is this: that since the emancipation of the workers will be their own work, they are the ones who should lead the revolution through their own organisations. As to the Communist International, I want to pose the question of its pretensions to have a predominant influence at our conference. I pose this fully recognising the Communist International's merits and its revolutionary work.

A French comrade, speaking about the situation in France, said that they had already had three revolutions but still the workers are in the same state as in other countries that had not had a revolution. Now this point is in contradiction with the political statements of the Communist International, which believes in state bureaucracy. This bureaucracy stands above the working class. The question is posed: Who are the individuals who will be the best bureaucrats? We know that workers are aware they are robbed, and we know that emancipation can come only from the workers themselves; they will certainly not rob themselves. They will demand ultimately that the means of production be turned over to them as members of an economic organisation, and that the economic organisation of which they are members will in turn then become the administrators of industry.

Russia is an example of that. I know that Russia has had a successful revolution, has overthrown the political power, and yet we find in all the statements of Lenin that the revolution in Russia will not be complete until the developing economy increases production to the necessary level. This is the conclusion of the representatives of the state capitalist theory: either industry attains a degree of development, or industry will go to other countries. Therefore, the question is posed there just as in any capitalist country. Economic emancipation of the working class must be made through industrial organisations. Trotsky says that we must be careful lest the revolution fail due to economic imbalance, which would push us back to start all over again.

Now, I maintain that industrial organisations are the only ones that can carry on production after the revolution. That is apparent all over the world, that the workers who produce items should take intelligent action on the distribution of them.

The position of the IWW toward the Communist International is that the revolution, once it takes place, must be of a purely economic character. Since the representatives of the Communist International place such a high importance on political power, I would advise them to conquer it above all in the small industrially backward countries, to thereby surround world capitalism.

As for the relations between the trade-union International and the Communist International, we must have reciprocal representation between these two organisations. Those who proclaim the supremacy of the Communist International must nevertheless recognise the need for a purely industrial International, composed of workers' organisations; otherwise it is impossible to explain the convening of this congress. We could in fact have drawn workers' organisations directly to the Third International, and thus avoided a waste of energy.

In conclusion, I would like to emphasise that the opposition of the IWW is from a purely American standpoint, as in America a considerable contingent of workers are deprived of the right to vote and excluded from political activity. Among our members are a large number of workers who migrate from state to state looking for work, and are deprived of the right to vote according to the electoral laws of certain states. These workers are all indifferent and sometimes even hostile to political activity, which is of no interest to them.

Nin: I give the floor to Comrade Reinstein.

Boris Reinstein: Comrades, the question now under consideration is an old one, which we have been fighting over ever since the First International. It caused a split in the First International, and ever since it has been the object of continuous debates.[15] The question can be reduced to this: Is the trade-union movement a sufficient weapon for the overthrow of the capitalist order, or is it yet necessary to unite the workers on the political level with the object of gaining control of state power, for the purpose of crushing all attempts by the bourgeoisie to re-establish the old order?

15 A reference to the debate with the anarchist current in the International Workingmen's Association (the First International) that was headed by Mikhail Bakunin. A split between the Marxists and anarchists occurred in 1872.

It was my lot thirty-two years ago, when I was still an immigrant, to be present at the First Congress of the Second International in Paris in 1889, and I remember at that congress how the representatives of the trade unions from different countries – France, Switzerland, and Spain – used the same arguments that some of the comrades are using now, and tried in different ways to build a fence around themselves, so as not to participate or have anything to do with the political struggle. At the three following congresses in Brussels, Zurich, and London, fights took place between representatives of Marxism and anarchism, between partisans of Bakunin and partisans of Marx, and in the end it was seen that these two currents cannot coexist; both of these movements cannot go hand in hand. At the London Congress in 1896 it was decided not to work together with the elements opposed to political action.[16]

I hoped and still hope that our comrades, the Bakunin partisans, have not lived through the years of war and revolution in vain. I hope that they have truly learned the lessons of the revolution, that they have understood that the political and trade-union spheres must not be confused with the social-democratic movement of the failed Second International. I hoped and still have hopes that they understand that the Communist movement in Russia and in all other countries is based on the fundamental principles of Marxism and that it stands without question, first of all, for the unconditional overthrow of any and every form of oppression. This is plainly embodied in the programme of the Communist Party and also in the Constitution of the Soviet Republic, as well as in all the literature of the Third International. The syndicalists should understand that the international Communist movement alone is able to develop that strong progressive power that alone will realise the social order, and in which the oppressive state mechanism can no longer exist. I hoped and still hope that the comrades who came here from countries where, for one reason or another, the Bakunin prejudice against political action is still widespread, will learn from the experience of the Russian Revolution that before you can destroy a capitalist state, it must be first wrested from the hands of the bourgeoisie.

But it would be stupid after wresting the guns from the bourgeoisie to throw them aside. No, the workers must hold firm to those guns so that they can

16 At the Second International's congresses in Brussels (1891), Zurich (1893), and London (1896), small numbers of anarchist delegates opposed to political action caused disruptions in the proceedings. As a result, at the London Congress a resolution was adopted that recognition of political action was a precondition for participation in the Second International's congresses, thus excluding anarchists from future participation. For the text of the 1896 resolution, see Taber (ed.) 2021, p. 62.

always stand ready to smash any and every counterrevolutionary organisation. Only then will the possibility arise of realising and establishing the old hopes of all the best elements of society, when we shall turn swords into ploughshares through peaceful labour. So far we have not reached that stage here or in any other country. Whether the anarchists want it or not, the workers are ready to direct their efforts to disarming the capitalists and holding in their own hands the power of the state, and using it on their own behalf until the time when the old order of things shall be no more.

I remember when comrades of the opposing side who came out against close contact and joint work with the Communist International had, to a certain extent, a real cause and grounds to be opposed to the political struggle led by the social-democratic parties of the Second International. But they have no grounds to be opposed to revolutionary political action by the genuinely Marxist Communist parties of the Third International. I hoped they understood that for the workers not to try and gain control of state power – while at the same time saying that the question between labour and capital can be settled only by the trade unions and economic organisations – means that they do not understand our position. It means that they have not outlived their prejudices against political action based on revolutionary Marxism. It means that they let the great issues that shook the entire world pass them by, and remained the same blind and prejudiced people.

I hope that these comrades even now, during their stay in Moscow, will take advantage and get acquainted with the methods and action of the Russian workers, so that they might understand the causes of this struggle, that it is not a specifically Russian system of struggle, but is an inevitable system of struggle for all the oppressed masses of the world, wherever capital reigns. I hope therefore that in spite of their prejudices, in spite of their sometimes fanatically hurtful tactics against the Communist Party, they will understand that even with the possibility of being outside the Communist International, they will no doubt in the long run understand that for them, as fighters for the interests of the workers, working for the success of the Communist programme is not only their honorary right, but their sacred duty.

(*The session is closed until 11:00 a.m. on 11 July.*)

RILU-Comintern Relations (continued)

(*Session opens at 11:10 a.m. Comrade Lozovsky in the chair.*)

Lozovsky: The session is opened. We shall continue the debate on the reports of Comrades Rosmer and Tom Mann. Comrade Disch will speak now.

Johann Hermann Disch (Germany, General Workers' Union): Comrades! We are now in a period when the exploited are waging a revolutionary war against the exploiters. In this war the Russian workers and peasants, as the most oppressed class, have conquered the bourgeois state and established their own state. It is, then, a matter of course that in the international combat now going on, they have acquired a sort of supremacy, or dominant position. The initial stage of this supremacy became evident when the first steps were undertaken to create the Third International. The International is the framework within which are grouped all the forces striving to establish the economic and political equilibrium of the Russian proletarian state. This cannot be otherwise, and we are the last ones to make it a point of attack. What puzzles us are matters of quite a different sort.

Our Russian comrades are quite fond of quoting Marx on every occasion. Now, the basis of Marxism is historical materialism, which teaches us that the ideology of entire classes bears a quite definite relation to the conditions of production obtaining in a given society. It is certainly true, as Lenin himself stated as far back as 1919, that state capitalism for Russia is an advanced stage of improvement upon the forms of production hitherto prevalent in Russia. In that case it becomes quite clear why we, who come from countries where far more advanced forms of production predominate, cannot regard the Third International as a 'Communist' International. Hence comes our opposition to this sort of international organisation.

The comrades who try to mix up the theoretical conceptions of the IWW, the syndicalists, and the Unionists[1] with those of the Bakuninist opposition of fifty years ago are poor dialecticians. No serious and far-seeing political leader in the movement would now be willing to confine the struggle to merely

1 A reference to members of the German *Unionen*, such as the Free Workers' Union (FAU), the General Workers' Union (AAU), and the Gelsenkirchen Free Workers' Union.

 | DOI:10.1163/9789004712867_012

political or merely economic action. Such a view would be just as untenable as the view brought out here somewhat loosely during the discussion that the political International should at all times be let loose to rush in and out like an unsaddled horse. Only one International is entitled to last for a long time. The time has not come as yet for the Soviet International, but the time has come for concerted militant action on a communist basis and an international scale. If in the course of historical development economic and political problems have become merged into one, and economic conflicts have at the same time assumed the forms of political warfare, why then have two different Internationals? Our International should assume both functions.

If we recognise that the Third International is, during the stated period, the necessary instrument for carrying out the policy of the Russian state, we expect that the basis upon which the trade-union International is to be built will give us freedom of action to transform it into a real International. For this purpose we must be completely independent of the Third International.

The fact that we have thousands of adherents in different countries is certainly a development closely connected with the fundamental economic basis of those countries. When our Russian comrades inspired others to take the field against the Unionists, we can fling at them what a political leader, the other day, said in another connection: 'You are using historical materialism in this question as did the Negro who tied his suspenders around his naked body for display'.[2]

I have already pointed out that different economic conditions lead to different forms of the class struggle. I should like to point out something that is of fundamental importance in this connection, namely, that a given social system is never overthrown through the agency of an organisation built on the same fundamental principles. State centralism, for instance, swept away the last remnants of feudalism; the same is true of the rigid state centralisation of 1917, which did away with the underdeveloped forms of production prevalent in tsarist Russia. But the same centralisation will by no means overcome the highly advanced capitalism of Western Europe, with its enormous resources.

We have to develop new forms. We see new organisations organically shoot up alongside of political parties, trade unions, etc., which enter at once into

2 Disch is referring to Karl Radek's racially offensive remarks at the Third Comintern Congress. See Riddell (ed.) 2015, *3WC*, p. 414.

bitter combat against everything connected with bourgeois ideology. To these new organisations neither the conception of centralism, nor that of federalism, can be applied. Their growth will determine how fast 'power' and 'state power' will die off.

I come now to the concrete question. Those who sent us here did not think that we should have to listen to endless speeches about the advantages of the tactics of strengthening and creating cells within the old trade unions. We must note, in this connection, that the Moscow theories remain at present as unchanged as they have been hitherto. What has brought us here is the natural proletarian tie binding us to the Russian proletariat, and we are still facing the question of how to help Russia and ourselves.

How do the organisations represented here mean to carry out the common revolutionary struggle in the future? In what way do these cells in the old trade unions [*Gewerkschaften*] think to work in concert with our unions [*Unionen*] to destroy the powerful machinery of the counterrevolutionary trade-union bureaucracy?

If the syndicalists and Unionists of all countries were invited here to persuade them to go back to the organisations affiliated with Amsterdam, well then, we are much obliged, but positively refuse such company. We will never go back to a point of view that our revolutionary members have rejected. We must make this point quite clear at our congress. Either you form here an International of those who stand for the 'cell' tactics within the old trade unions; in that case, the revolutionary syndicalists, the Unionists, and the Industrialists [IWW] have no connection with this International; we shall go ahead and form a true International of revolutionary workers. This requires that we trace here the fundamental lines that will guarantee the trade-union International free play and development of all its energies alongside the Third International.

The choice is in your hands. You are taking measures to steamroll the independent revolutionary organisations at this congress. You thus assume a heavy responsibility for the decisions of this First World Congress. The Russian workers, who have offered us their hospitality, control you. Help them in achieving the victory written on the banners that welcomed us on our arrival: 'Workers of the world, unite!'

Lozovsky: Comrade Gieseler has the floor.

Emil Gieseler (German Seamen's Union): We have just heard a splendid report made by Comrade Disch, dealing with the views adopted by the independent revolutionary organisations. I shall therefore only make a brief statement as to the character of the views of the German revolutionary seamen.

Mention was made of the relation of both Internationals guaranteeing each other equal rights. We, revolutionary water transport workers, who are suspicious by necessity, cannot but ask ourselves what equal rights could mean under the present circumstances, when one of the organisations does not as yet exist.

The equality of rights really depends upon the equality of combat forces, but the trade-union International can only deploy its forces in the future. The equality of rights that the two organisations guarantee to one another ought to be created by the process of mutual work and struggle. This cannot be decreed in advance. The opinion that the Third International has frequently voiced in the press is that it is desirable to unite all genuinely revolutionary organisations independently of their political platforms. But now it becomes more and more clear to the representatives of the independent revolutionary organisations that what is actually meant by unity is the subordination of the organisations within the Third International to its slogans. The German seamen, being united in a revolutionary organisation, reject such a manner of obtaining unity, and we do so with well-considered arguments. To regard us on that basis as not being revolutionary would therefore not be right.

The German revolutionary seamen are in a most difficult position. The slogan 'Back to the old trade unions' is for us absolutely unacceptable. Confidence in the trade-union International can only be strengthened by the process of joint struggle and activity. To speak now about the relations of both Internationals would be the same thing as eating an apple you do not have. The trade-union International has to develop its ideological content independently and without any pressure; it must show its revolutionary will.

Comrade Lozovsky thought it opportune to emphasise again the views of the political International of remaining in the old trade unions, as this method led to drawing two million workers toward the Communists [in Germany].

We too think it necessary that all members of the old trade unions inclined to communism should be drawn in. Perhaps it will also be possible to draw in the rest of the three million who were organised in trade unions before the war. The others, who have joined the trade unions after the war, are petty bourgeois who, hoping to be guaranteed peace as a result of the class collaboration proclaimed during the war, have rushed into the trade unions. To think it possible that those six million can be conquered for communism is overly optimistic. For the German seamen's union to follow the slogan of returning to the old trade unions would be equivalent to suicide for any revolutionary movement in its ranks.

The conclusions made by Comrade Lozovsky indicating the special importance of systematic organisation and agitation only strengthen our point of view, because systematic organisation and agitation is possible only when our independent organisations are preserved. Moscow must help us to create a living International. Moscow is doing so by convening the present historic meeting. It ought to prepare and make easier the way for us, but not pressure us. In the first case Moscow will deserve our thanks and will be guaranteed in the future. But if one speaks of tactics without having an organ in which to realise them, then it would only be wasted energy.

Such a case would mean to operate with a non-existent International, or with a second edition of the Communist International. It would be better to elaborate the tactics of the congress itself, and create the trade-union International despite all the obstacles.

Lozovsky: Comrade Tom Barker has the floor.

Tom Barker (Argentina): Comrades and fellow workers! I greet the congress in the name of the Federación Obrera Regional Argentina Comunista [FORAC] and the Federación Obrera Regional Uruguaya, both of which desire to unite on the economic field. The first organisation numbers over 250,000 members and is the largest industrial organisation in South America. It is militant, class-conscious, and revolutionary. The Federación Obrera Regional Uruguaya is much smaller, operating, as it is, in a much smaller country. Its membership is over 30,000 members.

Comrade Lozovsky has touched upon the Berlin Congress, and says that the tendency of the revolutionary syndicalist unions represented there was a change of front to the stand formerly adopted by organisations of this character.[3] It was quite true, for the concessions made towards political parties striving towards the same revolutionary end was a sign that the Berlin Congress attempted to find a road upon which the left industrial movement could travel in spite of ideological differences.

It is well known that the federalist form of organisation predominated in the Latin countries, while Marxist organisations were more evident in the North European and North American countries. This wide range of political and industrial opinions was largely caused by the varying conditions in different countries. In Great Britain, we had a working class subordinated to 200 years of capitalism. The love for capitalist institutions had, through generations, been bred into their bones. In Russia and Japan capitalism was much younger. Therefore, we would not succeed if we desired an immediate conjunc-

3 For the December 1920 syndicalist conference in Berlin, see p. 145, n. 19.

tion of advanced and revolutionary unions, unless a fair amount of elasticity was allowed. Rigidity in this regard would mar the success of the congress, for it would practically bar every militant union south of the Panama Canal from coming into the movement to which they properly belong.

When Gompers sent his call to the South American proletariat to rally to his Pan-American Federation of Labor at Laredo in Mexico, no organisation of any importance in South America responded.[4] Neither did any of them join or participate in the Amsterdam International. They had great hopes about Moscow, and Moscow could not afford to lose them by a rigidity that would leave the federalist revolutionaries of Latin America unallied to the world proletariat.

Speaking of the word *syndicalism*, it was a comparative term. Its meaning varied from country to country and from time to time. In 1912 Comrade Tom Mann was a syndicalist, living within the old moth-eaten unions. What was 'syndicalism' then is now the 'cell' system of penetration favoured by the Communist International. In Argentina a 'syndicalist' is simply an old-fashioned trade unionist, belonging to a yellow federation, who marches behind the local Gompers of his country. In Russia we are told that certain syndicalists are counterrevolutionaries. In Italy, however, the syndicalists are at the forefront of the industrial revolution. Therefore in this congress, with many nationalities present, we have to remember that when we mention the word *syndicalism*, we will have the word and our speeches interpreted in various ways.

The Berlin Congress did good work and it helped prepare the even more important congress that is now taking place. This congress can well afford to be as elastic as the one in Berlin, so as to unite actual revolutionary organisations and create a relatively strong organisation. Amsterdam was strong, and we needed something more than a shadow army in which there might be more generals than soldiers.

The FORAC instructed me to vote for separate organisations for the Communist International and the Red Trade Unions. The Uruguayan federation is also a purely economic organisation, and does not favour any political party. Anyone who knows South America is well aware that the genus 'politician' is not highly regarded there. Every year there are two or three political revolutions in Latin America, which merely means that the 'outs' throw out the 'ins'

4 On the initiative of the American Federation of Labor, a Pan-American Federation of Labor was organised at a conference held 13–16 November 1918 in Laredo, Texas, on the US-Mexican border. One significant Mexican trade-union formation did participate in the PAFL: the CROM (Regional Mexican Workers' Confederation).

by force, without waiting for election day. The working class of these countries does not interest itself much about these matters, as they affect its miserable position only to a very minor degree. They regard politics as a sleight-of-hand game.

This suspicion has been strengthened since the rise of the political socialist movement to some prominence. These gentry have sold out their class, or rather the class that they pretended to speak for. They became chauvinist, and in 1919, the socialist daily newspaper *La vanguardia* was used as a medium of advertising goods boycotted by all the union federations.

To confuse things these politicians covered up their treachery with tidbits of Marxist phraseology. Thus between the professional political parties and the yellow socialists, it has become a widespread opinion among the Latin American proletariat that politicians are anathema and that political parties are objects of suspicion.

The revolutionary unions therefore take great care to prevent political control, which in the past caused much division, especially in cases when union leaders were in the pay of the parties and precipitated strikes for the purpose of embarrassing a party in power to the advantage of a rival party. Therefore, in Latin America it took much work and propaganda to convince industrial workers that there was such a thing as a revolutionary party. Only in Argentina were there no difficulties between the Communist Party and the Federación [Obrera] Regional Argentina Comunista.

My instructions make it incumbent on me to urge the creation of a Red Trade Union International standing on its own two feet, and drawing from its own immense reservoirs the capable driving force for making itself strong and formidable. It would certainly accelerate the growth of the International, and attract to its banner organisations that would be worthy and would be an asset in every sense of the word. Cooperation between the party and the Red Unions would be desirable, and the separation between the economic and political organisations would attract such unions as those of Latin America.

In conclusion, I plead for elasticity so that the syndicalists of Spain, Portugal, and Italy and the revolutionary federations of South America can enter the Red Trade Union International and definitely smash both Amsterdam and the Pan-American Federation of Gompers. I call for the creation of one great industrial organisation of the workers of the entire world.

Lozovsky: Comrade Artem has the floor.

Artem [Fyodor Andreyevich Sergeyev] (Russia): Comrades, the fundamental issue that divides us at this congress is the question of the forms of our organisation. Should it be one organisation of the masses, of the revolutionary part of the proletariat that aims at freeing the broad masses of the proletariat from the influence of the reactionary leaders, and, having organised them, to prepare them for a successful fight against the bourgeoisie? Or is this going to be a small organisation only, a sect that is afraid to assimilate the poor, innocent masses that follow the yellow leaders, and that intends to create, within the shell of capitalist society, the embryo of communism? These two tendencies have been presented to us here very distinctly. Therefore, when we approach the question of relations between the Communist International and the trade-union International we must consider it from the point of view of these differences of opinion. Which point of view we accept – that of the vanguard or that of the sectarians – will determine our relationship to the Communist International.

The sectarian view has been clearly presented by Comrade Tom Barker. To our regret he failed to relate all the consequences that should result from such a viewpoint. Comrade Barker stated that we wished here to form a single industrial organisation for the working masses of the world; otherwise there was no benefit in convening one. We know Comrade Barker well. He is an old industrialist, an IWW member. His statements could not be construed otherwise than as a suggestion to the congress to limit its aims to an international organisation of small unions that for different reasons could not or would not join the large unions and remain outside of them. This recommendation is not a new one; it is the struggle of the old principle of the revolutionary elements leaving the large unions and forming sects.

Still we are not anxious to limit our work solely to the strengthening of the small chips that have broken away from the old labour unions, and who within the shell of the old society wish to create the embryo of a new society This new miniature organisation would not add anything, or would not increase the strength of the proletariat and its fighting power. On the contrary, had we taken such a step, it would have disrupted the labour movement, weakening its strength even more. Those small bodies of workers who are hostile to the bourgeoisie, if removed and isolated from the masses, would be a source of impotence and of insufficient strength for the labour movement. They would attract the attention of the enraged bourgeoisie, which, with the help of the yellow leaders of the large unions, would persecute them, with the absolute indifference of the broad masses. It is self-evident that it would be absurd on our part to demand of such numerically small groups to declare an open fight against the bourgeoisie. Such tactics would be detrimental, and therefore the leaders of these groups will be obliged to advise the workers – as they already do – to keep calm and cool, so as not to provoke an attack on the part of the bourgeoisie. Hence the leaders of these groups will have to play the part of pacifiers of the revolutionary movement, a role no less reactionary than the one played by the yellow leaders of the old unions.

Our divergence is not confined to the above-mentioned facts alone. Differences on structure also result in differences about the relationship of the vanguard to the masses as a whole. Our goal is to remove the masses from the influence of the reactionary leaders, and push them toward the overturn of capitalism. As opposed to the watchwords of bourgeois democracy, we put forward the dictatorship of the working class. As the revolutionary vanguard, we tell the masses who we are, what our aims are, and what our relations with the masses are. The revolutionary vanguard must acquaint the great masses with the principles of the class struggle and define these clearly.

It is not just a question of the masses. We must also have a clear and exact conception of the responsibility of the vanguard. We must penetrate the masses, win their sympathy, and awaken hatred toward our enemies. Only then can we expect to develop an organisation, a vanguard that would be able to unite all the masses and lead the fight.

Between such a vanguard and the sect suggested, there is a wide difference. The sect cannot recognise the part to be played by the vanguard, and does not share its tasks. The vanguard says to the masses: we are Communists; we are the leaders who are aiming at the organisation of the working class for the overthrow of the bourgeoisie. We come to the masses and say that as long as the power lies in the hands of the bourgeoisie, you are slaves, you cannot improve your positions, you cannot change conditions in your favour. We are for the dictatorship of the proletariat, which is necessary for the establishment of a new social order. We must take upon ourselves full responsibility for the revolutionary struggle, and do so at each and every step. We must put forward the choice – revolutionary vanguard on one side, and on the other, vanguard of the bourgeoisie and their lackeys, the yellow leaders of the labour organisations. We must win the masses' confidence; otherwise they will refuse to follow us and instead follow Gompers, Thomas, Jouhaux, and Company.

The question arises then: What say our leftist comrades, the sectarians? Would they call on the masses to distrust their vanguard? If that should be the case, we will fight them tooth and nail. They have not said anything new here. They are repeating the same old story of ten or fifteen years ago, without adding anything new to it. But it looks radically different now. At present, when the question of the Communist International's supremacy is being discussed, they conjure up the old socialists and petty-bourgeois groups, and appear to be saying that the Communist International, the revolutionary vanguard of the working class, is composed of fraudsters, villains, and good-for-nothings – in short, no different from the lackeys of the bourgeoisie who call themselves socialists. Our leftist comrades fully understand the great difference between the yellow socialists and us. Still, they do not realise that their antagonistic position toward us renders the yellow organisations invaluable help.

Tom Barker advises our trade-union International to stand on its own two feet. I ask him: When will he himself stand firmly on his own two feet? My answer to him is: he will stand erect only when he joins the organisation and the vanguard that expresses its uncompromising struggle against capitalism and the bourgeoisie. Otherwise he will be standing on feet of clay, constantly doubting and wavering as to whether to be or not to be with the revolutionary vanguard fighting against the bourgeoisie, for the dictatorship of the proletariat.

I know, everybody knows, that at present it is ridiculous to convince the workers that you are against politics. The bourgeoisie has laid bare the forms of its dictatorship and has made the workers anxious to destroy it and establish in its place the dictatorship of the proletariat. The sympathy of the working masses toward Soviet Russia is the approval of the dictatorship of the proletariat. It is therefore impossible to object to the dictatorship of the proletariat. Some of our leftist comrades have invented a new scheme – the dictatorship of the proletariat solely through the economic organisations, through vaguely organised masses. I ask you, comrades, tell me the meaning of this schema? You cannot at present get rid of this vital question by simply using empty phrases. We have four years' experience of the proletarian dictatorship in Russia, and we already know some of the immediate requirements necessary for each accomplishment. The recommendation of our leftist comrades would bring many problems, one of which is the following:

Does the watchword 'dictatorship through the economic organisations' mean that it would be necessary, every time the conditions of the struggle become unbearably heavy and the masses are panic-stricken, to make the dictatorship dependent upon the results of a vote of these panic-stricken and wavering masses? I say no, not under any circumstances. This is just what our enemies have demanded, when Russia was in a state of prostration. But this state of affairs did not affect us in the least. Nothing could hold us back; we could not afford to hesitate. We first introduced the proletarian dictatorship, and afterwards we have given ourselves over to the judgement of the masses.

You favour the opposite; you recommend that a vote should be taken first. Under such circumstances you are bound to find yourselves in the same boat with the yellow fakers in the big unions who use it whenever the power of the exploiters is endangered. Your last argument is the physical impossibility to explain to the masses the necessity of the supremacy of the Communist International over the other organisations and primarily over the Red Labour

International. You state that the role of the vanguard is all fine, but we cannot tell the trade unions to submit to this vanguard. However, I think we can approach the masses with these watchwords, and we will do so.

I am ready to debate with the leftist comrades over the need to give to the Communist International the leading role in the struggle that is unfolding. I am convinced that the majority of workers will be with us. Any worker of the rank and file will easily understand us, if we explain to him that despite the diversity of forms in our struggle, still the class struggle as a whole remains the same. The struggle of the masses in separate and different spheres of social life can be crowned with success only when the entire labour movement is united and has one aim in view, when it is directed by the more advanced and conscious organisations, the leadership of which is thoroughly and carefully tested.

What can comrades of the extreme left say in opposition to this? In my opinion nothing, save empty phrases that we must not trust the vanguard. As a matter of fact, many of their arguments rest upon this, which is a very dangerous slope. We cannot let it pass silently. We will fight against such prejudices, which can shake the masses' faith in the vanguard. This fight at present must be considered one of the principal tasks of our revolutionary work. When our leftist comrades go to the workers and tell them not to trust the vanguard because it is a party, they say and act the same way as the yellow leaders and are a menace to the revolution.

In general after the Kronstadt events,[5] it was unforgivable for a militant to counterpose the masses to their vanguard. In Kronstadt too some naïve anarchists thought they were doing a revolutionary deed by organising the masses under the watchword of 'dictatorship through the masses' instead of through the Communist Party. As a matter of fact, it was a platform drawn up with the consent of the Russian bourgeoisie to overthrow the proletarian dictatorship. And these great fighters for the proletariat against the vanguard found security under the roof of the Finnish hangmen. This lesson must not be forgotten.

Yes comrades, there are differences of opinion between us. There are two ways of approaching the subject, and it is up to us to make our choice. We must, under the present circumstances, cultivate a strong will power, in order to retain the leadership of the vanguard, which intends to consolidate its influ-

---

5 Soviet soldiers and sailors in the Kronstadt fortress, on an island close to Petrograd, mutinied on 2 March 1921, at a moment of grave economic crisis and widespread discontent in Soviet Russia. The revolt was forcibly suppressed by 18 March. Bolshevik opponents such as Mensheviks, Socialist-Revolutionaries, and anarchists pointed to the fate of the Kronstadt rebellion to bolster their opposition to the Soviet regime, as did openly counterrevolutionary and imperialist forces. Following the revolt's end, some 8,000 rebels fled to nearby Finland.

ence in the trade unions and unite virtually the entire working class. This can be accomplished only when the working class puts its entire confidence in the Communist International.

We must insist upon having elections in the trade unions under the following watchwords: Who is for the proletarian dictatorship and who is against it? Who is with the Communist International and who is with our enemies? We would not want to elect individuals just because they are honest; they must also be militants devoted to the interests of the working class and enjoying their confidence. We cannot defeat the bourgeoisie unless the broad masses put their confidence in the vanguard. The vanguard will succeed if the organisations are headed by responsible militants. As soon as this is accomplished, the relations between the Communist International and the trade-union International will be clear. It will be the relation of a part to the whole, of a section to the entire organisation. This is our aim; this is what we fight for. Without it a revolution is impossible, and we must clearly state this before the working class.

Lozovsky: Comrade Haidt has the floor.

Ernst Haidt (Austria): Comrades, in the pre-war period we had the opportunity of noting the ossification and breakdown of the social-democratic trade unions and their inability to fight. But the same phenomenon was seen in the syndicalist movement during this period.

First of all, I want to say that we must not completely discard the syndicalists' methods of struggle. On the contrary, I think that before the war, when the syndicalist organisations legitimately opposed the social-democratic trade unions, we propagated and applied the fighting methods of the syndicalists, thereby creating the first movement among them. During the course of the war, unity was reached between syndicalist organisations and Communist fractions in support of revolutionary action.

But it must be said that the point of view on which the syndicalists take a stand, namely to not take part in politics, is at the present moment very harmful to the struggle between labour and capital, for at the present moment every economic question is dependent on political conditions, as for instance, the refusal to pay taxes for the last few years in Austria. That was a purely economic question, which brought about revolutionary mass action.

The supposed neutrality of the central trade-union confederations is pure appearance. The activity of the social traitors and social pacifists, who try to make the masses impervious to all ideas in contradiction with theirs, must be defeated by us. When we were weak, the old trade-union leaders cared little about us. So long as the unemployed were the only ones with us, they didn't pay attention. But when we began to have influence within the unions, the struggle began. They have thrown down the gauntlet. 'Get out of the organisation; organise your own Communist trade unions'. We had to decline all these invitations, for fear that such a split would reduce our forces and our influence on the masses. We remained in the trade-union organisations with the intention of increasing the number of Communists, of conquering the organised masses, of defeating the old leaders in these organisations and compelling them to speak the truth on all questions and come out into the open.

Comrade Arlandis's assertion that the syndicalist organisations ought to receive first place, while other trade-union organisations should have only a consultative voice, is incorrect. The broad masses are not seen in the syndicalist organisations, nor in the independent organisations. We must first create the broadest foundation for revolutionary propaganda. I believe that the road we are taking is the one that will lead us to the revolution.

We need have no fear about the subordination of the Red International of Labour Unions to the Communist International. What are the demands of the Communist International? It calls the workers together for revolutionary action, and for the final liberation from the capitalist yoke, for the establishment of the dictatorship of the proletariat. If all the comrades understand this and are inspired by these principles, they need not fear the influence of the Communist International. Then together we will look for the final road to victory of the workers against capitalism, and we will find that road. In that way the congress will get the opportunity to create a firm organisation for the coming struggle. (*Applause*)

Lozovsky: Comrade Bouwman has the floor.

Engelbertus Bouwman (Netherlands): The delegates of the National Labour Secretariat have come to Moscow to attend the congress of Red Trade Unions with the sincere intention of taking an active part in creating one big consolidated Red International of Trade Unions. This International will carry on a vigorous fight, not only against the bourgeoisie, but also against the yellow Amsterdam International. 'Against Amsterdam' – this is the view of the vast 'independent' masses organised in trade unions.

Still, it does not yet mean that unanimity reigns in the Dutch trade-union movement with reference to the question of the Red International of Trade Unions. On the contrary, since the very moment of the Berlin conference of syndicalists in December 1920 a vigorous struggle began, under the leadership of the chairman of our central organisation, B. Lansink, Jr., against Moscow and the Red International.

The main subject of debate consists of the relations between the Red International and the Communist International. The opponents of Moscow try to say that the trade-union movement will have to submit to the dictates of the Third International and the Communist Party. In spite of this, the majority of the revolutionary trade unions of Holland are not against Moscow. Our comrades want to create a big trade-union International in opposition to Amsterdam. This International must be the refuge for all revolutionary trade-union organisations of the world.

Nevertheless, they do not agree that the trade-union International should be subordinate to the Third International or to the Communist Party. Taking this into consideration, comrades, I would like the executive committee of the Red International not to insist that the Red International of Trade Unions place itself under the guidance of the Communist International. Such different views should not serve as obstacles to creating a revolutionary trade-union International.

I want to say a few words about the Berlin syndicalist conference.[6] Clauses 1 and 5 of the declaration adopted by that conference are the most important.[7] With reference to the first clause, there was a prolonged discussion on the question of the 'dictatorship' of the proletariat. Against the 'dictatorship' were principally the German syndicalists, as they were of the opinion that by not recognising the proletarian dictatorship, the dictatorship of the party can be avoided. As a matter of fact, no one at the conference was against the dictatorship of the proletariat. But being against the term and trying to avoid it, you find throughout the whole resolution the word 'power' instead of 'dictatorship'. In my opinion it is only a form of expression.

Every sincere revolutionist has the duty of supporting the dictatorship of the proletariat. I therefore think that the vast masses of the revolutionary workers of Holland, united by the National Secretariat, will stand for the proletarian dictatorship, and there will be no difficulties in their joining the Red International.

With reference to clause 5 of the Berlin declaration, Comrade Lozovsky said that the syndicalists are against working together with the Communist International. That is not true. This clause says that the syndicalists are ready to work together with political organisations that share the views of the Berlin resolution. Nevertheless, the whole fifth clause was rather unclear. A representative of the Provisional International Council of the Red Trade Union International,

6 Bouwman himself was a delegate to the December 1920 Berlin syndicalist conference.

7 For the six points of the Berlin conference resolution, see p. 207.

Comrade Belenky suggested some amendments that in their essence led to the idea of the two Internationals working together in critical stages of the struggle. This amendment, supported there by me, was rejected by a majority.

In conclusion, allow me to state the unanimous view of the Dutch National Labour Secretariat:

The trade-union movement must and will in the future be closely connected with the Communist International, as this is necessary for making the revolution. It is, on the other hand, necessary to reckon with the reality and with the very different conditions in various countries. The history of the development of the trade-union movement of Britain is different from the history of other countries. The trade-union movement of Britain and Germany, for instance, has assumed a quite different character than in America, Spain, Italy, or Holland. We need not close our eyes before the difficulties prevailing in those countries.

I therefore appeal especially to the Russian comrades not to stick to their point of view as a dogma when this point is discussed. I hope that when the relations between the Red International and the Communist International will be considered, we may find a formula that will unite all the delegates. And this will give an opportunity to create a revolutionary trade-union International that will work in accord with the Third International.

Lozovsky: Comrade Heckert has the floor.

Fritz Heckert (Germany): When we approach the problem of neutrality of the trade unions in connection with the political organisations, we are faced with two questions: What are our capitalist enemies doing? What role is neutrality playing in these organisations, which Amsterdam represents as neutral?

Answering the first question, we find that our capitalist adversary does not think to be neutral at all. He is always prepared to rally his forces whenever there is a question of attacking the proletariat. We noticed this clearly enough during the negotiations between Mr. Walter Rathenau, the political representative of the German bourgeoisie, and Mr. Loucheur, the political leader of the French capitalists, on carrying out the provisions of the Versailles Peace Treaty. In spite of the fact that both of them were deadly enemies during the war, they at once came to a mutual understanding in their attitude toward the proletariat. They both declared, in spite of the agreement with the Washington Bureau of Labour at the League of Nations, that the workers and the workers' organisations should not take part in these negotiations.

With regard to Amsterdam, one may say that its neutrality is a downright swindle. In reality its adherents refuse to carry on the class struggle against the bourgeoisie. Their 'business-like' collaboration with the bourgeoisie shows this quite clearly.

Let us put this question to ourselves: What are the objectives of the Communists, and what are those of the workers who are striving to organise themselves in the Red Trade Union International?

The Communists find that in order to free the workers from capitalist slavery, it is necessary to overthrow capitalism, and by seizing power the proletariat creates possibilities for restoring the economic machinery of the country.

The Communists wish to carry out this fight rapidly and successfully by centralising in the most effective manner the forces of the working class. Therefore, we separate ourselves from Amsterdam and seek to unite in the Red Trade Union International. Thanks to their tactics of collaboration with the bourgeoisie, the adherents of Amsterdam are playing a double role, and are instrumental in supporting the dictatorship of the bourgeoisie. By so doing they dropped the struggle for the overthrow of capitalist exploitation. The revolutionary workers who are united in the Red Trade Union International wish to carry on the fight against the capitalist enemy. They wish to destroy the enemy with the objective of creating a new social order. For this reason they reject all compromises with it. Common sense tells us that if our capitalist adversaries, in spite of all contradictions prevailing within their class, are united against the proletariat, the workers should also submerge all their differences regarding their aims and tactics of the struggle and unite their fighting efforts.

It is easier for the capitalists to arrive at a uniform point of view on aims and tactics in the struggle against the proletariat, owing to the fact that the capitalists are defending their social system, their unlimited domination of the means of production. As for the large masses of the workers, they have at the beginning of the struggle no clear understanding of the substance and aims of the struggle. They attain this clearness only through long and hard trials and reflections. Therefore, it is the duty of the more advanced elements of the proletariat who are leading the revolution to point out to the labouring masses the real aims and tactics of the struggle, and not to make concessions to reactionary ideas.

The greater part of the syndicalists – the French syndicalists chiefly – say, 'We should not engage in politics; the workers do not wish that.' And the syndicalists refer to the fact that they are nearer to the masses. We Communists can answer them: the masses can never have clear points of view before they enter the struggle. The masses are always subject to wavering. An example of this was the chauvinism that took hold of the masses in 1914. Politics are repulsive to a large part of the revolutionary workers not as a result of deep understanding, but as a result of practical experience with a gang of bad politicians.

It is not sufficient to gather all workers who may seem revolutionaries in one mass. An unorganised mass, however large, can find neither unity nor uniformity of tactics or clearness of aims. It is the duty of the class-conscious element of the proletariat to serve as a leader, with clarity of understanding. This is an important condition for our victory.

If we listened to those like the French syndicalists, who say that the fact that the masses do not wish to have anything to do with politics and do not understand its significance must be taken into consideration – we would certainly be committing a crime against the revolution. Through hard trials workers will become convinced that we are right and they are mistaken, but this conviction will cost them the lives of the best revolutionaries. Even when a part of the proletariat does not understand our aims, we should say decisively: before the common enemy we wish to preserve the unbreakable front of the revolutionary vanguard – we stand for the Communist International on an international and national basis.

Where the road of neutrality in politics leads is shown by the direction that the development of German syndicalism has taken. The latter refuse to combat the bourgeoisie by violence. They are against the dictatorship of the proletariat. They are passive in the revolutionary struggle that the working class of Germany began against the capitalists and the adherents of Amsterdam, which has cost the lives of 20,000 German proletarians.

We read in *Der Syndikalist* (no. 19):

> Since before the war Prussia has been the centre of reaction … when you think of it you understand what a great change social life has undergone. One must be astonished and glad as to how extraordinarily quickly the mentality of the population has developed in such a short period.

Furthermore, the author of the article is attesting that Germany is the freest country in the world. Concerning the Amsterdam International, he says:

> The Amsterdam International of Trade Unions has included in its programme a well-planned organised campaign for the socialisation of industry. It declared war on capitalism and the capitalist state, and has adopted the general strike as a weapon. What is most important, Amsterdam has declared that only trade unions can be the creators of the

> socialist commonwealth, and they must be free and independent, not subordinated to any political party. Therefore, it is a mistake to look upon the Amsterdam International as a yellow organisation.

This development of German syndicalism proves to us that neutrality leads to the recognition of the capitalist state and the Amsterdam trade-union bureaucracy. We shall never take such a course. (*Applause*)

Lozovsky: Comrade Sirolle has the floor.

Henri Sirolle (France): It is not on behalf of the French delegation that I am going to present the French syndicalist point of view. It is only on behalf of a section of this delegation, although a section that includes a great number of trade unions, federations, and revolutionary elements. It has been possible for this section, in a short period of time, to affirm itself with vigour and clarity at this congress. We represent the tendency that Comrade Monmousseau introduced in a motion he presented that was carried at the congress of the railway workers' federation, and since then by different other congresses of departmental unions of syndicalists and of *minoritaire* unions through the resolutions of our Comrade Monatte. The comrades who do not share this conception will come afterwards to explain to you the reasons why there are various interpretations of French syndicalism.

Comrades, it is necessary first of all to clearly lay out our view of revolutionary syndicalism. All the interpretations given from this platform have borne a character of a systematic distortion of the syndicalist idea. In many Western countries – in France, Italy, Spain, and particularly in America – certain organisations sprang up that adopted the platform of revolutionary syndicalism, accepting its philosophy, its methods of action, and its ideology. It must be specifically stated here, when attacks against syndicalism are being put forward, that all the criticisms raised are directed against the purely corporative and narrowly trade unionist approach, and not against the organisations in the countries I have just mentioned.

French, Italian, and Spanish syndicalism, along with that of certain American organisations, is animated with a political spirit. Their struggles have always been political struggles. Anti-militarism, anti-parliamentarism, the organisation of production, the study of statistics, the study of economics and labour regulation – all this is included in the work of our organisation. We were always attacked not by the political proletarian groups but by the bourgeoisie of the different countries, which systematically and persistently persecuted us just because the syndicalist organisations occupied themselves with politics.

In France civic guards and civic unions are organised to break the effort of the syndicalist organisation, because its activity in the domain of politics expanded more and more.[8] In Italy the fascists have directed their raids against the working-class organisations, burning the labour exchanges.[9] In Spain, against whom is the attack of the defenders of the bourgeoisie directed? Against the militants of the syndicalist organisation, because they conduct an active fight in both the economic and political sphere.

When we talk about neutrality and independence of the trade-union movement, we must specifically point out one of the clauses of our doctrine. We consider that the syndicalists and Communists are linked together, because in our opinion syndicalism aims to abolish the wages system and to replace existing capitalist society by an organisation adequate to meet the needs of the working masses. We are marching toward communism. We gather in our organisation the vanguard of the proletariat, which has a clear vision of the aims of syndicalism. The vigour and vitality of our syndicalist organisations is determined by the presence of firmly dedicated comrades inside of them able to determine, explain, and lead the communist masses to the communist goal. We believe that a revolution is not the result of a party or a group, but the materialisation of the dissatisfaction of the masses. A revolution, no matter which one or in what country it takes place, is always made by the majority of the revolutionary people.

We revolutionary syndicalists say that it is the organisation of the masses, the proletarian masses and their most conscious elements – that only these elements are capable of driving forward the working masses and encouraging them to organise a society of the future that would give them fullest satisfaction. If we are against the moral influence of political parties, it is because we consider that these parties do not live with the masses, but are outside of them. They group together individuals with particular affinities, coming from different classes and different milieus. Because they do not know the everyday struggle, these parties cannot carry the necessary influence with the masses and lead the masses to their emancipation. We equally consider that our syndicalism develops on account of its continuous struggles directed at this aim.

8 For the Civic Guard in France, see p. 75, n. 23.

9 The labour hall, or labour exchange (*camera del lavoro*) was a local union centre that played a large and militant role in the Italian labour movement, going back to the 1890s. These centres became a major target for Fascist attacks. Between January and May 1921, 243 labour halls were attacked, with 202 workers killed and over a thousand wounded.

The war and the revolution have brought some changes in the spirit of syndicalism, and thus to its fundamental forms of organisation. We are ready to adapt those syndicalist organisations to new forms of activity, making the syndicalist organisation a powerful weapon of proletarian struggle and aspirations. Our syndicalist organisation is a fully developed administrative organ that has the same spirit as the soviet. In our country the organisation grows into two parallel branches. On the one hand, there are the departmental and local unions with their federative principle of organisation; on the other hand, we have centralised industrial federations.[10] We believe that the combination of these two types of unions forms a central popular economic organ, charged with the federal organisation of local unions and the centralisation of the country's economic life. As for other parts of the machinery in the transition period, they must direct the country's general activity. We believe that we must draw into these union organisations the elements responsible for organising a new society under our own control. This centre of popular economy, formed by the combination of local unions and industrial federations, will have the right to appoint and oversee all officials. That is why we say that our syndicalism and its spirit are determined by our economic realities.

We repeat again that the only true class organisations of the proletariat are the trade unions, and their spirit of transformation. This is the only form of labour organisation that could actually get the working masses together into natural groupings having common interests. Thus the ever-growing mass acquires the consciousness of its class interests.

Once more I must state that within this mass is a proletarian elite, carrying a class consciousness and spirit. All our activity consists of instilling class interests and consciousness in the masses. We believe that we alone, working with the masses and among the masses, can lead them in this direction. The driving power of our syndicalist organisation is indisputable; it was proved by the results obtained in those countries where it was applied.

Here in short – because for the development of the theory a quarter of an hour is insufficient – are the reasons why we cherish so much the independence of the syndicalist movement.

It is precisely the spirit of syndicalism in the above-mentioned countries that allows it, at the moment of revolutionary conflict, to organise violence by

10 This dual structure was a particular feature of the CGT. First, it was organised territorially around local unions in a particular area that were grouped together in intercraft '*bourses du travail*' (labour exchanges), with buildings made available to local and regional unions. Simultaneously the local union was part of a national federation of workers of the same craft. Thanks to Michel Pigenet for research assistance.

the proletarian forces for purposes of both offence and defence, which inevitably leads to the dictatorship of the proletariat over the exploiters. The transition period from capitalism to the proletarian regime is a period of destruction, and at the same time a period of construction, creating the organisations, organising the cadres. During this period it is absolutely necessary to destroy all counterrevolutionary action that attempts to restore the past, stand in the way of the revolution, and hinder its future advance.

The revolutionary elements looking to the future do not have to fear proletarian violence. To determine who are our friends and who are our foes, we shall turn to the masses. It is the proletariat, the masses, the working class, which organises the violence. They are the ones who know where the bourgeoisie is, or as our writer Flaubert says, 'The being that thinks basely';[11] this being can be found among the capitalists and working masses alike. Within the working class we recognise those with base thoughts; they always are dreaming of a return to the past, and our organisation of violence has a solid foundation because it rests upon the dictatorship of the union organisations.

The necessity of our independence from the Communist International arises from higher motives than we are usually credited with. We consider the interests of the revolution ahead of the interests of the party. Revolution is the action of the masses and not of the party. Therefore the interests of the revolution cannot be subjected to the interests of a party, but entrusted to the revolutionists of the world.

To emphasise more strongly what I have said, to show you our correctness, so that you understand our passionate opposition to the ideological leadership of the Communist Party and the Third International, I must remind you of a resolution adopted by the Russian Communist Party, at the same time as it is being proposed here and at other congresses to accept collaboration with the Communist International.

(He reads extracts from the resolutions of the Tenth Congress of the Russian Communist Party attacking syndicalism.)[12]

When such declarations, representing a systematic application of an opinion antagonistic to our view, are adopted, we cannot be blamed for our desire to safeguard our independence. We want to conserve our independence, because we learn from history how the left elements of the working-class movement

---

11 In a letter to George Sand, French novelist Gustave Flaubert wrote, 'I call bourgeois whoever thinks basely'.

12 For the original resolution drafted by Lenin, see 'Preliminary Draft Resolution of the Tenth Congress of the R.C.P. on the Syndicalist and Anarchist Deviation in Our Party' in *LCW*, 32, pp. 245–8.

now are used to create a mighty power, and then are discarded mercilessly when they are no longer needed. We do not want to be fooled, to be playthings, to be dupes and puppets.

This is why we urge you to conserve the full independence and autonomy for the Red International of Labour Unions. We openly warn you that any attempts to subordinate us to the Third International, to suppress working-class opposition, will be met by our ferocious and energetic resistance, appealing to the masses for the defence of our idea. Nobody has the right to utilise the proletarian masses for the realisation of the interests of a party, sect, or group. In the name of these masses, we, living among the masses, suffering with them, refuse to become playthings in the hands of a party.

Lozovsky: Comrade Tommasi has the floor.

Michel Relenque[13] (France): Yesterday I was put on the list of speakers after Sirolle. I consented to change places with Tommasi, but on condition that I would be given the floor after him, as I understand that the time only was limited but not the list of speakers. I absolutely insist on having the floor after Comrade Tommasi.

Lozovsky: After the speech of Comrade Tommasi, the congress will decide whether Comrade Michel may have the floor.

Michel Relenque: But I insist on having the floor after Comrade Tommasi.

Lozovsky: You cannot put conditions to the congress; the congress will decide.

Sirolle (*from his seat*): At the beginning of this congress I asked whether the number of speakers was limited. Why then do you refuse the floor to Comrade Michel?

Lozovsky: I ask you not to interrupt the work of the congress.

Joseph Tommasi (France): I have to excuse myself for having taken the floor at a moment when the French delegation has not yet reached agreement on the possibility of getting themselves in harmony with the congress. My intention is not to make a speech about theory and doctrine.

13 Referred to simply as 'Michel' in the proceedings.

I would not have taken the floor had it been possible for me to remain among revolutionary comrades, on the same grounds on which we met some days ago. But with deep emotion I have to state that after the speech of Comrade Sirolle, which from this platform expressed not only his own opinion, but the opinion of many comrades, I must take the floor to answer him.

What did Comrade Sirolle say in his speech? He said that we must distrust politicians. We must remove from the path laid out by syndicalism all those elements who do not emanate from it, but strive instead to subordinate its action to interests that are not its own.

Nevertheless, among those who wrote the Amiens Charter are many who can be put on the same plane as the politicians we fought against in the Socialist Party, at a time when there was no mention of a movement toward communism.

Unfortunately these declarations, made by Comrade Sirolle and Comrade Lemoine, are sometimes in complete contradiction with the needs of the moment. We could refer to the 1910 strike by rail workers and the response to its dramatic end by the newspaper *L'Humanité*, which was not at all revolutionary.[14]

In 1910 it was a question of implementing the Amiens Charter, at a time when a movement was launched that could be held within the strictly corporative framework. Those who were at the head of the organisation and had the responsibility of leading the movement were partisans of [trade-union] neutrality. This did not prevent them from being influenced not only by Socialist Party politicians, but even by a politician of the Radical Party.

If we follow the development of the workers' movement, we see that very often the actions of syndicalists in our country came about through successive negotiations between politicians and those who pretend to fight politics.

We agree with Comrade Sirolle and those who think like him that we are against the politicians, against those who many times attempted at different congresses to lay their hands on French syndicalism. Yet Comrade Sirolle is contradicting himself when he says, 'We do not want politics; we do not want politicians to lay their hands on trade-union action'. But then he says, 'We know that it is impossible to do without politics; we concede this point to you, and

14 The French general railway strike began 12 October 1910, led by the CGT's National Union of Railwaymen. In response, the government – led by prime minister and former socialist Aristide Briand – issued a mobilisation decree, putting all railway workers under military discipline, and making all those who failed to obey the summons liable to prosecution. The strike was ended 18 October. The Socialist Party and *L'Humanité* strongly opposed Briand's move, but largely restricted themselves to parliamentary protests.

even with this purpose intend to create within the syndicalist organisation a political party, a conscious minority that would play the leading part, which will have to act on the day its actions will be needed.'

Your syndicalism is imbued with a political spirit, and just on account of this we fail to understand how you can possibly profess to be politically neutral.

There are, alas, outside the syndicalist organisation a large number of workers who do not recognise the necessity of organisation, who believe emancipation is possible by means of a great revolutionary act. There are a large number of militants at the head of trade-union organisations, even reformist ones, whom Comrade Sirolle cannot see as likely to help on the day of action.

Recall the movement of 21 July 1919; recall how it was killed and in what a disgraceful way.[15] This purely syndicalist movement, aiming to lend its assistance to the Russian as well as the German revolutionaries, undertook to give us proof that politics was permeating it and even sapping its organism little by little. No politics in common with the Socialists, with the Communists – and at the same time our General Confederation of Labour was killing the movement with the help of the politicians. And you know this full well, Sirolle, since I said it on the floor of the Lyon Congress.[16]

On the evening right before the movement was killed, they went to the Ministry of Public Works, to which they were summoned by a vague telegram requesting Mr. Bidegaray come for a short talk with the minister of public works. Two days later, it was impossible for the French syndicalist organisation, professing its political neutrality, to act in a revolutionary spirit on 21 July, to stand against the policy of the governments of France, Britain, and Italy.

What do those men say in their defence? They say: We cannot follow you in the successive fields you attempt to involve us in; we are politically neutral, we stand for neutrality of the syndicalist movement. And Sirolle knows as well as I do that these men, three-quarters of those men, have at the present moment in their pockets the destiny of the political Dissident Party of France.[17] Sirolle even knows that among those who at the present time define themselves most sharply and say, 'No politics within the trade unions' are precisely the same ones who, when the Committee for the Third International in France and the Communist Party attempted to make the Twenty-One Conditions pre-

15 For the scheduled strike of 21 July 1919, see pp. 168–9, n. 10.

16 A reference to the CGT congress held in Lyon, 15–21 September 1919.

17 A reference to the French Socialist Party. The term 'Dissidents' was commonly used to describe the French SP minority that opposed the majority decision to affiliate to the Comintern in 1920 and rename itself the Communist Party. After the split, this minority retained the old party name.

vail without any amendments, were among those who voted for the motion and said, 'Excuse me, no reservations'.[18] Syndicalism is a movement that cannot remain politically neutral, and is obliged to be political. The next day we signed the motion of the Committee of the Third International. And these are the same comrades who say now: We do not want to occupy ourselves with politics.

Yet at a moment like this, when revolutionary action is nearer every day, when the different sections of the bourgeoisie are accumulating their weapons against us, when the possibilities of coercion are accumulating and threatening us in any possible action of ours – is it at such a moment that we're supposed to investigate whether one person or another is doing their duty? Has not the moment arrived to deliberately put aside personalities and face realities and events? I thought it was possible to come to terms with Comrade Sirolle, and in the course of a conversation I had with him we agreed that the moment had come to look for the possibility of agreement. I was therefore deeply affected to hear what Sirolle just proclaimed here.

The congress is not a place where one expects one's opinion to prevail, or else failing to obtain satisfaction, to smash the windows. Oh, there are plenty of bourgeois windows to be smashed. Let us preserve ours!

You assert that the French syndicalists will disavow us. Perhaps in any case we shall tell the syndicalists what they have never been told before. We shall tell them: If the moment has not yet come for you to look for possibilities of common action, well, we shall have to meet again face to face, and necessity will impose itself. You refuse to make the smallest concession at the congress; you refuse to let yourself be permeated with a spirit other than the spirit that animated you upon your arrival here. I hope this will not last.

There is one point to which all France will listen attentively: not to keep outside the International of Moscow, but to act in concert with all the revolutionaries of the world, to unite around an idea that has already given proof of not serving the interests of the enemies of the working class. We shall ask the trade-union International – we shall do it animated with a different spirit than yours, and hoping to make our spirit prevail on you – we shall request the International to not be as strict as it seemed to be at the outset; we shall ask it to look

18 The Committee for the Third International, formed in May 1919 as continuator of the Committee for the Resumption of International Relations (formed in 1916), helped campaign for the transformation of the French SP into the CP.

The 'Theses on the Conditions for Admission' to the Communist International approved by the Second Congress – referred to commonly as the Twenty-One Conditions or Twenty-One Points – can be found in Riddell (ed.) 1991, *2WC*, pp. 765–71.

over together with us the possibility of an attenuation of its statutes. We shall request that it take into consideration the particular situation of our country, to recall the fifty years of our history, often glorious and often also painful. We shall tell them that we too have achieved something, and we feel sure that this will be taken into consideration. You arm yourself with the statements of men like Monmousseau and Monatte, but we could just as well use these statements against you. But the moment should be well chosen for such a thing. It seems to me that we ought to have the courage, both sides, to acknowledge that the Amiens Charter, which was necessary to us in 1906, has now suffered two attacks – that of the war and of the Russian Revolution – and it is not something that should become fossilised, losing the ability to see what is happening.

Great events are developing. We did not come here to this congress in order to find satisfaction for our doctrines and conceptions. We have come here to meet revolutionists, to meet the men who decided to use all means in their power in order to attain the aim that we aspire and are devoted to. For our part, we desire that our fraction, the French syndicalist-communists, should take along with them at least the results of an effort that could allow us to start with new revolutionary work. I am deeply convinced that once and for all you will be willing to come to terms, that we will agree among ourselves and, taking heart, cast aside certain formulas we have used too much. We must decide not to have two formulas – one for the public, the other for ourselves. The formula ought to be indivisible. In spite of the right you possess to combat our ideas, to have a different point of view, we tell you that you have no right to proclaim that unless you find total satisfaction you will not remain …

Interruption: We must remain ideologically with the Red International.

Tommasi (*continues*): If your wish is to remain ideologically with the Red International, I wonder how you can pose questions such as, 'Should the syndicalist party be a political party or should it remain politically neutral?'

Sirolle: Ask the chairperson to let me put a question to you.

Lozovsky: Agreed.

Sirolle: Comrade Tommasi, I am sorry that you, whom I so often talked to, misinterpret in this way the spirit of French syndicalism. I assert again that French syndicalism contains a political spirit, since it pursues communist aims and since it draws all the elements within itself for the inauguration of communism. We are not reformists, whatever you may say to the contrary.

Tommasi (*continues*): Comrade Sirolle's remark does not embarrass me in the least; it leads me to my conclusion. We both agree that syndicalism is apolitical or politically neutral no more; moreover, we state that it includes all the elements of politics. The question should be, therefore, which is the political tendency that prevails within syndicalist organisations? But our mind does not work in this direction. You know full well the formula employed in the *minoritaire* resolution at Orleans: 'Collaboration with the political party that will act in a revolutionary way'. This was a formula that would have been impossible during the war.[19] The Russian Revolution seemed to make you waver and to shake your doctrinal basis. Some of you are inclined to take this step and declare that you are willing to enter into negotiations with the political party, acting in close cooperation with those who were acting in a revolutionary way.

Let me remind you of something that happened a while ago – you, who now accuse me of distorting the spirit of French syndicalism. While I was secretary of the union federation of the Seine, I called a meeting of the executive committee of which you, Sirolle, are a member, explaining the situation created by the government's military call-up of the Class of 1919,[20] the clamour of the war, the clouds accumulating on the horizon. It was I, a member of the Communist Party, who asked you to maintain certain forms of the call to action. It was you – politically neutral and who attacked the political party because you are afraid that it should take hold of the movement – who then said, 'Enough discussion, time is dear, let us head over at once to 37 rue Sainte-Croix de la Bretonnerie;[21] we are ready for action'. What more should we ask for? Did we not meet here to prepare for revolutionary action? There is no disagreement any more. When we have black sheep in our way, we shall know how to cast them aside. And we shall have to do it on both sides, as you know. We shall be so strict that nobody escapes. So cast aside your reserves. Keep your doctrines and tactics. I am not aware that at this congress any revolutionary element would refute your policy.

For my part I should not refute it. You say that the Communist Party is by no means qualified to start revolutionary action within the syndicalist organisa-

19 The CGT conference in Orleans, held 27 September to 2 October 1920, was the scene of an intense struggle between the reformist majority and the *minoritaires* of the Revolutionary Syndicalist Committees (CSR). The latter's resolution called for affiliation to the Moscow trade-union International then being organised, as well as expressing a willingness to cooperate with revolutionary political organisations, as long as trade-union autonomy was respected. The CSR's resolution received 602 votes, compared to 1,479 for the *majoritaires*.

20 On 3 May 1921 the French government called up the conscription class of 1919 – some 200,000 men who had reached draft age that year – to meet its manpower needs for occupying the Ruhr Valley, with the goal of forcing Germany to pay war reparations.

21 The central address in Paris of the French Socialist Party, dating back to 1912.

tion. I am entitled to answer you that I find again within the political organisation the most solid foundation of the trade-union organisations. The elements cooperating with you within union organisations belong likewise to the Communist Party, and under such conditions you have no right to underestimate our action, just as we have no right to undervalue yours. We have to look for points of contact. I appeal at the congress to our comrades – French syndicalists, pure syndicalists, anarcho-syndicalists. We must find points in common and remain within the trade-union International in order to be able at last to work in a revolutionary way.

Lozovsky: Comrades, a number of delegations have proposed ending the discussion on this question, and allowing the reporter to make his concluding remarks. We shall then read the resolution and those statements that may be made by separate delegations in connection with this resolution. The following question is to be decided now: whether we are going to continue or discontinue the debate. If the congress is willing to continue then they may do so, but if the discussions break off, then permission may be granted to the speaker to read his resolution. Or perhaps we should postpone the reading of this resolution to the night session? Comrade Rykov will speak on this question.

Alexei Rykov (Russia, All-Russian Council of Trade Unions): Comrades, a number of questions were raised in connection with the relations between the Red International of Trade Unions and the Communist International. This question embraces the whole practical work of the revolutionary movement. There is a special point on the agenda on the tactics of the revolutionary trade unions. Several delegates who have not yet stated their views have signed their names to speak on the question of relations between the Red International of Trade Unions and the Communist International. Comrade Michel wants to supplement Comrade Sirolle's remarks. I am afraid that there will be some other French delegates who will want to supplement Comrade Michel's remarks. There are more speakers from the national delegations who have not stated their views. We are not guaranteed that this will not be supplemented. The question as discussed by the majority of speakers has gone far beyond the limit of the narrow question of organisation that stood on the agenda. You will have the opportunity of hearing comrades from other countries when the question of tactics of the international trade unions will be discussed. I suggest we discontinue discussion on this question, and listen to the resolution. At any rate, a copy of the resolution can be handed in to the commission for its final drafting and to hear separate suggestions when the resolution will be discussed.

Michel Relenque: Comrades, I do not intend to expound the theory of syndicalism. It is only a question of clarifying a point that has been formulated here imprecisely. I don't have to give a very long speech; I actually wrote it down and can read it to you. When I registered on the list yesterday, I did so with the idea that all delegations could have all their members available to speak, and that only the time limit for the speeches was limited. I absolutely want to have the floor in my turn. I ask the congress that I be heard.

Lozovsky: It's not about you personally, Michel; these are the interested parties. There are still nineteen speakers registered. We must now decide whether or not to close the discussion.

Michel Relenque: I thought we were not closing the discussion yet. We are wasting a lot of time, in which I would have already had time to read my speech.

Lozovsky: Everyone has speeches in their pockets. It is not possible to consider the question from a personal point of view.

Michel Relenque: I believe that the congress is entitled to maintain that its bureau itself declared that the number of speakers would not be limited, but that only the time limit of the speeches would be limited. The congress is big enough to decide now that we give the right to speak to all registered speakers.

Godonnèche: The congress had also decided that it would be the delegations that would designate their speakers. However, you designated yourself. You were not even able to appoint a speaker for your fraction.

Michel Relenque: Someone spoke for closing the debate. Another speaker must speak for the continuation of it.

Lozovsky: Comrade Michel, I state once again that I still have twenty speakers registered. I cannot give the floor to one without giving it to the others. It is therefore a question of deciding a question of principle here.

I will now read out the countries. Whoever votes 'for' is in favour of closing the debate; whoever votes 'against' is opposed to closing the debate.

Austria against. Australia against.[22] Azerbaijan for. Britain against. Bulgaria for. Hungary for. Holland for. Greece for. Germany 11 for and 5 against. Den-

22 This is per the English, German, and Russian texts; the French version has 'for' here.

mark for. Far Eastern Republic for. Spain against. Canada: votes divided. Latvia for. Lithuania for. Luxembourg for. Mexico for. Holland for. Russia for. Ukraine: 11 for and 1 against. France: 7 against and 5 for.[23] Finland for. Czechoslovakia for. Switzerland for. Estonia for. Yugoslavia for. Argentina against.[24] Romania for. America: 13 for and 3 against. Sweden: 3 for and 5 against. Norway for.

A voice: What about Italy?

Lozovsky: The official representatives of Italy said that they had a formal mandate from the CGL to attend only for information purposes, but not to vote. We will discuss this matter tomorrow morning.

Comrades, the debate is closed. I propose to proceed as follows: we will give Comrade Rosmer the floor to end the discussion, and then a short resolution proposed by a number of delegations will be distributed to all delegations. At 8:00 this evening there will be a plenary session. We will start by voting on this resolution, and each delegation will make its proposal on the said resolution.

Michel Relenque: I ask the floor to conclude. Comrades, it is really astonishing to see this Communist congress sitting for so long, discussing all the questions for so long and deepening them; yet we who are gathered here for a constitutive congress are muzzled. These are very important questions where a position needs to be defined and where it is absolutely necessary that we say our piece. No, comrades, I find this unspeakable. The bureau itself considered that the number of speakers should not be limited. And now, when we see that it is a question of specifying the position of everyone, of giving free rein to the ideas represented here, our voice is stifled.

Sirolle: We want to know the number of votes for and against closing the debate.

Lozovsky: There are twenty countries that are for the motion; there are seven against. Thus the vast majority is for closing the debate. You will be given the exact figure in a moment, but there is in any case a majority of several hundred votes for closing it.

The discussion is closed. Comrade Rosmer will now conclude.

23 This is per the English, German, and Russian texts; the French version has 7 votes for and 5 against.

24 This is per the English, German, and Russian texts; the French version says 'for'.

Summary

Alfred Rosmer: Comrades, I shall not take up the attention of the congress for very long, as a considerable number of delegates have already spoken on this question, and the discussion on this point of the agenda is entirely exhausted.

We listened to speeches on the question of the relations between both Internationals from representatives of all countries, of all delegations, and of all possible currents. I shall only endeavour to establish two sets of opinions that were made clear soon after the discussion was closed. It is clear that a vast majority of delegates present here are in favour of the collaboration of both Internationals. It is left only to determine the formula by which these relations will be framed. But it seems to me that even this important point has already been made clear.

The question that provoked the most discussion and the sharpest disagreement was that of the relations between political parties and trade unions. On one side, the comrades from trade-union organisations that were connected with Communist parties, and for whom the collaboration of the two Internationals seemed to be simple and quite natural, have convinced the syndicalists to agree to the proposed formula of collaboration of the two Internationals. They have drawn attention to the fact that conditions following the war have changed, that the former disagreements between the Communist parties and the trade unions belong to the past, that the old political parties that have remained with the Second International are guilty of these conditions, that the question now is about new parties, about Communist parties, which undertake to resume the revolutionary fight all over the world.

The representatives of the syndicalists, on the other side, seem to have maintained to a considerable degree their old traditions. They have declared that in spite of the reconstruction of the old Socialist parties into Communist parties, and inside the new Communist parties, it is just possible that there is a dominating tendency on the part of the Communist elements with regard to the labour movement, and that the political party in its essentials will always seek to subordinate the trade-union organisations. It may be feared that after the discussions these two convictions still remain in the same state as they were prior to the discussion. But if one examines carefully all these syndicalist organisations hostile to the Communist parties and that express even a certain distrust toward the Communist International, then it is easy to become convinced that they have no single platform.

The following words were said by the representative of the German Seamen's Union: 'We will never accept the indications of the Communist International because it demands that we join the old trade unions. We have left them, and will never allow the new organisation created by us to be destroyed and to re-enter the old organisations'. We also heard the delegates of the General Workers' Union of Germany stating that the International does not take into consideration the prevailing conditions. We want first of all, he said, new forms of organisation, and not the rusty weapons of the past that the International is going to give over to us. The same spirit is also found in the speech by the representative of the IWW, and also by the representative of the newly formed French organisation [the CTM] that has withdrawn from the CGT.

On the other side we see that the minority of the revolutionary syndicalists of France have an entirely different opinion toward the representatives of the above-mentioned organisations. On the contrary, they support the idea of staying in the trade unions. They stand for the fight inside the trade unions, so as to bring them to the revolutionary position they were in before the war. We see that the opposition group is far from united.

I deem it necessary to recall the fact that a congress was held in London before the war aiming to create a new revolutionary trade-union International in opposition to the International Federation, whose secretary was then Legien. It seemed that the congress could easily achieve its aims, because the delegates who took part were in agreement on the main question. Still, after a very lively discussion – even livelier than the one we see here – no understanding could be reached between these fractions, and there was a sharp, brutal, and violent split.[25]

What conclusion can we draw from this fact? We can conclude that these organisations are powerless, are not able to carry out their work, and cannot even come to an understanding with each other so as to work out a general line of action. Why? Because these little groups, these little sects, first of all stick to their dead formulas, to their dogmas that seem, in their eyes, superior to others and are considered to be infallible. They imagine that they possess forms of organisation and high revolutionary conceptions so highly developed that they are striving to impose their methods of struggle on others.

The question that is to be solved here is quite a different one. There is a mass movement in all countries at the present time. We have an opportunity to create a powerful International that would indeed unite the whole working class, all the revolutionary groups of every country. We have an opportunity to create

25 The First International Syndicalist Congress was held in London from 27 September to 2 October 1913. The congress was unable to agree on the formation of a new International, but it did create the International Syndicalist Information Bureau as a vehicle of exchange and solidarity. For a detailed account of the conference proceedings, see Westergard-Thorpe 1979, pp. 68–99.

a powerful International that will be able to defend the workers' interests. Up to now we were compelled to note nothing but failures everywhere. After the war, in spite of some successes that were of a provisional character, we are in the same position, which makes it easy for the bourgeoisie to defeat the working class. When I hear the French syndicalists remind us what French syndicalism was, defending it with all their energy, I for one understand that they have grounds to be proud of their traditions. I believe, as they do, that the French trade-union movement will be considered, in the history of the world labour movement, as an epoch of glorious battles.

But when the French syndicalists insist today on preserving syndicalism intact, when they think it is sufficient to dig it out of the grave buried since 1914 by all the acts of treason, then I must warn them that they are making a great mistake. Instead of learning the lesson that the imperialist war and the Russian Revolution have taught them, they dream of leading the revolutions in a direction that may be excellent in theory, but that hardly fits in with the demands of the moment. When syndicalists counterpose their organisations to political parties, their position appears to me very shaky.

There is certainly a great difference between trade unions and parties. The unions unite workers only, and by their very existence they are realising the class struggle, pitting the workers against the bosses. Parties, on the contrary, unite elements who do not belong to the industrial working class exclusively, and it may therefore happen that they lose contact with the masses. Clearly in this case, they cannot claim to interpret the working class. But parties so composed – and we find many of them in this state – can become reformist.

If we wish, on the other hand, to take a very striking example, we had better turn to the Russian Communist Party. Can we deny that this party is a real party of the workers? I think that no one will deny this. Thus, if the Bolshevik Party has played such a prominent role, it is due to the fact that it has always been the exponent of the interests of the working class. Could this party have made the October Revolution, taken over entirely the organisation of the new order, as well as carrying on the struggle with the bourgeoisie, had it not been the faithful exponent of the will of the workers and peasants of Russia? Certainly not. I have heard from many persons belonging to different parties and very hostile to the Communist Party in the period of the October Revolution, that the Communist Party was undoubtedly the only one that expressed the real interests of the working class, and for this reason no one but this party could take upon itself the great task of leading the great Russian Revolution.

Two of the French comrades have quoted some passages of Lenin's pamphlet that, in their opinion, were so clear that they did not find it necessary to comment on them. I would say this is rather superficial. The pamphlet from which they quote the passages is part of a very big complicated discussion on the role of the trade unions, which was carried out last year in Moscow. By taking out one fragment only they are crippling the sense of the quotation that is brought forward. It is certainly impossible to go into details here on the dispute that was waged. I only wish to point out that the foreign comrades who were at this time in Moscow found great difficulty in understanding the shades of thought of different groupings that had been formed at the time within the Russian Communist Party. But the question that had to be solved could be put forward only at a time when the revolution was in progress; this was the question of the relations between the trade unions, soviets, and the party.[26]

I wish only to add here that the chief representative of the Workers' Opposition (one of the groupings at that time) is at the present time a member of the Central Committee of the Communist Party. He has defended his views, as any member of the Communist Party can do, but the party congress rejected his point of view. Nevertheless, he consented to become a member of the Central Committee of the party.[27]

The syndicalist comrades are somehow afraid that the Communist Party will not become really revolutionary; they seem to be afraid of competition. As some of our comrades have pointed out here, the CGT in its heroic period was a real revolutionary party that had very much in common with the Bolshevik Party. It was said here that the French syndicalists are not Marxists, but in reply to this I will bring forward the opinion of a person who takes a prominent place in the syndicalist movement. Comrade [Robert] Louzon, who is well acquainted with Marxism and syndicalism alike, points out in his article that the basis of syndicalism is Marxism. Is it possible to think today of resurrecting the old revolutionary party that the CGT was before the war?

Could it be that revolutionary syndicalism lost its spirit because Jouhaux happened to betray the workers' cause in 1914? But even after that betrayal by Jouhaux, many other betrayals took place, which caused heavier blows to the

26 The debate in the Russian Communist Party over the role of the trade unions began in early November 1920, in the context of the final stages of the civil war and difficulties caused by the system of war communism. It began with a proposal by Trotsky to reorganise the unions in order to accelerate the revival of industrial production. As people's commissar of communications, Trotsky had done precisely that earlier in 1920 with the railroad industry and unions in order to prevent the collapse of the Soviet railway system. Trotsky's trade-union proposal was rejected by Lenin and the Central Committee, and a debate on the subject ensued in the party, which was ultimately resolved by the Tenth Party Congress in March 1921.

27 A reference to Alexander Shlyapnikov.

workers' cause than Jouhaux did. After Jouhaux's betrayal had shown itself in all its malevolence, a good many went over to the *minoritaires* who opposed Jouhaux; but later on they abandoned the *minoritaires* and the working class too. However, one may presume that the reasons for the changes that have occurred in French syndicalism are of a deeper character than those betrayals.

After the war all trade unions have undergone considerable changes. Those changes have taken place not only in Britain and Germany, where the trade unions have had a strong footing, having been well organised with wide issues. But even in France, where the number of trade unions has never been too great, one noticed a tendency of the workers to flow into the unions. The CGT, which differed from what it was in the past not only by its numbers but also by its tactics, has developed into a large organisation, similar to the British and American trade unions and has become a reformist organisation, all the time masking its reformist activity. The use of these old syndicalist formulas, the meaning of which was never in doubt, nevertheless gave rise to different interpretations.

Shall we, under the present circumstances, dream of resurrecting the syndicalism that existed before the war in its full purity? Shall we direct our energies to carrying out this work and wasting part of our energy in disputes? It seems to me that the French comrades have forgotten that in France after the war, the working class especially has suffered great defeats. Even the strike of 21 July 1919, which I have just reminded you of – the only expression of sympathy of the French workers towards the Russian Revolution – failed, and under disastrous circumstances for the working class.[28] An order of the CGT on the eve of the day in which the strike was appointed was sufficient to break the action. The consequences of this failure were soon felt. The policy of strangling Soviet Hungary was adopted the following day. The bourgeoisie did not stop there. From that day on it decided to enter into an open struggle with the proletariat, knowing that the latter's revolutionary strength was broken. Has the revolutionary minority taken this into consideration? It seems this lesson has not taught the working class much.

When we examine the next great event – the general strike of May 1920[29] – we become convinced that this time the bourgeoisie could suppress the working class with even greater force. It should be clear to you that after these two great events, when the minority of the French syndicalists were fooled by the

28 For the planned July 1919 general strike, see pp. 168–9, n. 10.

29 For the 1 May 1920 general strike in France, see p. 169, n. 10.

majority of the CGT, the *minoritaires* probably came to the conclusion that as long as the CGT was not strongly welded in one united whole it would always be at the mercy of the manoeuvres of Jouhaux and his friends.

You may probably think this minority has considered nothing else but the question of its internal organisation, but it has also raised the more important question – the question of the events of the day. The discussion that has taken place here shows that although the minority has undertaken this necessary work, it has however not yet finished with the period of confusion. We see that there are a few currents within the minority of French revolutionary syndicalism that seem to be quite ready sometimes to work together, but sometimes they begin to attack each other furiously. The manifestations of the opposition clearly indicate that French revolutionary syndicalism has not yet fully solved its problems. I think that the French comrades understand very well that intentionally hazy formulas are not sufficient anymore. Thus we have the formula speaking of the decision to collaborate in the future with political parties that will carry on revolutionary work. Sometimes it seems that this formula says a lot, and sometimes it seems that it has no practical meaning. We only go back to the old counterposition of the workers' organisations to the political organisations, and the old dispute is on us again.

Under such circumstances the revolutionary syndicalist minority in France can find no solid foundation for action. That is the reason it has failed to rally the militant elements of the working class. The working class is aware of the drawbacks of the minority, and it never responds to appeals that are not founded on clear ideas or definite views. There is one call they never refuse to respond to – that of the revolution. And the simple formula that has often been resorted to is to speak of the Moscow International; this is the formula that the working class is able to understand, and therefore joins without any reservations.

The task of the militants of the trade-union movement consists in bringing home to the masses what revolution and affiliation to Moscow means. In the pre-war period we had leisure enough at our disposal to discuss the various forms of organisation, and everybody enjoyed the legal right to resolutely defend one's point of view. But the epoch we are living in now is in many ways entirely different from the pre-war epoch. Before the war capitalism was still strong; during the many years of its existence it had more or less adapted itself to the different transformations in the social structure, and it was not an easy task to overthrow it. At the present moment this system, once so strong, is now shaken to its very foundations, and we witness now how in many countries it strives to rebuild society on a new basis, still maintaining its predominance. We very often proclaim our assurance that capitalism will never again win back its position, but in our heart of hearts we can never be fully convinced of the truth of this assertion. Abstractly we can easily conceive that the capitalist system may still maintain itself for a certain time.

The question now before us is: Who is to restore social life: the bourgeoisie or the working class? This is no mere question for theoretical discussions, but involves practical tasks to be carried out.

Revolution is an accomplished fact in our life. It depends on us to decide what forms the new society is to assume. Either we shall be crushed by the bourgeoisie – and then this new system would be the regime of enslavement of the working class, more cruel even than before the war – or this new society will be built by our efforts, and then we shall be able to secure complete emancipation of the working class and the establishment of a genuine communist society.

In order to successfully cope with this task we must forge here – and this is the task incumbent upon this congress – an international organisation, qualified to direct the struggle of the working class. The resolution to be submitted to the congress will give the possibilities to unite in the new organisation all units represented here, and I hope that not one of them will allow itself to be carried away by petty considerations in comparison with our colossal task, and that they will not reject the formula presented here. I hope that we shall all prove able to create the first genuine revolutionary trade-union International. (*Applause*)

Chair: The session is closed. The next session convenes at 8:00 this evening.

Bergmann protests that the speech of Rosmer has not been translated into German.

Chair: All German comrades are gone; only five or six are left. The translation cannot be done for five comrades only.

SESSION 9. 11 JULY 1921, EVENING

RILU-Comintern Relations; Workers' Control

(*Session opens at 8:00 p.m. Comrade Lozovsky in the chair.*)

Lozovsky: We are to vote on the resolution regarding the question of the relationship between the Trade Union International and the Communist International. The draft resolution to be read now is signed by Comrades Mann, Nin, Lozovsky, Heckert, Rosmer, Tsyperovich, Rykov, Godonnèche, Tommasi, and others.[1]

(*The resolution is read in French, English, German, and Russian.*)

Lozovsky: The second draft resolution is introduced by the French delegation. Comrade Rosmer, please read it. (*Rosmer reads.*)

Resolution on the Question of the Relations between the Two Internationals

After a careful discussion of the question of the relations that are to be established between the Trade Union International and the Communist International, the congress decides to recognise the full independence of the Red Trade Union International and the unacceptability of the Communist International as the moral leader. At the same time, the congress, in order to consolidate all the forces, considering that the revolutionary strength of the working class depends upon its unity of thought and action, expresses the readiness to assure a lasting contact with the Communist International without subordination of either International to the other.

Signed G. Sirolle, C. Lemoine, Michel [Relenque], Boisson, Victor Labonne, G. Gaudeux, A. Lemoine.

Lozovsky: You have heard the two resolutions. Comrade Bartels and others wish to speak upon the order of voting. Comrade Bergmann has the floor to explain the reasons for his proposal.

1 For the text of the resolution, see pp. 602–3. The full list of resolution signers consisted of Lozovsky, Rykov, Knight, Mann, Hampel, Tsyperovich, Godonnèche, Tommasi, Rosmer, Heckert, Volan, Nin, and Maurín.

 | DOI:10.1163/9789004712867_013

Bergmann (*Reads*):

> We consider that the proposed resolution cannot be voted until:
> 1. The question of tactics has been discussed and decided upon.
> 2. After the congress has been informed of the decision arrived at by the Communist International on the question of the relationship between the two Internationals.[2]
>
> Signed: For the AAUD, Leopold Darekus;[3] for the FAUD, Bartels.

The theses are so clear that they hardly need any comment. It is evident that the relationship, to a certain degree, depends upon the tactics to be accepted by the Communist International. It is also very clear to us that a parallel decision of both congresses would create confusion and may even result in contrary decisions on one and the same question, which could easily be avoided had we before us the resolution of the Communist International.

Lozovsky: Comrade Nin will now speak against the motion.

Andreu Nin (Spain): I am against postponing the vote on the resolution on the relationship of the two Internationals. First, the question has been thoroughly thrashed out, and each delegate has already formed an opinion. Secondly, the Red International is free to devise its own laws and tactics. To wait on the decisions of the Communist International would mean subordination, to which we would not subscribe. That is why I recommend rejecting this motion and voting on the resolution.

Lozovsky: We will now vote on the motion to postpone the acceptance of the resolution until a similar resolution has been debated and issued by the Communist International. Those against the motion should raise their hands. There is a majority. The motion is rejected.

We will now vote on the resolution that should be taken as a basis. The question of amendments will be taken up later.

The resolution signed by Mann, Nin, myself, Heckert, and others – we will call it number 1; the French resolution will be called number 2.

---

2 For the Comintern Third Congress resolution on this question, see 'Theses on the Communist International and the Red International of Labour Unions'. In Riddell (ed.) 2015, *3WC*, pp. 953–65.

3 This is presumably a reference to Leopold Dautkus.

The vote is taken by countries. For resolution number 1: Austria, Australia, Azerbaijan, Britain, Armenia, Bulgaria, Hungary, Germany (11 votes out of 16), Georgia, Denmark, Far Eastern Republic, Canada, Latvia, Lithuania, Luxembourg, Mexico, Norway, Poland, Russia, Romania, United States (13 votes out of 16), Ukraine, Spain, Finland, Czechoslovakia, Sweden (5 votes out of 8), Estonia, Yugoslavia, Switzerland; the minority of the French delegation also voted for number 1 (5 out of 11).[4]

For resolution number 2: Argentina, Holland, France (6 out of 11) and minorities of German delegation (5 votes), USA (3 votes), Sweden (2 votes).

The Turkish and Palestinian delegations were absent at the time of voting. The delegations from Abkhazia and Korea expressed themselves in favour of number 1, but did not take part in voting, as their credentials are still in the hands of the commission. The same is true for the representatives of Palestine and Khiva.

Lozovsky: We will shortly announce the exact results of the votes on the first and second resolutions. Comrade Nin has the floor to explain the reasons for his vote.

Nin: The Spanish delegation desires to explain why we have added our signature to the list of those who signed resolution number 1 just carried. We have put the question about the International plainly and sharply: Amsterdam or Moscow. Efforts to create a revolutionary International outside of Moscow are doomed to failure. We are convinced that to unite all syndicalists, to establish one revolutionary labour International is a high service to be rendered to the proletariat.

We have another reason. The Russian Revolution is the burning torch of the proletariat; it may instil the masses with the same energy and spirit as the general strike did. To sever connections with Russia, the cradle of the world revolution, would be equal to suicide and the conviction of the world proletariat that there is nothing but death, with no hope for resurrection. Consequently, we must remain in the Red International of Moscow. Does this mean that it will be our International? Yes, if it is anxious to fulfil its duties, it must not become sectarian.

This is why with all the strength of our revolutionary authority – which nobody has a right to doubt – we ask our comrades of the left wing to give all their power and energy, their resources, to the new International. Shoulder to

---

4 The French and German texts say 5 out of 11; the English and Russian versions say 5 out of 12.

shoulder, let us work in harmony for the realisation of our revolutionary and syndicalist ideas to which we shall remain true. We also ask our Communist comrades not to transform the trade-union International into a sectarian party organisation.

All the delegations are in favour of mutual cooperation between the two Internationals, the logical sequence of which is the exchange of representatives in the executive committees of both. We Spaniards pay very little attention to mere words; only deeds count with us. If the Communist International is sincerely ready for revolutionary action, it will find us right with it.

In conclusion, I cannot let pass silently the accusations made against the syndicalists during the discussion of 'neutrality'. We are not 'neutral'. The revolutionary syndicalists are just the opposite of neutral; we believe our revolutionary and creative power, the history of our movement, proves that we are not at all 'neutral'. There is no persecution of the Communists in Italy. Their periodicals are freely published, while ours were stopped by order of the government; they enjoy the right of assembly, which has been taken away from us. Our comrades are being murdered in the streets by the white guards; our fighters are in the prisons. What does this mean? It means that the bourgeoisie sees us, the revolutionary syndicalists, as a direct threat, as a force capable of disturbing their peace, as a danger for the capitalist system. Hence we are very far from being 'neutral'. We always work hand in hand with those who are truly revolutionary. The Communists, in order to gain our trust, must convert their words into deeds, as there are many among them who are 'revolutionists of the future', 'revolutionary neophytes', and no more.

I would like to make a final statement. We are not afraid of subordination. We know that in great revolutionary upheavals the moral as well as the actual leadership belongs to those who deserve it. Taking into consideration the influence and the authority we possess, we know that the leadership of the revolution may fall into our hands and then slip out of our hands should the masses lose their confidence in us. We would deserve that; it would simply mean we are not up to the task. (*Applause*)

Lozovsky: The floor is given to Comrade Howie to explain the reasons for his vote.

Jack Howie (Australia): Comrades, an opportunity has been given to the Australian delegation to put their views before the congress regarding the relations between the Red Trade Union International and the Comintern. I have been requested to read this statement, but it seems somewhat strange that I have not been given the opportunity to express the views of Australia upon this all-important question in a manner that I desire to do.

Owing to the great distance that Australia is situated from Europe, very little is known of the activities of the working-class movement in that country. This is the first occasion that the Australian workers have been represented at an international congress, not because they have had no desire to participate in the international class struggle of the proletariat, but simply because the previous Internationals have had nothing to offer them.

The question under discussion – the relations between the Third International and the Red Trade Union International – has been solved in Australia not by theory, but in actual practice. I heard Comrade Barker speak from the platform this morning. I expected to hear from him remarks of a nature that would lead to a discussion of a more vital character.

From 1912 to 1916, in Australia, the IWW organisation was in full operation, but they claimed that they were working or advocating a purely industrial form of organisation. But during that period we find in Australia that the IWW was compelled to go into the political field and fight on more than one occasion. They were active in the anti-conscription campaign. In Australia we find the IWW standing up and fighting the cause of political freedom for the workers. In the free-speech fights in Australia, the IWW participated on every occasion. And yet when they were asked during these operations in Australia, they would tell you they were purely an industrial organisation. One of the differences among the delegates of the various countries concerns the definition of political action. The experience of the IWW organisation in Australia clearly shows that the economic organisations cannot keep out of the political fight, the fight in the interests of the mass of the people.

In 1916 the leaders of the IWW organisation in Australia were sentenced on a frame-up charge on the evidence of police agents; twelve men were sent to jail from ten to fifteen years.[5] The organisation that remained after these men went to jail said that they were going to fight for the release of our leaders, but it must be in the industrial field. The trade-union movement consulted on this with the IWW men, and I do not want to take any credit from these men – during their term in Australia they fought a gallant fight. But they said no, we will operate in the industrial field, we will go on fighting until we get the men out by purely industrial action. After the campaign, which continued for a short period, the campaign collapsed and the comrades recognised the futility of trying to get their people released.

---

5 During September and October 1916, twelve leading members of the Australian IWW were arrested, tried, and convicted for treason and sentenced to up to fifteen years of hard labour.

We find in the course of six months, several trade-union organisations in Australia were passing resolutions that the twelve IWW men should be released, and after six months of agitation upon the workers of Australia, the Sydney Trades Labour Council came and said that the twelve leaders of the IWW must be released, and the whole of the Australian trade-union movement took up the cry and agitated for their release. As a result of that agitation, these twelve men were released, proving correct the policy that the Red Trade Union International is adopting here tonight.

I want to mention another experience in Australia of the use of the two machines working together, which was seen in 1917. In 1917 a general strike took place in Australia in the principal cities of that country, and within a week 400,000 men were involved in the strike.[6]

The leaders of the movement in Australia failed to recognise the significance of the fight that was being waged in the industrial field, and they told the workers to be quiet and not take any drastic action, as this was an economic fight and not a political fight, and therefore we must fight it on the economic field. And what was the result? Through the leaders of the working class, the workers of Australia lost the strike. The parliamentary machine of that country organised their forces to throw them against the workers, and the campaign of 1917 was defeated.

In conclusion, I would say in regard to the relationship between the Red Trade Union International and the Comintern: I have studied Comrade Williams's statement. He stated that the IWW is a very serious organisation in America and that it advocates purely industrial action. And I think we can safely say that not only in Australia, but in America, the IWW organisation will also resort to political means for advocating the release of their imprisoned men. What is that if not purely political?

In conclusion, I would say that the Australian delegation endorses the principle of close relationship between the two Internationals, and I also say that they support the formation of a Red Trade Union International – but on the condition that the foundation that is going to be laid at this congress must be a sound one; it must not be a shaky one, because if we do not build on a sound basis it is going to collapse in the very near future.

6 A walkout by New South Wales railworkers occurred in early August 1917 over an attempted introduction of new cost-accounting systems and wage reductions. The strike soon spread to other rail yards in Australia and then to other industries. Mass demonstrations in support of the strikers occurred of up to 150,000 persons. In the face of government strikebreaking, the strike ended on 8 September without winning any gains. In some parts of the country, strikers refused to go back to work until December.

Lozovsky: The representative of the Dutch delegation, Comrade De Visser, will explain the reasons for his vote.

Louis De Visser (Netherlands): The Dutch delegation has voted against the first resolution and for the second one. The first resolution contains a great many points with which the Dutch delegation is in full accord, but we have voted against not because we didn't agree with it – just the opposite. But to our sorrow, its representatives have their hands tied by the mandates they have brought with them. As far as we ourselves know, the red trade unions represent a solid united front with the Communist International.

Lozovsky: The representative of the Romanian delegation, Comrade Turcescu, will explain the reasons for his vote.

Nicolae Turcescu [Nicolae Gorniski] (Romania): Comrades, the dictatorship of the proletariat is the only means for the liberation of the working class from capitalist oppression. This is recognised both by the Red Trade Union International and the Communist International. In view of that, we Romanians have voted for the first resolution, which makes its aim that of uniting revolutionary workers of the world against the capitalist order.

Lozovsky: Comrade Tellalov of the Bulgarian delegation has the floor to explain their vote.

Kirill Tellalov (Bulgaria): Comrades, the Bulgarian delegation has voted for the resolution because it stands solidly for unity between economic and political action, for the closest union between the trade unions and political organisations of the workers, and for close contact between the everyday industrial struggle and the general struggle for the dictatorship of the proletariat.

We are for a close unity between the trade unions and the Communist International for the very good reason that we wish the industrial movements may act under the political leadership of the Communist International in the general revolutionary fight for the dictatorship of the proletariat. The correctness of this political policy was demonstrated by the dazzling success of the Russian Revolution and by all the struggles of the working class in Europe and America after the war. The Bulgarian delegation protests with all its might against unwarranted attempts on the part of some of the syndicalists to picture the Communist International as a sort of political society guided by political charlatans, on the same level as the treacherous leaders of the Socialist parties and the Amsterdam Federation.

It is well known throughout the entire world that the Communist International has gathered under its banner millions of the most class-conscious revolutionary workers from all parts of the world, and remains in fact the only revolutionary International for working-class action. No wonder that the entire capitalist class throughout the world hates it and its agents. The Bulgarian delegation is convinced that the congress, with its deliberations, will demonstrate to friends as well as to enemies of the working class that the Red Trade Union International is not being created for the purpose of undermining the work of the Communist International in any way, or of disorganising the leadership of the fighting revolutionary proletariat. The RTUI is being created for the opposite purpose of strengthening the leadership of the Communist International, so that it may consolidate all the trade unions under the banner of communism in order to hasten the victory of the social revolution of the proletariat.

Lozovsky: The floor is given to the representative of the Georgian delegation, Comrade Kurulashvili, to explain the reasons for his vote.

Georgy D. Kurulashvili (Georgia): The Georgian delegation has voted for the first resolution for the reason that for the last three years we went through many experiences and struggles, so that we know the meaning of the 'independence of the trade unions' defended by the Amsterdam partisans and Mensheviks.[7] The results of that so-called 'independence' were such that in three years' time the revolutionary unions of Georgia were on the point of dissolving. The best of its workers, who stood at the head of the revolutionary unions, were put in prison; workers were beaten up at meetings. That is why we are at present standing for a closer union with the Communist International, which will be our only means of getting rid of the 'independents' who are trying to serve both capital and labour.

Lozovsky: The floor is given to Comrade Ozol of the Russian delegation to explain its vote.

Fritz Ivanovich Ozol (Russia): Comrades, on behalf of the Russian delegation, we have to declare that on signing the resolution we have taken into consideration the peculiarities of conditions in each country, and the state of the labour movement and organisations in the different countries. We think that the revolution has not brought us as close together as we would have liked.

---

7 A reference to the Menshevik-led 'Democratic Republic of Georgia' proclaimed in May 1918. It was toppled by Red Army troops in February–March 1921.

We render homage to our syndicalist comrades, who are fighting on our side. We hope that our meeting with revolutionary workers' organisations in struggle will bring us closer, so that at our next congress of revolutionary trade unions, the agenda will not include the debate we have had today on the question of relations with the Communist International. We are confident that at the time the next congress takes place our comrades, the revolutionary syndicalists, will have become convinced that the point of view defended here is without foundation. And like the Spanish comrades here today, they will declare that it is impossible to separate the economic struggle from the political struggle. The working class will overthrow the capitalist system only by joint action with the political organisations. Owing to this, we hope that long before the next congress all revolutionary organisations will work with us for the overthrow of the capitalist system.

Lozovsky: Comrades, there is a proposal to close the list of speakers on this subject. Is anyone against? The proposal is accepted. Permit me to announce the result of today's vote: for the first resolution, 287; for the second, 37. (*Loud applause*)

Now we shall have the following point on the agenda. The Presidium proposes to put on today's agenda Comrade Bell's report on unemployment. The question of trade-union tactics will be left for tomorrow, as we have only now received the French text and the majority of the delegates have not yet seen it. Are there any objections to this motion? No. Accepted. Comrade Bell will now speak on the question of unemployment.

(*Bell delivers his report on the unemployment question.*)[8]

Lozovsky: Comrades, it is moved that no discussion be opened on the question of unemployment, as this is not a debatable issue or a matter for discussion at this congress. It is proposed to receive Comrade Bell's report and elect a commission of seven that should, on the basis of this report and of the discussion that will take place in the commission, draw up a resolution on the above question. The motion provides that all delegations, as well as individual delegates, wishing to make any supplementary amendments or practical suggestions in connection with the above question, refer these to the above commission.

Are there any objections? Comrade Drewnitzky wishes to oppose the motion.

8 The text of Bell's unemployment report is not contained in the published proceedings in any language.

Viktor Drewnitzky (Germany, General Workers' Union): It is necessary to open the discussion. Though the question of unemployment is not a subject for debate at this congress, it is too important to be disregarded.

Thrashing out this question on the floor would lead to giving directives to elaborate a line of action for forming a solid fighting front in a number of countries severely affected by unemployment. I therefore ask the congress not to refuse to open this discussion.

Lozovsky: Comrade Nin has the floor.

Nin: I believe we ought to give all the necessary time for settling the question now before us, but no more than is absolutely necessary. A question of this sort cannot give rise to protracted discussion, as we can hardly expect widely divergent views on this matter. We should compile information on the extent of unemployment in various countries and suggest ways and means of fighting this evil. It seems to me that the result would be about the same if we refer this work to the commission, without taking up too much time for it at the congress itself. In view of this, I am against the motion to have the question of unemployment fully discussed at the plenary session.

Lozovsky: I shall put the motion to a vote. All those in favour of Comrade Drewnitzky's motion, please raise your hands. The motion is rejected, while the motion is carried to not open a general discussion, but to refer the question to a commission. This commission will consist of delegates representing Germany, Britain, USA, Poland, Spain, France, and Russia. Since Germany has a minority within a minority, there is a motion to give this country two votes. Comrade Bell will be the ninth member of this commission. The commission will thus consist of nine members. Moreover, Comrade Bell is charged by the congress to convene this commission, organise its work, and report to the congress any resolution adopted by it.

B. Glozman (France) (*from his seat*): The congress decided to have the Presidium redraft the manifesto to the workers of the world. What has been done in this connection?

Lozovsky: Delegates wish to know what has become of the manifesto referred to the Presidium for redrafting. I promise that its final draft will be ready by tomorrow evening. The proclamation on white terror is now ready. It was somewhat delayed because many delegations had not brought in the data they were asked for.

There will be a plenary session at 11:00 a.m. tomorrow, but not in the evening. Beginning Wednesday we shall have our regular morning and evening sessions.

Rosa Bloch (Switzerland) (*from her seat*): I move to have no plenary session tomorrow, whether in the morning or in the evening, as the Communist [International] congress takes up the question of its relations to the trade-union International at its day session tomorrow, and closes in the evening.[9]

Lozovsky: There is a motion to have no plenary session tomorrow, but to postpone it until 11:00 a.m. the day after tomorrow. The motion is carried. I declare the session adjourned.

(*The session is adjourned at 11:10 p.m.*)

Report on Workers' Control[10]

Grigorii Tsyperovich (Russia): After having heard the report of Comrade Varga,[11] I presume there is no need to dwell upon a detailed review of the characteristics of the crisis that all capitalist countries are now living through. This crisis is the most characteristic expression of the fact that the bourgeoisie is unable to overcome the anarchy of production, in which its organisation of production is a direct cause. This crisis demonstrates quite clearly to the whole working class that the capitalist class is unable to master the productive forces it has itself developed, giving them the opportunity to operate freely.

On the basis of the contradiction between the forces of production and their growth, on the one hand, and on the other the relations of industrial production – i.e., the capitalist system – a great class struggle is now developing, involving all the countries of the world. The causes of this struggle lie in a whole series of irreconcilable contradictions of the capitalist system itself. The more the crisis develops, the steadier grows the thought in the minds of the working

9 For the 'Theses on the Communist International and the Red International of Labour Unions', adopted by the Comintern's Third Congress at its final session, 12 July 1921, see Riddell (ed.) 2015, *3WC*, pp. 953–65.

10 This report was published in the official congress record, where it is identified as having been given during the Ninth Plenary Session. However, exactly where in the session it was given is not clear.

11 See pp. 115–29.

class that the capitalist system requires radical changes, that in the interests of all the toiling masses it is necessary to begin a radical reorganisation of the whole economic system.

The war itself, which was undertaken in the interests of the bourgeoisie, has already created a conviction among the advanced masses of workers that the hour of destruction of the capitalist system is approaching. During this war an extravagant waste of the forces of labour was evidenced. The workers who participated in creating the means of production were convinced, day after day, that both the raw materials and the output product had disappeared into the abyss of the destructive war. This contradiction between the true results of the gigantic war and what the bourgeoisie had promised during the war's duration, was accompanied by sharp social contrasts. At the same time as the masses were being ruined, the capitalist class was accumulating colossal fortunes. Out of this developed a striking contrast between the misery and despair of the working class and the luxury of the capitalist class. The working class began to understand that the capitalist system is a system of destruction and misery for the masses, that it is necessary to create a new form of relationship between labour and capital – a form that would do away once and for all with the existing system of oppression.

Out of all this the idea of workers' control has rapidly developed.[12] Of course, workers' control as it now exists did not originate overnight. In Russia workers' control originated here [in 1917] with the sabotage on the part of the employing class, because ever since the Russian bourgeoisie saw the first signs of the revolution, it began to obstruct and to destroy production, so as to prove to the workers that all strikes lead to disorganisation.

In a number of enterprises workers realised that the capitalists were trying to stop the growth of production, to hold it back. They at first introduced simple guardposts in order to prevent theft of factory materials. But these outside guards were soon convinced that their work should be transferred to inside the enterprise, because the outside control was not adequate for the duties required. But upon the establishment of inside control, it gradually became

12 The term 'workers' control' poses a special problem in English, given that the word *control* does not have the same precise meaning in English as its cognates in Russian, German, French, and other languages. Whereas in English the word usually connotes 'mastery' or 'authority', the meaning of the word as discussed in this agenda point is actually closer to 'oversight', 'monitoring', and 'supervision'. In other words, workers' control here refers to the idea of workers keeping close tabs on the financial and productive operations of factories and workshops under their capitalist owners, and through a process of struggle increasingly taking charge of these operations. Such an experience happened on a wide scale in Russia in the months following the February 1917 revolution.

clear that ordinary technical control would not suffice either, and that it was necessary to pass over to financial control in order to master the whole system, to have a complete understanding of all that was going on at each factory and workshop.

In this last phase, i.e., in the phase of financial control, the working class met the utmost resistance on the part of the bourgeoisie. The bourgeoisie understood perfectly well that should the workers succeed in reaching this phase of control, it would threaten the whole capitalist system. In reality financial control gave birth to the idea of unifying all forms of control by the workers' organisations, that is to say, to the dictatorship of the proletariat.

But what took place in Russia is just beginning to appear in the West, in a weaker form. The working class there, as well, had been under the influence of the old trade unions, which had been continuously trying to prove to the working class that they should confine themselves to the struggle within the limits of the existing capitalist system for ameliorating their situation. But under the influence of the war and the crisis, they began to realise that the whole capitalist system had become entangled in unsolvable contradictions owing to the economic struggle.

The development of workers' control in Russia coincided with the general revolutionary movement. In our country, the Communist Party was the leader of the working-class movement, which, having worked out a definite plan of action, has followed it firmly and unswervingly. For this reason our development of workers' control was rapid and accelerated. In the West this guiding nucleus is just beginning to emerge, and therefore workers' control there is still under the influence of the old conciliatory trade unions. While workers' control rapidly succeeded in our country, in the West the bourgeoisie, together with the trade unions, continues up to the present time to make successful attempts at perverting and turning workers' control into an appendage that would serve the interests of capitalism.

This is precisely the reason why the question of workers' control is particularly acute in the West, and this is precisely the reason why great attention should be paid to it. Attempts to establish workers' control in the West have taken place in a number of countries. We have seen quite an accelerated development of workers' control in Italy; we see a whole series of attempts to introduce workers' control in Germany; and in some cases we see attempts to establish workers' control in Britain. Everywhere, as a result of the workers' discontent, there develop in these countries new revolutionary organisations (factory and workshop councils, etc.) that have as their task either to replace the old trade unions altogether or to assist in reorganising them.

In Italy, only a few months ago during the widespread movement in connection with the occupation of the factories,[13] there also took place a strong growth of factory committees, and workers' control immediately went through a number of stages. The workers began with strikes, to which the employers responded with lockouts. In answer to this, the workers began to apply control in the most resolute way, beginning with taking possession of the mills and factories. In a whole series of the biggest enterprises, workers' and technical commissions were established, which worked in contact with the craft unions and began taking production into their own hands. The highest stage of workers' control that was taking place was the mastery of all production. Nevertheless, the opportunist leaders of the trade unions succeeded in distorting this spontaneous movement, so that it did not take the form of genuine workers' control.

I shall quote some passages from an article by an Italian reformist, Colombino, who sums up the work of the factory committees and gives the following characteristic of workers' control and its tasks.[14] He says, 'The role of factory councils consists of being an arbiter between workers' trade unions and employers' trusts, a role that sometimes may be very useful.' Colombino's point of view on workers' control is that of a true reformist. He looks upon the factory committees not as a revolutionary nucleus directing the will of the working class against capitalism, but as an arbitration board that straightens out disagreements between unions and industrial trusts and assists in production. In what sense does it assist? Of course, in the sense of retaining the domination of the employers over production. He then says, 'Workers' control sometimes may even improve relations of the workers to the labour they are performing, as they realise that they are not merely a working mechanism; that from being mere automatons, they are becoming true citizens, to whom society has entrusted the work.' And here, in this sentence, one feels the negative attitude of the reformists and syndicalists of the old type toward workers' control.

13 Beginning at the end of August and continuing through the end of September 1920, over half a million workers, led by the metalworkers, seized factories throughout Italy, creating a revolutionary situation in the country. Workers began to organise production under the leadership of factory councils, and in many places workers organised red guards to defend the seized factories. The strikes spread to the railways and other workplaces, and many poor peasants and agricultural workers carried out land seizures. The Italian Socialist Party and the trade-union federation refused to see the movement as anything more than a union struggle, however, and the movement eventually foundered.

14 From the pamphlet by Emilio Colombino, a leader of the CGL and PSI, titled *I Consigli di fabbrica nel Movimento Sindacale* [The factory councils in the trade-union movement], Varese 1920.

The reformist says, 'Control may improve the relations of the workers to their work.' According to his point of view, the main thing lies not in forcing the employers to abandon their leading role in production, in taking the productive posts away from them, in depriving them of the tools and means of production. According to him, the main point is not having the working class take production into its own hands, but simply in leading to a better relationship of the workers to their labour, i.e., making the workers work at a faster rate in the interests of capital. He understands the importance of factory committees in this way: they must be created so that workers will know they are responsible for the most successful exploitation of labour by capital. In practice this finds its expression in the fact that the bureaucracy of the old trade unions has succeeded up until now in reducing the role of the factory committees to such petty results. In Germany, by enacting a law on factory committees, these have altogether lost their importance and have been turned into organs for improving the situation of the enterprises in the interests of the capitalists themselves. The same thing happened in Italy.[15]

Notwithstanding the first unsuccessful steps, however, the idea of workers' control in the West did not disappear, because it is being engendered by the current economic conjuncture. The working class became convinced, out of its own experience – although often unsuccessful – that without controlling production, it will not be able to better its situation. The red trade-union movement needs to spread this conviction, so as to direct the trade unions onto a new path, toward the goal of workers' control. It should be turned into a powerful means of education of the masses on the basis of a practical study of the capitalist system. Comrades know what is now going on all over the world owing to the struggle between labour and capital.

From the very beginning, the attempts of the workers to establish control in the factories met with violent opposition from the capitalists. The capitalists then opened a furious counterattack, because they realised that to allow such new forms of the working-class movement to develop would mean to open the door to socialism, to the dictatorship of the proletariat. Now the question is not only about undermining workers' control, but about the destruction of the fact-

15 A Works Council Law was passed by the German Reichstag 18 January 1920, requiring enterprises with more than twenty workers to have an elected works council, and establishing procedures for how they were to function.

Coming out of the massive occupation of the factories in Italy in September 1920, Prime Minister Giovanni Giolitti signed a decree establishing a joint commission of unionists and capitalists charged with formulating a law on workers' control. The decree was never implemented.

ory committees as well, about crushing and doing away with the organisation of the working class, because the capitalists realise perfectly well that if they stop halfway, the working-class movement will sooner or later take revenge and sweep them off the earth.

But as this struggle develops, becoming more and more acute, it also becomes clear that if workers' control gives a certain direction to the working class, disclosing secret manipulations of the capitalist system, nevertheless control alone cannot attain the fundamental idea of the working-class movement: taking possession of production by establishing the dictatorship of the proletariat. The working class is beginning to realise more and more that it is precisely on the field of workers' control that the final and decisive battle with the capitalists will take place, not simply as owners of the tools of production, but as masters of state power as well. This is why workers' control inevitably acquires political forms and turns into a struggle for the conquest of the state apparatus. This is why in its last stage it turns into a social struggle for the dictatorship of the proletariat.

In cases where the working class is able to capture industry – as for instance, in Soviet Russia, in Hungary – workers' control begins the day after the social revolution, taking forms that more and more bring it nearer to the fulfilment of tasks of state as a whole. Experience has proved that workers' control isolated in separate enterprises can go off in a wrong direction. The Russian workers have had this experience when a 'factory patriotism' developed in the rush for raw materials, fuel, etc. The Russian workers were saved from this danger by transferring the factory committees and their controlling functions to the organised labour movement by means of their unification by industries and on a state scale. This control received new forms after the social revolution; it transformed itself into an organ of production, establishing new economic forms. This is the final stage, after which begins the development of socialist society by way of attracting the broad working masses to the general industrial reconstruction.

I believe that on the basis of these considerations, insofar as we already possess our experience [in Russia] and in the Western European countries, we can determine the practical approach to the problem of control. The forms of workers' control should be established by our congress. Workers' control is the inevitable consequence of the present-day economic position of all capitalist countries. There is therefore no need to abandon workers' control on the pretext that it failed in some cases. On the contrary, the red trade unions should issue the workers' control slogan. The attitude of different groups and parties toward workers' control will indicate their attitude to the working class itself. Every worker will easily determine, in connection with this question of workers' control, what the attitude is of these parties, groups, and trade unions to the very idea of the conquest of power over production by the working class.

But the struggle for workers' control cannot be carried out only by means of agitation, propaganda, or the issuing of definite slogans. It is necessary to work out detailed instructions, thanks to which workers' control will take concrete shape. It is necessary that the working masses should, in their everyday struggle, insist upon workers' control, learn by it, and prepare for the capture of production. The first experiences of workers' control – overseeing the quantity of raw materials, monitoring orders, supervising financial means, examining the reasons for shutting down factories or shortening the hours of labour – all these methods of control can give colossal results. We must, therefore, in issuing the watchword of 'workers' control by the trade unions', give concrete expression to this slogan, so that the workers may know that they are fighting not for formulas, but are taking part in the actual process of carrying out revolutionary principles in real life.

Workers' control must be placed on a strict class foundation. With the aim of crippling the principle of workers' control, the bourgeoisie, in full agreement with the yellow trade unions of Amsterdam, has advanced the idea of parity control commissions and the idea of state control and oversight. Such a form of control is based upon the idea that the legitimate master of the means of production and labour power is the employer, and that he and the state have the right to be represented by an equal number of votes. These parity commissions, based on the principle of equality, transform themselves into a representation of two votes against one. This is the reason why the red trade unions must oppose parity and state control and oversight. The trade unions must counterpose class control, i.e., control carried out by workers' organisations alone. It goes without saying that this way of solving the question will be met with furious opposition on the part of the bourgeoisie. That is one more reason to pose the question sharply.

This leads us to the question of who must carry out workers' control, and in what way it is to be carried out. I will not go into the role of factory committees in the matter of workers' control, because on this aspect of the question – and in general on the role of factory committees within the labour movement – Comrade Heckert will speak later. What interests me at the present moment and comes within the framework of my report is that the trade unions, owing to the development of the system of workers' control, will need to make a clear decision on the question of who will be elected to these control commissions, and consequently the factory committees as well.

Two different points of view crop up, as always: the revolutionary point of view and the reformist point of view put forward by the old trade-union movement. The leaders of the latter affirm that workers' control cannot be entrusted to unorganised workers who form an amorphous mass, thoroughly incapable of exercising control. This idea is quite transparent in a series of decisions and resolutions, one of which I will quote, from the article by Colombino that I just referred to.

He writes: 'I would be willing to grant the right of voting in elections for the control commissions and factory committees to unorganised workers in the centre, where they are always together with the organised workers. But it is utterly impossible to grant the right of voting to unorganised workers in elections to the leading committees of these bodies.'

Inasmuch as the matter concerns workers solidly organised, the trade unions, this representative of the trade-union movement says: 'I would be willing to', but inasmuch as the matter concerns the enormous mass of the unorganised workers, who suffer most of all from the results of the war and the world crisis, who most of all are anxious to join the trade-union movement, this right is not to be granted to that part of the proletariat. The bourgeoisie can only rejoice – they see the alienation of this most important section ripe for revolt, affected by the war, the industrial crisis, unemployment, and starvation. This is why the red trade unions must sharply insist that elections to control commissions and factory committees should be carried out by the whole mass of workers in the establishment, independently of whether they are organised or unorganised.

Workers' control must also be made use of as a means for the transformation of the trade unions into industrial unions. Workers' control can be systematically carried out only when all the workers within an enterprise are united in one body, when all the workers in the enterprise are united in this control, when they are not split into different unions in which every union acts on its own and for its own aims.

In carrying out workers' control, it is necessary to remember that while it in itself is unable to resolve the fundamental question of the expropriation of the means of production, it is nevertheless an excellent preparatory school for the final battle to capture the means of production, i.e., for the dictatorship of the proletariat. This is the reason why workers' control must be carried out as a demonstrative form of struggle that trains the greatest mass of workers. The task of control is a way to attract workers, interest them in the daily realisation of this control, and at the same time, thanks to it, develop the most active and qualified workers to manage production in the future.

As to the question that in practice will have to be solved after the congress is over – in what way should the work of the control commissions be connected with the factory committee, and through them with the trade unions – inasmuch as the congress has accepted the point of view that we must do our best to unify the trade-union movement and use it for further struggle, the control commissions as well as the factory committees must be united in a bloc with the trade-union movement. A control commission in an isolated enterprise can lose sight of general class and state interests. Our task consists therefore in foreseeing such a possibility and taking measures accordingly, directing our energies toward the creation of a system of workers' control from one enterprise to a series of enterprises of the same industry; starting from a single enterprise up to a series of enterprises in a given industry, to all of them on a national scale, and from a national scale to an international scale.

These, comrades, are the fundamental practical propositions that we must accept at this congress, and that should be followed by the trade unions everywhere. All these fundamental propositions indicate one definite line, but it would be impossible to determine in every separate country which form of control concretely should be adopted at a given moment. That should be the task of the local organisations of workers on the basis of the general considerations outlined above, taking into account the relationship of forces at any given moment and fixing which form of control should be carried out, which part of it should be strengthened, which control body should be set up, and so on.

The task of the Red International of Trade Unions consists in carefully and attentively following in what way the direction recommended by the congress develops in each country, showing mistakes committed, in bringing into a single whole the experience of the entire trade-union movement, to lead the entire movement as part of an international plan. This is why I limited my report to the general characteristics of workers' control, taking into account that the considerations that will be accepted at this congress will lay the foundations of our future work, and that the workers in every country will, through their initiative and their creative power, create the new forms of the trade-union movement on the basis of revolutionary workers' control.

SESSION 10. 13 JULY 1921, MORNING–AFTERNOON

Factory Committees; Italian Question

(*Session opens at 11:15 a.m. Comrade Lozovsky in the chair.*)

Lozovsky: The Presidium proposes to establish the following agenda: This morning we begin with the report on trade unions and factory committees, tying it to the report on workers' control. As the report on workers' control was delivered yesterday by Comrade Tsyperovich,[1] we shall begin our work with the report on the trade unions and factory committees. Comrade Heckert will present the report.

Report on Trade Unions and Factory Committees

Fritz Heckert (Germany): Comrades, before analysing the tasks of factory committees and their relation to the trade unions, let us go back to the period when the idea of such committees first originated in the trade unions, in order to give one or two references of a historical character. This is important in order to get a clear idea of the aims and meaning of workers' control as a historical necessity.

I am sharing the task with Comrade Tsyperovich of presenting at this congress the report on workers' control and factory committees. Unfortunately, the theses on this question are not yet translated into German, French, and English, and consequently our comrades are not yet acquainted with the theoretical basis of my report. That will be done in the next few days.

The creation of factory committees is the expression of the will of workers to have a voice in matters concerning the factory, workshop, and industry in general, and to limit the employers' absolute power over production. This idea, though, did not come about by accident and did not arise out of definite principles. Even earlier, during the [Russian] revolution of 1905–6, we saw the germ of this idea. After that revolution, it was forgotten. The factory committees at that time were to a certain degree not of an economic character, but were purely political.

1 The report on workers' control was given in Session 9 on 11 July.

 | DOI:10.1163/9789004712867_014

Since the war, the idea of creating factory committees has come to life again, this time to stay. Our economic relations, our attitude toward the capitalists, is based upon the following:

The capitalist state tried during the war to maintain production on the same level while sending the greatest number of men to the war front. This tendency to wrest the maximum number of men from production has created many difficulties for industry. In connection with this, it has become necessary to abolish all social laws that had been introduced during the last ten years. Collective agreements and fixed working hours are binding no longer. All this, as well as the restrictive laws in the employment of women and children, has been annulled. The population was mobilised pitilessly either for the war front or for work in war industries. The war has proved, however, that the military machinery has intensified the utilisation of human material to such an extent that people have perished far more of exhausting work in the rear than at the front.

From 1916 onwards, great difficulties in the economic life of all capitalist countries of Europe were observed. Production could not meet the needs of consumption. In Germany everything was sent to the front; what remained in the rear was insufficient. In consequence of that, the population endured great privations. But such suffering could not last long. On one side, owing to the fact that the means of production were employed for war industry, the people's consumption had been limited to the minimum. On the other hand, despite the undernourishment of the people and the introduction of longer hours, there was no possibility of keeping industry on a level necessary for the requirements of the front as well as for the needs of the country.

In the years 1916–17, we notice a stagnation in industry in Germany, Britain, and France, as the working population's capacity for work fell considerably as a result of poor nutrition, which resulted in a drop of production in various capitalist countries. The workers – who at the beginning of the war had fallen into a sort of nationalist trance, being told they were fighting for the fundamental principles of their existence – did not understand how such a state of things could last any longer. Under these circumstances, economic ruin was inevitable. But workers soon realised that they were heading to the abyss not only in Germany, but in other countries too. They began to understand that in addition to the economic struggle waged through strikes, they had to deal with other questions. The workers said to themselves: We cannot afford to have protracted strikes; we want enough food and clothes, we want houses fit for human habitation; otherwise we shall perish.

The trade-union leaders, however, opposed the workers' aim of bettering their situation. No wonder, considering that they had proclaimed a civil peace.

In Britain some of the trade-union leaders approved of a special law that was directed against the workers in the munitions factories; according to this law, workers participating in strikes were considered as deserters and had to be punished as such. Mr. Henderson was engaged by 'His Majesty' to impose this law on the workers. In France, Albert Thomas also opposed the workers' demands. In Germany, as we know, military catastrophe at the front was occurring simultaneously with the growing economic crisis. As the war dragged on, the economic position of the country grew worse, and so did the physical strength of the labour force. In 1918 it became clear that the war needed to end. Had the nations even desired to continue the war, it would have been impossible to carry it out, as this would have meant the total ruin of the national economy and the labour force.

In February, March, and April 1919, 800,000 people died.[2] In other words, the death toll was higher than during a similar period in ordinary times. This fact is to be explained exclusively by the decline of the physical strength of the population. We observe the same tendency in the Balkan states, in Austria, and in Italy.

But as production of clothing and footwear disappeared, the workers began to rebel. They elected their representatives in the factories, demanding a voice in deciding all questions. To halt the advance of the revolutionary movement, the capitalists made concessions to the workers. But the era of revolution had begun,

The workers in capitalist countries revolted and entered into a hard economic struggle. Demoralisation spread in the armies at the front. The trade-union leaders attempted to keep the peace. In 1917 the revolution broke out in Russia. In France, the masses began to move. In 1918 strikes broke out in Austria; and in February, in Germany.[3] With the exception of Russia, all other countries succeeded in calming down the workers, and the revolutionary situation ebbed.

As revolution broke out in Central Europe it became clear that the idea of workers taking over industry was increasingly popular, and assuming the form of action.

---

2 Many of these deaths were undoubtedly caused by the 'Spanish flu' epidemic, which killed an estimated 125,000 to 250,000 people in France alone.

3 Close to a million workers went on strike throughout Austria-Hungary in mid-January 1918, demanding better living and working conditions and an end to the war. At the end of the strike, numerous strike leaders were arrested or drafted into the army.

On 28 January 1918 close to half a million workers went on strike in Berlin calling for an end to the war. In face of government repression, and its threat to declare martial law in the factories, the strike ended by 3 February.

This will of the workers could be clearly seen in Germany already in October 1918, when the military power was still in the hands of the old regime. Hugo Stinnes, the powerful magnate of the Ruhr basin, appealed to Carl Legien with an offer to improve workers' conditions of life, reconciling the interests of capitalists and workers. This was the same Stinnes who formulated the idea of practical collaboration in production between the organisations of the workers and the employers:[4] 'We shall allow the workers to carry out their desire to participate in the reorganisation of industry. We shall give them a brotherly reception.' He did so not only because he was afraid of revolution, but because he was clever and careful, as shattered economic life has brought about the revolution in many countries. Thus, he tried to avert the tendency of the workers toward revolution. He spoke so sweetly to the workers: 'I am not your enemy, I would willingly give much more if only I could.' Such offers were made to the workers in other countries.

In general, the idea of business cooperation is not new; it has not been invented in any one particular country. The bourgeoisie has often applied this method of class collaboration as a way to avert revolution whenever it felt the ground shaky under its feet. In November 1918 the trade-union leaders declared that revolution was a great crime, and those who were for revolution were severely criticised. But revolution occurred in Russia, in Austria, and in Hungary. In most cases the bourgeoisie abandoned its factories, resulting in a great disorganisation and collapse. The workers of Austria, Hungary, as well as Germany, were ready to take over the direction of production. In many countries the capitalist system remained, but the bourgeoisie thought the revolution would crush them. In face of this catastrophe, men such as Stinnes and Thyssen in Germany did not lose their heads and kept on their feet. The bureaucracy had disappeared during this time – we don't know where – and in this way workers' committees in the factories came about, performing both political and economic functions.

Keeping your attention still on Germany, I wish to say that the above-mentioned committees would have soon tackled the economic functions imposed upon them, were it not for the powerful Social-Democratic Party and the influential trade-union bureaucracy, which opposed this and said to the workers, 'You should not seize the power and take over industry, as some ultra-clever and super-radical irresponsible elements wish you to do.' From the very first

4 The Stinnes-Legien Agreement of 15 November 1918 was signed by twenty-one employer associations and seven unions, outlining the policy of class collaboration between trade unions and capital in order to achieve economic reconstruction.

day of the revolution we heard from all the trade-union leaders, 'It is certainly necessary that the capitalists should stop being autocrats in industry; the worker must of course participate in the organisation of production, but you must not take away from them the right of property, otherwise they will lose their whole interest in the industry. But the workers are not yet able independently to organise production. It is therefore necessary that the workers should restore industry, in cooperation with the employers.' The theory of *Arbeitsgemeinschaft*, which later contaminated all countries, was thus born in Germany.[5]

At a time when the working class was waging an open struggle, Kautsky called the capitalist economy a stone quarry – not a quarry that could be worked, but a heap of fragments.[6] Capitalist production could not, in such a state, be transformed into a socialist system. A man of genius must make his appearance in order to draw up a new economic plan on an entirely new basis, and thereby restore the ruined capitalist economy. Hilferding similarly asserted that the capitalist system could not possibly be transformed at the current time by way of revolution. That could be achieved, in his view, only when capitalism had amassed and left an inheritance of dazzling wealth. Therefore, conclusions were drawn that we would be able to pass to higher economic forms only when capitalism was restored. If capitalist production is nothing but a heap of ruins, and the workers do not possess sufficient knowledge and capacity to restore the economy and undertake its management, this therefore means that we are still in need of the genius of the employer, and the necessity of practical collaboration with the employers. There should be no revolution.

But the worker who stood for the revolution answered these arguments of Hermann Müller, Hilferding, and Kautsky with the words, 'I want the working day to be shortened. I don't care to die as other workers have done. I've been starved long enough. Let the idle rich now open their pocketbooks, so that we might buy some bread.' Once such thoughts originate in the minds of the workers, and they rise in open revolt – as they did in the Ruhr district – they said, 'We shall take Stinnes by the collar and throw him into prison. We shall dispossess him of his coal mines. He should not own anything.' The workers who struggled in the factories agreed to the idea that property was not inviolable and sacred.

5 *Arbeitsgemeinschaft* (or more precisely, *Zentralarbeitsgemeinschaft*) was a body created 15 November 1918 through an agreement between German employer associations and the free trade union and Christian trade-union federations. The term was also used more broadly to refer to the policy of class collaboration between trade unions and capital in order to achieve economic reconstruction.

6 This would appear to be a reference to Kautsky's 1887 book 'Karl Marx' Oekonomische Lehren' [Karl Marx's Economic Lessons]. It was revised and published in English in 1903 as *The Economic Doctrines of Karl Marx*, and can be found in the Marxists Internet Archive.

However, this idea of the miners was ignored, and preference was given to capitalist production over workers' production. The leaders of trade unions, such as Legien, said in the first days of the revolution, 'Our revolution must not be transferred onto a purely economic field.' These so-called revolutionaries absolutely refuse to recognise the meaning of revolution, nor the objective experiences that occurred in the process of its development. And since the large masses of workers lacked consciousness and had only a vague idea of the revolutionary process, they allowed themselves to be convinced of the necessity of collaboration with the employer.

What is the *Arbeitsgemeinschaft* form of business cooperation? It is very important that it be known. In its essentials, it is the recognition by the workers of the stability of the foundations of the capitalist mode of production. But in this policy of business cooperation, they are entirely wrong, for under the present mode of capitalist production, articles are not produced in order to satisfy the urgent needs of humanity. The only aim of capitalist relations of production is profits. Capitalist employers are interested solely in the extraction of as much profit from production as possible. The moment the capitalist ceases to extract profits and begins to incur losses, he loses all interest in production. We are witnessing this in France, where a big French statesman and manufacturer was asked why he had extinguished his blast furnaces and thrown thousands of workers out into the street. He answered, 'I produce only when production is profitable. Otherwise I am unable to produce any more.' This is a very clear expression of the capitalist mode of production. These are the conditions under which our social democrats and Kautskys preach to the workers: 'You must cooperate with the capitalists'. In all cases where the cooperation of class organisations was brought into being, it proved to be fuel in the fire that greatly contributed to a complete re-establishment of capitalist domination. It deprived the workers at once of any real possibility of exercising influence over production, which they had for a moment conquered by such a hard struggle. Naturally, leaders of this kind are to be found only in purely capitalist governments.

If the capitalists enter into 'cooperation' with the workers, they do so only because the amount of profit they get in this way is much higher than, or at least equal to, the amount they could have received had they invested their capital otherwise. It is well known that capital tends to shift from less profitable fields into more profitable ones. This is the gist of the *Arbeitsgemeinschaft* form of business cooperation. Nevertheless, the social democrats continue to assert that business cooperation is the sole path toward the restoration and revival of the national economy, the only road leading to socialism.

Practical experience since the war has clearly and definitely shown whether socialism can be attained by such means. We witness something entirely different from what the leaders promised. The heap of ruins that we inherited from capitalism were not put in order; on the contrary, in such places where a certain order was preserved, it was destroyed, and disorder was transformed into complete ruin. Business cooperation failed to bring even the slightest order to this chaos. It was able to accomplish only one thing: to hamper workers' claims and to draw advantage for a more secure development of capitalism.

But the workers see things more and more clearly, for they are no longer the same after the war. Under the influence of an instinctive distrust, they say to themselves: when capitalists such as Krupp, Stinnes, Schneider, Armstrong, and Carnegie all declare 'Let bygones be bygones', it's clear that there's something in the air. These words undoubtedly conceal the intention to betray the working class, to bribe it and re-establish the capitalist economy. The latest events prove that these suspicions were not entirely groundless. Therefore, the workers were right in their conclusions when they said to themselves, 'We must not fall for the capitalist bait. On the contrary, our duty is to push the revolution forward. And we must not establish cooperation with the employers for an industrial democracy, but must establish our own power and take the reins of production into our own hands. We must take hold of the means of production.' To achieve production, not collaboration with the employing class, but solely the overthrow of capitalist domination is necessary.

The comrades who were sowing these thoughts among the masses did not, we regret to say, encounter sufficient attention among the workers. I already told you that the social-democratic movement, in agreement with the trade-union bureaucracy, strived to convince the masses of workers – and especially the revolutionaries – of cooperation with the employers in the field of production, and by such means hold them back from revolutionary action. When, in spite of this, the revolutionary upheaval made the bourgeoisie tremble, the latter shrewdly availed itself of the mediation of the trade-union bureaucracy and voluntarily promised the workers everything they had wanted to take by force. Of course, it would be naïve to expect sincerity from the bourgeoisie.

When, in March and June 1919, revolution thundered all over Germany, the workers were told: 'Have patience, you will be given control over production; you will be granted equal rights with the employers in the field of production and the right to form factory committees.'

The workers of Britain have also attempted to shake the foundations of the capitalist order by the organisation and activity of the Shop Stewards.[7] The bourgeoisie of Austria and Sweden, has suffered the same blows, and in the end was compelled under the pressure of the workers to promise some rights. The bourgeoisie told the workers that the capitalist order was a very complicated and difficult system, and any changes in its construction or any new introduction must be seriously weighed. In addition, the workers were promised a law on socialisation, the improvement of conditions in industry, and the creation of factory committees. All this was done, of course, to make the workers imagine that they are almost the sole owners of industry and induced them to think, naïvely, that socialisation of industry would come. It is necessary to recall how the revolutionary sections of the workers have acted.

When the revolutionary sections of the workers learned that civil peace was continuing after the war to the detriment of the working class, a great number of workers of various countries hesitated as to whether trade unions were necessary at all or were superfluous. Perhaps the labour movement as a whole is not worth much, they thought. You are aware of the experience at the time, when the capitalist class was weakened and depressed, when the workers did not ask their bosses whether they agreed to an eight-hour working day, but simply took it by force. At that time the idea arose of making use of factory committees as the nuclei of industrial unions, at the same time thinking that the trade unions themselves had outlived their time. Such a movement occurred among the vast masses of workers in Germany. And the direct action of the shop stewards was permeated with the same spirit.[8]

These ideas may also have evolved for the following reasons: Trade-union organisations originated at first as local craft unions of workers. These unions developed over time into a central confederation; in their essence, they remained organisations of the craft type. Capitalist production developed in the meantime on a different basis. The growth of capitalist production was not due, of course, to one enterprise uniting similar enterprises, such as locksmiths with locksmiths, carpenters with carpenters, etc. In capitalist production gigantic enterprises developed from one single unit by means of its organic growth. In these gigantic enterprises the raw material usually passed through all stages of production, until it was transformed into finished products. This

7 For the Shop Stewards' movement in Britain, see p. 140, n. 11.

8 The Revolutionary Shop Stewards (revolutionären Obleute) in Germany emerged out of mass strikes and antigovernment protests during 1917–18. In Berlin elected workers' representatives who had led these battles formed the Revolutionary Shop Stewards of the Large Factories of Greater Berlin. These militants, based largely among metalworkers, collaborated with the USPD and were generally aligned with its left wing. While the group was built in opposition to the trade-union bureaucracy in Germany, most leaders of the Revolutionary Shop Stewards nevertheless did not call for workers to leave the trade unions.

was the rule in capitalist countries. When the workers created their factory committees it became easier for them to fight the owners, because they were united in one committee instead of being divided into ten or fifteen craft unions.

The trade unions, owing to their structure, were not adapted for fighting against capital. We must make use of the factory committees in order to abolish the craft organisations, and to transform the trade unions into industrial organisations.

When the unions, with the help of the factory committees, are reorganised on an industrial basis, then these committees become the organs of industrial bodies, the very same bodies that industrial workers will rely on in the separate enterprises. During the revolutionary period, a number of new ideas enter into the minds of the workers; a number of wrong ideas are knocked out, and their heads become clear. The factory committees have not as yet become the mechanism for transforming the trade unions into organs adapted to the requirements of the class struggle. The bourgeoisie is too strong for that, and became stronger every day; on the other hand, the labour unions did not become what they should have become to carry out the struggle. I shall not dwell in any length on the fact that in different sections of the working class the idea and hope arose that all difficulties could be overcome by means of organisational schemes and experiments. This actually prevailed in various countries.

We must state the fact that the capitalist system is advancing toward ruin, and that this process goes hand-in-hand with the disintegration of the working class. Industry must be saved, and this is possible only on condition that the capitalists no longer are at the helm of economic life. Hence our primary problem is to fight the notion of class collaboration that has taken root in the working masses, of cooperation with their class foes in the matter of production. This we shall accomplish through the work we do in our everyday fights and struggles. It is beyond any doubt that the idea of the social revolution has already got a strong hold on the minds of a considerable section of the working class.

But we must not overlook the fact that while the working class was maturing, the bourgeoisie was not napping and was utilising this breathing spell. To our regret, we have at present no available proletarian force at our command of sufficient power and resistance urging it on to the revolution, as the state power has completely chained the proletariat. In a large number of countries there are all sorts of laws – especially laws and a whole mass of regulations dealing with cooperation between labour and employers' organisations in the field of production. All this legislation completely paralyses the development of the revolutionary struggle.

In this respect we now no longer have the same favourable terrain that we had during the formation of the first factory committees. In view of this, the question arises whether, under the given conditions, we could revive the idea of factory committees and carry out revolutionary work on this basis. There are many who maintain that this is impossible just now; that real revolutionary work can be carried out only when the revolutionary storm is in full force and capitalism totters and breaks down. Hence the inference that the idea of taming the bourgeoisie by utilising the trade-union machinery is reactionary, or rather a piece of sheer madness. Our answer to that is that the choice of the starting point of our revolutionary work does not depend upon us.

In order to deploy our forces and prepare them for revolutionary action in the future, we must start from the situation we are placed in by the given stage of historical development, irrespective of our likes and dislikes. And when we see that inevitable disaster is getting nearer with every hour and involves the working masses, we take as the starting point of our movement the vital interests of these working masses approaching the fatal point of extinction in order, amid the conditions created by the exploiters and the state, to fan the flame of battle and knock down the high walls that class collaboration has built around the proletariat.

We know that in many countries, unemployment has assumed frightful proportions. Hence the workers' leaders within enterprises have the very serious task before them of explaining to the workers that the stoppage of production, which arises from the capitalist conditions of wholesale unemployment, is not entirely due – especially now – to overproduction, but rather to underconsumption of the goods produced on the part of the impoverished masses.

We must show workers that cooperation with the employers in production is plunging them ever deeper into this disaster; that instead of the promised bait of restoring industry, the cruel fact in store for them is the most complete and irreparable paralysis of economic life. All this is very useful material for agitation. It can and must serve the cause of mobilising the masses and making them ready for militant action.

The battle is inevitable; it cannot be otherwise when capitalism is being drawn into the whirlwind of unparalleled unemployment growing daily with unheard-of rapidity. The reason for the growth of unemployment is due to underconsumption on the part of the masses, which in its turn leads to the further shrinkage of production, since every worker thrown out onto the scrap heap ceases to be a consumer. And so we are on the road to economic ruin. This must be made clear to the proletariat.

As for the unemployed, they must be made to realise clearly that their returning to the factory is not a mere personal question for each one of them, but it is a question of raising industrial production to a higher level. But here we clash with the employer, who says, 'I have no need of the unemployed, as I am not interested at present in the extension of my business.' If this is so, it is evident that the unemployed worker must return to his lathe irrespective of whether the employer agrees or not. The unemployed need food, clothes, and shoes, and cannot get them. The employer says: 'I have no need for factory hands in the present economic situation. Neither do I want nor can I pay for their work, considering that my aim is production for profit.' If we can take the point of view of the unemployed and develop our militant action on this basis – i.e., by demanding that the unemployed be returned to the factories – it becomes evident that the inevitable resistance on the part of the employers due to the capitalist mode of production must inevitably lead to a revolution. The workers would learn that their salvation depends upon their own initiative and mass action against their employer's will.

It is true that from the standpoint of many comrades it is inadvisable to create a revolution at present, basing their arguments upon groundless quotations from history and economics. The dead letter of a book has never created a revolution. The question now is: Which conditions are appropriate and which are inappropriate for a revolution? A revolution is inappropriate when the working masses are not revolutionary or class-conscious. A revolution cannot happen when the workers do not realise their miserable economic and social conditions. But as soon as the working class awakens to the fact that there is only one way to improve things, as soon as it begins to realise its conditions, its economic place, it is then ready for action. No power on earth can hold it back. The same idea can be expressed in another way: when the economic conditions of the proletariat reach a state beyond endurance, when its intellect is sufficiently developed to understand the economic reasons for these conditions, neither factory committees nor collective bargaining with the employers will have the power to hold the workers back from a victorious revolution.

Comrades, let us sum up our theses. Comrade Tsyperovich and I have put great stress on the importance of the present-day unemployment in the proletarian movement. It is incumbent on us to utilise these forces. I hope that we have also succeeded in showing you the right direction toward the realisation of our aim – the victory of the revolution. We consider that by utilising the factory committees and shop stewards, we can prepare and organise them for the proletarian struggle. We also hope that the trade unions will be renewed and, through factory committees, will continue the fight in defence of the social revolution. I ask you, comrades, to accept the theses proposed as a guideline for the immediate future in our struggle for a final victory over capital.

Lozovsky: Comrades, in connection with the two reports, on trade unions and factory committees, and on workers' control, there is a motion not to take up the questions for discussion, but to refer them directly to a commission composed of four delegates for each country possessing 16 votes, three members for countries with 12 votes, two members for countries with 8 votes, and one member for countries with 4 votes. Who desires to speak on this question?

Franz Grölig (Germany): In view of the exceptional importance of the question raised in connection with the reports of Tsyperovich and Heckert pertaining to the everyday practical activity of the labour organisations in the economic field, I propose to submit these questions to a general discussion.

Lozovsky: We thus have two motions. The first is to refer the question to the commission without taking it up for discussion. If the commission is unanimous in its findings, it will be up to the congress to open general discussion. If, on the contrary, two points of view are expressed in the commission, they must both be taken up for discussion at the congress. The second motion is to start immediately with a discussion of the reports. I put the two motions to a vote. Who is for referring the questions to the commission? Who is against? (*There follows a vote by the raising of hands, but it does not give a clear majority.*)

One of the Russian delegates (*from his seat*): What is the opinion of the delegations?

Lozovsky: The majority of the delegations is for transferring the question to the commission.

One of the German delegates (*from his seat*): It must be voted by delegation.

Lozovsky: I shall then have to vote by countries. I shall read the countries and each country will answer: commission or discussion.

Austria: discussion. Azerbaijan: commission. Armenia: no representative. Hungary: no representative. Far-Eastern Republic: commission. Canada: commission. Poland: commission. Ukraine: commission. Czechoslovakia: commission. Romania: commission. Finland: discussion. Sweden: commission. Korea: commission. Australia: discussion. Britain: discussion. Bulgaria: commission. Germany: discussion. Spain: commission. Latvia: commission. Russia: commission. France: commission. Estonia: commission. Luxembourg: discussion. Switzerland: discussion. United States of America: 9 for commission, 7 for discussion.

Comrades, as a result of the voting we have 95 votes for discussion, 201 for commission. So, the question is referred to the commission.

(*After hearing the results of the voting, a statement was handed in by Lithuania, which was omitted from the list; it also votes for commission. Thus, the number of delegates who voted for the commission amounts to 205.*)

Comrade Reinstein has the floor for a communication on behalf of the Credentials Commission.

Reinstein: Allow me to communicate to the congress that, although there has been no statement handed in or credentials presented, we are aware of the presence here of Comrades Bianchi and Azimonti, representatives of the General Confederation of Labour of Italy headed by D'Aragona. Should any documents in relation to this matter be presented to the Credentials Commission, the latter will draw its conclusion and submit them to the congress. For the moment we are unable to supply fuller information.

The Italian Question

Lozovsky: Comrade Tsyperovich has the floor.

Tsyperovich: Comrades, the question of admitting to the congress Comrades Bianchi and Azimonti representing the Italian Confederation of Labour is a very serious and acute question. The CGL delegates last year took part in signing, together with representatives of other countries, the agreement with the Russian Trade Union Council with regard to the organisation of the Red International. They assured us that the Italian proletariat was vitally interested in this important matter. Since then, however, the Italian delegates took no part in the work of the provisional International Council of Trade Unions. At the same time, they have been taking a very active part in the work of the Amsterdam International, in spite of the fact that at the formation of our International they emphasised very clearly that they were against the viewpoint of the Amsterdam International. A short time ago the Livorno Congress passed a very clear resolution to the effect that the Italian trade-union movement was in favour of the Red Trade Union International.[9] Nevertheless, the leading elements of the CGL have continued to orient toward Amsterdam and in every way evaded

9 For the March 1921 congress of the CGL in Livorno, see p. 144, n. 17.

working in common with the Red International. During the last few months the leaders of the CGL have made all possible efforts to have our congress postponed or to thwart it.

Taking all this into account, I find it necessary to request that Comrades Bianchi and Azimonti state the reasons for their actions, and in connection with their explanations, to hold a thorough discussion of the matter in order to bring out clearly to what extent their credentials reflect the revolutionary feeling of the Italian proletariat.

Lozovsky: Comrade Bianchi will now speak.

Giuseppe Bianchi (Italy, CGL) began his speech by explaining the reasons that prevented the Italian delegation from arriving in due time to the present international congress of red trade unions.

First of all, the Italian organisations have the habit of discussing prior to congresses all the materials on hand, and only after those discussions have taken place in their organisations and after the masses have pronounced their opinion, the General Confederation of Labour – which voices the state of mind and opinions of two and a quarter million workers – undertakes the task of interpreting the thoughts of these workers at an international congress. On the present occasion, the CGL lacked the possibility of getting the necessary materials; it was acquainted only with the agenda, but knew nothing about the reports to be delivered and was waiting, therefore, for fuller information concerning the forthcoming congress.

Having failed to receive the necessary information, the Italian delegation nevertheless still sent its representatives. The delegation was further detained in Berlin; Comrade Bianchi asserted that they were told by the Russian mission there that the congress was delayed until 10 July. On its arrival in Moscow, however, the delegation found that the labours of the congress were in full swing. Upon arrival in Moscow, the delegation became aware that representation at the congress was extremely heterogeneous. Comrade Bianchi adds, by way of explanation, that when the CGL addressed its request to the Russian comrades to adjourn the congress, it had in view that in this case there would be a greater possibility for homogeneous representation at the congress.

It was for the above reasons that the Italian delegation requested the Russian comrades to transfer the congress to any of the European centres.[10] These fears were justified. The organisations that ought to have entered into closer mutual

10 The 25 June 1921 issue of *Moscow* (no. 25) published the following telegram by the CGL received 15 June by the International Trade Union Council in Moscow: 'Confederation of

connections were not represented at the congress. The representatives of certain organisations – for instance the representatives of the Unione Syndicale [USI] – were not afforded the possibility of being present at the congress.[11] Taking into consideration the obstacles that the European governments were putting in the way of the delegates obtaining visas and passports for Russia, the CGL deemed it advisable to transfer the congress to one of the European centres.

In spite of everything they are here, be it only for purposes of information, so as to acquaint the Italian comrades with what has been going on at this congress. Bianchi said that they intend to participate in the work of the congress only insofar as they are able to give the necessary explanations to questions that might arise with regard to Italy. Owing to the fact that the Italian delegation was deprived of the possibility to discuss the items on the agenda beforehand, it was not given the right to actually participate in the discussion on these questions by the CGL. He further declared that the CGL embraces two and a half million workers, and that greater attention should therefore be paid to an organisation with so many members. He said that the Russian comrades usually obtained their information with regard to the Italian movement from indirect sources.

All the rumours that have been circulating about Italy are false. Bianchi asserted that before Moscow raised the question of an opposition to be formed against Amsterdam, Italy was the first to create it. At its Livorno Congress the CGL brought in the question of creating an opposition to Amsterdam. In 1919 the CGL took the initiative and organised protest strikes against the blockade of Russia. Comrade Bianchi, continuing, said that these actions could not excite the sympathy of Amsterdam, which naturally did not share their point of view; because of this the strike could not be organised on as large a scale as Italy had proposed.

The revolutionary character of the General Confederation of Labour amounts to the following: At the time of the occupation of the factories, shops, and lands, the movement had developed under the influence of the CGL, which started creating separate nuclei composed of soldiers coming from the front. It took advantage of their state of mind, directed the ever-growing movement

---

Labour proposes to hold the Congress of Labour Unions in Stockholm or Reval postponing it till August, so as to have the decisions of the Congress of the 3rd International and to extend the order of business, preceding it by a general discussion of the International position of labor unions and of the program of the 3rd International on these questions.'

11 The Italian Syndicalist Union (USI) did send a delegation to the RILU congress, but it did not arrive until the congress had concluded. See Tosstorff 2016, p. 266.

and, in the long run, got the possibility of support from wide masses of workers and peasants in order to achieve, de facto, by means of direct action, control over production. The movement began by the occupation of a whole series of factories and shops. The CGL therefore did not confine its aims to purely local actions taking place in Turin and Milan.

The confederation aimed at the seizure of all industry and taking possession of the land in order to re-establish the agricultural economy. But this movement was broken. The reason for this was not that the CGL failed to give proof of sufficient activity, but owing to the very same leftist tendencies that Comrade Lenin designated by the name of 'infantile disorder'. The defeat was due to the extremist tendencies that began taking root in certain sections of the Italian proletariat. Although a great number of comrades who later passed over to the Communist Party had a clear idea of the situation, they nevertheless tried to ascribe to the movement – which bore a spontaneous and elemental character – a political character that it did not have, and issued to the working mass the extreme slogans that resulted in complete defeat of the workers.

As to the charges brought against the CGL in general and its leaders in particular, it is said that the Italian CGL is tied to the bourgeoisie, that it can be easily confused with Amsterdam, and that its leaders are to be considered as members, on an equal footing, of the Amsterdam International. Nevertheless, referring to Comrade Gennari – a participant in the congress of the Communist International and now a member of its Executive Committee – Comrade Bianchi states that even the Italian Communists do not dare say that the CGL is to be put on the same level as Amsterdam. Bianchi quoted a passage from an article by Comrade Gennari in which the latter stated that the activity of the CGL is by no means as closely connected with the bourgeoisie and Amsterdam as it might appear at first sight. Comrade Bianchi stated that the CGL has nothing to hide, and that he was speaking openly in order to dispel all the misunderstandings and misrepresentations concerning the CGL.

He said that we had always maintained, and will continue to maintain, a revolutionary position. Since 1919 the confederation has had the goal of bringing about a social revolution, but it was handicapped by the extreme left elements, which were paralysing the movement at inopportune times. The most acute question – which had an enormous significance at the time of the occupation of the factories, and which acquired an even greater significance when the movement was strangled – was the question of control over production. Bianchi said that he has in his possession a whole series of documents drawn from the reports of the CGL for the last year, which can prove that all his assertions are not groundless. The question of workers' control was posed in the CGL as a concrete demand of the day, which it continues to fight for.

Comrade Bianchi stated that the movement was rendered helpless because it was localised and isolated in separate regions of Italy. The fault does not rest with the leaders. He said that during the powerful movement of 1919 revolutionary demands were put forward not only by him – Bianchi – who occupied a centre position and by left-wing elements, but even by [right-wing elements in the PSI such as] Buozzi, who was also a member of the CGL. But responsible people like me and other members had to take into consideration the real situation and to draw from it the necessary conclusions, and not allow ourselves to be guided by our own revolutionary sentiments.

He pointed out further that when the movement was in full swing, the question was very sharply posed: what to do? The factories and workshops had been occupied in many parts of the country; about 30,000 hectares of land were seized. A special commission was created to discuss tactical methods. It was like a military general staff that had to decide whether it was possible to pass over from the defensive to the offensive, as well as the possibility of creating a red army.

This commission contained military specialists sufficiently acquainted with the extent of available military forces and with the possibilities for creating a military organisation. The commission came to the conclusion that direct action was impossible, not only owing to the lack of a dependable military force, but also owing to the economic situation of the country, which indicated that the movement lacked a solid foundation. Industry was ruined and the branch of it that was still in action – the military industry, owing to the weakness of the general state of industry – could be shifted from a military to a peaceful basis again only with the greatest difficulty. At any rate, Comrade Bianchi thought, one cannot say that the CGL betrayed the movement just because the movement did not have the desired result. One cannot speak of treason in analysing the CGL's activity from September until today. Comrade Bianchi does not seek to defend the leaders of the CGL. He considers that they are not in need of this defence. He repeats again that a study of the situation in Italy can be done only on the spot.

Addressing the congress, he said that if they came to Italy and saw for themselves what is happening there, they would become convinced that the CGL, owing to the existing state of things in Italy and the historical and political condition, could not have acted otherwise than it did. The National Council is at the head of the CGL, constituting the heart and brains of the Italian working class. He pointed out the fact that separate labour exchanges and federations send their representatives to the National Council. This council is made up not just of federated unions, but also of unions composed of local district labour exchanges.

He said there was another obstacle that impeded decisive action. This obstacle consisted in the fact that the CGL's connection with the Socialist Party – a connection that was established at the insistence of the extremists and partisans of Serrati – had created a particularly difficult situation for the CGL. During the period when the movement reached its climax, the question was raised as to who was to take responsibility for this movement: the party or the CGL? It must be stated that in agreement with the party, the CGL leads the economic struggle, whereas the party leads the revolution. Therefore, the party ought to take the initiative. By virtue of the above, the CGL did not assume the responsibility for the movement, but for their part the Communists lacked the determination to continue the revolutionary movement.

Further, Comrade Bianchi expressed his displeasure at the entirely false light thrown upon the attitude of the CGL toward Amsterdam. Italy was in opposition to Amsterdam prior to Moscow's appeal, and was the first to respond to the appeal to create an organised opposition to Amsterdam in the shape of the Red Trade Union International. But a whole series of obstacles stood between Moscow and the CGL. These obstacles consisted first of all in incorrect information with regard to the activities of the CGL, whereas the work of the CGL within the Amsterdam International was exactly the same as the work of Moscow outside it. The Russian comrades confused their aim of destroying Amsterdam with the idea of solidarity with Amsterdam.

Bianchi expressed doubts as to whether the present congress really represents 17 million workers. He believes the figure to be exaggerated, and that if our congress truly unites such a large mass of workers, why then cry out for the destruction of Amsterdam from the inside? If the number in question is correct, why ignore the masses within it rather than leading them along the true path? It is necessary not only to gain new partisans among those remaining within Amsterdam, but also, in the course of everyday work, to struggle with the Amsterdam leaders, pointing out to them the sins against revolutionary policy of which they were guilty. Bianchi pointed to himself as one of the representatives of the CGL who, at the congress [of the Amsterdam International] in Switzerland, came out resolutely in opposition to Jouhaux.[12] Comrades who were present at that congress can confirm my statement. The point

12 This passage in the proceedings (in all languages) would seem to refer to the February 1919 conference of the Amsterdam International held in Bern, Switzerland. The CGL is not recorded as having attended that conference, however. Nor was there an Italian delegation at the IFTU's July–August 1919 Amsterdam Congress, as the CGL delegation was refused entry to France on route to Amsterdam. The CGL did send a delegation to the IFTU's London Congress of November 1920.

of dispute during the discussion at that congress was the question of socialisation. Socialisation cannot be realised other than by means of the conquest of power.

Comrade Bianchi finds that our policy with regard to Amsterdam not only abandons the masses in that organisation, but also creates very difficult conditions for the national trade-union organisations. For instance, at the present moment one part of the unions in Switzerland joined Amsterdam, whereas the other part affiliated with Moscow, breaking the unity of the trade-union movement in that country. Do you really desire to split with two and a half million workers [in the CGL], in the same way as the Swiss unions were split? Allowing simultaneous allegiance to the two organisations, giving organisations affiliated to Amsterdam the possibility of continuing their work, is a correct policy. Comrade Bianchi says he is not here to defend Amsterdam and its leaders, but he finds that the Russian comrades were not sufficiently objective in their appreciation of the relations between the CGL and Amsterdam. He said that we can prove with documents in his hands that the CGL is much more with the Communists than with Amsterdam. We have, said he, long since passed from words to action; we have declared our ultimatum to the government: 'The eight-hour day or strike'. We did not act through the intermediary of parliament, but exerted direct pressure on the government with the organised proletariat, obtaining the recognition of the eight-hour working day in Italy.

Matters stand in the same way with workers' control and factory committees, as well as a whole series of other questions. The difference is not in the aims but in tactics. Bianchi referred to the report he wrote last year when he returned from Russia.[13] He pointed out that on both the theoretical and practical level the Italian trade-union movement has taken up the ideas put forward by the Russian Revolution. He sees this report as a document fully confirming the revolutionary position of the CGL. In this pamphlet he endeavours to summarise all that was brought out by Comrades Lozovsky, Tomsky, and other leaders of the All-Russian Trade Union Congress.

Addressing Lozovsky, Bianchi said that, as he had already mentioned many times, information from Italy should be obtained from first-hand sources. Only then would it be possible to refute the charges raised today against the CGL. The voting at the Livorno Congress proved once more that the CGL does not in the least deserve these accusations. There is no doubt whatever that the

---

13 A reference to the report on trade unions in Russia given by Bianchi on behalf of the CGL's commission in Russia, composed of D'Aragona, Bianchi, Colombino, and Dugoni. Published as *Russia sindacale: Rapporto dell'on. Giuseppe Bianchi al Congresso confederale di Livorno* (Milan: Codara di Carlo Matti, 1921).

Italian masses have been greatly revolutionised during the last period, and at this actual moment the Italian proletariat is prepared to assimilate communist ideas. Yet, the vote at the congress resulted in only half a million votes being in favour of the Communists, whereas the overwhelming majority of votes were given to the CGL. Several labour exchanges that had been directly linked to the Communist Party came back to the CGL after its Livorno Congress.

Pointing out the difficult position the newly arrived comrades from Italy are in, Bianchi finds that two circumstances are contributing to it: on the one hand, as was already mentioned, incorrect information about Italy – first, the imprecise information on the situation in Italy; and second, the difficult situation currently of the Socialist Party, a party with which the CGL is linked. The day is approaching when a new split will take place at a congress of the Socialist Party, and it is very possible that three groups will come out of this split – the Communists (minority), the centre, and the right wing.[14] He considered himself to be part of the centre group. He said that the watchword of subordination of the trade-union movement to the party, presented before the Livorno Congress, not only thwarts the movement when the time comes for action, but at the current moment it harms the development of its activities.

To sum up, the delegates from the General Confederation of Labour are present at the International Red Trade Union Congress only for purposes of information with regard to the current situation. Bianchi says that Comrade Lozovsky, when answering the syndicalists of France, Germany, and other countries, stated that the existence of the Red International encompassed the possibility of spiritual links between it and the Communist International. Bianchi felt rather sceptical about that point and about its possibility. The Communist Party would try to win over the International of Trade Unions. Clearly there must be an interdependence of the political and economic organisations of the working class, but the Communist Party poses the question of subordination, which surpasses the requirements of the Socialist Party.

In concluding his speech, Comrade Bianchi said that the atmosphere of ill will that surrounds the CGL is based on entirely secondary considerations. The differences centre more on general considerations rather than the character of its activity.

Much has been said, and with great contempt, about the 50,000 lire received from the Amsterdam International, which were a form of alms. The 50,000 lire is part of the funds that Amsterdam collected during the white terror in

14 Over the next three years, the Italian Socialist Party would undergo two major splits. In October 1922 the reformist right wing was expelled. In 1924 a left-wing pro-Comintern minority split off to join the CP.

Hungary and other countries. Part of this fund was sent to Italy in order to aid the victims of fascism and the white terror. At any rate, Bianchi considers this 50,000 lire as a debt paid by certain organisations to the CGL.

The next accusation brought against the General Confederation of Labour was the agreement with the Fascists.[15] He says that he does not want to compare big things with little things, but nevertheless he wishes to remind us of the fact that even the great Russian Revolution had sometimes resorted to temporary compromises. He is not aware of the CGL having ever entered into an agreement with the Fascists, but he pointed out that the Russians concluded the Brest-Litovsk Peace Treaty.[16] He said that compromises are inevitable during an intense political struggle, because the necessity of a respite for the working masses is sometimes a condition for future victory. There was a moment when the Communists of Italy came to an understanding with the Fascists. After the murder of the secretary of the Communist Party,[17] when the terror was assuming an acute form, the Communist Party addressed itself to the chief of the police asking for a respite. (*A representative of the Communist Party present in the hall declared this to be false. Bianchi responded by offering to back up his statement by proofs before leaving Russia.*)

Bianchi stated once more that he came to the congress for the purpose of information. The fact that the representatives of the GCL came here as visitors but not as actual participants is the result of all the above-mentioned circumstances. Nevertheless, it does not prevent them from being heart and soul with Russia achieving its great revolution. They have always fervently supported the Russian Revolution and have always endeavoured to create an atmosphere of sympathy toward it, which is so necessary for a country fighting for the interests of the working class. Today they are unable to participate in the work of this congress, but in the near future they intend to convene a new congress at which the question will be categorically raised – which of the two worlds is to be victorious. It is clear, Bianchi says, that the Italian proletariat will be with Russia.

Rykov (chair): The floor is given to Comrade Lozovsky.

---

15 A formal agreement of the parliamentary representatives of the Italian Socialist Party and CGL with those of the Fascist party, including Mussolini himself, was signed on 3 August 1921. It was published the following day on the front page of *Avanti*, under the title 'Truce'. Mussolini announced the end of the truce in November 1921.

16 The Brest-Litovsk Peace Treaty between Soviet Russia and the Central Powers headed by Germany was signed on 3 March 1918. Under its terms, Soviet Russia ceded a quarter of the population of the old Russian Empire, as well as nine-tenths of its coal mines.

17 This is presumably a reference to Communist editor Spartaco Lavagnini, killed in Florence by a Fascist squad on 27 February 1921 at the offices of *L'Azione Comunista*.

Lozovsky: Comrades, the question that has arisen at the present time encompasses the whole activity of the Italian General Confederation of Labour and the relations that have existed in recent months between the CGL and the Red Trade Union International on one side and, on the other, the future of the trade-union movement in Italy. What interests us here is not why the Italian delegates arrived late, but why they came to this constituent congress in a consultative capacity, while they are going to the Amsterdam Congress with a decisive vote. This is a question of principle.

Let us look into the facts and documents in our possession.

When the Italian comrades were in Russia in July 1920, we started talks to create a Red Trade Union International intended to oppose the Amsterdam International, and differences were expressed. Our Italian comrades said, 'We cannot leave Amsterdam immediately. We are willing to sign a pact with you, an agreement, but we will stay in Amsterdam for a period of time to oppose and work for the cause you here are working for.'

Now, comrades, if we look at the past eleven months, if we go through the history of the trade-union movement in Italy and especially its international activity, we note first of all that despite signing an agreement with us, creating a revolutionary nucleus that was to fight Amsterdam, the CGL did absolutely nothing to link its actions with those in Russia. On the contrary, it did a lot to get closer to the Amsterdam International. Did not the very fact of signing a commitment with us obligate the CGL not just to put itself in opposition to Amsterdam, but also to take measures so that its actions have an impact internationally?

What have you been doing all this time? You'll remember, Comrade Bianchi, that our exchange of views dates back to October. It was in October that I wrote my open letter to the CGL, to which the CGL replied with a letter explaining the reasons why it was staying in the Amsterdam International, in order to work in opposition.[18] And on 23 November Italian delegates participated in the London Congress [of the Amsterdam International].[19] What were they doing there?

Bianchi: Working as an opposition.

Lozovsky (*continues*): I will explain what this opposition consists of. What did they actually do? A number of issues were discussed at the London Congress, notably the question of distribution of raw materials among the various

18 For Lozovsky's 23 October 1920 open letter to the CGL and the latter's reply to it, see pp. 97–98, n 7.

19 The London Congress of the Amsterdam International was held 22–27 November 1920.

nations, the question of socialisation, and the question of the insults that the Red International of Labour Unions had made with regard to the sacrosanct Amiens Charter. In the speech that the Italian comrades gave at the congress, they opposed – it's true – the chauvinistic spirit that reigned there. They repeatedly pointed out that the policies practised by the leaders of the international trade-union movement have had a poisonous impact internationally. But afterwards, comrades, when it came time to vote on the resolution on socialisation, there was only one organisation at the congress that voted against.[20] The Italian comrades voted with the Amsterdam people in favour of the resolution on socialisation.

What does socialisation mean for Amsterdam? This has been very clearly explained to us. In the letter addressed to Gompers, which you will find in issue no. 21 of *Mouvement Syndical* published by Amsterdam, Jouhaux and Company wrote, 'Socialisation should not be confused with socialism; socialisation is peaceful action and not revolutionary action'.[21]

The Amsterdam people say definitely and clearly that socialisation does not mean socialism at all. This should not trouble Gompers in the least. Is he not troubled by the question of collective ownership of the railways?[22] This explanation as to the difference between socialism and socialisation splendidly illustrates not only the essentials of the theory, but also the practice of the Amsterdam International.

And you, the representatives of Italy, sign a resolution that sows confusion in the minds of the masses of Italy; you sign it together with Jouhaux. And you say you have been in opposition. When you signed this confused resolution, you were an opposition in words, but not in deeds. And the other representatives said, 'Yes, on the practical question, we agree with the Italians.' I am well aware of the speech that Comrade Bianchi made at the congress. No doubt he said that one could not have socialisation without a revolution. That's true. But then why did the CGL sign a resolution on socialisation that is entirely permeated by this spirit of class collaboration, by this spirit that we can achieve socialisation without revolution and by simple class agreement?

---

20 The organisation opposing the socialisation resolution at the Amsterdam International's London Congress was the Norwegian Confederation of Trade Unions.

21 For social-democratic 'socialisation' schemes, see p. 84, n. 1.

22 At the June 1919 convention of the American Federation of Labor, Gompers opposed a resolution calling for government ownership of the railroads. Although the resolution passed, Gompers nevertheless continued his opposition, fighting against the Plumb Plan to extend the US government's wartime seizure of railroads.

Secondly, when the question of the Moscow International came up at the London Congress, when the Amsterdam people formulated a resolution directed against us, did the CGL vote against this resolution? No, it abstained. There was only one organisation – that of the Norwegian comrades – that said, 'To vote for this resolution means to engage in a counterrevolutionary demonstration.' I ask Comrade Bianchi to tell me frankly: Is this really opposition, or is it collaboration? No, comrades, this is not opposition; it is collaboration.

In all this, when a congress adopts a resolution violently opposed to the trade-union International that we have created together with your representatives, who signed here in Moscow the agreement founding this Red Trade Union International, you abstain, and say: 'Don't look. We sinned in Moscow; here we are in Europe and it no longer concerns us. We abstain.'

Comrade Bianchi, explaining to us the situation in Italy, spoke about the Livorno Congress [of the CGL]. What did this Livorno Congress do? What is its resolution? Here is the text:

> The CGL congress decides:
>
> 1. To affiliate wholeheartedly to the initiative to found a red trade-union International, subject to the condition that the ties between the Labour Confederation and the Socialist Party remain in place, and that the principle of unification of the Italian trade-union movement in the Confederation be recognised.
> 2. To break from the Amsterdam trade-union alliance, in accord with the decisions to be taken by the Moscow trade-union congress.

The resolution says, 'we affiliate'. But comrades, we need an expression of this affiliation. We need an expression that is not only abstract, but also concrete. Material evidence of this membership must be given. One cannot affiliate in words and not affiliate in deeds. How could you apply this CGL decision? Did you write to us and ask for our opinion on the question of the relations of the Socialist Party and the CGL? Instead of sticking to that decision that said, 'Join without reservations', you not only made many reservations, but you did much more.

From the Livorno Congress that took place in February up until today, you have gotten closer to the Amsterdam International. At the CGL's National Council in April,[23] you decided to address the Amsterdam International, asking the latter to come to the aid of the Italian movement. This was a rapprochement –

23 The CGL National Council meeting was held 22 April 1921.

not a platonic rapprochement, but a de facto rapprochement. The facts speak for themselves. The English have a saying, 'facts are stubborn things', and I think we have to stick to those facts. When the Amsterdam International sent proof of its good feelings toward our Italian comrades, whose good will and goodness of spirit I do not question, you replied to these 50,000 lire by a sweet note.

But comrades, we still have to understand how much impact this had outside Italy. When I take *Le Populaire* of Paris, an organ that combats communism and the revolution, I find there your exchange of letters, or diplomatic notes, with Amsterdam, followed by this little explanatory remark: 'While the Amsterdam International expresses its solidarity with Italian workers and sends them money, the Moscow International is hurling its anathemas and Papal Bulls in order to send the CGL to the pillory.'[24]

The spirit of this exchange of letters was well understood. Indeed, comrades, as long as you are in the Third International you must adhere to it alone. We can tolerate the ambiguous situation in which you find yourself after signing your treaty with us without having left Amsterdam for one, two, or three months, but not forever. You have to understand that this situation cannot last. Tell me, comrades, when you sent your delegates to London, they went as members like all the others. But when you come to Moscow, before you even came, you already put forward reservations. 'We are going to Moscow for information purposes only.'

When you signed a commitment with us in July 1920, did you not know that this committed you to something? Otherwise it was not a commitment. And if you come here on a purely fact-finding mission, it proves that you not only have reservations about one issue, but that you will formulate a whole series of reservations that we will discuss later.

In general we could translate the relations of the comrades of Italy in this way: they are legally married to Amsterdam, while they are flirting with Moscow. *Avanti*, the organ that directs the spirit of the CGL, commented on the donation of 50,000 lire.[25] It writes, 'We are moved by this gesture of solidarity. We know that among the people in this organisation, there are some with whom we do not entirely agree, and we could even formulate some criticisms of their past actions. But since they currently are making this gesture, now is not the time for criticism.' (Comrade Bianchi, do you have the text of this art-

24 An apparent reference to the article 'L'Internationale syndicale d'Amsterdam pour le prolétariat italien' in the 21 May 1921 issue of *Le Populaire*.

25 A reference to the 11 May 1921 issue of *Avanti*, which contained a front-page article on the Amsterdam International's donation of 50,000 lire. The title of the article was 'International Solidarity'.

icle? If not, I can give it to you; it is not signed.) When the central organ of the [Socialist] Party writes, 'We could criticise the past actions of these people' – that is to say, their actions during the battle – 'but we do not currently do so' – what does that mean in political language? It means, 'No doubt they sinned during the war, but now is not the time to discuss this'.

Comrade Bianchi, you said earlier that you are in opposition [to Amsterdam]. Does the action of these people after the war differ from their action during the war? It became even more villainous, more treacherous. And when the central organ of the party says, 'We could criticise their past actions', it is speaking a falsehood. And why? So as to consolidate the unity between Amsterdam and the Italian comrades. This will have bad results, because the Italian proletariat will not want to stay in this lovely company for long.

I now move on to the latest fact. We received on the eve of the congress (it was 20 or 25 June) a telegram in which the Italian comrades asked us first to adjourn our congress in August in order to find out the decisions that would be taken at the congress of the Communist International and to discuss these, and then to transfer the congress to Reval or Stockholm.

A number of delegates had already arrived, and we replied by telegraph: (1) that it was impossible to adjourn the congress; and (2) that there were already nearly 150 delegates who were here, and that if there were difficulties for the Italians, it was obvious that there were also difficulties for the others.

Comrade Bianchi says, 'We had difficulties; we could have come in greater numbers'. But there are comrades who came from Australia, and as you know, Australia is geographically a little further away from us than Italy. These comrades came anyway, because they wanted to come. For them it was not a matter of formalities, of diplomacy. They came because they had a burning desire to get together with all the revolutionaries and work out a single course of action, to counterpose to those who betray the workers' cause an organisation with the will and the power to fight world capitalism.

After the telegram in question, I received a letter signed by Comrade D'Aragona and dated 25 May. The telegram was sent after the letter, but it was received before.

In this letter of 25 May, D'Aragona expresses the wish that the congress be held in Reval or Stockholm. Well, we too would like the congress to be held in Reval or Stockholm, and not only in one of these cities, but also in Milan, Berlin, or Paris. But it does not depend on us. There is the bourgeoisie, which still exists, and which, as Comrade Bianchi knows well, would not allow our congress to meet in one of the cities under its control, a congress that deals not only with socialisation, but also with some other questions dangerous for world capitalism.

And when you offer to hold our congress in Reval or Stockholm, do you provide us with guarantees that we can transfer it there? Have you discussed this with the governments of Reval or Stockholm through diplomatic channels?

When our Russian delegates were in Kristiania [Oslo][26] we asked the Swedish government to give us permission to cross Sweden in order to enter Germany. After long deliberations the authorities granted us a visa under the following conditions, which we had to submit to: we promised not to devote ourselves 'to propaganda of any kind while on Swedish soil'. This alone was not quite satisfactory to the government, but in order to assure themselves of the fulfilment of our promise and obligations, the Swedish government placed four gentlemen with police faces in our car with the sole purpose of spying on us and seeing that we maintained perfect order and did not make Bolshevik propaganda during the journey through Swedish territory, that is to say, for fourteen hours by train. This fact alone explains, with sufficient clarity, that the motion to move the congress to Stockholm is ridiculous. Further you suggest 'Reval'. Now, did you inquire of the Estonian government whether they would allow such a congress? If not, your recommendation is simply a piece of diplomacy.

What then is the purpose of this proposal? If we think about it, and if we consider that the Italian comrades are at the head of a large organisation, we see that they must know well what they want. For my part, I believe that they wanted in one way or another to simply adjourn the congress. I do not know if they wanted anything more, but there was in any case among them the desire that the congress not take place now and be put off to the Greek calends.

And after this exchange of letters, the CGL meets and decides: 'We will send our delegates in a consultative capacity for information purposes only'. What do you want to inform about, comrades? If you want to find out if we are for the social revolution and the dictatorship of the proletariat, I think you already know the answer very well. But you did not come to investigate the situation in Russia; you came to a constitutive congress of the Red Labour Union International. What information do you want to draw from this congress? Do you not know that by signing the agreement with us you already laid the foundation for this organisation, which was the nucleus that was to oppose Amsterdam.

The Italian CGL comrades avoid clarity. They do so because the question is all too clear. Even the Livorno Congress, which decided unequivocally and unreservedly to affiliate, did not commit the CGL by its decision. I say this because this decision implies 'full membership'. Which means you have already

26 For Lozovsky's trip to Norway, see p. 592, n. 12.

chosen between the Amsterdam International and the Red Labour Union International. And yet after Livorno, the CGL still does not make its choice. It says: 'We will send our delegates in a consultative capacity, and we'll await events'.

What does all this prove? It proves the following: you have entered into a legal marriage with Amsterdam and you are simply flirting with us. But we want you to understand that we will never subscribe to such an act; there is no need for information. All such acts of this style are purely political, and by doing so, you are putting a weapon in the hands of our enemy – the Amsterdam International.

You state that you are fighting against the Amsterdam International. This, however, is not true. The Amsterdam International has been claiming a membership of 23 million, among them three and a half million Italian workers. The Amsterdam International speaks, writes, and acts in the name of so many members, in whose number are also included the Italians. The entire policy of Amsterdam is pointing against us. Amsterdam is under your protection. As members of that organisation, you dare not charge them with treason against the working class. You claim that you are making propaganda, that you are in the opposition bloc. To whom is your propaganda addressed? Jouhaux, Simon, and others. But these people and their teachings have long been discredited. When your representatives were in London, where 200 representatives of the 'tops' congregated, did you make propaganda to them? No, you have simply followed them. All the facts show that we differ radically in our methods and tactics.

And now, comrades, a few more documents.

Comrade Bianchi spoke of revolutionary action in Italy, of the action of September–October, during the occupation of the factories and the failure suffered by the workers' movement in Italy. We do not reproach you as to why you did not make a revolution in October. There are ups and downs in every struggle. If we reproach you, it is for your conduct during the month of October.

The question that arose for us during this movement was the lack of clarity, the indecision, that tainted this action. The comrade objected that there was a pact between the party and the CGL. The CGL, after examining the matter, said, 'We cannot take responsibility. We withdraw and leave this to the party.' The party said for its part, 'Since you have withdrawn and have not taken responsibility, we cannot do so either.' But during this time, the workers in the factories were carrying out this action. Can we say to the masses, 'We have a pact and it is not clear who bears the responsibility'? But when the blood flows everyone is responsible. What interests us, I repeat, is this lack of decision, this disengagement, this fear of making decisions: 'We are not yet organised enough, we cannot take responsibility'. It seems to me that this is not a tactic for fighting against the employers. I say this in all frankness and loyalty.

In his speech Comrade Bianchi said that the CGL delegates had come to the present congress knowing full well that their presentation here would not be very regular, that there would be difficulties. And when they got here they convinced themselves that they were right. Comrades, everyone knew there would be difficulties. We are creating an International in opposition to the already existing International. When you signed your pact with us, it was obvious that the situation was not clear. But what matters is not a question of form; it is a question of substance: How to assemble and organise all the revolutionary elements? How to create this body capable of fighting against Amsterdam?

And here Bianchi says: 'We fight in our own way; you fight on the outside and we fight on the inside. We are inside the house and are taking advantage of this to shake things up while waiting to shatter the Amsterdam International in the long run.'

Comrades, I fear that if you continue to do this, it is you who will be shattered. Among which elements will you make propaganda? Do you think Jouhaux and the others need to be informed about the social situation? Do you really believe that your action can affect the Amsterdam people? I even believe that Comrades D'Aragona and Bianchi said that at the London Congress were men who had long years of betrayal, and wavered in their stance toward the bourgeoisie. So we should not be playing petty politics with them, but must act against them. And you, did you write a single manifesto against them?

During these eleven months, what action did the CGL take in opposition to the Amsterdam International? I assert that in everything you have written as members of this International, you have been obligated not to upset the feelings of those who compose it. You cannot tell a person with whom you are in the same organisation that he is a traitor. You can say to him, 'You have slightly different conceptions than I do, but it will all get better over time.' You cannot speak any other language to him. But when we are sure that we are dealing with traitors, we slam the door behind us and leave.

This is why it seems to me that the policy and the actions of our comrades in Italy during these long months have proven that the CGL as an organisation was moving closer to Amsterdam, while the Italian working class was moving closer to Moscow. These facts are undeniable.

If the Livorno Congress decided to affiliate without reservation to the Moscow International …

Bianchi (*interrupting*): An initiative!

Lozovsky (*continues*): But the initiative found expression in this International. The initiative does not always remain an initiative; it takes on a material expression at some point. This material expression found its form in the organisation of the Red Trade Union International. Can we join the initiative without affiliating to its material form? These are subtleties, and I don't believe that Comrade Bianchi is using the subtleties of bourgeois jurisprudence.

Here is another argument: Do we, the Russians or all the comrades present, believe that we will separate from the Italian proletariat? Not at all. We are absolutely sure that the Italian proletarian comrades will be with us. And when Comrade Bianchi says, 'We will be with the revolution', it is the proletarian will of the working class of Italy that speaks through his mouth, because the Italian workers by their actions of the past as well as the present, cannot be with those who are for class collaboration.

But what are the causes of the action of the CGL comrades, what are the causes of their decline, of their legal, somewhat diplomatic, ambiguities? Why these ambiguities? I find an explanation for them in a speech by a delegate here, Comrade Azimonti.

Comrade Azimonti says that there is an opposition between the realistic conception of the working class and its dreams of insurrection. For us the Italian workers' dream of insurrection, their dream of the red flag, is the expression of the vitality of the working class; it is the desire of the working class to overthrow capitalism. It is this understanding, this idea, this somewhat extravagant dream that a certain number of workers have, that stands in opposition to the reformist conception. The counterposition of the two is completely false; it is completely dangerous and harmful in our international activity. And if there are even a small number of comrades among the activists of the CGL who are imbued with this spirit, then we can explain this decline and this incomprehension that currently exists between us.

We hope, comrades, that the CGL – which has done good work for many years and which wants to be with the working class (it cannot do otherwise) – will be with us against Amsterdam. It will be with us, and it will be with us against the will of those who will not be with us, because the Italian working class wants to be with the revolution. It does not have to choose between Amsterdam and Moscow, because it has already chosen. And you must also choose unequivocally and without reservations.

This is why, comrades, I express the hope that in two or three months, at your next congress, a large majority will vote to leave the Amsterdam International and affiliate to the Red International. And if you want the misunderstandings and the confusion that exist to disappear, the CGL must take steps to avoid sowing such misunderstandings in the future – because I believe that the representatives of the CGL have done much to compound these misunderstandings and sow this confusion.

But I believe that the Italian proletarians will correct these faults, and that we will be together to make the social revolution.

Rykov: The session is adjourned until 7:00 p.m. tonight.

Italian Question (continued)

(*Session opens at 7:10 p.m.*)

Lozovsky: Comrades, the Presidium discussed the question of how long approximately the congress will last. We were anxious to arrange our labours so that we might close the congress as early as possible. The following proposal was then made: No general discussions to take place on the question of trade-union tactics, but to refer the question to a commission, after which, if two standpoints are noted, they will be referred to the congress. As to the question of organisation, it is also to be reported to the congress after discussion in commission. We shall thus be able to speed up the labours of the congress, and on Monday [18 July] at the latest we hope to be able to close its sittings.

Bartels (Germany, Gelsenkirchen Free Workers' Union): It was said here that the question of tactics should not be discussed at the plenary session. We declare that under these conditions it was altogether unnecessary to come to Moscow. This question is the most important item on the agenda, and we insist that the plenary take it up for detailed consideration.

Lozovsky: Does anyone wish to speak on the question of whether the discussion on tactics should be taken up at the plenary session or be referred to the commission? Who will speak in favour of referring it to the commission? As no one seconds this motion [by Bartels] it is declared rejected.

Discussion will be opened at the plenary session. We shall now take up the Italian question. Comrade Ghioldi has the floor.

Rodolfo Ghioldi (Argentina): I wish to state my opinion on this question, as in Argentina we are quite familiar with its details. First of all, I wish to point out Comrade Bianchi's error, perhaps unintentional on his part, in saying that Comrade Lozovsky and his comrades are in favour of the independence of the trade-union movement. This is untrue, especially since the congress has already adopted the resolution on the relations between the Communist International and the Trade Union International, and decided to have mutual representation on the executive committees of each International.

Bianchi referred to the revolutionary past of the Italian CGL, as shown by its opposition to the war and by the fact that its delegates were present at the

 | DOI:10.1163/9789004712867_015

Zimmerwald Conference. But these facts are not sufficient for one to recognise a revolutionary spirit in that organisation. It is enough to be familiar with its general policy after the war and its stand as regards Amsterdam in order to prove that. Although we may give it credit for its pre-war conduct, we must now unreservedly condemn this organisation for its constant reformism. Besides, we should not forget that many of the participants at Zimmerwald are now dangerous counterrevolutionists, such as Merrheim, Jouhaux's right-hand man in France.

This morning Comrade Bianchi said that the CGL, through Comrade D'Aragona, had signed the agreement against Amsterdam, and has not changed its point of view since. But what does it mean to be against Amsterdam? It is not enough to oppose it with words while supporting it in deeds; it must be given no support, for it is the bulwark of the bourgeoisie. We must, in the name of the class struggle, fight the yellow trade-union International to the death, because this is the indispensable preliminary condition for defeating the capitalist system. To belong to Amsterdam means to serve its leaders, who are in the pay of capital.

The stand taken by the CGL is quite peculiar. It stands with one foot in Amsterdam and the other in Moscow, which enables it to turn both to the government and to the masses at the same time. For the government, affiliation with Amsterdam signifies social peace; the masses identify the word 'Moscow' with the idea of supporting the Russian Revolution. Such a false, erroneous position cannot last. There is only one course to follow for honest revolutionaries: against Amsterdam and for Moscow. The Italian Confederation of Labour must choose between the two. (*Applause*)

It was somewhat curious to listen today, at this congress, to the plea in defence of the CGL, which accepted 50,000 lire from the yellow Amsterdam bureau. How could such a donation be accepted with thanks? The Amsterdam International is an agent of capitalism, and this cash means nothing but financial assistance offered to the CGL by the League of Nations. Yet the CGL gives thanks to the League for such a courtesy and such 'solidarity'.

Bianchi maintains that the Russian point of view and that of the CGL are essentially the same. But he is profoundly mistaken. As long as the CGL keeps up its affiliation to Amsterdam and carries out the policy of D'Aragona, it remains an organisation for sabotaging the proletarian revolution.

Bianchi committed an even greater error in saying that the Fascists, the Socialist Party, and the CGL could come to a compromise agreement on the plea, that it was analogous to what the Russians did in signing the Brest-Litovsk Peace Treaty. No, Comrade Bianchi, compromises are not all of the same kind. The Brest-Litovsk compromise saved the Russian Revolution, and hence the worldwide revolution. Your kind of compromise, however, can save only the Italian bourgeoisie. (*Applause*) Enough hypocrisy and political trickery! (*Applause*)

I hope that this congress will pass a strong and clear-cut resolution that will ensure the masses are not to be deceived for long. The General Confederation of Labour must choose between marching shoulder to shoulder with Moscow – that is, with the revolution – or with Amsterdam, that is, with the counterrevolution. (*Applause*)

Victor Godonnèche (France): There is very much to be said on the Italian question. I should also like to express here the disappointment that was felt by the French revolutionary syndicalists when they learned of the final outcome of the occupation of the factories in Turin, a disappointment easily explainable when one considers the vast scope of this movement and the fact that from the economic point of view Italy was more revolutionary than other countries. Still, among those knowledgeable, the disappointment was less. We have known D'Aragona too well, and witnessed the CGL's participation in the Washington Conference. We therefore expected, to a certain degree, that during the development of these events the leaders would change their attitude, because the policy of timidity of D'Aragona and Baldesi was well known to us.

From the time of the Washington Conference, from the moment when the Italian delegation left the shores of Italy for Washington, we began to feel the deception. The participation in that conference was the first step toward the policy praised at this congress by Bianchi. They must have gathered there for the purpose of boring from within the yellow Amsterdam International. Baldesi produced before the Washington Conference a critical report, which partly satisfied us; still it did not remove the bad impression created by the acceptance of the invitation to the Washington Conference.[1]

We have placed side by side the behaviour of the Italian CGL, which disrupted a movement that was then in full swing, with the behaviour of Merrheim, who, during the events in the Loire district, for fear of responsibility and also from personal fear, prevented the spread of the movement.[2] D'Aragona and the

1 For the Washington Conference, see p. 62, n. 4. The statement criticising the Washington Conference by the CGL delegates there, together with Swiss and Polish unionists, was published in D'Aragona and Baldesi, *Rapporti internazionali* (Milan, 1921), pp. 6, 31. See also, 'Rapport de Gino Baldesi délégué de la C.G.T. italienne', in *La vie ouvrière*, nos. 30 to 32, 30 January to 13 February.

2 A reference to a series of strikes in the Loire Basin in the spring of 1918. A number of militants hoped to convert these French strikes into a general strike against the war, a perspective opposed by Merrheim.

leaders of the CGL had a very courageous stance during the war. Merrheim also took a firm stand at the outbreak of the war, but was not strong enough to maintain it. Merrheim, D'Aragona, and some other leaders of the Socialist Party in Italy were strong pacifists during the war, but their pacifism could not go to the point of revolution. Hence we must say today that these men, who have pulled back out of fear of the revolution, have passed over – or are in the process of passing over – to the other side of the barricades, and for this we must express our condemnation. We are convinced that at the present time we cannot find ourselves between Moscow and Amsterdam.

The suggestion of Comrade Bianchi to remain in the Amsterdam International for the purpose of infiltrating the yellow International sounds rather childish. The structure of the Amsterdam International is radically different from that of national confederations. We, representatives of the revolutionary minority in our organisations, have decided to remain inside the CGT [of France] in order to conquer it. We have not waited for instructions from Moscow. We started the ball rolling even before the formation of the Red International of Trade Unions. Our opinion was that it would be fruitless to sever our connections with the CGT and build a new organisation. We still join Moscow; this affiliation does not of course have the same value that it would have had we won the majority of the CGT. Once this is an accomplished fact, our first step will be to break off relations with Amsterdam. We are at present already doing plenty of propaganda against Amsterdam. Our formula is 'Leave Amsterdam and affiliate to Moscow'.

But you Italians, who hold the CGL of Italy in your hands, you, how do you explain your behaviour? While remaining in Amsterdam you considered yourself in agreement with the Provisional Council of Red Trade Unions and took an active part in creating it. Did you not join the Provisional Council? Did you not invite us here? Is not your name attached to the first manifesto issued by the Provisional Council? Now, after we answered your invitation with the purpose of participating in its deliberations, you tell us that your presence here is solely for the purpose of 'information'! (*Applause*) Do you at least understand your ridiculous position and the ridiculous position in which you have placed the whole congress? Do you not know that one of the main arguments of the French reformists consists in saying, 'But the Italian CGL is not with Moscow, it is with Amsterdam'. How could we answer that?

Comrade Lozovsky has correctly defined your attitude during the London Congress. Where are the revolutionary fruits you claimed you tried to implant in the yellow International? We in France have not noticed them yet, although millions of Italian workers were represented in London, as claimed by the yellow leaders. We, the French syndicalists, believe that the Italian CGL is on the wrong track. You play a double part; such a position cannot last long: you're either with Moscow or else with Amsterdam. As far as we're concerned, we shall leave Amsterdam entirely as soon as the majority of the French CGT is with us. In the name of the French delegation, I ask the Italian comrades to make an end to their false position, and openly proclaim, once and for all, whether they are for us or against us. You cannot remain in the middle of the road.

Lozovsky: Taking into consideration that the representatives of the Italian CGL are here for information, I am therefore glad to give the floor to the Italian minority representative, a member of the metalworkers' union, who is of a different opinion than the Italian majority delegates. Had the Italian majority come here with decisive vote, the Italian minority would not have been entitled to special representation.

Comrade Repossi will now speak.

Luigi Repossi (Italy, Communist fraction in the CGL): I must announce, to my sorrow, that I represent only a minority in the CGL in Italy. Had it not been for those who are now the leaders of the CGL, I would have represented here the majority. At the last congress of the CGL held in Livorno in February 1921, thanks to the policy of the old leaders, the number of votes was incorrectly distributed and did not represent the wishes of the Italian proletariat. The half million votes given to the Communists do not really reflect the exact number of Communists among the workers, just as the other 1.2 million votes accredited to the CGL [majority] do not attest to its support among the masses.

Bianchi's speech today did not surprise me in the least; he presented what all the leaders of the CGL have been presenting. They are unable to speak differently. I want to call your attention to the charge made by him against the Communist Party, which is worthy of serious attention. Bianchi stated that the unsuccessful end of the occupation of the factories was the fault of the Communists, that fascism was the creation of the Communist Party, as a reaction that shows the Communists to have played a provocative role. There is no need to waste many words to prove the fallacy of his statements and charges. Granted, for the sake of argument, that such was the case. Why then did not the revolutionary CGL seek to weaken the reactionary influence of the Communist Party? In reality, the situation was entirely different. It was not the Communist Party that is responsible for the growth of fascism, but the opportunism and indecision of the CGL during the critical moments in the life of the Italian working class.

I cannot calmly think of that moment when the revolution was in the hands of the Italian proletariat, when the shops and factories were actually in the hands of the workers, when the land was practically under workers' control. During that period production did not stop. Things were running in perfect order. Great effort had to be made in order to destroy this movement, and it was the CGL that did it. What forced them to undertake such a job? The CGL was afraid that were the social revolution to begin, there would not have been a sufficient stock of prime necessities of life because of the breakdown of industry. They believed that after a certain lapse of time there would inevitably come a crisis, and the condition of the working class would be worse than it was before the revolution.

In its desire to get hold of a surplus of the prime necessities of life, the Confederation of Labour endeavoured to convince those who held in their hands the destinies of the revolution that the revolution was premature, that a moment should be chosen when there would be no risk incurred, when one might be assured that after the revolution there would be sufficient supplies of products in the warehouses of the workers' cooperatives, etc.

The leaders of the General Confederation of Labour were not satisfied with this. They brought forward other arguments, and declared that the revolution is likely to stop the tilling of the land, and this in its turn would threaten the population with famine. The comrades from the CGL should think less of the accumulation of the prime necessities of life and of good crops for the bourgeoisie, and be more preoccupied with the thought that this movement, created by the working class, would result in a good crop for the working class itself. At the moment when the working class clamoured for action, they were too entangled in doctrinairism. That is the framework within which you find occasion to bring charges against us that we handicapped the movement. And we, in our turn, have the right to say that you deprived us of any possibility of bringing this movement to success.

All the successes that Bianchi referred to and that he attributed to the CGL are by no means to be considered as the results of its activities. All we succeeded in achieving – the movement itself, the occupation of the factories and the land, the famous workers' control, the eight-hour day, the increase in wages, the introduction of collective bargaining – all these gains were not the achievement of the CGL, but the result of concessions made by the bourgeoisie under the pressure of the working masses, led by the most radical elements within the CGL and outside of it.

I do not believe these conquests can be attributed to the CGL, nor to the Communist Party, for the movement was spontaneous. The Communist Party was too young and weak to take hold of the movement, while the CGL lacked the capacity and will to do so. The fundamental flaw of the CGL, if we examine its deeds on the tactical field of action, is its constant talk about political action, but whenever its theory had to be carried into action, it was entirely unable to give to any movement a political basis.

Bianchi recalls that the CGL, in a whole series of articles, in parliament, and at meetings, has presented the viewpoint of proletarian struggle, insisting that we ought to strive to secure, through the medium of parliament, all the reforms that would provide the workers with better conditions of life. How then can Bianchi say that the eight-hour day was the revolutionary achievement of the CGL? How can he say that this organisation is noted for its revolutionary activity? The eight-hour day, like the rest, is the result of the struggle by the working masses. Is this the sum total of the CGL's revolutionary actions?

At the current time, the Italian working class – despite the obstinate struggle it has waged for ten years and despite all its sacrifices – has been forced far back compared to where it might have been had the revolution been accomplished.

There is another question worth taking up, an object of special attention at this congress. Why is the CGL still affiliated to the Amsterdam International, and seemingly to Moscow too? One may think that this is what the masses demand, and so the CGL, which is so attentive to whatever the masses want, simply obeys their dictum – to soothe the masses it stays with Amsterdam and also flirts with Moscow. But this is not so. The masses – and there is plenty of documentary evidence to bear out my statement – made it quite plain, at numerous conferences, meetings, and congresses, that they stood absolutely for unconditional affiliation to Moscow. On these occasions there was no mention of Amsterdam, because it was quite plain that affiliation to Moscow meant a break with Amsterdam. But the CGL, good diplomat that it is, when the question came up for definitive settlement at the Livorno Congress, made the following addition to the formula: 'Without withdrawing from Amsterdam'. The Livorno formula retained the sense voiced by the insistent demands 'to unconditionally affiliate to Moscow', but there was an additional proviso 'if the Socialist Party is recognised by the Communist International'. The additions to the original formula did not come from the masses, but were suggested by the leaders of the CGL.

As regards the 50,000 lire that the CGL received from Amsterdam, things are not the way Bianchi tries to paint them. Bianchi calls this donation 'debt repayment'. He says that all the organisations affiliated to Amsterdam made contributions at various times for the relief of the victims of political terror all over Europe, and now Amsterdam is paying the debt. I don't think that the agents of the League of Nations are paying back to the Italian proletariat the loan of 50,000 lire it has made to them, but rather is sending the cash that the

League of Nations squeezed out of the German proletariat as well as of the proletarians of other countries. This is not a debt, but a bribe given to the Italian proletariat; it is intended to pacify the leaders and soothe the passions of the proletariat.

Returning to the question of the occupation of the factories, I remind you that we had then a clear understanding between us to resort, if need be, to extreme action, so that what we had begun did not turn into a farce. We felt the tremendous risks we were imposing on the Italian proletariat. This was no idle experiment, but quite serious business. We therefore agreed that it was necessary to take the most energetic revolutionary measures. But when it came time to act, then as always they were more concerned about the interests of the bourgeoisie than the interests of the proletariat. Do you remember, when the movement was in full swing after our negotiations with the CGL and its leaders, when everything was thrashed out and decided, when the Socialist Party seemingly was inclining to the view that the movement was assuming a revolutionary character – what did D'Aragona declare at that moment? He said, 'If such a line of action continues, I decline to retain my position as secretary of the General Confederation of Labour and resign.'[3] How shall we characterise such a method of intimidation, used at such decisive moments? There is only one answer: it is treason to the working class and the revolution. But it is not the term that matters; what matters is that this had deadly consequences.

The Communist fraction within the CGL never rejected the idea of uniting all the trade-union forces. Quite recently we appealed to all the Italian unions to end all internal dissension and create a single united front of struggle in face of the dangers threatening the proletariat from the bourgeoisie, which had already recovered from its fright and had regrouped its forces. In making this appeal, we acted consciously.

To create this unity, we have to not only coordinate our efforts, but also reconcile the different tendencies that can be reconciled, while completely breaking with those who are going in a different direction. Only then shall we be able to demand a straightforward and clear answer to the question: Amsterdam or Moscow?

Convene your congress as soon as possible; but do not organise it as you did your previous congresses. Then we shall clearly see what the masses want.

---

3 In the midst of the September 1920 factory occupations, D'Aragona and other leaders of the General Confederation of Labour threatened to resign their positions. The threat was made at a 9–10 September joint meeting between the leaderships of the CGL and the Italian Socialist Party.

Then there is the question of strikes. For the CGL this question is not a means but an end. They think that strikes lead to a predetermined result. For us it is the reverse; strikes are a means and not an end. If we considered strikes to be our end, we would be afraid, like you, of depriving the employers of their profits by tying up the factories or robbing the landowner of his harvest by leaving the land fallow. But a strike is not a fetish to us.

Finally, we must take up the question of fascism. This evil would now be impossible in Italy were it not for the defeat of November–December 1919,[4] if the CGL had not proved so spineless in face of the events that were then advancing on us; and if the bourgeoisie had not succeeded in recovering from the fright it felt in face of the unexpected conquests of the working class. It was only because the movement was completely routed, and the armed force of the working class was defeated owing to lack of political unity and the empty talk of the CGL, that the bourgeoisie became convinced it could easily defeat the working class. It created an army, to have a force at hand capable of defeating the workers. Fascism is nothing other than the bourgeoisie's white guard. It is the iron fist that the bourgeoisie seeks for use in breaking the head of the proletariat. The revolutionary movement in Italy is in decline, despite having had the revolution in its hands. The proletariat let it slip through its fingers because the CGL and the Socialist Party clung to their old preconceptions. True revolutionaries ignore preconceptions; preconceptions about parliament and constituent assemblies do not exist for them. The revolutionary necessarily gets rid of these preconceptions, as happened in Russia. But the Italian CGL has not outlived them yet, and still repeats this liberal nonsense.

Adopt the revolutionary point of view. Proclaim your affiliation to Moscow and your departure from Amsterdam. Our disagreements will then cease to exist, and the great gulf existing between yourselves and the working class will immediately disappear.

Rosa Bloch (Switzerland): Comrade Bianchi has asked today why they are considered as traitors and are treated as such. I must answer Bianchi, as I do not know him just from today. You are declared to be traitors because you as leaders of the CGL have betrayed us all. Because there was no other country in such a favourable situation, and you spoiled it. You acted against us.

4 On 1 December 1919 Socialist Party members of Italy's parliament walked out in protest when King Emanuel came to deliver a speech before the body. The walkout sparked a general strike by Italian workers on 2–3 December, with semi-insurrectional battles in some places. But on 3 December the PSI and CGL called off the general strike, telling workers to return to their jobs.

You ask us where are the 95,000 Swiss workers? The 95,000 Swiss workers are in favour of Moscow; it is only their leaders who are against Moscow. Just as in Italy all the workers are for Moscow while their leaders are against it. And you, the leaders, have the audacity to come to Moscow and make the same statements as Serrati did last year at the Second Congress of the Communist International. Like him, you say today, 'We have no information, and we therefore don't know what this is all about.' Then I want to ask you: What kind of information can there be at such a congress? We are creating here a Red Trade Union International. It's not a question of information, but rather having a firm will. And a review of the resolutions of the last world congresses would make it quite clear that you have deceived and betrayed the Italian proletariat. In no other country were the masses so revolutionary as in Italy.

If you wish to hold onto your title as leaders, then go back as quickly as possible to Italy and convene your congress immediately. This congress should make quite clear whether you are with Moscow or with Amsterdam, because to remain here and listen to the congress discussions, having already decided this question, is meaningless. You must let the Italian proletariat distinguish between what is white and what is black, and to draw the necessary conclusions.

Any leader who will then not remain with the masses will have no right to remain on these premises any further. Bianchi, you told us very much about the past, but you said nothing about the present. What happened in the past does not interest us today; the question at issue is the present. You were not the only ones who went to Zimmerwald. Your trip to Zimmerwald does not mean anything; we're talking about the present. You must say clearly whether you are for the revolution or against the revolution. (*Applause*)

Jesús Ibáñez (Spain): Comrades, on the day we received the telegram from our comrades from the CGL, we were extremely surprised by their proposal to transfer the world trade-union congress from Moscow to Stockholm or Reval. Yes, we were very much surprised, as we didn't think it was necessary to make the journey. But this morning, after listening to the speech of Comrade Bianchi who spoke of the situation in the CGL, I changed my opinion. I at once understood the gist of the Italian proposal, and understood that this would be a good chance to listen to some eloquent and flowery speeches, nicely put together, but unfortunately lacking frankness and a revolutionary spirit.

Comrade Bianchi, describing the present-day activity of the CGL, affirmed that its activity has always been revolutionary. He has shown us a series of actions carried out by the CGL during the war, and reminded us of the fact that it participated at the conferences of Zimmerwald and Kienthal, where a new revolutionary movement was born. My dear Comrade Bianchi, it is useless to remind us of the past; we are talking of the present. We cannot count on the past to make a world revolution, nor to come to the aid of the Russian Revolution. We must speak about present-day action, on what can be done today, and of the help that could aid the Russian proletariat, which is endangered by world capitalism. We cannot hide behind what happened before or during the war.

One must stick to the revolutionary reality at all times. And you, Comrade Bianchi and all those comrades who are at the head of the CGL, did not meet the revolutionary requirements of the circumstances. You lacked the necessary spirit; you lacked precise decisions so as to lead the working class to the goal it has chosen to follow, that is, to the social revolution and the establishment of communism. In Italy you had a splendid chance to show your revolutionary mettle. You boasted about it this morning, but you did not want to take advantage of the opportunity. At the very same time that the workers in the factories were fighting the police and the carabinieri, who were serving the capitalists, you were occupied with dealings with the Italian government and the Socialist Party. You trampled on the revolution, trampled on the Red International, on the principles that you say you defended, the principles of communism.

This is the reason, dear comrades, why you wanted to transfer the gathering to Reval or Stockholm. In order to justify your opposition to revolutionary action during September 1920, you say, 'We were doing revolutionary work, while at the same time negotiating compromises with the capitalists to give us control of industry. In this we acted as revolutionaries.' But I would say this – and I think all the Spanish comrades would agree with me – you cannot talk about revolutionary work if control of industry is in the hands of the capitalist class. No, such tactics will never build a revolutionary movement, but will instead divert the working masses toward reformism and class collaboration. We think that control over factories and products in general must not be the result of an agreement between the capitalists and the workers, but must be imposed by the working class organised in unions, as is the case in Spain. We too have established control, but it is against the will of the powers that be. We have carried that control in the factories, in order to keep up the fighting spirit of the organised workers.

You are complaining about the reproaches that are made against your behaviour with regard to the Moscow International, and also that you are being taunted with doing counterrevolutionary work. Have you not promised to affiliate to the Red International of Trade Unions? And now you raise objections about the leaders of the Moscow International, and are saying that the Russian Revolution is not a revolution of the working class, but is a revolution of some Bolshevik elements. And the persons making this cowardly propaganda are the most prominent figures in the CGL and the Socialist Party. I presume that D'Aragona and Company, who were at the head of the labour organisations and of the Socialist Party, always speak not on behalf of these organisations, but in their own name, expounding their personal views. In this they have betrayed the working class.

If you want an example of your revolutionary [*sic*] work, it is what you cited this morning in response to objections regarding the agreement between the CGL and Socialist Party, on the one hand, with the Italian Fascists. This agreement is the strongest proof that the CGL, as well as the Italian Socialist Party, have allied with bourgeois elements to betray the principles of the social revolution. And we cannot comprehend how the part of the CGL that professes to be devoted to the cause of revolution could sign a compromise with those who are murdering our comrades, the revolutionary syndicalists, in the streets, with those who take up arms against legal workers' organisations, who compel the Italian proletariat to resort to mass emigration. By signing the agreement with these elements, by these very means, you have trampled on all revolutionary principles and you have trampled on your own dignity.

We too have fascists and white guards in Spain, but the Confederation of Labour in Spain [CNT] would never fall so low as you when you signed the agreement. (*Applause*) Your behaviour in this matter, comrades, shows clearly that you have not been up to the requirements of a revolutionary. You state that the September revolutionary movement was betrayed not by you but by the Communist elements in the country. But the comrade who has just spoken pointed out that the blame lay not with the revolutionaries, but with the reformist elements, of which you are the representative at this congress. Of course, I have more confidence in Comrade Repossi than in counterrevolutionary expressions by those representing the interests of the bourgeoisie. I say this because you represented the CGL in Amsterdam, and also at the Washington Conference, where most participants were representatives of the bourgeoisie.

We told you just now that at the Livorno Congress you betrayed the revolutionary principles held by the comrades of the CGL who wanted to establish relations with Moscow. The leading elements of the CGL, who you represent, deceived the masses. Such a thing can never occur in Spain. There, if this happens among us, a leader who betrays the principles of the revolution, of the CNT, is immediately expelled and leadership is given to those truly revolutionary elements who are ready to sacrifice life and liberty for the cause of the social revolution.

Comrades, I will abuse your patience no longer. I believe there should be fewer revolutionary phrases and more revolutionary action. Comrade Bianchi concluded his speech by saying, 'Long live the social revolution!' I prefer working indefatigably for the realisation of the social revolution. Only when it is achieved will I cry out, 'Long live the international social revolution!'

Carlo Azimonti (Italy, CGL): I am taking the floor on a personal matter. This morning Comrade Lozovsky, in making general points on the so-called Italian question at this congress, quoted the following from the speech I delivered at the opening of the People's University: 'Revolutionary workers with little consciousness should think less of red banners and more of reality.'

This sentence cannot be understood unless the comrades understand what the People's University is in Italy. In the past the proletarian institutes were in the hands of the Catholics, and they served the purpose of educating the masses in a reactionary sprit. Even Turati and his supporters contributed to them to a certain degree. The cultural and educational work we undertook had to create an entirely new type of proletarian school. The people's school must be transformed into trade and technical schools, where the workers develop true class consciousness. So my words must not be taken literally but rather figuratively. They should be understood as meaning that the question is having a realistic outlook toward life and a rational way of envisioning it. Turati and the comrades who took part in founding the university have always been ardent partisans of the Russian Revolution at the meetings in the People's University, in order to instil among the Italian working masses a deep feeling of admiration toward revolutionary Russia. I am not a diplomat and do not play with words. I always express my convictions sincerely. This can be attested to by Repossi here.

Repossi (*from his seat*): This is true. But tell us, are you a reformist, an opportunist, or not?

Azimonti (*continues*): Yes, I am a reformist, and I never made a secret of it, but the question here is not at all whether I am a reformist or not. I have always sided with the right wing [of the socialist movement], nevertheless I have said that it is absolutely necessary to adhere to Moscow, because Moscow is the centre that at present can unite the entire proletariat. On the other hand, I say that it is impossible to affiliate to Moscow until the Socialist Party is accepted by the Third International.

It must never be forgotten that the trade-union movement is closely linked to the political movement; unity of the two can be achieved only by experienced leadership on the part of proven militants. Only in this way can the Italian and international workers' movement go on the offensive.

Besides the personal matter, I also consider it necessary to emphasise the general situation that is being discussed here. Why did the revolution not take place in Italy? The fault for this is not ours; and it is not yours, the Communists. Our revolution was not carried out to a successful end because we and you were powerless. We lacked capable people at the head of the movement.

I again call upon your sincerity, Repossi. If you admit it, then have the courage to state that the old story of our being traitors to the working class is only a fiction. This should not be repeated, as neither the working class nor the workers' movement will benefit by it. This will not make easier the solution of the question before the congress. Yes, I side with the right wing of the socialist movement, but Comrade Repossi knows that I have always been a disciplined member of the party and of the CGL. When I was invited to Milan by Comrade Repossi, telling me that we must be prepared for an insurrection, I was the first to respond to his appeal, and I prepared weapons and combatants in my town to prepare the insurrection. And if this was not done, if we were not given the necessary signal, then it is not the fault of my comrades or me.

There were also references here to fascism. It is attributed to the reformists; some attribute it to their counterrevolutionary activities. But in reality fascism is the fruit neither of one nor the other. Fascism is the consequence of the power that the ruling classes received after the suppression of the revolutionary movement.

Concerning the 50,000 lire, this was simply repayment of a debt. Amsterdam has repaid these 50,000 lire to the Italian workers who contributed to the relief fund designed to aid the victims of the political terror. Amsterdam is simply returning the money that had been put in its coffers.

There is another question that provokes much animated discussions. One speaks a great deal about the unity of the trade-union movement. Yes, we reformists have always been for such unity. And now when the railway workers and seamen have decided to join the General Confederation of Labour it is, to a certain degree, the result of the success of the CGL's work over many years, which should be recognised. It is the work of the General Confederation of Labour itself. Of course the railway workers and seamen, who support your views, will give you the majority, and we will probably become the minority. We are not afraid if in the near future you have the leadership of the CGL in your hands. If you are at the head of the CGL, then you will have to lead the working masses. You will also be compelled to act as we have done up to now.

I shall not speak about all the gossip that accumulated in the course of the polemic. It is not the time and place to speak about it; we can talk about it under different conditions when we return home. Here we must speak of what may be important to the trade-union movement as a whole.

In conclusion, I consider it necessary to say a few words with reference to the question of the occupation of the factories. We took the initiative. We began the movement and were ready to continue it. It was a joy to deploy all our forces so as to lead the working class to victory, but the historical conjuncture was against us. The misfortune of both us and you was that we did not correctly appreciate the moment. We overestimated our forces. I am among those who realised what the situation was. But we also yielded to the temptation to see the victory of the working class realised.

I repeat that the failure was due only to the historical conjuncture, and the absence of capable leaders among the ranks of Socialists as well as Communists to carry out the revolution. I believe that the moment will come when unity will be achieved with our organisations. But we will not be united internationally until the Italian Socialist Party is in the ranks of the Third International. And when that party is accepted, then the CGL, which depends upon that party, will automatically enter the Red International of Trade Unions.

Tom Mann (Britain): Comrades, the movement in England is an old one; it has been in progress for more than generations, and this explains why we are in ruts and it is so difficult to extricate ourselves, but we are determined to do it.

We are living in a country with very little sun, and that is probably the cause of our being phlegmatic people, but we have always looked to the people of the Latin race as being the main sources with regard to revolutionary strength and the exhibition of those characteristics that put strength and vim into the movement. The Italian people set the pace in revolutionary propaganda, and we admired them for their activities in trying to keep the country out of the war, and we, who have not been blessed with such a fine country as Italy, we have often looked on the Italians as examples.

When lecturing in the past, I have always asserted that Italy has the most radical trade unions in the world, the most genuinely revolutionary, the most capable, and I have quoted them as worthy of being looked up to, as in all probability Italy would be amongst the first of the countries to bring about a revolution.

Now it comes to me and to the English delegation as a source of disappointment. The Italian people who had set such a good example, whom I had always thought of as worthy, and advocated that some of us try to imitate them, then to find that they complied with their bourgeois government, cannot command our admiration. We lauded the Italians that they were successful even long before entering the war, and I have quoted the Confederation of Labour as being the organisation from which we would have much to learn. To me it comes as a deep disappointment that those whom I had learned to love and appreciate so thoroughly are now occupying the position with regard to the Red International that we know that they do occupy. To learn also that at the conference at Livorno it was decided that the Italian Confederation of Labour should participate in the formation of a Red Trade Union International – that gave us again courage. And during the past few months a number of us have been quoting the fact, with the greatest belief that they would be here in large numbers, declaring that the Italian Confederation was with the reds.

Now it is a source of disappointment to find comrades like Bianchi explain, as he has explained, why they are not with us. It is indeed a pitiable position to occupy. It is not worthy of the ideals and militancy of their past; they can accomplish better things. And I am confident that it is the dabbling with plutocracy and politicians that is the direct cause of this temporary degeneracy.

I knew Comrade Malatesta well. I remember him living in England and before he went to Italy. We watched his activities in Italy up to his arrest, and we learned something of the movement that we thought was fully prepared to take action when the time arose. We expected the Italians to decide upon revolutionary action; but it was not done. It seems that the plutocracy outmanoeuvred them and continues to be the dominant factor. What can we say to the people at home when they ask, 'Were the Italians there? In what numbers were they there? Did they take action with you that you caused us to expect that they would take?' We shall have to say no, and we deeply regret this. We want to see solidarity exhibited amongst the Italians. And we may at least call on the Italians to mend their ways. We ask them not to leave this congress in the same fashion that they have entered it – some saying yes, some saying no, some saying, 'We just came to Moscow to explain why we are allied with Amsterdam.' The work has to be done in Italy itself; change the mentality there and the trade unions will follow with regards to the alliance with Moscow.

Our delegates request the comrades from Italy to weld themselves together and become identified with the Red International. To be ready to set the pace again, or at least to be equal to the first in the race; there is a great and glorious opportunity. Now that we have reached the stage when in at least one country the revolution is actually an accomplished fact, how difficult it is for me to picture that Italy of all countries should lag behind. I am sincerely hoping that Italy will not lag behind, that Italy will come up to the top. We strongly urge comrades that you do your utmost to bring your movement over to the Red International, that you will not be half and half, but line up in the front ranks of the glorious Red Trade Union International.

Heinrich Farwig (Germany): In the name of all the German delegates I declare that we fully agree with Comrade Lozovsky's statement as regards the question under discussion. We shall limit ourselves to only a short statement, as we do not wish to prolong the discussion and take up unnecessary time of the congress. But we must say to Bianchi and his comrades that political wavering and looking about is little short of treason, and it must be looked upon as a counterrevolutionary act. You must come out in the open and state whether you are for Moscow or against it. For the revolution or against it? (*Applause*)

Lozovsky: Comrades, the chair has received a number of notes from different delegates asking for the discussion to be discontinued. Is there anybody against that? No? Accepted.

Bianchi (*from his seat*) asks to speak.

Lozovsky: Comrade Bianchi wishes to speak. Owing to the decision just carried to discontinue discussion, I suggest that he should hand in his statement in writing to the Presidium. It will be attached to the stenographic report. I propose the same thing to the representative of the minority of the confederation. As a result of the discussion, there is a resolution, signed by the Russian, Bulgarian, Ukrainian, Polish, British, Spanish, French, and Czechoslovak delegations.

A voice from the congress: The American and Canadian.

Another voice: And Swiss.

Lozovsky: The American, Swiss, and Canadian; so much the better. Then it is the entire congress. The resolution will be put to a vote by groups at the same time in the Russian, French, English, and German languages. We shall put it to a vote. Who is against the resolution that is brought forward? None. Who abstained from voting? Nobody. Who is for the resolution? The resolution is carried by acclamation.[5] (*Stormy applause by the entire congress*)

Comrade Bianchi has the floor for a declaration.

Bianchi: I would mostly like to answer Comrade Lozovsky. At the present moment I shall limit myself to stating only that it is not true that the Confedera-

5 For the text of the Resolution on the Italian Question, see pp. 604–5.

tion of Labour has betrayed the working class. We remain true to our aims, and come here for informational purposes, as we were bound by the line laid down by our congress. This is not our fault. On our return home we pledge to remain active and hope in the end to come together with our Russian comrades. If the congress of the Third International had decided that the Socialist Party would remain in the Third International, our consultative mandates would automatically have become decisive ones. But this did not happen.[6]

We believe that the near future will create more favourable conditions, and that at the next congress our aspiration will be realised.

Lozovsky: So then if I understand you correctly, Bianchi, you are saying that at the London Conference you voted against the resolution? (*Bianchi from his seat, makes an affirmative gesture, pointing to a pamphlet*).

The corrections made by Bianchi do not correct anything. Here is the exact statement made at the London Conference, in the words of D'Aragona:

> The attack of the Russians against the Amsterdam Congress is the expression of a protest against the behaviour of some of the national trade-union confederations during the war, and with regard to the Russian Revolution. The Italian delegation agrees with this point of view. But the Italians cannot approve of the use of the Russian political procedures, which are used in a way that judges facts without having sufficient information and that seeks to impose on all nations the same methods of social struggle.
>
> However, the Italian delegates will not vote for the proposed resolution, for the reason that it can be misinterpreted as approving the past action of the leaders of some of the national trade-union confederations who all are now at the head of the Amsterdam International. And they will not even vote against, because it might be considered an approval of the [Russian] accusation brought against Amsterdam. This is the reason why they abstain from voting.

Do you call this a vote against the resolution?

Lozovsky (as chair): Comrades, this question has been thoroughly discussed. There is a proposal to add one point at the end of the resolution to the effect

6 The Third Comintern Congress discussion on the PSI's relations with the Comintern can be found in Riddell (ed.) 2015, *3WC*, pp. 339–86.

that the congress considers it necessary that the General Confederation of Labour should in the shortest possible time call a congress for the purpose of deciding this question.

Boisson (France) (*from his seat*): Who will issue the call for the congress?

Lozovsky: It is understood that the congress will be called by the General Confederation of Labour, and only by that body.

Is there anybody against the amendment? I hear no opposition. The amendment is carried. Comrades, I propose that we have the Presidium formulate that amendment. Is there any opposition? Adopted.

Comrade Malzahn has the floor.

Disch (Germany) (*from his seat*): A point of order.

Bartels (Germany): Comrade chair, there is another declaration from the German *Unionen* on the Italian question.

Lozovsky: Please read your declaration.

Bartels (*reads a declaration by the German unions*):

> The delegates of the German unions [*Unionen*] state that they support the resolution of the German minority oppositions insofar as it will demand of the Italian trade unions a clear decision: Moscow or Amsterdam. They are putting their demands to all the organisations participating in the congress that, like the Italian organisations, are tied to Amsterdam. What is asked of the Italian organisations is the verbal acknowledgement in the resolution, as established by the opposition minorities.
>
> (*Signed*): Gelsenkirchen Free Workers' Union;
> General Workers' Union of Germany;
> German Seamen's Union

Lozovsky: Comrades, the question raised in this statement about the minorities is a question of tactics, and that will be taken up when we get to the discussion on tactics.

Comrade Malzahn wishes to speak upon the further work of the congress.

Heinrich Malzahn (Germany): I wish to say, at the outset a couple of words about the decision you have just passed.

Lozovsky: No debating, Comrade Malzahn.

Malzahn: I wish only to state that we well understand this resolution, and will give our response during the debate on the question of tactics.

I wish to state that we, the German delegation, after serious deliberation, have decided to introduce the following proposal:

With a view toward creating a sound foundation for the debate on tactics, the German delegation proposes for the second time to discuss Comrade Lozovsky's address in the Commission on Tactics. After the commission's report, this item on the agenda will have to be presented to the plenary sitting in the following manner: one reporter will speak for each tendency; 45 minutes will be allocated to the reporter and 15 minutes for the summary.

The question of tactics is of such importance that unless there is serious preparatory work performed, we shall risk much repetition. It is in our interest to prevent useless talk, so that points of difference can be thoroughly clarified. I believe this to be the wish of all the delegations, and that our proposal will meet with everyone's approval.

Lozovsky: Speaking against Comrade Malzahn's proposal is Schüppel.

Willi Schüppel (Germany, Gelsenkirchen Free Workers' Union): We are obliged to oppose the German delegation's proposal. It is precisely because the question of tactics is so important that we cannot agree to only 45 minutes being given for the report and 15 minutes for the summary, while the question itself is to be referred to a commission. Although it may sound convincing at first sight, we already know by bitter experience that the debate is soon cut off. We are therefore against this proposal. In addition, we are not so sure that the commissions always give sufficient attention to clarifying the questions under consideration. As early as last Friday our union, together with other *Unionen*, expressed the desire for a co-report on the question of tactics. So far we have heard nothing on the matter. The question of tactics could, of course, be referred to a commission, but we are against the closure of further debate.

Lozovsky: We shall now proceed to the vote. There are two proposals: one, to not discuss the question and refer it to a commission; and the other, first to open the debate on the general question and then refer to the commission.

The majority has expressed its wish to open the debate in the plenary.

(*The session is declared closed at 11:25 p.m.*)

SESSION 12. 14 JULY 1921, MORNING–AFTERNOON

Debate on Tactics

(*Session opens at 11:15 a.m. Comrade Lozovsky in the chair.*)

Lozovsky: Comrades, to direct the discussion on tactics in a rational manner, the Presidium proposes to go into the question of winning over or splitting from the trade unions. Six organisations represented at our congress defend the splitting standpoint: the Gelsenkirchen Free Workers' Union, the German syndicalists, the Industrial Workers of the World (IWW), a small fraction of the French labour movement (the Travailleurs du Monde), and finally a small fraction of the American trade-union movement, the Workers' International Industrial Union (WIIU).[1] The proposal of the Presidium consists in giving 15 minutes to each representative of the respective organisations to define their point of view. Thus the comrades from the German Free Unions will have 45 minutes.

A voice (from the German *Unionen*): This question was already discussed yesterday.

Lozovsky: Yes, but now it is modified in that the German representatives will have 15 minutes each, or 45 minutes altogether.

Leopold Dautkus (Germany, General Workers' Union): At the time we received the invitation to Moscow, we were also told not to delegate leaders, but simple workers. By the way, we haven't got any leaders, (*interruptions and laughter*) we have only workers. We here are workers from the job, industrial workers. We state that we are categorically opposed to the American trade unions. During the war we waged a strenuous fight in Germany against the unions of that country, and we founded our model unions.

At this congress we have not been given a chance to fully develop our views, and we consider that 15 minutes, or even 45, is absolutely insufficient for this. Taking this into consideration, we must state that it was useless to tear away workers from the job and bring them to Moscow, and that in the future we will refuse the floor altogether. (*Exclamations: 'Very good.'*)

---

1 The delegate to the RILU congress from the Workers' International Industrial Union – linked to the US Socialist Labor Party – was Adolf S. Carm.

 | DOI:10.1163/9789004712867_016

Bartels: Comrade chairman, we have made a proposal; it was signed by the following German unions: the Seamen's Union, the Agricultural Workers' Union, and the Union of Hand and Brain Workers. Our proposal is quite different from yours. We maintain it and ask that you put it to a vote.

Chair: I have already said that for these debates …

Comrade from German *Unionen*: We assert that based on the agreed-upon procedure, we be given 1 hour and 30 minutes for the report and 10 minutes for the summary. You yourselves adopted that procedure.

Chair: The question was put in the following way: if we consent to this proposal of the three delegates from the German *Unionen*, then the IWW and the French delegates will have the right to request the same thing. But it is inadmissible that such a small minority take up all the time at this congress.

Comrade from German *Unionen*: It is to be regretted that the German question is counterposed to the other countries.

Chair: If you can agree with the other comrades and with the comrades of the IWW, you may be permitted to present a full co-report; otherwise, as stated before, the IWW may make the same claim, because as you know, this organisation is five or six times larger numerically than yours.

The floor is granted to Comrade Malzahn.

Malzahn: Considering the fact that at this congress we can trace two main tendencies, namely, the revolutionising-the-unions-from-within and the revolutionising-them-from-without. (*Exclamation: 'No, not from the outside, but to divide them even more.'*)

Yes, to smash the trade-union organisations and revolutionise them from the outside. The German delegation agrees that Comrade Bartels should be permitted to have the floor as a co-reporter, and that the other delegations be given 15 minutes each for discussion. If this is accepted, the incident is closed. Had the proposal come in yesterday, the question would have been settled. (*Exclamation: 'But it is necessary to have 15 minutes for a summary.'*) You will also have 15 minutes for a summary. We do not intend to avoid this question; we too are very interested in deciding it here.

Lozovsky: Comrade Malzahn, I will ask you not to open the debate.

Disch: I wish to explain our proposal. We are delegated to present a co-report with the revolutionary syndicalists. We favour the proposal so far as to authorise Comrade Bartels to read the report; he will speak on behalf of the German Free Unions: i.e., the General Workers' Union, the [Gelsenkirchen] Free Workers' Union, the Seamen's Union, the Agricultural Workers' Union, and the Union of Hand and Brain Workers. In case this is not allowed, each one of us will independently express his views during the discussion.

Chair: It is impossible that the co-reporter on behalf of the Gelsenkirchen Union … (*Shouts: 'No, for all the German Unionen'*).

Rosmer: I move the following proposal: we should grant one hour to the co-reporter and half an hour for the summary. Each one of the German Unions should be given 30 minutes. (*Shouts from comrades of the German Unionen: 'No, the others are yielding their speaking time to Comrade Bartels.'*)

Grölig: (Germany, General Workers' Union): I would like to state the following as an explanation: Comrade Dautkus protested against limiting our time to 45 minutes. The motion made to grant Comrade Bartels 1 hour 30 minutes solves the problem, as he can also speak in our name.

Chair: This is possible. Comrade Bartels, you have not handed in copies of your theses, which are necessary for distribution among the delegates.

Bartels: I will do this later.

Heckert: Comrade Maciejewski has the floor.

Józef Maciejewski (Poland): Last night we dotted our 'i's on all points. We have completed half of our task with regard to the tactics and aims of the trade-union movement. I do not think there are any more misunderstandings among us on the question of tactics. We must make clear to ourselves which road to select and what means to use to reach our goal.

The motion accepted yesterday with regard to the recognition of the ideological leadership of the Communist International, and that in the future we should continue working in coordination with the Communist International – gives a sound and unequivocal answer on the question of the economic and political struggle. According to this viewpoint, the economic and political phases in our struggle are interwoven. There is one united general fight, the fight of the entire proletariat against the entire bourgeoisie, one mutual struggle to destroy capitalist power and establish the dictatorship of the proletariat. Our success depends solely upon harmony and unity in our actions. An economic victory is possible only after complete destruction of the old governmental political machine. Without this an economic victory is impossible.

This is seen in the everyday struggle. At the slightest provocation governments direct their entire apparatus against the working class during strikes, putting strikers into prison. Such instances unmistakably prove the danger of disassociating the economic and political struggles. Our decision to wage a common struggle with the Communist International for the establishment of the proletarian dictatorship and the social revolution clearly defines our attitude. It is unlike that of the utopians, who are trying to separate out the workers into two halves, an economic half and a political one.

Our goal is the dictatorship of the proletariat and the social revolution, and there should no misunderstanding on this. It must be done as a class, and not as a small group. The social revolution cannot be made by a group of workers, even a very conscious one, but only by the working class as a whole. Therefore, all the workers must be trained in this struggle.

The question arises: How do we get closer to the workers, and what should we do so that they come to the conclusion that they must be part of the fight to take power, overcome the bourgeoisie, and establish the dictatorship of the proletariat? We will arrive at this result only if in the daily struggle waged by the working class, we demonstrate to them that workers can improve their position only through this struggle against the bosses, and only if the bourgeois state apparatus is destroyed. And we can do this only if we are where the workers are.

Isolated struggles waged by the working class against the bosses cannot improve the situation. In the course of these everyday struggles of the working class, we tell workers that victory is not possible waged by isolated workers, but only when the working-class masses join and support this struggle.

I shall cite an example: during the month of February 1920 the workers in the Warsaw stone quarries went out on strike – a most inopportune time for a strike. The woodworkers joined them, as did the metalworkers; the strike lasted five and a half weeks. The employers did not even think of a settlement. A general strike was then declared. All the military factories stopped working, as did the electrical stations. The government responded by militarising the electrical workers. The Communist Party then issued a call for a general strike all over Poland. The miners ceased working; the railroad workers threatened to go out. Only then did the government settle, and the strike ended in a complete victory for the workers. This also proved that the success of the workers in the class struggle depends entirely upon their solidarity, that the success of a strike depends on the support of the entire working class against the bourgeoisie.

Only with such examples from the everyday struggle can we teach the workers how to use their power, how to attain their aim, overturning capitalist power and establishing the dictatorship of the proletariat, upon which we can begin building a better and more wholesome future. In order to educate the working class in the course of the day-to-day struggle, we must be with them in the factories and their organisations. The workers at present are already organised, with a membership running into the millions. We must utilise this power. Should the workers simply confine themselves to the fight for an increase in wages, their condition will not be improved; on the contrary, their situation will become worse. We must convince the workers that only an organisation that is trying to unite the entire working class is a true defender of the interests of the working class. We must nevertheless remember that at present we cannot succeed in uniting all the workers' organisations. Under bourgeois rule this is an impossibility. We can hope for that only after the dictatorship of the proletariat has been established.

Many comrades claim that the Communist Party is numerically too small, and therefore could not become the leader of the workers' movement. That argument can be refuted simply by stating that neither do the unions embrace the totality of the working class. If one claims that the unions express the needs of the working class, we shall answer that the Communist Party, which includes the most class-conscious workers, should therefore lead the struggle. The task of every class-conscious worker is to enter the organisations of the workers, with the purpose of influencing them and transforming them into conscious Communists. The workers must be convinced in practice that only the Communist Party is their true support. Those who recommend turning the unions into small revolutionary organisations risk the loss of their influence on the masses, and play into the hands of the bourgeoisie. The Communists are being driven out of the unions by the police, the bourgeoisie, and the reformists. The Communists who take this position are following the road of the Second International. They are unconsciously fighting against Moscow and against the dictatorship of the proletariat. They are playing into the hands of the bourgeoisie and Amsterdam.

Nat Watkins (Britain): Comrades, the British delegation, of which I am a member, wishes me to express their general agreement with the theses as presented by Comrade Lozovsky. But although we are in general agreement with the principles embodied therein – especially the one of working within the unions – we entirely disagree with the views expressed by him with regard to the movement in Britain, and this disagreement I wish to express in no uncertain fashion.

Comrade Lozovsky must either be very much misinformed or not at all acquainted with the movement in Britain. I have therefore to endorse Comrade Bartels's observation that Comrade Lozovsky's knowledge of the labour organisations in the Western countries is not such as to inspire confidence in the Eastern critics of the Western movement. To be really acquainted with the movement in England it is necessary to be inside it. Well, those who are here representing the British movement have from ten to forty years' membership in the unions, and we want to tell you that Comrade Lozovsky is not only wrong with regard to his estimate of the immediate situation, but that he and Heckert are wrong on the question of the origin of the workshop movement. The incidents they cite are very interesting incidents in which the factory committees acted separately from the trade unions – in fact the 1905 example cited by Comrade Heckert meant the birth of a union movement.[2] But in the West, especially in the English movement, they can be traced almost to the middle of the nineteenth century.

They [factory committees] grew up within the union movement. It was the extraordinary conditions of the war period that brought them to the front as actual leading organs of the struggle. These organs have not always been the same in form, and so far as we miners are concerned, the unofficial miners' reform committees – now a section of the National Workers' Committees[3] – came into being during the miners' struggle against the Cambrian Combine in 1911. Then we struck right against the employers and the union bureaucrats. It was a great fight in which we paid in the lives of men.[4] It was on this occasion that A.J. Cook, N. Ablett, and W. Mainwaring came to the front as leaders of the South Wales Miners. The first two are Communists and now members of the EC of the Miners Federation of Great Britain.

2 For Heckert's reference, see p. 292.

3 The National Shop Stewards' and Workers' Committee Movement emerged in Britain in the course of militant struggles during World War I, although with roots in pre-war formations such as the Miners' Reform Movement. In January 1920 a National Conference of Shop Stewards' and Workers' Committees, representing some 72,000 workers, voted to affiliate to the Comintern.

4 The Cambrian Combine was a mining cartel in South Wales. A year-long strike against it by miners was waged from August 1910 to September 1911. In what became known as the 'Tonypandy Riot' in November 1910, some 500 miners were injured in an attack by police; one miner died from his wounds.

These facts alone show how wrong an impression of the British movement has been conveyed to this congress by Comrade Lozovsky.[5] His position is much like that of a spectator in the grandstand of a football match, an interested onlooker, but one who knows nothing of the teams engaged in the struggle.

The Shop Stewards and all the workers of the Workers' Committee movement have worked in the trade-union movement from their inception. Indeed, it was because the revolutionists were against the policy of leaving the unions that the movement came into existence, and to a very large extent have worked along the lines laid down by the Communist International before there was a Communist International.

That we have been successful in this direction is beyond question, just as it is beyond question that the unofficial movement has been the backbone of the miners' struggle, which has lasted for thirteen weeks. Even the leaders of the miners will admit that, as well as Mr. Lloyd George. And when Comrade Lozovsky talks about it not being a well-conceived fight, we would remind him that this was a lock-out forced upon us, and we were not in position to determine all the steps leading up to that. We simply had to fight, and we know that if we can accomplish the task of getting a million and a quarter men to stand firm as an organised force for a period of thirteen weeks, we have every confidence in workers and in ourselves that we shall acquit ourselves, leaders and men alike, as creditably as any other nation in the hour of revolutionary struggle.

Again, when Comrade Lozovsky states, as he has stated, that the Workers' Committee movement is outside the unions and takes no part in their work, I deny the truth of that statement. For we have not only been responsible for the election of the miners' leaders I have named, but the Workers' Committees were directly responsible for the election of Tom Mann to be general secretary of the Amalgamated Engineers Union. So I want to put my foot down emphatically upon such assertions as made by Comrade Lozovsky. If you choose to analyse the work of the Communist Party, the National Workers' Committees, the statements in the press, you will find that they all support my statements.

I believe that the British movement will play no insignificant part in the world revolution. When Comrade Mann stated the other night that 20 per cent of the British workers were on the side of the Red Trade Union International, I thoroughly agreed with him, in spite of the fact that they are not all represented here. We are on the move to the revolution; we are conquering the unions. Turn to any part of the country and you will find the young men of the

5 Lozovsky's remarks on the British trade-union movement in his report on tactics can be found on pp. 139–41.

revolutionary movement steadily getting to the leadership of the unions. Go to the Northern districts and you will find Harvey and Kirker, both members of the Communist Party, coming to the front. Go southward to South Wales and you will find the Workers' Committee movement has repeatedly led the way in strikes, in curtailing production, to such an extent that they have become a power to be reckoned with in that part of the country, and have practically become the dominant force in the South Wales Miners Federation. And don't forget that Herbert Smith said to Lloyd George that although he did not agree with the policy of the unofficial movement, he confessed frankly that the unofficial movement had been the backbone of the miners' fight. Make no mistake about it, the workers of Britain are moving forward rapidly to their decision, which will be, I am confident, in favour of the Red Trade Union International, in favour of the revolutionary movement that today has its centre in Moscow.

Dashkevich (Ukraine): Comrades, I am very surprised by the statement of Comrade Bartels, who, when referring to Comrade Lozovsky's theses, said that they were too superficial and lacking in serious thought. I will not touch on the theoretical side of the theses; they speak for themselves, as they very clearly and deeply take up the question of tactics in the trade-union movement. As to the practical application of these theses, they were brilliantly confirmed by the activities in Ukraine last year. There is virtually no other country where these tactics were more effectively tested than in Ukraine.

There were a whole series of counterrevolutionary governments in Ukraine in the final months of 1920. In the general development of the revolutionary struggle, the position of the trade unions and the participation in the trade unions of our Communist nuclei is especially interesting. I will go over some of the experiences of our trade-union revolutionary struggle in Ukraine in the past.

Let us take, for example, the fight against the government of the Central Rada during 1918, when the trade-union movement followed the same road as happened in Russia under Kerensky. After the October Revolution, the Communist nuclei started their work in our factory and shop committees. In January 1918, when the first decisive battle was waged, our trade-union nuclei, together with the Communist Party, led the struggle on the barricades for the conquest of power.[6]

---

6 In Ukraine the bourgeois-nationalist Rada, under the leadership of Simon Petlyura, waged a war against the soviets that started within weeks of the October Revolution in 1917, declaring a 'People's Republic of Ukraine' in January 1918.

Then we come to what our European comrades no doubt remember: the tremendous struggle led by the Ukrainian proletariat at the time of the hetman Skoropadsky.[7] Just remember the big railroad strike, when the Communist Party and all other left elements were represented by a very small minority. But this minority succeeded in taking hold of this chaotic movement, and the leadership of this strike passed over to the revolutionary groups that had been working in the trade unions. Many other examples substantiate the same thing: the enormous significance of penetrating the old unions, with the purpose of taking the leadership of the trade-union movement, discrediting the old leadership, and directing the old trade unions into the revolutionary struggle.

For this kind of work, the revolutionary enthusiasm of our syndicalist comrades is not sufficient. The merit of our great teacher Karl Marx consists in the skilful coordination of the consciousness of the working class with the political activity of the party. If the trade-union movement aims at the conquest of power and the establishment of a socialist order through the dictatorship of the proletariat, then it cannot reach this goal without the closest cooperation with the political party of the working class.

Within the trade-union movement we must always fight for backward elements that propound neutralism. Politics and economics cannot be separated. The organisation of factory and shop committees is of enormous importance for the trade-union movement. These committees are the initial nuclei linking together the masses with production and creating an atmosphere of revolutionary struggle among the working masses. Only the coordination of political and economic activity will enable the working class of the world to establish the dictatorship of the proletariat, not only in some isolated republics, but a world federation of Soviet republics.

Borden [William Z. Foster] (USA): In the name of the American delegation, I wish to state that we fully agree with the principles drawn up by Comrade Lozovsky in regards to tactics within the unions. But before I express the opinions of our delegation on this subject, I must make a few remarks on the speech delivered by Comrade Williams representing the IWW. His viewpoint is this: should the unions become revolutionary the bosses will disrupt and destroy them; should they unify with the American Federation of Labor, their leaders will immediately be bribed. Such arguments will not stand criticism. It

7 Pavlo Skoropadsky was a Ukrainian aristocrat and tsarist general who became a puppet of the German occupation forces that overthrew the Ukrainian Soviet republic in April 1918, establishing Skoropadsky as hetman. In December of that year Skoropadsky was ousted and fled to Berlin. Soviet power was established for good in Ukraine by early 1919.

is one thing to have business with unions whose membership runs into millions, and another thing to have business with little revolutionary unions. We must understand the situation. Comrade Williams states that in general the IWW is not opposed to entering the large unions, that there are merely some technical differences between us. This is not so. They simply refuse to join the large unions because it is against their principles. In this respect the IWW and the Communist Workers' Party of Germany [KAPD] are against the theses of Lozovsky.

In America, the situation at present is as follows: we have the strongest and most militant bourgeoisie there on the one hand, and a very disrupted working class on the other hand. The fault here certainly lies with the theories that the revolutionary element of the working class has followed for the last twenty-five years. We did have strong revolutionary organisations, but that was twenty-five years ago. The Knights of Labor at one time was a very revolutionary organisation. The American worker is revolutionary by nature and environment. The American working man will go on strike at any time; he thinks nothing of staying out for months, and if he has to he will strike with a gun on his shoulder. The argument that the American worker is not revolutionary is nonsensical. We merely have to refer to the strike in the year 1886, which no European strike had at that time equalled.[8]

After 1886 a change took place in the American labour movement. The teachings of De Leon and his disciples began to foster and take root. The followers demanded that the revolutionary elements leave their organisations;[9] this has brought great splits in the organisations and many of the revolutionaries have practically gone under. The results were a conglomeration of different elements. The left wing was broken up, and hardly had a membership of 60,000 organised workers. Had the revolutionary workers not accepted such ruinous tactics, the result would have been radically different. The American movement is in a terrible situation, and the revolutionaries are responsible for it. Hence we must accept the decision of the Communist International: we must join the masses and their organisations.

However, a new difficulty arises here. In order to enter the unions we must get the sanction of the IWW. The delegate of the IWW claims that his organisation has been leading the left wing of the labour movement, but the IWW

8 As part of a movement throughout the United States for the eight-hour day, 350,000 workers went on strike on 1 May 1886.

9 In 1895, supporters of the Socialist Labor Party, led by Daniel De Leon, formed the Socialist Trade and Labor Alliance as a left-wing alternative to the American Federation of Labor, encouraging revolutionary-minded workers to leave the AFL.

does not represent even a small part of the left wing in the labour movement in America. There are many times more revolutionary workers in the large unions than in the IWW.

I will simply cite one example. The United Mine Workers has a membership of about 600,000. Seventy per cent of the workers in that industry are foreigners. These workers are rebels; they had many conflicts with the bourgeoisie. Still they have separated from the IWW, which has a membership of only 300 in that particular industry.

Only those who accept the viewpoint of the Communist International, only those who will join and work in large unions will do revolutionary work. That revolutionary work could be done in the big unions has been proven time and again. It is enough to refer to the struggle in Seattle and Winnipeg to learn what a revolutionary minority can accomplish in the American unions.[10] For twenty-five years we have stood outside of this movement, and so it is no wonder that we have such results, and the bourgeoisie had its hands free. We should no longer carry out such a wavering policy. This wobbling in two directions cannot be tolerated any longer. We must work either within or outside of the American trade-union movement. It is only necessary to eliminate all doubts, all wobbling ways, and accept the thesis that only through tireless work within the unions shall we get results. Then there will be no doubt that we shall achieve a tremendous success in the American movement.

Chair: Comrade Müller has the floor.

Richard Müller (Germany): The delegation of the Communist trade unions of Germany agrees on the whole with Comrade Lozovsky's theses, but would like to have some of the questions discussed in the commission. We are very glad that Bartels, who represents the Free Unions [*freie Unionen*], was given the opportunity to present his views before you. I got the impression that the speech you heard by him only discredited the organisations on whose behalf he spoke. Had he kept on speaking, he would have driven a stake into the Free Unions.

Well, what did he say? He said essentially as follows: 'The proletariat must carry out the fight right now while capitalism is crumbling. It must take the

10 The Winnipeg general strike lasted from 15 May until 26 June 1919. It was called by the Winnipeg Trades and Labor Council in solidarity with striking building trades workers. Some 35,000 workers took part, the big majority of the city's working class. Sympathy strikes took place in Calgary, Edmonton, Toronto, and other Canadian cities.

For the Seattle general strike, see p. 166, n. 9.

offensive, and for this purpose it must prepare adequate armament.' What does that mean? On the one hand, he thinks it necessary to go into an immediate open fight; on the other hand, he thinks we must first begin to prepare our munitions of war. How long, then, does he think it will take him to smash the old unions and how much time does he need for converting the present Free Unions into suitable machinery.

Bartels's ideas in their practical workings are counterrevolutionary, because in his opinion, as it seems, the struggle should be put off for a long time until the arms are ready; but this means to shelve the revolution for a long time. Bartels does not want to win over the trade unions, and he even thinks it impossible. First, he said he was going to give you a historical account of his Free Unions in order that the delegates of other countries better understand our situation in Germany. I am extremely sorry that he has not confided to us the history of the Free Unions. Had he done so, he would have given himself a slap, because he would have thus given the last proof that the job of smashing the old unions or conducting the revolutionary fight was beyond his depth. We therefore lost a great deal when Comrade Bartels failed to reveal the history of the Free Unions.

These unions were organised in 1919. Well, what have they accomplished up till now? Their representative claims that they have managed to bring up their total membership to 300,000. During this time the membership of the old unions rose to 9 million. According to Bartels these Lilliputians carry on a spirited fight against the old trade unions. Does this not remind you of the puppy barking at the moon? At any rate, the Free Unions are mere clowns alongside of the great masses organised in the old trade unions.

Bartels said further that the Free Unions must win over the masses. But where are the masses? According to his own figures, 10 million are organised in the old trade unions, and 11 million are still outside of any labour organisation. My dear comrades of the Free Unions: Have you just found this out today? What have you done to bring these unorganised hosts under your sway? Your ridiculous puny membership shows how comparatively weak your slogans are, what little magnetic force there is in your theory. Your influence even on those masses, for whom you do not have to fight the old trade unions, is next to nothing.

We must decidedly reject the theories that the representatives of the Free Unions try to force on us. We think that their slogans, as far as Germany is concerned, are tantamount to postponing revolutionary class action for an indefinite time. But anyone who sees the employers in Germany arming themselves and advancing against the workers, the drop in wages, the lengthening of the working day, the conditions of labour getting ever worse, cannot but recognise the imminence of revolutionary conflicts on a grand scale. Anyone who sees all this must definitely reject the slogan of 'Smash the old trade unions!'. We must keep in close touch with the masses and lead them in the struggle until the revolution is triumphant. What does the slogan you flung at the masses amount to for us? It surely means the fight of labour against labour, especially when the employers are taking the offensive. But we can say to the comrades representing other countries that we are not the only ones who came out against the Free Unions.

What is the attitude of the members of the Free Unions toward the theory of their leader Bartels? I maintain that Bartels does not express the views of the bulk of the members in his organisation. It is improbable that the members of the Free Unions should want to put themselves in decided opposition to the rest of the working masses and endorse the slogan of 'Smash the unions'. One of the speakers of the Free Unions has stated today that they have no leaders. And still Comrade Bartels acts here as a leader in determined opposition to the will of the masses.

Only last January we reached an agreement with the Executive Board of the Free Unions by which they bound themselves to give up the 'Smash the old unions' slogan. The members agreed to this decision. And still, after the March Action,[11] their Executive Board allowed a break of discipline by refusing to abide by the above agreement, on the strength of which they were admitted to membership in the Red Trade Union International. The rank and file has not had any occasion as yet to pass judgement on the conduct of their executive organ. Here Comrade Bartels himself stated that they had resumed the tactic of splitting the trade-union movement. He wants to confront this congress with a fait accompli. But what will the rank and file say to this?

I know that meetings were held in May at which the following resolution was adopted: 'Having heard the direct report about the completed negotiations, this meeting declares that the Executive Board of the union has broken the agreement. This meeting calls upon the Executive Board to put an end to such breaches of discipline affecting the conditions of admission laid down by the Red Trade Union International and the party. Otherwise, this meeting demands the resignation of the Executive Board.'

On Sunday, 22 May, there was also a meeting of the 'North Star' Union, where a resolution was passed, which in part reads as follows: 'The meeting held 22 May 1921 … expresses its lack of confidence in the Executive Board of the Free Workers' Union of Gelsenkirchen and demands dropping the slogan "Get out of the old unions!"'

11 For the March Action in Germany, see p. 215, n. 7.

In the same way, a meeting at the Dirhardt mine resolved as follows: 'The meeting held at the Dirhardt Mine 22 May 1921 decidedly condemns the slogan of the leading organs of the party, "Out of the old unions!"'

I also know that a meeting at Loberg unanimously passed the following resolution: 'The meeting held by the members of the free unions of Gelsenkirchen condemns the slogan raised by the union of "Out of the old unions!"'

I could cite a dozen more such instances, which prove that the representatives of the Gelsenkirchen union here present do not reflect the views of the rank and file.

We demand that this congress make no concession to Bartels's theories. All organisations affiliated with the Red Trade Union International are duty-bound to abide by the decision of this congress. We further demand that the revolutionary class struggle not be sabotaged by such slogans as are being raised by Bartels. Our task is to carry out the revolutionary struggle with all the means at our command up to the triumph of the revolution.

Adolf Kunte (Czechoslovakia): The trade unions of Czechoslovakia have a membership of about 1.5 million workers. Therefore, the assertion that the Red Trade Union International includes only 200,000 does not correspond with reality, the more so given that the Communist Party of Czechoslovakia counts about 400,000 members.

We have neither syndicalist nor independent trade unions, but we have trade unions on two parallel national lines: Czech and German. I am glad that this congress has come out for the amalgamation of the two. I am authorised to declare, on behalf of the two organisations, that they fully accept the theses by Comrade Lozovsky. We accept unreservedly the point of view of conquering the trade-union movement through the formation of Communist nuclei in the unions.

On the question of the relationship between the Red International of Labour Unions and the Third International, we are of the opinion that the relationship should be of the same character as existed between the old trade unions and the Social-Democratic Party.

We wish to, and we must, win the confidence of the masses – this is our policy on these questions. At the same time, however, we think that our Russian comrades do not pay sufficient attention to the special character of the Communist parties of the West. We are weaker numerically, and therefore the formation of Communist nuclei is difficult. Owing to the general political character of our country, we have succeeded in winning to our side – which means also the side of the Red Trade Union International – the Union of Agricultural Workers, the largest Czechoslovak union, as well as the Union of Chemical Workers.

We in Czechoslovakia very often read in the newspapers of appeals to leave the trade unions. However, we do not follow these appeals and we shall certainly ignore them in the future. The Czech press, and those who are behind it, pursue a threefold aim: (1) separating the revolutionary elements from the masses; (2) bringing economic harm to the revolutionary elements; by this method they are being thrown out of the industries, which has a terrorising effect upon the hesitant element of the workers; and (3) hindering the adoption of resolutions of trade-union conferences and congresses directed against the trade-union bureaucracy.

We on our side are acting in the following way: all groups excluded from the old unions united in independent organisations, but this did not continue long. We at once began an energetic propaganda among them to re-enter the unions. At the same time, we saw to it that the excluded workers did not lose their jobs. Very often they had to work in such a way that the workers, victimised for their convictions, were sent to unions favourable to the Communists, regardless of one's trade. Thus they may be sent to our Agricultural Workers' Union although they are metalworkers. We also might find it necessary to organise nuclei of trained and disciplined comrades with the objective of combating the old trade unions.

Our chief purpose is to permeate the masses of workers with the revolutionary spirit. This is not our ultimate goal, but is only a means to make them capable of carrying out systematic revolutionary action. The workers must become convinced that everything we are doing is being done in their interest, and in the best interest of the revolutionary struggle.

I have said already that in general we accept the theses of Lozovsky, but we wish to propose the insertion of a separate point on the question of the excluded workers in the course of the fight for revolutionising the trade unions. It runs as follows:

> Workers driven out of the unions through the terror of the bureaucracy should know that they are strengthening the position of this bureaucracy by leaving the unions without a fight, without trying to join their comrades again, or by appealing to their comrades to leave the unions. On the contrary, revolutionary workers should take the view that the fight against such exclusions, the fight for readmission in the unions, and not pulling the revolutionary elements out of the old unions, is the best means to develop class consciousness and the revolutionisation of the masses. The conquest of the trade unions does not mean capturing their funds, but winning the confidence of the workers. It goes without saying that the excluded groups must have the full support of all revolutionary workers.

These are our principles, which the congress will certainly agree to and for which we will fight.

This fight will require much energy, forbearance, and patience, as we are well aware of the power of the trade-union bureaucracy at present. We consider that at present this bureaucracy is the last refuge and support of capitalism in the West. Therefore, our immediate aim should be to wage the decisive battle. (*Applause*)

Chair: Comrade Bartels will speak.

Arthur Bartels (Germany, Gelsenkirchen Free Workers' Union): Comrades, we have before us the theses of Comrade Lozovsky on the tasks and tactics of the trade unions. I have already remarked that in the course of the day we shall submit our theses. The proposals of Comrade Lozovsky, from our point of view, require serious criticisms. I wish to remark from the outset that, in our opinion, the proposals of Comrade Lozovsky do not refer to what we usually connect with the idea of tasks and tactics of trade unions. We think that Comrade Lozovsky does not touch on the problem in its real sense. He is engaged in recounting the events within the trade-union movement, in criticising and omitting those questions that most interest us.

His 'report' – and his 'theses' are nothing but that – I would call the part that refers to the Free Unions superficial and even light-minded. When one reads his criticisms of the independent unions of Germany and America, one comes to the conclusion that the treatment of the question is the outcome of his own particular point of view on the subject. Lozovsky writes in *Moscow* that the Free Workers' Union is half a Communist creation. This expression of Lozovsky can be explained only by the fact that he is not fully informed about the trade-union movement in Germany. As I said, he ignores the fundamental problem. My purpose will therefore be to touch upon why this movement came to be formed and how this came about, and to explain in detail our basic principles and spirit, so that our foreign comrades can get a clear idea of the real state of things in our country.

Comrade Lozovsky has recently been very preoccupied, so we shall not blame him for not developing his theses, which are not very deep or thought out.

If we now take the liberty of criticising them, we will certainly provoke the dissatisfaction of those who applaud and say 'amen' to everything that comes out of the bureau. When the other day there was a question on the relationship between the Red International of Trade Unions and the Third International with reference to the struggle in Germany, Comrade Lozovsky used the following comparison: What the Unionists want, he said, is very similar as if someone, anxious to take possession of a house, would instead of driving out its masters, pour oil into it and attempt to burn it down.[12] ('*That's true.*') Maybe, from your point of view, this may be the right thing to do. I wish to speak on the fundamental principles. If you put a new roof on an old house, if you put in new panes, the house will still remain old. This old house we do not want. This old house is no longer good for use. It is neither a refuge for defence nor a place from which to attack the enemy. We must have a building that can stand the attack of capitalists and white guards – a modern building that can stand against modern weapons.

We will now take a closer look at the basic problem. I will later touch on the question of the tactics of the trade unions, the most important question.

The role of the trade unions, in comparison with the pre-revolutionary period, has changed very much. Formerly the trade unions, owing to their nature and the character of the conditions under which the workers lived, were more adapted for a defensive struggle. This nonrevolutionary period involved the whole period up to the beginning of the World War. During that period the initiative of the fight had always come from the employer, who dictated to the workers and their organisations the methods and means of the struggle.

In the transitional period – which I consider the whole period of the Great War – it appeared that those old methods were becoming ineffective. The capitalists changed their methods in the fight, but the workers' organisations did not follow their example. This is best proved in the methods by which the leaders led the German workers down the wrong path. This period can be characterised as a period of betrayal, even when compared to the previous period. For during the pre-war period the central union offices relied to some extent on the class consciousness of the workers, and the leaders sought to maintain the class character of the workers' organisations.

How did this betrayal happen? You are very well acquainted with the state of things in France, Britain, and Germany. During the transitional period the methods of the struggle imposed on the workers by the capitalists themselves became a brake on the development of the revolutionary class struggle.

We have analysed this occurrence in our attempt to get at the truth. We have attempted to find the causes that made such a betrayal on the part of the bureaucracy possible. We have come to the conclusion that, unfortunately, the workers have not tried to secure their influence within their unions, to force the officials to take into consideration the will of the workers. The main thing is that

12 For Lozovsky's remarks, see p. 106.

the structure of the present trade unions has been the cause of the betrayal. A betrayal becomes possible when the mass of workers have no influence on the administration of their trade union. But if we condemn a system, we simply ask ourselves what other methods will help us to solve the question, to reach the desired aim. Inasmuch as the betrayal in the organisational period has become evident, the old weapons of the class struggle have become antiquated. The workers must adopt new methods of class struggle.

We are now coming to the revolutionary epoch in the real sense of the word, which was started by the Russian Revolution in 1917, when the proletariat showed itself able to resist the attacks of the enemy. At the same time that the revolutionary class struggle was becoming acute, capitalism entered into a period of decline, whose symptoms could already be traced to the pre-war period of boom. It is clear that the downfall of capitalism is subject to dialectical oscillations.

With the beginning of the attack on capitalism, the workers pass over from the defensive onto the offensive. As the defensive does not create anything new for the working class, it is conservative and needs to be replaced by the offensive. But the proletariat did not change its methods of struggle. It did not take the offensive. This is a new page in the history of struggle that developed within the organisations. This is a struggle we are waging at present against the tendencies that find an echo in this hall.

Once we recognise that the proletariat must take the offensive and that the old methods are holding back the attack on capital, it is necessary for the proletariat to adapt to the new conditions of struggle. It must completely change its tactics and methods of struggle, which were fine for defence, but not for the attack. The proletariat must create a true attack apparatus. This apparatus must first of all find its expression in the unity of revolutionary forces. Are the methods and tactics of the old organisations sufficient for the new times? This is the principal question that must engage our thoughts. Can we be satisfied with the organisations that the workers have at present? I say no. These organisations are not sufficient; they are old, rusty weapons. They are an old house in which the proletariat barricades itself and from which it cannot escape. This is but an old fortress that cannot stand the firing of modern cannons.

During the struggle it is necessary to see that what has been gained should not be easily relinquished. We must hold our gains at all costs. When the general succeeds in beating the enemy at the front, but at the same time all his reserves are used up and there are no possibilities for him to fortify his new positions, his success may be but a Pyrrhic victory. The proletariat must be prepared beforehand if it wishes to attain the victory for which it strives and to make it durable. That is why the workers' organisations must be adapted to the requirements that are necessary after the battle has been won. These requirements are control of production, creation of new forms for the expropriation of property, organising new detachments, Communist education, and so on. The Russian comrades better than anyone can tell us what needs to be done on the day following the conquest of power.

Have we the organs that are needed to bring this about? What does our experience teach us? We cannot live with the present; we must look to the future. In other words, we have to adapt our organisation not only to the present but also to the future. Taking into consideration the struggle that is to follow the conquest of power, we have to pay attention to the industrial organisations. The industrial organisations alone are capable of realising control of industry. We are confronted with the necessity of forming new organs of workers' struggle. The struggle for power inevitably requires organs of political rule.

We believe that the Free Unions are constructed in such a manner, making them real fighting organisations. It must be clear to you from what I have said that we attach great importance to form. In opposition to the views of the United German Communist Party and to those of Zinoviev, Lozovsky, and others, we pay much attention to the form of organisation of the class struggle. In accordance with what I have said, the form is to us a thing of great importance, which we must not forget for a moment.

For instance, we have to create a special trade-union apparatus for carrying out the control of industry. How can the existing trade-union organisations realise this control? Recall Russia: here from the very beginning they thought of creating new forms of the political class struggle, and these new organisations are neither craft nor trade unions but rather industrial unions.

They now wish to mechanically transform the craft unions in Germany into industrial organisations. That is exactly what is said in the theses by Lozovsky. What does this mean? That we have to build a roof, and after the roof is ready, erect the foundation. But we must say that it is impossible to create industrial unions in such a mechanical way. It is sheer utopia. An industrial union must have an industrial basis; otherwise, it would mean nothing. What is to be done? People who think themselves very clever – and there are plenty of them in Germany as well as in all countries, and whom Lozovsky has also joined – advise the transformation of the trade unions into industrial organisations, making use of the factory committees. These wise men wish to build, at the same time, both the roof and the foundation, that is, to unite the semi-unions with industrial unions, thereby transforming the units of production.

Obviously this will not succeed. First of all, the trade unions do not want it. The remarkable thing is that this work is to be done within the old trade unions themselves. To unite the semi-unions with industrial unions is nonsense. (*Protests*) You must forgive me for this expression; after all, you consider my theory also to be nonsense. We say: first the foundation, and afterwards the roof; not the other way around. You've never heard anything like this before, because you disdain the Free Union movement without being acquainted with it. Heckert also said that we have to create industrial organisations, and at the same time mechanically unite the halfway unions. As far as the rest is concerned, he simply repeats well-trodden truths.

I now take up another question, comrades, which is closely related to what I have just told you. We are told that it is necessary to take hold of the whole apparatus of the trade unions in order to impose our conceptions on the organised workers in the unions; that's how you penetrate the masses – by going where they are. It is understood that we have to do this. But can that be done from within the trade unions? They say the unions have to be conquered and cite the example of Russia. If in Russia the trade unions were conquered by means of the Bolshevik nuclei, we cannot draw any conclusion from that for Germany. The Russian trade unions – created in 1905 and some of them as late as 1912 – had neither stable traditions nor a well-organised apparatus, as is the case of the German trade unions. The Russian trade unions were not as solidly built and structured. It was therefore easy to penetrate them. The Russian workers were at a low level (thanks to the educational work, matters have now improved) and those who had the best means of propaganda were not seen by the masses. In Germany the greatest success is very often obtained by those who carry out the best agitation. (*Applause*) I am not used to being applauded here. The partisans of the nuclei applaud evidently because they expect to get the occasion to fling something at the Free Unions, taking advantage of my words. We know this by our experience in Germany. But these taunts are arrows that will turn around and hit those who shot them. It is impossible to conquer the German trade unions.

I must likewise express my doubts about how far Tom Mann is correct in stating that the British trade unions can be conquered. When they speak in Germany of the conquest of the trade unions as meaning the capture of the trade-union apparatus without having to break it up, such a conception is simply ridiculous. But even if we succeed in this, I must say that we have no interest in preserving or conquering these old organisations. We want to get rid of them, because they are organically defective. The trade unions are a state within a state. This is particularly true for the German trade unions, and is not contested even by the partisans of the nuclei.

Marx, Engels, Lenin, all who swore allegiance to Marxism, say rightly that the state cannot be conquered, it must be smashed and replaced by newly created organs of proletarian rule. Marx speaks of it in his *Eighteenth Brumaire*.[13] The heavy losses and defeats of the working class have given us one thing: we have at least found the concrete forms and organs of proletarian rule. Those who are acquainted with the history of the Paris Commune of 1871 should know that through it the soviet system made its entry into history.[14] The Russian comrades went through the same experience. It's true we have submitted this system to criticism, but that's not the essential point. The trade unions, as a state within a state, must be treated in a Marxist fashion. What Marx said about the state also applies to the trade unions. They cannot be conquered; they must be smashed. The Free Unions are soviet organs; they become such in the process of their development. It is simply a piece of nonsense to assert that the Free Unions are formations that have 'dropped from the sky'. Do you wish to turn back the wheel of history?

Comrade Müller voices the opinion that the Free Unions should be reined in. In the opinion of Comrade Béla Szántó, they must be put under the supreme control of the Communist Party in order to obtain the same results. See for yourselves now what your Marxism looks like. The whole system must be toppled. The industrial organisations with a soviet superstructure are the foundations of the future. This is our opinion, which, if not at this congress, will win out in the end.

And so, comrades, I go on to the next point. It seems to me that I have traced the methods that should be applied in the international workers' movement. Now the question arises irrespectively of the need for new forms: Are we in a position to do new forms of work within the old trade unions? We could argue the matter for hours, but I will just touch on the most important and essential points.

It is quite clear that trade unions, such as the German trade unions, the British trade unions, the Gompers union in America, and the General Confederation of Labour have nothing in common with the revolutionary proletarian movement. They are the simple tools of capitalism and its last stronghold. They combat the Communists in the cruellest manner, as was shown during the

13 'This executive power with its enormous bureaucratic and military organisation, with its extensive and artificial state machinery, with a host of officials numbering half a million, besides an army of another half million, this appalling parasitic body, which enmeshes the body of French society like a net and chokes all its pores, sprang up in the days of the absolute monarchy, with the decay of the feudal system, which it helped to hasten .... All revolutions perfected this machine instead of breaking it.' In Karl Marx, 'The Eighteenth Brumaire of Louis Bonaparte', *MECW*, vol. 11, pp. 185–6.

14 For the Paris Commune, see p. 209, n. 5.

recent March uprising in Germany. I ask: When and how have the Communist nuclei done anything positive? I maintain that they exercised a negative influence on the revolutionary movement, while their positive achievements were only of benefit to the treacherous game that the big German trade unions were playing. They have done nothing to create or develop the revolutionary struggle in Germany. The same is true of the German trade unions and the General Workers' Union of Germany [ADGB], which played the same role as those who took up arms against the proletariat, helping to subdue the March uprising. The March movement was led exclusively by the independent revolutionary organisations.

Malzahn (*from his seat*): This is not true.

Bartels (*continues*): Comrade Malzahn, you'll speak later. Remember your own statistics.[15]

While the independent organisations always bring out their own men, at the moment of combat the nuclei have proven their lack of capability. They were able to lead only an insignificant number of unions, while comrades under our leadership were almost everywhere in revolutionary combat.

The trade unions, as we understand them, have had their day. You are asking the impossible, and you will be compelled very soon to recognise your mistake. Our time will come; the weakness of the nuclei is becoming clear.

Now, I'll get to the so-called theories of the masses. It's true that Marxists say that revolutionists must have the support of these masses. But I will ask you: Where are the masses? The trade unions are pointed to. But this is incorrect, and I'll prove this to you by some statistics.

In Germany, according to statistics, there were 21.4 million workers employed in 1920, including women and youth; in 1918 there were 18.1 million, and in 1907 14.4 million workers. Out of these 21.4 million workers according to the 1919 statistics (at present there are no new statistics) in the free trade unions [*freien Gewerkschaften*] of the General German Federation [ADGB], there were 7,338,123 organised workers. At the end of 1918 there had been only 2,866,012. It follows, thus, that from the end of 1918 to the end of 1919 the number of organised workers increased by 4.6 million. But at the beginning of 1921, and up to the present moment, the number has been rapidly decreasing, with a decline

15 A reference to Malzahn's speech at the Comintern's Third Congress, where he gave statistics on the number of workers participating in the March Action. See Riddell (ed.) 2015, *3WC*, pp. 260–2.

of one million workers. Comrade Müller, in *Der Arbeiter-Rat* and *Der Kommunistische Gewerkschafter*, substantiates these facts. If despite this decline we put the membership of the free trade-union organisations at 8 million and allow about 2 million for all other trade-union organisations, we have 10 million organised workers out of a mass of 21 million.

I ask you: Where then are the masses? It is obvious that the big majority of the workers are unorganised and stay out of the big unions. So when we are told that we must get the support of the masses, we should not limit ourselves to the trade-union movement, as is done by United Communist Party of Germany, but go where the masses really are.

Exclamation: Where are the masses? Where should we go?

Bartels (*continues*): You are asking where they are: in the shops and in the factories. That's where we should go; there we must spread our influence; there we must build the cornerstone of our organisation, win the sympathy of the masses, educate them and enlighten them, spread our literature. But not in the old trade unions, where the influence of the top leaders is still strong because of the indifference of the masses, where it is poisoned by the yellow bourgeois press. I repeat: if we want the support of the masses – and we all want it – we must look for the masses where they really are: in the shops and factories. Those whom you meet at the gatherings of the union are not the masses, but only a part of them.

Your slogan, 'Everyone into the trade unions!' is simply an appeal to Amsterdam. By the dues you'll pay to Amsterdam, you will strengthen it materially; you will support the bourgeoisie. You will also strengthen it morally, because the Amsterdam Federation boasts of the number of its adherents, and you are going to strengthen it morally by your presence.

Owing to this fact, we say to the workers: 'Out of the trade unions – your place is in the factory committees'. By this we don't intend to say that everything that is created by the independent unions is sacred and unalterable. We don't want to create any sanctuaries, because we know that all this is the result of the process of development and is subject to the development of the revolution. We are not like the others, who consider themselves infallible. But we must recognise and admit whatever is necessary for the proletariat in a given situation.

What is the importance of coming to Moscow and saying, 'We are Communists in body and soul'? Anybody can say this. I want to remind you of the Italians – Bianchi and his friends. We must severely judge by deeds; mere talk is worth nothing.

The nucleus of Gaspari failed to come here to Moscow, but went instead to Amsterdam. (*Noise*) *Die Rote Fahne* in its issue no. 203 writes, 'If at present in Germany there are a million organised workers in the trade unions who favour the Red Trade Union International, but formally adhere to Amsterdam, we consider it erroneous to advise them to formally join the Red International. ('*That's right.*') Because such a step will give a pretext to the bureaucracy to split the trade unions.'[16] ('*That's right.*')

Comrade Malzahn stated before the Credentials Commission, 'At the present time we cannot ignore Amsterdam.' Consequently you have one foot in Amsterdam and the other in Moscow.

We say: we must sever connections with Amsterdam. Yesterday you adopted a resolution on the Italian question; you concluded it with a request that the Italian workers clearly decide whether they are for or against Moscow. If this resolution should be applied to Germany (*noise*) … if this resolution is considered applicable to Germany, then we are with you. (*Commotion*)

Now Comrade Lozovsky states in his theses that our standpoint is counterrevolutionary. (*Cries of 'That's stupid!'*) It's written right here. This is an insulting outrage. (*Cries of 'Stupidity!'*) The secret of success, according to Lozovsky's words and theses, lies in standing firm. That's fine; we have experienced it ourselves at this congress. But this does not render any great service to the international workers' movement. What is going on here? Those standing on the basis of the nuclei have the possibility of mistreating their opponents. This standing-firm policy is already being applied to Germany. Many connections with the working class were broken by this policy, and at this congress the same policy breaks connections with the revolutionary workers of the world. We must admit this with sorrow.

Comrade Murphy foresees the danger of bureaucratisation. We must face this danger with open eyes. It can neither be denied nor can it be compelled to disappear by black magic. You must carefully strive to make the trade-union bureaucracy disappear, and first of all you must not allow it to get a firm foothold in the International. The International shall not exercise a dictatorship over the proletariat. We want a dictatorship of the working class and not of its leaders.

George Williams (USA, IWW): On the question of tactics, I have noticed that there are many situations in various countries. And also that the programmes

16 This is apparently a reference to an article by Jacob Walcher, 'Der dritte Weltkongress und die Gewerkschaftsfrage', in *Die Rote Fahne*, no. 252, 6 June 1921.

advanced by various elements consist merely in a statement that we should get in the reactionary unions and capture them. Now, that is perfectly agreeable to everybody, I suppose; at least it is in America. I want it understood, however, that what I say applies only to America. I know nothing about the conditions in other countries, and leave the settling of this question to them. My objection to the matter is the question of the tactics that are to be used in America, and I question the carrying through of the programme that would bring these tactics from its point of inception to its logical conclusion. The only thing that I can find from the speakers, and from the theses of Zinoviev and Lozovsky, is a mere statement to get in the unions.

In America, owing to the different conditions, the Communists have a more definite programme. They are agreed in America that the A.F. of L. should be captured. But the various elements in the American movement disagree as to how to capture the A.F. of L. The American Communists plan to form a nucleus in the A.F. of L. and are working on the plan now. Then there is another element in America that is trying to capture the A.F. of L. They are semi-radical and are more or less political. They seek to capture the A.F. of L. by degrees, converting it into a revolutionary organisation. Then again, there are members of the IWW who are members of various A.F. of L. unions, who are carrying out a persistent campaign.

Many people are under the delusion that the IWW does not believe in getting into the A.F. of L. That is not correct. The IWW does not say to any of its members that you cannot belong to the A.F. of L., nor do they put it as a condition of membership that a member of the IWW should withdraw from the A.F. of L. The difference between the IWW and the A.F. of L. is that the A.F. of L. form of organisation is craft – one craft is organised against the interests of all other crafts. The IWW maintains that the workers should be organised according to industry, and not crafts; and on these lines they fight the A.F. of L. between the three elements that are mentioned as boring from within the A.F. of L.

I want to discuss first the Communist nucleus. I want to ask some questions regarding this programme. Now, I want to say that the question of boring in the A.F. of L. and propagating revolutionary programmes is a good one, and nobody has anything against it. There is no objection of going into the A.F. of L. and boring from within. If any organisations want to bore, it is not for anyone to deny them the privilege. But when a general policy is advanced along these lines and put forth as a substitute for the IWW programme, then we must be shown some definite programme if we are to agree on a certain policy.

Now, the question of forming cells in the A.F. of L. I speak now regarding the question of forming cells in the A.F. of L. with a certain handicap, because I know that nearly everyone here does not understand properly the nature of this organisation, and I hope that those who do understand the A.F. of L. will be able to get my points and place more sense on the question than those from other countries who are not acquainted with the A.F. of L. I state here without fear of contradiction that the meaning of 'trade union' in America is entirely different from that of Germany or England, and anybody who understands the American labour movement will appreciate that point.

Now as to the question of forming cells. After cells have been formed in these unions, what is going to be their aim? Who is going to be the director of the cells? Is it intended to work through some particular labour organisation in America and transform it into some economic organisation, or is it intended to create a political organisation? If so, what organisation is it going to be? I maintain that the question of cells in the A.F. of L. is important because it is purely an economic question. Therefore, those who start boring from within should be directed by an economic organisation, because if it is a political organisation they will naturally subvert what they accomplish into a political programme. What are the aims of these cells? Are they going to capture the A.F. of L. and convert it into a proletarian economic union or industrial union? Or is the purpose of this boring from within to capture the leadership and machinery?

Now, there are two points that deserve a lot of discussion. If they are boring merely to set up new leaders, then I would suggest that the tactics adopted in Chicago by the labour leaders of that city be adopted.[17] But as that is a destructive method and no results [are] possible, then it stands that the Communist plan of forming cells can only have for its purpose the capturing of the A.F. of L., and the establishment of a revolutionary economic organisation. But here their programme is brought to a halt, because the capitalist class together with the reactionary leaders of the A.F. of L. immediately get busy and set up new craft unions in the very places of the unions captured by the revolutionaries.

I want to cite here instances that occurred in Vancouver, B.C. and the State of Washington. In Vancouver, B.C., the One Big Union of Canada succeeded in capturing the entire metal trade locals of that city. Within a very short time, the capitalists together with the international officers of the trade unions, which had gone over to the new organisation, set up new A.F. of L. locals, and forced the members who had gone over to the OBU of Canada to rejoin the new locals

17 Presumably a reference to the Chicago Federation of Labor, led by John Fitzpatrick. At the time, Fitzpatrick was attempting to present a left-wing alternative to the Gompers leadership of the AFL.

and pay over again a high initiation fee. The seceding members were confronted with the situation of either joining the new locals that were set up or lose their jobs. The affair ended in all of them abandoning the OBU and coming over to the A.F. of L.

In the State of Washington, the State Federation of Labor, which is an A.F. of L. organisation, was instructed by its convention to issue a ballot among the various locals of the state calling on the members to decide whether or not they should form or consolidate all the locals into a One Big Union. On the eve of the elections, the officials of the Washington State Federation were ordered by the Executive Committee of the A.F. of L. to withdraw the ballot, which they did, and nothing more was done towards merging the workers of that state into a better and more effective organisation.

Now I want to take up the question that was discussed regarding the revolutionary leaders at the head of these organisations. I want to know what is the difference between what is called a revolutionary leader and a conservative leader. The theory of putting revolutionary leaders in the organisations in place of conservative leaders, and that these revolutionary leaders would be trustworthy is false, as it supposes that the emancipation of the workers depends on the leader. But what assurance is there that these leaders would be sincere? We would have only their word, and I want to point out that words are cheap. The history of the world is full of false leaders who before acquiring power showed all the symptoms of being sincere. Some people suppose that revolutionary leaders and reactionary leaders are born, that is to say, men are reactionary or revolutionary according to where they are born. But it is not the reactionary leaders that we want to remove; it is the reactionary form of unions that we want to remove. Revolutionary leaders become reactionary, because as soon as they get into the movement and get power they are corrupted by their environment. I argue that the individual is not the question in this revolutionary movement. It is not the question of the quality of the individual, but the quality of the organisation he belongs to.

Now, if the Communist nuclei are going to form industrial unions, isn't it logical to suppose that the unions they form will become detached and will suffer the same fate as the IWW has suffered in all its years of repression? Is it logical for us to form such unions that will be destroyed as fast as they come into existence? The programme of the nuclei will have to be so arranged that the whole A.F. of L. movement will be captured at the same time. It is impossible to define the independent element that is trying to capture the A.F. of L. They are of so many shades that it is hard to tell where one starts or the next begins. All these people having a progressive programme say they will remove the machine of the A.F. of L., but we see these leaders, so-called independent revolutionary leaders, as soon as they get into power they subject their various theories to their own ends. I can point out no end of officials in the West of America that have gone in as progressives in the labour movement with the result that now they are bound in and their organisations are trying to get them out. The independents join as leaders, never as workers, and as soon as they acquire power they become corrupted, if – as is generally the case – they were not corrupted before.

I question individually the possibility of capturing the A.F. of L. as an institution. It is entirely capitalistic and is nothing more nor less than a chamber of commerce, that is, most of its members are mechanics who join the A.F. of L. merely to sell their skilled labour for as much as they can get. And it is proved by the fact that whenever the membership of the union becomes greater than the jobs available, the unions immediately close the books. I would like to point out more of the difficulties of boring within the A.F. of L., but the obstacles are so many that they can only be appreciated by somebody who has great experience with the A.F. of L. I have no time to explain here, or go into details, about the A.F. of L. The A.F. of L., as a labour organisation in America, amounts to something like three and a half million according to the latest report, and those people who claim the IWW as a dual organisation with no right to be in the field fail to point out that there are fields in the labour movement of America that the A.F. of L. does not attempt to organise.

For instance, there are three and a half million workers in the A.F. of L. There are in America 30 million wageworkers. What is going to be done with the 27 million wageworkers who are not in the A.F. of L.? There are the lumber workers, the agricultural workers, and a vast army of unskilled labour that travels around the country. The A.F. of L. never attempts to organise these workers. It is possible for the IWW to organise these skilled workers. In fact, these workers will not have anything to do with the form of unionism that is advocated by the A.F. of L., and it is not our intention to invite the A.F. of L. and its corrupt officialdom into the field to organise these unskilled workers under the banner of the A.F. of L. These workers are all revolutionary in spirit, and to even suggest to them joining the A.F. of L. would be to invite trouble.

Lozovsky: Comrade Michel will now speak.

Godonnèche (*from his seat*): Comrade Michel is speaking in his own name, as he has received no instructions from the French delegation. I consider it an elementary rule that a member of a delegation, before taking the floor, should consult his delegation. But neither Sirolle nor Lemoine nor Michel followed this elementary rule. I wish to inform the congress about this state of things before I have the opportunity to report the matter to the higher body of the Confederation [CGT].

Lozovsky: Comrade Michel has the floor.

Michel Relenque (France): Comrades, the policy that the parties and organisations follow in order to go into action very often, if not always, has its origin in the theoretical conceptions which this or that movement professes. As to political parties, their activity is on a general level and is essentially political. As Comrade Lenin puts it, they may be either flexible or wise; sometimes wiser than flexible; and too often not wise and too flexible. The wisdom of political parties very often has a rubbery backbone. Owing to lack of time, I shall give only a short sketch of the tactics and functions of the revolutionary syndicalists.

Comrades, the International we are now creating should be the expression of the working class, organised in unions. It must likewise reflect the true spirit of revolutionary syndicalism.

You will concede the point, comrades, that nowhere could the history of syndicalism be as richly instructive as in Western Europe and also in America. And if we desire to construct the trade-union International, the predominant position must be assigned to the old union organisations of Western Europe and America that forged fighting organisations, trained them theoretically and practically in the experience of daily struggle against employers who are acutely conscious of their class interests, against the organised power of the state and its support.

I believe we all agree, comrades, that this International council is to be the spokesperson, the guiding power, and the driving force of the international working class. But if we desire it to be such not in words but in deeds, we must endow it with the necessary authority, and not handicap it from its very inception by ambiguities that would render it powerless and unpopular, would impede it in its action, and transform it into a bureaucratic machine. In order to avoid this, an active and real force must give it a robust constitution, allow it to fulfil its task, to have its own policy so that the Red International of Trade Unions may grow, develop, and gain the confidence of the workers all over the world.

What must we do in order to obtain this? I already stated it, comrades – a robust constitution. To obtain this, the elements that compose it should refuse to define themselves as belonging primarily to this or that party or school, but should first of all proclaim the principle of revolutionary syndicalism. In order to fulfil the tasks of syndicalism, in order to set its tactics, one should be a revolutionary syndicalist.

What is a political party? A group of people who have come to an agreement on a certain theory on the construction of society, and on an ideal to be pursued. Outside this theory and this ideal uniting them, the party is a heterogeneous body; it's composed of individuals belonging to different classes of society, with different positions of life. All too often these differences create a rivalry among individuals, a divergent conception of the movement and tactics to be employed. It follows that, as the Germans say, *Der Hund ist begraben.*[18] The Third International, with its new organisation, and which because of the revolution itself, is revolutionary, wishes, as the saying goes, to stir the dead – or more precisely, to stimulate life in the affiliated parties. It issues decrees and dictates conditions, which each party accepts.

But when it comes to fulfilling these clauses, we begin partially to not understand one another. The discussions within the party grow venomous, and the disputes degenerate, owing to the fact that the parties lack the solid basis of life; or more precisely, they lack the living basis of the class struggle. They split into two, three, or more fragments, and the whole party organisation falls to the bottom, as happened in Germany, Italy, and Britain, and will inevitably occur in other countries. A political party depends on the fluctuation of general national and international politics of the bourgeois state, the more so when it is called to lead the country.

Such is not the case with trade-union movements – which are class organisations that group the wageworkers for their vital interests and in their struggle against the exploiting class. So long as it exists, the capitalist class will perpetuate the class struggle with all its accompaniments: violence, revolts, and as the struggle's final aim: revolution to organise the communist society. Since socialism, or communism, is a doctrine of the liberation of the working class from the yoke of capitalism, it is only natural that the workers, after their long and painful experiences, feel inclined in many countries to accept these doctrines, adapting them to their own specific field, the field of syndicalism. To whom, then, would this task be incumbent if not to producers organised in unions in the true field of the class struggle? This is why we entertain the hope that the Red International of Trade Unions will go down in history as absorbing within itself all human elements on a national and international scale, and that it will propagate the social revolution.

Starting from this argument, comrades, we may state that now, more than ever, we are entering a stage when syndicalism itself is bound to suffice. We

18 'Here lies the buried dog.' This colloquial saying is roughly equivalent to 'This is the heart of the matter.'

shall have to develop the spirit of the Amiens Charter, which answered the requirements in 1906, and now in 1921 responds to the same needs. But it is also necessary to develop and enlarge its basic economic and political spirit, in accordance with the conceptions of revolutionary syndicalism, which takes its place in battle for the abolition of capitalism and the organisation of a new society that will reflect its basic spirit.

Yes, comrades, we must loudly proclaim the truth that our experience has verified: that as long as syndicalism exists and is coveted by political parties that seek to make use of it and subordinate it, syndicalism must violently resist such attempts, as we do right now, and guard its character, its autonomy, and its independence.

Are these union organisations so young that they require guardians? Are they not old and experienced organisations with their past of martyrs (Villeneuve–Saint Georges, Chicago, etc.)?[19] And haven't they, in the course of the long history of their struggles, acquired a clear conception of the political and economic role they must play in their central organ – the Red International of Trade Unions, the emanation of and true expression of the revolutionary spirit of the workers? No, comrades, we need no other organisation whatever except our own, except the Red International of Trade Unions, as a moral leader.

We state that we would gladly join any Communist organisation that acts in a revolutionary way, and all those groups that in their revolutionary actions on a national and international scale are standing for the class struggle. Let us, as brothers in arms, advance in closest ranks with the watchword, 'Conquer the common enemy: capitalism and the state', and establish the dictatorship of the proletariat, carried out by union organisations from top to bottom. Our watchword should be: Those who want to eat must work; those who work must lead. And all should be subordinated to one platform freely agreed to and maturely

19 The martyrs of Villeneuve-Saint-Georges were victims of attacks by gendarmes against striking quarry workers in June–July 1908, in which nine were killed and sixty-nine were wounded.

The Haymarket martyrs in Chicago were victims of a judicial frame-up coming out of the 4 May 1886 rally of striking workers in Haymarket Square. At the conclusion of that rally, a bomb was thrown at police officers by an unknown person, after which the police opened fire on the crowd, killing a number of workers. The incident was used to stage a frame-up against the workers' leaders, who were anarchists. Eight were tried and convicted of murder. Four were hanged and one committed suicide before his scheduled execution. The Haymarket martyrs were defended and honoured by the workers' movement throughout the world, and they became associated with the establishment of May Day as an international workers' holiday.

deliberated. Such is our position, our policy, our task. In stating this, I believe I am interpreting both the West and America with their old union organisations. And I believe that in this short review I have not neglected their revolutionary syndicalism.

To conclude, comrades, I shall read the resolution adopted by the Seine Federation of Unions [Union des syndicats de la Seine],[20] which accurately reflects the spirit of French revolutionary syndicalism.

> The Seine Federation of Unions, which reflects revolutionary syndicalism and acts in accordance with its principles, recalls that the immutable aim of the General Confederation of Labour always tended toward the creation of a trade-union International based on revolutionary principles.
>
> During 1900, the year of the World Exposition,[21] the Confederation invited the central trade-union federations of all European countries to an international congress with the purpose of creating a trade-union International. But these central organisations, being under the influence of social-democratic parties, did not respond to the appeal.
>
> During the following year, 1901, the Legien craft organisations of Germany convened the federations of Northern and Central Europe to a conference to be held in Copenhagen. The secretaries of various general confederations of labour met there in order to come to an agreement and organise a purely defensive trade-union platform, whose framework was set on a narrow basis.[22]
>
> In 1902 ten labour secretaries met again in Stuttgart and were joined there by the representative of France, who had not been invited to the Copenhagen Conference.[23] At this conference the French motion was rejected, according to which international connections had to be established between trade-union organisations with the purpose of developing revolutionary union actions. At this congress a contradiction arose on the question of organisation between the syndicalists and the reformists. These differences were an expression, on the one hand, of an immature movement of the working class politically subordinate to the Social Democrats and suffering under the limits of bourgeois legality and, on the

20 The Seine was a department of France that included its capital city (Paris) and its suburbs.

21 The Paris World Exposition of 1900 was held from April to November 1900.

22 The Copenhagen Conference of 21 August 1901 founded what eventually became the International Federation of Trade Unions (IFTU).

23 The Stuttgart international trade-union conference was held 17–18 June 1902.

other hand, revolutionary syndicalism, animated by a spirit of autonomy and independence, ready to rebel against the fetters of parliamentarism and the established capitalist system.

This discrepancy between the two tendencies within unionism, so different in their nature, did not weaken or abate during the war.

Since the trade-union International that sprang from the brain of Legien could realise its unity only within the bounds of legal unionism and backed by an apparent revolutionary phraseology – although hollow in its essentials – all the actions of this International are of a negative character. The homogeneity of its composition finds its expression in the International Labour Bureau holding its sessions in Geneva, created by the Versailles congress of governments.

Saluting, with great joy, the creation of a trade-union International whose revolutionary action draws its power from the realisation and extension of Soviet Russia;

The [Seine] Federation proclaims the evident truth that despite the different conditions that are determined by environment and circumstances, sovietism and revolutionary syndicalism come from the same ideological source and aspire to the same aims: the power and hegemony of the producers and the absorption of all human elements into social production.

This identity of aims signifies that the Russian Soviet revolution is the sister of Western revolutionary syndicalism, that in Russia the revolution has entered into the stage of full realisation. At the same time, in the West, the working-class movement is developing under tremendous difficulties, and is directly influenced by the Russian revolutionary events.

Arising out of these considerations, the Revolutionary Syndicalist Committees express the ardent wish that the international congress of trade unions to be held in Moscow should create an International of producers, which would be the reflection of the ascending economic might of labour.

We desire that this International, whose task is to unite the workers of the world, should extend across borders, eliminating all separate national existence on the basis of the class struggle, proclaiming the inevitability and necessity of the hegemony of the producers. It should declare that the first obligation of the producers is to constantly work in the economic field, the foundation of society. The International should strive to accelerate revolutionary activity, as it has been defined by the workers' movement of all countries, and that it should above all present the truth that the producer in the factories and fields embodies all the conditions for the emancipation of humanity. The Moscow congress should draw its attention to the fact that, particularly in France, the revolution – whatever its nature may be – will be realised following the guidance of revolutionary syndicalism, and by means of its organs: the General Confederation of Labour, the trade-union federations, and local trade unions.

The Federation of the Seine asserts that the new International, bearing in mind the watchword of 'the emancipation of the workers must be achieved by the workers themselves', will be the mother of the social revolution.

The Seine Federation of Unions states, in addition, that the French revolutionary syndicalists are closely linked with the organisation of which they are an inalienable part. They will participate in the collective life of French syndicalism, as they feel assured that they will succeed in introducing the above organisation into the new trade-union International.

The federation commits itself to ardently work for the realisation of the above aims, and expresses its assurance that economic events will accelerate the decay of the capitalist state and the development of the revolutionary power latent in the mass of the producers.

The federation brings forward the following problems for solution: to wrest the proletariat of France from the Amsterdam International, so that it might join the Moscow International and participate in preparatory revolutionary work now in full swing.

In conclusion, the federation addresses all the organisations that are to take part in the Moscow congress with an appeal to take into consideration the above-stated opinions. By following them, they will reinforce the Western proletariat's power of action.

Heuchel: But he speaks about the International, and not about tactics.

Lozovsky: The speech is his 'revenge' for yesterday.

(*The session is adjourned until 7:00 p.m.*)

SESSION 13. 14 JULY 1921, EVENING

Debate on Tactics (continued)

(*The session opens at 7:00 p.m. Comrade Lozovsky in the chair.*)

Lozovsky: Comrade Boisson has the floor.

Louis Boisson (France, CTM): Comrades, the French labour movement, from the time of the ending of the accursed war, has assumed an entirely different character. We will have to go into the history of our unions so as to have an opportunity to clarify the debate over the situation that faces our pro-split organisation in France.

After war hostilities ended, a revolutionary movement began in France, and the working class joined the trade-union organisations in great numbers. So that you may picture for yourselves what took place at that time, we'll have to return to the month of March 1919. At that time, there were successive general strikes in the provinces.[1] That movement coincided with the Black Sea mutiny within the French squadron; the sailors did not want to participate in an anti-constitutional war against our Russian comrades.[2] At the same time, dissatisfaction arose in France around demobilisation, including mutinies throughout the country. We wanted to take advantage of the general strike movement that broke out in the south, with the goal of unleashing a general revolutionary movement that could give aid to our Russian comrades. But that movement was channelled into a court of arbitration that was cunningly conceived with diplomatic covering, owing to the events that had taken place.

1 The spring of 1919 saw the beginning of a massive strike wave throughout France. In 1918 a total of 499 strikes took place involving 176,187 workers. In 1919 that figure ballooned to 2,206 strikes involving 1,160,718 workers.

2 A reference to the April 1919 mutiny among French sailors in the Black Sea, who were part of a French military intervention to oppose the Bolsheviks and support White forces in the Russian Civil War. The events started on the battleship *France*, as sailors refused to work as a sign of protest. After some of the protestors were arrested, the majority of the ship's crew of 1,200 men, raising the red flag and singing the 'Internationale', took over the ship. Among their demands were an end to the war against Soviet Russia and improvement of conditions for sailors. Similar mutinies took place on other ships. The French general staff concluded from these events that the French forces were unreliable and withdrew its fleet. Two of the leaders of the mutiny – André Marty and Louis Bedina, who became members of the Communist Party – were later prosecuted and jailed for these events, along with a hundred other sailors.

 | DOI:10.1163/9789004712867_017

After the end of that movement, we continued to work in the trade-union confederation. We also participated in the preparations for an international movement that was to have taken place on 21 July 1919, together with our Italian and British comrades. We suffered a great let-down on 19 July, when we received a telegram asking us to postpone the general strike. Immediately a meeting of representatives of the workers' organisations was called, including the pro-split comrades, who put forward demands for the resignation of the leaders of the CGT.[3]

We thus come to the time of the Lyon Congress of the CGT, which was held in September 1919. At that meeting, members of the bureau of the confederation again displayed their treason. How did things go at the 1919 congress? It only touched on the question of the July strikes; but we were able to account for the betrayal only when the examining magistrate, Mr. Jousselin, began the case to dissolve the CGT.[4] This is why all the debates at Lyon were concentrated around the June and July strikes. Once again we had harsh arguments with the people who are leading the CGT. These people are functionaries who do not know the poverty and need of the working class. They themselves have never experienced such poverty and need. During the war they collaborated with the capitalist government. They are unable to work for the liberation of the proletariat because they are tied to the bourgeois government.

A completely revolutionary resolution was passed at the Lyon Congress by a great majority. And what did the leaders of the CGT do? A few months after the passing of that resolution they left for America on their way to the Washington Conference, and worked to start up the Amsterdam trade-union International and work out a 'Charter of Labour', with the aid of the governments and of representatives of business interests.[5]

Let us now pass to the new period, that of March 1920. The railroad workers, out of solidarity with the militant trade-union workers who were being persecuted in Paris, announced a general strike on the entire railway system. The leaders of the CGT did not want to grab the bull by the horns and take down the main enemy – the government. What happened then? The railway workers singlehandedly were able to gain a victory. How did that victory come about?

---

3 For the scheduled general strike of 21 July 1919, see pp. 168–9, n. 10

4 Following the strikes by French railworkers in 1920, investigating magistrate Louis Jousselin brought a court case against the CGT, claiming the strikes were 'political' (an 1894 law restricted strikes to economic questions only). On 13 January 1921 the court ordered the CGT's dissolution, although the order was never carried through. The dissolution order was finally withdrawn only in 1924.

5 For the Washington Conference, see p. 62, n. 4.

They took the railway companies by surprise. That victory put to shame the leaders of the CGT, and a decision was arrived at in favour of a general strike in May 1920. All the comrades know very well what that strike was like. It wound up as a most shameful defeat. The leaders of the General Confederation of Labour did not perform their duty at the time of the general movement.[6]

Every time we are confronted with such a situation in our country, our trade-union organisations, built as they still are on craft lines, lead to the majority of votes always being cast for the treacherous leaders at the congresses of the federations or the CGT. They have been able to gain Pyrrhic victories; they were able to create artificial majorities in their favour, and our *minoritaire* comrades in the end have to continually pay for it. And now after all their betrayals, we declared ourselves opponents of the CGT and decided to part company and split from the federations and the central labour organisations.

When we began building our own organisations we tried to avoid imitating the structure that the unions have stuck to in the past. On the contrary, we tried to create something that would be in accordance with the times, remembering the experience and object lesson of such organisations as the Shop Stewards, the factory councils, and industrial unions. By this we meant to reflect the spirit of revolt that existed in the CGT at the time of the historic struggles of 1906–14.

I must call your attention to the fact that owing to the Lapierre plan, the CGT choked off the spirit of revolt prevailing in the local decentralised organisations.[7] Before the war, the CGT was composed on one side of purely trade-union federations, and on the other side of sections of labour exchanges. On one side there was an ideological movement; on the other there was the movement for centralisation, which was to give considerable power to all these movements.[8]

At the present time the CGT has been reorganised in a centralised body. Bureaucracy is rampant. Every time we organise for action, the responsible leaders escape the workers' judgement. That is the reason why we wanted to change the structure of our organisation. On this point we disagree with our comrades of the CSR. We did not want to remain in the CGT, since by remaining side by side with those who are selling out the working class we would be compelled to

6 For the May 1920 French railroad strike, see p. 169, n. 10.

7 Jules Lapierre was an assistant secretary of the CGT, in charge of overseeing regional and industrial federations. At its 1919 congress, the CGT reorganised to give its national centre, dominated by reformists, more power over the regional and industrial federations, which were often led by revolutionary syndicalists and which up to that point had been relatively autonomous.

8 For the CGT's dual structure, see p. 255, n. 10.

take responsibility for their action. When we pay our dues, we enrich the treasury for reformist propaganda among the working class, and at the same time fatten the Amsterdam International's treasury for propaganda. That is why we have chosen to place ourselves in a categorical position of split.

From all the discussions that have taken place at this congress, it appears that most comrades think that those who split have acted wrongly. We do not think so. The fact that we have left the central confederation on account of the treacherous activities of the old leaders who had captured it poses a paradoxical question. We have sought to create revolutionary organisations with the help of the masses themselves, in opposition to the reformists' organisations. We are among those who declare that if revolutionary unity is dear to us, we nevertheless believe that unity with reformists is impossible. We cannot unite with those who sell us out, and who stab us in the back during an action.

Comrades, I want to say a few more words. When I was on my way to the dining room this morning, my eyes fell upon a paper called *L'Atelier*, the collaborators of which are active leaders of the CGT. I emphatically protest against all the dirt filling the pages of that paper against our Russian comrades, because I consider that our Russian comrades have fallen into the situation they are living through at the present moment due to the cowardice of the members of the CGT. Every time there was a proposal to build a solidarity movement with the Russian Revolution, these people – whether through weakness or cowardice, or perhaps because they are traitors – cheated the Russian Revolution. And that gives me an occasion to rise against all this ignominy, against all this slander. I think it necessary to make this protest right from this platform.

But on the other hand, I also find it necessary to make clear the following: In all the cases where for some reason we cannot reach a common decision at this congress and have to listen to insults, we are often called counterrevolutionaries, as happened in the discussion on tactics when we were not in agreement. Comrades, we are among those people who did not try to save themselves, who took part at all times in the revolutionary movement, and who have fulfilled all their duties. We therefore believe that when we philosophically disagree, owing to our syndicalist views, we have a full right to demand from this gathering that a fair hearing be given to all the different tendencies. We come here above all as revolutionists who are fighting for the revolution.

Lozovsky: Comrade Gliński has the floor.

Gliński [Stefan Królikowski] (Poland): Comrades, our congress has reached one of the most important questions, that of tactics. In the first place, I wish to say that as far as we can judge, all the speeches and advice given to us here by the syndicalist comrades are meant to convince us that the tactics in the trade-union movement that we have adhered to thus far are wrong, harmful, and even counterrevolutionary. When our comrades of the Communist International drew up tactics for the trade unions, they put into one resolution and one set of theses the entire practice and experience gained by one section of the revolutionary proletarian movement in Russia, Poland, and other countries. What the Communist International laid out last year for the trade-union movement was only a synthesis of the methods practised up to that period by the different parties in the trade-union movement.[9]

When we come to the theoretical part of this question, we find ourselves in the throes of the social revolution, i.e., a revolution of the proletariat. The mass trade unions are proletarian organisations, and consequently we are convinced that if the social revolution is a proletarian revolution and the trade unions are proletarian unions, then sooner or later these unions will come over to our side, as we win the working class for the revolution.

A year has passed, a year of practice, a year of experience on almost a universal scale, and what result did we get – good or bad? The best example of the results of these tactics is the position that was taken by Amsterdam and our enemies, against whom we are waging a fight in the area of the trade-union movement. They appreciated the results of our work better than our comrades of the German Communist Workers' Party [KAPD] did. The Amsterdam leaders considered our work as very dangerous and harmful, and understood that if this work continues in the same manner, it will mean the absolute and inevitable downfall of Amsterdam. And in order to avoid this danger, they came to the conclusion that they must save themselves and, with all their strength and might, oppose our efforts, whether by means of the police, or by way of organisations and ideological methods in order to throw us out of the trade unions.

It seems that the comrades of the Communist Workers' Party have come to the same conclusion. The representatives of the counterrevolution came to the conclusion that all Communists must be thrown out of the trade unions. And here comrades, supposed revolutionists, say the same thing: 'Out of the trade unions!'. There is a danger for the revolution here. When the comrades of the Communist Workers' Party take the floor here, they must explain to us how it happened that they are in agreement with our enemies, the counterrevolutionaries from Amsterdam, on the essential question. If the comrades do not believe us, they must come up here and say that during the last year, owing to our tactics, such-and-such unions betrayed us, that we have lost our influ-

9 For the Second Congress trade-union theses, see p. 417, n. 3.

ence on the masses, that the influence of Amsterdam has increased, and give us concrete proof of this. They say: We cannot fight against the trade-union bureaucracy because it is powerful. We agree with this; it really is powerful, but we know that the working masses who are united in trade unions are a hundred times more powerful. Therefore, to speak of the might of bureaucracy and to have no faith in the power of the organised workers is not the correct position to take.

We speak seriously to these comrades not for the sake of convincing them, but because they have 300,000 organised workers behind them to whom we must say, 'Comrades, those who appeal to you on behalf of the revolution to abandon the trade unions and create small, tiny unions work for the good of Amsterdam and for the good of the counterrevolution.'

Now I wish to touch on another question. We are living in an era when the capitalists have come to the conclusion that in order to somehow adjust the economic situation of the capitalist world, in order to re-establish the decaying industrial situation, two things are necessary: first, the workers must be forced to work more diligently, and their labour must be more productive and beneficial to the capitalists. The second problem is to put the entire devastation and ruin that was wrought by the war upon the shoulders of the working class. For this they deprive the workers of the right to strike, they wish to install overtime work, they are making an effort to tax the workers wherever possible – not only indirectly, upon necessities of life, but to also tax the workers' income. We see thus that the working class, while conducting an economic struggle, is also drawn into the political struggle between two classes, because the government backs the employers.

Owing to the fact that the working class is in such a situation, we must come to a clear understanding as to what our tactics should be in the struggle against the employers. Life has given us the answer: first, not trade unions, but industrial unions; secondly, not a strike in one or another concern, but a strike of all the workers, because the fight that the textile workers are waging today has a decisive importance to the railway workers and to the metalworkers.

We had such an example in Britain during the strike of the coal miners. They carried on a fight for over three months while the other workers took no part in it. And not only were the coal miners defeated, but so too were all those who calmly looked on at this fight, thinking it was no concern of theirs. I wish to state that in the struggle that is becoming imminent between the workers and the capitalists, the tactics of the trade unions must be such as would not allow the capitalists to break the workers up into small sections, so that they know that if they commence a fight against one part of the working class, the entire working class will rise up and defend its interests.

The Polish delegation approves and supports the proposed theses on the question of tactics, because it finds that these theses are in accord with the tactics set by the Communist International and the tactics practised in Poland for some time already.

Lozovsky: Comrade Haywood has the floor.

William D. Haywood (USA): Comrades: I am not speaking here as a representative of the Industrial Workers of the World. I came credentialed by the American Labor Bureau.[10] Before leaving the United States I carefully went over the ground with the American Labor Bureau, giving my opinion as to the methods that should be pursued in the United States to build up a revolutionary working-class organisation.

I have been very much surprised in this convention to see the manner in which various delegates have referred to the only revolutionary organisation in the United States of America, namely the IWW. Comrade Flynn remarked that the IWW was pure Marxist, an ideal organisation, a perfect industrial union. On the other hand, Comrade Lozovsky refers to the IWW as purely anarchistic, antiparty in its point of view. Comrade Borden [Foster] comes as an expert on labour unions; he is the 'medicine man' who is pointing out a new method to be adopted in Russia. Hence in the A.F. of L. – and the A.F. of L. is something that I want to describe to you, because in the way of labour organisations there is nothing equal to it or similar to it in any other country on the face of the globe.

The American Federation of Labor is a loosely affiliated organisation of from 110 to 120 international unions. It is officered by Samuel Gompers, who has been the president for thirty-nine years, elected now for the fortieth time, or the thirty-ninth time, because he was defeated once. This organisation has its headquarters in the city of Washington, where Sam and his henchmen, his satellites – the seven vice-presidents and the officials of the industrial unions – have access to the ear of capitalist politicians. Never in the history of the American Federation of Labor has that organisation done one single thing for the working class. I do not mean by this to include the unions that are affiliated with it. Officered by a president who gets twelve thousand dollars a year for chiefly, now, signing documents harmful to Soviet Russia, these documents are not written by Samuel Gompers himself, but by renegade socialists like William English Walling and Chester Wright and others of that particular stripe.

10 A reference to the American bureau of the International Council of Trade and Industrial Unions formed in January 1921.

These 110 or more international unions have no consolidation, no agreement with each other; they comprise 346 craft unions. The craft unions have an autonomous right; that is, they can enter into agreements with their employers. Sometimes these agreements extend from the craft to the international, but these agreements are never made with a sense of working-class interest, never made with a revolutionary perspective. The international, the craft, if you will, have no other conception, no other idea, than that of improving their own immediate condition. They build up walls around themselves that prohibit the possibility of organising the working class of America.

The American Federation of Labor in conference now, or last month, claimed a membership of 3.8 million. Compare this, if you will, with England or Germany, with one-half the population yet two or three times the membership in organised labour in each of those countries. So far did these internationals go in this idea of protecting their own interests that they closed their books against further membership. This is true of the bookbinders. It is true of the painters and decorators. It is true of the carpenters. With the aim of closing the books, they have other methods.

Some will put up their initiations. I inquired of the British delegates what was the largest initiation fee in their country, and was advised that it was £5 ($25). He stated that this was outrageous, and they are making efforts in Britain to have this exorbitant initiation fee reduced. Imagine, if you will, that a $25 initiation in the United States is extremely low. Most of the organisations charge 75, 50, 200, 300, and as high as 500 dollars. The photo engravers, $500. The electrical workers no. 134 of Chicago, $250; the moving picture operators everywhere, $300. This is not a labour organisation; it is a job-trust organisation for the protection of those who are well enough to keep outside of the fees.

That is not all. They have another scheme in effect in almost all the building trades of nearly all the large centres. They won't allow the men to join the unions, but they will issue them a permit to work, and for this permit he pays $1 to $1.50 a day for the privilege of working. This by the unions, understand, and this money goes to the business agents and probably finally to the officials of the union. They want to make a union man out of the man who holds the permit, but they simply use it as a craft perhaps. But this is not all.

There are unions that refuse to admit a woman, not because she is not just as good a worker – and there are women in all phases of industry in the United States. The Barbers International refuses admission to a woman because she is a woman. And there are other unions that close their doors to black men, to Japanese, to Chinamen, to the Hindus. Why, because of their colour? Yes, because of their colour, not because they are not as good workers as the Irish and Scottish and whatever nationalities go to make up unions. This is the American Federation of Labor. This is the labour movement in the United States.

I believe there are members of the IWW in that union notwithstanding what Borden [Foster], the medicine man, may have said to the contrary. There are members of the IWW in the A.F. of L. and they are there, first, for the purpose of getting their bread and butter, they have to have a membership. They are there for the express purpose of carrying out their revolutionary agitation and education in the ranks of the A.F. of L.

I want you to understand that the IWW is the only labour organisation of the United States that was invited to the Communist International congress, and in that congress there was a man who spoke about my having taken the platform to advertise the IWW.[11] The IWW does not need advertising in the Communist International. I was there by invitation, and who was this man who harangued me on the platform?

Allow me to read you the following clipping from one of the American papers:

> And so the IWW travelled everywhere, and everywhere the IWW came to be considered as the storm bird of the revolution. When the Russian revolution came, the IWW came to Russia. Not the idea, but men, lots of them. Those who had come to America had some time or other been members of the IWW, and went back to Russia with the fall of Kerensky. They came by the hundreds and by the thousands. It might be said that when the tide was changing there and a small number of men counted finally, that if it had not been for the IWW the Russian Revolution might have been lost.

That might meet with disbelief. That is because people who disbelieve it have never seen the revolution. When you have seen something like we have, you will know that revolutions are both made and stopped by minorities. So the IWW has a name in Russia. Those IWWs who went back to Russia began everywhere to push organisation. In Kharkov they adopted the preamble intact.[12] Everywhere they organised unions, and these unions organised by the IWW became the backbone of the soviets. But there came a time in the Russian Revolution

---

11 Haywood is evidently referring to the speech at the Third Comintern Congress by Marshall (Max Bedacht). See Riddell (ed.) 2015, *3WC*, pp. 726–9.

12 In *Ten Days that Shook the World*, John Reed writes: 'In Kharkov thirty thousand coal miners organised, adopting the preamble of the I.W.W. constitution: "The working class and the employing class have nothing in common".'

when these IWWs were put to the test – just as all things are put to the test – just as the soviet which they formed was itself put to the test. Some took the anarcho-syndicalist position and some went with the Communists, but all have come clean, though I am of the opinion that those who went with the Communists and took part in the dictatorship took I think the most scientific stand. It was an American IWW who was sent to sign a certain treaty, and an IWW in command of Russia's greatest city when Yudenich mustered his forces at the gates of Petrograd;[13] when the officers of the army of defenders were in a conspiracy to deliver up the capital to the counterrevolutionists, it was an IWW who discovered the plot and lined the generals against the wall. There are many of these people. But an American delegate will remember that speech.

Now, in America, in the United States there has been a programme adopted and the Communists have stated this, that they are comrades in the battle with the IWW.[14] Do not forget that. That is the position of the Communists in America. That is the position of the industrial unionists. And we are after those craft unions. We are going to make Communists out of them. We are going to send them home, better men, than they came to Russia.

Just one word about the steel strike. Aside from the fact that it mentions the Americanisation of the workers to prove it, they printed their membership cards in red, white, and blue.[15]

Lozovsky: The floor is given to Comrade Malzahn.

Heinrich Malzahn (Germany): During the discussion on the question of tactics, one should by no means base one's arguments on a morbidly exaggerated organisational egotism. If we, as Communists, are striving to develop the revolutionary class struggle and to crush the whole capitalist system by that struggle, we should by no means deceive ourselves as to the extent of the exist-

---

13 Haywood is referring to Bill Shatov, a former IWW member who returned to Russia after the February 1917 Revolution. Shatov became a leading Red Army officer in the Tenth Army, playing an important role in the defence of Petrograd in 1919.

14 The programme adopted at the 1921 Joint Unity Convention of the Communist Party of America and published in *The Communist* of July 1921 stated, 'The Communist Party regards the workers in the ranks of the I.W.W. as comrades in the class war.'

15 A national strike began in the largely unorganised steel industry on 22 September 1919, eventually involving over 350,000 workers. The strike lasted into January 1920, finally collapsing on the eighth of that month. The central leader of the strike was William Z. Foster.
The mention of red, white, and blue membership cards would appear to be a reference to Foster's social-patriotic stance during World War I, when he gave support to the US war effort and publicly promoted the sale and purchase of war bonds.

ing power of resistance. On the contrary. The first condition of reaching one's aim is to take into account the actual condition of things. All those comrades who, at the Comintern congress, heard the report of Comrade Trotsky on the world economic situation and the report of Comrade Radek on tactics,[16] and who regard themselves as revolutionists to any extent whatever – such comrades must admit that as Communists we must consider the revolutionary struggle of the workers' organisations to be of utmost importance, and we must appreciate such struggle independently of the particular person who is playing the leading part in this or that organisation.

What do we see in reality? On the one hand, we see the fortresses of the capitalists, who are defended by the powerful machinery of the contemporary state and by the white guard army. On the other hand, we see 10 million workers organised in trade unions. The whole machinery, the material means, the whole press of these organisations are wholly in the hands of the Amsterdam followers. And these Amsterdam followers have sold their body and soul to the class of the exploiters by the fact of their accepting a business collaboration with them.

I ask you: What is more rational: to break with the masses and try to build new organisations, or to remain in the midst of these masses, to raise the level of their class consciousness, to make them realise the inevitable necessity of the class struggle, and to deliver them from the influence of Amsterdam? I ask further: What is more difficult, what requires more boldness and greater efforts: to hold a discussion among an intimate circle of followers on Amsterdam's betrayal and to pronounce revolutionary speeches in a closed circle – or to engage in an open fight against the trade-union bureaucracy and to chase the enemy from his own camp?

And if you say that by remaining within the old trade unions we continue to stand under the banner of Amsterdam, we will say in reply to this that it is you who entrenched yourselves in your insignificant independent organisation, that the bureaucracy of the trade-union movement is not at all afraid of you and does not take you into account. This bureaucracy is afraid only of that internal enemy that is represented by the Communists remaining in the old trade unions, and that gains a strong foothold day by day. We shall not be mistaken if we say that our workers within the old trade unions have dealt quite a number of telling blows to Amsterdam. It is proved by the fact that a few hundred of our comrades who occupy responsible positions were driven out of the

16 Trotsky's report to the Third Comintern Congress on the world economic crisis can be found in Riddell (ed.) 2015, *3WC*, pp. 102–33. Radek's report on tactics and strategy can be found in Riddell (ed.) 2015, *3WC*, pp. 406–45.

old trade-union organisations. As a result of this, it proved detrimental not to us, but to Amsterdam itself. (*Voice: 'That's true.'*) As to the expelled comrades, they remained as before ideological leaders of the Communist nuclei within the trade unions.

During the half year since December 1920, when the conference of the United Communist Party in Germany took place,[17] the opposition crystallised more and more, although prior to and during the war we of course already led an opposition within the trade-union movement. Did we not succeed once before in overthrowing the bureaucracy in a considerable part of the trade-union organisations adhering to the Social-Democratic Party of Germany, replacing it with the more revolutionary elements from the ranks of the Independent Socialists [USPD]? This, as you know, has taken place in the big central federations of the woodworkers, metalworkers, textile workers, railway workers, and so on. Something similar must be repeated on a wider scale. At present our opposition enjoys a certain moral support of the Red International of Trade Unions and of the Communist International.

Over the course of half a year we have been building up our network of nuclei throughout Germany, systematically and in accordance with a worked-out plan. We created secretariats according to trades and branches of unions on a general and national scale. Thus we have spread our nuclei over the whole breadth of the country; they lead their daily revolutionary work within the bounds of a mass movement. During the half year gone by, a number of very significant elections have taken place in a whole series of trade unions, by which we can judge the productivity of our work. We succeeded, thanks to our attacks, in making known the true nature of the Independent Socialists of Germany, which, after all, did not much differ from the Social-Democratic Party of Germany and from Amsterdam. The Independents and the Social Democrats have been acting, all throughout, in perfect solidarity against the Communists. However, the latter succeeded in overcoming the resistance and winning over a number of important positions in the trade-union movement.

It was mentioned here that there are 2.2 million workers under our influence; these figures are not at all exaggerated, but rather are underestimated. (*A voice: 'Too modest!'*) As far as the future is concerned, we must say that the general situation in Germany, the class battles that are now taking place there, the general offensive of the employers against the working class, of which my friend Richard Müller has already spoken today – all this will facilitate our struggle,

---

17 The unification congress of the KPD and the USPD majority was held 5 December 1920. The congress created the United Communist Party of Germany (VKPD).

because the Amsterdam supporters gave themselves away entirely when they joined the government, when they declared the necessity of satisfying all the demands of the Entente at the cost of an increased exploitation of the workers. All this deprives them of the possibility of resisting the attacks of the capitalists. All the strikes of the last months – as for instance in Waldenburg, at the docks of Elbing, in Central Germany – were crushed by the trade-union bureaucracy. The Social Democrats and Independents did everything to make them fail. And in all these cases, the struggle developed as a result of the widespread unorganised will of the working masses. These strikes by the workers, this continuous betrayal on the part of the leaders of the trade unions, and side by side with it, our clear programme of action with which we shall now return home from the congress of the Red International of Trade Unions and of the Communist International – these will give us the possibility to infuse the trade-union movement with a revolutionary spirit in the shortest possible time.

Now, addressing myself to the comrades of the General Workers' Union and Gelsenkirchen Free Union, I must say that they will hardly be able to refute my statement as to their weakness and unpreparedness during the fighting that the workers were compelled to lead in the Ruhr District, in Hamburg, and in Berlin. It became clear that they had no means at their disposal for participation in this struggle. All of us were painful observers of the way the revolutionary miners tried in vain to protect themselves from the increased tax burden that fell on the shoulders of the workers, from the seven-shift working-week system,[18] which lasted many months, the way the old Miners' Union betrayed their cause. Various leaders showed themselves not as defenders of the interests of the working class, but as a kind of heavily weighted object that pulled the proletariat to the bottom.

If you, comrades of the Free Unions, will not reconsider your views, you are condemned to impotence. As far as we are concerned, we shall at any rate be guided by the instructions of this congress, and we shall then undoubtedly be the pioneers of the social revolution.

Lozovsky: Comrade Godonnèche has the floor.

Victor Godonnèche (France): Comrades, the theses of Comrade Lozovsky, on the whole, satisfy us. There are but a few points regarding which we want to give some explanations, as for instance on sabotage. We think that sabotage, although not a mass action, is at the same time a weapon that we should not

18 The seven-day shift system is one of rotating shifts to enable non-stop production.

repudiate formally as is done in the theses. I might point out one case, when a skilful application of sabotage rendered great services in attaining some successes. Sabotage does not necessarily mean 'destruction'. I might give as an example a printshop, where the material may be made unusable for a period of time, without spoiling it. The same with the postal and telegraph service, where, as we have seen in practice, the organised workers succeeded, under certain circumstances, in hindering the sending over the wires of mobilisation decrees during the strikes. That happened with the decree on the militarisation of railroad workers during strikes. And last but not least, the intentional reduction of production is also one of the forms of sabotage under certain circumstances, which we cannot formally condemn. And then there are cases when it is necessary to stop the transportation of troops into a strike situation, when it is necessary to sabotage the telegraph lines in order to isolate this or that district in which the strike of the workers is spreading.

These are all cases where sabotage has been practised, if not widely, at least skilfully. All this relates to the field of revolutionary tactics, and we might have cited many examples taken from our everyday practice to demonstrate that sabotage cannot be categorically excluded as a means of struggle, provided, of course, it is intelligently applied.

Arising out of these considerations we propose to reconsider point 53.

On the most interesting question in the discussion on tactics, Borden [Foster] has already refuted most of the points put forward by Bartels in favour of leaving the old organisations. When Bartels says that it is necessary to widen the basis of the trade-union organisation, to have deeper roots in the very places of production, I agree with him. This is the reason why we are carrying out propaganda in favour of creating factory committees. But to entirely destroy the old organisations, to create new ones, would be an error that the workers of all countries would have to pay too much for. This would alienate the workers from us for a number of years, and would thus retard the advance of the revolution.

The old system of trade-union organisation does not of course answer the requirements of the present time. But by fighting within the old trade unions, we remain in contact with the masses, and by directing all our efforts toward the widening of our base and our cadres, we give to these old trade unions the necessary organisational forms and organs that will deepen their roots with the masses. I have in view factory committees and shop stewards. This is the way we in France understand the regeneration of the old syndicalism.

As to our French adherents of splitting, the representative of the CTM pointed out in confirmation of the correctness of its tactics – during the discussion of the Credentials Commission report – the disaffection of the masses with the traitorous leaders, the membership drop in the unions that took place after the great strike of 1919. Out of two million, he said, there remained six- to seven hundred thousand members in the CGT. This is a serious argument, in his opinion, for leaving the old trade unions. The growth of the membership in the trade unions that was registered in the period after the war should have been used to build a revolutionary movement, and there is no doubt that energetic and resolute leaders would have availed themselves of the people's dissatisfaction in order to accomplish great things. But if the failure was directly connected with the betrayal of the leaders, then the membership reduction is in no way connected with it, because such a reduction is always noticed after any action. If his assertion was true that the masses left the trade unions because they understood the betrayal of their leaders, then they would have joined a different organisation, a more revolutionary one. But out of the 1.2 million members who, according to the representative of the CTM, left the Confederation – did many join this split-off organisation?

Boisson informed us that they have a total membership of 1,000. I do not want to laugh at him in connection with this information. But if this figure is correct, it stands as a formidable refutation of his theory of splitting.

In France, cunning leaders of the CGT made use of the CTM leaving the confederation by declaring war on the revolutionary minority, accusing the latter as a whole of provoking a split. At the same time, it was their desire that we follow the example of our French adherents in the idea of leaving the trade unions. The best proof of this is their decision to expel us, in order to get rid of us, a decision from which we can also see that they do not take into consideration the loss of dues that threatens them in case of our expulsion. Whereas Boisson and his friends attribute great importance to this question, it has no bearing on the topic. Our leaving the confederation would have afforded the greatest pleasure to the reformists after the Orléans Congress.[19] We, on our part, resolved to stick with all our might to the organisation that they intended to steal from us, and we can already mark some successes attained, which foretell greater ones.

The resolution on expulsion, passed several weeks ago by the Amsterdam Bureau, is proof that we are on the right path.[20] And we shall stick to it as long as we can. Let those who assert that they work in favour of the revolution and to gain victory together with us, let them bring about, together with us, the unity

19 A reference to the CGT congress held in Orléans, 27 September–2 October 1920.

20 In May 1921 the Amsterdam International's leadership body decided that any organisations affiliating with the Red Trade Union International would be automatically excluded from the International Federation of Trade Unions.

of all revolutionary forces – first of all in opposition to those who betrayed the spirit of the class struggle against capitalism, the last support of which is Amsterdam.

We call on the congress to condemn the methods that are preached here by Bartels and his adherents from other countries. The congress must speak in this sense if it does not want the Red International of Trade Unions, from its very birth, to return to the store selling all kinds of useless things – the Amsterdam International.

Boisson: Can you tell me whether you speak on your own behalf or on behalf of the delegation?

Godonnèche: I speak on behalf of a part of the delegation.

Lemoine: Not in my name!

Godonnèche: Allow me to read the amendments offered by us. In point 51 it would be necessary to delete from the end of the first sentence the words, 'which must be put on a much higher level than prior to the war'. Point 53 should be formulated as follows:

> In the struggle with the employers, sabotage can sometimes be used, such as partial damage of machines and means of production. Such methods of struggle should be used with care, not only for the reason that the proletariat is heir to the bourgeoisie and is thus interested in getting the property undamaged, but also because the destruction of machines does not help the cause. It may sometimes artificially hold back the renewal of work in the factory and make the scabs leave work, but it may also become a double-edged weapon in unpractised hands. The supreme criterion of any new method of struggle is the consideration of the consequences which this or that action may have for the workers – will it or will it not serve to enlighten and organise the masses?

Lozovsky: Comrade Murphy has the floor.

Jack Murphy (Britain): Comrades: I do not intend to dwell on the English situation, as I understand Comrade Watkins dealt very fully with that this morning. There is only one more thing that I want to add to his remarks, and that is, I hope, that those who have anything to say with regard to the English movement will take greater pains to become more fully acquainted with the data before arriving at any conclusions than is evident in these theses. Not that we object to criticism. Let us have criticism by all means, but let it be criticism that gives positive results to the movement. We know quite well that there are many weaknesses in the English movement. Chief among these are the lack of coordination of the revolutionary forces, and the lack of a strong leadership right through the crisis. These things we will readily admit. But do not let us have inaccurate reports.

Now, comrades, turning to the problems in general, I want to pass on the observation that the level of the discussions up to now has not proved very high. We seem to have much pride and prejudice with regard to our organisations; we have been so busy defending them one against the other that we have almost forgotten what we are attempting to do – and that is to examine the tactics for the trade-union movement of the whole world.

There have been two policies put forward. The policy known as boring from within, and the policy of building separate unions. You have heard many arguments with regard to these two policies, but we have not yet heard anyone point out that we may create of the policy of boring from within a new fetish, a mistake against which I want to warn all present at this congress. There is great danger of placing the idea of the preservation of organisations before that of prosecuting the revolutionary struggle. Once that becomes the dominant note in our work, once we are obsessed with the idea that we must at all costs preserve the organisation, then our policy of boring from within sinks completely into the old policy of the socialist parties, which are nonrevolutionary. Now let us beware of that policy.

What we are out for, what we must place before everything else, is the development of the revolutionary forces. That is our foremost task, and we say that it is far better to prosecute that policy within the organisations than to leave those organisations alone. Old organisations and new ones, whatever their form, are thrust into the struggle in spite of their backward political development, and we must strive for the leadership of the struggle. This cannot be done by remaining outside of the unions.

This is clearly evident when we have such large situations as the miners' strike in England, and such as the general strike in Germany at the time of the Kapp Putsch. I would particularly refer to the latter. I remember I was in Germany at that time, and I never before witnessed an incident so full of striking features as that. Every worker had stopped work. The strike was as tight as a drum. The government, after three or four days, called the strike off. There was no response. The trade-union leaders called the strike off, and there was no response. The fight continued until the central committee of the factory committees in Berlin determined on the conclusion of the strike. We cannot ignore those situations, for out of these situations will rise that leadership that can lead the workers to the victory we have in view.[21]

I will pass on from this argument to other matters in the theses, and to things that have been omitted. I see no reference, for example, throughout the theses, as to what tactics we are to pursue with regard to women in industry. Now, there are unions that do not admit women into their organisations, and there are unions trying to drive out from industry women who came in during the war. The employers are using the women as a type of cheap labour, while the men attack the women instead of the employers because of this. That policy should be combated and we should aim at fighting all policies introduced that tend in the direction of emphasising any economic domination of men over women. These methods should be very strenuously and definitely fought.

I see no reference in the theses to all the problems of America. Here let me say that I am somewhat surprised at our comrades of the American delegation for pursuing the methods of slamming each other. America presents the most complex problem. In America there are more organisations than the IWW or the A.F. of L. You have only at most 30 per cent of the workers of the United States organised. You have in addition to this all kinds of unorganised labour. All kinds of unskilled labour pouring into the country that presents a tremendous problem to solve. You have in addition the Negro problem in America, out of which we see at times the class struggle assuming the appearance of a racial struggle, from which the capitalist class is deriving the benefit. You have also the problems arising out of immigration. The capitalist class studies the situation, and sees the differences in the national psychology and the racial psychology, and uses them to set one section of the workers against another.

In addition to this, we have not only failed to look closely into the United States, but have ignored the workers in the Latin American countries. Here we have most of the working-class forces opposed to the A.F. of L. They are mostly anarcho-syndicalists tending definitely in our direction. The IWW is also there, somewhat obsessed with sectarian ideas, but viewing the situation as a whole – there are all those forces outside the A.F. of L., and no work is being done in this great field to bring these forces together. So we simply allow these organisations to drift, and talk as if there is only the American Federation of Labor and the IWW in the whole of the American continent. We have got to face all these problems, and see to it that we bring all these forces together and lead them towards the Red International.

21 On 13 March 1920, Wolfgang Kapp and Walther von Luttwitz led a military coup in Germany against the republican government headed by the SPD. While the SPD itself offered little resistance, officials of the SPD-led trade-union federation called a general strike that was observed by 12 million workers, virtually the entire proletariat. In the face of the general strike and developing armed workers' resistance, the coup collapsed by 17 March.

We have heard so much talk of Amsterdam that we have almost forgotten that the American unions do not touch upon Amsterdam at all. We have also forgotten the thirty-two secretariats that exist partly connected with Amsterdam and partly independent.[22] All of them are pursuing the policy of Amsterdam. Some of them are paper organisations, some are real organisations led by reactionary men. Take for example the transport federation. We all know the attitude they took in regard to the sympathy strike in England. We ought to definitely outline our policy with regard to these thirty-two international secretariats and pursue a policy that will break them or make them contribute to the building up of the Red International.

One point further. While we have heard in this congress some reflections about small unions, we have not recognised altogether the Eastern problems. We have almost forgotten that the East exists, and we find workers are being drawn towards organisation of one kind or another. Shall we get in contact with them? Shall we invite them here? How shall we approach them? Tactics should be outlined for pursuing our work in these different countries of the world. And we hope that in our further congresses, we will give more attention to these problems.

Hence, the main question is more than that of boring from within or building from without. It is that of mobilising the masses for revolutionary action. In pursuing this task we have got to examine the peculiar conditions in every country that we approach and apply our fundamental principles of revolutionary action, and rally the masses to Moscow, which challenges not only Amsterdam, but all other reactionary forces opposing the working class of the world as it marches to victory.

Lozovsky: Comrade Grölig has the floor on a point of order.

Grölig: Although I asked to speak long before Comrade Malzahn, I was not allowed to make any statement so far.

Lozovsky: Considering that the representatives of the German delegation have already spoken on the question of tactics, it is desirable to grant the floor to other members of this delegation only after the floor has been given to delegates of other countries.

22 Beginning in the 1890s, international trade secretariats were organised by branch of industry, eventually affiliating to the International Federation of Trade Unions. The relationship between the secretariats and the IFTU was never entirely formalised, however, although the trade secretariats did receive minority representation in the IFTU leadership.

A voice: These are the methods of a Turkish pasha!

Grölig: In this case, allow me to ask whether Comrades Müller and Malzahn are representatives of two different countries. I should very much like Comrade Lozovsky to be impartial to all the delegates, and not prefer those who share the views of the theses presented.

Lozovsky: The accusation made by Comrade Grölig is utterly absurd. Comrade Bartels, in the name of his group, has spoken an hour and has another thirty minutes for summarising, while the majority of the German delegation spoke only 15 minutes each. One's brains must be quite topsy-turvy to accuse me of partiality. I use such a strong expression because I was accused of running things like a Turkish Pasha. I suggest the congress say whether I acted correctly.

Comrade Nin has the floor.

Andreu Nin (Spain): While reserving the right to propose amendments to Comrade Lozovsky's theses, which in our opinion are indispensable, we still feel we must emphasise, from the platform of the congress, the extraordinary lack of comprehension of revolutionary syndicalism shown by the comrades and a number of speakers who have taken part in the debate. In fact, they present syndicalism as a doctrine that has failed, and even as a 'disease'.

Revolutionary syndicalism is a doctrine with sound foundations, with a very precise and determined aim. Marxist and Proudhonist at the same time, it takes from the fundamental principles of scientific socialism the class struggle, which considers the union as its most living expression, and adopts from Proudhon and from anarchism the spirit of criticism, federalism, and opposition to the state. Revolutionary syndicalism considers itself to be the most powerful instrument of the direct struggle against the bourgeoisie, and as the only force capable of building up on new foundations the communist society of tomorrow.

Revolutionary syndicalism, contrary to Comrade Lozovsky's theses, has not failed. You must not condemn a doctrine because of the defection of a few men. If you do, you must also proclaim the failure of socialism, because the immense majority of socialists have betrayed it shamefully. Just as the Bolsheviks in Russia saved the honour of socialism, so in France, Italy, Holland, Spain, and America there have been revolutionary syndicalists who, in spite of the disgraceful betrayal of socialism and syndicalism by some sections, have known how to make revolutionary doctrine stand upright. These revolutionary forces are a power of the first order today, an element that cannot be ignored in Western Europe and in America if the social revolution is to be something more than the revolution of a party.

It must be understood once and for all that revolutionary syndicalism in most of our countries is not a lifeless force, containing half-dead names, but a force with a real active personality. To try to stifle the movement – without which the revolution would be impossible – would be to serve the interests of the bourgeoisie.

As regards the tactics to be used against Amsterdam, we are quite of the opinion that these organisations must declare once and for all and quite definitely either for Moscow or for the yellow International.

We are told that we must be in contact with the masses. Agreed. But will you find the masses in the office of the unions, in meetings? No. It is in the workshop and in the factory that the revolutionary workers must accomplish this work of attracting them to Moscow.

This is what we have done in Spain, and with the best results. In 1914 we had about 60,000 members; at the beginning of 1920 we had a million. If we had tried to do propaganda work inside the General Union of Workers [UGT], an ultrareformist organisation, we would surely still be awaiting a congress to know whether we affiliate to Moscow or not. Further, absorbed by the struggle against the reformist leaders, we would not have been able to constitute our industrial unions, of which we are proud. Nor would we have instituted our shop stewards, with whom we carry on an obstinate struggle against the bourgeoisie, and whose value is recognised in the unprecedented ferocious repression of which we are the object. Is not the combat value of the small revolutionary organisations sometimes superior to that of the big organisations?

I will give you only two examples from our experience. In Barcelona, in 1902 we had only 8,000–10,000 organised workers; still we declared a revolutionary general strike, which lasted eight days, during which the proletariat fought heroically against the public forces. In Catalonia, the most industrialised region in Spain, we had some 8,000 organised textile workers in 1913. Nevertheless, more than 150,000 workers – men and women – rose up and waged a fight that lasted several weeks. This means that although our organisations were weak, the masses followed those who were the more audacious and determined in interpreting their aspirations.[23]

---

23 A strike of Barcelona metalworkers that began in December 1901 became a general strike on 17 February 1902, lasting until 24 February. Some 100,000 workers participated in the strike. The government declared a state of war, killing and wounding hundreds of workers.
The Barcelona textile strike of some 20,000 workers lasted from 30 June to 15 Septem-

The workers' mentality is simple; they don't understand subtleties. For them it would be incomprehensible to speak daily about the Jouhauxs, the Merrheims, and the Oudegeests being traitors, and at the same time to strengthen the funds of the yellow federation. Therefore, I think that contrary to what you fear, when the problem is placed quite clearly before them to decide either for Moscow or Amsterdam, the proletariat will march with the Red Industrial International of the revolution.

There is a fear that the split will separate the workers from the organisations, and that their combative power will be reduced. I think the important thing is that they don't separate themselves from the revolutionary spirit, a spirit that can be drowned in votes and resolutions. I can tell you that with us something much more important has happened to separate the workers from the organisations. They have closed the unions, they have declared a state of siege, they have imprisoned those who held a membership card in the National Confederation of Labour. In spite of this, the proletarian masses have followed the orders of the committees; they have declared general strikes. There has been the censorship of the bourgeois press, but they have not given up a single inch of ground; the proletariat has stuck to those who have a revolutionary spirit. Therefore, let us bear the revolutionary spirit and we will destroy the old organisations, and with them the Amsterdam International. Let us direct our efforts so that our Red Trade Union International shall not be an organisation that groups the 'cells' without cohesion, but a living International in which the various tendencies rival one another in their interest in and love of the social revolution.

In conclusion: I think that our discussion is fairly useless. Amsterdam has understood that it can no longer maintain the equivocation, and that it is ready to hunt out the friends of Moscow. So in spite of the opinion of some of the comrades, we must carry on the fight against Amsterdam not inside the old unions, but outside these unions.

Lozovsky: Comrade Rykov has the floor.

Alexei Rykov (Russia): Comrades, the congress vote on the Italian question has demonstrated unanimity on the question of tactics, and only declarations by isolated delegates were in contradiction with the general trend of the congress. If we consider our constituent congress at the current stage of its development,

ber 1913. The largely female work force demanded shorter hours and an increase in wages. Massive popular demonstrations of thousands of workers occurred during the strike.

after the debate on the question of relations with the Communist International, after the debate on tactics and on the Italian question – we shall not meet with such differences as to make us susceptible to a split among the organisations represented here, nor even to any serious differences at a period when the working class of the world is passing more and more resolutely to a direct revolutionary struggle.

Differences have arisen between the majority of the congress and the revolutionary syndicalists like the IWW. I don't mention the speeches of individual delegates, inasmuch as they are not characteristic of the trade-union movement in their country. The most serious differences with the trend of the congress arose between the majority and the revolutionary syndicalists of France. The last speech of Comrade Nin, was to a considerable degree, in solidarity with the views of Comrade Sirolle. I must state, to my regret, that in his speech Comrade Nin showed that the errors that the Russian trade unions committed in their illegal revolutionary struggle are not yet fully grasped.

We Russians have many times worked underground, but I cannot recall any period in the history of the development of our revolutionary movement when any of the participants or organisers of this movement made the proposal to organise exclusively in underground work. We never had the slightest doubt that it would be criminal from the point of view of organisation of the working class, of its trade-union and economic struggle, not to avail oneself of any legal possibility to support illegal work. In the course of many years, in the economic as well as political field, there were two main currents in the activity of the Russian working class: the legal and the illegal. This we carried out even in parliament. Many times the workers' deputies in our bourgeois parliaments were sent to hard labour and thrown into prisons for having availed themselves of the legal Russian tribune for the expression of the illegal revolutionary movement of the working class. Just the same, in the field of the trade-union movement, if there is no possibility to work legally, it is necessary to resort to illegal organisations. But these organisations should consider it their immediate task to utilise legal organisations in order to propagate their slogans, their platform, to avail themselves of these legal organisations for purposes of supporting illegal revolutionary movements.

As a reflection of Comrade Nin's fundamental point of view, we find his attitude toward leaving Amsterdam. He simply recommends that we withdraw from Amsterdam. But this would by no means settle the question. Of course, it would be easy for us to decide here to withdraw from Amsterdam, but what we want is for the millions of workers who adhere now to the Amsterdam International to leave it together with us. When it is said that the workers don't work in Amsterdam but in the factories, this is simply a sophisticated evasive argument. Unionised workers discuss the trade-union movement at their meetings, inside their unions – not in the factories and surely not in the private offices of Amsterdam. These questions are debated at the assemblies of union members, and our presence there should be obligatory to combat the influence of Amsterdam.

Comrade Watkins has absolutely misunderstood when he stated that we reproach the British movement for having formed organisations within the trade unions that did not obey the leaders. We don't go to Amsterdam to observe their leaders, but in order to compel the mass of workers there to go against Amsterdam and not follow its leaders. Comrade Watkins and his friends have succeeded in undermining the authority of the leaders by their system of shop committees. The work should be organised in such a way as to throw off the trade-union leaders.

Insofar as the Western European movement is only now entering the stage of revolutionary struggle, our Western comrades should take into account the experience of other countries. I am by no means inclined to object to the assertion that the Western European proletariat is more class-conscious, and has a long history. But I assert that in the majority of Western European countries, the working class lacks great consciousness. Its numerical force and its long history are not enough to put into practice the means and methods to prepare the struggle for the dictatorship of the proletariat.

In this respect, it would be the greatest error to neglect to take into account the experience of the red trade unions. The syndicalist comrades expressed their desire that the doctrine of syndicalism should be officially and formally adopted as the foundation of our tactics. This was claimed by a minority consisting of thirty or forty delegates. I was not aware that anybody, when appearing at this podium, had moved to officially establish as the foundation of the Red International of Labour Unions the doctrine of Marx or Engels. It is clear that the revolutionary organisations that struggle for the dictatorship of the proletariat, independently of the philosophical theories they base their struggle on, should be represented at this congress. If the majority of the congress did not seek an official acknowledgement of this doctrine, what right has the minority of the delegates to claim from this podium that their philosophical historical thesis should be formally accepted as the basis for the organisation of the International?

I believe that before Marxists can persuade syndicalists, or syndicalists can persuade Marxists, the revolution will have broken out in several countries.

In the process of the struggle with world capital, we must take into account the fundamental factor that our comrades who have not experienced all the difficulties of the communist revolution do not see as clearly. The remarks of many delegates and their references to Lenin's statement that our turn toward state capitalism has been caused exclusively by our backwardness are absolutely incorrect.[24]

Comrades, this reference is wrong, because Comrade Lenin has underlined many times that our change of orientation is not determined only by the backwardness of Soviet Russia and the economic situation but also by the state of the international revolutionary movement. It is determined by the fact that we have a state with a dictatorship in the hands of the working class, but one that is also surrounded on all sides by capitalist countries. This circumstance plays a greater part in determining our line of action than the backwardness of our economic life.

I must also underline the falsity of Comrade Sirolle's statement about the resolutions of the congress of the Russian Communist Party. He indicated that in the resolution against the so-called Workers' Opposition,[25] syndicalist tendencies were condemned. I must state that in taking this resolution, our party had in view specific manifestations of the syndicalism that the Western European countries, with a more highly developed capitalist system, will have to likewise experience. In the transitional period we passed through, separate factories and shops were inclined to pass fully into the hands of the workers, where there was a tendency to elect their factory administration by the general vote of the workers. We stood, in this case, before two alternatives: to put the interests of the class as a whole above the interest of specific groups, or to leave it to the agreement of separate factories and shops to decide the question. This syndicalist tendency will inevitably develop during the transitional period in a whole series of countries, and the statements made here by various comrades that centralism is obligatory in Northern countries and that in the Latin countries there will be federalism – this view is wrong in its essentials, as syndicalism and

24 A reference to Lenin's report on the policies of the Communist Party of Russia, given to the Third Comintern Congress. For the specific reference mentioned concerning state capitalism, see Riddell (ed.) 2015, *3WC*, pp. 667–8.

25 The Workers' Opposition was a group within the Russian CP led by Aleksandr Shlyapnikov, Alexandra Kollontai, S.P. Medvedev, and others. Formed in September 1920, it called for trade-union control of industrial production and greater autonomy for CP fractions in the unions. After its position was rejected by the Tenth CP Congress in March 1921, the Workers' Opposition subsequently raised criticisms of measures adopted introducing the New Economic Policy. Following its censure at the party's Eleventh Congress in March–April 1922, the Workers' Opposition ceased organised activity.

For the Tenth Congress resolution on the Workers' Opposition, see Lenin, 'Preliminary Draft Resolution of the Tenth Congress of the R.C.P. on the Syndicalist and Anarchist Deviation in Our Party', in *LCW*, 32, pp. 245–8.

federalism are defined by the economic conditions of the country concerned. The greater the links between isolated economies in the process of production and distribution, the less is it admissible to have such a syndicalist deviation as you are experiencing just now.

In Britain, for instance, where the life of every worker, of every party, depends upon the organisation of economics as a whole, upon the work of all factories, if you do not take this into account you will arrive at autonomy, to an entire independence of the factory committees, and will fail completely. The tendency to take hold of separate branches of the economy will inevitably develop everywhere. It would be reckless to believe that it is enough to bring about a communist revolution, and everything will come by itself. Undoubtedly in the process of the development of the workers' organisations and formation of the proletarian state, we shall stumble upon many complications and conflicts between separate groups.

To sum up, I should like to point out one of the stages that our state lived through. There were times when, at the frontiers of Soviet Russia, there gathered under one command detachments of British and French soldiers. The organisation and consciousness of the representatives of the bourgeois countries attacking us was very developed. The discipline of these masters of the world's destiny was strong, their unity, irrespective of their nationality, was extraordinary.

If we want to defeat the imperialists and the bourgeoisie at the present stage of development, we need to introduce, besides general tactics, the same iron discipline we now witness among our enemies. Otherwise we shall fail to defeat our enemies and shall inevitably be defeated.

Lozovsky: Comrade Flynn has the floor.

Flynn (USA): It has been stated here that the intellectual level of discussions this evening has not been very high, and I am very sorry that I am not going to contribute in any way towards elevating that level. My primary purpose in taking the stand is to answer a speech made here tonight, and as the level of that speech was not very high, I myself cannot rise much above it. The only thing I hope is that the chairman will be as lenient with the bell in my case as he was in the case of the individual to whom I will reply.

Comrade Haywood laid a great deal of stress upon the point, in opening his speech, that he was not here as a representative of the IWW, which is quite correct. He is not the official representative of the IWW, but in the mind of anyone who is familiar with the history of the development of the IWW, it is impossible to separate the names of the IWW and Haywood; they go together; they are like

Siamese twins. If you think of Haywood, you think of the IWW. They are inseparable, and William D. Haywood is largely responsible for and is in a position to speak on the position of the Industrial Workers of the World. It is true that he was sent here by the American Labor Bureau, and he was sent here for the purpose of advising the congress upon tactics and the attitude to be adopted here towards the American labour movement. The most important question that this congress is going to decide in the American labour movement is the question of staying within the mass organisations or withdrawing from them. Comrade Haywood, in speaking on the subject, ducked that issue completely. He did not refer to that at all, and nobody knows whether William D. Haywood is in favour of going into the trade unions or withdrawing from them.

Now, he places a statement into my mouth in a speech that I made in the early part of this congress on the report of the Credentials Committee. He attributed to me the opinion that the IWW is Marxian. I do not pretend to be a Marxian myself,[26] but know enough about the Marxian theory to know that Marxism plays no part whatever in the IWW programme. I do not think of the IWW as a Marxian union, nor do I think it is a pure union. I was using those terms in a sarcastic sense.

The most important thing Comrade Haywood talked about was, of course, the A.F. of L. One of our comrades was attacked because he has come to Russia as a medicine man, to introduce new methods into Russia. I wish to call attention to the fact that there is not a member of the American trade-union delegation who has come to Russia with any idea in mind of introducing or inducing them to adopt new tactics. We are leaving that kind of attitude to Comrade Haywood himself. The IWW has been invited to participate in the Third International's congress. That invitation was sent out at the time of the First and Second [Comintern] congresses, and it has been repeated for the Third Congress. On the first two occasions it was never responded to. Now, there has been a lot of misinformation circulated regarding the revolutionary character of the IWW, regarding its general make-up and its actual importance in the labour movement. I am very thankful for the fact that we have in Moscow today some real representatives of labour and that, together with the actual representatives of the IWW, I think they will puncture the Industrial Workers of the World bubble for all time in Russia.

The steel strike has been spoken of here this evening in a rather contemptuous manner. The steel strike has been referred to as nothing in the American

26 This formulation is taken from the proceedings. From the context, it's possible that 'Marxian expert' may have been meant.

labour movement. The book published about the steel strike has been quoted to us that it was a loss.[27] I wish to call attention, for those of you who are not acquainted with the American labour movement, of its activities, that the United States Steel trust, against whom the strike was aimed, is the largest corporation in the world. Now, an American large corporation means something. They have their own army, their own police force, their own detective agencies. It is practically a little state within the big state of the United States. And that strike was called against this largest corporation, and it was the largest mass movement of organised workers in the history of the United States of America. In the course of this strike 21 men were killed, 10,000 at least were clubbed and beaten up by the police, and at least 25,000 were arrested. And we have an American labour leader who can only see a red, white, and blue membership card. He has that card so close to his eyes that he fails to appreciate the significance, the magnificence, if you please, of a gigantic mass movement. He neglects to see it; he does not see it, but is blind to it. During the course of the steel strike it was impossible to carry out public meetings; it was impossible to have free speech or anything else. Nevertheless, those men were out and stayed out for weeks on end, fighting against the efforts of the United States Steel Corporation. It is practically the only strike in America that tied up the industry from top to bottom.

The A.F. of L. is a rotten organisation, it's rotten to the core. That's all that you can say about it, and we who are working on the inside have known worse things about the A.F. of L., and know fully how rotten it is. We are not here carrying any credentials or briefs from the bureaucracy of the American Federation of Labor. We are here carrying briefs for the four million workers who are inside this organisation. It is known that the A.F. of L. has been officered by Samuel Gompers for thirty-nine years. It is known that it has been split up into craft unions. It is also known that William English Walling is a pen prostitute for Samuel Gompers. What is responsible for this? Now if you are to have an organisation for any good purpose, you have got to leave the revolutionists in it. What has the IWW been doing? They have been pulling out the brains of the movement. They have been saying this is a rotten organisation, that if you stay in there you will get rotten too. It comes then to the same end as the tactics being used by the leaders of the A.F. of L. in throwing the brains out of the movement. That is where the two extremes meet.

We hear a lot of talk about high initiations and closed books. The photo engravers, the moving picture operators, excluding women, and all this. What

27 A reference to William Z. Foster, *The Great Steel Strike and Its Lessons* (New York: B.W. Huebsch, Inc., 1920). For the 1919 US steel strike itself, see p. 386, n. 15.

are these organisations? Remember that at this time there are just a little over four million workers in the American Federation of Labor. All of these organisations together only form a very small fraction of the American Federation of Labor. None of them are any larger than the IWW itself.

You have heard mention on this floor of something about the United Mine Workers of America. This organisation is industrial in form and militant in character. At the present time in the State of West Virginia the members of this organisation have guns upon their shoulders battling against the hired army of the mine owners.[28] The IWW representatives were there in favour of working within the American Federation of Labor. What did they do in the case of this organisation? The organisers of the IWW are at this very moment making efforts to disrupt the United Mine Workers organisation. In the State of Pennsylvania they have organisers pulling small groups of ten and fifteen men out of the union and building up industrial union locals. That is the method of the IWW within the A.F. of L.

We have representatives here of the metalworkers section of the Industrial Workers of the World, an organisation with 1,292 members. In America we have organised at least a half million metalworkers. Their method here is to break the large organisations and organise new industrial unions. In the railroad brotherhoods of America we have at least one and a half million organised. There the IWW is working in an effort to disrupt this large organisation, and pulling out groups for the benefit of the Industrial Workers of the World. Their work has the same effect upon the unions as the work of the employers. Their slogan, as well as the slogan of the manufacturers' association, is to smash the unions.

The inference given here is that the IWW attitude has the endorsement of the Communist Party of America. Such is not the case. Time forbids me from reading the Communist Party programme upon this point. Nevertheless, at their last convention they adopted a programme that condemns the policy of building dual unions, and accepting the policy of working within the mass organisations in America.[29] The Communist Party of America realises that in order to gain control of society they must first gain control of the mass of organised

28 A number of armed battles were taking place in the summer of 1921 between coal miners in West Virginia and an alliance of company gun thugs, police, and army or national guard troops. One such confrontation was the Battle of the Tug of 12–14 May 1921, in which members of the United Mine Workers fought a gun battle with deputy sheriffs, police, mine guards, and national guardsmen, during a struggle to unionise coal mines in southern West Virginia; three persons were killed in the fighting. Then in late August, the Battle of Blair Mountain occurred, in which up to a hundred people were killed.

29 The Unity Convention of the US Communist Party in May 1921 adopted a programme that was published in *The Communist*, no. 1, of July 1921.

labour. The method of pulling members out of these large organisations has been shown to be a failure. The test of all things is history, and history proves conclusively that this policy of dualism does not work. Twenty-five years of activity in America has proven that beyond a doubt.[30]

We are here to do something to replace that policy and to build an organisation that will train and organise the working class for a revolutionary conquest of political power.

Lozovsky: The session is closed. The next plenary session will be tomorrow at 11:00 a.m.

(*The session is declared closed at 11:00 p.m.*)

---

30 For the Socialist Trade and Labor Alliance founded in 1895, see p. 352, n. 9.

SESSION 14. 15 JULY 1921, MORNING–AFTERNOON

Debate on Tactics (continued)

(*Session opens at 11:00 a.m. Comrade Hampel in the chair.*)

Adalbert Hampel: I declare the session open. Comrade Repossi will now speak.

Luigi Repossi (Italy): I fully agree with the theses of Comrade Lozovsky. I speak simply to explain certain points.

The phrase 'exceptional circumstances' very often makes us suspicious, as we have been used to hearing such apologetic expressions from the mouths of reformists and the Italian Confederation of Labour. It is, of course, self-evident that Comrade Lozovsky is using it in a different sense. Not through parliament, but outside parliament do we intend to improve the life of the workers. The workers must demand publicly of parliament the promulgation of the necessary labour laws. Such laws, carried under the pressure of the direct action of the proletariat, would be a real victory for the proletariat, struggling against the bourgeoisie.

The reformists are trying to convince the workers, for instance, that they, the workers, are contributing only one-third toward insurance and sick benefit funds. But in reality they pay the whole sum, as the part contributed by employers is added to the cost of production. Against such a system, therefore, we must fight by all means.

There are a few points in Comrade Lozovsky's theses that I do not fully agree with. I am in full agreement with the resolutions of the Communist International that we must draw into the workers' councils not only the organised workers, but all workers in general. If the existence of class enemies among many of the labour organisations is quite evident – as for example in the Catholic unions – still, we have a great number of partisans among the unorganised masses.

Further, I consider it dangerous to sanction the keeping of agreements, even for short periods. The bourgeoisie breaks its agreements without hesitation. Why should we not follow in their footsteps? We must fight against a decline in wages by all means at our disposal. Today the bourgeoisie has begun to lower wages, invoking a drop in prices that has not happened yet. In the past, the price of commodities dropped first before wages were cut.

We do not recommend sabotage as a method of struggle. To sanction it would be dangerous. It is hard to find people who would offer their willing-

 | DOI:10.1163/9789004712867_018

ness to destroy the things they themselves have produced. Sabotage leads to lockouts or the occupation of the factories by gendarmes.

Obstruction, on the other hand, is sensible; it brings the desired results. This method of fighting is causing great losses to the employers with no loss to the workers, who receive their wages in full. I am a metalworker myself, and my comrades and I have used this method occasionally. In one factory where we put obstruction into practice, the employer suffered a loss of 14,000 lire in the first day, and 12,000 the second day. This method undoubtedly gives the workers an opportunity to widen and strengthen the labour movement. During obstruction, production becomes difficult and disorganised, while the workers stick together and their spirit of solidarity grows.

We do not approve of sympathy strikes on economic grounds, because we only advocate large political battles. We advise the workers to organise themselves in industrial unions and consolidate all the trade and industrial unions into one proletarian organisation for the purpose of the class struggle.

Amsterdam or Moscow: these are the two counterpositions that mean either opportunism or revolution. This is how the theses of Comrade Lozovsky should be understood. We have, for instance, proposed to the railroad workers – contrary to the reformists and syndicalists – to group themselves in an industrial union. If we continue our work in such a direction, we shall succeed in rooting out reformist tendencies from the trade unions of Italy.

Hampel: Comrade Knight has the floor.

Joseph R. Knight (Canada): Comrades, before dealing with the problem under discussion at this session, I just wish to make a brief statement in reply to some inferences that were made by Haywood. For instance it was inferred – not charged but inferred in an insidious subtle manner – that I was not a member of a trade union. The comrades know that I have never since the age of nineteen been outside of a trade union, and Haywood knows that I am a General Executive Board member of a revolutionary union in Canada. Also, the statement was made that I was not a Communist. At the same time, he knows that in the country that I came from there was no Communist Party when I left. And he knows also that I belong to a revolutionary socialist organisation that has, since I have been in Moscow, become part of the Communist International. (*Applause*) I may state further that I have a full endorsement of the Communists of the American section; the complete section of the American Communists in Moscow endorsed me. So I reply to the canards of Haywood. The fact is, when you have no principles to discuss, or have not the intellect to discuss a speech made, then the one method is to try and slag your opponent in the absence of intellect. Such were the methods of Haywood. (*Applause*)

I have nothing to add, not one word, in regard to Haywood and the IWW. They have come to Moscow and have written their own epitaph, and so we still say, 'let the dead bury the dead'. We have too much important work to do to waste any more time on such a fraction.

In regard to the principles that we are here discussing, there is one question that must first be answered. What is our purpose? For what purpose are we gathered here in this congress, thirty-six different nationalities representing organisations of the working class? When we can agree on our purpose, then the other is very easily settled.

We are here to do our all, with our movement. But in the east there was very little response. The workers there still clung to the old organisations, and we were forced to realise that much preparatory work was necessary, that boring from within was the only tactic to advance the revolutionary movement. This is the result of experience and not simply taken from a book. We are faced with a choice of either becoming a small sectarian party or a part of the great revolutionary movement, and we chose the latter.

One speaker, in an attempt to justify the creation of petty world unions, stated that Russia had found it necessary to adopt new forms of industrial organisation. There is no comparison to be made between the workers' economic organisations in Russia and the trade unions of countries yet under the domination of a bourgeois dictatorship. In Russia the unions and industrial organisations are built up under the protection of the proletarian dictatorship, and it is positively droll and absurd to attempt a comparison with the slave organisations of the bourgeois state.

Men, there is one thing that we must always bear in mind. We are yet slaves, and if we would free ourselves from slavery, all our energies must be exerted to organise our class to conquer the capitalist state. To dissipate our energies in juggling with various forms of ideal industrial organisations that might be serviceable when we are free from the bonds of slavery is a crime against the movement. Let us first settle with our masters; let us first overthrow the capitalist system and establish the dictatorship of the proletariat. And then under its protection we will have time and leisure to formulate systems of economic organisation that will lead to our greater comfort and happiness. Let our slogan be: 'The unity of the political and industrial organisation of the workers merging in one mighty revolutionary proletarian organisation'. Let us put forth every possible effort toward the establishment of the dictatorship of the proletariat. There is no being in this congress that does not see the necessity of the dictatorship of the proletariat.

Some have spoken in a manner that would make one think it possible, through a purely industrial organisation, for the workers to obtain control. Can they not see the conditions that face them today? The master class is united through the social, political, and economic organisations into one cohesive force against the mass of the working class. This is a very definite fact, and we of the working class are divided into so many different small organisations. We must have the dictatorship of the proletariat. It is necessary to overthrow the capitalist state and to suppress counterrevolution. How can this be accomplished without the mass of the working class? Why, it is absurd to think of such a thing.

Then, if we must have the masses, we must go where these masses are. It is absurd to say that the leaders of these unions are rotten and corrupt. That is common knowledge. You are not telling the revolutionaries anything by saying that. We know they are corrupt. We know they have betrayed the working class again and again. It is childish to say we want to overthrow the capitalist system, we want to overthrow the capitalist state and establish the dictatorship of the proletariat, but oh, we cannot conquer the trade unions. Yet this is the language of some who deem themselves revolutionists. They boast of their revolutionary purity, which they fear to tarnish by contact with the trade-union organisations, and then talk loudly of conquering the state, of overthrowing the system. Why, it is ridiculous, inasmuch as the masses are in these organisations. If we would have the masses with us, we must go within the reactionary unions and, by our knowledge, by our revolutionary spirit, win them for revolution, win them for communism. It is simple, it is clear, and those who refuse to understand are not revolutionists, but they hamper the work of the revolutionists.

It was mentioned here by one speaker – and it amused me at the time – that in Canada, in Vancouver, the A.F. of L. had forced the working class back into their organisation, that money was spent to break the One Big Union of Canada. That is very true, but these people don't understand the significance of revolutionary tactics. I know more about that than the one who related it. It was during the Vancouver strike that was called in sympathy with the Winnipeg general strike.[1] It was declared during a trade depression, and the employers, seizing the opportunity, arranged with the A.F. of L. that no employee could return unless he first took out a card in the American Federation of Labor organisation. This was done to break, if possible, the One Big Union organisation. And seeing that to resist meant to victimise several good revolutionists, a meeting was called by the OBU Executive at which it was decided that the men take out an A.F. of L. card and go back to the job and continue a general tactic of boring from within.

1 For the Winnipeg general strike, see p. 353, n. 10.

The One Big Union of Canada is not like the general run of 'little one big unions'. It was not engineered by a few revolutionists who were attempting to build an ideal industrial state within the shell of the old. Nothing of the kind. The organisation was born in struggle and baptised in blood. It came into being immediately after the Armistice [of 1918], when the persecution of the state drove the workers into open revolt against the reactionary policy of the old trade-union officials. The whole of Western Canada was seething with discontent and mass strikes, which automatically severed them from the A.F. of L., ranging from Winnipeg to Vancouver. The organisation was literally forced into existence, and we hoped at the time to sweep the whole of Canada.

Hampel: Comrade Earsman has the floor.

William Earsman (Australia): Comrades, on behalf of the Australian delegation, I want to say that the theses on tactics were fully accepted. We do not only accept them because we think they are correct theoretically, but because we have found them correct by the test of action being applied to them in the past year.

When we got the theses laid down by the Second Comintern Congress last year, the organisation that was then at work among the trade unions, known as One Big Union Propaganda Committee, was spreading the ideas of industrial unionism among the crafts. They made it part of their programme to apply the theses on tactics that had already been drawn up by the Communist International. During the following months in the conflicts that were arising throughout the country, the workers engaged in the struggle – though not yet organised in a political party – nevertheless recognised the full value of those tactics and on several occasions used them effectively, not only in assisting the workers in the everyday struggle, but in particular acting and using them for the benefit of educating the workers. That was particularly true regarding the unemployed.

We recognised that we could do nothing for the unemployed under capitalism, and the workers in Australia are like workers everywhere else. They recognised that the Labor [Party] government could not remedy or alter the position that they found themselves in. But those who understood the position, who were at the head of the movement, recognised that the unemployed should be used for the specific purpose of educating. What happened? After playing to the fullest extent with the unemployed, the government ultimately said they could do not a thing. So we commenced to apply our tactics to individual capitalists, and this is what we did. We got the unemployed workers organised, not into different organisations, but into one organisation. And two or three of the leaders of the trade unions took them into different restaurants throughout the city and got free food for them, and then informed those managers to send the bill to the minister in charge of that particular department in the government. In Brisbane pennies were distributed among the unemployed, and they were sent to the refreshment shops buying penny buns that had been sitting there a whole day. The result has been that these individuals who were so unfortunate in that particular period are now recognising the benefits of that experience, and now are working for all they are worth in the old craft unions for the formation of industrial unions.

We in Australia were also fortunate in another direction. There were practically no outside organisations such as the IWW and others. The IWW members recognised some time ago the futility of attempting, in Australia at least, to build up an outside independent organisation, and we are happy today that the former members of the IWW are now operating sincerely inside the craft organisations. But I want to have registered here that though the IWW failed as an outside organisation in Australia, nevertheless they did not fail in propaganda work. In fact the seeds that were spread by the IWW bore fruit that we are reaping today in the different industrial unions that have been formed in that particular territory.

On looking over the views as have been represented by the different sections of the American movement, I can only say that even yet, and as far as I am personally concerned, in America they have not yet been able to prove that there is more of a field for operation for the IWW. But I do say this emphatically, that there is a very great misunderstanding among members of the IWW themselves in their refusal to recognise the development of recent years. They seem to refuse to recognise or to accept the lessons that they must recognise, if they are going to have any success in the development of the Russian situation.

To say that political action and parliamentary action are the same is only to put the stamp of a fool on yourself. We know today that no matter what action the working class may take, it ultimately finishes in a political fight, that the power of the state for the last six or seven years has on all occasions, in any mass movement of any description – it has finished in a fight against the political state. The position is clear. Then why not get down and recognise the situation and get away from the false basis? If the IWW and the WIIU of America would only sit down and calmly review the whole situation and cease pretending to be revolutionary and recognise the facts that exist in the everyday struggle, they would arrive at a sound base and we would find them inside the Red International working and preparing for the final struggle.

Returning again to the movement in Australia, I want to put this point particularly to our German comrades, because as I said to the Comintern congress, it had been said that the working class of Australia was conservative.[2] That is not true. But it is true that this is the first time we have taken any part in international affairs. Not because we were conservative by any means, but because past Internationals had nothing to offer us. Past Internationals, in particular the Second and the Two-and-a-Half Internationals – their programme is even more reactionary than that of our Labour Party, and at the present moment the working class of Australia has travelled beyond them. Therefore, we will have no connection with them.

When there is an International to be formed upon a sound, solid, and scientific basis, I can say without any fear that the working class of Australia will be inside that International. I have not the slightest doubt that not only will the different individual organisations in the country, but the different federations and labour councils throughout the length and breadth of Australia will also be here. And in saying that, I want to say on behalf of the Australian delegation that we do not want any 'Yes, No' International – one that is looking both ways – but clear-cut principles that will show to the IWW and the craft unions where we stand. We want it definitely to be laid down then that those who cannot accept these principles must go outside. Failing to come inside, they will soon recognise that we are right and they are wrong. It is the only possible way that we can build up a sound International to avoid mistakes of the past, to recognise these mistakes and to make full use of them, to see that they are not embodied in principles and in our tactics.

The same applies to the independent unions of Germany. We desire them inside, but they must change their tactics. And if they cannot recognise the situation, well, in the course of time they will certainly do so, that is, they will only be forced to recognise it when the trouble comes. And then, they say, they will stand by us. If we are one, it enables us to build up that sound organisation, which will be able to grapple with all situations as they arise. It is impossible to do this with the present difference, for the simple reason that they have been working in another direction. They often attempt to use tactics that we cannot accept. The result is then that we have a new element, which may mean reorganising.

I ask those independent organisations in Germany, syndicalists in France, IWW in America, WIIU in America, to also sit down and realise the development of the past few years, and to recognise what is taking place in Russia, what is taking place throughout Europe, in which most of the workers must finally

2 For Earsman's remarks at the Comintern Third Congress, see Riddell (ed.) 2015, *3WC*, pp. 648–50.

recognise the activity of the bourgeoisie in the political state. When they have done that, there is only one conclusion that they can arrive at, and that conclusion is to accept the theses that have been laid before this congress.

Hampel: Comrade Dimitrov has the floor.

Georgi Dimitrov (Bulgaria): Comrades, after having decided the question of the relations between the Red Trade Union International and the Communist International, our congress has to decide another question, no less important for the further development of the labour movement: that of the aims and tactics of the trade unions under conditions of an economic crisis and the process of the proletarian revolution already begun.

The detailed debates that have taken place up until now have unfortunately dealt only with one side of the question, our attitude toward the old trade unions, wheras the problem in this particular case is obviously much more comprehensive. The problem not only concerns the existence and further development of the trade-union movement, but has a critical significance for the issue of the gigantic struggle now going on between the proletariat and the bourgeoisie, between the proletarian revolution and the bourgeois counterrevolution. I do not wish to repeat what was already said by other comrades. I only wish to emphasise the essential point connected with the fundamental problem that requires solution.

The question now consists of transforming the trade unions into fighting organisations of the proletariat, so that they may successfully fulfil their mission. No special proofs are needed to understand that under the present political and economic conditions the trade unions have only two ways: either to follow the old reformist policy of compromising with the capitalists, to make collective bargains, to support civil peace, and thus to support the domination of capitalism and exploitation – or to accept the revolutionary platform for the overthrow of capitalism, i.e., to link their daily struggle to the fight for the dictatorship of the proletariat. There is no middle road, and there cannot be one.

The whole movement of the large proletarian masses of Germany, Britain, Italy, and other countries has clearly proved that the new conditions place before the proletariat and its labour organisations the iron necessity of solving the new revolutionary problems and of carrying out the new revolutionary policy. The basis of this new problem is that the trade unions should, with all the means and strength at their command, serve the interests of the revolution. As to the new revolutionary policy, its wisdom consists in coordinating the economic and political fight of the proletariat against the bourgeoisie, and in carrying out this fight for the establishment of the dictatorship of the proletariat, which alone can overthrow capitalism for good.

The fruitlessness of the reformist policy of the old trade unions and their powerlessness to conquer anything, or to improve somehow the workers' position within the framework of the present capitalist order, is becoming daily clearer and clearer to the vast masses of the working class of all countries. The necessity of taking state power into its hands and organising production on a socialistic basis also becomes clearer to the proletariat. The victorious revolution in Russia has best shown the way, clarifying the new problems and the new tactics of the trade unions.

This experience has not only proved to the proletariat how disastrous reformism is within the trade-union movement, but it has at the same time clearly disproved the theory and practice of syndicalism. We heard a statement from the doctrinal syndicalists that they are also for the political struggle and for the establishment of the proletarian power. But this, according to them, must be the immediate and direct task of the trade unions themselves, which are, it seems, the only real workers' organisations that could conquer and establish the dictatorship of the proletariat.

In comparison with the old syndicalists they have made a step forward, but this step is, after all, a false one. The platform supported by them considers, in its essentials, that they wish to transform the trade unions into a sort of syndicalist party that would carry out the political fight of the proletariat. And yet the fact is clear as daylight to any active worker well acquainted with the history and essential points of the labour movement, that the trade unions, however revolutionary they may be in their essentials, are compelled to act within the limited bounds of the given industry, and in their daily activities and struggle are compelled to reckon first of all with the conditions and with the special interests of the workers of the given industry. They themselves, as trade unions, are not in a position to organise and guide the general revolutionary fight of the proletariat, which is always a political fight.

Another proletarian organisation is needed to achieve this aim, for which the dividing lines of separate industries and the sectional interests of the workers are of little significance, and which is in a position to unite the most revolutionary elements of all industries and make its influence felt upon millions of the unemployed and of workers remaining outside the trade unions, and which alone can have the leading lines of its activities and struggle for the general interests of the proletariat and its emancipatory movement. This is what would be the true political organisation of the proletariat, its Communist Party in each country and the Communist International on a world scale.

To defend the view that the trade unions must have the practical initiative, that they must organise and guide the general revolutionary fight for the overthrow of capitalism and the establishment of the dictatorship of the proletariat, proves the full lack of comprehension of the essential points in the class struggle and in the rules of the proletarian revolution.

It would be just as if on a battlefield separate units of an army, operating on separate sectors and carrying out special tasks, would pretend to organise and lead the joint operations of the whole army, work out and carry out a general programme of tactics on the entire theatre of the war. Every soldier knows very well that this is the task of the general leading headquarters and not of separate units. It is just this simple truth that our evidently very pretentious doctrinal syndicalists are unable to grasp with reference to the social class war.

As to the attitude toward the old-style large trade unions, our German *Unionen* and the American comrades of the IWW, proclaiming the slogan of the destruction of the old unions and the creation of new organisations from the separate revolutionary trade-union groups, are clearly arguing from a purely metaphysical standpoint. They are clearly not in a position to see and understand the dialectical process that is going on within the old trade unions, a process that is revolutionising them more and more each day under the pressure of the masses organised within these unions.

To identify the American Federation of Labor with the reactionary bureaucracy within the trade unions themselves is untrue and does not hold up to criticism. The American Federation is the headquarters of the bourgeois agents and traitors of the working class, while the trade unions that are affiliated to it are nevertheless proletarian class organisations. Against these bourgeois agents within the unions we will ceaselessly carry out the fight until we are able to completely wipe them out, while within the trade unions we will work to prevent them from falling under the influence and dependence of the bourgeoisie and its agents. We shall transform the trade unions into revolutionary class organisations, indispensable for the complete triumph of the world proletarian revolution.

To withdraw from the trade unions, to demand their destruction for the sole reason that they are guided by social traitors and counterrevolutionists, means completely to misunderstand the historical importance of the trade unions for the proletarian revolution. This would assume the nonsensical supposition that the success of the revolution is possible without the participation of the trade unions, or even with their opposition to the revolution, i.e., without the great masses of the proletariat or with their negative and hostile attitude. Comrade Lozovsky is quite right when he declares that the slogan of withdrawing from the trade unions and fighting for their destruction is a counterrevolutionary slogan.

Moreover, now, when the Amsterdam leaders themselves have put forward the question of expelling the revolutionary elements from the trade unions, an appeal to withdraw from them would simply be a crime toward the emancipatory task of the proletariat. To such an unwise policy, the enemies of the working class could only applaud. Therefore, it is the duty of the congress to emphatically condemn and to reject such a policy, as was already done last year by the Second Congress of the Comintern.[3]

The Bulgarian delegation supports the theses on the tasks and tactics of the trade unions presented by Comrade Lozovsky, because the basic provisions of these theses fully correspond to the historical role that the trade-union movement is called on to play in the world proletarian revolution.

Against the treachery of opportunism, against the prejudices and errors of syndicalism, against sectarianism and the sentimentality of revolutionary romanticism, and for the transformation of the trade unions into real fighting organisations of the proletarian revolution – this is a clear and unambiguous practical programme that ought to be presented to the proletariat organised in its trade unions by the constituent international congress of revolutionary trade unions in Moscow.

And we are deeply convinced that this programme will be adopted by the congress, to the misfortune of the enemies of the working class, and to the benefit of the world proletarian revolution.

Hampel: Comrade Tiura has the floor.

Tiura [Leo Laukki] (Finland): Comrades, there are three fundamental problems that have been discussed on the question of tactics as outlined in the speech of Comrade Lozovsky. These questions are: (1) the relations between the Communist International and the Communist parties on one side and the revolutionary trade unions on the other; (2) the question of the attitude of revolutionary workers in general, of Communists in particular, and also of red

3 Point 6 of 'Theses on the Trade Union Movement, Factory Committees, and the Communist International' states, 'Shunning the union movement by choice poses an enormous danger for the Communist movement. So too do attempts to create separate unions artificially, unless this is made necessary by unusually outrageous actions on the part of the union bureaucracy (the disbanding of individual revolutionary union locals by the opportunist central leaderships) or by narrow-minded, aristocratic policies barring the great masses of less-skilled workers from membership in the organisations. Such actions threaten to separate the most advanced, most class-conscious workers from the masses who are on the road to communism, leaving them at the mercy of opportunist leaders, who play into the hands of the bourgeoisie.' In Riddell (ed.) 1991, *2WC*, p. 628.

trade unions toward the old trade unions, in other words, the question of the two tactics: that of boring from within or fighting outside the unions; (3) the question of the plan of action of the revolutionary trade unions.

The Finnish delegation is in agreement with the theses as drafted by Comrade Lozovsky. Some changes in the theses are of course necessary. At the same time, it agrees with a number of statements made by Comrade Murphy when describing the present situation in America.

As to the theoretical basis on the question of tactics, the Finnish delegation is in full agreement with Comrade Lozovsky and not only accepts his theses from the theoretical standpoint, but intends to carry them out in practice. As a matter of fact, these principles were already accepted in Finland before the beginning of the civil war.

The trade unions that existed in Finland before 1917 and that had a membership of 400,000 were crushed by the white terror.[4] After the crushing of the revolution, when the first critical moments had passed during which the white terror spread over the whole country, the Finnish trade-union movement again began to revive. The membership rose to 60,000. But the question of the Finnish trade unions is marked by the fiercest struggle, and you know, comrades, that there is no country where the working class had to suffer as much as in Finland. Wholesale imprisonment and isolation in concentration camps were the order of the day. Dozens of members of trade-union organisations and of political parties were killed outright or tortured by starvation or the most medieval inquisitorial methods.

You understand that after such an experience, the entire working class of Finland is taking a very keen interest in the question and the problem of tactics, forms of organisation, and so on. You must understand still more that the Finnish working class had to reconsider, in its foundations, the entire field of previous tactics, because the tactics of the leaders and the Social-Democratic Party had failed in the civil war and demonstrated their complete sterility. At the same time, the tactics of the labour organisations during the civil war showed their complete incapacity, compelling a search for new ways and new methods of struggle.

---

4 The following statement was inserted into the minutes by the Finnish delegation: 'In Finland, until 1917, the unions contained not 400,000 but 140,000 members.'

In January 1918 workers in Finland, granted independence from Russia following the October Revolution, organised a Red Army and declared a proletarian republic. The Red Army was able to seize most of southern Finland, but it was defeated by counterrevolutionary forces. The number of victims of the ensuing white terror is uncertain, but some estimates are that 10,000 were summarily shot and over 100,000 were sent to concentration camps, where some 12,000 died of disease or starvation.

What were our considerations with regard to these three main points?

The question of working within or outside the unions could easily be raised in Finland, for the reason that the Finnish labour movement has always been working in harmony and hand-in-hand with the working masses. But the question of tactics and of the plan of action are at a critical stage in our country. The Finnish trade unions have entirely reorganised themselves along industrial lines, in accordance with which we decide all the tactical questions as well. The question of the general plan of action, of the general strike, of partial industrial strikes, of control over production – in one word, everything that interests our congress – all this is included in the programme of the Finnish trade unions.

Let us go over to the question of relations between the unions and the political parties. The Finnish Social-Democratic Party, which together with its leaders had betrayed the common cause, is now working shoulder to shoulder with the white government, becoming a powerful tool in the hands of that government. But the Finnish trade unions trust the Communists. They want the Communist Party to take over the full leadership of the trade unions. From the point of view of our unions, the entire work of the trade unions must be directed by the Communist Party. The Finnish trade unions will not sympathise with the ideas and points of view of the syndicalists, who have sidetracked the working-class movement on the wrong path. The Finnish trade unions have the definite point of view that only under the guidance of the Communist Party will they work, create, and bring about the revolution. The Finnish workers are aware of the fact that a political action such as a revolution cannot take place without the participation of the political party. They know this not from theory, but by bitter experience.

Now I wish to say a few words on the opinions that were here expressed on the movement of the Industrial Workers of the World. I lived in America for about fourteen years and took an active part in party work, as well as in organising the workers of the IWW.[5] I was a member of the Socialist Party of America for several years, and consider the question of the IWW not only from the point of view of trade unionism, but from the point of view of political struggle. Two remarks have been made here with regards to the IWW, and I wish to deal with the two of them.

The first remark was made by one of the American comrades, who pointed out that Haywood evaded the question of entering the unions with the

5 Tiura (Leo Laukki) was among the ninety-three IWW members who were convicted in the mass frame-up trial in 1918, including William D. 'Big Bill' Haywood, and sentenced to up to twenty years in prison. Like Haywood, Laukki jumped bail and went to Soviet Russia, along with seven others.

object of revolutionising them from within. But Comrade Haywood has handed over his theses on tactics to Comrade Lozovsky, in which he quite definitely approves of joining the trade unions with the object of revolutionising them from within.[6] With regard to the attitude of the IWW towards the necessity of entering the unions: we know there are fractions that are against joining, but there are others – and they represent the majority – who agree with the point of view expressed in Comrade Lozovsky's theses.

With regard to the question of political guidance, I think it is solved in the affirmative sense. If the French comrades think that the IWW in America is opposed to political struggle, they make a great mistake. If the French comrades think that the American IWW will be against political action, against Communist leadership as described by Comrade Lozovsky, they will be disappointed. It may happen that as an organisation it will take such a stand, but it will then be bankrupt. I say this not as an onlooker from outside, but as one who was within their organisations.

The question of entering the trade unions with the object of revolutionising them from within is a question of great importance to the American working-class movement, and arose at the time when I was a member of the American Socialist Party, at the Chicago Convention in 1908.[7] As a matter of fact, Comrade Haywood first became known at this convention in the debates on the question of entering the unions. At the present, as far as I know, the solution of this question in the affirmative is gaining more ground.

These are the considerations that the Finnish delegation has found necessary to put before the congress.

Hampel: Comrade Ramírez has the floor.

Manuel Díaz Ramírez (Mexico): The tactical methods of struggle of the organised labour movement have drawn the attention of the whole congress. The reason for this is self-evident, because upon those methods depends the final aim toward which we are all striving.

On the question of tactics, we discern two tendencies that at first glance seem to be diametrically opposed. One, which offers to concentrate the revolutionary forces within the old trade unions; and the other, to organise new revolutionary trade unions, which by their own example would revolutionise the working masses. In order to be able to judge which of the tendencies is

6 No theses on tactics by Haywood have been located for this volume.

7 The Socialist Party of America's convention in Chicago was held 10–17 May 1908.

better, we must find the reasons that have engendered these tendencies. We ask the question: Are the conditions absolutely the same in all countries? Of course not. Conditions under which purely proletarian organisations are built up in this or that country are different.

A great deal was said here about the attitude of the Industrial Workers of the World towards the American Federation of Labor. The opinion I will express will be impartial, because this problem does not concern me directly. I am able to judge, as I took an active part in the work of both organisations. Many insist upon the absolute necessity of going into the old trade unions in order to conduct a revolutionary struggle there. Others say that it is impossible to work there, and they propose to leave them and create new organisations. I presume that the reasoning of both is quite correct to a certain extent, but the former as well as the latter do not wish to listen to different opinions. I wish to remind you, comrades, that for us revolutionists there is nothing absolute but the revolution itself.

I shall try to prove that both sides are reasoning correctly to a certain extent. There are places in the United States where it is absolutely impossible to revolutionise the trade unions. In other places, we may meet in the trade unions a revolutionary element of the same type and the success of revolutionary work is guaranteed, as for instance, along the Coast. We must bear in mind those years when these trade unions were to some extent the brains of the petty bourgeoisie. I do not mean by this that it is impossible to change the psychology of these trade unions, but I only want to say that it is impossible to do it quickly. I don't know the conditions of other countries, but I fear that something similar to the United States is going on there.

The second point of view is also correct to a certain extent. This is an evident fact, of course, provided the split takes place for some definite reason, and not on account of mere capricious personal considerations or haphazardly.

These two opposing tendencies need to be reconciled. This is the problem we need to solve. This is why we're here. They both must work for the benefit of the revolution. Even if the tactics are different, the final aim is the same. One cannot say that the revolutionary workers who left the big trade-union organisations have failed. This may be proved looking at the syndicalist unions of Italy, Spain, etc., as well as by unions in America.

For instance, it is true that the membership of the Industrial Workers of the World has decreased in number, but in the struggle against the bourgeoisie and the capitalist regime the IWW has justified its existence. If we want to be up to the task, we must go ahead without getting hung up on secondary details. For me, I consider quarrels over words to be hair-splitting discussions.

The congress must prohibit admission to the Red Trade Unions of those who are under the influence of social reformers or avowed reactionaries, and should open widely the doors to the other elements. We should not dwell upon trifles and refuse admission to real revolutionary elements, no matter what they call themselves. Their place must be among us. Such action on our part will prove that we have fulfilled our duty and have done something for the world revolution.

Hampel: Comrades, a motion to close the discussion on the question of tactics has reached me. I put it to the vote. Who is in favour of the motion? The motion is carried. Comrade Dautkus of the *Unionen* is the last to speak.

Leopold Dautkus (Germany, General Workers' Union): Comrades, I consider that at a congress like ours, mutual accusations are out of place. That is why I do not care to take up what Comrades Müller and Malzahn have said here concerning the German nuclei.

With reference to the charge made against us, I must, on behalf of the Free Workers' Union, take exception to the statement made here that some local groups had come out against the central leadership. This however did not take place as far as the union was concerned. There was a meeting of those members who were partisans of Levi; they discussed the question of the alleged decision of the Executive Board of the Free Workers' Union to withdraw from the United Communist Party of Germany. As a matter of fact, the Executive Board passed no binding resolution of any kind, as it did not even have the right to a vote. I want to explain to the comrades of other countries that our union is built from below, and our board has only executive functions, so that all decisions must be sanctioned from below.

Comrades, I wish to say something in the interest of historical truth; it ought to have been said by the comrades from the German nuclei. We read in Rosmer's report and in Lozovsky's pamphlet[8] that the revolution in the trade-union movement began with Comrade Lozovsky's appearance [in Germany]. Comrade Melcher inferred from this that Comrade Lozovsky's work was instrumental in making the first breach in the counterrevolutionary trade unions. For the sake of truth, I want to sketch the birth of the *Unionen* in Germany. The revolutionary movement did not at all start with Lozovsky's trip, though it must be said that the nuclei did begin to form after his appearance. The great bulk of

8 A reference to *The International Council of Trade and Industrial Unions*. In English this pamphlet was serialised in *Industrial Pioneer* in its February, March, and April 1921 issues, and it appeared in several other pamphlet editions.

the workers, at any rate, were not waiting for the elixir that Comrade Lozovsky brought along with him, and should he now come to Germany, he would find that his medical potion had become very much diluted with turbid water from Levi's march. The nuclei in Germany have drifted away from the course contemplated by Lozovsky.

The *Unionen* grew up during the war owing to the dissatisfaction of the working masses with the reactionary tactics of the trade-union leaders. The bulk of the workers became convinced that the reactionary work of the trade unions made it impossible to carry out revolutionary work of any kind. They also found that by remaining within those unions they could not fight against the reaction prevalent there. They therefore left these unions and organised new Free Unions, which rested on the dissatisfaction of the workers, and, based on it, their activities ceaselessly intensified this dissatisfaction. These Free Unions began to form during the war and grew up especially during the revolutionary period. There was a time when the Spartacus League put forward the slogan of 'Leave the trade unions and join the Free Unions!' and this slogan served as a point of departure for the Communist Workers' Party of Germany [KAPD], on the assumption that this slogan reflected the will of the workers. Hundreds of meetings were held under this slogan.

At the Heidelberg party congress, Levi, whom we already considered a traitor at that time, came out, under Radek's influence, against this slogan.[9] Many comrades agree with me that Levi, at Heidelberg, committed the greatest crime against the revolutionary movement in Germany by substituting the slogans of 'Back to the old trade unions!' and 'Out of the Free Unions!' for the slogan 'Out of the old trade unions!'. Imagine what impression this sudden change of tactics – which ran counter to the will of the masses – must have produced on them. This was a great blow against the revolution and the Communist movement.

Comrades, the Free Unions are a historical event. They got a firm footing in spite of the war waged against them by capital and the old trade unions, which in this fight stooped to the most despicable and dirty means. The Free Unions held their ground against the authority of the Third International and against the nuclei too. Were the nuclei not to possess this moral and financial assistance, they would not have withstood this battle so long. The Free Union movement became rooted in the German labour movement. In Germany, the

9 The KPD's Heidelberg Congress was held 20–24 October 1919. Paul Levi led a narrow majority in rejecting ultraleft positions on the trade unions and on participation in parliamentary elections. On Levi's initiative, the congress then resolved to exclude from the party those who did not accept these decisions. The expelled forces later formed the KAPD.

revolutionary workers are in these unions. You cannot tell them, one fine morning, to go back to the old trade unions. They would not do so even if resolutely pushed in the manner done earlier by the Spartacus group. The Free Unions are a product of historical development, while the nuclei – as Lozovsky himself admits – are a hothouse plant artificially brought to life by Comrade Lozovsky.

The tactic of the nuclei is meant to incorporate the great masses. You also say that you have grouped within the trade unions two-to-three million partisans of Moscow. Lozovsky says in his pamphlet, 'What importance can the proletariat attach to verbal recognition? What sense can many promises, programmes, and ambiguous declarations have?' And a few lines further he says, 'Reference to great numbers is of no moment; arithmetical guarantees mean nothing if they have no fighting value'.

Comrades, when the trade unions voted for Moscow or for Amsterdam, what was it if not verbal recognition? Let us decide by a test whether it is idle talk. This can be verified only when they have to show their attitude to Moscow or Amsterdam – not by mere resolutions but by actions. The answer to this question is still to come.

If the comrades, after the close of this congress, should wish to solve it in Germany, they would find that only a small fraction of the two-to-three million would follow Moscow. If three million were really in favour of Moscow, the March rising would have had a different character; more than 200,000 would have come out in the open fight, and the movement would have spread all over Germany. In many places where the tactics of the nuclei were especially pronounced, there were no mass risings.

The March movement speaks precisely in favour of the Free Unions. Hörsing, formerly a trade-union leader and now a hangman of the workers, also proved by his statements that the slogans of the Free Unions were correct. Hörsing brought the SiPo detachments into Central Germany, as the workers no longer obeyed their shop councils.[10] In his proclamation Hörsing said: The workers no longer follow their trade unions, nor do they submit to the authority of their legally elected shop councils. They elect 'wild' committees of action of 'savages' that force the employers to pay their employees for the time they were on strike. These 'wild' committees of savages followed the slogans of the Free Unions and of the Communist Workers' Party of Germany [KAPD]. Thus, Hörsing bears out

10 The Sicherheitspolizei (SiPo) were a militarised security police force set up in a number of German states in 1919.

Otto Hörsing, an SPD member, was governor (Oberpräsident) of Prussian Saxony. On 16 March 1921 he ordered the Prussian police to occupy the province, ostensibly to combat strikes, looting, and acts of violence.

the statement that the workers follow our slogans, while the fact that only a small fraction of the three million participated proves that these millions do not follow Moscow. Were this different, the movement could have developed on a far larger scale.

The great danger is that we rely too much on such statistics. Before the war Germany had 4.5 million socialists. Where did they go when the war began – the very millions who on May Day festivities and at meetings always came out against war? The organisations of nuclei are worth just as much. When the Red Trade Union International is compelled to lead these masses, it will find out that they do not follow it. It can count only on those masses who have broken entirely with Amsterdam.

I want to sketch briefly the way our unions are built, as many comrades are not familiar with the structure of the Free Union movement in Germany. True, we have presented to this congress our theses as a basis for the structure of the Red Trade Union International, but these have not as yet been translated into other languages, so that the comrades who do not understand German have had no chance to get to know these theses. I wish to think that the delay is due to technical reasons, and that the matter will be taken care of. I also handed in theses on the tactic of forming nuclei; our views are stated in these theses more clearly than I could do here in a short time.[11]

The Free Unions did not spring up all at once. They have as yet no answer to every question and are far from perfect; they are just developing, and I wish to acquaint you with the stage of development they have already reached.

The Free Union is based on the factories and is built on the industrial principle. On this point we agree with Lozovsky, who finds it necessary that organisations, in order to fight capitalism successfully with a view of remaining in power after the victory of the proletariat, should be built not by craft but by industry. And we, who have been doing just this, were attacked more than anybody else, and among our critics, the comrades from the Communist nuclei did not take a back seat. In Germany we carried out this principle long ago. From the very beginning our unions were organised such that there was no dictation from the 'top'; the initiative came from below, while the bureaus only carried out the decisions of the rank and file. The success of the revolution demands that the great masses realise the necessity of building up their organisations precisely on these lines. Lozovsky admits this. Thus, we have been correct up to now. Why then are we wrong now?

11 Presumably a reference to the 'Theses on the Tactic of Communist Nuclei' proposed by the General Workers' Union and the Gelsenkirchen Free Workers' Unions, read out to the congress later the same day by Artur Wille. See pp. 453–7.

As to the nuclei, their aims are quite different, as shown by Malzahn's speech at the congress of the Communist International.[12] He said there that it was necessary to win over those elements in the trade unions who dominate at meetings and in executive boards. Consequently, he wants to get on his side not the masses but only the upper crust.

Comrades, who will accomplish the revolution: the leaders or the rank and file? We organise the masses from below, cultivate their class consciousness; we care nothing for the upper strata. We know that the revolution in Germany will call for great individual effort on the part of every worker, because this revolution will be far more bloody than it was in Russia. It needs fighters convinced of the justice of their ideas, and not party leaders sitting in their offices. We must be within the shops in order to be able to draw the masses after us from the factories. (*Explanations and interruptions*) My time is limited, while Comrade Lozovsky will be able to defend your standpoint.

For lack of time, I only wish to read our programme to you.

> The aims of the Free Workers' Union are essentially as follows:
> 1. To unite the proletariat as a class through the factory and workshop.
> 2. To conquer the means of production.
> 3. To manage production.
> 4. To organise the system of production on a collective basis (soviet society).
>
> The immediate tasks of the Free Workers' Union are:
> 1. To revolutionise the factories by means of propaganda and action.
> 2. To lead partial strikes, mass strikes on a large scale, every form of struggle in the factories, and steer the movement in communist channels. As methods, the union recognises strikes, uprisings, passive resistance, factory occupations, systematic sabotage.
> 3. To support all types of revolutionary movements.
> 4. To use propaganda and militant action in favour of revolutionary councils of action within the factories.
> 5. To keep in closest touch and in active solidarity with the unemployed.
> 6. To establish and maintain international communication, especially with Western Europe, with a view toward widening on an interna-

12 Malzahn's speech to the Third Congress on the trade-union question can be found in Riddell (ed.) 2015, *3WC*, pp. 705–8.

tional scale the foundations of the struggle, if possible through the medium of the Red Trade Union International.
7. To show active solidarity with Soviet Russia.
8. To educate the proletariat for passing from words to action.
9. To fight with the greatest energy and determination for the realisation of points 4–8.
10. To consolidate the Free Workers' Union for uniform theoretical and practical action, for successful leadership in the struggle, for carrying out the decisions of the majority, etc.

Comrades, this is a part of our programme. You see that a good many things have been attributed to us incorrectly, that there is a tendency to show us in the wrong light. We are constantly told that we are a small sect.

Well, the Bolsheviks were also a sect, and we take them as a model. The Bolsheviks had 825 members in 1903, 46,046 members in 1907, 172,625 members in 1917, and 705,245 members in 1921. Therefore, the reproach flung at us that we are few means nothing. Just like the Bolsheviks, we maintain that in order to conquer the masses we must have a clear understanding as to our actions. When the fight is on and the masses realise that the Mensheviks betray them, they at the same time fully realise that our organisation suits them best. In spite of the struggle waged against us by the Third International and the nuclei, we have become stronger and numerically surpass the Bolshevik organisation of 1917.

These arguments prove nothing, no more than the claims that we are not among the masses. Are Malzahn and others in the masses? They sit in their central national trade-union bureau and most of them, in addition, are expelled from their unions. And so even they have no chance to work in the trade unions. Where, then, are their masses? Are they at the union meetings, so little attended by the workers? It is a well-known fact that out of one-to-two thousand members of any trade union, only twenty to thirty members come to the meetings. We find in the factories that the masses there are really united. There we, the workers in the factory, are nearer to the masses than the comrades from the centre. This argument is thus also wide of the mark.

We must take stock of historical experience. All revolutions up to the present time have shown that the masses constantly find their true way by instinct. The theoreticians who try to ignore the will of the masses and steer the movement into more rational channels have always proved a drag on the revolution; we fear that the same thing is going on now. The masses follow the right track, and the Russian Revolution is a splendid lesson in this connection.

At the congress of the Communist International, Lenin and others argued that they were forced, in the interest of restoring economic life, to make concessions to capital, since Russia lacked both trained men and technical equipment necessary for restoring its industries.[13] In Germany we have the masses capable of restoring industry, but only on condition that we organise not merely the upper crust – in that case, we would get a dictatorship from above. We admit that we are facing uphill work. But we in Germany do not want to take up the job of organising leaders isolated from the masses.

It is far harder to rebuild industry than to capture political power. As Russia lacks the necessary economic prerequisites, its economic life cannot be put into shape and hence concessions to capital become imperative. Germany and other European countries have workers capable of managing industries; all that is necessary is that they should be united in organisations capable of assuming the management of production. Lozovsky says in his pamphlet that small organisations find no home anywhere, and therefore are compelled to join Moscow. By this he wanted to hint that we did not count.

We, the Free Unions of Germany, have always helped communism in Soviet Russia by word and deed. We took no account of the manner in which we were treated. As long as Soviet Russia is the moral bulwark of communism, we shall follow the same path in the future. But if, under pressure of circumstances, Soviet Russia begins to slide down the slope toward capitalism and becomes an obstacle for the communist revolution, we will unhesitatingly take our stand against Russia.

Hampel: Comrade Lozovsky will now give his summary.

Summary

Lozovsky: Comrades, the discussion on the question of tactics shows that many speakers, instead of speaking on tactics on an international scale, approached this question from a very limited standpoint of their national horizon. This method of considering world problems from the point of view of local interests is a wrong one. An international congress is not a mere arithmetical sum of so many national affiliations, taking account of the internal tactical situation in each country, and compiling them to construct a resolution, which nobody is

13 Lenin's report to the Comintern's Third Congress on the policies of the Russian Communist Party can be found in Riddell (ed.) 2015, *3WC*, pp. 656–71.

obliged to act on. No, an international congress is an organic amalgamation of different trade-union organisations, and its tactics must consider the world experience, whether positive or negative, that we possess in each country. Only then can a congress find the proper expression, the real line of conduct, for the revolutionary trade unions of different countries.

Listening during a whole hour to the co-report of Comrade Bartels, I remembered the ironical words that his compatriot Goethe put in the lips of Mephistopheles: 'When one lacks thoughts, words replace them. Debates are led by words and out of words systems are constructed'.[14] To listen to Comrade Bartels, one would think that there is not in the world a more terrible beast than the trade-union bureaucracy. During one hour he tried to show us how bad and treacherous it is. I don't think that the congress should lose time over such arguments; we all know it, we all agree that the bureaucracy has always betrayed the working class. Talking about it represents merely a useless waste of time. Are we concerned with arguing about it? No, we don't argue as to whether the trade-union bureaucracy is good or bad, whether it has betrayed the working class or not. What we are concerned with is how we shall gain the working masses, the masses who are within the unions.

Comrade Bartels would have been justified if, instead of tracing in black colours a picture of the bureaucracy, if instead of giving an account of his very limited experience of the small Gelsenkirchen union, he had told the congress, on the basis of experience in France, Italy, Britain, and other countries, what tactics should be employed by the trade-union International. It would then be worthwhile talking seriously with him. There are some countries that, on the basis of their practical experience, tactics, and methods, have admitted that the bureaucracy is unconquerable. But if you think this way, then how do you expect to overthrow capitalism? Why do you dream about the social revolution? How will you destroy the bourgeois state? You intend to destroy them all, but you are unable to dislodge Gompers. This is a 'pauper's oath'; it shows that you have not the slightest idea of the internal mechanism of the social struggle. It shows your pessimism, your disappointment in the masses. But if the working masses are hopelessly lost for you, then what is the use of talking? You may talk your head off, but you will not accomplish the revolution. This is why your standpoint is theoretically wrong, and in practice utterly ridiculous.

I will go further. I will ask you: What results would have been brought about if the congress had accepted your slogan? I want to ask you: Who led the struggle

14 A paraphrase from Goethe's *Faust*. The exact words were 'Denn eben, wo Begriffe fehlen, Da stellt ein Wort zur rechten Zeit sich ein. Mit Worten lässt sich trefflich streiten, Mit Worten ein System bereiten'.

of the miners in Britain? The miners. But was the Miners' Federation at the head of the movement? Yes it was. Did other organisations lead this struggle? Did the Shop Stewards direct this struggle? No, the struggle was led by the old organisation of the miners. Why did it lead this struggle? Because the spirit of the working masses is such that despite the treacherous attempts of the leaders, the united and stubborn resistance of the working class compelled them to follow it and unwillingly lead the miners' strike. I ask you: Would we have such brilliant results in Britain, one million miners striking, if we had followed the advice of Bartels? Would we have the spirit, the solidarity, the bravery, and revolutionary inspiration that we have just witnessed in Britain?

Imagine that, at the time of the attack of the employers, at the moment of reducing wages, in a period of economic depression and crisis, we came to the workers and told them: 'Smash the unions, get out of them; we promise you small unions composed of saints'. Then you would be advancing a counterrevolutionary slogan, not because you are counterrevolutionists, but because this slogan is objectively counterrevolutionary. A contemporary union is forced to fight against the policy of wage reduction. It is compelled to organise the masses, fight the old bureaucracy, which always betrayed the masses and will not hesitate to betray them again. This bureaucracy, under the pressure of events, will either have to go with the masses, or it will be cast aside in a scrap heap by the labour organisations. It would be sheer madness, during the period of capitalist crisis and decomposition, to say: 'Down with this organisation, let us build other unions, let us leave these unions without our revolutionary criticism, without our revolutionary influence, without the communist consciousness that we must carry into the masses, by which alone we can raise the masses to the understanding of the big problems of our great heroic epoch.'

I think that no matter how many blocs our Gelsenkirchen comrades will construct, no matter how many resolutions they sign, they will remain fairly isolated, finding perhaps sympathetic feelings among the IWW only. They maintain that their activity will bring about the splitting of the old unions, the creation of new unions. But show us first what you are capable of creating, and then smash the old unions – and not the other way around. It is utterly absurd: 'First get out of the unions, and we promise you the Kingdom of Heaven by and by.' It is utterly absurd, and by acting in this way you will accomplish nothing.

Comrade Watkins, of the British delegation, expressed his agreement with the part of the theses that concerned Russia, but he does not agree with the part regarding Britain. Other comrades say the same thing with reservations regarding their own country. Comrade Watkins even goes so far as to state that he considers the theses to contain a certain Oriental violence with regard to the Western European labour movement. 'Lozovsky', he says, 'reminds me of a spectator at a football game who does not understand the play at all'. This may be a comparison for Watkins, who is a perfect sportsman. I myself am not.

The objection of Watkins reveals the mistakes of the Shop Stewards at present. The worst tactics are when we don't know our own strength and when we overestimate our abilities. A workers' organisation cannot say, 'We will do this and that'. Let us have fewer declarations about what we will do, and more facts of what has already been done. If we follow the history of the Shop Stewards for the last three years, we will see that the influence of the Shop Stewards has diminished. Why? Because they have accomplished their task. They are within the trade-union movement, and to the degree that the masses get revolutionised and their consciousness awakened, the question of little groups and Shop Stewards loses its significance when considered in the light of many millions attracted to the movement. If Comrade Watkins will try to attentively observe the movement, he will admit the correctness of my statement.

Comrade Murphy approached this question more correctly and critically. Our problem does not consist in stating at all times and under all circumstances that everything is fine in our movement, that there is nothing to change or to add. No, everyone must severely criticise our actions. Only then will we be in a position to develop and improve the workers' movement in all countries.

In America again we have two extremes. One side, the IWW, claims as much glory as would suffice for twenty other organisations. This is really exaggerated; they may have performed very big acts in the past, but to maintain, as some are inclined to do, that the IWW is the only organisation in America capable of achieving the revolution means to overestimate by about 95 per cent the real relationship of forces in America. On the other hand, there are comrades who are bending the stick too much in the opposite direction. Those who say that the IWW is of no importance at all are also exaggerating; this too must be avoided.

We should not overestimate the IWW and praise it to the skies, because this sun is not without its spots. What does the IWW lack? First, this organisation has no definite clear-cut policy; its policy is undetermined; they have no theory or practice. I will read you a small quotation from an appeal issued by the IWW in March 1921 that bears the title, 'The Principles and Methods of the IWW'. This appeal was published by the General Headquarters of the organisation in Chicago. It replies to the accusation that the IWW intends to overthrow the democratic order and carry out a social revolution similar to that perpetrated by the Russian 'Robber-Bolsheviki'. This is what it says:

> The I.W.W. is not a revolutionary organisation in the usual sense, like for instance the Sinn Feiners. The I.W.W. never instigated or practiced violence, never preached or practiced destruction of private property, never aspired to and will not aspire in the future to overthrow the government of the United States, its Constitution and its laws.[15]

The fact that one can reach such a stage in which a leaflet is issued in the name of the central body, discrediting the organisation itself, shows that there is no theoretical stability in the organisation, no stable programme. For in reality, how can there be stability when such wavering is possible – when the organisation says today that it is making a social revolution and tomorrow issues such a disgraceful circular. Our task consists in saying, at this congress, 'Comrades, we must have a more stable programme and theory and a clearer method of approaching the question before us'.

Now I come to the last part of my reply. When we consider the workers' movement of the different countries, we come into contact, from the very beginning, with various historical situations and in connection with the form of the social struggle. It would be absolute madness were the congress to settle the tactics of each organisation in advance and for all time. But the congress can and must decide that insofar as we all are going toward the social revolution and toward the opposition of one class against the other in a more acute form, unity in tactics and benefiting from the experience of other countries is absolutely necessary. Otherwise there can be no victory, but only defeat. The theses on tactics are written on this basis. Of course, theses will be altered, because they cannot be faultless, but the arguments of the opposing comrades were absolutely incorrect. Comrade Bartels spoke only from the heights of his small organisation, and the representative of the IWW dealt only with the heroic deeds and merits of his small organisation. But comrades, can we make decisions on the movement as a whole from the merits of a small organisation? How can we tackle the question from such an angle? This only bears witness to the fact that the brains of many of our international comrades have not yet freed themselves of their national experiences. This fact only proves that there is a great deal of work to be done within our organisations in order to free them of all sorts of preconceived notions, and to use the political experiences of each country to find the appropriate methods of struggle in all the other countries.

15 An apparent reference to *The I.W.W., Its Principles, Objects and Methods* by John Sandgren (Chicago: General Defense Committee).

Only from this angle can we approach the question of French syndicalism. When the comrade [Michel Relenque] delivered his speech – which I called his 'revenge speech' – he said that revolutionary syndicalism is the most important movement in the world, that only revolutionary syndicalism can make a revolution and organise the public economy. During the entire course of his speech, in all that he said, we perceived a purely French point of view. First, a certain national tendency of a German character was visible to some extent, and now a national tendency of a French character.

What is it that really interests us at present? Is it the question of who is going to organise the public economy after the social revolution? And why in the course of all your resolutions, in all your rules, do you all the time give three-quarters of your space to the question of what you will do 'after' the revolution? But we are interested in the question of what you will do now, in order to hasten the social revolution, and not what you will do afterward. And in the course of hastening the social revolution, what did you propose other than those famous 'small' revolutionary unions?

Comrade Boisson, who is also in favour of a split, has already created his organisation. It has a membership of 1,000 throughout the whole of France, and for that reason, most likely, it is called the 'Confederation of Workers of the World'. Generally we witness a passion of these organisations for names: the smaller the organisation they succeed in building, the louder and more fantastic its name. This passion for loud names and fancy phrases of which Boisson is a victim – as are very many of the 'industrialists' of America – was revealed here when he spoke from this platform of the reasons why it is necessary to leave the unions. He left them because he did not trust the leaders of the union. But is there a single person in this hall who trusts them? No one, because they are real rascals. But the question does not consist of the fact that we do not believe in them, but in the fact that there are hundreds of thousands of workers who, to our sorrow, still do. To shatter workers' belief in them, to hammer it out of their heads – this is the problem before us, and not to come and say, 'We wrote a very good declaration fifteen years ago, and there were leaders who betrayed it. Therefore, we are gathering our belongings and shaking the dust from our feet, because we are righteous people and do not wish to side with philistines.'

All this will lead to the fact that Comrade Boisson will deliver 99 more speeches during his life on the benefits of syndicalism, but the membership of his organisation will not increase or perhaps in about fifteen or twenty years another fifteen or twenty people will join. If you think that the social revolution can be prepared by such a system, if you believe that by such work you can aid the Russian proletariat, you are greatly mistaken, comrades. You are pushing the revolution back, you are holding back its course. And the French comrades, and other comrades who disagree with me, have proved this in practice. For example, the comrades of the Free Workers' Unions or the comrade from Gelsenkirchen, whose point of view is excessively nationalistic.

In conclusion, I wish to say a few words on the question of principles that Comrade Michel and other comrades of his put forth on revolutionary syndicalism.

We do not intend to declare war on revolutionary syndicalism. We consider that revolutionary syndicalists and Communists are two regiments of the same fraternal, revolutionary proletarian army. Their problem consists in finding one general language, so that our struggle in the different countries might bring the maximum results.

If we raise a theoretical argument against the syndicalists as to whether the CGT in France will make a revolution or not, it will be an utter waste of time. We are interested in the fact that the revolution must be made; that's what interests us! The question as to whether the CGT, Bartels, or someone else will make it is of secondary importance. The point is to make the revolution. Instead of dispersing the various revolutionary forces of the different countries, we must unite them. Instead of wasting your time on absolutely metaphysical arguments that economics is everything and politics nothing, the bourgeoisie – which is wiser than you – knows that both economics and politics are one and the same thing; it does not separate its economic organisations from its political ones. It does not separate its organisations from the whole bourgeois state, and for this reason it inflicts defeats on us.

This, comrades, is why I think that the less our comrades, the revolutionary syndicalists, waste their time on metaphysics, on what they will do after the social revolution, the more they will work on the preparation of the revolution in their country, the more they will learn from the experience of other countries. The less they look down from their summits, the sooner will we come to victorious results and the overthrow of the bourgeois system. Only then shall we settle many debated questions.

The revolution is a great furnace in which all preconceived notions will burn. At the present time the revolution proved that we must learn. If the originators of the Amiens Charter had been told in 1906 that in 1921 the French revolutionary syndicalists would declare themselves in favour of the dictatorship of the proletariat, they would have looked at you as upon an insane person, and it would have been quite natural of them to do so.

As I already said before, facts are stubborn things. Life will teach you. It draws you to us, as it draws us to you. We cannot break up into enemy camps. We have called a congress in order that, at the end of this congress, a strong, welded revolutionary family is formed, so that all internal political differences can be settled jointly by us at moments of danger. Then we will win. Otherwise we will be destroyed, and the social revolution will be delayed for years. (*Applause*)

Hampel: Comrades, the discussion is closed. Before we adjourn I have to inform you that today, from 6:00 to 8:00 p.m., there will be a meeting of the German-speaking delegations, and at the same time the comrades speaking Russian will meet in the Blue Hall to hear Comrade Lozovsky's report on the question of organisation. Please come on time. The plenary session will take place at 8:00 p.m.

(*The session adjourned at 4:25 p.m.*)

SESSION 15. 15 JULY 1921, EVENING

Organisation Report; Women in Unions

(*The session opens at 6:00 p.m. Comrade Hempel in the chair.*)

Chair: Comrade Lozovsky has the floor for his report on the question of organisation.

Report on Organisation

Lozovsky: Comrades, the question of organisation, as it is posed at this congress, is the logical conclusion on the question of tactics and of those basic principles that we have established, on the one hand, in relation to the Communist International and, on the other, with respect to the tactical problems that we have just discussed. The question of organisation is the practical adaptation of our theory. The revolutionary unions must therefore consider it in a different light than do the reformist unions, although both revolutionary and reformist unions have similarities in their organisational tasks.

If we consider the reformist unions in the pre-war period and after the war, we shall see that they had as their task to rally dispersed working-class forces, with the aim of opposing individual employers and groups of them. To unify the workers, to introduce discipline among them, to prepare them for collective struggle – such was then the task of the reformist unions.

The same fundamental tasks face the revolutionary unions. Where then begins the difference between our unions and the reformist ones in the realm of organisation? The difference begins with the methods to accomplish these organisational tasks. The assembly of forces must be achieved by means of a revolutionary struggle and by following revolutionary principles.

If we take as the starting point of our struggle the tactical principles we've established in relation to the Communist International during the period of the struggle against capitalism in its period of dissolution, the whole machinery of the unions, their internal and external structure, need to be adapted to the new tasks posed before the working class in its entirety.

In one of the clauses of my theses dealing with the organisational question,[1] I pointed out that revolutionary unions must develop a spirit of solidarity, class

1 For the Resolution on the Organisation Question adopted by the congress, see pp. 635–48.

 | DOI:10.1163/9789004712867_019

consciousness, and discipline among the workers. If you would ask me to formulate it, I should refer to point 4 of my theses, in which I stated that experience in the struggle is the best school of solidarity, discipline, and class consciousness. It's worth emphasising constantly that organisation is not an end in itself, but only a means to that end. You are wrong if you believe that this last point is something new in the practice of our organising work.

Even among workers in the revolutionary trade-union movement we very often witness a somewhat religious attitude toward the organisation itself. In opposition to this tendency we also have the other extreme – the tendency to conserve forever the unions in their present state. Therefore, in the education of the union's members, we have always borne in mind the aim and not the means. And inasmuch as the means cease to serve our aim, we reject them. The end – the social revolution – remains unchanged, whereas one means can substitute for others.

What then are the new methods we are to introduce on an international scale from the organisational point of view? What are we to oppose to the old trade-union movement? What is the struggle to centre on in the field of organisation? Which slogans are we to put forward?

The best thing is to advance the idea of organising unions by branches of industry. In effect, to oppose the old trade-union movement with its age-old traditions – the movement in America, for example, with its craft unions, its narrow guild interests, its particular hostility toward other categories, and its deeply aristocratic tendencies. To this we counterpose the idea of organisation by branches of industry, of drawing in all the workers without distinction of category into one and the same union. This would signify a deepgoing revolution in the world trade-union movement. The principle of union organisation by branch of industry should be adopted by all revolutionary unions, and should be applied and carried out. This is at the centre of trade-union activity in all countries.

For the Russian trade unions this is an elementary truth, and had the congress been composed of Russian delegates only, the question would be settled at once. The Russian trade unions have already gone through this painful stage of their development, and their experience is an extremely valuable and edifying one for trade unions of other countries. For there is no use in creating an International if the workers of one country do not learn the lessons that other countries are teaching them.

We must recognise that workers' organisations lag behind the employers' organisations in this respect. This is particularly true if we consider the world organisation of the bourgeoisie.

In America, for instance, we find that the employers do not organise by companies, but by trusts in entire branches of industry. The steel trust in America amalgamates, without exception, all the metallurgical companies of all varieties, with all kinds of categories of workers and employees. The factory is nothing but a link in this organisation of employers, and the trust is a type of bosses' federation comprising all enterprises in a given industry.

So what do the American trade unions possess to oppose this? A series of small craft unions and a whole host of 'labour unions' in each company, which serves to weaken and disperse workers' forces and to waste energy.

We must remember that if we consider how matters stand in this respect in Germany, France, or let us say, Britain, we find the same backward state of the labour organisations in comparison with those of the employers. In France too, we find the Comité des Forges, which groups the whole of the metallurgical industry. In Germany we have the colossal amalgamation of the metallurgical factory owners and of the mine owners. This unification of the employers, going beyond the limits of the company and embracing a series of companies, should be a good lesson to the workers. But at the current moment, we regret to say, the workers are at a lower stage of development in comparison with the employers, and therefore are up to the present moment in a state of wage slavery, whereas all the power is concentrated in the hands of the employer.

There is another characteristic trait relating to the way the employers have surpassed the workers in the field of organisation. Already during the war, when it might have seemed that the world was divided in two, when the bourgeoisie of one country was fighting the bourgeoisie of another – even then the spirit of class solidarity of the bourgeoisie was a hundred times stronger than the same spirit among the workers.

Let us cite some examples.

When the German army entered the Briey basin, which possesses iron mines, the French capitalists – as has been proven in numerous documents – easily came to terms with the German capitalists, and they proceeded with their joint exploitation of the mines with the aid of German bayonets. The same thing happened in Belgium. Even now, in the occupied regions of Germany, production is proceeding with the aid of French bayonets.

All this proves that the degree of class consciousness is incomparably higher among the bourgeoisie than among the workers. The capitalists never separate politics from economics. They would consider this question as ludicrous; they know full well that politics and economics are the same thing, and that a class that dominates in economics prevails in politics as well. It is only among the workers that we find heated debates on this question, whereas the capitalists do not waste their time on such metaphysical matters.

In addition to the transformation of craft unions into industrial unions, there is yet another form of union organisation that Western Europe must adopt – a profound change in the very structure of unions: factory committees. What is the connection between factory committees and the working masses? Within an enterprise 10–20 per cent of the workers are organised, with their own representatives and delegates and their own leading committee. But the working masses as a whole have no organ to serve their interests, to reflect their will, to be the expression of the workers' hopes and aspirations. Such an organ needs to be created. We should adopt the watchword of factory committees, and put it into practice.

I have already noted in my report that the bourgeoisie not only understands the nature of its interests, but possesses to perfection the art of drawing lessons from every revolution, and in particular from the Russian Revolution. The bourgeoisie has drawn more lessons than the workers of Western Europe and America did. The great working-class movement that spread in a mighty flood all over the world led to the spontaneous creation of factory committees by the working masses.

I must draw your attention to the fact of how the bourgeoisie reacted to this event, how it approaches this question. The German bourgeoisie adopted forms of organisation in order to render harmless the movement in favour of factory committees. In this the bourgeoisie was at all times aided by the Social Democrats. But the question of factory and shop committees was posed in Germany differently than it had been with us [in Russia]. There, the factory committees are connected with workplace councils. There, they are not called factory committees but 'Betriebsrat', i.e., 'works councils'.

At the time of the revolution in Germany, the election to factory committees depended on the creation of a soviet system, and the fundamental idea was to develop the workplace councils into national soviets that would become the basic economic organ of the entire country. The struggle against the soviets was long and fierce, and resulted in the abolition of the political soviets with the assistance of the Social Democrats and a part of the right wing of the Independents. As for the factory and shop committees, these were given legal recognition.

The same crisis came about in Italy during last year's occupation of the factories, when the movement was kept within the legal framework. The Italian workers also came to the conclusion of the need to create factory committees. In general, the idea of drafting a constitution for factories and workshops is currently popular, and the employers are now arguing in the same way as monarchies did when they were confronted by the danger of a revolution: it's better to declare a constitutional monarchy than to risk having a republic. This policy of concessions is being practised with regard to factory committees.

The revolutionary ferment, which took the concrete form of factory and shop committees, has led to the proclamation of a constitution, the aim of which was to give workers the appearance of certain rights, and to channel the movement into harmless legal bounds. We can see what these limits are from the first paragraph of the law on factory committees in Germany, which reads that they aim to contribute to the successful development of the enterprise.[2] Thus the workers' organisations created for the purposes of fighting capitalism are transformed into agents of capitalism, the aim of which is to contribute to the successful development of the capitalist enterprise.

This is not the moment to discuss the value of the above law. We are concerned only with the practical question – how to replace these bad factory committees with better ones, and what attitude to assume toward the legal shop committees. Some of our revolutionary comrades believe that once the legal factory committees are created, one has to run away from them as from a plague, simply because they move within legal boundaries. This fear of legal bounds is noticed among many of our extreme left-wing syndicalist comrades, who believe that participation in these legal bodies constitutes a deadly sin against the revolution. This is not true. The sin against the revolution consists not of participation in an election to the factory committee in accordance with the law, but of participation in it in the wrong way, and behaving not as revolutionists but as philistines. This is the real sin you are guilty of. For in itself the legal framework is not an insuperable difficulty. The law exists, as we are aware, to be violated. And the proletariat may violate the law if it is well organised.

We must state in a clear and precise way that it is our duty to enter into all the legal factory and shop committees created by the bourgeoisie, using all opportunities to enlarge their functions, develop their activity, and combat the law by means of the law itself. This tactic is a very complicated one and requires flexibility, energy, and revolutionary firmness – qualities that not everybody possesses but which must be acquired in the struggle itself, or else we will not be able to gain victory. That's why the question of utilising these legal factory committees, and other similar institutions, is a practical one and can by no means be disregarded.

It is a characteristic fact that in Germany some of the partisans of the factory committees – especially the General Workers' Union and others – have come to the following conclusion. They say, 'Of course we stand for the creation of factory committees, but in what way do you want us to create them? Are the workers themselves to elect them? But are there not among them Scheideman-

2 For the Works Council Law of 1920 in Germany, see p. 287, n. 15.

nites, Independents, and non-party forces? If the workers are to participate in the elections, it would not be a revolutionary or communist factory committee, but a committee where even Scheidemannites would be represented.' They then devise a trick. They summon their followers to a private meeting (very often only a hundred workers are present out of ten thousand), and these hundred workers elect a 'committee'. They call it 'Betriebsratorganisation', i.e., works council organisation.

Well, it must be said that these councils are merely your party nuclei, but by no means factory committees. Of course, under present conditions, a factory committee is not a great thing, but nevertheless it is the product of the whole mass that works in the factory. In spite of the theory of our extreme left, we must proclaim the following slogan: 'All workers, independently of their political and religious beliefs, must participate in elections to the factory committee'.

It is curious that the extreme left agrees on this question with the Scheidemannites. At a conference of factory committees that I took part in, I heard the Scheidemannites say, 'Only members of political parties may take part in the election. The members of the Christian unions and others are not to participate in the election. It would be opportunism to adopt any other decision.' The Scheidemannites, collaborating with the bourgeoisie, refuse to participate with the workers of the Christian unions in the election of a common body. And this is quite natural; they fear that if all the workers of the given enterprise are to vote, these people would lose their influence and revolutionary workers would win the majority sooner or later. The same narrow views are observed among our comrades of the left who expect to create a factory committee with the help of a hundred followers. This point of view is, of course, ridiculous, and we should oppose it.

The same thing is to be observed in Italy. Again we have the same strange combination of forces. In Italy the Communists stand for the participation of all workers in the election to the factory committees, whereas the Italian Socialist Party and the CGL insist that only workers organised in trade unions should take part. Why then are the Communists, whom no one can suspect of collaboration, partisans of a general election? It's not because they want to collaborate with the Christian unions, of course, but because they want to draw the working masses into the struggle. The election to the factory committees is to be carried out by all the workers, and we must struggle within the organisations and not isolate the revolutionary workers into separate organisations. The question of factory committees is a very important one for the progress of the trade-union movement.

Thus we must break the old traditions. To reach the most backward, it is necessary to come out in favour of factory committees as a powerful means of revolutionary struggle. Revolutionary unions must put forward this slogan not only as a principle, but as the practical problem of the day.

Let us take up the following question, which agitated our congress for many days: What is our attitude toward the old unions? When I heard the long speeches of the comrades in which they were stating that the old unions are counterrevolutionary organisations, I always felt that it was a philosophy of weakness, which finds its expression in revolutionary phraseology. I cited one instance that perfectly illustrated all the absurdity of this point of view. If the slogan 'Leave the unions' was really dangerous, would the Amsterdam International have taken the decision to expel from the unions all followers of Moscow as well as all Communists? Does it not strike you as absurd that the same slogan is proclaimed by Amsterdam and by the comrades of the extreme left? We must tell the comrades, 'Your slogan coincides with that of Amsterdam. Therefore think it over thoroughly before you propose it to the unions.'

We must lead the most resolute and energetic struggle against such pessimistic views, against such distrust of the working class. For if we are really to believe that withdrawal from the trade unions is necessary, would it not mean that the workers of these unions are entirely lost for the revolution? But if 10 million German workers organised in trade unions are lost for the cause of the revolution, by what means would you accomplish the revolution? That's why this slogan, in spite of all its apparent revolutionary spirit and the effect it is apt to produce, does not breathe the revolutionary spirit and contains not a bit of revolutionary practical sense.

In Germany we found two extreme points of view on this question. On the one hand, there are comrades who say, 'Leave the trade unions at any cost'. On the other hand, we have Communists who shudder at the mere thought of a split in the unions. This is a fetishism that will only bring harm. With us the unions are only the means for the achievement of a certain aim. And inasmuch as it is so, we may, in the one case, stand for the complete unity of the organisation; in the other case, for splitting it if there is no other way out. This point must be firmly established at our congress, composed of revolutionary unions that base concrete practical activity and tactics on an accurate assessment of conditions.

If from these general problems we are to pass immediately to the problems before us, especially in the big countries, we must say that they are defined by the development and of the struggle that has taken place and the relations between the social forces within these countries at the present time.

In Britain, for instance, the question is quite simple, much simpler than in Germany. The trade-union movement in Britain is now undergoing a great transformation. Within the gigantic British trade unions a powerful fermentation is going on. The economic breakdown, the world economic crisis, finds its reflection within these unions. And in the same way as at sea the waves smooth the rocks, the separate outbursts, the separate economic conflicts and crises, smooth and sweep away the old tendencies within the trade unions. A new world outlook is being formed, new devices, new methods of work; finally a revolutionary spirit begins to animate the old craft-union machinery.

The task incumbent on the trade-union movement in the Western European countries consists in working within the unions. By no means are tiny organisations to be created, even if they bear the name of 'International Confederation of Labour' or 'One Big Union', etc., as we often observe in the Anglo-Saxon countries. It is necessary to work within these organisations. Our work should develop organically with the growth of these organisations.

If we consider the British trade-union movement, we note that among the 20 per cent of metalworkers that, according to the statement of Tom Mann, are disposed in our favour, we still lack any organisation and support within that union. From case to case, from meeting to meeting, our resolutions gain the majority, but this attitude in our favour among the working class is not organisationally consolidated. Our task should be to provide an organisational form, and to reinforce the unofficial organisations, such as nuclei and workers' committees within the union. We must try to bring these into the working-class movement and little by little extend their influence, sweeping away the trade-union bureaucracy and replacing it with workers animated by a revolutionary spirit and conscious of the historical problems before them.

In France the labour movement was on the whole developed in the right way in the field of organisation, and the syndicalist comrades took the right position by declaring themselves against a split. And when the council of the district unions decided to withdraw from the CGT on account of the betrayal of its executive committee, our comrades declared themselves unanimously against it. They were quite right, for by no means is an organisation to be destroyed on account of betrayal by its leaders; the betrayal should be taken advantage of only for the conquest of the workers and securing our influence in the unions. But withdrawing from the union, causing its destruction, can by no means be resorted to.

We have an instance in France of how such a withdrawal affected a union bearing the high-sounding name of Confederation of Workers of the World. This organisation boasts of having 1,000 members, but we rather doubt the truth of that statement. Even if it really contained 1,000 workers, however, this number is ridiculously small for France as a whole. And this dwarfish organisation entertains the pretension of substituting, neither more nor less, for the General Confederation of Labour. These ridiculous pretensions prove clearly that people show no discrimination whatever in considering the great problems before them. They deem it sufficient to organise several hundred workers, and imagine that one fine evening they will be able to achieve the social revolution with the support of this handful. Such a humorous conception of the social revolution clearly exists in France among many of our comrades. Such a conception ought to be uprooted entirely. The social revolution is a difficult task requiring an enormous preparatory work and detailed, systematic, stubborn activity. The above-mentioned attitude toward social revolution shows a total lack of comprehension of the epoch we are now living through.

The state of things in Spain is a very characteristic one. Spain is a country permeated by a syndicalist spirit. There are two organisations: the revolutionary syndicalist one, which is represented at our congress, and the reformist one. In 1920 an attempt at unification was made, but this unification was not realised in the economic struggle and was unsuccessful. The Spanish syndicalists are great opponents of centralism, because they believe it to be very much akin to communism, whereas they are faithful adherents of Bakunin. They have abolished all their national structures organised by branch of industry. They have no Spanish national union of metalworkers, textile workers, and so on, because such organisations, in their opinion, are apt to develop bureaucratic tendencies within the labour movement, as the result of a central committee. In their view, it is better to destroy the central committee. It reminds me of the German proverb about pouring out the baby together with the bathwater. What are we to think about this abolition of the central committee? This is federalism reduced to an absurdity. The organisations are, in fact, built on the following principle: they have a local union, then a council of unions, and nothing else. No national federation of metalworkers, and each province organising itself independently. In short, they have no centre.

I tell them: Let us admit that it gives you a certain advantage in the struggle against the bourgeoisie, although I have my doubts about that. But what about the social revolution? You hold the view that the CNT will be the instrument to organise the effort of the masses. But how are you to organise propaganda? Are you to develop your actions by province? You lack the organs that would unify industry on a national scale. It is sufficient to put this question forward to become convinced at once that the fears of centralisation are leading our Spanish members too far, and that they are cutting off the branch on which they are sitting. We must point out that a federation of this kind is greatly detrimental to the realisation of the social revolution, and particularly on the day after it, when the question of economics will be raised. These are the reasons why we must declare ourselves against this irregular and distorted federalism.

As to Germany, its situation is a very complicated one. There are too many organisations there. On the one hand, we have the reformist organisations, the so-called free trade unions [*freie Gewerkschaften*, a reference to the ADGB], comprising 9 million members. We have the Christian unions embracing 2 million members. And lastly, the workers' unions with syndicalist tendencies with 600,000 members. Within the free trade unions a strong revolutionary Communist movement is observed, embracing approximately 20 per cent of the workers. The Free Workers' Union has adopted the revolutionary syndicalist view. It has inherited the principles that were proclaimed in France some fifteen to twenty years ago. Now they are frozen in the old position, and have not been taught any new lessons during the last fifteen years.

On the other hand, there exists the Gelsenkirchen Free Workers' Union. This organisation had its origins in 1912[3] and embraces 150,000 workers, animated with a very revolutionary spirit, and having somewhat vague ideas and sometimes rather confused practical views. The representatives of this organisation, present here, also proclaim the slogan 'Leave the unions!' and believe that solely in this way, by splitting and smashing the unions, the workers' movement of Germany is to be cured from the ulcer of reformism and opportunism.

Lastly we have the General Workers' Union [AAU] under the leadership of the Communist Workers' Party of Germany [KAPD]. This organisation also shows very revolutionary tendencies and stands for smashing the trade unions.

This panorama of shadings is by no means a sign of strength of the revolutionary left in Germany, but rather attests to its weakness. At a time when the bourgeoisie, in agreement with the Social Democrats and reformists, presents a united front, on the left we have the above organisations, which instead of joining together in a struggle against the common enemy, are biting each other's noses, as the French say, and are doing it very successfully.

Besides the above organisations there are, at present, tens of thousands of workers expelled from the unions. Whole local branches of unions have been expelled. In Chemnitz, 3,000; in Halle, 4,000. What is to be done with these expelled branches and with the expelled in general? The question is rather complicated. To leave them unorganised and dispersed, to abandon them to their own fate without paying any attention to them – this would be inadmissible in the revolutionary movement and among revolutionists. They must be organised. But how?

3 The year 1912 appears in all languages of the proceedings. It is unclear what Lozovsky is referring to, however, since neither the Free Workers' Union of Germany (FAUD), nor the Gelsenkirchen split-off from it dates from that year.

In Germany we observe a tendency to outline these questions in the following way: In each trade a union is to be formed composed of the expelled workers. We shall have thus an organisation of textile workers, an organisation of those expelled from the metalworkers' union, an organisation of those expelled from the woodworkers' union, and so on. Later on these groups will amalgamate and form a national federation that is to lead the struggle, having for its slogan, 'Down with the splitters!'. Whether this slogan is adopted or not isn't important. That is a secondary question. The essential question is: By what means can we compel the working class to reflect on the fact that workers who had for many years paid their membership dues to the treasury of their union are now deprived of the support of this union, are thrown out, are expelled merely for their adherence to the Moscow International. Each worker should oppose this violence toward the members of the given union. If we organise them in this way, they will no longer be a dispersed mass. It would be a group of about thirty-to-forty thousand linked organisationally. It would be an organisation that helps in breaking down the old trade unions, encouraging the workers to reflect on the violence and brutality that the trade-union bureaucracy is committing.

Is there another way out of the difficulty? Some comrades have great doubts on the matter. If some of them shout, 'Out of the unions!', the others refuse to organise themselves even if they are expelled. Comrades, if you're expelled – organise yourselves! It's not just the Communists who were expelled. When the Communists are expelled, they still have their own organisation they belong to. But when 4,000 metalworkers were expelled in Halle, not all of them were Communists; they were just revolutionary workers. They will not all enter the party and will consequently remain unorganised. You risk losing several thousand workers. For the sake of what will you lose them? To this they answer: 'If we organise them, we shall play into the hands of the splitters.'

A new course of action must be brought forward, and it is brought forward by life itself. It must be carried out whatever the cost. The very fact that expelled comrades will be immediately received into the United Trade Union of Germany will make the union bureaucrats think about it. These people would not expel workers so lightly. The expulsions would lose their character as epidemics, and this organised action would render us an enormous service in the struggle against the trade-union bureaucracy, and contribute to strengthening the revolutionary movement within the old trade unions.

I still have the question of Italy to touch upon. The situation of Italy is a very peculiar one, which was already mentioned at this congress. The General Confederation of Labour [CGL] sends us its delegates for purposes of information. The Union of Railway Workers also sent its delegates for the purpose of information. In short, the thirst for information is very great in Italy. All three types of trade-union organisations in Italy have sent their delegations, expressing their warm sympathies to the Red International of Labour Unions. But up to now these sympathies have not inspired any concrete acts. There is in Italy a CGL comprising 2.3 million members. Then there are two independent unions: a union of railway workers and transport workers, embracing 600,000 workers; and the Italian Syndicalist Union [USI], comprising approximately 200,000 workers. The latter unions are purely revolutionary syndicalist organisations.

What are we to tell the Italian workers on the question of organisation? The Italian proletariat, contrary to the German, British, and American working class, is animated with a deeply revolutionary spirit. It is full of energy, and we must show at this congress that there is no serious reason for these organisations to remain outside the CGL, even if this organisation is headed by waverers, reformists, and so on. The task of revolutionists is to enter this organisation, to defend their views within it, and to revolutionise the unions. The economic unity of the working class in Italy is a very urgent matter. The latest events that have taken place in Italy showed to what degree the Italian working class is disorganised in the face of the bourgeoisie.

The situation in America is already known to you, comrades. The American proletariat consists of 30 million workers. Approximately 12 per cent of them constitute the forces of the American Federation of Labor, i.e., about 4 million workers; and 30,000 belong to the IWW. Thus 10–12 per cent of the American proletariat is in the American Federation of Labor; 10 per cent of this 10 per cent are organised in the IWW. Besides the above organisations there are independent unions, and within the American Federation of Labor some local organisations are affiliated to us. What is to be done in so complicated a situation, given the reactionary character of the AFL?

Given the reactionary spirit of people like Gompers and Company – who consider even the Amsterdam International to be red – it is not surprising that American workers begin to believe it necessary to smash this federation. If we were to decide that there would be no revolution in America, we might then give up not only the AFL, but the IWW as well, which works for the destruction of the former. But if we acknowledge that the objective conditions for a revolution exist in America, we must adapt our work so as to go where the masses are, to keep in constant touch with them, and by no means to isolate ourselves as our comrades from the IWW do. True, they have worked out a good plan in the field of organisation, with many provisions that we carried out in our unions after the October Revolution. They want to build their unions on the industrial principle; they want to create an organ that would regulate the public economy.

This is their merit. But the masses do not follow them and are estranged from them; they probably believe the revolution can be made exclusively with their 30,000 members.

We must fight against their error in a fraternal, comradely way. We can give them the advice: (1) that all comrades, members of the IWW, should remain members of the other organisations affiliated to the AFL; (2) that the actions of the workers, members of the IWW, should be coordinated with the organisations that belong to the AFL but already share our views and therefore should be considered as revolutionary unions. We cannot admit that the organisations that have proclaimed here their adherence to the Red International of Trade Unions would, on their arrival back in their countries, stab each other in the back instead of organising a coordinated action against capitalism.

Approaching the end of my report, I want to draw your attention to one of the most complicated questions that we have to decide in the field of organisation: this is the question of the international federations by branch of industry.[4] On the eve of the war we had about thirty such international federations: the international federation of textile workers, cap makers, miners, woodworkers, etc. These federations were destroyed in the course of the war and re-created after the formation of the Amsterdam International. But they took the form of international information bureaus for purposes of mutually forwarding each other statistical data and their materials. How can we be satisfied with this role in the epoch we are living in?

If these international federations were to have any value at all for us, it would be only if they are organisations for revolutionary purposes, as we need no organisations of a purely formal character. Therefore, the task of the international federations should consist in instilling a revolutionary spirit, a programme of battle, and a course of action based on our struggle and our everyday activity. We should participate in all the congresses of textile workers, of metalworkers, etc., and raise at these congresses the question of Amsterdam or Moscow, and all other questions posed before the trade-union movement in all countries.

The question is complicated by the fact that some of our comrades follow the slogan of 'Out of the unions!', while the yellow unions, for their part, are preparing to expel all the unions that adhere to Moscow.

In view of this, we have to consider whether we are now to create red international federations of transport, textile, and metalworkers, etc. – yes or no?

4 For the international trade secretariats affiliated to the Amsterdam International, see p. 395, n. 22.

I believe that to create such federations at the present time would be premature. It might suffice for us to create ten or fifteen international propaganda committees among the textile, transport, wood, metalworkers, etc., and begin propaganda in the respective unions in various countries in order to win them to our cause. Only when we have secured sufficient forces and selected a definite quantity of organisations can we develop these propaganda committees into larger and more important groupings and turn them into something more.

I will pass on now to two questions touched on in my theses on organisation: these are the question of the trade-union press, and the question of work and propaganda among young people. These questions are very simple; everybody understands that a good press is necessary. As to the work among the youth, I think it necessary to say a few words on the subject.

Many trade unions paid insufficient attention to young people, and did no propaganda work among them. The old unions confined themselves to trade and technical education. But our task is different: we must work at the political-communist education of youth. It is quite different work, and we must draw the attention of the revolutionary unions to this point. It is significant that in all countries the youth organisations were the first to declare themselves against the war and for the Third International. This was not accidental. Young people naturally respond quickly to events. If we intend to secure firm ground for our proposed work, if we want to go within the working masses, as revolutionary unions, we have to pay particular attention to the young generation that is working in the factories and workshops. We must pay attention to them not only because they are our allies who march with us toward the revolution, but because the old generation has seemingly grown weary and a new generation will replace it, one better prepared for the struggle for our cause.

The last question is this: What does our International of Red Trade Unions represent? Is it similar to the old International, where one can enter or leave as one wishes? Does the Red International of Trade Unions freely grant entry to any group of workers simply because they have employment papers? No, we cannot share such a formal point of view. If we adopted such a view, we would be transformed into a second edition of the Amsterdam International, to which anyone could adhere on very formal conditions without assuming responsibility for the decisions taken, or any obligations with regard to the class struggle of the proletariat.

We have formulated five conditions. They are simple, but have the character of ultimatums for organisations that wish to affiliate to the Red International of Labour Unions. These conditions, comrades, are the following:

1. Not just verbal recognition of the class struggle, but genuinely carrying it out in the daily struggle. The class struggle was recognised even in the old constitutions of the unions and has become a cliché. We believe it necessary for the class struggle to be realised in the day-to-day struggle.
2. Recognition of the dictatorship of the proletariat. Our organisation is a non-party one. It admits Communists, non-communists, revolutionary workers, anarchists alike – to all those who want to destroy the old system. Nevertheless, a certain minimal agreement is indispensable in order to fight. Without such an agreement, without a common basis of unity, some would be shooting in one direction, while others would aim the opposite way. One such condition is recognition of the dictatorship of the proletariat, recognition of the need to forcibly destroy capitalism, and the need to break the resistance of the exploiters by means of the united forces of the working class. What forms it would assume is a secondary question. What is important for us is that the workers' organisations affiliated to the International should know that only through the overthrow of capitalism and the establishment of the dictatorship of the proletariat is there a possibility to achieve our aims, to lay out the tasks before us.
3. Prohibition of simultaneous affiliation. You remember, comrades, our discussion on the Italian question, and how some of the organisations were trying to sit down with both sides. One of the two must be chosen: either Amsterdam or Moscow.

Today I had very interesting news from Berlin. We have lately become so important a power that our enemies now resort to new slogans. They proclaimed before: Either Amsterdam or Moscow. Now they proclaim: 'Moscow *and* Amsterdam'. This is a recognition of our strength. They recognise that we have become a real power, forcing them to come up with a new slogan. They believed formerly that we were just a bunch of Bolsheviks who had invented some kind of a Red International of Trade Unions, whereas now they're afraid to put the question squarely: Moscow or Amsterdam. And they begin talking of 'Moscow *and* Amsterdam'. They want to find a synthesis of these two organisations.

In this period of the struggle, to be in both organisations at the same time should be absolutely inadmissible. The break from the Amsterdam International and a formal withdrawal from it should therefore be the necessary condition to be fulfilled before affiliating with the Red International of Trade Unions.

4. I already spoke of the need for unity of action by the trade-union organisations, and this, comrades, should also be one of our conditions. At this congress some of the countries have sent representatives from three, four, five different organisations. Why not? They can all be members of the Red

International. But can we now admit them to vote with us for our resolutions, and then return home and wage a struggle against each other instead of working on the basis of the platform adopted by our congress? We must put as a necessary condition the coordination of action in each country for a joint struggle against the bourgeoisie. If not, the same situation would be created as in Germany when, during the March days, the Communists struggled arms in hands and were shot, while the syndicalists indulged in mud-slinging at them and abused them in the press even more than the Scheidemannites did. We create our International not for purposes of joking or singing 'The Internationale' together, but for the guidance and coordination of our work and action.

5. What then are the conditions upon which we are to build this International? Everyone must acknowledge international proletarian discipline. It is inadmissible for us to adopt a decision today and then tomorrow each organisation would begin to act in whatever way it chooses, every way other than the way adopted by the congress. The congress establishes international proletarian discipline and considers its decisions binding and obligatory: whoever disagrees with these decisions, finds them inadequate, etc., can carry on discussions within the respective organisations in a friendly, fraternal, comradely way, up to the next congress, but unity of action should not be violated. Submitting to the decisions of the congress should be obligatory. It is the fifth and last condition of affiliation with the International.

The general conclusion to be drawn from this examination of the question of organisation is the following: we must carry out our work in the Red International according to an international plan. In each country we should do this in such a way that every day the smallest actions prepare the consciousness of each individual worker of the necessity of a revolutionary dictatorship of the proletariat, and that each step forward in the field of organisational work within the union aspires to the same aim. This is the sole aim that guides us in our practical everyday activity, which we can and must achieve.

As I stated at the beginning of my report, the organisational question is the logical consequence of the premises we made when we debated and defined our line of action. Our organisational tasks are the logical consequences of the course of action we have adopted. The entire organisational structure of the unions, our everyday activity, our approach to individual workers and groups of workers – all our work within the old unions should be directed toward one aim: to prepare the workers' organisations for the social revolution, so that each separate small union, each small organisation should, in its everyday work, always have this great aim in view. Only then will we be able to put on a proper basis our understanding of the organisational tasks of the revolutionary unions in the period we are now passing through.

Chair: We have a quarter of an hour left before the opening of the plenary session in the Great Hall. Time is too short for a wide discussion on the question. All that is stated and developed here on an international scale is the simple formulation of the path we have taken, the obstacles we have surmounted during the last three years of our revolution. I believe that this consideration gives us, as well as the reporter, full freedom of action at this congress and allows us to be in a privileged position. I therefore take the liberty to move that the report of Comrade Lozovsky be adopted as the foundation in the course of our further debates and discussions on it. (*Adopted*)

Lozovsky: I move in the name of the Russian, Lithuanian, and Baltic delegations that no general discussion be taken up at the congress, as the question of organisation is a logical inference from the tactics, and that this report be referred to the commission. The report will be translated in the four languages.

Chair: Is there any objection to Comrade Lozovsky's motion? No. Adopted. I declare the session closed.

(*The session adjourns to the Great Hall.*)

Session in the Great Hall

Lozovsky: Comrades, at this morning's session we closed the discussion on the question of tactics, and now we put to a vote the theses on this question before referring it to the commission for further discussion. The question is whether the congress should adopt the theses [on tactics] moved here as the basis of further discussions in the commission, or whether it would adopt other theses. Up to the present moment no other theses have been handed in, although the comrades from the German *Unionen* intended to bring in a counter-draft.

Bartels (Gelsenkirchen Free Workers' Union) (*from his seat*): Our theses on the organisation of nuclei and the structure of the Red International of Trade Unions have been given to the Presidium.

Lozovsky: Who is assigned by the Free Unions to read your theses?

Bartels (*from his seat*): Comrade Wille.

Lozovsky: Comrade Wille has the floor to read the theses.

Artur Wille: Comrades, the German *Unionen* propose the following theses on the question of the formation of nuclei:

Theses on the Tactic of Communist Nuclei Proposed by the General Workers' Union and the Gelsenkirchen Free Workers' Union

I *General Considerations*

1. Since the Second Congress of the Communist International, experience has demonstrated that the creation of Communist nuclei within non-communist unions or organisations with the object of winning over those organisations to our side may be useful only in some cases and under certain conditions. The fundamental condition consists in that the dialectical law of the development of contradictions has not yet manifested itself. The nuclei may be formed only in such organisations where the relations and ideology are of a primitive character, where the revolutionary striving of the workers is vague, and where they do not yet understand that their traditional ideology is in contradiction to a clear communist consciousness.

The second condition is when the workers in question, for one reason or another, come into open struggle with their exploiters. The Communists can under such circumstances, influence the struggle to the extent possible, or when in a country the struggle cannot take place yet and the Communists have to limit their activities to pure propaganda.

2. These conditions are absolutely necessary. But even with these conditions, it is essential to carefully examine the position to see that the danger arising out of the formation of nuclei should not be greater than the gains from an organisational point of view.

The dangers of this open policy of creating nuclei with the object of conquering the unions becomes quite apparent in countries with a highly developed industry and a conscious workers' movement, even if dormant through disuse. These factors are the following:

(a) In countries with a highly developed capitalist system the chief support of capitalism is the democratic illusions of the masses, their belief in the unconquerable power and stability of the capitalist system. These illusions are reflected in almost all workers' organisations. To belong to such organisations (trade unions, cooperatives, etc.) means to strengthen them as well as these illusions, instead of propaganda for their destruction. Thus, under such circumstances, these open tactics of the nuclei lead to the strengthening of the domination of capital and have a negative, counterrevolutionary influence.

(b) In all countries with a highly developed capitalist system – especially in those where the workers' movement has long been in existence – the workers have an entirely incorrect idea of their position and of the course of action that is necessary. These ideas are so deeply rooted in them that they have a uniform opinion on all questions. In such case the law of development of contradictions manifests itself. If the Communists intervene under such circumstances, they will quickly replace the groups, giving rise to a new view on all questions in contradiction to the old ideas of the last ten years. If the Communists, in order to avoid the consequences of such a position (in the form of 'militant' nuclei), strictly adhere to the old form of organisation, they will, by so doing, arrest the development of the contradictions and of the old ideology, i.e., instead of helping to develop class consciousness in the working class, they will retard the development of this consciousness. Therefore:

(c) Under such conditions the Communists using this (open) tactic of conquering through the nuclei begin to be in contradiction with themselves, because, on the one hand, they carry out propaganda to preserve and fortify the old organisations, renounce every intention of splitting the unions, and defend the unity of organisations against the yellow bureaucracy, and, at the same time they create inside these organisations their own separate organs. Such a tactic, as proved by the experience of the whole workers' movement, leads toward the inevitable destruction of the organisation. The workers look upon such an action as disloyal toward their interests. A disloyal attitude toward the capitalists and their agents would be no reproach to the Communists, but disloyalty toward the broad working masses separates the Communists from the masses to a far greater degree than an open and deep divergence of views.

II *The Nuclei in the Trade Unions*

3. From the theoretical point of view, the above-mentioned tactic of creating nuclei can succeed, with regard to trade unions in countries with a highly developed capitalist system, in two directions. It may lead either to their capture, or toward splits and collapse. In the first case the Communists gain an important weapon for the social revolution; in the second case, the Communists destroy a weapon of the counterrevolution.

4. The conquest of the yellow trade unions on a large scale by the Communists is a matter upon which one need not be very hopeful. The events in the German free trade unions [the ADGB] show that the bureaucratic officials have begun to expel from the unions the main leaders of the nuclei in order to destroy the movement at its root. They base their action upon the objective factor of the destructive work of nuclei, and upon the subjective view of the workers as to the disloyalty of those who advocate the creation of the nuclei.

If the Communists wish to avoid such reproaches, they will have to keep within bounds of time-honoured trade-union policy. But in that case they would retard the development of the masses' revolutionary consciousness and would risk falling into absolute opportunism. The participation of members of the Communist Party in trade-union leadership bodies does not constitute the conquest of the unions for communism. The general condition of the life of the trade-union official separates him from the worker and draws him nearer to the petty bourgeoisie. The hope of obtaining an important post will always attract elements who are nothing but specimens of the social-democratic petty bourgeoisie. In a great majority of cases it appears that people accepting positions in trade-union leadership bodies are not Communists and do not understand the responsibilities of such workers toward communism.

5. If it happens that a union is conquered by the tactic of the Communist nuclei, it is apparent that the machinery of such a union inevitably will represent a weapon that is useless for the working class and for the revolution.

(a) The masses in the trade unions, owing to traditional democratic methods employed there, are not prepared for battle, but only for a policy of reconciling differences, negotiations, and passivity. The struggle to win the majority in the unions, as far as it is carried out within legal bounds, reinforces this tendency. Merely belonging to the Communist Party does not guarantee against strengthening this tendency.

(b) The whole machinery of the trade unions is adapted to leading peaceful, legal strikes.

(c) The funds of the trade unions that are being utilised in cases of strikes, unemployment, accidents and death, etc., have an even more counterrevolutionary influence than the laws of state insurance. Thanks to this, the idea of a true revolutionary movement is foreign to workers. They have gotten used to adapting their struggle to the amount in their strike fund.

(d) In revolutionary periods each strike must rapidly take on a direct revolutionary form; otherwise it will soon lose its strength and will be suppressed. It is therefore necessary that it should begin at once, that its development should proceed quickly, and that at the very beginning the most effective means should be exercised, up to drawing in the masses through sympathy strikes. But the trade unions are not fit for such activities at all. The preliminary negotiations that take place in various executive units on the eve of a strike make the policy of sudden action impossible and weaken the combative energy of the workers.

The application of illegal means in the strike is impossible owing to the legalistic spirit of the masses and the utter weakness of the trade-union machinery in face of the government apparatus. The participation of the masses is hindered by the existence of separate craft unions, by the statutes of the unions ratified by law. If the movement develops despite all this, it inevitably leads to the ruin of the organisation and the exhaustion of the strike funds. Thus, the trade unions during every serious strike are exposed to the danger of debacle. The masses and the Communist leaders are therefore compelled to avoid serious actions in order to preserve the organisations. The organisation becomes an end in itself, and precisely for this reason, is not suitable for the revolutionary struggle.

(e) The organisation of the trade unions gets workers used to thinking that someone else is to act for them, that they themselves can remain passive. Thus it holds back the propagation of the idea of soviets. In times of revolution, in order to successfully fight capitalism and overthrow it, real revolutionary organisations are necessary that are imbued with the spirit that the emancipation of the workers must be achieved by the workers themselves.

6. The old trade unions would likewise be completely powerless to organise the restoration of the economy during the dictatorship of the proletariat. So long as they exist they would preserve their social-pacifist, Menshevik ideology, which is impossible to cover with Communist phraseology. The machinery of the old trade unions, no matter who governs these, would inevitably stand in the way of the formation of soviets, and would prepare the ground for handing the proletariat back over to the bourgeoisie. Ultracentralised and competing with each other, craft unions that exclude the active participation of ordinary workers are not capable of reorganising a complicated economy of countries with a highly developed industry.

7. Inasmuch as the above-mentioned tactic leads either to destruction or split, it only removes an obstacle to the revolution but does not create anything positive. Isolated Communist nuclei are obliged to limit their activities to certain localities or trades. They do not possess the apparatus that could be adapted to modern conditions of isolated economic struggles, not to mention the revolutionary struggle for power. They will, as in the past, hinder the manifestation of the initiative of the workers, and will thus be an obstacle in the development of soviets. It is necessary to destroy all illusions among the workers that it is possible to achieve anything by such methods. The complete incapacity to answer the question of what is to be done after the destruction

of the unions by the revolutionary nuclei proves that such a destruction is no victory on the way to the social revolution.

8. Taking into consideration the dangers that cannot be counterbalanced by the corresponding advantages, the First Congress of the Red International of Trade Unions categorically rejects the tactic of nuclei for countries with a highly developed industry, and binds the organisations affiliated to the Red International of Trade Unions to cease every attempt begun in this direction.

Wille (*continues*): Comrades, we have handed in these theses to the Presidium, and we were promised that they would be translated into Russian, French, and English. We hope that this will be done and that the different delegations will be able to define their attitude toward them. At the same time, I wish to remark that I have handed in our theses on the structure of the Red International of Trade Unions to Comrade Lozovsky. We are surprised that it has not appeared in the newspaper *Moscow* up to now, so that the delegates might become acquainted with them.

Lozovsky: We have thus two sets of theses: one proposed by the Russian delegation; the other introduced by the German *Unionen*. We shall now take a vote as to which we shall take as a basis.

Bartels (*from his seat*): I propose to accept both sets as a basis.

Lozovsky: It is impossible to accept two resolutions that are diametrically opposed to each other. The theses of the German unions exclude the Russian theses and vice versa.

We go now to the vote. The Russian theses will be considered as the first; the theses of Bartels and his comrades will come second. The vote will be taken in the usual form, according to the numerical representation of countries.

Permit me to announce the result of the vote: for the first theses (Russian delegation): Britain, Germany (11 out of 16), Poland, Russia, France, Czechoslovakia, Austria, Hungary, Bulgaria, Yugoslavia, Ukraine, Norway, Australia, Switzerland, Canada, Greece, Sweden, Denmark, Finland, the Far Eastern Republic, Azerbaijan, Armenia, Georgia, Latvia, Lithuania, Luxembourg, Estonia, and 13 delegates of the United States. Altogether 270 votes. The Spanish delegation has abstained from voting; Romania, Belgium, and Mexico were absent during the vote. Thus the first theses are adopted. Tomorrow morning it will be referred to the commission.

A declaration signed by six organisations has been handed in to the Presidium. Comrade Bartels will read it.

Arthur Bartels: Comrades, our motion reads thus:

> The First World Congress of the Red Trade Union International considers the organisations of the revolutionary syndicalists, the Industrialists [IWW], and the [Free] Unionists to be revolutionary class-struggle organisations. All organisations that have joined the Red Trade Union International must therefore cease all propaganda and agitation that may be detrimental to the development of these organisations; in other words, must not stand in the way of their activities.
>
> General Workers' Union of Germany
> German Seamen's Union
> Confederation of Workers of the World
> Swedish Workers' Central Organisation
> National Labour Secretariat of Holland
> Spanish [National] Confederation of Labour

Comrades, by this motion we wish to compel the congress not to create difficulties for the development of independent organisations existing in the different countries. We are of the opinion that it is just these independent organisations that are the true nuclei of the trade-union movement, and only they can effectively fight against Amsterdam. We have gained the impression that it is the tendency of the congress to put these organisations against the wall, leave them without rights inside the Red Trade Union International, and subordinate them to the 'minority groups' that remain affiliated to Amsterdam. We believe that the congress does not desire what we want and strive for: that is, the creation of unity among all the revolutionary trade-union organisations.

You may reject our motion and make an effort to push us aside – perhaps because you think that our organisations will, despite everything, remain inside the Red Trade Union International – which, by the way, is a correct supposition. If you do so, the only reasons you can give is 'the unwillingness to grant our organisations an importance that the general state of things does not seem to justify'.

Comrades, we are of the opinion that passing our motion does not signify any sort of 'concession' toward our organisations. There are no concessions in a revolution. The revolution does not need concessions; that would be an absurdity. The revolution takes its course whether concessions are made or not. We maintain that our independent organisations have at least as much right as anyone else to be part and parcel of the Red Trade Union International, and on this basis we demand the preservation of our right of complete freedom to develop in the future.

For this reason we ask you to vote for our proposal. Rejecting it would give an impression that you are barring the independent organisations from participation in the Red Trade Union International.

Hampel: Comrade Lozovsky will speak now against the motion made by Comrade Bartels.

Lozovsky: The motion made on behalf of several delegations contains a demand of loyalty and toleration toward the syndicalist organisations on the part of the Red Trade Union International.

We, on our part, have emphasised several times that we want to reach full agreement. Allow me to point out to you how our comrades, the syndicalists, understand loyalty, and how they put it into practice with regard to the Red Trade Union International. I will read a circular, dated 14 July – that is, yesterday – which was issued by Comrade Bartels and two syndicalist organisations present here. This document is of extraordinary interest. Allow me to draw your attention to it:

> To the representatives of the independent revolutionary organisations of all countries forced to remain in a minority at the First Congress of the Red Trade Union International.
>
> Comrades:
>
> The revolutionary trade-union organisations of the world have remained in the minority at this congress. They are outnumbered by the trade-union minorities that are still organisationally affiliated to Amsterdam, minorities that are outside of any control. All decisions made by the congress thus far have come from these groups, and they all have the same character.
>
> In reality our organisations have lost all rights in this International. They have been made dependent upon the Third International and upon those who by their dues and by their numbers strengthen the influence of Amsterdam. This subordination demands nothing less than the renunciation of the independence of our organisations on a national as well as international scale. It even demands a partial dissolution of our unions. It demands that the revolutionary organisations dig their own graves.
>
> We must close ranks and defend ourselves against these attacks. The interests of the world labour movement necessitate the creation of an International of independent organisations firmly linked to each other, and not an International of nuclei and groups. It is our firm belief that

it would be harmful to the revolution if the representatives of kindred revolutionary organisations should head home without any results.

On the other hand, we are convinced that international unity of independent organisations outside the Red International of Labour Unions would cause a further dispersal of energies of the working class, which we must not allow until we have utilised all means to ensure our influence within the Red Trade Union International, and the triumph of our principles.

Furthermore, given the fact of the predominance of the nuclei within the Red Trade Union International, we propose that all independent organisations that are in opposition at this congress agree among themselves within the Red Trade Union International, to observe unconditional solidarity and uniformity of action, in case the central leadership committee of the Red Trade Union International expels one or another organisation or persecutes it in any way. The fundamental aim of this agreement must be to transform the Red Trade Union International into a real International, to secure its independence, to further the practical revolutionary activity of the International, mercilessly fighting against all reformist and opportunist tendencies detrimental to the International.

We ask all representatives of independent organisations to unite for the good of the revolutionary labour movement of the world.

Moscow, July 14, 1921
Gelsenkirchen Free Workers' Union
General Workers' Union of Germany
German Seamen's Union
Signed by Bartels and Dautkus

I believe, comrades, that circulars should not be issued proclaiming our International a fiction, that our International tends to destroy the labour movement, and then declare from the platform, 'We demand a loyal attitude toward us'. Such actions are hypocritical, demagogic, and absolutely inadmissible. I believe nothing of this sort has ever occurred at any other workers' congress. This is politics of the worst stripe, and is nothing more than demagogy of the worst type. On the one hand, they demand that we not fight them, that we not object to their principles, which are utterly incorrect in the view of many comrades. On the other hand, they call our International a fiction; they consider it mired in reformism, and consider it necessary to fight us.

I believe that this 'loyalty' and demagogy should be properly judged by the comrades. The only thing I am sorry about is that among the signatures to the declaration [of six organisations] were those of our Spanish friends, who are not demagogues but workers who honestly defend their point of view, while seeking agreement with us whenever possible.

Allow me, comrades, to warn you against this demagogy, which threatens our unity and which may lead not to the creation of a workers' International, but to something sterile and miserable. I move to reject the motion of those who stab us in the back, as their demand of loyalty is neither loyal nor sincere, but merely demagogy.

Bartels (*from his seat*): I wish to speak. (*Protests from the German delegation*)

Hampel: One orator spoke for and one against the motion. Discussion is closed. Let us vote. All those for the motion of Comrade Bartels and his comrades, please raise your hands. The motion is defeated by all against the votes of the German Free Unions.

Disch (*from his seat*): I demand that a vote be taken according to countries.

Malzahn (*from his seat*): If we accept Comrade Disch's demand and vote according to countries, I demand that the vote be taken according to groups, as a majority of the German delegation is against the motion.

Hampel: Owing to the demand of one of the comrades, we will vote by delegations. (*Vote taken*)

The voting by countries gave the following results: for the motion of Comrade Bartels, 5 votes of the German delegation and 9 votes of the Dutch delegation – total 14 votes; 3 members of the American delegation, Spain and Argentina abstained from voting. Belgium and Greece did not participate in the vote. All the other delegations voted against the motion. Total against the motion – 260 votes.

The motion is defeated.

Bartels (*from his seat*): I ask to be allowed to make an explanation.

Lozovsky: Comrades, we defeated the motion of Comrade Bartels because the character of the motion was inadmissible. But this does not mean that we intend to take any special measures against the minority of the Red Trade Union International. I take this opportunity to impress upon you once more the fact that our policy toward the minority will be a policy of absolute loyalty and tolerance. (*Applause*)

Bartels (*from the seat*): I ask to speak.

Hampel: All discussion on this question is closed. If you wish to make an explanation, submit it in written form and it will be entered into the minutes.

We are ready for the next question on the agenda. Comrade Sturm will report on 'Women in the trade-union movement'.

Report on Women in the Trade Unions

Hertha Sturm (Germany, Central Union of Clerks in Commercial Enterprises): If the aim of the Red International is to spread the ideas of the revolutionary struggle among the broad masses of the working class, we must not forget that women make up a large part of the proletarian masses. Women represent over half the proletariat; after the war there are 15 million more women than men.

If trade unions represent an organisation of the working class as a whole, for women the unions are unique organisations. The woman worker, on account of her situation, differs greatly from the housewife. They are both exploited by capitalism, and are, generally speaking, apolitical and antisocialist. Nevertheless, the woman worker stands on a higher level than her sister, the housewife. The housewife suffers from capitalism indirectly, while the woman worker is exploited directly, and is therefore more conscious. The housewife is always alone, and her consciousness develops slowly. The woman worker not only suffers direct exploitation, but she comes in direct contact with hundreds of class comrades within the workplace – both men and women – and she is able to discuss things and concretise her impressions.

In order to have a clear view of the part played by women workers in the trade unions and the tasks of Communists inside the trade unions, we must first of all make clear the social and economic position of women in the process of production. Women work alongside men, and become interested in participating in the class struggle on an equal footing with men. Each woman who joins our ranks is a new centre for agitation. Great battles are coming, and women's participation in the struggle, their unity and their bravery, will serve us greatly, both today and after the conquest of power, in building communism.

But in order for the woman to be able to take her place in the movement, we must make clear our attitude to the following questions: Do we accept or deny the usefulness of women's participation in the class struggle? Do we favour the reactionary viewpoint of Amsterdam, or should we form and express new views on the matter? To answer these questions we must review the history of women's labour within the capitalist system, a direct result of the development of capitalist production.

Before the war, women were drawn into capitalist production. This was not the result of their greater abilities or of the lack of men. The modern system of production introduced first in Britain, then in America and Japan, has facilitated the use of female labour power. Mass production became so highly organised, with a division of labour so minute, that the demand for skilled labour dropped, facilitating the use of untrained labour. The result was that women began to appear in great numbers in the factories and mills. The adoption of the newest types of machines has forced the rapid proletarianisation of the middle class.

The World War precipitated the use of female labour, as the capitalists moved to war production and millions of men were torn away from their jobs. The production of cartridges, sandbags, and similar items was done almost exclusively by women's labour power. In many trades the employers hired exclusively women, especially when no experience was required. These were the main reasons for the increase of women in the industrial field.

In Germany, before the war, we had, as women workers: in 1882 – 10 million workers, or 24 per cent. In 1917 the figure was 30 million, or 72 per cent. Out of this total, 46.2 per cent were married, divorced, or widowed. On a world scale, women's labour in industry expressed itself: in Germany, 1.4 million women workers; in Great Britain, 3.2 million; in France, 2.2 million.

Besides these quantitative changes with regard to women employed in production during the war, a qualitative change must also be emphasised. Women entered branches of work that had traditionally been closed off to them. They were employed in the production of steel, in the railways, etc. – in other words, in the fields of work requiring a great expenditure of physical force. They also found employment in transport, in commerce, in offices, and in state services. And not only did they find jobs, but they held their own in the places they occupied. Statistics on this question are unnecessary.

How much the female labour force increased in Germany during the war is evident from the number of hospital-fund contributions [medical insurance payments] for men and women.

In February 1914 the ratio of contributions by men to women in Germany was 2 to 1; in February 1917 it was 1 to 1; since then the number of women has increased over men. In many trades the ratio became 4 to 1 in favour of women. Among construction machine workers, the number of women was five times greater than men.

In Britain and France during the pre-war period, women workers were from a third to a fifth of the entire number of workers there. During the war the woman worker was more exploited than in the past, taking into consideration the greater intensity in production and the annulment of many factory laws. The record shows that during 1914 there were 44 million night shifts by women; in 1918 it reached 47 million.[5]

The work of women in branches of industry dangerous to life and health – such as work in printshops, chemical factories, etc., involving great expenditures of physical effort, done outdoors in all weather conditions, in the heat and cold – was to the highest degree harmful to their health. Many women perished who were unaccustomed to such working conditions.

The war ended; there were some changes. Above all, one notes a change of attitude among the working masses with regard to women in the workforce, as some viewed female labour with hostility. In addition, men were returning from the war, and the women had to give up their jobs. In some cases the abandonment of work by women was done voluntarily; in other cases they were removed by force.

Everyone is aware of the work that has been accomplished in this regard by the demobilisation commissioners. The war industry threw millions of women into the street because, deprived of this work, women could not return to the major industries where they had been employed prior to the war. The global economic crisis broke out because of a lack of raw materials, among other reasons, and a large number of workers were thrown out of work. One might have thought that the widespread use of female labour power was over, and that a new phase was opening in this field.

This shutdown of production cannot be considered as a total stoppage of production. Capitalism knew how to conform to the new conditions and, as always in periods of its weakness, increased the exploitation of the female labour force, using it as a cheap way to achieve its past prosperity.

In many cases, the bosses left the women in the places they occupied during the war, and replaced the men who had worked there before. They did not do this because women work better, but because women's work is cheaper and easier to apply harsh conditions of production to. The capitalists have taken all measures to push the exploitation of female labour to the utmost, and the demobilisation commissioners have given them complete freedom in this regard. The new law intended to regularise female work, which will be studied in the near future by parliament, will have considerable consequences for women, because it contains far fewer 'protective measures' for female labour than the ones in pre-war law.

5 This is per the English version; the French and Russian texts say 41 million.

Besides the unscrupulous exploitation of women, it is necessary to underline the attitude of the working class as a whole toward this issue. We must note that the working class is not unanimous on this question, and different tendencies have different views, from the bourgeois tendency defended by Amsterdam up to revolutionary tendencies. However, even within these latter tendencies there is no unanimity.

The old trade-union movement saw women in the workforce as undesirable, although unfortunately inevitable. It was opposed to the admission of women into trade-union organisations, formally closing its doors and forcing them to create their own organisations. This point of view was preserved during the war period, and even today it is not uncommon to see unions dominated by petty-bourgeois conceptions on this issue.

When workers became convinced by the weight of events, they began to organise the women on the basis that women cannot be rejected from production, as they already constitute a large percentage of the working population. They began to organise them despite the fact that women, driven by very difficult living conditions, had contributed to the unemployment of men.

But the old view arose again, and there was a competitive struggle between men and women. There are clearly men who are oblivious to the need for solidarity with women.

To highlight the point of view of the Communists on this question, it is necessary to ask: Is the woman a comrade enjoying the same rights as men in work and in the class struggle? Or should she be considered a competitor? How we respond to this question depends on our attitude toward women in the trade-union movement.

Workers begin to realise the danger of women being left unorganised. The employers have been using women to their own advantage against the male workers. There is no solidarity yet between the two, and great competition of labour exists between them. It is up to the Communists to define their attitude on this question, upon which depends the future work of women in labour organisations.

Many women would prefer housework to work in a factory, and the same point of view is held by many men. At a meeting of shoemakers held in Berlin, the decision was in favour of women staying at home.

Such a theory is utopian. It is wrong from the individual point of view, and also from the political-economic one. Millions of women workers are active in all industries. In Germany alone there are ten million women workers. More than half of them are single – either unmarried or widows. To prohibit them from working would mean privation. From the economic point of view this is impossible, as in many trades – such as garment, textile, and food – more than half the jobs are filled by women. The removal of women from industry would cause a decrease in production, in other words, fewer items for proletarians to maintain themselves.

On the other hand, we cannot allow the employers to abandon women to unlimited exploitation. The new law concerning protection of female labour is a step backward. Women need greater consideration and protection with regard to night work, wages, etc. The war industry has led to such horrors that not just the social workers and doctors, but the whole public realised the crime of such negligence.

There is another reason why we cannot remove women from the factories at present. The workers are exhausted, the crisis is widening, capital is threatening ruin and resorting to measures of exploitation that it usually employs during crises. At such a time, to remove women workers from production would harm large-scale industry. From the revolutionary point of view this would be a mistake, as we must prepare women for the economic activities necessary in a communist state. Still that does not mean that we should leave the woman worker at the mercy of her exploiter. Of course, the definitive solution of this question, and the disappearance of the contradictions associated with it, can be accomplished only by the destruction of the capitalist system and the establishment of communism. It is nevertheless important to prepare for the future and start the work of organising women. We should not limit our activity to propaganda among women involved in production. The Russian Revolution has shown that a great deal of agitational work is necessary to attract to the building of communism women who were not employed in industry before the revolution. I hope we will profit by this lesson. It is up to the women workers to take the responsibility upon themselves.

These questions cannot be solved by the Amsterdam International. They can be resolved only by the Communists.

The fear of unemployment in all countries has bred the idea of removing women from industries, but this is a great error. The trade unions have based their ideas upon the fact that in some families every member is working, while in other families wives and children are all idle. They believe in an equal distribution of labour – which is a practical impossibility. The removal of the woman from the shop would be dangerous. Instead of participating actively in the struggle, women would express their hatred against their male comrades. Due to their unemployment, one part of the working class would become inactive and removed from the class struggle. By removing women from the revolutionary movement, the working class weakens its struggle both quantitatively and qualitatively.

Here are some figures on the number of men and women in the trade unions:

In Germany the free trade unions have 9 million; out of this number 2 million are women. In Yugoslavia, 300,000, of whom 20,000 are women. In Switzerland (five big unions), 40,000 women. In Britain (tailoring trade), 82,898 women. In America (ladies' garment only), 5 million workers, of whom 700,000 are women. In Australia, 43,000 women. In Sweden, 300,000, of whom 26,000 are women. In German Austria, 193,000 women.

These figures prove the important part played by women in the process of production. Hence, women must be on an equal footing with men in the economic struggle.

What is the present attitude of unions to women? Is it of a rivalry character or one of close comradeship? What are the means for the establishment of mutual relations between them?

Here are yet more statistics:

In Germany in eleven unions women's membership is from 50 to 99 per cent. In German Austria there are 29,000 women metalworkers, 28,000 hotel workers, and 23,000 clerks. In Britain (in the needle trades) there are 82,000 women. In America (ladies' garment workers), 700,000. This makes the percentage of women in the organised trade unions quite a factor. The percentage of women in comparison to men is as follows: in Germany in 1914, 9 per cent – 2,483,661 men and 215,777 women. In 1919, 21 per cent – 8,010,262 men and 1,685,911 women. In Austria in 1913, 11 per cent; in 1919, 25 per cent. In Australia, in 1913, 4.1 per cent; in 1917, 8.7 per cent; in 1919, 18.6 per cent.

We have no statistics about women workers in Britain. We do know that the number of women in the textile industry has increased by 32,000; the number of sales clerks has increased by more than 17,000. It is also interesting to know that in these trades the predominant element consists of women. The increase in female trade-union membership was due not solely to the absolute increase in the number of women workers, but also to the fact that the war and the revolution fundamentally changed their views. During the war women took part in production in large industry and became convinced of the importance and the advantages of organisation. Particularly after the revolution, women began to be interested in all kinds of questions.

Here are the figures on the proportion of women party members to the number of women in trade unions: Germany, 40,000 out of 1.6 million; Switzerland, 1,000 out of 40,000; America, 25,000 out of 400,000; Sweden, 2,200 out of 26,000; Yugoslavia, 5,000 out of 20,000.

It would be a mistake to believe that these figures are very advantageous for us. The main thing is that women have a revolutionary spirit. We know how difficult it is for women to do housework alongside their other work. Women usually do not have time for trade-union activity. Were we to make the attempt to attract women to this activity, the attempt would be successful. The woman feels the exploitation of capital more than the man; she constantly displays solidarity with men; she is disciplined and could be placed at the centre of the struggle. But women very rarely hold trade-union office and are rarely elected as delegates.

At the congress of the workplace councils of clerks in Berlin, out of 950 delegates there were 8 women. Although there are 40,812 women members among the metalworkers, still at the special congress called for the purpose of agitation among the women, only 80 were present. Why are they so passive? The excuse that they are too busy is insufficient; the main reason is insufficient propaganda among women.

The question now is: Who is going to approach the woman first: the Communists or Amsterdam? Communists must warn her about Amsterdam. We must arouse the interest of the woman and win her confidence.

The content of the propaganda should be general questions of the workers' movement. We know that Amsterdam is spreading counterrevolutionary propaganda through the Women's Committee in Washington.[6] We must pose the question of the prohibition of married women from holding jobs. The congress of metalworkers held on 6–7 May in Berlin adopted the following resolution, over the objections of the union leadership: (1) to prevent women from getting jobs whose husbands are able to earn a living; (2) to forbid, in the future, the hiring of men together with their wives.

The question of wages should play a large role in our propaganda. According to German social security statistics, the wages of women are from 52.6 per cent to 59 per cent of the wages of men. Umbreit's journal *Industrie* gives the wage ratio before the war as 1:2; this proportion stands now at 2:3.

Among commercial employees there is a separate rate for women and men. This rate is established for employees from eighteen years of age, and the wage difference between men and women ranges from 60 marks at the bottom of the scale to 200 marks at the top of the scale. As for teachers and women employed in state service, the state pays lower salaries, because they have a lower civil service ranking than the men, even though the work done is the same. In the textile

6 In October 1919 the International Labour Organisation helped sponsor the First International Congress of Working Women, held in Washington, D.C., in conjunction with the ILO's first International Labour Conference. A second congress of the ICWW was held in Geneva in 1921. At the Third Congress of 1923, held in Vienna, the delegates voted to join the IFTU (Amsterdam International), and dissolved as a separate organisation.

industry we find the same hidden form of wage reduction. Women are forced to use slower textile machines, and due to piecework they obviously earn less than the men using faster machines.

In Britain women receive from 5/8 to 3/4 of men's wages. In Switzerland, even in highly skilled work, women get a lower wage than men. In France the wages of men in the lingerie industry are twice as high as women's. The average wage of women in comparison to men is 62-70-80 per cent.

Concerning unemployment assistance, women get a lower allowance than men in Germany and in Switzerland. In Berlin the men's allowance is equal to 6-8-10 marks according to family situation, while for women it is 4-6-8 marks – in other words, less by 2 marks at each rate. It is interesting to note that the bill brought into the Reichstag by the Independent Social-Democratic Party and the Social-Democratic Party about increasing the unemployment allowance preserved the difference of 2 marks between the sexes. In Britain the allowance was 15 shillings for men and 10 shillings for women; at present it is 20 shillings for men and 16 shillings for women.

At a time when the Amsterdam Women's Committee's methods of action push women into the hands of the reactionaries, it is necessary to create in Germany a special organisation for propaganda among women and show them who their real enemy is. We must acquaint women with the meaning of a strike, and teach them solidarity.

Strikes are the best weapon in the hands of workers. But they cannot be successful unless women are sufficiently disciplined. In the past, women have never been active militants. During economic strikes, women sometimes found it difficult to understand why they should suffer privations; all the more so in political strikes. Thus during the miners' struggle in Germany against the introduction of overtime work – a strike that was of international importance, in that the overtime work of German workers caused the wages of French and British miners to drop – women sought to convince men to accept an agreement to return to work because of the increased earnings from overtime. Women therefore will have to be prepared for certain privations as consequences of the strike.

In France last year during a big strike, women replaced the strikers.

Among the many general questions, there are some that are of particular interest to women. In Germany, as in many countries, the practice of trade unions does not correspond to the principles of class solidarity; for example, women printing workers are prohibited from occupying well-paid jobs. Cases like the one I mentioned earlier – the resolution of the union of technical workers – do not contribute to feelings of solidarity among women and do not increase their confidence in trade unions.

How should we solve the problem of organisation? The question is not to organise them separately, but to develop an organisational plan to unite women on the platform of the Red International. This work can be done within the unions, as well as in the factories and at the work bench. Trade-union cadres should therefore seek to interest women in questions that touch on them in particular. For this it is necessary to utilise lectures and assemblies. Choose topics of particular interest to women, and have them take part in the discussion.

It is necessary to form committees in each union for the purpose of coordinating their work, based on the position of the Red International.

The revolutionary and labour press should be distributed widely among women. The German Communists are issuing a periodical, *Die Kommunistische Fraueninternationale* [The Communist Women's International]. The same thing was done by the Communists in Czechoslovakia.

In all this work the revolutionary workers must not lose sight of the need to win the confidence of women and to interest them. The Red International is the only organisation capable of grouping all workers, including women, for the class struggle. And the woman deserves very serious attention because she is capable of playing a very active role in the world revolution.

Equalising the wages of women and men is not only a matter of women's interests. In any case, women themselves sometimes betray this tradition according to which they apparently have less need than men. If the woman spends less than the man, it is simply because she saves or avoids spending.

There are still a whole series of questions on which revolutionary workers will have to decide, for example, night work and Sunday work, maternity protection, etc. It should be emphasised that the conference dealing with labour protection opposed the prohibition of night work for women, despite the fact that it was pointed out how defending women contributes at the same time to defending men. But even the resolutions adopted by that conference have not yet been implemented everywhere (with regard to child labour and the protection of women before and after childbirth).

Evidence of the extreme importance of these issues is given by the British Labour Party's women's conference in Manchester, which adopted no fewer than eleven resolutions on the government's inaction in the area of protecting women workers.[7]

The Seventh Women's Congress in France drew up a bill on maternity protection, to which revolutionary workers' organisations have presented a counterproposal based on the measures taken in this area by the Russian Soviet government.

---

7 The Labour Women's Conference was held in May 1921.

As regards the duties of housewives, they can be alleviated by thorough application of the collective principle in the domestic economy.

Lozovsky: It is proposed not to open the discussion, but to refer this report to a commission of seven members with the purpose of drafting a resolution. Is anybody against the motion? It is accepted. The commission includes Comrades Sturm, Bloch, Heuchel, a woman representative from the Russian delegation, and one from the British delegation. It will meet tomorrow at 11:00 a.m.

Allow me to make the following announcement: Tomorrow and Sunday morning the committees will meet. Sunday evening, a concert will be given in honour of the members of the congress. The plenary session will take place on Monday. There is a proposal to finish up the work of the congress on that day.

Are there any objections to the proposed order of business? None. It is accepted.

Tomorrow at 11:00 a.m. the commissions will meet. We shall draft a resolution on tactics, unemployment, and the woman question.

Hampel: I declare the session closed.

(*The meeting is adjourned at 11:35 p.m.*)

Commission Reports; War Victims

(*The session opens at 11:30 a.m. Comrade Heckert in the chair.*)

Heckert: The session is open. On the agenda are the following three reports: (1) report of the Credentials Commission; (2) report of the Commission on Workers' Control; (3) report of the Organisation Commission, appointed to work out the statutes. Comrade Szántó has the floor to report on behalf of the Credentials Commission.

Report of Credentials Commission

Béla Szántó (Hungary): The Credentials Commission has given many reports, and therefore I shall be brief. I will not dwell on the protests and disputed points that have already been resolved by the congress. I shall limit myself to indicating the number of representatives who are present at the congress.

The commission has verified all the credentials presented here. The following countries are represented at the congress: Germany: five delegates of the independent organisations; besides those, by delegates of the revolutionary minorities [within unions and federations affiliated to Amsterdam] representing thirty-two unions and territories. Austria: by representatives of the minority groups of ten unions. Hungary: by representatives of minorities. Czechoslovakia: represented by one union and by minorities of six organisations. Switzerland: by representatives of two trade unions, town councils, trade unions in Geneva, Zurich, and Basel; and also by eight organisations of the minority groups. Poland and Eastern Galicia: by representatives of the minority groups. Estonia: by representatives of unions and of the minority groups. Latvia: by representatives of the minority groups. Lithuania: by representatives of two organisations. Finland: by delegates of the minority groups. Sweden: by representatives of three organisations and by the minority groups. Norway: by representatives of one organisation. Denmark: by representatives of two organisations and the minority groups. Holland: by representatives of the organisations and of the minority groups. Luxembourg: by representatives of the minority groups. France: by representatives of one organisation and of the minority groups. Spain: by representatives of the National Confederation and of one independent union. Italy: by representatives of the minority groups. Yugoslavia: by rep-

 | DOI:10.1163/9789004712867_020

resentatives of the Central Council of Trade Unions and of seven organisations. Romania: by representatives of the Central Council of Trade Unions. Greece: by representatives of the minority groups. Turkey: by representatives of one organisation. Bulgaria: by representatives of eleven organisations. Britain: by representatives of the minority groups and of two independent organisations. Australia: by representatives of forty-four organisations. South Africa: by representatives of one organisation. Palestine: by representatives of the minority groups. Japan: by representatives of the minority groups. China: by representatives of the minority groups. Java: by representatives of one organisation. Korea: by representatives of one organisation. Russia, Ukraine, Azerbaijan, Armenia, the Far Eastern Republic, the Caucasus and Georgia: by representatives of the amalgamated trade unions. The United States: by representatives of five organisations, three amalgamated unions, four local groups, and minority groups. Canada: by representatives of two organisations. Mexico: by representatives of one organisation. Argentina: by representatives of one organisation.

The delegates are classified according to countries in the following manner:

Country	Delegates with decisive vote	Delegates with consultative votes
Germany	71	9
Austria	10	2
Hungary	3	–
Czechoslovakia	10	–
Switzerland	10	5
Poland and East Galicia	9	–
Latvia	5	–
Estonia	5	–
Lithuania	3	–
Finland	14	–
Sweden	11	–
Norway	9	–
Denmark	3	1
Holland	8	0[1]

1 This is per the Russian and French texts; the English has 1.

(*cont.*)

Luxembourg	4	–
France	13[2]	–
Spain	5	1
Italy	3	–
Yugoslavia	11	–
Romania	5	–
Greece	–	1
Turkey	1	–
Bulgaria	13	–
Britain	7	8
Australia	4	–
South Africa	–	1
Palestine	2	0[3]
Japan	–	1
China	–	1
Java	1	–
Korea	1	–
Russia	64	5
Ukraine	8	–
Azerbaijan	2	–
Armenia	2	–
Far Eastern Republic	3	–
Abkhazia	1	–
Georgia	4	–
United States	6	9
Canada	2	–
Mexico	1	–
Argentina	2	0[4]

Thus, at the congress 380[5] delegates from 41 countries were represented, among whom 336 had decisive vote and 44 had consultative vote.

2 This is per the Russian and French texts; the English has 14.
3 This is per the Russian and French texts; the English has 1.
4 This is per the English and Russian texts; the French has 1.
5 This is per the French and Russian; the English has 370.

In addition, the Credentials Commission, after looking into the motion of the Spanish delegation, decided to propose to the congress formation of a new fifth group of countries composed of Turkey, Korea, Palestine, Bukhara, Abkhazia, and Khiva, giving to each country of this group one decisive vote. As for India, the Credentials Commission proposes to include it in the group of countries that [each] have four decisive votes.

Heckert (Chair): Does anyone wish to speak on the report of the commission? As no one wishes to speak, the report of the Credentials Commission is taken as confirmed by the congress.

(*After the vote is taken with regard to the report of the Credentials Commission, the following declaration of the Azerbaijan delegation was handed in.*)

To the Presidium of the First Congress of Red Trade Unions:

During the discussion of the report of the Credentials Commission, Comrade Arlandis, on behalf of the Spanish delegation, the German group (of Gelsenkirchen and others), and some syndicalists, said in his speech, among other things, 'Such countries as Azerbaijan, Bukhara, India, Palestine, which are represented here, and the activities of which we are not in a position to judge, shall not have a decisive vote'.[6] With regard to the above, I am instructed to declare the following:

Azerbaijan, with its capital Baku, is a country with an old labour movement. Baku, the oil town, has long been known as the centre of the labour movement on the Caucasus and in the south of Russia. During the dark times of tsarist reaction, the Baku workers were always in the front ranks among the fighters and wrote a good many pages in the history of the movement for Russia's liberation.

At times, in the 1890s and at the beginning of the twentieth century, they provided an example to the Russian proletariat. After the great October victory, the Baku workers, in 1918, were the first in the Caucasus to raise the banner of Soviet power. But not for long, as the Baku Commune existed for only five months. At the end of July 1918, it fell under the blows of the British and Turkish imperialists due to the low treason of the Mensheviks, Social Revolutionaries, Dashnaki, and Müsavatists.[7] It fell, and together with it the leaders

6 For the remark on this by Arlandis, see p. 173.

7 The Baku soviet regime, known also as the Baku Commune, lasted from 11 April to 25 July 1918. Under pressure from invading British and Turkish troops, it was ousted by a government of right-wing Socialist-Revolutionaries, Mensheviks, and Dashnaks. The new government arres-

of the Caucasian proletariat later perished: Comrades Shaumyan, Djaparidze, and others – a total of twenty-six martyrs. The names of the martyrs of the Baku Commune may be put alongside those of the Paris Commune and the recently crushed Hungarian Soviet republic, the history of which in many ways reminds us of the life and death of the Baku Commune.

At the end of April 1920, with the approach of the Red Army and after the destruction of the white guards, the Baku proletariat, with the aid of that army, again raised the banner of the soviets over the whole of Azerbaijan.[8]

Azerbaijan is now an independent Soviet country that is connected by close ties with its elder sister, the RSFSR [Russian Soviet Federative Socialist Republic]. In the Azerbaijan Council of Trade Unions there are now more than 150,000 organised workers. The Baku proletariat now works on Soviet construction and in every way possible helps the Azerbaijani villages, under the leadership of the Azerbaijan Communist Party – which now has 16,000 members. It stands, as before, in the oil fields, sending the oil to Soviet Russia and other friendly Soviet countries, and thus is doing its work for the world revolution and for the Red trade unions of the whole world. It seems that all this gives them the right to have a decisive vote at the First Congress.

[Signed.] *Mikh. Kakhiani*
Delegate of the Azerbaijan trade unions

Heckert: A motion was handed in to adopt the resolution without discussion, as it was also unanimously adopted by the Credentials Commission. Are there any objections? There are none. Consequently the resolution is adopted.

Before the second point on the agenda, that is, the report of the Workers' Control Commission, is dealt with, the floor is given to the commission on the question of women in the trade unions.

Comrade Rosa Bloch has the floor.

---

ted twenty-six soviet leaders – most of whom were members of left-wing parties other than the Bolsheviks – who fell into the hands of anti-soviet forces. The SR leader in charge ordered them shot, and they were executed the night of 19–20 September 1918, most likely encouraged by a British liaison officer.

The Dashnak Party in Armenia and the Müsavat Party in Azerbaijan were nationalist parties that had fought against oppression by both tsarist Russia and the Ottoman Empire. In the years after 1917 they each opposed the October Revolution and Soviet Russia.

8 In late April 1920 a rising by Communist forces overturned the pro-imperialist regime and founded the Azerbaijan Soviet Socialist Republic.

Report of Commission on the Women's Question

Rosa Bloch (Switzerland): Comrades, after the report of Comrade Sturm, a commission consisting of women delegates was appointed to work out a resolution on this question. The commission understood its task as follows: All that we can say on various questions – as for instance on the question of women in industry, on the question of women in the trade unions – is to be entered in the minutes.[9] In the theses of Comrade Lozovsky on the question of organisation, before section 10, which refers to the work among young workers, a new paragraph should be inserted on the work among women. We shall move this proposal when the question of organisation is discussed.

(*Bloch reads the resolution on the women's question.*)[10]

Comrades, we propose that the congress adopt this resolution, but it is not sufficient just to adopt it. I think that the moment has come when adopting resolutions for the solution of questions is not sufficient; the actual protection of the interests of women should be our task. The moment has come to act, and not only to speak here at the congress. Talking has been done at all other congresses, but nothing has been undertaken to protect women, and women until now have remained isolated in the background. We have to choose a new path. We should not only adopt resolutions, but carry out all that is said in them.

Heckert: Clara Zetkin is given the floor to speak on the report of Rosa Bloch.

Clara Zetkin (Germany): After the report of our friend Rosa Bloch, in which she briefly but clearly expressed the essentials of the question, I will be able to limit myself to a few words only.

Our duty, comrades, is not only to adopt resolutions, but to give them life. Above all, we should not be satisfied with the idea that there are existing organisations that would act for us. Let us ask ourselves: What really is an organisation? It should be clear to you that an organisation is nothing but you yourselves taken as a whole, you yourselves expressing your individual consciousness, your will to act, and the action itself. An organisation is nothing but an amalgamation of separate men and women workers united in a compact fighting unit, in a force that brings victory. And into these fighting ranks you should bring the woman worker. You cannot do without her, as the tend-

9 A report on women metalworkers in France by Louise Heuchel was published in the French version of the congress proceedings, but was not included in any of the other languages. Heuchel's report can be found in the Appendix, pp. 684–6.

10 For the text of the resolution, see pp. 656–7.

encies of social and economic development draw women more and more into industry. Recently the World War, and the economic crisis that is a direct outcome of it, has to a great extent reinforced these tendencies, developing them further and making them understood.

In those countries that passed through the furnace of the war there are millions of women who lost their breadwinners. Those women now have to carry out the duties with regard to their children that through the process of the division of labour have historically fallen to the lot of the father. At the same time, we notice on the part of the capitalists an effort to restore their shattered economy on the back of cheap women's labour, whose price is becoming lower and lower and affects wages in general.

Our task, therefore, is not only to draw women into the trade-union movement, but also to prepare every woman separately for the struggle against capitalism, against capitalist exploitation. We shall attain victory only when we succeed in forming a single united front of men and women workers under the banner of the Red Labour International. And this is all the more necessary because in the labour movement the friends of the working classes of yesterday – friends only in words – have now been transformed into traitors and enemies of the working class, who work in the yellow International in the interests of the employers. The more the yellow International displays initiative and activity, the more essential will the question become for the Red Trade Unions of drawing the women workers into its ranks. This question will be a matter of life and death for it. As long as we do not succeed in drawing the masses of women workers into the red trade unions, they will form an unlimited source that the employers will utilise for cheap labour, and from which the yellow International will recruit its adherents.

I call upon you, comrades, to work among the women and with the women. Only under the banner of the Red Labour International will women workers find their place as legitimate participants in the great endeavour that is bringing us nearer to new and higher forms of social life.

Heckert: Comrade Tsyperovich is given the floor to report on behalf of the Workers' Control Commission.

Report of Workers' Control Commission

Grigorii Tsyperovich: Comrades, the questions of workers' control and factory committees has been divided into two parts. Part 1 is on the question of workers' control, based on my theses. Part 2 is on the factory committees, based on the theses of Comrade Heckert insofar as they are related to workers' control. The work of the commission has followed the same plan. First it dealt with the question and theses of Comrade Tsyperovich on control, and then with the theses of Comrade Heckert.

You will remember, comrades, that in general it was agreed by the congress that the draft of the theses on workers' control should not be dealt with at the general plenary session, but should be directly handed over to the commission. I thought, however, that it was necessary before dealing with the theses to propose to the commission the opening of a preliminary discussion for an exchange of opinions on the draft in general. This proposal was unanimously rejected by the commission, and after that we started to deal with the separate points of the theses. Discussion on separate points showed that there were no differences in matters of principle on any part. There were but two or three amendments that were of a more general character.

Permit me, therefore, to dwell on these essential amendments.

The first amendment, the more serious one, refers to point 7, to the passage, in the first part, that reads 'At such a [revolutionary] moment the role of mass organisations, including not only the vanguard of the proletariat (the Communist Party), but also the great masses not affiliated to a party, assumes a very important and almost decisive influence.' Well this short phrase, which emphasises the vanguard role of the more class-conscious members of the working class, the role of workers in the ranks of the party, imbued with a revolutionary spirit, in the revolutionary struggle with capital – this passage drew objections from Comrade Leval, the Spanish delegate, who considered this point of the theses from the viewpoint of the situation in Spain. He pointed out that to emphasise the leading role of the Communist Party in the revolution would not be quite correct, as in some countries – as for instance in Spain – the Communist Party, in terms of its membership and influence, is very weak, while the syndicalists, according to their membership and organisations, are much stronger. He finds it inopportune therefore to refer to the leading role of the party in all countries.

This question has been thoroughly dealt with, and the representative of the German General Workers' Union has partially approved this amendment. He pointed out, however, that it would be impossible to delete the whole passage, and that instead of the 'Communist Party' the word 'Communists' should be inserted. Comrade Gliński, the delegate from Poland, responded to him, pointing out that the word 'Communist' does not say anything regarding the relationship of forces of the two groups, that one could not imagine a Communist who did not adhere to the Communist Party, and therefore it would be more opportune to point out clearly and definitely the role of the Communist Party as the vanguard in the coming battles. After discussion the question was put to the vote and its original formulation was accepted by the whole commission, with one against.

With regard to the same question in a more general form, the representative of the Free Union of Germany pointed out that our draft theses has the defect of overly emphasising the connection of the organs of workers' control with the red trade unions. However, inasmuch as the theses were unanimously accepted as a basis, and inasmuch as the commission did not discuss this question from the standpoint of principle, this question was put to the vote and the result was that the majority (minus one) supported it. I must point out that after the vote was taken, these representatives did not appear at the sessions of the commission any more.

The next question that interested us was that of the relationship between the factory committees and the trade unions in the process of realising workers' control. A motion was made on this question that the commission accepted, and point 7 was divided into two parts. Thus the seventh item in its final form goes down to the last paragraph, which begins with the words, 'But the unions can be reorganised in the interests of the social revolution only …'. This part became point 8, with the following words added to it: '… in opposition to the yellow and counterrevolutionary trade-union bureaucracy, [only if] there is created in each industry a firm and determined revolutionary nucleus to counteract the policy of this bureaucracy, and to keep the organised masses in the factories on the path of the revolutionary struggle for control.'

This new paragraph was put in to underline clearly that where the unions are in the hands of yellow leaderships, it is necessary to establish a nucleus of revolutionary elements in the heart of the unions that would direct and press upon the yellow unions, winning them over and directing their struggle for workers' control according to the demands of the general revolutionary struggle.

This motion was accepted, thus adding point 11, with point 8 becoming point 9. In considering the general results, we decided to change the last points 7, 8, and 9, which were combined. They were formulated anew, reading as follows:

> It is necessary that the trade unions direct the work of the factory committees, while the trade unions must coordinate the work of the locally based control committees of the same industry, in such a manner as to avoid any attempt to create 'factory patriotism' on the basis of localised control.
>
> 8. For the guidance of the work of the factory committees, the trade unions must from the outset issue special instructions, discussing the

> questions of workers' control, carrying out a propaganda in the daily press and in factories, not only by explaining the tasks of workers' control, but also through reports on the results of workers' control by enterprise and groups through factory and local assemblies and conferences, etc.

In this connection we had to expand point 9, which is part of the general statement of reasons that I gave as a special supplementary point to the text. This point reads as follows:

> With a view of carrying out these aims in trade unions that do not accept the principles of the Red Labour Union International, it is necessary to organise strong revolutionary nuclei that will lay special stress on reconstructing the unions on an industrial basis and will maintain the revolutionary character of the struggle for workers' control.

These, comrades, were all the changes made during the three sessions of our commission. I did not call your attention to some important additional changes because they were purely a matter of editing and style and did not change their essence.

The theses of Comrade Heckert, being a component part of Comrade Tsyperovich's theses, went through considerable alteration. The original draft of the theses took up no less than twelve pages. The first eight pages were devoted to proving the necessity of revolutionising the labour movement, including the need to create factory committees, placing these revolutionary factory committees in the heart of the trade-union movement with the goal of winning it over. After the discussion on the tasks of the red trade unions, on the organisational questions, on the question of tactics, and the discussion of my theses, it was obviously superfluous to repeat in a general form the ideas and considerations that underlay the theses on these questions. The commission therefore decided, with the consent of Comrade Heckert, to omit all the introductory and theoretical parts as an unnecessary burden to the theses.

That left us with only four points on theoretical questions, which dwell on the general nature of the relations between factory committees and unions during the development of the revolutionary struggle. Besides that, there remained a number of practical proposals about the form that workers' control should take through the factory committees, and how the factory committees should carry out the daily struggle under the circumstances I described earlier, how they should carry to the working masses a clear understanding of workers' control, which is necessary for success in the struggle for this control. These proposals were also boiled down to several points. They read as follows:

> The concrete tasks before factory committees are as follows:
>
> 1. To draw the unemployed into the process of production. For this it is necessary: (a) to clearly determine the productive possibilities, taking into account and controlling the available supplies of raw and other materials necessary for production; (b) to shift the available labour force into such branches of industry in which a shortage of hands is felt; (c) to secure sufficient aid to the unemployed, paid for by the employers, until they return to work; (d) to establish connections with the distribution organisations in order to get acquainted with the exact needs of the working masses and to conform production to these needs.

Point 2 deals with the organisation of the distribution of fuel to the factories as well as to the workers, not forgetting the possibility of having to fight sabotage in the factories. Then comes the point about stopping all unuseful production, especially that of arms, ammunition, and articles of luxury. Point 4 deals with the control of transport. Point 5 takes up the control of finances. Point 6 deals with the matter of controlling production and the distribution of food by establishing systematic relations between the workers of the city and the villages, and particularly by organising an exchange of commodities in order to mutually provide for the needs of agriculture and industry, beginning with manufactured goods and raw materials. Point 7 speaks of controlling the price of farm products and manufactured goods needed by the workers. And point 8 deals with the matter of control of exports and imports.

All these points – which are directly connected with the general theses that we have adopted on other reports – on the one hand deal with the question of sabotage and the struggle against it, and with lock-outs by companies; on the other hand, they are in full harmony with the resolution on unemployment. In short, they fully agree on a number of theses that I took up in my report.

Thus Comrade Heckert's report is in a way an outcome of my theses. We therefore decided to put our theses together, so as to make them appear like parts of one and the same report. This is why my resolutions and those of Comrade Heckert will appear in the form of general deductions about workers' control and the tasks confronting the factory committees in general and the matter of control, in particular workers' control.

The theses of Tsyperovich make up part one, and Heckert's report on factory committees and their role in the trade-union movement makes up part two. In view of the fact that in considering all the points – made by me as well as by Heckert – the commission raised only those objections that I mentioned before. After reading through it point by point, no essential objections or changes were raised. The commission therefore found it advisable to present this short report and asks the plenary session of the congress to accept the amendments and to approve the theses as final.

Heckert: The commission, represented by the speaker, moves the acceptance of the commission's report on workers' control without discussion. The Presidium supports the motion. Are there any objections? No. (*The motion is passed with two negative votes.*)[11] Comrade Lozovsky has the floor to report on behalf of the Organisation Commission.

Report of Organisation Commission

Lozovsky: Comrades, the Organisation Commission considered the statutes in several sessions and proposed a number of practical changes, of which I am going to speak now in my report.

First, that in the very preamble to the statutes, the clause that reads, 'The International of impotence, and subservience to the bourgeoisie must be opposed by a militant International that organises the working class …' had the following added to it: 'that together with the Communist International will organise the working class for the overthrow of capitalism'.

Thus the overthrow of the bourgeoisie is framed in the statutes as a joint task of the Communist International and the Red Labour Union International. Further, the name of the 'International Council of Labour Unions' was changed to the 'Red International of Labour Unions'.

The seventh section omits the second part, which states that the Red Labour Union International enters into contact with other international class organisations. This paragraph was considered superfluous, for it is understood that the Red International will enter into relationship with all organisations with which it needs to make connections, and it is unnecessary to name them in advance.

The most serious debate in the commission involved the third section of the statutes, which deals with the conditions for membership in the RILU. You are aware that during the preliminary sessions, point 5 of the statutes, 'Recognition of the ideological leadership of the Communist International' brought about a big debate. In view of the fact that the congress definitely fixed the relations between the Communist International and the Red Labour Union International by its resolutions, and the question of recognising the ideological leadership of the Communist International has been decided, I moved

11 For the resolutions on workers' control and shop committees, see pp. 625–31 and 632–4.

the deletion of point 5 of the statutes in order to avoid lengthy discussions on the question. Point 5 has been taken out and replaced by the following: 'To become a member of the Red Union International it is necessary to recognise all the decisions of the congress, for without recognising these decisions, it is, of course, impossible to be a member of the International.'

Important changes were made in the part dealing with the international congress. You remember the debates on the question of allotting votes. You realise that some countries are represented out of proportion to their importance. To avoid this happening again at the next congress, the commission defined with great precision the future conditions of joining and representation. The conditions are as follows: at the next congress of the Red Labour Union International, national union federations having 10,000 members will get consultative votes. Those having from 10,000 to 25,000 members will get one decisive vote. Those having from 25,000 to 100,000 will have two decisive votes. Those having from 100,000 to 250,000 will have four decisive votes. Those having from 250,000 to 500,000 will have six decisive votes. And above that, one additional decisive vote for every 500,000 members. Such a representation cannot be said to be truly proportional; still to a certain degree it reflects correctly the relationship of forces of the different union organisations.

Regarding section V dealing with the organs of the Red International of Labour Unions, the commission decided to establish two organs: one decision-making body and one executive body. The decision-making body, according to the statutes, is the Central Council of the Labour Union International, which consists of four representatives of Russia; two each from Poland, France, Spain, Italy, Germany, Britain, Czechoslovakia, and the United States; and one from each of the other countries. Countries having less than 25,000 organised workers each have a consultative vote in the Central Council.

The Central Council elects a Secretariat of seven, of whom two are from the country where the council is situated, which is in the same country as the Red Labour International.

The functions of the Secretariat are defined by the statutes and it is not necessary to speak of this here. Section VI did not call forth any objections, but section VII on financial means was debated at great length.

With regard to financial resources, the situation is as follows: Until now all the expenses of organisation, publications, and the congress itself, were borne by the All-Russian Central Council of Trade Unions. It is necessary to have this movement financed not only by the Russian unions, but by the entire working class of the whole world. For that purpose the unions of each country will have to make some effort, and the draft of the statutes originally proposed that each organisation affiliated to the Red International contribute 5 per cent of the income of its central treasury. But this point was contested in the commission, because the dues paid by the local organisations of the various countries to their respective central treasury differ greatly with each country and organisation. There are some central organisations getting 50, 75, and 100 per cent of the total membership dues, so if they pay out 5 per cent, it will make quite a considerable sum. On the other hand, there are organisations whose central treasury gets only 10, 15, or 20 per cent. In general, if every organisation were to be assessed 5 per cent, there would be great inequality. It would be too much for some and too little for others. Therefore the subcommittee elected by the Organisation Commission, consisting of five representatives from Britain, America, Bulgaria, Scandinavia, and Germany, worked out the following formula, accepted by the commission:

> Organisations whose Central Committee receives from 50 to 100 per cent of membership dues pay a minimum of 1 per cent. Organisations whose central treasury receive from 25 to 50 per cent of membership dues pay a minimum of 2 per cent. Organisations receiving from 10 to 25 per cent of membership dues pay a minimum of 3 per cent. Organisations receiving less than 10 per cent to their central treasury pay a minimum of 5 per cent of their income.

Section VIII, concerning an international strike fund, gave rise to debate and hesitation. In the first place, some delegates found that the institution of an international strike fund would bring about the illusion among workers in all countries that this fund was for the purpose of supporting all strikers and all specific strikes. Such illusions, though groundless, could come back to haunt the Red Labour International in the future. A number of comrades, therefore, decided to formulate this clause more carefully and name the future fund an 'International Militant Solidarity Fund'. The money collected will be offered only in exceptional cases, where a clearly revolutionary struggle takes place, so that the workers of every country might know that there is a strike fund on which they can count in every revolutionary – but only revolutionary – strike. To emphasise that, the commission adopted for this fund the name 'International Militant Solidarity Fund'.

In section X, relating to the connections of the Red International of Labour Unions to the Communist International, only one change was made: The directing bodies of both Internationals are to be mutually represented by three, instead of one, members of the other body with decisive vote, and thus our resolution coincides with that adopted by the congress of the Communist International.

Section XI, regarding our connections with the international labour federations, has not been changed.[12]

A radical change was made in section XII, on the bureaus and their powers.[13] We deleted this altogether for the following reasons: What are the 'bureaus' and their 'representatives', and what have they been until now? These were the local organs for coordinating the work of the Red Labour Unions on a national scale. In the countries where the local organisations were not sufficiently strong, where they could not organise a centre and direct this work of their own accord, we would come to their aid by creating bureaus, etc. But this was a transitional form of organisation. It is desirable to have the trade unions of each country democratically elect at their meetings their centre and leaders, so that the Red Labour International might be confronted by the task of organising such bureaus, 'planted' so to speak from above, in exceptional cases only. Had we introduced 'bureaus' in the statutes, big misunderstandings might have arisen. We therefore omitted this point, leaving it to the Central Council and executive body to decide the necessity of creating an executive bureau in this or that place, for this is a purely practical question, and it is better not to decide it once and for all and embody it in the statutes.

The naming of the departments of the International Council of Labour Unions, which had been part of section XIII – dealing with internal structure – was omitted, for this again is of a purely practical nature. Insofar as departments need to be organised, the Red Labour International will do so, but determining their number in advance would tie the hands of the executive body.

These are, on the whole, all the amendments that were introduced into the statutes distributed to you. Without changing the substance of the statutes, these amendments brought into it some practical corrections and gave a more finished form to the Red Labour Union International itself.

I consider the central point of the statutes that we are presenting to you for approval to be the following: We have created a new organisation. It will be strong only if the revolutionary unions of which it is composed will carry out the resolutions adopted by us. The substance of the work consists in giving concrete form to the confused and spontaneous revolutionary impulse of the masses, channelling it into a single current, concentrating the revolutionary energy of the separate red unions, and leading the movement in all countries.

---

12 In the published version of the statutes, this is section IX.

13 Prior to the RILU founding congress, the International Council of Trade and Industrial Unions had set up bureaus in Berlin and Baku, as well as British, American, Far Eastern, and Mexican bureaus. See Tosstorff 2016, pp. 313–23.

The amendments proposed are the result of our collective experience, and the commission therefore moves their adoption without discussion, for each point has already been discussed in detail.

Heckert: The Organisation Commission unanimously adopted the draft of the statutes, just reported on by Comrade Lozovsky. There is only one additional clause proposed by the French delegation, which is to be put into the statutes as section XVII, and which reads as follows: 'The permanent location of the Red International of Labour Unions is decided by the congress. The time and place of the congress are designated by the Central Council'. In reality it is hardly necessary to state this; it ought to be understood.

Another motion has been made besides: the Central Council is to be situated in Moscow until the next congress.

Let us take up the question. This amendment moved by the French delegation is to be voted on first. All those in favour of letting the congress determine the centre of the International Council please raise your hands. Approved.

Those in favour of having the time and place of the congress of the Red Labour Union International fixed by the Central Council of the trade-union International, please raise your hands.

Who is against the motion of the French delegation? None. The motion is passed.[14]

Let us now take up the question of the statutes in the form reported by the commission. Those who wish to approve it, raise your cards. Who is against it? Eleven voted against it. The draft is therefore adopted. Those voting 'no' are the German Seamen's Union and General Workers' Union, two French delegates, one from Sweden, and two IWW delegates.

A voice (one of the representatives of the German *Unionen*): The count is wrong; we ask to vote by countries.

Heckert: Comrades, we will vote again by countries in order to fix the precise number of votes. Comrade Lozovsky will announce the list of the countries in the order of their voting.

Lozovsky: Britain for. Germany 11 for, 5 against. Italy absent. Spain for. Poland for. Russia for. France … . (*Noise among the French delegates*)

---

14 This is section XVI in the final published version.

Victor Labonne: We wish to make an announcement. We do not reject the draft as a whole, but we cannot accept the part that is entirely unsatisfactory to us, stating that the RILU sends three representatives to the Executive Committee of the Communist International, and the RILU Central Council includes three representatives of the Communist International, although the mention of the Communist International as being the ideological leader has been omitted from another clause. We believe that the inclusion of the three representatives already restores this 'ideological leadership', as we see it. We demand that the International of Labour Unions and the Communist International be two independent organisations and not one International, which the theses makes them, according to our understanding of them.

Heckert: I ask the delegates to put aside their quarrels until they return home. At present please keep quiet and give the Presidium an opportunity to find out who is for and who is against.

Labonne: They want to sidetrack us. We wish to put a stop to that. We do not reject the draft as a whole, only section 2.

Michel Relenque: I agree with everything said by Comrade Labonne.

Lozovsky: Comrades, it is necessary to understand, after all, what you are voting on. The theses as a whole are being voted on and not separate paragraphs. To vote for or against is your own affair.

Lemoine: In the French delegation there were two abstentions on all votes. I ask that this be noted.

Heckert: We will continue the vote. France: 6 for, 3 against, 2 abstentions. United States: 13 for, 3 abstentions. Czechoslovakia, Austria, Hungary, Bulgaria, Yugoslavia, Ukraine, Norway, Australia: all are for. Argentina against. Belgium absent. Holland for. Mexico: 5 for, 3 abstaining.[15] Greece absent. Sweden: 5 for, 3 against. Denmark, Finland, Far Eastern Republic, Azerbaijan, Armenia, Georgia, Korea, Latvia, Lithuania, Luxembourg, Turkey, Estonia, and Abkhazia: all are for.

The final vote is as follows: for approving the draft of the statutes, 301 votes, against 23, abstentions 11. The delegates of Belgium, Italy, Greece, and Palestine were absent.[16] Comrade Bartels has the floor to explain his vote.

15 This is per the minutes, but Mexico had only one vote.

16 For the text of the statutes, see pp. 649–55.

Bartels: On behalf of the German Miners' Union, I want to announce that we voted against the draft of the statutes not for reasons of principle. We voted against it only because the changes proposed in the final version of the statutes were, except in the rarest case, not considered.

Heckert: Comrade Gliński has the floor to explain his vote.

Gliński (Poland): We voted for the draft of the statutes, although we considered it wrong to delete point 5 of section III of the statutes, which speaks of the recognition of the Comintern as the ideological leader.

(*Heckert leaves the chair, which is taken by Comrade Rosmer.*)

Appeal on Behalf of International Union of War Victims

Rosmer: Comrade Tiedt has the floor for reading the resolution brought in on behalf of the International Union for relief to war victims.[17]

Karl Tiedt (Germany): Due to the great number of issues taking up the attention of our congress, we have failed to give due attention to the organisations engaged in securing relief for the war victims. I therefore ask the congress to give me a chance to present the question to you and draw your attention to its two principal demands. Our Russian comrades may not be interested in the matter, since Russia has successfully coped with this problem by giving those disabled in the war suitable employment or some other form of relief. We cannot say the same in the case of capitalist countries. This is borne out by the fact that organisations to aid the war victims sprang up in the belligerent countries even before the close of the war, demanding that their governments make good their former promises in this connection.

The partisans of Amsterdam at once realised the full importance of this movement, and are taking an active and even conspicuous part in the above organisations in Germany, France, and other countries.

Germany has a national centre for securing relief to soldiers disabled in the war,[18] with a membership of 750,000, which is entirely under the influence

17 An International Union of War Victims, also known as the 'War Veterans' International', was founded 1 May 1920 at a congress in Geneva, with affiliated organisations in eleven countries. Among its central leaders were Karl Tiedt and Henri Barbusse, the latter of whom was elected its first secretary general.

18 A reference to the Reichsbund der Kriegsbeschädigten, Kriegsteilnehmer und Kriegshinterbliebenen (National Association of Disabled War Veterans, Ex-Servicemen, and War Dependents).

of Davidson and Baumeister (notorious head of the magazine *Die Glocke*) – partisans of Amsterdam widely known even beyond the borders of Germany. The tendencies of this organisation are shown by the fact that its leaders were instrumental in organising the white guards. A part of the membership came out against this, which brought about a split in Germany. We then organised the International Union for Aid to the War Victims, whose membership is constantly growing. Amsterdam's influence is felt in all other similar organisations, not only in Germany, but also in the other former belligerent countries.

The section for securing relief for those disabled in the war, which the International Labour Bureau in Geneva felt compelled to form, called upon all similar organisations to get in contact with it. We received the same invitation, but of course declined it. Henri Barbusse, leader of the French organisation, gave the same negative response. But the International Labour Bureau is still supplying us with all its publications. Its work is more or less successful, as is shown by the fact that the German union of war victims, with its 750,000 members, is affiliated to it. The same is true in other countries. The International Labour Bureau is utilising its position to acquire influence in the organisations of war victims. In this field the social traitors have full scope for action. We must keep in mind the fact that 50 per cent of the disabled soldiers are not just members of these organisations; half of them are also members of trade unions. These are the ones who have a chance of resisting the ideological influence of Amsterdam, to the extent that the Red Labour Union International replaces this influence. The millions of disabled soldiers making up the other half are fully under the sway of Amsterdam. This fact makes them lost to the cause of the social revolution, and fills their heads with the ideas of Amsterdam. I must add that Germany has a widespread network of employers' organisations catering to the needs of disabled soldiers. Their influence is considerable. Here we have wageworkers mixing with employers, an example of class collaboration on a small scale.

We should note here the legislative provisions for relief to disabled soldiers that are operative in Germany and other countries. One of these laws provides that disabled soldiers taking any part in the revolutionary movement are subject to discharge if employed, and should be deprived of relief. There is another law compelling employers to hire those who have sustained serious injuries in the war. But this law is applied in a very peculiar manner. When employees struggle for a rise in wages, the disabled are ordered to keep away from the fight or else incur the penalty of being deprived of what protection they could otherwise get under the law. Such are the efforts of the ruling class to sow disunion between the disabled and the able-bodied wage slaves, and to turn the former into strikebreakers.

During the month of April of the current year we merged into a single organisation four unions of war victims, with a total membership of 1.25 million, in order to combat the above attempts to turn them into union-smashers and corrupt their feelings of class solidarity. The only condition for admission to the union is recognition of the principle of the class struggle and participation in the revolutionary actions of the proletariat. All the other organisations repudiate the above principle. We therefore recommend that this congress adopt the resolution embodying the following two demands:

The two demands in the resolution were:

1. To enter into relations with the International Union of disabled soldiers holding the above reformist views, with the object of training them in the spirit of militant class action against capitalism, with its inherent predatory wars.
2. The General Secretariat of the Red Labour Union International and the Central Trade Union Councils of the countries affiliated to this International are to organise their respective sections for dealing with matters affecting war victims.

The congress must endorse the above demands. They will serve to free the war victims from the tutelage of their class enemies and the Amsterdam International. But the above resolution demands close connection with the International Union of War Victims, and this fully warrants the congress in advancing the question as to whom and what this union really represents. This is why I have asked for your attention.

Our International Union of disabled soldiers was organised in May of last year in Geneva. Henri Barbusse appealed to all similar organisations to take part in that first congress. The representatives of different countries who met there were unanimous in grasping the full importance of the issues before that congress.

(*At this juncture the chair tells the speaker that his time is up.*)

I cannot close my remarks in a few words in spite of my efforts to be brief. I therefore, appeal to the congress to allow me to finish my speech. (*The chair puts the question to a vote of allowing the speaker ten minutes more. The motion is carried.*)

Comrades, I can present in broad outline the ideas that are inspiring the International Union of disabled soldiers by citing the speech delivered by Barbusse at the Turin Chamber of Labour in Italy. He said, 'War on war is a meaningless formula unless it means war against capitalism'.

At the first congress of disabled soldiers, Barbusse said:

> All through its sessions, the congress was animated by a powerful revolutionary spirit. We all felt that we were dealing here not with sterile pro-

> nouncements thrown into the wind, but with tangible and significant efforts. We had here delegates representing Italy, Germany, Austria, France, Britain, and Alsace-Lorraine. They were men who had fought one another on the battlefields, and now present a spectacle both solemn and sublime in their unified front against the folly and madness of war. At this moment our eyes open to the glorious vista of the world as finally shaped by the master-builders of the future, since all of us who were sent to this congress by the will of millions feel impelled to lay the cornerstone of this edifice with our own hands.
>
> Moved by a welling up of feeling at the close of Comrade Tiedt's speech, I gave him a hearty handshake. The delegates of the congress and the public rose in a body and cheered – not us personally, I am quite sure of that. They applauded the idea that we were symbolising. We sealed an alliance characterised by nobility and honesty, as well as its lasting nature. The declaration of principles underlying our union admits of no ambiguous interpretation. We gave, it is true, a good deal of attention to technical questions concerning legislation affecting the war's disabled, widows, and orphans. We took up all questions directly affecting war victims – questions that form the basis of our union. At the same time, we laid special emphasis on the necessity of fighting against war and capitalist bondage, and embodied this idea in our programme around two questions: (1) The propaganda for our demands should be carried out in a systematic manner and expose the danger of the existing institutions. This work should be done hand in hand with workers' organisations. (2) We must take part in the general strike in the countries affected, a strike that must precede the revolution. This is the only thing capable of making war disappear.

These words of Henri Barbusse clearly and unmistakably voice the feeling shown at that congress in favour of fighting for the interests of the war victims hand in hand with the revolutionary workers' organisations. At that congress there were also representatives of the pacifist tendency, but the majority was not on their side – a fact that was proved when the congress repeatedly demanded its affiliation to the Third International. Such direct affiliation was, of course, out of the question, as the International of war victims is an economic organisation.

Then the further question came up of affiliating directly to the Red Trade Union International. But this was objected to on the grounds that our organisation is not purely a trade-union organisation and, consequently, cannot directly join the Red International. This objection was well taken, and so we only demanded the establishment of close connections and the formation of special sections with the General Secretariat and the central labour union councils in various countries. This would facilitate joint work with the revolutionary proletarian organisations.

Our aims and tasks can be best represented by means of the following comparison: We have in the medical field general practitioners and specialists. Now the Red Labour Union International is the medical practitioner for the professional treatment of disease in general, while our organisation is the specialist striving to deal directly with the specific question of securing relief to war victims. Such contact as we propose could be effected by sending a representative of the Red Labour Union International to our next congress, which will probably take place in Italy, where this representative will have the opportunity of getting first-hand information bearing on our specific aims and tasks. We shall thus remain under general leadership and guidance as a part of the great army of proletarian fighters.

We must conserve a united front, and though we march separately, we shall be fighting together and deal the enemy a common blow. We call upon you to aid us in the above sense and adopt our two demands. Help us in the struggle that the war invalids are waging all over the world for securing a human existence. We showed at our Magdeburg Congress that we have an intelligent grasp of our aims.[19] Many comrades rejoined our ranks at this congress, comrades who up to that moment had taken part in other organisations fighting the proletarian battle, thinking them much more important than our interests. Many of our leaders are now in prison or in exile. This fact brings out most clearly to what extent our organisation is hated. It is not enough that the male war victims are thrown into prison, but in addition their wives and children are refused any relief on the grounds that their husbands and fathers have taken part in revolutionary movements of the proletariat.

For the benefit of our Russian comrades in particular, I wish to read here the resolution passed at our congress:

> The members of the International of veterans protest against the war with Soviet Russia. They pledge themselves never to take up arms against the proletarian revolution in Russia or in other countries, and send their warmest greetings to the heroic Red Army and the government of Red Russia.

---

19 The Magdeburg Congress of the War Veterans' International's German section, which Tiedt headed, was held 26–27 March 1921.

I close with these greetings, which I am transmitting to you on behalf of the millions of war victims, who are imbued with one desire: to be the soldiers doing their share of the fighting in the world revolution.

Rosmer: Comrade Lozovsky has the floor on this question.

Lozovsky: I move to adopt in principle the resolution on the question of the war victims as brought in by Comrade Tiedt, with the exception of point 2 calling on the Red Labour Union International to organise special sections for securing relief to the war victims, which I regard as impossible. The Red Labour Union International cannot do anything of the kind, and so this point cannot be adopted. But the resolution as a whole should be referred as a basis to the Presidium for its further elaboration and final drafting. We shall, in addition, have the Central Council give its special attention to this question. (*This motion is carried.*)[20]

I suggest on behalf of the Presidium that the delegates elect their representatives to the Central Council so that it may meet tomorrow night for the first time, as we shall probably close the congress by 4:00 p.m. tomorrow.

Declaration of the German *Unionen*

Rosmer: Comrade Bartels has the floor for an explanation.

Arthur Bartels: The General Workers' Union, the Gelsenkirchen Free Workers' Union, and the Seamen's Union in Germany feel bound, in connection with Comrade Lozovsky's remarks at the Friday session, to make the following statement:

> Comrade Lozovsky referred to the spreading of our circular as an act of disloyalty, and added that under these conditions the above organisations could not expect this congress to treat them on terms of loyalty. This led us to establish the fact, beyond any doubt, that the chairman at the congress session openly voiced what, for a long time back, had been no secret to the representatives of the organisations in opposition to the majority at this congress.

20 For the text of the Resolution on the Question of War Victims, see p. 661.

We have been watching the proceedings of this congress, noting its one-sided stand dictated by the views of the comrades who, up to now, have been the leading elements in the Provisional International Council, and this arouses our deepest alarm as to the future destiny of the Red Labour Union International. We feel bound, in this connection, to register the profound discontent felt by the organisations represented here.

We must also state that a great number of organisations – including nearly all independent unions – will find it impossible to join the Red Labour Union International, feeling that their independence and their opportunities for carrying into effect their revolutionary tenets are at stake and are seriously menaced by the narrow and intolerant stand taken by the majority at this congress due to the above influence.

For this reason we could not but obey the imperative need of making the attempt to have these organisations stay within the Red Labour Union International, provided they are allowed the possibility to defend their rights and views within its bounds. Judging by the way matters now stand, this could be accomplished only in the form of practical collaboration as provided by our circular.

Whether the above attempt succeeds or not will depend, above all, on a reasonable attitude on the part of this congress and its leaders. Otherwise, if these elements fail to materialise, this attempt will prove abortive, and the above independent organisations will find it impossible to stay in the Red International. As a consequence, the dangerous forecast voiced in the above circular will become a fact. That means this International will become a mere fiction, uniting as it will primarily various groups – and that in name only – belonging de facto to the Amsterdam International.

We hold this congress and its leaders responsible in advance before the revolutionary section of the working class of the world for all the hardships, trials, and defeats that are inevitable if they fail to adopt a broader policy free from the straitjacket of a doctrinaire spirit that dictates, on the one hand, total subordination to the Communist parties of the Third International, and, on the other hand, is indissolubly wedded to the tactic of forming nuclei within the trade unions.

On the above grounds, we energetically reject the rebuke of disloyalty. We think it not only our right, but our revolutionary duty as well, to unify the oppositional forces within the Red Labour Union International.

Rosmer: Comrade Heckert has the floor.

Heckert: The Gelsenkirchen Miners' Union, or, rather, Comrade Bartels, on behalf of all the Free Unions in Germany, has come out here with a declaration. In this connection I must declare: (1) The Presidium is not convinced that Comrade Bartels, and those with him who have drawn up the above declaration, really have the right to speak on behalf of all the Free Unions in Germany. (2) It is utterly out of place, and in very bad form, to present to this congress a declaration as ambiguous and as full of contradictions as the present one.

The third paragraph says that the independent organisations find it impossible to affiliate to the Red Labour Union International. The very next section, however, says that they will nevertheless join the International, but in the form of some sort of 'practical collaboration'. We are entirely in the dark as to how this collaboration is to be realised, since the declaration says absolutely nothing on this point.

And so, comrades, we see from this declaration that, on the one hand, they do not care to join, and on the other hand, do not wish to separate from the Red International of Labour Unions. (*Loud protests from the floor*) Yes, it is just as I said. In the third paragraph they want no affiliation, and in the fourth they want it again. (*From the floor: 'No, you're wrong.'*) The declaration says, 'We have been watching the proceedings of this congress, noting its one-sided stand dictated by the views of the comrades who, up to now, have been the leading elements in the Provisional International Council, and this arouses our deepest alarm as to the future destiny of the Red Labour International'. (*Noise from the floor*) And then further, 'We feel bound, in this connection, to register the fact of profound discontent felt by the organisations represented here. We must also state that a great number of organisations – including nearly all independent unions – will find it impossible to join the Red International of Labour Unions.' So it clearly says that nearly all independent organisations cannot affiliate. But it also follows that some of the independent organisations want to stay in the Red International, and even want to stay there without you.

It also became clear that among the representatives of the Free Unions there are differences of opinion. (*Loud protests*) Yes, it is quite so, as is best shown in the fourth paragraph where it expressly states: 'For this reason we could not but obey the imperative need of making the attempt to have these organisations stay within the Red Labour Union International'. This passage also shows that they wish to defend their rights within the Red Labour Union International. But it is not clearly stated whether they all wish to affiliate to our International. It rather follows that not all the independent organisations are of this opinion. (*Loud protests*)

Still, this congress is interested to know whether or not all the independent unions want to stay within the Red International. (*Voices: 'This is not clear.'*)

That is obscurely worded in your declaration. (*Voices from the floor: 'We came out only against Comrade Lozovsky's written statement.'*) But we must, at any rate, establish exactly what this declaration does say. (*Indignant shouts of 'Demagogue!'*)

When Comrade Grölig fires off his cry of injury, it does not affect us in the least, since we are used to it. But we must still say before the whole congress that all of this is inadmissible, the cries of 'demagogue', 'swindler', and other names of this ilk. We are here at this congress where we can freely express different opinions, and it is entirely indecent for a tiny minority to hurl at the majority such epithets as demagogues, swindlers, and the like. (*Noise and excitement*)

Comrades, all this is stated in the declaration. I shall read it again. 'We hold this congress and its leaders responsible before the revolutionary section of the working class of the world for all the hardships, trials, and defeats that are inevitable.' I shall not read the entire paragraph just read by Comrade Bartels. Here we read of leaders, and they are held responsible as if they were bosses. (*Objections from the floor*) Well, we are not going to have a split over this. It's your way of doing things for the benefit of the revolutionary family, which is not the least inclined to follow you in your experience. (*Shouts: 'Your ranks in Germany include anti-Bolsheviks.'*) The anti-Bolsheviks are found in your ranks. Your organisations are the homes of Laufenberg, Wolffheim, and Rühle. (*Arnos from his seat: 'And where is Levi?'*) We threw them out. (*Noise*)

We are not going to debate with you over this matter, as this will lead us nowhere. What matters here is whether you recognise this congress and accept its decisions as binding on you or not. In the first case, we should be able to work together. If not, we have nothing more to do with you. Here, at this congress, is just where you are duty-bound to give a straight and clear answer, but no evasive equivocal declarations. I tell you once more: we want to know what you are doing, or rather, what you intend to do. This you must tell us, so that everyone present here will understand you.

Rosmer: Comrade Lozovsky has the floor.

Lozovsky: The Presidium suggests the following order of work. No session tonight, but finish up commission work. Plenary session at 11:00 a.m. tomorrow for adopting the reports of the commissions on organisation, tactics, unemployment, and for taking up current business. There are no objections and the motion is carried.

(*The session adjourned at 4:10 p.m.*)

Trade Unions in East; Commission Reports; Russian Anarchists; Congress Closing

(*Session opens at 11:45 a.m. Comrade Lozovsky in the chair.*)

Lozovsky: Comrades, we have the following questions on the agenda for today: (1) adoption of the resolution on the report of the Provisional International Council of Trade Unions; (2) resolution on the trade-union movement in Eastern countries and in the colonies; (3) report of the Organisation Commission; (4) report of the Commission on Tactics; and (5) resolution on unemployment.

The following resolution was brought in on the report of the Provisional International Council. Are there any objections? There are none. The resolution is adopted.[1]

Here is the proposed resolution on the second question: the trade-union movement in Eastern countries and the colonies. This resolution will certainly not arouse any objections. Let me read it. (*Reads*)[2]

Comrade Nor-Yono from the Island of Java has the floor on the question of the appeal to the workers of the Eastern countries and the colonies.

Nor-Yono (Java):[3] My command of German is poor, and therefore I ask you to listen to me with patience. I have studied too little to speak well.

I wanted to tell you that for us Communists it is very hard to carry on propaganda in the colonies. The economic conditions in the colonies are different from those in the Western countries, while the agitation of the nationalist parties is far more successful than ours. Among the masses race hatred is very strong; for us Communists it is very hard to convince them that this hatred is wrong. In order for the masses to understand communism, it is necessary to explain to them the entire social structure of contemporary society.

1 For the text of the resolution on the activity of the Provisional Council of Red Trade and Industrial Unions, see p. 601.

2 For the text of the Resolution on the Labour Movement in the Near and Far Eastern Countries and the Colonies, see pp. 662–3.

3 There was only one delegate to the founding RILU congress from Java. Files from the Comintern archives contain a single mandate from that country: Raden Darsono, who is almost certainly the speaker here.

 | DOI:10.1163/9789004712867_021

The Communist movement in the colonies is quite young. In Java it began in 1913.[4] It is very hard for us to work there, as the Dutch government supports the nationalist parties and thus also fosters race hatred. It is our duty to turn this race hatred into class hatred. This is all the harder because the masses are too backward to understand the social interrelations as do the workers of Europe.

It would be very useful to us if the workers of all countries would reach out to these masses by means of a special appeal to the colonial masses, extending to them a fraternal hand so as to help in diminishing this race hatred: otherwise it may happen that the world revolution may take the form of a race revolution. In that case all the whites living there may be massacred. This is not our aim; we are not against the whites, but against the capitalists, against the oppressors. A manifesto should be drafted and translated into all the native languages in the colonies, in order to have them understand that the oppression of the colonial nations does not come from the whites, but from the capitalists. Capitalism jointly with the government is always striving to create a gulf between whites and blacks. Whenever black workers go on strike, the strikebreakers have always been whites. In this way the policy of capitalism, which consists in creating discord among the workers, has strengthened and intensified race hatred. Therefore, I heartily endorse your intention to issue an appeal to the colonial peoples in order to weaken race hatred and turn it into class hatred. (*Loud applause*)

Lozovsky: Comrades, Tom Mann has the floor to answer our brothers from the exploited colonies.

Tom Mann (Britain): Comrades, I should like to occupy this tribune for a short time in order to voice, on behalf of the British delegation as well as of myself, the feeling of deep satisfaction experienced by us at the meeting of Western workers with workers of the East, to which we have just been eyewitnesses. It is a joy to get the conviction that some of the nations of the East, in spite of all difficulties, have already taken definite and determined action for uniting with the labour movement of the world.

From the talk I had with the comrade from Java, I learned how hard it is for them to fight for organising labour; nevertheless, they have already achieved definite and undoubted success. For example, most of the railroadmen, to whom the comrade himself belongs, are already organised. The workers in the sugar industries are also organised.

4 Presumably a reference to the First Congress of Sarekat Islam on 26 January 1913.

But I was deeply grieved to hear about the mean part played by the whites in the labour movement of Java. As the comrade was telling me, the white people very frequently act in opposition to the Malayans and act as strikebreakers during strikes. But I hope that this will soon change, and that the race hatred of which our comrade spoke will cease and turn into class hatred and class struggle. At any rate, we heartily wish success to our comrades from Java and assure them that there are many white people who desire in no case to hinder the people of other colours in their struggle for emancipation.

I shall not occupy your time any longer, comrades. I only wish to express, on behalf of the British delegation, our great joy that Java, too, is present at this meeting of the world proletariat and that the working class of Java is organising. (*Applause*)

Lozovsky: Comrade Rosmer has the floor to make a special statement.

Rosmer: The American trade-union delegation makes the following proposal: Comrade George Andreytchine, one of the IWW leaders and a member of the Communist Party of America, who was sentenced to twenty years in prison, has just arrived at this congress after having successfully evaded arrest.[5] The American delegation proposes to greet him. (*Applause*)

Lozovsky: Comrade George Andreytchine has the floor.

George Andreytchine (USA, IWW): Comrades: Thanks to the Communist International, I am happy to find myself today in your midst and greet you in the name of the revolutionary workers of the United States. As you all know, there are hundreds of IWW workers and members of the Communist Party of America languishing today in the prisons of this 'democratic' republic of our most hypocritical ex-president Wilson. The Third International will fight for their liberation; they cannot be abandoned to a living death.

I do not want to abuse your patience by making a speech on the general situation in the United States, but I would like to say a few words about the labour movement in the United States and of the profound sympathy that the

5 Andreytchine was one of the defendants convicted in the mass frame-up trial of IWW leaders that included William D. Haywood. Together with eight other co-defendants – including fellow RILU congress attendees Haywood and Leo Laukki – Andreytchine jumped bail and went to Moscow rather than report to prison.

great masses of the workers in the United States feel for the great proletarian revolution that happened in this country. Great sympathy, which is so deep that Samuel Gompers cannot speak another word to the masses of the large industrial centres in the United States against the Russian Revolution. In Seattle, Butte, Minneapolis, Chicago, etc., Samuel Gompers would be shouted down, and so he is afraid to utter one word there against the Russian Revolution. Through my journey in the last few days that I spent in the United States; on my journey from New York to the Pacific Coast, to Seattle, I have witnessed the deepest and most profound sympathy and solidarity for the Russian Revolution and for the dictatorship of the Russian working class in the mass of the IWW members as well.

Some of the members of the IWW who are here have spoken and have uttered words against the tactics used in this great revolution. I speak in the name of the Communist opposition within the IWW, which will fight always not only against open treason, but also against every renunciation of revolutionary principles and traditions. The future will prove that our organisation is composed of revolutionists and not traitors and renegades. The time is near when the organisation will come out and fight against capitalism, just as the Russian workers did.

I can state that the Russian Revolution dominates the spirit not just of the best elements of the IWW, but also of the great masses of organised workers in the American Federation of Labor. At numerous union meetings and conferences, workers in the A.F. of L. have expressed their most profound sympathy and solidarity with the Russian Revolution, and they are ready to come to its aid.

Black workers in the United States are entirely devoted to the Russian Revolution. Thousands of these toilers, who are oppressed, who are beaten and lynched by the American bourgeoisie, by the American capitalists, are deeply in sympathy with Soviet Russia and the Red International of Labour Unions in the struggle to free the working class from the capitalist yoke. It's true that the economic development of the country has not yet reached the stage where the workers will be driven by despair and starvation to embark on revolutionary struggle.

In conclusion, I want to greet the congress in its effort to organise an International of industrial unions that will work alongside the Third, Communist International, to deliver the decisive blow to the capitalist system. I greet the fellow workers and comrades who have come from the different countries. In the name of the American revolutionary workers, I wish all success to the Red International of Labour Unions, as well as the Communist International. (*Applause*)

Report of Organisation Commission

Heckert: The congress is going to take up the report of the Organisation Commission. Comrade Lozovsky has the floor.

Lozovsky: The Organisation Commission had four sessions. The question they were concerned with is directly connected with the question of tactics. The question of organisation naturally corresponds to the basic lines that determine our tactics, conforming to the decisions adopted. Therefore, I won't take up your time by a lot of detail, but will rather go over straight to the amendments and changes brought in at the sessions of the Organisation Commission.

The first of the amendments was brought to point 19 dealing with the trade-union movement in America, especially with Canada, which is linked with the American Federation of Labor. The amendment states that so-called international unions that link the Canadian workers with American workers prevent the creation of a nationwide centre of Canadian unions that would fight against reformism in both America and Canada.

The second amendment was to point 21, dealing with Spain. The Spanish delegates expressed their full accord with the paragraph concerning them, but insisted on the amendment that stated that all unions that split from the reformist General Workers' Union [UGT] of Spain must affiliate with the National Confederation of Labour [CNT], and recommends that Communist nuclei working within the reformist unions get in close contract with the CNT.

Most of the debate arose around point 22 concerning Germany. The discussion revealed a very important difference of opinion within the commission, and almost led to a split in the German delegation. The question was what to do with the expelled unions – shall we create a separate national organisation or not? The majority of the German delegation was against the creation of any separate organisation. After a very long discussion and mutual compromises, a common opinion was formed: the main organisational problem for Germany consists in getting the expelled workers together and connecting them with an organisation that works within the unions and leads them to the conquest of the unions under the slogans: 'Down with the splitters!', 'Down with the trade-union bureaucracy that expels revolutionary workers from the unions!'

Minor corrections were brought in to point 35 dealing with the expulsion of whole unions, the necessity of organising them during the time period until their return to the industrial unions. Many comrades objected to this type of organisation, stating that as far as it concerns the workers who will return to the old organisations, the provisional unions must be organised on the same principle as the old ones. A formulation was adopted allowing for the creation of unions by craft or industry in conformity with local conditions and the aims of each union.

Finally the commission submitted a new section, number 37, concerning the organisation of women workers. You know that following the report of Comrade Sturm the commission decided to amend our organisational theses with such a special point. I will just read it; it's very short: this is one of its merits; the other one is that it is very clear and will not require any explanations. (*Reads*)[6]

All these amendments and changes are brought into the organisational theses. No other changes in principle were made for the simple reason that the theses, as I said here before, are the organised expression, the logical conclusion of the general policy established by us before and adopted by the congress. This is all I have to say on the organisational question.

Nin: We will put to a vote the theses on the organisational question. We are going to vote by country. Comrade Lozovsky will read the list.

Lozovsky reads the list of the delegations and groups of different countries.

Nin: The resolution is adopted by a majority of all the votes against six, with three abstentions. Voting against: three delegates from the United States of America; three from Canada have not voted at all; three delegations were absent pending the vote – Austria, Belgium, Germany (three delegates were out for deliberations pending the report of Comrade Lozovsky.) Results of the voting: 311 for and 6 against.[7]

Dautkus (Germany, General Workers' Union): The draft of amendments on the organisational question was not given to us, and this is why we refuse to vote on the amendments.

Lozovsky: In that case, you'll inform us about your decision later on.

Report of Commission on Tactics

Nin: Comrade Lozovsky has the floor to report on behalf of the Commission on Tactics.

---

6 For section 37 of the organisational theses dealing with 'Organisation of Women in the Trade Unions', see p. 646.

7 For the resolution on the organisation question, see pp. 635–48.

Lozovsky: Comrades, discussion in the Commission on Tactics did not run off so smoothly as in the Organisation Commission, since, by going thoroughly into the tactical questions, we have practically settled in advance all the questions before the Organisation Commission. The amendments made by the Commission on Tactics essentially amount to a more detailed formulation of some points that I am about to take up.

Points 9 and 10 aroused lively debates. The end of this clause says that revolutionary syndicalism took shape under the influence of anarchist ideology and has all the defects peculiar to anarchist radicalism. The syndicalists took strong exception to this wording, and proposed to reformulate this clause in the sense that revolutionary syndicalism is a definite attempt to reconcile Marxism with Proudhonism. The majority of us thought such a formulation wrong and therefore agreed to change only the phrase that the syndicalists wanted stricken out, as follows: 'The theoreticians of revolutionary syndicalism claimed it to be the synthesis of Proudhonism and Marxism'. By this version we simply state a definite fact and no more.

A substantive change was made in point 11, as suggested by the Spanish delegation. This point says that revolutionary syndicalism was formerly imbued with the idea of neutrality and independence as regards communism. The Spanish syndicalists – I lay stress on the word Spanish, because the other syndicalists and especially the French variety were conspicuously absent and took no part in the work of the commission – protested that they never professed any neutrality as regards communism; they were neutral only insofar as political parties were concerned. In connection with this statement, we modified this point to the effect that syndicalism was neutral as regards all political parties, including the political party of the proletariat, and declared itself opposed even to the proletarian state. The theses in the original wording said that syndicalists were in principle opposed to every state. We deleted this, because far from being the exclusive monopoly of syndicalism, opposition to the bourgeois state is the chief characteristic of every revolutionist.

Slight changes were made in point 12, where it speaks of trade unions and where, in its present version, it indicates more precisely that the traits of adaptation to capitalism – which were so characteristic of the past period – enabled the bourgeoisie, especially during the war, to utilise the trade unions for its class aims. By this we want to say in the theses that the patriotic enthusiasm that gripped the working masses, and that was responsible for the fact that the proletariat supported the bourgeoisie over the course of four years, was not accidental. It was instead the definite legacy of this period, and the traces of this horrible legacy were borne also by the workers' organisations.

The most substantial changes were made in the subsequent points. Without dwelling on these, I pass on to point 19, where the entire point was deleted. It said that the two currents struggling for supremacy in the French trade-union movement both claim the Amiens Charter. We deleted this in order to avoid repetition, because the same thing was said in one of the preceding points.

Next, very important changes were made in the points dealing with the condition of the trade-union movement in Britain. In the corresponding points we emphasised the part played by the factory committees, and pointed out that the weakness of the opposition within the British trade-union movement did not consist in its incapacity to conquer any unions, but in the lack of coordination in their activities and movement, in its separate organisations and groups in the trade-union movement.

On Germany we had a conflict with the German *Unionen*. The comrades of these unions, as you well know, as a general rule, create conflicts easily where there are no grounds for them. This conflict was due to the fact that we declared the slogan 'Out of the trade unions!' to be counterrevolutionary. When these comrades protested, I said that we would not insist on this word and should replace it by another, and indeed we replaced it by pointing out that the slogan concerning withdrawal from the unions is contrary to the interests of the working class and of the social revolution.

They then protested just as energetically against the affirmation in the theses to the effect that the German *Unionen*, rather than uniting, were fighting among themselves. This affirmation seemed to them so monstrous that they decided to leave the session of the commission, slamming the door and taking no further part in the commission's work. They explained their action by saying that here they were all united, and that all their organisations and separate little groups were closely coordinating their activity. To this I answered as follows: 'You comrades united to fight against us, but in your own country you failed to unite other than against the Communists.'

At any rate, they left the commission. In order to show clearly that the congress considers it necessary, in any case, to give the opportunity to every labour organisation that stands for our fundamental principles to remain in the ranks of the Red International of Labour Unions and work, we also deleted the passage in question and replaced it as follows: 'They did not coordinate their struggle against the capitalists'. We leave it to the judgement of the members of these unions to determine whether our tactics and theses are correct. For us, we responded to their exit from the commission by passing on to the next order of business and continuing our work.

Modifications and precisions were also made in point 42, at the end, where the tasks of the Red International in the shops were, as suggested by Comrade Nin, more precisely formulated to the effect that it was necessary to carry on the struggle, draw the unions into it, and pose the question of Moscow or Amsterdam – i.e., revolution or collaboration with the bourgeoisie – and thus unremittingly to draw the attention of the working masses to the decisions of our congress.

Next, an important addition was made to section VIII of the programme of action. The commission, first of all, thought it necessary to delete entirely point 52, concerning sabotage. The question of sabotage is differently understood even by those who belong to the same tendency, and so we feared that this question would take up more than one session. We therefore decided to delete this altogether, so as not to encumber our programme of action.

Instead of this, we replaced it with a new formulation, as follows:

> The employers are making use of any means in their power to bring about a split in the ranks of the labour movement. They fully made use of women's labour during the war, and continue to use this cheap labour power for the purpose of cutting men's wages. Instead of fighting the employers, the workers in a number of countries have called for removing women from industry and expelling them from the unions. This policy should be met with determined resistance by the red trade unions. Revolutionary unions must fight for equality of working conditions for men and women and for equal pay for equal work.

This point was introduced in the programme of action at Comrade Murphy's suggestion and was unanimously adopted.

The second addition in this programme was made by a comrade of the German delegation and dealt with three questions: militarisation of labour, taxation of wages, and compulsory arbitration. This point became number 59 and reads as follows:

> In order to paralyse and eliminate the fighting force of the working class, the bourgeois governments, under the pretext of defending vital interests of the nation, work to militarise separate enterprises and even whole branches of industry. Under the cover of preventing, as far as possible, economic crisis, they introduced, in the interests of capital, obligatory arbitration courts and conflict commissions. Still in the interests of capital, some countries introduced withholding taxes on earnings, with the aim of throwing the weight of the war wholly on the shoulders of the working class – the tax collectors being the employers themselves. It is incumbent upon the trade unions to lead fights against these state measures, which exclusively serve the interests of the capitalist class.

These, comrades, are the changes made by the Commission on Tactics in the draft submitted to you.

I can say that the Commission on Tactics exerted its utmost efforts to find a common language satisfactory for all comrades. Our aim is that the line of action mapped out by the congress should not just be adopted formally. We do not want any group or organisation to feel offended on formal grounds or some idle pretext and say, 'We don't want to work jointly with you because such-and-such clause is offensively formulated.' That aim was realised.

In any number of differences that sprang up in connection with the proposals made by the Spanish delegation, the German delegation, and Comrade Murphy, the commission mandated me, jointly with the authors of the above proposals, to work out a conciliatory formulation, and we found such a formulation in every case. We took out all formulations that seemed offensive to anyone and left unchanged only principles and the substance of the theses. The commission unanimously adopted the theses embodying the above amendments. The commission adopted the theses unanimously, and proposes that the congress do the same.

Nin: Before putting the theses on tactics to a vote, I give the floor to Comrade Arlandis for reading a declaration signed by several delegations.

Hilario Arlandis: A few days ago, when we discussed the tasks and tactics of the trade-union movement, many members of the delegations now present could not banish their fears that some delegates, owing perhaps to their failure to understand the ideology and the characteristic traits of the labour movement in Western Europe, might draw conclusions far from beneficial to our syndicalist movement.

On account of the fact that we have come here with the firm determination to forge proletarian unity necessary for bringing about the approaching world revolution, we think it necessary to come and speak before this congress for the information of those delegates who are poorly informed about our movement. The object of our declaration is to prevent the adoption of decisions that are too rash. Such decisions would first of all cause a disruption among several delegations present here, and would then have as their result that in some countries it would be physically impossible to carry out many decisions of the congress, even if the delegates present here who represent those countries were to submit to the opinion of the majority. Although it is rather late just now to make this declaration, I still want to read it so that it may be incorporated in the minutes of this congress, and serve us as justification and a guarantee. This declaration, together with the discussion at the congress, will serve in the future for the syndicalist organisations of the whole world as a starting point for their activity. The declaration reads as follows:

Whereas:

1. The Red International of Labour Unions should represent all revolutionary currents found in the trade-union movement;
2. Every attempt on the part of any one current to assume the dominant position must be looked upon as detrimental to the interest of the revolutionary proletariat;
3. Revolutionary syndicalism is the living embodiment of the class struggle and cannot be forced into a narrow sectarian framework;
4. The chief aim of our Red International of Labour Unions is to strengthen the workers' organisations that have already broken with Amsterdam;
5. In view of the fact that the tactics of organising nuclei cannot be applied equally in all countries, and that in several countries – as for instance in Germany – our chief aim should be the creation of a single strong organisation, for which the now-existing Communist nuclei groups with their two million members and all the other organisations that have broken with Amsterdam and have a membership of 1.5 million may serve as the basis, and that such a situation may arise in other countries as well;
6. It is necessary to respect the opinions of the revolutionary organisations that have broken with Amsterdam, and that every pressure on the part of the congress compelling them to go back to the reformist unions may prove fatal to the Red International and create, as a result, an International consisting exclusively of nuclei;
7. One of our tasks is to destroy the old reformist unions and to draw the masses into our revolutionary unions by means of energetic propaganda and action in the factories and shops, amidst the very heart of the working masses.

Therefore:

We call upon the congress to recognise that tactics of one sort or another as regards the reformist unions should be applied in accordance with the conditions and the development of the labour movement in each given country.

On the other hand, we declare before this congress that although we firmly wish to achieve the unification of all revolutionary forces, a too-rash decision adopted to the detriment of independently existing organisations may bring about a dangerous rupture in the movement that may prove fatal for the revolutionary movement as a whole. We hope that this will not happen and that the spirit of solidarity will triumph.

Moscow, July 15, 1921

Signed:
National Confederation of Labour (Spain)
Gelsenkirchen Free Workers' Union (Germany)
Workers' Central Organisation (Sweden)
National Labour Secretariat (Holland)
Hand and Brain Workers' Union (Germany)
Free Agricultural Workers' Union (Germany)
Communist Labour Federation (Argentina)
Federation of Labour (Uruguay)
Confederation of Workers of the World (France)
General Workers' Union (Germany)
German Seamen's Union
Syndicalist Union (Italy)
Members of the French delegation: Michel Relenque, Henri Sirolle, Jean Gaudeux;
Cascaden, delegate of Canada;
Williams, delegate of the IWW (USA);
Ramírez, delegate of Mexico.

As I said, this declaration is somewhat tardy, as the decision of the congress has already been formulated. The commissions on organisation and on tactics have already submitted their conclusions, which are a compromise among various currents represented here. We think that just now the rights of the minority will be sufficiently respected if we continue on the road of the revolution.

In view of the fact that the work of the congress is coming to a close, we think that our present aim should be to carry out in our country the general guidelines adopted by this congress.

We are concerned not about particular interests and resentments of small local organisations that may be more or less justified, but about the interests of the world proletarian revolution. For this reason, we Spanish syndicalists and those from other countries have come here not to defend at any price our point of view, but to establish revolutionary agreement and coordinated action in all countries.

On the one hand, we encourage our comrades who call themselves extremists to reflect on the question of whether or not their actions are detrimental to the revolution by applying obstructionist tactics. On the other hand, we call upon the comrades of the Communist majority to put a stop to the continual disputes with the revolutionary minority that holds a different point of view. We repeat, for the benefit of both, that our aim is to establish revolutionary unity in all countries.

The most important task at the present moment is to put the interests of the world proletariat above all quarrels and suspicions of ideological sects.

We therefore say to the delegates of this congress, on behalf of the Spanish proletariat just now engaged in a desperate, implacable fight with the bourgeoisie, that our sacrifices must not be in vain, but must serve the cause of the revolution. It is a vital necessity to create a united front to seize the means of production, to break the chains of the capitalist system, and establish the dictatorship of the proletariat.

Lozovsky: Comrade Dautkus has the floor for a statement.

Leopold Dautkus: Comrade Lozovsky in his report on the work of the Commission on Tactics represented the matter in such a light as if we left the session of the commission senselessly, as if we left the hall because it was said there that the Gelsenkirchen Free Workers' Union and the General Workers' Union are fighting among themselves. This is not quite the case, and I want to explain just what made us leave the meeting.

We intended to work together and took part, considering Comrade Lozovsky's draft on the tasks and tactics of trade unions up to point 22 of section IV on trade unions before the war.

In examining this point, we did not accuse the partisans of the nuclei of being counterrevolutionaries. We did not demand the deletion from this point of the passage speaking about oppositional nuclei by Communists within the trade unions. But we did insist on deleting the passage in which we were declared to be counterrevolutionaries. We thus propose to delete the following words: 'the pessimistic view provoked by the trade-union bureaucracy found expression in the slogan "smash the unions", which is contrary to the interests of the working class and the social revolution.'

Next, we objected to the following passage: 'The Gelsenkirchen Free Workers' Union and the General Workers' Union, and the Syndicalist Union – is working in its own way instead of conducting any coordinated struggle against the capitalists and their trade-union agents.' Whether or not we fought against the capitalists and their agents in Germany is a question that we shall calmly answer to the German workers. We protested the assertion that we are fighting against each other, and we declared that the Gelsenkirchen Free Workers' Union and the General Workers' Union of Germany never fought one another, and that, on the contrary, as early as last April we started negotiations on the question of fusion. We thought it necessary to establish this fact, because the theses contain a flagrant error, misinformation that speaks of our alleged dissensions and quarrels, and in the part evaluating our activity as counterrevolutionary. And only because we did not want to be an accessory to this untruth embodied in the theses and subsequently spread throughout the world, we left the session, not wishing to assume responsibility for this untruth.

Now I will say a few words about the positions that the German *Unionen* will take in the future. Even now the question is arising whether they will affiliate with the Red Trade Union International or not. In this connection I may state that we leave the decision of this question to the members of our unions. As soon as we return to Germany, we shall call a congress jointly with the Gelsenkirchen Union and submit this question for decision.

I would like to again speak about Comrade Lozovsky's theses on the question of organisation dealing with factory committees. Here is what it says in point 8:

> The gathering of the revolutionary forces in the trade-union movement must proceed under the banner of organisation of factory committees. Factory committees must be elected by all the workers of a given enterprise, independently of their political or religious beliefs. The attempt to create factory committees at meetings of fellow party members, as practised in Germany by the General Workers' Union, is only a caricature and discredits the very idea of such organisations in the eyes of the large working masses. As a matter of fact, under the false name of factory committees, the General Workers' Union established its party fractions. This, of course, is within the right of any organisation, but there is no need to give such high-sounding names to these nuclei.

Comrades, I declare before the entire congress that this whole point is a lie. All the comrades of the nuclei, if they are honest, will confirm the fact that when the factory committees were being elected in Germany we fought under the slogan that they should be elected by all the workers of the enterprise, irrespective of their opinions. In the theses we presented to the Organisation Commission, we clearly said that all workers in the enterprise should participate. Thus our theses propose precisely the opposite of what Comrade Lozovsky's theses ascribe to us.

I must say that if all these wrong passages remain in the theses, when we return to Germany and say that the congress has approved this, then, when we submit these theses to a vote, the vote will not be in favour of the Red Trade

Union International. I further declare that we shall invite to our congress a representative of the Red Trade Union International, and I guarantee that he will have full opportunity to speak without any time limit.

I thought it necessary to state this, and I repeat again that the decision on the question of affiliation to the Red Trade Union International shall be left to our members in Germany.

Bartels (*from his seat*): We propose to delete all the disputed passages.

Lozovsky: So, comrades, the representative of the Gelsenkirchen Union moves to delete point 22 from the theses on tactics. Who is in favour of this motion? All are against. In this case I shall put the theses as a whole to a vote.

Britain for. Germany: 11 for, 5 against. Italy for. Spain for. Poland for. Russia for. France: 14 for, 2 abstaining. United States: 13 for, 3 against. Czechoslovakia for. Austria for. Hungary for. Bulgaria for. Yugoslavia for. Ukraine for. Norway for. Australia for. Argentina for. Holland for. Switzerland for. Romania for. Canada: 5 for, 3 against.[8] Mexico for. Sweden: 5 for, 3 abstaining. Denmark for. Far Eastern Republic for. Azerbaijan for. Armenia for. Georgia for. Korea for. Latvia for. Lithuania for. Luxembourg for. Turkey for. Estonia for. Abkhazia for.

The vote will be immediately counted.[9]

Comrade Cascaden has the floor for a statement.

Gordon Cascaden (Canada): Fellow Worker Andreytchine, in his speech, whether by a slip of the tongue or not, left the impression that members of the IWW present in this room were against the Russian Revolution.

I am not here as a representative of the IWW, but I am also a member of that organisation. I have never heard one man here who is a member of the IWW make any attacks on the Russian Revolution, and I believe that we all are wholeheartedly in favour of it. As a professional writer I have at all times written in favour of the Russian Revolution, and expect to continue in this attitude when I return to Canada and the United States. My articles in favour of Russia are known to several fellow workers in this room.

We may differ with you on forms of organisation, but we always will support the Russian Revolution.

Lozovsky: Comrade Williams has the floor to make a statement.

---

8 This is per the minutes, but Canada had only two votes.

9 For the text of the Resolution on the Tasks and Tactics of the Trade Unions, see pp. 606–24.

George Williams (USA, IWW): Comrade Andreytchine in his speech said that 'members of the IWW here in Russia were attacking the Russian Revolution'. For the representatives of the IWW present and on behalf of the organisation I represent, I wish to deny entirely that this statement is true. Comrade Andreytchine, when questioned by me, stated he did not mean the IWW delegates who are present, but was referring to John Sandgren, who, as is well known, was removed as editor of the *OBU* magazine for his attitude towards Soviet Russia.[10]

I recognise that Comrade Andreytchine in his speech may have overlooked the fact that his statement, being couched in general terms, would be construed as meaning those of the IWW who are present here as delegates. Therefore, it would be highly advisable, so that justice be done to the IWW as an organisation and the delegates present, to strike out of the stenographic records that part of Comrade Andreytchine's speech which is objected to here, and I hereby offer this as a proposal.

(Statement also signed by Krause, Samuel Bolotin, M. Belinkis.)

Lozovsky: Comrade Flynn has the floor to make a statement.

Flynn (USA): Comrades, I wish to read to you a certain matter in connection with the accusations against John Sandgren. It has been denied or has been affirmed that John Sandgren, editor of the *One Big Union* monthly organ of the IWW, was removed because of his attitude. I wish to read to you from page 6 of the minutes of the last convention of the Industrial Workers of the World,[11] under the General Executive Board Report of the fourth day session as follows: 'One of the unpleasant problems that the board had to meet was the removal of the editor of the *OBU* who also had failed to keep in accord with the policy laid down by the board at the previous sessions. So much hostility had arisen against the paper because of the controversial articles he had published that the name was changed to the *Industrial Pioneer*.'

We emphatically deny that John Sandgren was removed from office because of the attitude against the Communist elements. We emphatically deny that there has been any change in the policy of the organ, as will be shown by statements made by the editor who succeeds him.

10 For the Sandgren affair, see p. 588, n. 8.

11 The IWW's Thirteenth Convention was held in Chicago 9–27 May 1921.

Unemployment Question

Lozovsky: We still have to discuss another two or three questions, the question of unemployment included. Comrade Tsyperovich has the floor.

Grigorii Tsyperovich: The question of unemployment had been on the agenda. As we did not think it necessary to devote a special session to the matter to open a discussion on the subject, we decided to draft a resolution and propose it to the congress for a vote. The drafting of this resolution was entrusted to Comrade Bell. The Presidium has, however, found the comrade's draft to be not sufficiently clear and complete. The redrafting of this resolution was entrusted to Comrade Leve, who did so.

We were unable to reconcile the two drafts, and a special commission was designated to work out a new draft. Only at the close of the congress have I managed to look through the theses presented by this commission, but unfortunately it has not been translated into any other language. For this reason we are unable to present a sufficiently worked-out resolution on such an important question.

In view of this, the Presidium has charged me to make the following proposal: 'All material on the question and the resolutions drafted by the commission are to be handed in to the council, headed by the new bureau, for redrafting and publication of it on behalf of the congress.' Signed by Comrade Bell and the council.

This is necessary, as the importance of the resolution in question requires it to be well worked out and well founded, so that it produces the desired impression.

Lozovsky: Comrade Bell has the floor to make a statement.

Thomas Bell: Comrades, it is necessary to make an explanation concerning the work of the Unemployment Commission.

After I presented the theses to this congress, they were sent to the commission, to edit all the points of the resolution and to get it translated. But I discovered that the theses I had presented had been modified and abridged. They set aside the theses I presented and proceeded with the translation of the modified theses. The consequence was that when the commission met we could not get a translation of the theses that I presented to this congress. No translation of it has yet been received; consequently it was impossible for the commission to go through the theses point by point and to do what was proper.

We did the next best thing. I quickly drafted a resolution and presented it to the next session of the commission on Saturday, as the basis for discussion. The commission went through this resolution and made some modifications. It was generally agreed, after discussing the different points that were subjected to criticism in the resolution, that the resolution should be expanded; it was expanded and finally presented to the commission meeting this morning. After going through the resolution and making new modifications, it proceeded to make the translation into German and French, although it was unable to get a translation into Russian.

So you will understand that if there is any delay, the fault is not with the commission or on my part, but with changes done by somebody in the Press Bureau, interfering with things they had no right to interfere with. I wish to declare that I accept the decision of the Presidium, and I dare say that the commission also will accept the decision of the Presidium, and that no reflection should be cast upon me for this delay.

Lozovsky: Comrade Drewnitzky has the floor.

Drewnitzky (Germany, Gelsenkirchen Free Workers' Union): Comrades, when the question of unemployment was brought in before the congress and the reporter gave sufficient references for his theses, we made a proposal to open a discussion on this question, but our motion was rejected. It was clear to us that without discussing the question of unemployment, without comments by the congress on this matter, nothing will be done in this direction.

The majority of the congress does not pay us much attention, but in spite of that we elected a commission that we assigned to deal with this question. After a whole series of plenary sittings, this commission worked out a resolution agreed to by all. The Presidium does not like this resolution, but I find that insofar as this resolution has been unambiguously accepted by the commission, we have the right to present it to the congress. I repeat and insist that we may bring before the congress something other than that which pleases the Presidium. The key thing is for it to be of use for the unemployed. We insist upon taking a vote on the resolution, as we consider that something must be done with regard to this question before the end of the congress. I advise everyone present to accept the resolution in its final form.

Lozovsky: Comrades, any proposal can be utilised demagogically, as the representative of the German delegation has done just now. The congress elected a Presidium of eleven members – people whom it trusts. The resolution is not translated yet, and therefore the Presidium as a whole has not had the possibility of familiarising itself with it.

Commissions with a number of members have been working all the time, and yet they have managed to finish their work on time. All of a sudden a commission of seven persons has found time to present theses just five minutes before the report was delivered. A session of the Central Council will take place tomorrow, and it will adopt the draft on behalf of the congress. But to say that the Presidium wishes one thing and the proletariat wishes another is demagogy, which cannot be allowed at an international workers' congress. Such a thing aims to create incidents where there it is no basis for doing so.

Lozovsky (as chair): Who here is for referring the resolution accepted by the commission to the Central Council, which will have its sitting tomorrow morning, for adoption of the resolution on behalf of the Congress? Who is against? The proposal is accepted.[12]

Comrade Haywood has the floor.

William D. Haywood (USA, IWW):[13] Comrades, one of the members of the American delegation present here stated something that needs correction. Delegate Flynn read here a paper containing, as he claimed, the decision of the National Executive Committee of the IWW to the effect of discharging John Sandgren from his editorial post on the staff of *One Big Union*, the IWW monthly. But Flynn added a few expressions not contained in the above-cited source, which entirely change the gist of the matter. Comrades, I am a Communist and also a member of the IWW. I was chairman at the first IWW convention when this organisation was at its inception, and so I won't stand for any false assertions and insulting sallies flung at an organisation that invariably and constantly led the class struggle in the United States. I know, and Flynn also knows, that hundreds of IWW members are at present pining away in American jails for the fight that they have been carrying out against the capitalist class and the war.

Allow me to tell you about the movement that started against John Sandgren and its causes. As stated by the editor who took Sandgren's place, he was discharged on account of one of his articles. Here is what the new editor says:[14]

12 For the text of the resolution on unemployment eventually adopted, see pp. 658–60.

13 The identification of Haywood as representing the IWW is from the published proceedings. Such identification was not given when Haywood spoke in session 10.

14 Sandgren was replaced as editor of the *Industrial Pioneer* by Henry Van Dorn.
Haywood appears to be quoting here from several sources, including Van Dorn's report to the Thirteenth Convention of the IWW in May 1921, published in *Minutes of the 13th Convention of the IWW* (Chicago: IWW, 1921).

> After I had worked a few weeks with Sandgren, he was discharged as editor for his hostile attitude towards Soviet Russia, which came out in very bold relief in the editorial published in the December issue of the monthly under the caption of 'Wrangel and the Bolsheviks'. One of the most unpleasant duties that fell to the lot of the Executive Committee was to discharge the editor of the *One Big Union* for his failure to act in accordance with the instructions of this Committee. The tenor and the tone of his articles antagonised the readers of this monthly to such an extent that its further publication had to be resumed under the new name of *Industrial Pioneer*. At the convention, Sandgren was given the floor for explanations, which called forth the joint protest on the part of Comrades Smith and Murray to the effect that Sandgren was enjoying special privileges in getting the floor. Then followed the joint motion made by Jackson and Donnelly calling for the endorsement on the part of the convention of the decision of the Executive Committee to dismiss John Sandgren from his editorial post. This motion was carried.

Now I can understand why the non-communists are so much against the IWW. I have not heard Communists coming out from this rostrum against the IWW. Like the comrade who spoke here this morning, I am in Russia for the same reason that formerly made our Russian comrades leave Russia and emigrate to America. It was only thanks to the Communist Party that I did not land a twenty-year term in jail. I hope that, if in the course of the next year, the IWW takes a correct tactical line, the number of Communists in this organisation will rise during that year to 10,000, and every one of them will be a fighter on whom you can safely rely, because these men fear neither jail nor execution. They fear nobody and nothing. I can assure you that every member of the IWW is body and soul with Soviet Russia.

Lozovsky: Comrade Crosby has the floor.

Jack Crosby[15] [Pascal Cosgrove] (USA): Comrades, I shall claim your attention for only a few minutes. At this congress a great deal of time was spent in discuss-

15 The identification of Crosby as the speaker here – included in all languages of the proceedings – is problematic. The stenographers record Crosby as saying that he represents the 'revolutionary workers of Seattle'. But the delegate representing the Seattle Central Labor Council at the RILU congress was Hulet Wells, so it's likely Wells was actually the speaker here. Crosby, on the other hand, had credentials issued from within the Amalgamated Metal Workers, the Amalgamated Food Workers, the Boot and Shoe Workers, and the Amalgamated Clothing Workers.

ing the American question. The reason is that in America, as well as in many other countries, there are two antagonistic points of view on the question of the form of labour organisation. One is based on the purely craft principle. The other, on the industrial principle. I want to say that I was delegated to this congress not by the A.F. of L., nor by the IWW, but by the revolutionary workers of Seattle. I also want to point out that in America, irrespective of the two above-mentioned points of view prevailing in the labour movement, there are labour organisations on a mass scale fully in sympathy with Soviet Russia.

I shall refer to Comrade Andreytchine, who quite correctly pointed out that Sam Gompers would not dare to come out openly in some cities of the United States against Soviet Russia. Comrades, I think that the time is not far off when persons of the Sam Gompers and Sandgren type will not dare to say anything against Soviet Russia. The discussion that was started here on this question was a pure waste of time, which is to be regretted.

As to the IWW, I must say that Sandgren was discharged for the reasons already stated. But I must say in addition that one of the reasons was that the Communists in the IWW did not want to buy this monthly and even mailed it back to the editorial office. There is in this organisation, beyond any doubt, a sound current of opinion, because propaganda against Soviet Russia among the ranks of the working class in America, both within the IWW as well as the A.F. of L., must be a complete failure. The reason is that the American working class realises that Soviet Russia – or rather, the Communists in Soviet Russia – have, for the last few years, done for the working class of Russia, as well as for the world proletariat, far more than anybody on the face of the globe.

A question was put here by the syndicalists present as to who was going to head the Red Labour International. I must say that this International has sufficiently shown its capacity for and the right to lead the proletariat, and no one can deny this. Neither the syndicalists nor the IWW can draw the masses along with them, as can the red appeal of the International in Moscow. When I am back home from this congress, I shall tell everyone of what has been done here in Moscow. I shall also point out the Amsterdam International, explain the difference between the two, and show what our goal is.

Statement on Russian Anarchists

Nikolai Bukharin: I must make the following statement in the name of the Central Committee of the Russian Communist Party. Insofar as it is known to all comrades, some among those present here are concerned about the question of the Russian anarchists, some of whom are now in prison and have called a hunger strike.[16] Our Western European and American comrades have an exact idea on the essentials of anarchism. Russian anarchism is, however, of an entirely different nature than the Western European and American variety, which, as a social tendency, has drawn in a section of the proletariat. Russian anarchism, on the other hand, finds its support in social layers other than the proletariat.

The main tendencies of Russian anarchism are not the product of the working class or a considerable section of it, but of a certain definite section of our peasantry, which uses anarchist phraseology as a cover. We live in a situation under which the proletariat, as the minority of the population, is compelled to rule the state. The majority of the population are peasants, and in some parts of our enormous country a section of the rich peasants are geographically concentrated.

We have an instance of this in Ukraine. The fact that Ukraine is the clearest expression of genuine Russian anarchism is no accident. On the contrary, it is the essential basis for it, finding its real embodiment – as must be known to you – in the guerrilla gang of the famous Makhno.[17] It is no less clear why the anarchist form finds the most sympathy among the wealthy, exploiting peasantry.

When we arrive in the countryside, invested with proletarian power – and all the more so in a rich village – we first of all demand bread from the peasants in order to give it to the starving workers. Up until now we could only use the method of requisitioning. Now we obtain bread by means of a tax in kind;[18] we dispossess the peasants of a part of their grain and are compelled to do so in the interests of the working class. But at moments when the counterrevolution was raising its head – it especially manifested itself with the advance of General Denikin and other white generals – these generals also took bread from the

16 On 2 July 1921 thirteen imprisoned anarchists affiliated to the 'Golos Truda' group started a hunger strike at the Taganka prison in Moscow.

17 Nestor Makhno was a Ukrainian anarchist who built a partisan army of 20,000. In 1918 and early 1919 his forces fought German, Austrian, and White Army forces, at times in collaboration with Bolshevik units. In late 1919 and early 1920, however, his forces were waging war against the Red Army. The Makhnovists were largely defeated by the time of the RILU founding congress, and in August 1921 Makhno himself escaped across the border, eventually winding up in Paris.

18 The New Economic Policy (NEP) was a series of measures first introduced in Soviet Russia in March 1921, aiming to restore economic relations between city and countryside. Replacing the previous system of grain requisitioning with a tax in kind, the NEP permitted peasants to freely market their grain, restored freedom of commerce, provided scope for small-scale capitalist enterprises, and subjected state-owned enterprises and administration to budgetary controls.

peasants. So when the Red Army arrived, the peasants were against the reds; when the whites arrived, they were against the whites. This was the terrain on which anarchist phraseology arose.

By its external forms, it is a specifically Russian anarchism. Insofar as it is directed against the whites, it is advantageous for us Communists, because it destroys the foundation of the former class structure in Russia. But when it is directed against the proletariat's economic management, it plays the role of the Vendée of the rich peasantry against the proletariat.[19] I have already explained to you the reason why this Vendée was bound to assume a purely Russian form of anarchism. If our appreciation of this movement is accurate, then this anarchist revolution should be defined as objectively counterrevolutionary. Under the difficult situation of our economy and the current political conditions, this tendency presents a big danger.

I want to cite some facts to help give you an idea of the Makhno movement and its significance.

On 5 June at the Fairsevo station, Makhno cut the telephone and telegraph wires, destroyed the tracks, and derailed train no. 423. It carried away the valuables that were in the train, and put all the Communists to the sword.

On 8 June at the Vassilievka station, Makhno destroyed the railway line.

On 18 June Makhno made a raid on the Grishino station, where he stayed for three hours, ordered the shooting of fourteen prisoners – Soviet employees and workers – destroyed the telegraph wires, and pillaged the railway food storage warehouses.

On 26 June Makhno broke into the Constantinograd district, and in the course of two days put to death eighty-four Red Army soldiers.

On 12 August Makhno made a raid in Senkovo and killed two members of the district party committee and seven Soviet employees.

On 16 August at the Mirgorod-Gogolev district, Makhno destroyed the railway in three places. In Mirgorod Makhno's gangs pillaged during two days all the food depots of the district, destroyed all the buildings of the soviets and workers' organisations, as well as fifteen telegraph machines. Killed in the most barbaric way were twenty-one red workers and soldiers. Makhno's anarchists were assisted in their plunder by the wealthy peasants of the vicinity, who arrived there in their carts.

On 12 December 1920 Makhno was in Berdiansk. His men, under the command of Makhno himself, massacred, in the course of three hours, eighty-three

19 Vendée is a department in northern France that was a centre of royalist and peasant insurrection against the French Revolution from 1793 to 1795.

Communists, among them one of the best workers of Ukraine, Comrade Michelovich. They tore off arms, cut off limbs, disembowelled, pierced with bayonets, and hammered people to death.

This is a short summary taken from the communications by the Ukraine general staff. Many more cases might be cited.

The economic ruin might have had heavy consequences. As to the political side of the question, we must say that Makhno committed all the brutalities under the slogan 'death to Communists'. The Kronstadt revolt had the same slogan too, and we had to pay for it with the lives of Communists, of many of the best forces we had, for it is the Communist Party that leads the proletariat.[20]

In the dynamite attack on the Moscow [Party] Committee – where among other comrades I too was in danger – we can find traces of exactly the same political orientation. Fifteen employees were killed, and among those who perished were women with children.[21]

Many among them [the anarchists], if we can put it this way, belong to the labour aristocracy.

In our relations with our adversaries, there is no place either for sentimentality or a desire for vengeance. We merely follow the law of political utility. No revolutionary in the world can expect us to spare our enemies when they attack us with bombs and grenades, and so on. It is the law of war.

Since many of our comrades – the French in particular – identify the Ukrainian anarchist movement with that of Western Europe – quite erroneously, in our opinion – they participated in actions in defence of the Russian anarchists. In connection with this, some have bound themselves by certain obligations.

We declare once more that we will do our utmost to comply with the request of these comrades, but they should not forget that they are bound by certain obligations that they will have to fulfil. I cannot enter into details here, and the comrades who have had to observe conspiratorial activity will be able to understand us. If we do not go into the 'facts' of this affair, it is not because there is nothing to say – and when I say that the practical side of the question is not to be discussed, it is because this question bears the character of secrecy. I repeat again that all revolutionaries who have had to resort to conspiracy will understand me.

Therefore, the declaration I have made in the name of the Central Committee is to be considered as a declaration by our party.

---

20 For the Kronstadt uprising, see p. 246, n. 5.

21 On 25 September 1919 anarchists threw dynamite into the headquarters of the Moscow Committee of the Russian Communist Party. Twelve were killed and fifty-five were wounded, including Bukharin himself.

Lozovsky: We now take up the following point on the agenda. (*Noise and shouts from the seats of the French and Spanish delegations.*)[22]

Sirolle (*from his seat*): I demand to be given the floor to make a statement on the declaration of Comrade Bukharin.

Lozovsky: I put to a vote the question of giving the floor to Comrade Sirolle. The majority of the congress decides to grant the floor to Comrade Sirolle for the statement. Comrade Sirolle has the floor.

Henri Sirolle (France): Comrades, we had not the slightest wish that discussions take place at the congress on this question. Since the moment of our arrival in Russia, based on our mandate by large French organisations, we considered ourselves duty-bound to obtain the widest possible amnesty for our anarchist comrades. We coordinated our actions with the Spanish delegation, with the Italian Syndicalist Union, with our Canadian workers, with comrades from the Communist Workers' Party of Germany, and with Comrade Tom Mann. We agreed to form a committee charged with investigating the question in order to submit to the Soviet government our request for amnesty. Along these lines we applied to the respective representatives of the government. We discussed the question with Comrade Lenin and defined the main lines of it.

Comrade Lunacharsky was assigned to receive us in order to establish the final concrete measures to be taken in the best interest of all. We determined the necessary concrete decisions together with the above-mentioned comrades, and in the presence of delegates of the Russian anarchist movement, we signed together the report on the question. It was agreed that all the questions should not be given publicity.[23] And if we have been compelled to discuss

22 This brief reference in the minutes greatly understates the tumult in the hall following Bukharin's report, which, according to Cascaden, caused 'the greatest uproar of the whole Congress. Delegates stood on chairs singing the "Internationale" when Lozovsky endeavored to speak. For several minutes the convention floor was not unlike the New York stock exchange with every one shouting, including spectators who rushed from their seats onto the convention floor itself. When many delegates were about to walk out it was decided to give the floor to Sirolle.' In Cascaden 1922, p. 82.

23 On Lenin's suggestion, a joint committee representing the Soviet government and foreign RILU delegates met to find a mutually agreeable solution. An appeal to the prisoners was issued to them signed by Arlandis, Leval, Sirolle, Michel [Relenque], A. Shapiro, and Anatoly Lunacharsky asking for an end to their action; the prisoners ended their hunger strike on 14 July. They were released 17 September and deported to Germany in January 1922.

the question at this congress, if the world counterrevolution should attempt to utilise this discussion, the responsibility for it rests not on us but on those who raised the question from this podium. After what I have said just now, our declaration and our protest should be considered as solidly based.

Of course, the anarchist movement in Russia should not be equated with the anarchist movements in France, Italy, Spain, and America. Nevertheless, anarchism has its philosophy common to all countries. There are anarchists and anarchists. Here in Russia the entire anarchist movement is associated [by Bukharin] with the Makhno movement. I declare that not all Russian anarchists participated in the Makhno movement, that many among them had even condemned it. Therefore, when we undertake steps, when we enter into negotiations trying to serve the cause of the anarchist movement, we do so in order to defend the ideological theories of those anarchists who fought in the front ranks of the revolution, who participated in all the revolutionary battles, who were loyal to all soviet organisations, striving in the meantime to obtain the adoption of their views, for that was their right based on the victory of the proletarian revolution and as members of the proletariat.

The anarchists we are now speaking of are well known in Russia; the character of their movement is known as well. Nobody has any right to identify them with those who carry out an armed struggle in order to discredit their ideas and say they were pursuing personal ends.

We have in Russia a group of universalists, the 'Golos Truda' group. These are anarchists who actively work for the cause of the revolution, and who never took up arms against the Soviet government. Just the opposite; many actively participated in and devote all their forces to the cause of the Soviet Republic. There are also anarcho-syndicalists, who in their everyday activity contribute all their knowledge and initiative. Among these there are left Communists whom we got in touch with and who likewise lend their collaboration with the Russian Revolution. These are all elements whose actions are indisputable, and which the Russian Revolution can rely on and draw its forces from.

It is precisely these living forces that we are now concerned with. And I tell you, comrades of all countries, never and under no circumstances would our delegation have spoken in defence of Makhno's gangs. Neither would our comrades, the Russian anarchists, have done so.

We presented the Soviet government a list with the names of those imprisoned. We said, 'Here are the names of the comrades. We request you free them in the name of peace and welfare of the revolution.'

We likewise submitted our documents and proofs. We might have expected other documents and arguments to be presented, but that did not take place.

At last an agreement was obtained that the imprisoned anarchists would be set free and get a permit to go abroad, guaranteed by all the delegations that had solicited their freedom. The document was signed and accepted by the designated comrades, who pledged themselves to carry out its provisions, even though these ran counter to their feelings as Russians. They consented to this voluntary exile according to the decision that we sent them the same day and which was signed by the French, Spanish, and other delegates, as well as by the Russian anarchist comrades.

Why then did you come here today and put them on the same level with the Makhno gangs, when we declare ourselves against and have resolutely condemned this gang. We have resolutely declared that there was nothing in common between these gangs and anarchism. At the committee I spoke to you about, we asked that freedom should be granted to the anarchists. Why did we do so? Because the anarcho-syndicalists had struggled for the cause of the Russian Revolution; because we pursue the same communist aims in the field of the economy; because we are communists ourselves and because communism and anarchism never excluded, but only complemented each other. We may argue the particulars of our doctrines, but it does not mean that we are enemies in our practical activities because of these divergences in our revolutionary conceptions.

This is why we believe that the anarchist comrades ready to serve the cause of the revolution should be freed and should not be confused with the Makhno gangs. In all sincerity, we should be able to draw a distinction between those who were struggling in Ukraine for the interests of the wealthy peasants, as Comrade Bukharin has been telling us, and those who fight for revolutionary aims and for the complete emancipation of the proletariat.

These are the reasons that induced us to intervene with declarations and protests. We do not want to be accused later, on the grounds of documents of some kind, that we have impeded the work of this congress, and we therefore decline all the responsibility for this painful discussion. Up to the present moment we have been trustful, yelled no distrust, but now we have been shown that we have no right to be trustful. We accept the challenge and are ready to discuss the question of the anarchists.

We now request such a discussion with the members of this congress. The question has already been touched on in a general discussion, so it is no longer within the scope of the committee. We request all delegates of the proletariat to suggest to the Soviet government, with the aim of making peace, to apply the resolution adopted jointly by the representatives of the delegation and the representatives of the government. In other words, to settle as soon as possible the question of the anarchists without mentioning the Makhnoists, and to allow the other anarchist group to proceed with their own political work. Revolutionists participating in the Soviet government should be allowed to apply all their forces independently, and without the constant threat of being charged with being counterrevolutionaries.

On behalf of the anarcho-syndicalists of France who play a sufficiently important role in the union movement, on behalf of the anarcho-syndicalists of Spain, on behalf of the Italian Syndicalist Union, on behalf of the Canadian comrades, on behalf of all those who participated in our work, we request you to support our solicitations and to help carry out as rapidly as possible this measure of peace, which at the same time is an effort for fairness.

Allow me now to make my second statement. In order to prove to you that the anarchists are not Makhnoists, but that there exists here a genuine anarchist movement, we invite you to listen to the responsible representative of the anarchist group from this podium. They will give you the strongest proof that there is fundamental opposition between the Makhno groups and the anarcho-syndicalists.

Gliński: Comrades, the Polish delegation moves that the congress take note of the speeches of Comrades Bukharin and Sirolle and move on to the next order of business.

Lozovsky: Any objection to this motion? Hearing none, the motion is adopted. Now we read the manifesto to the workers of the world.

Manifesto to Workers of the World

Lozovsky: Comrades, the congress authorised the Presidium to draft an appeal to the workers of the world. Comrade Rykov will read it. (*Rykov reads.*)

Comrades, we shall put to a vote the appeal just read in all languages. Anybody against? None. It is accepted unanimously.[24]

Greetings to the Russian People

Lozovsky: Comrade Godonnèche has the floor for the reading of an appeal.

---

24 For the text of the 'Manifesto to the Workers of the World', see pp. 597–600.

Victor Godonnèche: Allow me to read the draft of greetings by the Congress to the Russian people, which I hope will be adopted unanimously. (*Applause*)
(*The text is read. Loud applause*)

Lozovsky: Are there any objections to this appeal? No objections. Carried.[25]

Greetings of Comrade Lenin to the Congress

Lozovsky: Comrade Rykov will read a letter received from Comrade Lenin.

Rykov: Comrades, a number of delegations have appealed through me to Comrade Lenin, inviting him to participate in the last session of our congress. To our sorrow, Comrade Lenin is ill and authorised me to read the following letter addressed to the founding congress of the red trade unions.

> Please be so kind as to convey to the delegates of the International Congress of Trade Unions the following:
>
> I thank them from the bottom of my heart for the invitation to the congress sent through you. I deeply regret that I am unable to accept it because of ill health, for on doctor's orders I have had to leave Moscow for a month's holiday.
>
> Please convey to the delegates my greetings and heartfelt wishes for the success of the congress. It is hard to find words to express the full importance of the international congress of trade unions. The winning of trade unionists to the ideas of communism is making irresistible headway everywhere, in all countries, throughout the world. The process is sporadic, overcoming a thousand obstacles, but it is making irresistible progress. The international congress of trade unions will quicken this movement. Communism will triumph in the trade unions. No power on earth can avert the collapse of capitalism and the victory of the working class over the bourgeoisie.
>
> Warm greetings and confidence in the inevitable victory of communism.
>
> N. Lenin (*Vigorous applause*)

Lozovsky: Comrades, I would kindly ask you to keep your seats for a little longer.

25 For the text of the Greetings to the Russian People, see p. 672.

Closing of Congress

Lozovsky: Comrades! Our congress closes. Before bringing it to an end, allow me to briefly summarise.

We worked for a rather long time and with great passion. Our debates often assumed a stormy and acute character, for no reformist water flows through our veins, only revolutionary blood. But the passion and ardour of our discussions, the impetuousness of our debates, which sometimes led to brusque exchanges of words, cannot in the least darken the great cause we are serving. We have laid a solid foundation for the Red International of Labour Unions, which tens of thousands of workers already adhere to.

Simultaneously with our creation here of the Red International of Trade Unions, industrial federations have formed international propaganda committees, and we now witness here in Moscow fourteen international propaganda committees for each respective industry: the international propaganda committee of metalworkers, miners, farmworkers, lumber workers, and so on.[26] Thus, alongside the trade-union movement formed by the congress, we now have another structure. We have the organisation of the Red Trade Unions, which is the framework upon which the world economy should later be built after the complete victory of the social revolution.

Bringing to an end the work of the congress, we express the wish that all our energy and that of our followers, all the blood in our veins, should be devoted to the cause of the social revolution; that all the passionate debates and exchange of rough language that was inevitable should by no means slow our common work. Let our congress represent a strong phalanx, strong and intimately united for the destruction of imperialism and for the well-being of the international proletariat.

Long live the world proletarian revolution!
Long live the Red International of Trade Unions!
Long live the Communist International! (*Shouts of 'Long live!' and applause*)

---

26 For the international propaganda committees, see p. 448.
The Russian-language edition of the congress proceedings includes an entire bulletin (number 17) devoted to the proceedings of a number of conferences of various international propaganda committees that took place during the course of the RILU congress.

Statements Handed in to Presidium and Attached to Minutes

Declaration of German *Unionen*

The undersigned delegations have once more analysed the work of the congress. These delegations have been sent by the members of their respective organisations with definite instructions to participate in the work of creating a trade-union International independent of but working in cooperation with the Communist International and composed of all independent revolutionary proletarian organisations, formed according to the requirements of the present conditions of production.

The formation of such an International required however the following premises:

1. It is necessary to accept the fact that conditions in various countries are different, and that these differences must be taken into consideration.
2. With regard to tactics, detailed discussion based upon principles is to take place, and if no agreement is arrived at, this question is to be resolved in accordance with the further experience of the revolutionary movement.
3. The decisions of the congress should not be influenced by the votes of those who merely declare adherence to Moscow, but who are organically and ideologically still bound to Amsterdam.

We declare, however, that the work has not been carried out in accordance with the above premises.

The method of verification of credentials from the very beginning gave a numerical preponderance to those organisations that, under the influence of erroneous judgements, do not want to entirely break with Amsterdam.

The influence of the independent organisations that had broken with Amsterdam or had never belonged to it has, through manoeuvres, been systematically diminished at the congress. We respond to the erroneous view that the masses are united only in the old Amsterdam trade unions by saying that the masses may be organised in the factory, and the unemployed by employment bureaus.

These important arguments of ours have not been considered in proper fashion. The struggle against us was not carried out upon the essentials of the question, and it found its vivid expression in the fact that our organisations were characterised as counterrevolutionary.

 | DOI:10.1163/9789004712867_022

Further, the congress has allowed in its theses assumptions contrary to the truth. For instance, in point 22 [of the Resolution on the Tasks and Tactics of the Trade Unions] it is said that the Gelsenkirchen Free Workers' Union and the General Workers' Union are fighting each other rather than waging a common struggle against the capitalists and their henchmen in the trade unions. In reality, the above-mentioned organisations are not only *not* fighting each other, but on the contrary they showed great discipline in the struggle with capital and the yellow bureaucracy in the trade unions, acting as the vanguard in Germany.

Point 8 of the theses again also says, with reference to the General Workers' Union, precisely the opposite of what it has defended in its past activities and what it will defend in the future.

The independent unions of Germany long ago adopted the slogan of point 7 regarding the second thesis on the question of organisation – one shop, one union – and have formed their organisation in accordance with this principle. In spite of that, they are called counterrevolutionaries.

Summing up the results of the work of the congress, we proclaim the following, fully aware of our responsibility:

1. The attempt to bring the revolutionary movement back into the framework of purely dogmatic economic schemes by means of an artificial majority cannot but fail.
2. The course of action adopted by the congress, and consequently in effect until the Second Congress, the tactics of the Red International, at least with regard to Germany, are to be considered opportunistic. Considering this course of action to be an obstacle in the way of development of the revolution, we must reject it.
3. After having exhausted all means to influence the work of the congress, we are obligated to transmit the results and our assessment to the members of our organisations, for their sovereign decision.

Gelsenkirchen Free Workers' Union
General Workers' Union

Statement by Part of the French delegation

In spite of the differences that have come to the surface among members of the congress, as within the French delegation itself, we, the undersigned members of the French delegation, declare that we fully submit to the decisions of the organisations that form the majority of the constituent congress, and bind ourselves to carry out in our country an active propaganda for the adherence of all proletarian forces to the Red International.

Godonnèche, Tommasi, Heuchel, Gaye, Glozman

Statement by Comrade Petermeier

I wish to add the following statement to the stenographic report of the session in which the declaration of the General Workers' Union of Germany was made:[1] 'Comrade Petermeier, the representative with consultative vote of the Rhine-Essen industrial district, does not concur with the above-mentioned declaration.'

Statement by Dutch delegation

The Dutch delegation expresses its great joy that it was able to make a contribution to the creation of a single revolutionary world front of the organised workers at this founding congress of red trade unions.

The delegation is not yet authorised to declare the affiliation of the National Labour Secretariat in the Netherlands to the Red International of Labour Unions, but it declares that upon its return to Holland it will insist in the most energetic manner before the workers of the trade-union movement in Holland on immediate affiliation. It expresses at the same time its firm belief that in the near future the National Labour Secretariat in the Netherlands will become part of the Red International.[2]

Statement by Georgian delegation

(*In the last report of the Executive Committee and in the report of Comrade Rosmer, information on the trade-union movement in Georgia was omitted. I therefore beg to append to the records of the congress the following statement:*)

The revolutionary minority of the trade unions in Georgia joined the Red International a year ago at the very outset of the organisation of the ITUC [International Trade Union Council]. Over the past year the revolutionary part of the trade-union movement in Georgia carried out a hard struggle for revolutionising the masses and conquering the trade unions from within. At the time of the dictatorship of the Mensheviks,[3] the work had to be carried out illegally, at a time of great repression, when hundreds and thousands of active workers as well as those from the rank and file were in prison or exiled from the republic. But in spite of that, many of the trade unions were conquered. During the last months before the fall of the Mensheviks, neither repression, nor repeated

---

1 It is unclear which declaration by the German *Unionen* Petermeier is referring to.

2 A congress of the National Labour Secretariat (NAS) of the Netherlands met 25–26 March 1922 and voted in favour of conditional affiliation to the Red International of Labour Unions. Put to a membership referendum, however, affiliation was defeated by a vote of 5,826 to 4,458. Affiliation was finally agreed to in 1923.

3 For the Menshevik regime in Georgia and its overthrow, see p. 280, n. 7.

arrests of the leadership of the revolutionary unions, nor splits in the trade unions, nor formation of parallel trade unions, nor pressure exerted at general assemblies, could halt our work. The Georgian Mensheviks have entirely lost the ground under their feet; they have lost all influence among the workers, and the minority has become the majority. To this the Georgian Mensheviks could certainly not agree, and they preferred to destroy the unions rather than having Communist ones. In this they have partially succeeded. On the eve of the capture of power by the Georgian workers, the trade unions fell to pieces, thanks to the systematic repression.

Genuine trade-union activity began in March 1921 after the overthrow of the Mensheviks, when the workers began to breathe freely. It was possible to start work on a wide scale by means of organisation and propaganda among the workers, without meeting any repression (when all political parties were able to carry on their work freely, as the Mensheviks were amnestied and had a free field for their activities). We then succeeded in winning influence in the trade unions and making them the base of support of the workers' power in Georgia.

At present the trade unions in Georgia stand as a whole for the Red International of Labour Unions. The question of joining either the Moscow or Amsterdam International has been widely debated in individual unions, as well as in local and district interunion conferences, where the Mensheviks and other parties participated. Everywhere resolutions were adopted in favour of the Red International.

On 12 June 1921 a general Georgian conference of trade unions took place in Tiflis [Tbilisi], at which the question of leaving Amsterdam and joining Moscow was discussed. A total of 220 delegates with decisive vote and 30 with consultative vote were present at the conference, which represented all unions, with a total membership of 100,000 to 110,000 workers and employees. Mensheviks as well as other socialist parties took part in the discussion at the conference, but being well aware of the state of mind of the workers, none of them could take an open stand for Amsterdam, using as an argument that it was not worthwhile to form a new International and to split the world workers' movement. The conference adopted, with 4 votes against and 4 or 5 abstentions, the resolution to immediately leave Amsterdam and join Moscow, and to announce this to the workers of the whole world. It stated that the trade unions of Georgia have nothing in common either with Amsterdam or with those who ran away from Georgia and call themselves representatives of the Georgian workers, spreading tales about Soviet Georgia. I should add that the Georgian workers long ago took away this right from the self-proclaimed leaders.

The number of workers and employees in Georgia amounts to 120,000 to 130,000. The number of those organised in trade unions is 100,000 to 110,000.

There are twenty unions organised on an industrial basis, with sections throughout the republic. The most important among these is the union of railway workers, consisting of about 18,000 members. All the unions are affiliated with and under the leadership of the Trade Union Council of Georgia.

G. Kurulashvili, congress delegate, secretary of Trade Union Council in Georgia.

Statement of Russian delegation on speech of Comrade Sirolle at 19 July session

We hereby state that some of the principal persons who were mentioned in the above speech directly or indirectly participated in the Makhno movement and held leading positions in these gangs. We are in possession of all necessary documents, and this was also known to Comrade Sirolle. Certain other groupings were obviously connected with the counterrevolutionary Makhno movement, as well as with the Kronstadt affair.

On behalf of the Russian delegation:

A. Rykov
G. Tsyperovich

Statement of Canadian delegation on speech of Comrade Sirolle at 19 July session

I protest against the statement of Comrade Sirolle that the Canadian delegation joined the commission for the investigation of the arrested anarchists. That is false. Only Comrade Cascaden declared himself for the formation of the said commission.

J. Knight

Congress Commissions and Central Council Session

Organisation Commission

Session of 26 June

Comrade Lozovsky (chair), after a short introduction, points out that the task of the commission is to make amendments to the draft of the statutes of the Red International of Trade Unions that are to be approved by the congress, and also to consider the theses brought in by the delegations.

On the motion of the chair of the commission, a temporary technical bureau was constituted, consisting of Comrades Ramírez,[1] Ibáñez, Handlíř, Hubacher, and Meller.[2]

Those present at the meeting were questioned, and it was made plain that no concrete amendments to the statutes drafted by Comrade Lozovsky had been presented up to now.

Session of 27 June

Comrade Lozovsky (chair): Amendments to the draft of the statutes have been made by representatives of some delegations.

Bartels (Germany, Gelsenkirchen Union) suggests in point 6 of section III (aims) to replace the reference to material aid. This proposal was accepted by the commission.

The five amendments made by Comrade Maciejewski (Poland) caused an exchange of views, but a decision on these was postponed on a motion by Comrade Lozovsky, stating that all amendments are to be considered, if presented in written form. Comrade Lozovsky's suggestion was adopted.

Next, the commission took up the question of the name of the Red International. The following names were proposed instead of the present name (International Council of Trade Unions): 'International of Revolutionary Unions' by Godonnèche; 'International Federation of the Revolutionary Workers Organisations' (Britain); 'World Federation of Revolutionary Trade Unions' (Mexico); 'World Federation of Labour' (Australia, America, Canada); 'Red International of Trade Unions' (Denmark); 'International Red Revolutionary Unions' (Italy). It was decided to leave this question open temporarily.

The following amendments were consequently discussed and rejected.

1 This is per the German text; the English says 'Rosmer'.

2 This may be a reference to Richard Müller.

 DOI:10.1163/9789004712867_023

1. Motion to substitute 'communism' in the preamble for 'socialism' (Godonnèche).
2. Motion to put in the third section instead 'the revolutionary economic organisations – Trade Unions' and to delete the word 'communist' from 'revolutionary communist'. As it was explained by the speaker, Comrade Glozman (France), 'to leave the door open for all workers'.
3. Motion by Glozman (France): to delete from point 5 in section III, 'the recognition of the International as an ideal leader'. Voting for the motion: France, Gelsenkirchen, Denmark, Britain, General Workers' Union of Germany. Against: Russia, Poland, Canada, Australia, Italy, Switzerland, Czechoslovakia, Far Eastern Republic, United States. Not voting: Mexico, Australia.
4. Motion by Knight (Canada) to replace the above-mentioned formula of the fifth point by the words 'In contact with the Communist International'.
5. Motion by Bartels: (a) to merge the executive and the administrative organs of the trade-union International; (b) to appoint for the congress ten members to consider all questions connected with the statutes; (c) proposal by Godonnèche to delete from the statutes the section 'Relations with the Communist International'.

Session of 7 July

Comrade Lozovsky in the chair.

Comrade Lozovsky proposes that the commission proceed without any preliminary reports or introductory speech directly to the consideration of the statutes drafted by him. Comrade Lozovsky emphasised that the statutes reflect at one and the same time our experience, as well as the expression of those principles upon which the methods we employed up to now inside the international trade-union movement were based.

On the other hand, the statutes attempt to find a common ground for the various tendencies and currents that prevail in our trade-union International, so as to enable us to work hand in hand in order to lead a common struggle against our enemy. It is especially from this standpoint that the statutes should be considered, because in their essentials they allow wide possibilities for united action to different categories and groups of trade unions of various countries, to independent labour organisations, as well as to those trade-union bodies that are leaving the Amsterdam International and that have already defined their position.

Comrade Lozovsky proposes that the examination of the statutes, which are closely related to the work of the whole congress, should follow the order in which the statutes were drafted. Such a system will give the possibility of introducing amendments and additions, leaving the questions of principle upon which no agreement could be reached to the decision of the plenary sitting of the congress.

Howie (Australia)[3] seconded Comrade Lozovsky's suggestion and emphasised that the commission should give the fundamental outline upon which discussions should be started at the plenary session of the congress, subjecting the debatable questions to a preliminary discussion. The congress, of course, will have to arrive at the final decisions.

The commission passes to consideration of the first paragraph of the statutes, that of the name of the international organisation of industrial unions which until now has been called the 'Provisional International Council of Trade and Industrial Unions'.

Comrade Lozovsky states that in connection with the old name, the following new ones have been suggested: 'World Federation of Trade Unions', 'International of Revolutionary Trade Unions'. America suggests 'International of Workers Federations'. Mexico suggests 'International Confederation of Trade Unions'. Finally, 'Red International of Trade Unions'.

On Comrade Lozovsky's request, no debate is opened on this issue, with the proposed names brought to a vote immediately. But allowance is made for one person to speak in favour of each name, if requested.

The majority of the commission requests that the designation 'Red International of Trade Unions' be retained.

Comrade Polonsky speaks in favour of the adoption of the name 'International Council of Trade Unions', in view of the fact that at the present time there is a marked tendency for the organisation of councils in general, which also include the councils organised in factories and workshops. And whereas the shop stewards councils and the factory councils will have to be swallowed up in the long run by the trade unions, it would be more advisable to call the new body 'International Council of Trade Unions', thus covering the existing workers' councils. Moreover, this new name is diametrically opposed to that of the Amsterdam International.

On the voting procedure, Comrade Lemoine (France) moves that the question be voted on separately by delegation. This motion is rejected by the major-

3 This is per the Russian text; the English says 'Bowie (England)'; the German says 'Boigy'; not in the French.

ity of the commission, due to the existing differences of opinions on this question within the delegations themselves.

The result of the vote is 11 votes for the name 'Red International of Trade Unions', 4 votes for 'International Confederation of Workers', and 1 vote for 'International of Revolutionary Trade Unions'.

The name 'Red International of Trade Unions' is thus declared adopted.

The commission then passes on to the discussion of the preamble of the statutes.

The representative of the Swiss delegation declares that they accept the text of the preamble as drafted by Lozovsky.

A similar declaration is made by the Austrian delegation, which notes the necessity of some small editorial changes.

The French delegation moves to substitute in the text of the preamble the words 'socialism' and 'socialist' by the words 'communism' and 'communist'.

Comrade Lozovsky explains that he purposely used in some places the word 'socialism' and in other places the word 'communism', in order to lay stress upon the fact that there is no material difference between one and the other. Dissension existing between the leaders of different parties are not based upon different interpretations of socialism; they simply refuse to accept socialism. The methods proposed by them do not bring us nearer to socialism. He therefore does not find the proposed correction necessary. The British and German delegations state that from their point of view, there is no difference between 'socialism' and 'communism'.

Williams (USA) favours the amendments of the French delegation, and speaks of the necessity of having the words 'socialism' and 'socialist' changed to 'communism' and 'communist'. He indicates that the Socialist Party in America is recognised by the labour movement throughout the world as 'yellow'. He thinks that the same conception of the word 'socialism' as a 'yellow' type is also prevalent in Germany. The use of 'socialism' would lead to misunderstandings. It is advisable to replace it by the word 'communism'.

The French amendments are adopted. In the phrase 'the conquest of the means of production and the realisation of socialism', the word 'socialism' is replaced by 'communism'.

The commission then passes to the discussion of section II of the statutes about 'Aims'.

Comrade Murphy moves that after point 1 of this section, where it reads, 'to organise the large working masses', add the following new clause: 'to unite the international trade-union movement in a world organisation of the proletariat capable of leading the struggle against class enemies, and capable of assuming, after the conquest of power by the proletariat, the management of the world industries'. In formulating his motion, Comrade Murphy remarks that it does not in the least change the 'aims' as formulated in the first and third paragraphs. It is simply a necessary broadening of it. It is necessary to do so in order that this new organisation should become more accessible to the minds of the vast masses of the working class. For them the question of the management of industry in the future society is of primary importance.

Comrade Lozovsky, closing the debate, moves that the question of the internal organisation of the commission be first settled, as it has been postponed on account of the late arrival of many members of the commission, who came at 11:30 instead of 11:00. The full commission has only now assembled.

He moves that a presidium of two or three secretaries be elected, in view of the fact that the commission will have to be in session throughout the congress. The commission consists of eighty members and will have to decide upon very serious questions.

No objections are raised against this motion. With regard to the question of the number of secretaries, the British delegation moves to elect one secretary for each language, i.e., four. The French delegation seconds the motion. At Comrade Lozovsky's motion, the speaker is included as the fifth member.

As a result of this decision of the commission, the following delegates are elected members of the presidium: Murphy for the British delegation; Hubacher[4] for the French; Malzahn for the German; and Artem for the Russian.

Comrade Lozovsky, summarising the discussion, takes up Comrade Murphy's amendment, which seems to him quite unacceptable and should not be adopted, both on theoretical grounds as well as from purely practical considerations. Indeed, Comrade Murphy's amendment already foresees the economic part that is to be played by the international organisation. To include the organisation of production in your area of responsibility would therefore be tantamount to deciding in advance the question at issue for the different revolutionary groups: how and in which country the organisation and management of industry should be set up. This question will have to be answered in due course. The answer will be given by the comrades of each country in their resolutions.

A general answer to the question will be given in the theses. But to introduce into the statutes a statement that our confederation will be the leading economic organ would be pretentious and premature. Our fundamental task is to accomplish the social revolution, and then we shall see the part that each organisation will have to play. There is no need to be in a hurry to settle the

4 This is per the German, French, and Russian texts; the English says 'Glorman'.

question of principles: Who will organise the industries? It will be thoroughly discussed in the period between the first and second congresses [of the RILU]. The question will have to be raised and a definite decision taken at the second and even the third congress.

Gliński (Poland), on behalf of the Polish delegation, declares himself against Murphy's amendment on more than formal grounds. He points out that the statement that the trade unions shall be charged with managing the Soviet economy is entirely unfounded. This is the task of the Soviet government of the workers and peasants, which avails itself of the support of the trade unions, but not the other way around. Comrade Gliński is of the opinion that this should be firmly and definitely stated.

Comrade Williams (USA) supports Murphy's amendment. Over the last few years the programme and action of the IWW among the working masses had for its main object the advocacy of the principle of control over production in order to lead the masses to an immediate seizure of the means of production. True, the question as to how the roles will be distributed in this matter, between the labour organisations and the government, will be discussed together with the question of control over production. But in the presentation of the aims of the red trade-union movement in the statutes, it is necessary to indicate that the trade unions are not merely tools in the hands of the government for the capture of the power; their purpose is to achieve an immediate control over production in factories and workshops.

Comrade Batt (USA)[5] fully agrees with the opinion of Comrades Lozovsky and Gliński in that the amendment proposed by Comrade Murphy is premature and unacceptable. Comrade Batt is of the opinion that the said amendment shows that its author does not understand Marxist theory, according to which future society grows out of the framework of the present form of society. The introduction of such an amendment would weaken the position of the future International and obscure the fundamental aims of this organisation. In the opinion of Comrade Batt, such an aim consists in the conquest of political power, while any other activity would be of a mere subsidiary and secondary character. As to the question of which body will in the future be entrusted with the control over production, Comrade Batt finds that the three years' experience of Russia does not as yet give an exhaustive answer to the above question. This is another argument why he declares himself against the insertion into the statutes of Comrade Murphy's amendment.

---

5 This is per the published English and Russian texts; the German says 'Flynn'; the French says 'Flink'. For a discussion on the question of Flynn's identity, see p. 164, n. 8.

Comrade Murphy expresses his readiness to introduce changes in his proposed amendment in order to remove the misunderstanding revealed in the speeches of his opponents in connection with his proposition.

In reality he is very far from the idea of establishing in the future a trade-union organisation in opposition to a soviet organisation, but he considers it necessary to note that the syndicalist organisations are pursuing their own particular aims. In some countries their actions influence economic development. The growth of the economic influence of the trade unions is quite noticeable in many countries even now, within the framework of capitalist society. The leading role is gradually passing into their hands. This, of course, should by all means be supported. To establish a hard and fast rule as to what will happen first – the capture of political power or that of economic domination, is, according to Comrade Murphy, rather a difficult task.

As to the Russian experience, he considers that had Russia had a better developed and prepared staff of technicians and skilled workers, the control of the labour organisation over production would have been much stronger in Russia than it actually proved to be over the three years. Insofar as America and Europe are concerned – where there is a sufficient supply of skilled technicians and workers – the role of the trade unions in the matter of control and administration will undoubtedly be much stronger than in Russia. He therefore proposes to modify the initial text in the sense of his amendment, i.e., that the trade unions are not to be the 'future organs administering production', but 'organs of the Soviet power dealing with the administration of production'.

The British delegation moves that there be a break in the session so that the delegates can discuss among themselves whether the point of view taken by Comrade Murphy actually expresses the stand of the entire delegation.

Comrade Lozovsky objects and suggests that those already on the list should be given the chance to speak, especially the syndicalists of Spain and others. Let them all speak on the question, which will have to be taken up by the entire congress anyhow, so that it would be better to avoid unnecessary disagreements.

Comrade Ibáñez, on behalf of the Spanish delegation, speaks in support of Comrade Murphy's motion and the stand taken by him, which is that of revolutionary syndicalism, the very substance of which consists of the entire control of industry by the trade unions, remaining actually in the hands of the workers. Like Comrade Murphy, he does not intend to contrast trade-union organisations with soviets.

Furthermore, he considers that the actual organisation of the soviets is impossible without the active support of the Red Trade Union International, embracing all the revolutionary workers who accept the dictatorship of the proletariat.

But it is necessary to note that the workers will hold the industries in their hands and operate them to suit themselves. The statement of Comrade Lozovsky is mere sophistry. To say that the industries cannot be given over to the unions because of their small membership and undeveloped state is equivalent to saying that a child is not able to become an adult. The baby will eventually develop, and will become as wise as others.

The question refers to a declaration of principles and not to hard and fast practical rules for the present day. Murphy's thesis may therefore, without fear, be included in the statutes.

Comrade Artem speaks against the amendment introduced by Comrade Murphy not only in its original but also in its altered form, which throws an entirely wrong light upon our labour movement during the revolution. Instead of reflecting on the most important issue, the amendment merely advances questions of detail.

The aim of the working class is to defeat the bourgeoisie and establish the dictatorship of the proletariat. Inasmuch as the proletariat overthrows the bourgeoisie and becomes the ruling class, it cannot become merely the directing force of industry, since it is confronted with many other difficult problems.

The rule of the proletariat does not simply consist in industrial control; it must oversee the entire governmental apparatus. The contention of Comrade Murphy that with a greater number of skilled workers it would be easier to rule is absolutely untrue.

Our task during the revolution, being that of a ruling class, is to conserve our power. Revolution is a class struggle. The biggest assurance of victory that our enemies have is a split in our ranks; our victory can be assured only by the unity of the working class. The trade-union organisations serve to group together the entire working class. The form of organisation supported by Comrade Ibáñez underlines especially all those prejudices with which the 'antipolitical organisation' seems to be affected. They are dreaming of a 'democracy', which will simply mean oppression and violence.

Comrade Bartels (Gelsenkirchen Free Workers' Union) says that the question of power and government should not be put into our statutes. We may simply touch on this question but not introduce it as a special clause. He therefore considers the amendment of Comrade Murphy to be quite out of place at the present time.

A motion is made to close the debate. Discussion is ended.

Comrade Lozovsky puts the amendment of Comrade Murphy to a vote.

The French delegation suggests that matters pertaining to the motion of Comrade Murphy be first translated and distributed among the delegates.

Comrade Lozovsky is against this, saying that if this method is adopted, our work will never come to an end. It is necessary to explain the substance of the question and then vote upon it. Should the amendment be accepted, it will then be formulated exactly as outlined; no formulation of it is necessary.

The motion of the French delegation is put to a vote. The motion is defeated, and Comrade Murphy's motion is then put to a vote. The amendment is defeated, with 11 votes in favour (4 Spanish, 4 French, and 3 British).

Comrade Bartels reads the amendment to point 2:

> The world confederation of labour aims to organise the proletariat of the world in order to transform the economic system of capitalism into a communist one through the dictatorship of the proletariat. It aims to destroy capitalism, remove the chaotic forms of production and install instead a scientific form of production, based upon national and international needs, destroy the principle of the sale of labour power and replace it by universal labour conscription, regulate conditions of labour and production as a whole, and establish the control of the producers over distribution. To achieve this end, the following means and methods are to be used:
>
> 1. Energetic propagation of its ideas and of revolutionary mass action.
> 2. Carrying out active international solidarity.
> 3. Explaining the danger of conciliation, class collaboration, social peace, and the possibility of a peaceful transition from capitalism to socialism. In connection with this propaganda, it is necessary to wage a decisive fight against the Amsterdam International and the International Labour Bureau of the League of Nations, bulwarks of the international bourgeoisie.
> 4. The organisation of international proletarian action, taking advantage of all events in the class struggle.
> 5. Opening of relations among revolutionary organisations throughout the world, and the creation of a central organisation among them.
> 6. The convocation of conferences and exchanges based upon the experience of the international class struggle in the process of introducing control over production.

Comrade Lozovsky proposes opening discussion on the proposed amendments. He moves that in the future the discussions of amendments should be limited to two speakers: one for and another against the amendment. The motion is adopted by a majority vote.

A discussion of Comrade Bartels's amendment then takes place.

Comrade Lozovsky speaks against it. He points out that the amendment does not contain either practical or theoretical criticism. To state in the statutes that the Red Labour International will occupy itself with the conscription of labour or the organisation of labour is all pure trade unionism, which it is unnecessary to mention. The International is confronted with the problem of organisation of the masses. We must put forward slogans that are comprehensible to the masses. Regarding the conscription of labour, we will defend it after you have been successful in making your revolution and are in power. It is useless to have it embodied in the statutes.

Comrade Bartels, in defending his amendment, says that in his opinion the amendment makes the problem of international organisation clearer and more precise. Such questions as unemployment, etc., are of vital interest to the working masses. To limit ourselves to a resolution of the commission is insufficient; the discussions of this question must be included in the statutes.

The proposal of Comrade Bartels is voted upon and rejected by a majority of votes.

Comrade Lozovsky moves that henceforth new amendments should be presented in writing, translated into the foreign languages, and distributed in advance among the committee members. The motion is accepted.

The next session will take place 8 July at 11:00 a.m.[6]

Session of 16 July

The morning session opens at 11:00 a.m. Comrade Lozovsky in the chair.

The discussion on the statutes of the International of Red Trade Unions is resumed.

Comrade Lozovsky moves to put at the end of the preamble on the first page of the printed copy of the draft of the statutes in the seventh line from the bottom instead of the word 'organisation' the words 'that together with the Communist International will organise'. The motion is carried.

Comrade Nin moves to replace, in the third line from the bottom on the same page, 'socialism' by the word 'communism'.

In section II, point 7 is struck out on the proposal of Lozovsky. No other amendments are introduced.

In section III (Membership), a series of amendments are introduced:

6 No minutes of a session held 8 July were published.

The beginning of section III is to read as follows in place of the former text: 'Any revolutionary economic class organisation is eligible for membership in the International of Red Trade Unions if it accepts the following conditions.'

Comrade Lozovsky further moves to delete point 5 of section III. This motion raises a heated debate.

Comrade Maciejewski does not see the slightest need to delete this point; on the contrary, the ideological leadership of the Comintern must be emphasised.

Comrade Nin considers that the retention of this paragraph may prove an obstacle to the creation of an International of mass labour organisations: 'We, the revolutionary syndicalists, have made and are still making many concessions in order to get a united International. But if you insist on such conditions, we will find them absolutely unacceptable. By your requirements you leave aside the syndicalists of Italy, France, Spain, Portugal, and South America. It will be a great mistake to retain this point, because it would prevent the organisations of these countries from joining the International of Red Trade Unions, and would thereby nullify the work of the congress. We would have left this congress with painful feelings, because only Communist organisations could have joined us, and no others'.

Comrade Godonnèche supports the motion to delete this paragraph, because not being of any use, it will only harm the movement.

Comrade Murphy addresses himself to the Communists who insist upon retaining this paragraph, stating that the large masses are only sympathetically inclined toward communism, but are not entirely communistic. It would therefore be inadvisable to retain that questionable point. Many of the unions, even if they reject this point, will anyhow endorse collaboration with the Third International. Our aim is to build up a strong International of Red Trade Unions, gaining over to our side the large masses, who are not yet communistic. This is why I call upon you not to reject the multitude of comrades in all countries who will not be able to join the Red International if this point remains.

Comrade Lozovsky puts the question of deleting point 5 of section III to a vote. The result is as follows: for deletion: Russia, Spain, France, Britain, United States, Australia, Switzerland, Holland, Canada, Norway, and Yugoslavia. Against: Hungary, Bulgaria, Finland, Germany, Poland. Comrade Lozovsky's motion to delete point 5 of section III is thus carried.

It is moved and carried that instead of the point just deleted, the following new point be inserted: 'Recognition and application of the decisions of the Red Trade Union International'.

Point 6 of section III is adopted as follows: 'rupture with the yellow Amsterdam International'.

The commission then goes over to the discussion of section IV (International Congresses).

Comrade Pollitt moves that special congresses be convened upon the demand of 'one-third' and not of 'one-half' of all the members of the Red Trade Union International. The amendment is carried.

Comrade Lozovsky, regarding the part concerning the distribution of representatives of national trade-union bodies, proposes the following changes: 'Every national organisation having less than 10,000 members receives one consultative vote; those having from 10,000 to 25,000 will send one delegate with a decisive vote; those having from 100,000 to 250,000, four delegates; and each additional 500,000 members, one additional delegate.'

The changes proposed by Lozovsky are accepted.

Comrade Lozovsky further proposes to decide whether a consultative or decisive vote should be given to representatives of international industrial federations. He himself considers that it would be possible to allot two votes to each international organisation of that kind.

Comrade Nin speaks against the allotting of decisive votes to such federations, because then they will virtually get double representation; each country would be represented directly and again through the industrial federation.

Comrade Lozovsky puts the question to a vote. For allowing the industrial federations a decisive vote: Russia, Bulgaria, Poland, Estonia, Finland, Australia, Britain, America, Germany, Sweden, Austria. For giving them a consultative vote only: Far Eastern Republic, Canada, Spain, Czechoslovakia. By a majority vote it is thus decided to give them a decisive vote.

The commission passes to the discussion of section V (Organs of the Red International of Labour Unions).

Comrade Lozovsky reports that until now the executive organ of the International Council of Trade Unions was called the 'Executive Bureau'. He now proposes to call it the 'Executive Council'.

Comrade Maciejewski proposes 'Executive Committee' instead of 'Executive Bureau'.

Comrade Lozovsky states that it is advisable to adopt the term 'Council' and call the 'Executive Bureau' either 'Executive Council' or simply 'Council'.

Comrade Dimitrov moves that the 'Executive Bureau' should be called the 'Central Council of the Red International of Trade Unions'. Comrade Dimitrov's motion is adopted, and changes are made in the statutes accordingly.

As to the second paragraph of section V concerning the composition of the Central Council, Comrade Lozovsky moves to draft it with the following idea: eight important countries other than Russia (Poland, France, Spain, Italy, Germany, Britain, the United States, and Czechoslovakia) have two representatives with decisive vote in the Central Council. All the other countries with a membership of at least 25,000 have one representative with a decisive vote, and those that have less than 25,000 members have one representative with a consultative vote. As to Russia, its trade unions must have four representatives, because the weight of the work will fall on them. Comrade Lozovsky's motion is adopted.

The British delegation moves that the Central Council include one representative with decisive vote for each international industrial federation.

Comrade Lozovsky is opposed to this proposal, and moves to introduce representatives of international industrial federations with a consultative vote. Comrade Lozovsky's motion is adopted.

The Spanish delegation moves the following: The Central Council includes, with decisive votes, representatives of each group of countries; for instance, the Balkan group sends one representative with decisive vote; the Near Eastern group, one representative with a decisive vote; a decisive vote to the Far East, South America, etc. In short, small countries unite themselves into groups, and are granted one decisive vote.

The British delegation declares that this would be inconvenient and it would be unnecessary. If various countries would be given votes in the indicated manner, they would only quarrel with one another.

Comrade Dimitrov also speaks against the motion of the Spanish delegation, and says that if the Central Council would have representatives of various countries, according to Comrade Lozovsky's motion, then the representation makes no sense. This would already be a double representation.

Comrade Lozovsky puts the motion of the Spanish delegation to a vote and it is rejected.

Comrade Lozovsky, on the question of the General Secretariat, moves it should be called simply the 'Executive Bureau'. Comrade Lozovsky's motion is adopted, and amendments are made in the statutes accordingly. Comrade Lozovsky moves that the point concerning the Secretariat should read as follows: 'The Executive Bureau consists of seven members elected by the Central Council, including two members representing the country where the Central Council is located.'

The British delegation declares that it should be mentioned in the statutes that the Executive Bureau is carrying out its work under the guidance of the Central Council.

Comrade Lozovsky points out that it is superfluous to speak about it in the statutes, as it is self-evident.

The Swedish delegation moves that the Central Council should meet not less than twice a year. The motion is adopted, and point 4 of section V is formulated thus: 'the Central Council meets at least twice a year, dealing mostly …'.

The commission proceeds to consider section VI of the statutes (Unity of Action and Unity of Organisation).

Comrade Murphy, on behalf of the British delegation, moves to insert into the clause that speaks about separate organisations that trade-union minorities or separate organisations affiliated with the Red International of Trade Unions must coordinate their activities with the aid of a special national bureau attached to the Red International of Trade Unions.

Comrade Lozovsky thinks such an insertion unnecessary and moves to reject this motion. He says that if such a bureau were created in any country, it would not guide the trade-union movement, but would only be a transmitting centre. Therefore the motion of Comrade Murphy cannot be adopted, because otherwise the local organisations would have a bureaucracy represented by the bureau that would guide them, and this is absolutely inadmissible. The German delegation also spoke against the motion of the British delegation. Comrade Lozovsky puts the motion made by the British delegation to a vote. The motion is rejected.

No other discussion was raised on this section. Section VI is endorsed as originally drafted.

The committee proceeds to section VII on financial means.

Discussing the section, Comrade Lozovsky points out that the total financing of the International Council was done until now by the Russian trade unions. If we wish the work to be regular in the future, the affiliated national organisations should not only think of the means for their own existence, but should also furnish the means for the existence of the Red International of Trade Unions, because each rouble furnished by the Russian trade unions is given under the most difficult conditions. The Russian proletariat has to suffer for each rouble spent by it. These, comrades, are common resources, and we have to speak about them, because labour organisations can exist in any country only by their own means. And if we wish for normal conditions, then it is necessary that comrades should understand and remember that there exists an International that was created by them, and it is necessary to support it by dues, however little they may be. Under such conditions we can have not only financial relations, but also other relations.

Comrade Flynn[7] says that, as regards section VII, such dues should be fixed not at 5 per cent, but at 1 per cent, because this raises considerable trouble in America. At a 5 per cent assessment, every union would have to pay very large

7 Earlier in the minutes of the Organisation Commission, the English and Russian versions refer to 'Batt' while the French and German versions attribute the very same remarks to 'Flynn'. In this case, however, all four versions identify the speaker as 'Flynn'.

amounts. The miners' union would have to pay $300,000 a year. Thus they will have to bear the onslaught of the enemy, who will do all in their power to agitate against us on economic grounds, by saying that the Red International taxes them with heavy dues. This would create big difficulties in America.

Comrade Lozovsky explains that the question was only about the central treasury receiving assessments from local organisations. If, for instance, the central treasury received 1 per cent from every union, it would remit 5 per cent of the total receipts to the Red Trade Union International, so that on the whole this would amount to a small sum.

Comrade Flynn further says the condition of things in America is such that every member of the union pays $2 a month and even more, $1 of which the local remits to the central treasury. He insists on his first motion that only 1 per cent of the central treasury's receipts be remitted to the trade-union International not because he thinks 5 per cent too high a rate – even 10 per cent would not be excessive – but because we ought to think of the hue and cry this would arouse that the Red International of Labour Unions was plundering the workers, and this would supply the reactionary elements with agitational material against us.

Comrade Volan of Norway moves to form a subcommittee for discussing the question of international dues. First, we must distinguish between regular and emergency resources of the organisation. Again, we must distinguish the fighting fund from the propaganda fund. According to the bylaws, 50 per cent of the International's assets would go to the strike fund. It was also necessary to discuss the question whether international dues should be paid in gold or, for instance, in German marks at the current rate of exchange. All this should be discussed in subcommittee.

Comrade Lozovsky proposes to adopt Comrade Volan's motion to refer the question to a subcommittee, which should take it up today after discussion is closed. The question is complicated by the fact that in different countries different dues are paid to the central treasury. The collective experience of different countries should be coordinated. He moves to elect a subcommittee of five to solve the financial question. The motion is carried.

The following members are elected: Comrades Flynn (USA), Murphy (Britain), Volan (Norway), Punza (Germany), Dimitrov (Balkan countries).

The commission now takes up section VIII on strike funds.

Comrade Lozovsky moves to delete the last four lines of the third paragraph of section VIII, since the entire secretariat is responsible, and so there is no reason for choosing one person out of the whole body.

Comrade Flynn, on behalf of the American delegation, states that in general they are against a strike fund. He therefore moves to delete the entire section. American practical experience shows that strike funds do not play any important part. Workers on strike get more help from other workers in the same country and of other countries than from strike money. Instead of a strike fund, he proposes to form a fighting fund, not in the sense of giving monetary relief to strikers, but in the sense of extending them comradely help.

Comrade Maciejewski says that organising a strike fund was of no importance at the present time, when the class struggle is becoming more acute. Trade-union congresses were passing resolutions against organising such funds. The only help that is essential to the workers is to support them in their struggle by deeds, by calling upon the workers to enter the fight, but not by monetary contributions. Only such action can influence the government. Therefore the above section should be deleted.

Comrade Howie, on behalf of the Australian delegation, declares against a strike fund, as experience has shown it to be both ineffective and unnecessary.

Comrade Repossi (Italy) says that in the case of small strikes the strikers can help themselves, but in large strikes it would not do anyway; it therefore has no practical value.

In this connection, Comrade Lozovsky remarks that this fund is not meant for material relief, but for its agitational value.

Comrade Malzahn (Germany) says the German delegation is for deleting the strike fund from the statutes and replacing it with a fighting fund, because not every strike deserves financial support, nor can we provide it for every strike. But at the same time a fighting fund is necessary in case of conflicts that might be transformed into political battles and for furnishing means for agitation and for supporting one form of struggle or another. Therefore, this fund should be called 'Fighting Fund' instead of 'Strike Fund'.

Comrade Lozovsky fully endorses Comrade Malzahn's motion to call it the fighting fund. He says, 'When I formulated this section I had in mind to create some fund in order to emphasise our solidarity more strongly. The fighting fund has a practical value not in the sense of strike relief. If I had the slightest illusion on that score, I would not have put that point in the draft. Its purpose is to show that the Red Trade Union International is responsive to any revolutionary movement and comes to its assistance.'

Comrade Ries[8] shares Comrade Malzahn's opinion.

The British delegation is in favour of organising a fighting fund and thinks it necessary to add the proviso that the Bureau of the Secretariat has discretion in spending this fund whenever and wherever it may find it necessary.

---

8 This may be a reference either to Alf G. Rees of Australia, or Jakob Riehs of Austria, both of whom were delegates at the RILU congress.

Comrade Dimitrov says he thinks a permanent international fund necessary for showing constant solidarity, and proposes the following wording: 'An International fighting fund is created for offensive help in cases when workers fight with their employers. This fund is to be raised by means of appropriations, special collections, etc.' He proposes to call it the 'International Solidarity Fund'. This motion is carried.

Comrade Lozovsky moves to redraft the clause about the international strike fund so as to be able to come to the aid in every case where the workers come out in militant action. We hold that at the present state in the development of the international movement, it is impossible to create such a strike fund. 'This congress provides for the creation of an international solidarity fighting fund, out of which … etc.', and the rest of the paragraph should be redrafted accordingly. Motion carried.

Section IX (Connections with International Trade and Industrial Federations) is adopted without debate or amendments.

Section X (Relations with the Communist International)

Comrade Dimitrov proposes to change point 1 of section X so as to read 'three representatives with decisive votes' instead of one representative; mutual representation of both Internationals to consist of three members from each executive committee. Comrades Ries, Malzahn, and Arlandis are against Dimitrov's motion, which is adopted by the commission by majority vote.

Section XI (Relations with the International of Revolutionary Cooperatives).

Comrade Dimitrov moves to delete the entire paragraph about the relations with the International of revolutionary cooperatives, as there is no such body yet.

Comrade Flynn says this section could be adopted, only adding at the end 'as soon as it will definitely constitute itself'.

Comrade Lozovsky proposes to carry this motion, the more so since the question is about representation with a consultative vote.

Comrade Nin states ironically that we then get united with a metaphysical quantity not yet in existence. If we go on at the same rate, we might as well unite with some St. Paul the Apostle.

Comrade Lozovsky puts the motion to a vote to give representation to the Cooperative International.[9] The motion is carried by majority vote.

Section XII (Bureaus and Their Representatives)

Comrade Lozovsky says he received a motion to delete this section entirely. He makes the following remarks: I defend this proposal. I myself wrote the sec-

9 A reference to the Cooperative Section of the Communist International, formed in 1920 following the Second Comintern Congress to organise Communist work in the cooperative movement.

tion on the strength of our experience, but this experience is of a double nature; there are positive as well as negative sides to such bureaus. Since some local conditions may highlight the negative sides, it may be more prudent not to fix in our decision these 'bureaus' as 'obligatory' organs of the International. Instead of bureaus, it would be safer simply to send one to three members as representatives.

Comrade Malzahn says that in his opinion point 3 should be left as is, which says that in those countries where the general trade-union organisation is affiliated with the International Trade Union Council, etc. The rest may be deleted.

Comrade Maciejewski declares that we should retain point 4, which speaks of establishing a bureau of representatives, and delete the rest.

Comrade Kunte agrees with Comrade Maciejewski.

Comrade Flynn moves to delete the entire section since the Central Council, even without any specific instructions or statutes, has the right to appoint a bureau in any country in which it finds it necessary to do so.

Comrade Lozovsky puts the question to a vote. The majority are in favour of deleting the entire section XII.

Section XIII (Expulsion)

Comrade Lozovsky says that a proposal has been received to the effect that expulsion can be done only by the congress and not the council.

The Spanish delegation thinks that the Central Council cannot issue expulsions; only the congress can do it. In cases where such expulsion becomes necessary, the Central Council should refer this to the next congress.

Comrade Malzahn moves to adopt section XIII with the following supplement: 'The expelled organisation has the right to appeal the decision of the Central Council at the next international congress, which may confirm or annul the expulsion'. This motion is unanimously carried.

Section XIV (Internal Structure)

Szántó's motion is carried without debate to delete in section XIV the five lines beginning with 'should create the following sections' etc., until the end of the paragraph, and to put instead 'and organises sections and branches in accordance with the requirements and the decisions of the Central Council'.

Sections XV and XVI are carried without debate or amendments.

Session of 17 July, Morning

The session opens at 11:00 a.m. Comrade Lozovsky in the chair.

Lozovsky opens the session. He asks the gathering not to introduce any amendments of an editorial character, and to limit themselves only to amendments [to the organisational resolution] on questions of principle, as the style of the text will be improved by an editing commission. As there are no amendments in the first and second parts, the commission passes on to the third section, 'Factory Committees'.

Comrade Nin declares that the Spanish delegation cannot under any circumstances agree with section III, which reads, 'To take part in the elections in those factory committees that are established by law, as for instance in Germany or Italy', as this is nothing but the recognition of these laws. This is the same as if we were to take part in parliamentary committees and in other departments. This in its opinion smells of Amsterdam, and under no circumstances can the Spanish delegation take up this point of view.

Comrade Repossi says that in Italy the syndicalists, together with the Communists, take part in elections in order to pull the legal factory committees away from the reformists, and in his opinion the tactics proposed here are right, and he hopes that the comrades of other countries will take the same point of view.

Comrade Nin states that with such reasoning, one should also collaborate with bourgeois governments.

Comrade Lozovsky remarks that there is a great difference between the two things.

The amendment is rejected.

Comrade Malzahn proposes adding the word 'Austria' in the passage where the bourgeoisie of Germany and Italy is spoken of.

Comrade Lozovsky proposes no discussion of the fourth section, as the principles on this question are already established. He proposes to take up the fifth section – the most important part of the thesis – on the organisational problems in the principal countries. There are no amendments to points 16 and 17. Point 18 is then dealt with.

Comrade Pollitt proposes modifying point 18, because in Britain the IWW counts only 300 members. To speak of this organisation with reference to Britain therefore would be incorrect.

Comrade Lozovsky speaks against this. He points out that in Holland, for instance, the same organisation counts not more than 200 members, and nevertheless this paragraph ought to remain in order to express clearly our negative attitude toward the creation of such small international organisations.

Comrade Pollitt proposes in such a case to drop this point altogether, as these unions are so small that by mentioning them we only advertise them.

The majority is for leaving in this point.

Comrade Lozovsky proposes to deal with point 21, which refers to Spain.

Comrade Nin declares that the Spanish delegation is for this point as a whole, considering it useful for the Spanish movement, but proposes, in addition, to note that the nuclei – the adherents of the Red Labour International – who are in the reformist organisation, and also in those organisations that have broken or are on the way to breaking with Amsterdam, are invited to join the Confederation of Labour.

Comrade Lozovsky accepts the amendment, but under the condition that it should refer only to those who have already broken, without mentioning those who intend to break. Let them gather more members and then affiliate to us.

Comrade Nin points out that the UGT had 135,000 members before the December strike, when it betrayed the revolutionary workers.[10] Now the number of members has declined; many Communist groups have already left the UGT and are distinctly inclined toward us [the CNT]. The Spanish delegation does not think that these groups will join us immediately, as in three or four months' time the congress will take place. The Spanish delegation does not insist that these groups should join us now, but in the future they must do so.

Comrade Lozovsky proposes inviting the UGT to coordinate activity with us without mentioning immediate affiliation of those who have not yet broken with Amsterdam, and to limit ourselves for the time being to this, but at once to invite the representatives of the Spanish Communist Party to the first session of our Central Council, so that they could explain in detail what is really happening there, and after that to adopt a special resolution with regard to Spain.

The commission then takes up point 22 (Germany).

Comrade Malzahn finds that the beginning of point 22 is certainly correct, and that the position of Germany is really the most difficult and complex. The German delegation has dealt fully with this question, and after discussing it over three sessions, came to the conclusion that it must be altered in some parts, in accordance with the actual state of affairs in Germany. He points out that the general position of the trade-union movement in Germany is very acute owing to the fact that the bourgeoisie has taken the offensive along the whole front. The Communists have successfully organised nuclei within the trade unions that embrace the mass of the workers and office employees, but the trade-union bureaucracy has replied to it by mass expulsion of the Communists. In different trade unions there about 500 comrades have been expelled, without including two departments in Halle and Chemnitz that each have 3,000 members. These expulsions have created a very favour-

10 On 12 December 1920 the CNT had proclaimed an indefinite general strike. Two days later the UGT's National Committee voted not to observe the strike, dooming the action to defeat.

able feeling toward the Communists, which must be utilised. But the formation of an all-German grouping of expelled trade unions would complicate to a great extent the work started by the Communists. He therefore proposes replacing the text of point 22 by the text worked out by the German delegation.

Comrade Lozovsky finds that the text proposed by the German delegation is not acceptable. Firstly, the insertion of the paragraph devoted to the question of organisation – the question of why and under what circumstances we can accept the independent unions. The question of the conditions of affiliation is a separate matter, and it is out of place here. This insertion has too much of an internal and fractional character, which the congress cannot accept in any way. With regard to the question of affiliation, there are statutes and if they cannot submit to them, they will not be able to affiliate.

The second point that is very unclear is the question of the expelled unions and local groups. One cannot quite clearly see from Comrade Malzahn's proposal what the German comrades really mean to do with these expelled. It is said of the Communists that it is necessary to organise them into unions, but concerning the non-communists nothing is said at all. But if they will not be organised, they will go over to the independent unions, and part of them will return repenting to the old unions. Thus, on the one hand, the independent unions will become stronger, and on the other hand, the unions that are carrying out revolutionary propaganda will dissolve.

Comrade Lozovsky therefore believes that the German delegation has taken an incorrect point of view. In the draft of the thesis that is proposed to them, the unification of all the expelled members in a union is spoken of as the 'union of the expelled', and of getting it to fight for readmission to the old trade unions. The fear of such a measure testifies that the German comrades are taking the line of least resistance and are afraid that the trade-union bureaucrats would somehow benefit from this step. But how can they benefit from it? How would it be detrimental for us to raise the slogans of 'Down with the splitters! Return to the unions!'? Comrade Lozovsky is therefore in favour of the initial version, emphasising the need to carry out the struggle for readmission to the unions of the expelled workers by trade.

Comrade Dimitrov proposes handing over this paragraph to a special commission that will edit it, taking into consideration the proposal of the German comrades.

Comrade Malzahn declares that he made his proposal on behalf of the German delegation.

Comrade Kunte (Czechoslovakia) says that although in Czechoslovakia they acted as Comrade Lozovsky advocates, he nevertheless proposes leaving the solution of this question to the Germans themselves, without interference from other countries, as the Germans know the situation in their own country much better.

Comrade Lozovsky replies by pointing out that the task of the commission is precisely to resolve the issue jointly, and this in no way can be considered as 'interference'.

Comrade Malzahn declares that he certainly does not share the opinion of the Czechoslovak comrades who said that this question refers exclusively to Germany, and that neither the commission nor the congress can or should interfere. We are at the international congress of the Red Labour International, and it is clear that all present here can and must deal with questions concerning Germany. As to the subject in question now, the insistence with which it is being pursued is to be explained by the fact that over three sessions the German delegation discussed it thoroughly, as the delegation considers the question to be a vital one.

With regard to the independent unions, the delegation is prepared to withdraw this amendment if the question is taken up in some other section. But they consider the question of forming new unions of the expelled members to be of extraordinary importance and propose that the commission deal with it fully. The German delegation in its insistence is guided by the following: Up to now experience has proved that nearly all expelled members are Communists, and once they are Communists they are sure to be in the factories and in the nuclei, and they work under the leadership of the Communist Party. If the expelled include non-communists, the Communists will work to organise them into nuclei of sympathisers. Such organisations exist already, and they work under the direct guidance of the Communist nuclei and the Communist fractions.

The German delegation therefore finds that this question relates in practice to the present organisational forms. The expelled individual members reach the number of 500–600, all of whom are Communists. In addition, in local branches there are local groups that number 3,000 expelled members, and which are also under the guidance of the local Communist groups. In view of this, the delegation is of the opinion that the creation of new organisations could give the trade-union bureaucracy an opportunity for utilising them to the detriment of the Communists. They will bring forward accusations to the effect that the Communists split the workers' movement, and so on. Of course, the Communists will be able to explain their purpose to the workers, but this will take several months.

He therefore insists that when dealing with the question, the commission should take into consideration the view of the German delegation, inasmuch as this does not depart from the directives on the general course of action of the Red International of Labour Unions.

Comrade Lozovsky proposes setting up a special subcommittee composed of Lozovsky, Dimitrov, Malzahn, Heckert, and one representative of Spain for the purpose of dealing with the question of those expelled.

Comrade Malzahn withdraws his candidacy and moves instead that the Germans assign two members to this subcommittee. (*The motion is carried.*)

The commission passes over to point 23. This section does not raise any debates.

The chair announced the session closed until the following morning.

Session of 17 July, Evening

The session opens at 7:00 p.m., Comrade Lozovsky in the chair.

Comrade Lozovsky opens the session and proposes passing over to the sixth section, on 'The International Organisation by Trade and by Industry'.

Comrade Kunte makes a proposal concerning Czechoslovakia, and asks for it to be inserted in point 23.

Comrade Lozovsky objects to this motion in view of the fact that point 23, dealing with national unions, also deals with the national organisations of Czechoslovakia, Poland, America, and so forth; to mention it again in point 23 would be superfluous.

Comrade Kunte withdraws his motion.

Comrade Murphy points out that in Latin America three types of unions are fighting: the moderate trade unions, the IWW, and the anarcho-syndicalist organisations. The American Federation of Labor utilises the fact that the above three organisations are fully engaged in the struggle with the bourgeoisie, which is particularly bitter in Latin America, and do not pay due attention to the growing strength of this federation. Murphy thinks it necessary, as a matter of great urgency for the revolutionaries of South America, to call upon them to unite all these organisations for combating capitalism under the banner of the Red Labour International.

The Spanish delegation also stands for a more precise formulation on the relations among the unions.

Comrade Lozovsky opposes this motion as insufficiently clear and unable to give a practical answer to the question. The amendment would have some sort of sense if it were possible to define exactly what the structure or form of the trade unions in question is, as to what are their tendencies, and in general, how they can be united. This would bring some practical results. But as long as there is no such clear wording, it is much better to preserve the general form in which the question of federations is put in the theses.

Comrade Murphy declares that he did not insist and is prepared to withdraw his amendment.

Comrade Lozovsky draws the attention of the commission to the entire section that refers to the international industrial federations. Up to now there have been about thirty such international federations: of textile workers, miners, and so on. All of them are officially affiliated with Amsterdam. At the present moment it is doubtful we would be able to oppose them with new international federations. We would hardly be in a position to form new sufficiently powerful organisations for that purpose. It is necessary to approach the matter carefully. This was taken into account by the projected formation of 'international propaganda committees' of textile workers, miners, and so on.

After a few months of the work by these committees, during which they will bring under their influence a good number of trade unions, we will have the possibility of convening international conferences and founding national groups of such-and-such branch of industry. We had this in mind when composing the careful and 'diplomatic' wording of the section in question.

The German delegation agrees entirely with Comrade Lozovsky.

Sections VI and VII are carried without amendments. In section VIII on the expelled unions, Comrade Malzahn proposes some amendments to point 34, similar to those he proposed around point 22.

Comrade Lozovsky objects, pointing out that in section VIII there is point 33, which is specifically devoted to Germany, and this question is put in the theses in a general form that cannot in any way bind the German comrades. They can act independently, based on the concrete circumstances in their country. The aim of the theses is to establish general guidelines so that the trade-union bureaucracy should know that in case of mass expulsions they will have to deal with the unions of the expelled members that will fight against them.

Comrade Malzahn agrees with Comrade Lozovsky on the whole, but finds it necessary to delete the words 'especially in Germany' in point 33, and proposes, on behalf of the German delegation, (in point 34) instead of the words 'in such cases to organise by trade' to put 'organise themselves by industry', as this principle must guide the organisation of the masses in general. Besides this, it will give a certain stimulus to the reconstruction of the German trade unions on industrial lines.

Comrade Knight finds that the organisation of the expelled unions on new lines would be in direct contradiction to the slogan proposed of returning to the old trade unions. He therefore considers the amendment by Malzahn as inexpedient.

Comrade Lozovsky thinks the fears of Comrade Knight legitimate, and taking them into consideration, proposes giving a more careful and flexible wording, proposing the formulation that 'the expelled unions should speedily organise in accordance with the conditions of struggle, by trade or industry'.

Comrade Knight agrees with Comrade Lozovsky's proposal.

Comrade Lozovsky points out that the commission that edited the resolution on work among women decided to request the Organisation Commission to include in the organisational theses a special section on work among women, as there is in the theses a section on 'The Work among Young Workers', and so on. (The commission took this request into account, and entrusted Comrade Lozovsky with drafting the section on work among women.)

No objections are raised to sections IX and X, and the commission examines section XI.

Comrade Lozovsky expresses confidence that it can be carried without discussion, as the question on the conditions of admission into the Red International of Labour Unions has been thoroughly discussed and various objections have already been made.

Comrade Arlandis draws attention to the deficient wording of point 42, where the remark on the German syndicalists attacking those fighting on the barricades from behind may be taken as an accusation against all the syndicalists in general as being counterrevolutionary. He proposes adopting a more precise formulation to prevent the syndicalist organisations from breaking with the Red Labour International as a result of such careless wording.

The commission decides to delete from the last sentence of point 42 the word 'syndicalists'.

There were no other amendments.

Comrade Lozovsky closes the session in view of the fact that the question has been exhausted.

Commission on Tactics

Session of 16 July, Morning-Afternoon

The session is opened at 2:00 p.m., Comrade Lozovsky in the chair.

The Presidium consists of Stetter (Germany), Flynn (USA), and Lundström (Sweden).

The business of the commission begins with the consideration of Comrade Lozovsky's draft theses.

The amendment of Comrade Bartels (Germany) to change the wording of the end of point 1, which speaks of the impossibility of renewing the pre-war equilibrium by methods of capitalist exploitation, is rejected.

Comrade Arlandis (Spain) moves that in point 10 the part that speaks of the shortcomings of syndicalism due to its anarchist radicalism be changed. The final formulation of this paragraph is entrusted to Comrades Lozovsky and Nin.

Comrade Nin (Spain) moves to delete from point 11 the part that attributes to syndicalism the idea of independence and neutrality toward communism and an opposition to any kind of state. He also considers wrong the suggestion that the characteristic feature of syndicalism consisted in the separation or even opposition of politics to economics.

Comrade Godonnèche (France) considers that Nin does not put the question correctly. The syndicalists must confine themselves to economics and the political parties to politics.

Comrade Lozovsky, summing up the differences of opinion, moves that the disputed point be changed so as to simply emphasise that syndicalist ideas, in spite of their seemingly obvious revolutionary spirit, were in fact playing into the hands of the bourgeoisie.

After the approval of Comrade Lozovsky's proposal, Comrade Nin continues to insist upon the point that syndicalism embodied both politics and economics.

Comrade Lozovsky reminds Nin that pre-war syndicalism never synthesised economics and politics, always pretending to lead the economic and social struggle only. The commission votes to accept Comrade Lozovsky's point of view.

Comrade Nin moves that point 12, in which revolutionary syndicalism is put on the same level as Anglo-Saxon and German-Austrian trade unionism, be changed. To his mind, only the last two mentioned were guilty of adapting to capitalist society.

Comrade Repossi (Italy) does not see in Lozovsky's thesis any contradiction to the actual state of affairs prior to the war and during the war.

 | DOI:10.1163/9789004712867_024

Comrade Dimitrov (Bulgaria), agreeing with the last speaker, finds it necessary to point out the fact that it helped the bourgeoisie to make use of the trade unions in their own interests.

The commission accepts Dimitrov's motion, attaching it to the motion presented by Comrade Maciejewski, who considers it possible to speak not about three forms of the trade-union movement, but about the trade-union movement in general.

In accordance with the motion of Comrade Dautkus (Germany, General Workers' Union), point 13 is changed in the sense that during the war, in the majority of countries, the trade unions ceased to exist as militant class organisations.

As to point 14, Comrade Lozovsky does not agree with Murphy (Britain), who moved that instead of speaking about the disorganisation of the trade unions, one should rather speak of the disorganisation of the bureaucracy of the trade unions. Pointing out the fact that the war could not have been waged for four years if only the bureaucracy had been affected by disorganisation, Lozovsky moves that the word 'decay' be replaced by 'moral decay'.

Comrade Lezhava points out the fact that among the leaders of the trade-union movement, not all of them proved to be traitors to the workers' cause, and moves to point out that it does not refer to all of them, but to the great majority of them.

Point 15 is agreed to without changes.

Points 16, 17, and 18 are agreed to without significant changes, which do not alter them at all on matters of principle.

In point 19, referring to the General Confederation of Labour, Comrade Michel [Relenque] (France) moves an amendment that emphasises the fact that the reason for the CGT's weakness lies in the lack of inner unity.

Points 20 and 21 are agreed upon with insignificant changes that do not alter their fundamental meaning.

In point 22, on Michel's motion, the words characterising the activity of the Gelsenkirchen Free Workers' Union, the General Workers' Union, and the Syndicalist Union as counterrevolutionary are replaced by the words 'contrary to the interests of the working class and of the social revolution'. The representatives of the Gelsenkirchen Union, notwithstanding the changes made in this paragraph, express their protest made after its acceptance by a majority of the commission and leave the session.

Point 23 is agreed to without changes.

Murphy (Britain) moves an amendment to point 24. Considering that the motion carries no change of principles, the commission entrusts Comrade Murphy to formulate it in conjunction with Comrade Lozovsky.

Point 25 is accepted without changes.

As to point 26, Comrade Knight (Canada) moves an amendment to the effect of defining the tactics of the revolutionary trade unions of Canada in their attitude toward the American Federation of Labor. Comrade Lozovsky moves that this amendment be referred to the editing commission, without making any objections to it. An additional amendment moved by Comrade Murphy with reference to Latin American countries is rejected by a majority of votes.

Points 27 and 28 are accepted without changes. The amendments to the latter point moved by Comrade Kunte (Czechoslovakia) and Comrade Kurulov (Georgia) are rejected, as having no bearing on the question under discussion.

Session of 16 July, Evening

The evening session is opened at 7:00 p.m. with Comrade Lozovsky in the chair.

The evening session begins with the consideration of the section on 'neutrality, independence, and socialism'.

Points 29, 30, 31, 32, and 33 are accepted without discussion, with insignificant editorial changes.

In connection with point 33, Comrade Nin moves an amendment to the effect that the unification of the trade-union movement must be effected not with the Communist Party, but with all advanced revolutionary organisations. The amendment is rejected.

The whole of section VI was then agreed upon without changes.

Discussion of section VII brought out disagreements on point 42. Comrades Nin and Arlandis consider that the Red International must increase its propaganda also in those countries where there are big organisations adhering to Amsterdam. It must attract the workers to the international revolutionary organisation and to leave their old unions. This amendment is accepted only insofar as its first part is concerned. As for its final part, Comrade Lozovsky says that it might be acceptable for Spain only.

Point 43 is referred to the Editing Commission for final drafting.

In section VIII, Comrade Lozovsky accepts an amendment to point 44 deleting the last sentence, in which the decisions of the International of Trade Unions are to be considered in the light of the decisions of the Comintern. Comrade Dimitrov disagrees with this amendment. Comrade Nin insists on its importance; otherwise it will create the impression of absolute dependence of the International of Trade Unions on the Comintern. The amendment is carried.

Comrade Murphy moves to delete in point 45 the passage referring to armed insurrection as hindering the propaganda among the masses lacking consciousness. Despite the support of the German delegation, the amendment is defeated.

Points 46, 47, 48, 49, and 50 are accepted with minor corrections.

Upon a motion of Comrade Lozovsky, in point 51, where mention is made of the slogans of the economic struggle, the words 'to a level much higher than that of the pre-war period' are deleted. The motion of Comrade Murphy, to include in the aims of the revolutionary trade unions the fight for the equality of conditions of labour of both sexes and against the attempts of the bourgeoisie to utilise women's labour as a weapon against the interests of the working class, is carried by the insertion of this motion as a separate point 52.

Point 52 is accepted as it stands and becomes point 53.

Comrade Lozovsky moves to delete point 53 about sabotage. The motion is carried. For this reason the numbering of the points remains unchanged.

Points 54, 55, 56, 57 are accepted as read.

Szántó (Hungary) makes a motion to introduce a point after 57 about militarisation, courts of arbitration, and taxes on salaries. The motion is carried.

Points 58 and 59 are accepted as read.

Comrade Lozovsky moves to appoint an editing commission for the final working out of the theses in all the languages; this is carried. The following are appointed: Godonnèche and Marchand[1] for the French text; Kunte and Heckert for the German text; and Reinstein and Dixon [Browder] for the English text.

---

1 A probable reference to René Marchand.

Commission on Workers' Control

Session of 16 July, Morning-Afternoon

The session opens at 11:00 a.m. Comrade Tsyperovich in the chair. The commission decides to accept the theses presented by Tsyperovich as a basis for discussion, to discuss them point by point, and then take up Heckert's resolution point by point.

Comrade Tsyperovich reads his theses.

Point 1 is accepted unanimously.

Point 2. Comrade Leder proposes to add Luxembourg to the list of countries. Comrade Leder's amendment is accepted unanimously.

Comrade Grölig (General Workers' Union) says that the theses state that workers' control can be established under the capitalist system, although in another passage it says that this is impossible. It is absolutely necessary to state clearly and directly that it is impossible to establish a control system under the capitalist system.

Comrade Heckert states that Comrade Grölig's motion proves his inability to think dialectically. It is not correct to say that under the capitalist system it is impossible to establish the beginning of workers' control. There is no doubt that workers' control can be effectively established only when the proletariat takes the power into its hands, but we cannot imagine that capitalism will fall in a day or two. It will fall only as a result of a revolutionary struggle in a period when the workers will take control over production. He proposes to reject the motion made by Grölig as contrary to the revolutionary spirit.

Comrade Tsyperovich points out that Comrade Grölig, it seems, has not understood the theses correctly. In point 6 there is a statement that at the present stage of workers' control there is a contradiction – pointed out in point 1 – which finds its solution in the struggle for power between the bourgeoisie and the proletariat – that is, in the social revolution. This part shows that we do not wish to convince the workers that control, as understood by the bourgeoisie, can be achieved at the present time. We see in control a mighty means of education of the masses in the methods of management of industry.

Comrade Gliński considers it necessary to emphasise Tsyperovich's ideas by the following: the question of workers' control of industry for us is a question of political struggle, which we are carrying out. Capitalists will treat this point with special attention, as it gives a blow to their holy of holies: the right of ownership. This is why the question is posed, although control will not be fully established under the capitalist system.

 | DOI:10.1163/9789004712867_025

Comrade Király (Hungary) recognises the fact that workers' control is of great importance as a means of struggle against the capitalist system, but points out that the factory committees are in the hands of opportunists, and instead of a means of struggle against this system they may become its support and saviour. He indicates the work that should be carried on within the factory committees by the revolutionary elements – and mainly by Communists.

Comrade Matta (Italy) says that factory committees can become tools to support the government if they are legal institutions recognised by the government, supported by the employers, and are in the hands of the opportunists and trade unions.

The chair notes that this argument applies not to the point discussed but to Comrade Heckert's motion on factory committees, and partly to the following points. Therefore he asks not to discuss this question now, but only the questions raised in point 2.

Comrade Tom Mann calls attention to the fact that the question raised by the Italian comrade is mentioned in point 3.

Comrade Tsyperovich: Comrades, two amendments or additions have been made. One of them agrees with Comrade Király, and the second one cannot be accepted because it does not deal with this point. Therefore there is no objection to this point. I will take a vote. Accepted, Comrade Grölig voting against.

Point 4 is accepted with several editorial corrections proposed by Comrade Leder.

Point 5 is accepted without corrections.

Point 6 accepted without corrections.

Comrade Leval (Spain) proposes a change in point 7 where it says, 'At such a moment the role of mass organisations, including not only the vanguard of the proletariat (the Communist Party) but also the great masses not affiliated to a party, assumes a very important one'. The proposal is to delete the words 'Communist Party', because this mention of the Communist Party has not been agreed upon by the congress.

Comrade Tsyperovich speaks against the motion of Comrade Leval. It is necessary for the theses to note, in their analysis of the historical process, that up to the present time the vanguard of the working class, which directed, roused, and led the working class toward the conquest of the dictatorship of the proletariat, was the Communist Party, the Communist International. To say that this has not been proven means that you do not know the history of the workers' movement, as there is not a single country where the initiative for the conquest of power did not belong exclusively to the Communists. Therefore, to exclude these words from the theses would be antihistorical.

Comrade Leval (Spain) supports his amendment because, in his country, which he particularly knows, and in several other Latin countries, a great part is played by the revolutionary syndicalists, while the Communist Party plays no part. The leading role at the time of revolution will not be played by the Communists, having a membership of about ten thousand and divided into two currents, but by the syndicalists. It is not correct, therefore, to speak in the general theses of the leading role of the Communists. He does not demand that the theses should mention the role played by the revolutionary syndicalists, but in that case you must not talk of the role of the Communist Party, as its role is great only in those countries where the revolutionary syndicalist movement in the trade unions is weak. To generalise this fact, to make it a general rule, is not correct. He decidedly objects to the words 'Communist Party' remaining in the theses.

Comrade Grölig proposes to simply have the word 'communists'. He believes that this correction will be acceptable to Comrade Leval, as revolutionary syndicalists can call themselves communists, as their aim is also the establishment of the communist system.

Comrade Farwig speaks sharply against Comrade Leval's motion. In his view, the revolutionary syndicalists do not play such a leading role as Leval says. The Communist Party of Spain at the present time is undoubtedly weak, but as the revolutionary movement develops, it will unavoidably have to take the leading role. Besides, we should not discuss this question exclusively from the point of view of narrow nationalism, but rather in its international outlook. We must not forget that the struggle in Spain is only one part of the international struggle. The leading role in this international struggle belongs and should belong to the Communist International, the Communist Party. This was recognised by Comrade Leval himself, as well as by other comrades here at the congress from the platform. Therefore he is surprised at the insistence of Comrade Leval and categorically protests against it.

Comrade Gliński speaks against the motion of Comrade Grölig to substitute the word 'communists' for 'Communist Party', because in his opinion there can be no communists who are not members of the Communist Party. And if there were such, they could not represent people who lead the proletariat, as it is impossible to play a leading role, to be the leading organ, by itself.

Comrade Leval repeats his argument, objecting to Comrades Gliński and Farwig. Of course, the revolutionary syndicalists of Spain know very well that their struggle is only a single act of the world struggle of the proletariat. He, as a revolutionary syndicalist, cannot allow the Communist International to take the leadership to such a degree as to demand that the revolutionary syndicalists reject their doctrines. The revolutionary syndicalists and the Confederation of

Labour [CNT], whom Comrade Leval represents, expect to play the leading role in the revolution themselves. He objects to the statement that the revolutionary syndicalists do not play this part, as they did previously. On the contrary, the role is greater now than ever.

As there are no more speakers, Comrade Tsyperovich takes the floor for his summary: I must say to Comrade Leval that the theses do not state that this is the case in absolutely every country. At every moment different relations are possible. It is stated here that in cases where the Communist Party plays the leading role, it plays a most important part; but this is also true of the trade unions. Then what is the argument about? Of all the countries represented here, only the Spanish delegates point out the difference, and insofar as the theses define the general condition of things, it is absolutely clear that pointing out the leading role played by the Communist parties does not in the least decrease the role played by the trade unions, which have done a great deal. That can be accepted as a general rule, with the exception that has been mentioned here. In this way, all discussion on this question is closed and the question settled. The leading part in the revolution made by the masses is played not only by the vanguard, but also by the organised power of the workers. Comrade Tsyperovich, therefore, fully supports the original text of his thesis.

Comrade Leval proposes that instead of the words 'Communist Party' we substitute the words 'revolutionary-syndicalist organisations or the two united forces according to circumstances'.

Comrade Gliński proposes to put 'organised in revolutionary trade unions' after the word 'non-party'.

The commission passes to a vote on the amendments made by Leval, Grölig, and Gliński. All three amendments are defeated by a great majority of votes. Grölig proposes that in the part reading, 'this necessitates the utilisation of the machinery of the trade unions and their reorganisation by means of the committees, and making them in this way a mighty power of mass control and taking over the industries', the words 'by means of the factory committees' should be replaced by 'by means of industrial unions'.

Comrade Tsyperovich does not wish to raise objections to that, as this will occur on the day after the revolution.

Comrade Heckert supports the original text because the discussion is not only about the postrevolutionary period, but in the second part we speak of the preparatory period before the revolution. If we accept Grölig's amendment, it will mean that an artificial split will be effected among the industrial sections of the trade unions, the factory committees, and the trade unions.

Comrade Leder believes that Grölig's motion is insufficient. It is not enough to make the organisation of the factory committees dependent upon the trade unions or the industrial unions. But it is a question of avoiding the danger of turning the organisation of control bodies – the control committees, factory committees, or special control commissions – into a tool of the yellow trade-union bureaucracy, now carried out by the trade unions. Leder proposes either to insert a separate point or a separate phrase, in which it is stated that wherever the trade-union movement is in the hands of the yellow union bureaucracy, it is necessary that the revolutionary vanguard of the trade-union movement create special organisations to direct these organisations for control of the factories.

Comrade Gliński supports the motion made by Comrade Leder, and adds that the latter part of the theses is based on a very clear idea, but it is not clear enough. It is not even stated exactly who has the control functions, the factory committees or a special control commission elected by each enterprise. It is necessary to state exactly whether we have two forms of organisation or one. And if we are to have two forms, just what their relations will be.

The discussion is closed, and the commission passes to a vote on the amendments: (1) of Comrade Grölig that the words 'trade unions' be substituted by 'industrial unions'; (2) of Comrades Gliński and Leder, that we include a separate point in the theses in which the relations between the trade unions and the factory committees during the preparatory period of the proletarian revolution are determined, with an emphasis on the fact that we must not allow the factory committees as revolutionary organs to fall into the danger of being utilised by the bureaucratic trade unions of the old type.

Grölig's amendment is defeated by all but two votes. The amendments of Leder and Gliński are accepted, with the final wording to be formulated by the authors of the amendment.

In accordance with Comrade Mann's motion, which was carried, the floor will hence be given to one for and one against each amendment.

Point 8 is read and carried without amendment.

The commission takes up for discussion the question of 'General Conclusions'.

Comrade Tom Mann finds it necessary to make the following addition to point 1. Either after point 1 or in some other place, it makes no difference where, but it is necessary to insert that the trade unions must decidedly aim to allow workers' control to develop more until the time when the entire responsibility of the organisation of production in all its forms will be turned over to the trade unions.

Points 1–6 of this question are read and accepted one after the other. In point 7 Comrade Tsyperovich proposes that the words 'control commissions' be replaced by the words 'factory and shop committees', so that point 7, in its new wording, will read: 'For the efficient functioning of workers' control in each locality, it is necessary that the trade unions direct the work of the factory committees, while the trade unions must coordinate the work of the local control committees of the same industry, in such a manner as to avoid any attempt to create "factory patriotism" on the basis of localised control.'

Point 7 in its new form, as well as all the preceding points, are voted on and adopted. The corrected text in full is adopted unanimously. An editing commission is elected for the final drafting. The commission consists of Comrades Leder, Tom Mann, and one of the members of the French delegation. Comrade Tsyperovich, as the fourth member, is elected chairman of the commission.

The session adjourns at 3:20 p.m.

Session of 16 July, Evening

The evening session is opened at 8:00 p.m. Comrade Tsyperovich in the chair.

Comrade Tsyperovich says that Comrade Heckert's theses were written just before the question on tactics was discussed, and also the reports on the organisation of control. Therefore, more than half of Comrade Heckert's theses are a repetition of what was included in the theses of Comrade Tsyperovich.

It was agreed with Comrade Heckert to delete the general part of the resolution and to leave only points 6 and 7, because these points are on the mutual relations between the factory committees and the trade unions, from the point of view of control.

Owing to the fact that Comrade Heckert's theses were not issued in sufficient copies, and the Italian and Spanish delegates could not acquaint themselves with them prior to the discussion, it is decided to give them the theses printed in French for their perusal. It is decided that the session of the commission be adjourned until 17 July at 12:00 noon. It is requested that all amendments be prepared in written form before the opening of the session.

The session adjourns at 9:15 p.m.

Session of 17 July

The session opens at 12:00 noon with Comrade Tsyperovich in the chair.

Owing to the absence of Comrade Heckert, Comrade Tsyperovich presents the report.

Comrade Tsyperovich proposes to discuss the report on factory committees point by point. For amendments, to allow one speaker for and another against. The motion is carried.

Point 1 is unanimously adopted, but on the proposal of Comrade Leder, it is agreed that point 1, beginning with the words 'Factory committees cannot take the place of trade unions' to the end of the phrase, be made into a separate point, number 2.

Point 2 then becomes point 3

Point 3 then becomes point 4.

In point 4 the following amendment is made by Comrade Gliński: The passage beginning with the words 'the trade unions supported by the factory committees' until the end of the point be changed into: 'Trade union reconstructed on the industrial basis and supported by factory committees will familiarise the workers with industrial problems, will prepare the more experienced among them for the management of the enterprise, and effect control over the technical experts. Thus, under the general direction of the workers' government in cooperation with other economic organisations of the workers, the trade unions will carry out the fundamental principles of a socialist commonwealth'. Gliński's amendment is adopted.

After point 4 adding a special point on the concrete objectives of the factory committees is accepted.

Point 2, after being amended, is adopted in the following wording: 'Organisation of distribution for securing the normal functioning of the factories and the standard of living of the workers, that is, for the systematic supply of the factories as well as for the needs of the workers'.

The theses on the factory and shop committees as a whole, after proposed amendments and changes, are adopted unanimously.[1]

---

1 For the text of the Resolution on Factory Committees, see pp. 632–4.

Central Council Session

First Sitting, 20 July

(*The meeting opens at 1:15 p.m. Comrade Lozovsky in the chair.*)

Lozovsky declares the opening of the first meeting of the Central Council of the Red International of Trade and Labour Unions and announces the results of the elections to the Central Council. As ordered by the congress, the Central Council is to be formed as follows: four representatives from Russia; two each from Germany, Britain, France, United States, Italy, Spain, Poland, and Czechoslovakia; from all the other countries, one each; countries having less than 5,000 organised workers to have only a consultative voice, no vote.

According to the reports from the delegations, the following were elected:

1. From Russia: Lozovsky, Nogin, Rykov, Tsyperovich
2. From Germany: Maier, Richard Müller
3. From Britain: Tom Mann, Watkins
4. From United States: George Andreytchine, Dixon [Browder] (consultative)
5. From Spain: Nin, Arlandis
6. From Czechslovakia: Hampel, Kunte (consultative)
7. From Austria: Haidt
8. From Bulgaria: Dimitrov (proxy Popov)
9. From Yugoslavia: Pavlović
10. From Ukraine: Dashkevich
11. From Norway: Madsen
12. From Australia: Howie
13. From Switzerland: Wirth
14. From Canada: Knight
15. From Mexico: Ramírez
16. From Switzerland: Kilbom
17. From Denmark: Johnsen
18. From Finland: Lumivuokko (proxy Tiura)
19. From Far Eastern Republic: Kasparson
20. From Azerbaijan: Kabanovsky
21. From Armenia: Fiurstian
22. From Georgia: Kurulashvili
23. From Korea: Chin Min
24. From Latvia: Anderson

 | DOI:10.1163/9789004712867_026

25. From Lithuania: Girinis
26. From Luxembourg: Rosmer
27. From Estonia: Bleimann
28. From Abkhazia: Korolev

Rosmer announces, on the question of French representation, that the mandate given to the French delegation did not include the right to be elected a member of the council.

With regard to Italy, the council, taking into consideration the vague position of the General Confederation of Labour (CGL) and the presence of two organisations (the CGL and the Syndicalist Union) who aspire to representation in the council, it was decided, upon the recommendation of Comrade Lozovsky, to temporarily grant one seat to the Syndicalist Union and one to the CGL minority, with the understanding that after the next congress of the CGL, there should be only one representative of all the united trade unions of Italy, and representation should not be given to isolated and parallel union groupings. In agreement with this decision, the following were elected: Comrade Pagani for the Syndicalist Union and Comrade Massiano for the CGL minority.[1]

The Hungarian seat remains vacant, as the delegation could not agree upon the designee.

Lozovsky asks the delegates to the Central Council to report in detail as to the number of workers each one of them represents in his respective country.

The agenda for the meeting is as follows:

1. Election of an Executive Bureau and a general secretary
2. Personnel staff
3. Resolution on unemployment
4. The situation in Spain
5. On the representatives from Italy and an appeal to Italian workers
6. Congress of the French CGT in Lille
7. The Far Eastern countries
8. The situation in Germany
9. The international structure of the Trade and Labour International
10. Agitation and propaganda

---

1 An apparent reference to Duilio Mari and Luigi Repossi.

The two USI delegates at the RILU congress (who did not arrive until the congress had ended) were Duilio Mari and Nicola Vecchi. A delegate questionnaire filled out by 'Pagani', found in the RGASPI archives, matches Mari's biography.

The three delegates at the congress with decisive votes from the CGL minority were Luigi Repossi, Enea Matta, and Giuseppe Lattuada. As Repossi was the leading member of the delegation, 'Massiano' almost certainly refers to him.

After a short discussion, a motion by Comrade Tsyperovich to take up at the meeting only questions 1, 2, 3, and 5, which are of immediate importance, was adopted. All the other questions are to be referred to the Executive Bureau for study, after which the Central Council will take them up in plenary session.

In accordance with the adopted agenda, the council takes up the election of a seven-person Executive Bureau. On behalf of a group of comrades, Lozovsky proposes the following list: Comrades Lozovsky, Nogin, Tom Mann, Arlandis, Andreytchine, and Anton Maier. The seventh seat remains vacant on the motion of Comrade Rykov; the seat will be occupied by France or Italy, whoever will first send a permanent representative. Before a vote is taken, Comrade Rykov proposes to discuss each candidate separately.

The first candidate proposed was Comrade Arlandis. The Spanish delegation states that Comrade Arlandis has for many years been active in the labour movement not just in Spain but also in France. He possesses honesty and a solid theoretical education. His comrades point out his revolutionary zeal. His revolutionary record dates as far back as 1905. In particular, when the white terror was raging in Valencia, Arlandis showed his strength of character, courage, and devotion to his comrades. He is a member of the Communist Party.

The second candidate is Comrade Maier from Germany. As described by his comrades, he is still a relatively young militant in the revolutionary trade-union movement. Still they see in him a revolutionary power, and they have full confidence in him. He has proven his revolutionary character many times in his practical work, and possesses the theoretical training required to lead the movement today.

Comrade Andreytchine from America is a member of the IWW, also of the United Communist Party. He has been very active in the above-mentioned organisations in the front rank. According to his comrades, he is the living embodiment of the goal of the unification of the proletarian movement in America. He has the absolute confidence of his collaborators, as well as of the workers. He was closely connected with the RILU bureau there.

The council unanimously finds it unnecessary to discuss the candidacy of Comrade Tom Mann, as he is very well known to everybody.

The first of the two comrades proposed by the Russian delegation is Comrade Nogin, who comes from the generation of old revolutionary workers for whom the revolutionary struggle was a profession. He has been active in the revolutionary movement for more than twenty years. He was always in the left wing of the Social-Democratic Party (Bolsheviks), and was often on its Central Committee. He has served prison sentences many times on account of his revolutionary activities, and was deported to Siberia. He is a textile worker, and worked in England, where he learned English; he knows the English labour movement. After the October Revolution he became people's commissar of labour and has been active in the organisation of the economic life of the republic. He is one of the best authorities and critics of the labour movement.

The council need not spend much time on the candidacy of Lozovsky, as he is known by all as an old militant in the political and trade-union struggle, as one of the Russian experts on the union movement. He is author of a number of books on the workers' movement. Finally, he is a member of the Executive Bureau of the All-Russian Central Council of Trade Unions.

The motion to elect these six candidates is unanimously accepted.

The council takes up the question of the Secretariat. Tsyperovich moves to elect a general secretary to lead the work, and two assistants. He personally nominates Comrade Lozovsky as general secretary, and Comrades Maier and Tom Mann as his assistants. The motion is adopted unanimously.

The following resolution introduced by Comrade Tsyperovich was also unanimously adopted:

> On behalf of the First International Congress of Trade and Labour Unions, the Central Council of the Red International expresses its hearty thanks to the typographers, translators, the entire staff of the Press Bureau, and all other collaborators who, through their devotion and energy, have made the fulfilment of the obligations of the Red International of Labour Unions possible. Fraternal greetings!
>
> The Central Council of the Red International of Trade and Labour Unions

The council takes up the next question, which is the resolution on unemployment. Taking into consideration that the translations from the German text into other languages were unsatisfactory, the council decides to hold off adoption and to assign its final editing to Comrade Rykov and the Executive Bureau.

The last order of business was an appeal to the Italian workers. The motion of Comrade Lozovsky is to have the Bureau draft an appeal to be ready for presentation and discussion at the next session. It was also agreed to have a brief appeal by radio sent to the congress in Lille.[2]

The next session [of the Central Council] is set for 1 July at 12:00 noon.

The session of the Executive Bureau is set for 20 July at 7:00 p.m.

---

2 The 'Message to the Lille Congress' and 'An Appeal to the Italian General Confederation of Labour' were published in *The Red Labour Union International: Bulletin of the Executive Bureau*, no. 1, 30 August 1921, pp. 40 and 36.

Second Sitting, 21 July

(*The session opens at 1:00 p.m. Comrade Lozovsky in the chair.*)

Lozovsky: Comrades, the second sitting of the Central Council is open. The first question on the agenda is the question of the Spanish trade-union movement. Yesterday the Executive Bureau looked through the position in Spain. There is the National Labour Confederation (CNT), which is affiliated with us, and a reformist organisation – the General Union of Workers (UGT). With regard to the UGT there are the Communist nuclei, as well as a number of organisations that have left it.

The Executive Bureau has decided that the organisations that left the UGT should affiliate to the CNT. The date for this fusion will be set later, depending on the conditions of the struggle in the country and on the possibility for the CNT to come out into the open from the underground, where they have been driven by reaction.

It is further decided that the Communist nuclei that are working within the UGT should continue their work. At the next congress of the CNT, the revolutionary unions should participate, without formally breaking their ties to the old reformist organisations. After examining this agreement, the Executive Bureau recommends to the Central Council the following motion:

> The Central Council of the Red International ratifies the following agreement in principle, based on resolutions adopted at the First Congress of the Red International, between the delegations of the Spanish National Confederation of Labour, the Spanish Communist Party, and the Spanish Communist Workers' Party:
>
> 1. All trade unions that have separated from the reformist organisation – the UGT – should join the CNT. The date of this affiliation will be set by a special convention and will depend on the conditions of the struggle in the country and upon the possibility for the CNT to establish a legal existence after having been driven underground by violent reaction.
> 2. In accordance with the decisions adopted by the congress, possibilities will arise to make a bloc for common work. The Communist nuclei will remain in the reformist unions and coordinate their activities with those of the CNT.
> 3. In the event that the Communists have a majority at the next congress of the UGT, the fusion of the two organisations must take place. Otherwise, the Communists should remain within this organisation

and continue their work to conquer it. Departure from the reformist organisations will depend on a prior agreement of the two parties concerned. In the event that the revolutionary minority is expelled from the UGT, the expelled organisations will automatically affiliate to the CNT.

4. The revolutionary unions affiliated to the UGT are to participate in the congress of the CNT.

This agreement, which has been concluded between them, will be signed this evening. After that we will propose it to the Central Council for adoption.

Yesterday the Spanish Communists declared officially that they have up to now been opposed to affiliation with the CNT because the latter did not join the Red International. Insofar as the CNT declares that it accepts unconditionally and without any reservations the decisions of the congress, they agree to this fusion, as the basis for disagreements has now disappeared.

Thus the proposal is that the Council shall in principle approve of the agreement between the organisations.

Who is against? The agreement is ratified.[3]

Now we shall deal with the second question, concerning the German *Unionen*. At the last session we did not announce the declarations made by them, but decided to print them in the stenographic proceedings, which was done in Bulletin No. 15. In that issue there is a declaration signed by the Gelsenkirchen Union and the General Workers' Union.[4] It is said there that an artificial majority was created in favour of those who are still under the influence of Amsterdam, and that this was done by a trick. But this is not important; of more importance is the following declaration. (*He reads.*)

1. The attempt to bring the revolutionary movement back into the framework of purely dogmatic economic schemes by means of an artificial majority cannot but fail.
2. The course of action adopted by the congress, and consequently in effect until the Second Congress, the tactics of the Red International, at least with regard to Germany, are to be considered oppor-

3 Following the Moscow congress, the communist-syndicalist elements within the CNT became embroiled in a fight with an anarchist wing of the organisation, in which the question of affiliation to the RILU became a key issue. By early 1922 the anarchists had become dominant, and affiliation to the Profintern was rejected.

4 For the text of this declaration, see pp. 528–9.

> tunistic. Considering this course of action to be an obstacle in the way of development of the revolution, we must reject it.

The representatives of the two unions thus declare that our decisions are opportunist, that it will harm the revolution, and so on. By such declarations they show that they stand outside of the Red International. We must put to these comrades the following direct questions:

1. Do they accept the decisions of the congress in full, or do they not?
2. Do they bind themselves by the decisions adopted by this congress?

If they declare that they are not bound by these decisions, then we shall tell them that they are not members of the Red International and that they stand outside this International.

(*Upon the proposal made by Comrade Richard Müller, the declaration of the Independent Unions of Germany is read.*)

The floor is given to Comrade Bartels.

Bartels: The Gelsenkirchen Free Workers' Union, as is known, adheres to the Red International. In the sphere of revolutionary activities in the trade-union movement, the hopes placed in the oppositional nuclei within the reformist unions, the nuclei that are being organised and led by the United Communist Party in Germany, have not been fulfilled. Experience has proved to us that this system does not give the desired results, at least in those industries where the members of the Free Workers' Union are well represented. The formation and continued existence of the nuclei in the old unions should be condemned, especially after the shameful treachery by the trade-union bureaucracy during the March events.[5]

As a result of this, we are again compelled to return to the slogan 'Out of the unions!' and to accept once and for all that this slogan is to remain in effect. If the Central Council will not give sufficient freedom to the Free Unions, which is necessary in the judgement of the latter to carry out revolutionary work, the council will have to exclude them. But they do not intend to leave the International on their own. With regard to this, the delegates have received categorical instructions from their organisations. The slogan 'Out of the unions!' stands as firm as ever. Upon their arrival home, the delegates will, of course, give to the members of their organisations a full report on the congress and will put the question as to their attitude toward this slogan.

Very soon, comrades, a congress of the Gelsenkirchen Free Workers' Union will take place. Measures will be taken in order to coordinate our revolution-

5 For the March Action in Germany, see p. 215, n. 7.

ary work with that of the General Workers' Union and to establish some sort of organisational connection with this union. Our next step will be an attempt to influence the National Trade Union Office of the oppositional nuclei in order to realise a more definite expression of its organisational unity. Were the latter to be affiliated to Gelsenkirchen and to the General Workers' Union, it could create a true revolutionary trade union in Germany. This is our next task and our next objective. But in any case, it is out of the question that the independent unions will change their point of view on the need to leave the old trade unions.

Hampel (Czechoslovakia), analysing the considerations of Comrade Bartels, finds that the representatives of the independent unions refusing to submit to the decisions adopted by the congress put themselves outside the Red International. By doing so, they simply show their desire to bring about the destruction of all other organisations of Germany and those of other countries.

In Czechoslovakia, the work of the *Unionen* has been of a more demoralising character. Instead of organising the trade-union movement, they insert disorder into the communist spirit of the workers. Better that they follow the example of our Spanish comrades, who also have their own particular point of view but still wish to preserve the revolutionary unity of the workers' organisations. For the good of the revolution, the Spanish syndicalists agreed to a compromise resolution with the Red International and made certain concessions. Consequently the question of excluding the *Unionen* from the International is not posed, not even with the declaration made by them, which is equivalent to recognising themselves as standing outside the Red International. This fact cannot be hidden by whatever phraseology they may use. If the Unionists would succeed in their work, we would have to wait too long for the coming of the revolution in Germany.

Richard Müller expresses his astonishment with regard to the declaration of the Unionists. There was a definite question put as to their attitude toward the decisions of the Red International. We have received no direct answer. In his reply, Comrade Bartels tries to evade. Comrade Hampel has rightly declared that every organisation that does not submit to the decisions of the congress is putting itself outside the Red International. That is indisputable. Comrade Bartels has said here that the independent unions will not leave the International, but will wait until they are thrown out. They need it as a means for propaganda among the German workers, that they have done everything in their power to join the Red International, but in spite of that they have been thrown out. However, there is no need to throw them out as they have excluded themselves.

Can there be any question of exclusion when they have announced here that not only will they not submit to the decisions of the congress, but that they will enter into direct opposition to the policy of the Red International.

But there arises a new question. One must assume that the delegates leaving for the congress did not ask the point of view of the rank and file, as the latter would not have authorised them to disorganise the trade-union movement. They have received their credentials from the leaders of their unions.

Comrade Bartels, referring to the future, proposes to create in Germany a general union of all organisations represented here, for mutual work and to draw into this union the whole mass of our nuclei. It is however necessary to say firmly that the German Communists will not follow the leaders of the independent unions but on the contrary will oppose their destructive work with creative work. It is very doubtful that Bartels would have the right to make declarations on behalf of all workers belonging to the independent unions. What will become of those who are also members of the Communist Party in Germany? Well, they cannot but submit to all decisions of the Red International.

The independent unions have no wide perspectives. They are doomed to remain a little group, deserted by the rank and file, who will leave them and participate in the creative work of the Red International. There is no need to put the question of exclusion, as after the declaration of their delegates, they automatically are leaving the Red International.

Emil Gieseler (German Seamen's Union) states, in the name of his union (7,000 members), that he is in favour of the declaration read at the session of the Council by the Free Workers' unions' delegation. Personally, as a representative of a small organisation, he is thankful to the Russian comrades for the invitation to the congress. He judges from this fact that not the number of members, but the revolutionary spirit of each organisation is the guarantee. To his disappointment, he learned, after he reached Moscow, that votes had been distributed according to the membership of each organisation, irrespective of whether it is revolutionary or not. Comrade Gieseler concludes, therefore, that the Russians are not well informed about the current situation in Germany.

The Seamen's Union, part of which he represents, is a good example. Somebody stated yesterday that we can fully rely upon the German seamen. This is mistaken. We cannot guarantee that the German seamen will follow the resolutions adopted by the congress. There are very few Communists among the sailors, although they have been shedding their blood for the cause of the revolution. It is unnecessary to tell you how the sailors behaved during the German revolution. A great number of his personal friends died for the proletarian cause. I see that you have created a fake majority in favour of the Communist Party, which in Germany too seeks to impose its dictatorship. But the masses don't want such a dictatorship. What benefit can be derived from the privilege of expressing our opinion, when the question has already been decided in advance, and that we are hopeless. Many a time we tried to unite our revolutionary forces, but with no success. In conclusion, he declares that he desires unity with all his soul, but so far I have not found a practical way to bring it about.

Lozovsky, answering Comrade Gieseler, says that the International is not a debating club. The congress holds a discussion, everyone makes a decision, which after returning home must be carried out. If we had formed an international debating club, we could, of course, after long discussions return home and act as we please.

Andreu Nin, the representative of the Spanish CNT, says that the experience of the Russian Revolution has proven the need of proletarian discipline in order to lead the workers to victory. That makes proletarian unity and the acceptance of the congress resolutions necessary and binding. Sects, small groups, will not be able to lead the proletariat to victory; only the entire proletariat when it stands united.

I would like to say a few words to the comrades of the *Unionen*. The Spanish delegation, perhaps more than any other, defended its point of view and tried to get its views to prevail. But at the same time they have recognised that the proletariat must be unified, and this has led to concessions. For its part, the congress did so too, and this made it possible for the Spanish syndicalists to remain within the organisation and continue fighting for the revolutionary cause.

We appeal to the German comrades, continues Comrade Nin, with the following proposal: it is essential to call a congress of the Free Unions and decide once and for all whether they accept the decisions of the [international] congress. On the other hand, we ask the Central Council and the Executive Bureau to send their representatives to that congress for the purpose of presenting the viewpoint of the Red International. We are certain that should our platform be loyally presented, the workers will accept it. The revolution in Germany may break out very soon; it may also be postponed for several years yet. One way or another, we must prepare ourselves, and for that the proletariat must be united.

Dario [Duilio Mari], representative of the Italian Syndicalist Union [USI], states that he fully agrees with the opinion of Comrade Nin on the German question and advises the German delegates to abide by the resolutions of the congress in the name of proletarian unity. He also asserts that the USI associates itself with the decisions of the congress, as the Red International, in his opinion, is entirely independent of the Communist International. Taking all these things into consideration, he does not see why the German revolutionary unions should refuse to accept its decisions.

Girinis, the Lithuanian representative, insists that it is not necessary to resign from the old trade unions; we must win them over to us. The slogan of leaving the unions given by the German comrades is the same thing that Amsterdam wants: the exclusion of the left wing from the old trade unions. We directly feel the changes that are taking place in Germany. The reaction in Germany has greatly affected Lithuania. Still, we notice sadly that according to their statements they exclude themselves from the Red International. I think it advisable to leave this question open to the next German congress. At the same time, the Central Council should authorise the Executive Bureau to issue an appeal to the members of these unions, showing them the fallacy and danger of their actions to the cause of the social revolution by their split policy, and to call for them to submit to the decisions of the Red International congress.

Disch (General Workers' Union of Germany) says that they have not as yet affiliated with the International Trade Union Council. A long time before the congress, when they received the invitation, they took a general vote among the members, and over half of them were against sending delegates to Moscow. But shortly before the congress, they called a new conference, at which they tried to induce the comrades who had come to change their opinion in favour of sending delegates here, who should state their point of view and subsequently present all the decisions of the congress for discussion by all the members. It was said here that the General Workers' Union was under the influence of the KAPD, and that was sure to tie the union's hands, since the KAPD had assumed certain obligations at the congress of the Communist International. Comrade Disch therefore states in this connection that they have in their union not only members of the KAPD, but also members of other revolutionary parties, and that the number of Communists is no greater than one-fifth. Consequently it would be wrong to speak of the ideological preponderance in the General Workers' Union of the ideas advocated by this party.

In spite of the fact that we are not yet members of the Red Trade Union International, we nevertheless assume the obligation to submit all its decisions to the judgement of our members, and it will be up to them to decide whether or not to join the Red International.

Lozovsky: The list of speakers is exhausted. The explanations and statement we have heard show that the representatives of these three organisations, while taking part in our congress, evidently thought that the international congress meets for purposes of discussion and adoption of decisions of small organisations. The International cannot be a discussion circle. After debate, definite decisions must be adopted. Those who think they can come to the congress as to a show or a circus are very much mistaken. I therefore propose to the Central Council to adopt the following resolution, which makes a perfectly clear and precise distinction between the statement of delegates and the opinion of those workers in Germany who probably did not give them a mandate to not submit to the decisions of the international congress of Red Trade Unions (*reads*):

> The Central Council, having heard the declaration by the representatives of the German *Unionen* about their attitude to the decisions of the congress, resolves:
>
> 1. In accordance with the decision of the First International Congress of Revolutionary Trade Unions, only organisations that abide by the decisions of the congress can be members of the Red International.
> 2. The delegates of the Gelsenkirchen Free Workers' Union, of the General Workers' Union, and the Seamen's Union – Bartels, Disch, and Gieseler – have stated on behalf of the members of their organisations that they will not abide by the decisions of the congress.
> 3. The workers organised in these unions and bound by ties of blood with the Red Trade Union International did not, as far as we know, instruct their delegates not to submit to the decisions of the congress.
> 4. The Central Council therefore proposes that a congress of the above unions be called within two months on the basis of direct representation of the members of these organisations. It demands that this congress state clearly and definitely with whom the revolutionary proletariat of those organisations side – whether with the Red Trade Union International or with those who want to wrest them from the revolutionary trade-union movement of all countries.

Dimitrov, in stating his opinion on the resolutions proposed by Comrade Lozovsky, thinks it necessary to include in the resolution a refutation of the declaration made by the German Unionists to the effect that a sham majority was engineered at the congress. Comrade Dimitrov categorises such an assertion as slander.

Nogin supports Dimitrov's motion, as Comrade Lozovsky's resolution leaves out the main factor and the main charge proferred against the congress by the German Unionists. This does not mean that one need go into a detailed examination of the entire declaration.

Lozovsky: Comrade Dimitrov proposes to add to my resolution point 5, which reads as follows: 'As to the statement made by the representatives of the German *Unionen* about the sham majority of the congress, the Central Council decidedly repudiates this slanderous assertion.' Who is in favour of this addition? Carried.

I propose not to discuss the resolution in detail, but to adopt it in principle and refer it to the Executive Bureau for final draft.

Arlandis proposes to the German Unionists to withdraw their assertion about a sham majority. (*The Unionists decidedly decline to do so.*)

Lozovsky: The Central Council agrees to adopt in principle the resolution with Comrade Dimitrov's addition and refer it to the Executive Bureau for final drafting. Unanimously carried.[6]

The American question comes next on the agenda. In view of the fact that the American comrades are absent, it is moved and carried to adjourn this session until 12:00 noon tomorrow.

Third Sitting, 22 July

(*The session opens at 1:00 p.m. Comrade Lozovsky in the chair.*)

Lozovsky: I declare this third session opened. I presume it will be our last session. On the agenda are the questions of: (1) the US; (2) Norway; and (3) some secondary questions.

Before we get to business, I must make the following statement: The trade unions here in Russia, over the past year donated 35 million roubles in connec-

6 A conference of the General Workers' Union (AAU) in November 1921 formally broke with the Red International of Labour Unions. But a section of the German *Unionen* were eventually won to the RILU. In May 1922 the Seamen's Union declared its affiliation; a syndicalist minority split off and established its own union. For its part, the Gelsenkirchen Free Workers' Union participated in a September 1921 merger with the Free Association of Agricultural Workers and the Hand and Brain Workers' Union; the fused organisation joined the RILU.

tion with the lockout of the Swedish metalworkers. It is understood that this money collected in Russian currency was very difficult to exchange and send over to Sweden. Now we are informed that the reformists have undertaken a propaganda campaign in the foreign press, saying that this money was turned over to the Communist Party and spent for party needs. On behalf of the All-Russian Council of Trade Unions, I declare that all the money collected was turned over to the International Council, where it is still kept. We have not been able to send it over on account of the impossibility of exchanging it in cash. The Executive Bureau of the Central Council has now decided to turn this money over to the International Solidarity Fund created by the First Congress. This sum will be the seed money for the International fund. Is there any objection to this proposal? Hearing none, it is accepted.

We will now take up the American question. I consider it necessary to inform the Central Council about the following: the delegate of the IWW to the congress, Comrade Williams, had two meetings with me, and at both he told me of the decision of the last convention of the IWW, held in May, which sent him here as a delegate and gave him definite instructions as to how to conduct himself at this international congress. These instructions, he told me, were given to him in writing, and that these instructions contain the standpoint of his organisation on the world trade-union movement. Insofar as such instructions are available and were adopted by the convention of the IWW, even were it in closed session, these ought to be communicated to the international congress. Even if the delegate did not deem it possible to inform the congress, he ought to at least communicate them to the directing organs of our organisation.

At our first meeting Comrade Williams promised me to hand in this document during the week. But a week has elapsed, and he still carries it in his pocket. I don't think that pockets were made, after all, for concealing convention decisions. I requested Comrade Williams to give me a copy of it. He promised me the copy, but until now I have not gotten it. I did not want to raise that question at the congress, but the Central Council should know that one of the delegates, having special instructions from his organisation, did not consider it necessary to make them known to us. We cannot judge if the conduct of Comrade Williams corresponds with the instructions received by him. Let him say why he cannot produce his mandate instructions. Let him say whether he considers that the Red International deserves to know the decisions of his organisation, which considers itself a part of the Red International.

The Bureau deems it necessary to request an explanation from Comrade Williams.

Comrade Williams has the floor.

Williams: What Comrade Lozovsky said in regard to the interviews with me is correct. That is, literally correct, but Comrade Lozovsky does not state that I, through an interpreter, had, at the first interview, told him that what I had in my pocket was merely an official endorsement of the convention of the Industrial Workers of the World on the six points adopted at Berlin in December 1920.[7] He did not mention that I stated to him through an interpreter that my instructions – a copy of which I had – were nothing more than an endorsement, instructing me that the IWW attends this international congress on the basis of the six points of Berlin, and I stated to him that there was nothing more in them. I did promise to give him a copy of the instructions; in fact, instructions are issued by an organisation as a proper guidance to a delegate to the congress. It is not official. Therefore, I did not deem it necessary that Lozovsky should have a copy, but I was not unwilling to give him one.

The minutes of the IWW Convention were given to Lozovsky and later on they were turned over by him to the American delegation, without my knowledge. This American delegation apparently went through these minutes picking all the points they could find with which they could smear the IWW. They have examined these minutes, and we have seen them come into the congress at the last session and deliberately mistake the facts in the Sandgren case. They quoted sections of the General Executive report and used that as a basis to attack the IWW. Now these people got the minutes from Lozovsky.

When I requested Lozovsky as to why he turned these minutes over to the American delegation he said that, as he could not read English, he gave it to them to interpret. But that was rather strange, as these people do not speak Russian, and there are plenty of English-speaking Russians here who would readily interpret. Lozovsky gave these minutes without any intention of having it used as a basis of attack, but they were used for such a purpose. I have nothing more to say on the instructions other than that they are based on the Berlin points, and I am going to read these instructions so that you can see for yourself that there is nothing in them that I am ashamed of, or that they contain anything that I could wish to hold back.

(*Reads the resolutions of the Berlin Conference.*)

An explanation is apparently needed on one point of the Berlin convention, which reads, 'That the Revolutionary Industrial International be based on the class struggle and the domination of the working class.' I have not the minutes of the closed meeting of the convention, but the opinion was unanimous that

7 For the December 1920 Berlin syndicalist conference, see p. 145, n. 19. For its six points, see p. 207.

the stand taken by Russia on the dictatorship of the proletariat was absolutely in accord with the preamble of the Industrial Workers of the World. And it is impossible for any revolutionary organisation to stand for anything else. But it is entirely unnecessary for an organisation like the IWW, working under the conditions that exist in America, to continually proclaim from the housetops their belief in the dictatorship of the proletariat. So in order not to hamper the activity of the IWW of America it was considered unnecessary to go proclaiming the question of the dictatorship of the proletariat from house to house. It was not necessary at the convention to state that you believe in the dictatorship of the proletariat and rush downstairs shouting, 'we believe in the dictatorship of the proletariat'. We think that the preamble of the convention is clear.

I was instructed to point out that the history of the IWW proves absolutely that the IWW is no yellow organisation. Labour organisations must to a degree keep out in the open. It is impossible for the IWW to be a secret organisation. As a labour organisation we must stay in the open. We must maintain halls, run our press, and run halls in the open, where delegates can receive their supplies. Therefore, we have got to act in accordance with the conditions in that country. Naturally we observe the conditions that are inflicted on us by the bourgeois dictatorship. When we get to power, we inflict the same on them. But this is no reason why we should stand with our heads above the trenches and create good targets for them to shoot at.

At our convention we endorsed the principle of the dictatorship of the proletariat. Now I have nothing more to say, but if there is any question that anybody wants to ask, I shall be glad to answer.

Lozovsky: Comrades, the Presidium proposes that speeches be very brief and not extend over five minutes. But before that, I must make the following statement: Comrade Williams in his speech said that I betrayed his confidence by turning over the document to the American section, which discussed it. This is not correct. He returned to me the printed minutes and decisions in English already published in Chicago and New York. Not knowing the language, I handed them to the American Section, where such comrades as Reinstein, knowing English and Russian, could have done some translations of the decisions for my use. I had not the slightest belief that printed minutes might be considered a conspiratorial matter, and there was no breach of confidence on my part. I think that Comrade Williams himself committed the same breach of confidence by handing in this material for translation.

Nin: During the congress it was clear that the position of Comrade Williams was somewhat shaky and indefinite. This can in no way be construed as meaning the IWW itself is confused. It seems to me that Comrade Williams did not express the true opinion of the IWW. He reminds me very little of the true spirit of the IWW, always determined in action. Comrades Haywood and Andreytchine better reflect the true views of the IWW. At present, hesitation and silence of any kind are inadmissible, and at the congress this kind of secret diplomacy should be all the less permitted than anywhere else. We believe that the conduct of Comrade Williams does not correspond to the real situation, active work, and general principles of the IWW.

The question was put straight, and we are requesting a definite reply. Comrade Williams must give his response to the Red International of Labour Unions.

Andreytchine: After hearing Fellow Worker Williams's statement and having read the secret instructions given him by the IWW convention, I'd like to make the following statement: It appears now that his conduct at the trade-union congress was not what we would expect from a representative of the IWW, which in the past was known for its unequivocal and categorical stand on all questions. His instructions are vague and imprecise, and his attitude and actions have helped to create more confusion and indecision, thus discrediting the name of the IWW.

His negative vote on the statutes of the Red Trade Union International was contrary to the instructions he received direct from the convention. He states that the convention's instructions are merely an endorsement of this International. What a pity. I cannot see how he could vote against the following six fundamental principles of the Red Trade Union International: (1) Endorsement of the principles of the revolutionary class struggle. (2) To bring those principles into effect in the everyday struggle with capitalism and the bourgeois state. (3) Recognition of the necessity of the overthrow of capitalism through the social revolution and the establishment of the dictatorship of the proletariat in the transition period. (4) Recognition and submission to international proletarian discipline. (5) The rupture with the Amsterdam International. (6) United action with all revolutionary and Communist organisations of a given country for the purpose of defensive and offensive struggle against the bourgeoisie.

Even the French anarcho-syndicalists and the Spanish and Italian syndicalists voted for these principles. The only ones voting against it were Williams and Cascaden of Canada. I have heard the French syndicalists rebuking Williams for his irresponsible attitude during caucus meetings of the opposition elements. As far as the reasons advanced by him and supported by the instructions are concerned, they do not make the situation any clearer.

Why this deplorable condition in the midst of the IWW now? We must seek much deeper reasons than those in the superficial statements made by him. The IWW is passing through a critical period, a process of dissolution, a profound crisis in its very existence as a revolutionary union. This has lasted long enough – over three years. It is high time that it should define its position in the class struggle in America, as well as its relation to the international proletariat.

The counterrevolutionary articles in the *One Big Union Monthly* and the *Industrial Worker* were not the spontaneous and casual manifestations of hatred for the Russian Revolution by their respective editors. The very fact that they were tolerated for several months by the Executive Board shows that they expressed the general attitude of that body. Sandgren was removed by the Executive Board only when the Communist minority inside the organisation made it impossible for the paper to exist any longer or for the Board to remain in office. I know that the Board countenanced all his counterrevolutionary agitation, because in the same issue of the *One Big Union Monthly* where Sandgren, in his article 'Wrangel and the Bolsheviks', says 'that as far as we are concerned there is no difference between the terrorist Soviet government and the Palmer-Burleson regime in America', there is a statement of the Executive Board endorsing the attitude and policies of the editor.[8]

Yes, this painful affair with Sandgren is the outcome of the morass into which the present leaders have led the rank and file of our organisation. These leaders are neither syndicalists, revolutionary socialists, communists, or simple trade unionists.

We of the communist minority cannot stand by and silently see the name of our organisation be disgraced in front of the international proletariat. We categorically state that a great portion of the rank and file is not a part of this disgraceful spectacle, and we pledge ourselves to make the attitude of their delegate known, so that they can remove the stain from the name of the IWW. We know that they will endorse and join the Red Trade Union International without any reservations or equivocations.

---

8 The exact quote from Sandgren's article 'Wrangel and the Bolsheviki', published in the December 1920 issue of *The One Big Union Monthly*, was '… we fail to see the difference between the Lenin-Trotzky regime in Russia and the Wilson-Palmer-Burleson regime in America, as far as the workers are concerned'. The same issue of the magazine contains a statement signed by IWW General Secretary-Treasurer George Hardy and Roy Brown, chairman of the General Executive Board, on the invitation received by the IWW to participate in the RILU founding congress. While expressing their gratification for the invitation, the statement declares that 'the I.W.W. does not want an industrial international that is tied up with, or subordinated to a political international'.

The only difficulty is the distance separating us, and that the best and most qualified militants in the communist minority are languishing in prison today. But I have no doubt that the rank and file will repudiate the stand of their delegate to the Red Trade Union International.

Arlandis: I consider it necessary that Williams give a straight reply as to whether the IWW agrees with the decisions of the congress or not. We must know what policy to adopt in regard to it.

Williams: How can I make a statement as to how the Industrial Workers of the World thinks on what has taken place at the congress over here and what the congress has done? The organisation does not know what was adopted at the congress. I can only report to the organisation on what the congress has done, and I cannot say what the members of the IWW think of what has been done here. I can only speak as an individual. I am here as a delegate of the IWW to take the proceedings to the IWW and to let them see what they think of it. Why isn't this question asked of anybody else?

Dimitrov: We do not care to know the personal opinion of Comrade Williams. If he is not in a position to express the standpoint of the IWW, then it is altogether useless that he should speak. It is obvious that the IWW does not have a correct opinion regarding the Red International of Labour Unions. Comrade Williams has a written declaration and instructions that are directly opposed to the decisions of our congress. Other comrades, members of the IWW, maintain that the majority of the members are in favour of our position. We consider that the IWW is, in fact, not yet admitted to the Red International.

I move to issue an appeal to the workers of this union inviting them to decide whether they accept the decision of our congress. In case the majority accepts the decisions, they will be admitted to the Red International. Otherwise we will admit any minority of this union standing with us. There is no use in nourishing the illusion that the IWW is affiliated with the Red International. In general this organisation does not represent any definite idea; at the present moment this organisation is a very confusing one. We must require the IWW to accept a clear-cut resolution on this question, and after the decision of their convention we will know how to act in regard to them.

Lozovsky: Comrades, the discussion is closed. No concluding speeches will be allowed; otherwise we will never be through with it. I move to adopt the following decision:

> After hearing the explanation of Comrade Williams on the reasons why he did not turn in to the Bureau of the Red International or to the congress the text of the instructions he received from the convention of the IWW, the Central Council considers his explanation insufficient and decides to address an appeal to the IWW, inviting them to cast aside their hesitations and unreservedly affiliate with the Red International of Trade Unions.

I propose to draft the special appeal. Any objection? Hearing none, carried.[9]

Now we are going to move to the next item on the agenda. In Argentina, in the near future, a unity convention of two great organisations competing between themselves will take place: the so-called Communist Confederation composed of anarchist organisations with a syndicalist orientation, and of syndicalist organisations of a reformist character.

Comrade Arlandis has the floor to read the appeal to this convention in the name of the Red International of Labour Unions.

Arlandis (*reads*):

> To the united convention of the Workers' Organisations of Argentina.
>
> Comrades:
>
> The Moscow congress of workers' organisations of the whole world representing over 15 million organised workers has already constituted the Red International of Trade Unions. Our aim is to unite all the organised revolutionary forces of the working class and reinforce their combat strength in a relentless struggle against capital.
>
> The Argentine bourgeoisie, despite its neutrality during the last imperialist war, has adopted, at present, all the plundering methods of the bourgeoisie of the warring countries. Imitating the capitalists of Europe and North America, it undertook an organised offensive against the working class and has sown death and famine among the workers' families. They are unable to re-establish normal economic life within the capitalist system. The capitalist class is resolved to save their old privileges, not refraining from any atrocities. In all countries the bourgeoisie has cre-

9 Following the RILU congress, George Williams remained in Europe for five months, where he collaborated with anarcho-syndicalist forces. Following his return to the US, the IWW's General Executive Board took up the question of RILU affiliation in December 1921, and voted to reject it. The pro-communist wing of the IWW, however, continued the fight for affiliation. The IWW's Fourteenth Convention in November–December 1922 rejected the RILU's invitation to the IWW to send a delegation to the RILU's Second Congress.

ated its white guard: the Patriotic League in Argentina, the civil guard in France, the Orgesch in Germany, the Fascists in Italy, and the Somatén in Spain[10] – in all these countries they have created a united front against the working class. It kills them by starvation. It puts them in prison. It assassinates the most conscious representatives of the proletariat.

Under such conditions, any division in the ranks of the proletariat is absolutely inadmissible. To the united front of the capitalists, we must counterpose a united front of the revolutionary proletariat. Against the yellow Amsterdam International, we must counterpose the Red International of Labour Unions.

Long live the united proletariat of Argentina!

Long live the Red International of Trade and Industrial Unions!

Long live the world revolution!

The Central Council of the Red International of Trade Unions

Members of the Executive Bureau:

A. Lozovsky, general secretary
Arlandis (Spain)
Tom Mann (England)
G. Andreytchine (USA)
Nogin (Russia)
Maier (Germany)

Lozovsky: Is there anyone against this appeal? No. Adopted unanimously.[11]

Now we move on to the next item on the agenda. We have just received an appeal signed by the National Confederation of Labour and by both Communist parties of Spain. No changes in the text read yesterday were made, so I move

---

10 The Argentine Patriotic League was a paramilitary group created in January 1919, which, in cooperation with the police and army, attacked working-class and Jewish neighbourhoods in Buenos Aires.

The Orgesch was an armed German counterrevolutionary group formed in Munich in August 1920 to fight Bolshevism, with a claimed membership of 300,000. Led by Georg Escherich, it was officially disbanded in June 1921, although many of its units remained active, especially in Bavaria.

For the Somatén in Spain and the Civic Guard/Civic League in France, see p. 75, n. 23.

11 A conference of the communist-anarchist FORA-Comunista in August 1921 refused to merge with the syndicalist FORA, and also condemned the pro-communist faction within FORAC. Tom Barker, the Argentine delegate to the RILU congress, was eventually disavowed by the FORAC. (The word 'Communist' was removed from the organisation's name in 1923.) As for the syndicalist FORA, it too rejected efforts by pro-communist forces to affiliate to the RILU.

to adopt it without a reading. Any objection? No. The agreement arrived at by the Central Council of the Red Trade Unions is approved.

Now we move to the last item on the agenda, the question of Norway. The Norwegian trade unions found themselves in about the same situation as the trade unions of Italy. The central federation of Norwegian unions participated in the last congress of the Amsterdam International in London and formally did not leave it. We need an official statement by the delegates on how they intend to handle this question, because their answer will determine our future common action.

Madsen: In Norway thirty-seven trade and industrial unions have created a central labour federation, which sent ten delegates to the congress. The question you are discussing now was raised in our country around 1911, and since that time we have built up an opposition in the unions and put the question sharply of whether to smash the reformist unions or to leave them and create separate organisations. The opposition minority decided to stay inside the unions. In 1915–17 we were still in the minority, but at our last congress we had a very considerable majority, which proves that our tactics were correct.

A letter was addressed by the National Trade Union Congress to the Second Congress of the Third International, expressing our complete sympathy with the policy of the Red International. When in 1911 the leaders of the trade-union movement joined Amsterdam, the rank and file knew very little about this move, and very few people were interested in the question. After the war, there were two tendencies in the left wing on the question of Amsterdam: one to leave Amsterdam, and the other to stay inside and carry on the same policy adopted before. Personally I supported the first tendency, and not long before the arrival of Lozovsky in Norway I published a pamphlet proving that Amsterdam is no more a trade-union organisation but a political weapon in the hands of the social reformists.[12]

At the time of the London Congress of the Amsterdam International, our five delegates were instructed to formulate an opposition on all questions on the agenda.[13] Returning from London, our five delegates defended the stand-

12 Lozovsky arrived in Norway in late August or early September 1920, as part of a delegation from the leadership of the Russian trade-union movement. The delegation's plan was to travel to Britain, but when the British government refused entry permission, they went on to Germany.

The referred-to pamphlet by Alfred Madsen appears to be *Den faglige internationale* [The International Federation of Trade Unions] (Trondheim 1921).

13 For the IFTU's November 1920 London Congress, see p. 146, n. 21.

point of immediately leaving Amsterdam. The ten delegates present here share the same point of view. But there are various differences of opinion among us. Some say that we must leave immediately, but that affiliation with the Red International must proceed slowly. The majority of the delegation, in any case, support immediate affiliation with the Red International. We expect, when we return to Norway and put before the workers the decisions, resolutions, statutes, etc., that the working masses will express their willingness to join the banners of Moscow and not Amsterdam.

In reply to a question from Comrade Lozovsky, Madsen says that the thirty-seven unions of the Central Committee of Trade Unions of Norway number 145,000[14] workers. Outside of the central organisation there is a little syndicalist union having not more than 2,000 members with no influence whatever upon the working masses.

As to the question of affiliation with the Red International and leaving Amsterdam, that question can be settled directly by the Central Council and will not be delayed; the question of affiliation with Moscow depends on the national congress. The next national congress is to be called very soon. Right now an energetic agitation and preliminary work to call an extraordinary congress will be undertaken. Local conditions may slow some of this work, but Comrade Madsen has no doubt that the Norwegian workers will recognise the Red International of Labour Unions as their sole leader.[15]

Lozovsky: I move the following: Organisations taking part in the congress and not having yet determined their position must, during the three months after the congress, take a definite stand and then express unequivocally whether they are in accord with the decisions of the congress; those decisions also involve the question of double affiliation. Failing to do so will automatically put them outside the Red International of Labour Unions.

If there is no objection in principle, I move to instruct the Executive Bureau to formulate this proposal in final form. Any objections? Carried.

So the agenda is exhausted. All the other questions – such as organisation of the Bureau, representation, agitation, propaganda, publishing, and so on – I move to refer to the Executive Bureau of the Central Council for practical implementation.

14 This is per the English and Russian. The French says 135,000.

15 The Tenth Congress of the Norwegian Confederation of Trade Unions was not held until February 1923. For a history of the Norwegians' relations with both RILU and the Amsterdam International, see Tosstorff 2016, pp. 425–7.

Haidt (Austria) speaks on this and says that the question of propaganda and agitation must be decided by the Central Council itself, because of its great significance. In case this proposal is not accepted, it would be desirable that some delegates who consider it necessary should be given a chance to discuss those questions with the Executive Bureau and come to an agreement. It is also necessary to receive instructions on this question.

Lozovsky: Comrades, we have two motions. The first is that all questions be referred to the Executive Bureau, and the second is the motion of Comrade Haidt. Who is for my motion? Who is against? My motion is carried.

Any delegation that has some questions of principle to raise can discuss them with the general secretary and bring them to a special session of the Executive Bureau.

I declare the session of the Central Council of the Red International of Trade and Industrial Unions closed.

Resolutions

Manifesto to the Workers of the World

The criminal war started by the capitalist governments of Europe and America, which shook the foundations of the old world, has come to an end. The monstrous aftermath of the horrible crime committed against humanity is revealed in its full dimensions. True, ten million murdered are buried; their corpses do not disturb the peace of those who condemned them to death. But there are yet eleven million wounded and crippled, on whose bodies the capitalists have acknowledged their unprecedented crime by machine guns, bayonets, and bullets.

The blockade is over. With the signing of the so-called Peace of Versailles, the destruction on the battlefields of the people's wealth, created with the sweat and blood of the proletariat, appears to have also ended. But who can count how many more years of suffering, degradation, starvation, and destitution will be the price the toiling masses of all countries will have to pay for the destroyed wealth, estimated at many billions.

The war is over, but in all countries there is still a greater number of soldiers under arms than before the war; the expenses on armaments in all the impoverished countries are also greater than before the war. Humanity came out of the war not only diminished by ten million people, but also greatly impoverished and ruined. In addition to this, after a short and speculative revival of trade and industry, the world is passing through a most terrible and unheard-of industrial crisis: the price of the imperialist war. Not only did the war break down the productive forces of world capitalism, but it also tore to pieces the economic ties thanks to which an equilibrium between the capitalist national economies existed before the war. The capitalists of industrial countries, headed by America, are unable to sell their products owing to the absence of markets. Impoverished countries cannot buy them; the workers have not the means to purchase the necessary products.

The result is the extraordinary wave of unemployment in every country and a horrible waste of productive forces. Ten million able-bodied workers are thrown out on the street in all countries of the world; the machines are at a standstill and deteriorating; billions' worth of goods rot in warehouses or are deliberately destroyed by the capitalists, in order not to sell them cheaper to consumers; millions of men and women are thrown into the clutches of hunger and suffering. And at the same time capital is making a ferocious attack against those of the workers whom it graciously permits to stay in its factories. In all countries wages are cut, conditions of labour are worsened, and the squeezing of sweat and blood out of the workers reaches a climax. Sustained by the

 | DOI:10.1163/9789004712867_027

power of the capitalist government, army, police, hired press, courts, religious hirelings, and its lackeys of the yellow Amsterdam International, the capitalists feel sure of their domination.

What is to be done?

Brothers and comrades of the working class, you who follow the Amsterdam Federation of Unions and the old union leaders! The constituent congress of Red Labour Unions appeals to you, in the name of many millions of organised revolutionary workers of all countries, with whom you are working in the same shops, and with whom you will be together – we are quite sure – in the final struggle; the congress appeals to you to ask yourselves this question. To answer it, look soberly and attentively around, without trusting words but only deeds and facts; look at what your leaders of the Amsterdam International have done and what they are still doing. When the World War started they, together with the leaders of the Second International, called upon you to go obediently into the barracks and onto the battlefields. During the war they appealed to you for civil peace, to refrain from strikes, to make sacrifices in the name of the war. Louder even than the capitalists themselves and the corrupted press did they yell about the recompense that is awaiting you after the war. Is this your recompense – when the capitalists pay all their pledges by cutting prices, by terrible lockouts, by closing factories, by unemployment, by police violence, and by organising yellow gangs and scabs? Only the vanquished have to pay. And who then is vanquished – defeated, fooled, subdued – if not the working class?

What are the Amsterdam leaders doing – these alleged defenders of the working class? Do they demand, together with the working class, that the capitalists should pay? No. These people do not intend to speak on this question. On instruction from capital they repeat to the workers one and the same thing: work with all your might to rebuild the ruins of the war. But if the fakers keep quiet, it means the fooled must speak. Let them express their will; let the indignant cry of the proletariat call out one single watchword: Down with the yellow Amsterdam International! Down with the domination of the bourgeoisie!

Capital is attacking, keeping in reserve a huge army of unemployed. Step by step it takes away all the conquests of the past period. By a stubborn struggle the proletariat must defend every inch of its position. What are the merits of the Amsterdam International in this economic struggle of the working class? Did it successfully lead you in your struggle? That is the question to which all organised workers, even if they are indifferent to the cause of socialism and the revolution, must receive a clear and concise answer on behalf of their immediate needs.

Up to now the Amsterdam International either surrendered the working class to capital without a fight or, by its cowardly tactics, assured one defeat after another. The history of the latest heroic strike of the British miners clearly illustrates how the trade-union leaders betrayed the working masses who were repelling the attacks of capitalism. Instead of moving to support the miners under attack – new forces of the organised proletariat – and by a solid united front crush the enemy, these leaders refrained from the struggle and at the decisive moment kept back the proletarian reserves, thus giving the capitalists a chance to destroy the working class bit by bit.

Up until now, as long as the majority of the organised workers in the trade unions were led by Gompers, Jouhaux, and Henderson, it could not be otherwise. We are engaged in an epoch of merciless and terrible class struggle. And those leaders who are afraid of strikes, who are scared of expanding them in order to spare capital, who fear for the fate of capitalist industry more than the capitalists themselves – these leaders who dare not and don't want to lead workers to victory will inevitably betray the working class. All your savings, gathered by long years of privation, will be wasted in unsuccessful strikes due to the treacherous tactics of the yellow leaders. These leaders are only able to do the things they did during the period of the peaceful development of capitalism, i.e., to sell labour power on behalf of their unions. At a period when the working class was in need of fighting leaders, these traitors always sold the workers for the price offered by Morgan, Stinnes, and Creusot. All the leaders of the Amsterdam International who are putting obstacles in the way of the proletariat, striving by a united front to defend its rights against the attempt of the exploiters, are nothing but an international organisation of scabs.

Every day the number of cases increases where isolated groups of workers, unwilling to wait until they will be betrayed, chaotically go on strike and into revolutionary struggle. Faithful to their class instincts, they break the discipline imposed upon them by the traitors, break the discipline of capital, and keep up the sacred right of every proletarian unwilling to surrender to the enemy without a struggle. Get rid of the treacherous yellow leaders selling out the cause of the working class. The international congress of Red Trade Unions calls upon all workers still attached to Amsterdam to drive away, whenever and wherever they can, the bureaucrats and traitors standing at the head of the yellow unions and join in an organised manner the International of revolutionary unions. Two-fifths of the organised workers of the world have already joined the Red International of Labour Unions. The time has come when the international army of labour must unite under the red banner of the proletarian revolution.

In the ferocious struggle between labour and capital raging all over the world, the bourgeoisie is acting in a more organised, more conscious, and more decisive manner than the proletariat. And nowhere did the skill and superiority of the bourgeoisie reveal itself so obviously as in the possibility of keeping in bondage and subjection the many millions of workers with the hands of the working class itself, with the help of those of its leaders who, like knaves, stab the proletariat in the back and do not let them throw the capitalist superstructure off their shoulders.

If the capitalist order still exists, if the capitalist class is still able at the most critical moment, when the war ended and demobilisation began, to remain in power and still defeat the working class in skirmishes, this is due to the heroes of Amsterdam and the Second International. But everything has an end. Workers throughout the world are every day becoming more convinced that capitalism is not all-powerful, that the power of capital is due solely to their own weakness, their lack of organisation, and their willingness to endure. A new epoch of glorious struggles has begun, when the proletariat becomes worthy of better leaders than the scabs of Amsterdam. The new leaders will know how to defend the proletarian trenches and will take the offensive. The Red International of Revolutionary Labour Unions will very soon have the overwhelming majority of the working class all over the world, and then the proletariat of all countries will present the capitalist class with its bill, demanding full and immediate payment.

Workers all over the world! The First International Congress of Revolutionary Labour Unions, gathered on that bit of the globe that was wrenched by the Russian proletariat from the hands of capital, in the name of the millions of those crippled and murdered in the criminal war, in the name of the sufferings that the working class has gone through under the dictatorship of capital, in the name of the victims of bourgeois terror, in the name of your defeats suffered under the leadership of the yellow traitors, in the name of the future victories under the revolutionary banner of the Red Labour Union International, and lastly in the name of the Russian working class, steadfastly keeping up all alone, for the fourth year, the red flag over the land of the soviets and waiting for help from its comrades beyond its frontiers – we are calling upon you to join our ranks. We call you to the last and decisive battle.

Workers of the world, unite!
Long live the proletarian revolution!
Long live the dictatorship of the proletariat!
Long live the international Soviet republic!
Long live communism!

Resolution on the Activity of the Provisional Council of Red Trade and Industrial Unions over the Past Year

Having heard Comrade Rosmer's report on the International Council of Trade Unions, the First Congress recognises that:

1. The formation of the International Council of Revolutionary Trade Unions meets the most vital needs of the revolutionary working masses in their struggle against capitalism.
2. From its inception, the International Council has pursued a correct policy with regard to the dictatorship of the bourgeoisie, counterposing to it the slogan of the dictatorship of the proletariat.
3. The International Council has thus correctly assessed the role of the Amsterdam International, connected with the International Labour Bureau linked to the League of Nations, carrying out a determined and merciless fight against it.
4. During the eleven months of its existence, the International Council has, under the most difficult conditions, made propaganda efforts to accomplish its fundamental aims.
5. The fact that millions of workers in forty-two countries have affiliated to the International Council bears evidence of the great attractive power of the council and of its slogans, and proves most vividly the importance of the task it has performed.

Taking all the above into consideration, the congress resolves:

To approve Comrade Rosmer's report, as well as the line of action pursued by the International Council against the harmful and dangerous slogan that is detrimental to, and in glaring contradiction with, the interests of the revolutionary working-class movement, i.e., of destroying the old reformist mass trade unions.

 | DOI:10.1163/9789004712867_028

Resolution on Relations between the Red Labour Union International and the Communist International

Whereas: The struggle between labour and capital in all capitalist countries has assumed, as a result of the World War and crisis, an exceptionally acute, implacable, and decisive character.

Whereas: In the process of its everyday struggle the working masses realise ever more clearly the necessity of eliminating the bourgeoisie from the administration of industry, and consequently from political power.

Whereas: The above result can be obtained solely by establishing the dictatorship of the proletariat and a communist system.

Whereas: In the struggle to preserve the bourgeois dictatorship, all the capitalist ruling classes have already succeeded in consolidating and concentrating to a high degree their national and international organisations, political as well as economic, in a solid front of all the bourgeois forces, both defensive and offensive, against the onrush of the proletariat.

Whereas: The logic of the modern class struggle demands the greater consolidation of the proletarian forces and the revolutionary struggle, and consequently means that there must be the closest contact and organic connection between the different forms of the revolutionary workers' movement, and primarily between the Third, Communist International and the Red Labour Union International. It is also desirable that every effort should be made, in the national field, toward the establishment of similar relations between the Communist parties and the Red International of Labour Unions.

Therefore the congress resolves:

1. To take all steps to unite together in the most energetic manner all the trade unions in one united fighting organisation, with one direct international centre – the Red International of Labour Unions.
2. To establish the closest possible contact with the Third, Communist International as the vanguard of the revolutionary workers' movement in all parts of the world on the basis of joint representation on both executive committees, joint conferences, etc.
3. That the above connection should have an organic and business-like character and be expressed in the joint preparation of revolutionary action on a national and international scale.

 | DOI:10.1163/9789004712867_029

4. That it is imperative for every country to strive toward uniting the revolutionary trade-union organisations and to establish the closest contact between the red trade unions and the Communist parties for carrying out the decisions of both congresses.

Resolution on the Italian Question

Having heard the explanation of the representatives of the Italian Confederation of Labour, Bianchi and Azimonti, and after discussion, the First International Congress of Revolutionary Trade Unions resolves:

1. The Italian Confederation of Labour (CGL), which signed the agreement with the All-Russian Central Council of Trade Unions and other organisations for the formation of the Red International, has done absolutely nothing during eleven months for the consolidation of the newly formed organisation. Instead of attempting to strengthen the new organisation – the revolutionary trade union International – and to oppose the yellow Amsterdam International, the CGL in Italy participated in the Amsterdam International, maintaining its connection with the leaders of that organisation. The CGL even went so far as to attend the London Congress of the Amsterdam International with a decisive vote, and did not cast its vote against the resolution adopted opposing the Red International of Labour Unions.
2. Instead of weakening its ties with the Amsterdam International, the General Confederation of Labour in Italy on the contrary made them stronger by applying in April to the Amsterdam International for help in their struggle with the Fascists.
3. The congress of the General Confederation of Labour at Livorno decided 'to take part without reservation in the creation of the Red International and to break with the Amsterdam International in accordance with the decisions that will be arrived at by the congress of trade unions in Moscow'. In spite of such a decision, the Italian Confederation of Labour sends its delegates only for the purpose of information. Thus the confederation deems it possible to take part in the congress of the Amsterdam International with a decisive vote, while sending to the congress of the organisation that the Livorno Congress decided to join without reservations delegates for the purpose of information only.
4. At the last moment, in order to delay the congress, the General Confederation of Labour attempted to postpone it by proposing to transfer it to Reval or Stockholm, under the pretext of greater convenience in the verification of credentials of the arriving delegates.

Stating all the above facts, the First International Congress of Revolutionary Labour Unions considers that the Italian proletariat is not to blame for such detrimental duplicity, harmful to the Italian proletariat itself and to the interests of the world revolution; that the entire responsibility for this seesaw

 | DOI:10.1163/9789004712867_030

policy lies with the leading elements of the General Confederation of Labour, who endeavour to keep the Italian proletariat aloof from the revolutionary unions of all countries.

Such a situation, in which the central trade-union organisation of the country gives lip service to the Red Trade Union International but de facto belongs to the Amsterdam International, can no longer be tolerated. The First Congress of Revolutionary Trade Unions therefore requests the revolutionary proletarians of Italy, all local unions, labour exchanges, and national federations, to state their position on the question as to which organisation the revolutionary unions of Italy will join – the International of revolutionary struggle, or the International standing for class collaboration. Will they go hand in hand with those who stand for the social revolution and the dictatorship of the proletariat, or with those standing for social peace and the dictatorship of the bourgeoisie – with the Red International of Labour Unions or with the Amsterdam International?

This congress feels quite sure that the revolutionary proletariat of Italy will very soon make its choice, and even before the next international congress the Italian General Confederation of Labour will take its place – which the Italian proletariat fully deserves – among the revolutionary unions.

Resolution on the Tasks and Tactics of Trade Unions

I The General Situation of the Struggle

1. The tasks and tactics of the trade unions are determined by the conditions and intensity of the class struggle on an international and national scale. As a starting point of this struggle is the irrefutable fact that contemporary capitalist society has entered a stage of decomposition and dissolution. The symptoms of this decay are revealed by ever-increasing national indebtedness; by temporary prosperity in some branches of industry followed rapidly by a sharp industrial crisis; by perpetual war on many fronts; by economic instability in many of the oldest capitalist countries of Europe; by the atrocious industrial crisis raging throughout the world; by the enormous growth of unemployment; by the ruin of agriculture; by the mountains of goods piled up in some countries while at the same time there is a total lack of commodities in others; by the inevitability of new wars for gaining immediate advantages over their neighbours; by continually cutting wages and worsening conditions of work; and finally by the absolute impossibility of re-establishing economic stability and political and social equilibrium through the normal methods of capitalist exploitation.

2. With the background of this growing economic crisis and the unparalleled devastation caused by the long years of war, the social struggle grows sharper in all countries, acquiring a severity never yet seen. Strikes of unheard-of size are breaking out in one country after another, as the proletariat attempts by means of them to maintain its position against the assault of capital. But the proletariat is conducting its struggle in scattered, isolated groups, thus condemning its best-organised ranks to total defeat and destruction.

3. The struggle of the working class and its organisations is complicated by the fact that the bourgeoisie has fully availed itself of the lessons of the war and the revolution, and is strenuously creating and strengthening its organisation for the material destruction of the revolutionary movement. There is not a single bourgeois country that besides the usual, normal organisations for repression (such as the army, police, department of justice, etc.) has not created new organisations – voluntary bodies of representatives of the ruling classes for the armed suppression of the rebellious workers and prevention of their uprisings.

4. In this struggle against the increasing dissatisfaction among the masses, the bourgeoisie presents a united front, throwing into this fight all of its eco-

 | DOI:10.1163/9789004712867_031

nomic and political organisations. It realises perfectly well that only the highest degree of unity and concentration of forces, centralised organisation, and the moral and material support of its state machinery and the creation of special combat organisations can save it from defeat, or at least put off the approaching social revolution. The bourgeoisie never separates politics from economics.

5. The problems of the unions in the period of the peaceful organic development of capitalist society consisted in raising through mass organisations the standard of living of the workers, in improving the conditions of labour, and, relying upon the gains already obtained, to gradually move forward toward the realisation of socialist society. The reformist unions consider a slow and gradual transition from capitalism to socialism possible by means of the transformation of bourgeois democracy into socialist democracy. The revolutionary unions hold that without the overthrow of capitalism by force, the working class cannot abolish the system of wage slavery.

6. The revolutionary unions have always aimed at uniting, disciplining, and training the masses as their basic tasks. This problem is especially important in the present period of disintegration of capitalist society. The trade unions are a school of communism. Their task is to prepare the workers for the overthrow of the capitalist system.

The main question consists in knowing how and on what basis of the everyday struggle the masses can be united and prepared. The question must be put before the working class of how to organise its everyday struggle and link it up with the general problems of the working class, toward the definitive struggle with its class enemy. The conditions of this struggle have become considerably more complicated at the present time.

The interrelations of its many elements are entirely different than they were before or during the war. Therefore the task of the trade unions is different, and the methods and means of struggle must also be different.

II Trade Unions before the War

7. During the latter half of the nineteenth century and the beginning of the twentieth there were three main types of trade-union movements: the Anglo-Saxon ('trade unionism'), the German-Austrian (social-democratic reformism), and the French-Spanish (revolutionary syndicalism). These three types in the international labour movement differed from one another in methods, as well as in their character. They presented three different ideologies and programmes of action.

8. The basic feature of Anglo-Saxon 'trade unionism' was narrow craftism and political neutrality with regard to socialist parties, concentrating its entire attention upon the immediate concrete problems of the day. 'Trade unionism' accepted the social struggle only from the narrow craft point of view, and from this angle it approached the solution of all economic and social questions. The trade-union movement included chiefly the aristocracy of the working class. The very philosophy of 'trade unionism' is the philosophy of the labour aristocracy.

Capital and labour were considered by the theoretical and practical exponents of 'trade unionism' not as two deadly class enemies, but as two factors mutually supplementing each other. It contended that the development of society depends entirely upon harmony between capital and labour, and the just distribution between them of the social and public wealth.

9. The German-Austrian trade-union movement, which appeared later than the Anglo-Saxon type and formed under different circumstances, was imbued from the start with socialist ideas. The Social Democrats of Germany and Austria stood at the very cradle of the trade-union movement, thus transmitting to it the social-democratic spirit. But the social-democratic programme and tactics with regard to the trade-union movement have assumed the character of social reformism. The trade unions of Germany were the cradle of reformism, the very substance of which may be reduced to the following: they advocate gradual and peaceful development through democracy to socialism; they obscure class consciousness; they fear revolution and white terror, hoping at the same time that the development of democratic forms would automatically bring about socialism without revolutions or social conflicts. With reference to the purely trade-union field, their intentions are to keep them out of the political and revolutionary struggle; they advocate neutrality toward revolutionary socialism, and are closely bound with reformist socialism. Apart from that, they greatly overestimate the benefit of collective bargaining and the system of conciliation boards. In this manner they expect to establish social relations under which the workers would enjoy, in the political and economic domains, equal rights with the capitalists, while the system of exploitation is maintained.

10. Revolutionary syndicalism, which developed as a reaction against the opportunism of the French Socialist Party, had as its basis a certain number of revolutionary traits. It advanced the idea of direct action, immediate struggle of the masses, advocated the general strike and the forcible overthrow of capitalism; conducted antimilitarist agitation and propaganda; and proclaimed the anti-state theory. It also created a theory according to which the trade unions are the only organisations capable of making the social revolution, and will

themselves build the socialist society. The theoreticians of revolutionary syndicalism claimed it to be the synthesis of Proudhonism and Marxism.

11. Revolutionary syndicalism has brought to light a number of ideas – and this has been its merit – which placed it high above all the other forms of the trade-union movement and brought it nearer to revolutionary socialism. Direct action, revolutionary pressure of the masses upon capital and the state, abolition of capitalism through the social revolution – all this must be placed to the credit of the revolutionary syndicalists and their theories. On the other hand, we find in syndicalism the principle of independence and neutrality toward all political parties, including the political party of the proletariat, the negation of the proletarian state, the overestimation of the general strike, and an incorrect attitude toward the palliative demands of the workers. Economics and politics are two different things for the revolutionary syndicalists, although it is quite clear that 'politics is nothing but concentrated economics'. These latter ideas, in spite of their seemingly revolutionary spirit, are, as a matter of fact, being made use of by the bourgeoisie, although the latter has never recognised any difference between politics and economics in its own struggles.

12. The trade-union movement grew up and took shape chiefly during the period of peaceful, organic development of capitalist society, and it therefore possessed the features that permitted the bourgeoisie to utilise it, especially during the war, for the benefit of its class interests.

These peculiar features – narrow craft unionism and exclusiveness, the fight of some unions against women's labour, a nationalist and patriotic spirit, etc. – found their maximum expression during the war, when class interests clashed with national interests.

III Trade Unions during the War

13. The World War, resulting from the antagonism of national interests of the capitalist classes of different countries, demonstrated to the fullest extent the influence of bourgeois society upon the working class and its organisations. The trade unions in most of the largest countries of Europe, immediately on the declaration of war, ceased to exist as militant class organisations, and turned at once into organisations of imperialist war, whose task consisted only in assisting the government and bourgeoisie to smash its competitors for the world market by joint efforts and at any cost.

The old alignments of the trade-union movement disappeared. The leaders of trade unions of every country, with very few exceptions, despite the fact that they were fighting on opposite sides of the firing line, found a common language with their own bourgeoisie. The national interests of the bourgeoisie triumphed over class interests.

14. The period of the World War was a period of moral decay of the trade unions in all capitalist countries. The overwhelming majority of the leaders of the trade-union movement were agents of the government. They took upon themselves the function of smothering all attempts of revolutionary protest; they repeatedly sanctioned measures that rendered the conditions of labour worse. To please the capitalists, the leaders many times sanctioned the imprisonment of workers in the factories. They permitted the privileges gained by years of struggle to be annulled. In short, they executed submissively all the commands of the ruling classes.

15. The growing discontent with the war led to a number of demonstrations; these were nipped in the bud primarily by the very leaders of the old trade-union movement. The fear of revolution, which for many years had kept back the ruling classes from war and military adventures, disappeared, for not only the bourgeoisie but organised workers themselves on the side of the bourgeoisie were against the revolution. This conversion of the leaders of the trade-union movement into watchdogs of capitalism was the greatest moral victory of the ruling class, and at the same time the greatest defeat of the working class during the World War.

16. The nationalist propaganda of the trade-union leaders caused deep demoralisation in the masses. Instead of preaching the ideas of class struggle and class solidarity, the only appeal of the leaders to the working class that was heard for years was that of urging the workers to strain all their forces against the national foe, appealing for defence of the fatherland, for the 'sacred union' of classes. This treacherous work, carried on with the support of the bourgeois press and the financial aid of the government, was the principal reason for the war's duration and the enormous sacrifices that the working class was compelled to make as a result of the international slaughter.

The war was the manifestation of the unparalleled bankruptcy of all three forms of the trade-union movement. The leaders of the trade unions of Britain and America, of Germany and Austria, and the revolutionary syndicalists of France rallied to the platform of the betrayal of the working class.

IV Trade Unions after the War

17. The post-war policy of the trade-union leaders in various countries had the same basic features as their policy during the war. It consisted in prolonging the

'sacred union' concluded during the war, in tending to subordinate the interests of the working classes to the interests of re-establishing the capitalist economic order.

18. In France this policy assumed a most odious character, because its spokespersons were the revolutionary syndicalists of yesterday, anarchists, and anti-militarists.

The leaders of the General Confederation of Labour (CGT) are strenuously striving for the honour of sitting in the Versailles peace commissions. They take the initiative in making the German workers pay to France indemnities for the losses inflicted by the war, of sabotaging the revolutionary strike movement. Side by side with the government and the bourgeoisie, they are fighting against even the idea of social revolution. They proclaim the principle of the reconstruction of capitalism on the basis of collaboration of all the 'vital forces of present-day society': the workers, the capitalists, and the state. This policy inside the country leads to strengthening the bourgeoisie, demoralising the working class, and sowing distrust of revolutionary slogans. The more the CGT is linked to the bourgeoisie, the more it cries about the 'independence' and 'autonomy' of the union movement based on the Amiens Charter.

19. On the basis of this scandalous treachery and shameless betrayal of elementary revolutionary and class principles, a strong movement has grown up in France that expressed itself in the organisation of the Revolutionary Syndicalist Committees (CSR). The revolutionary opposition has already consolidated about half of the members of the CGT, but in spite of its numerical growth it is weak because of insufficient internal unity.

The entire opposition is united in its struggle against both open and masked treachery of the interests of the working class. But while the opposition is conducting this struggle and is even gaining victory, owing to its single front, still it has not yet made quite clear its concrete tasks, its programme, and its militant slogans. The opposition, consisting of anarchists, revolutionary syndicalists, and Communists, proclaims the slogan, 'Back to the Amiens Charter'. This slogan is insufficient, as the majority of the CGT also refers to the Amiens Charter.

20. The Amiens Charter, which was the result of the workers' protest against the opportunism of the socialist parties, cannot be considered as a basis of our activity. Not only was it written fifteen years ago, before the war and the revolution, but even in that period it did not answer all the questions posed before the working class. The World War, the disintegration of capitalism, the revolution, all taken together, absolutely dictate to the minority of the CGT not to stay within the framework of the antiquated Amiens Charter, but to draft a new one in accordance with the new circumstances.

21. The leaders of the German trade unions after the war have played essentially the part of saviours of the German bourgeoisie and the German military clique. The revolution of 1918 scared the German bourgeoisie so much that it turned to the trade-union movement for protection against the transformation of the bourgeois revolution into a social revolution.

These German trade-union leaders have concluded an agreement with the bourgeoisie for creation of parity commissions composed of workers and employers, around which the entire activity of the German trade-union movement is based. The activity of these parity commissions consists of discussion of social reforms. The result of this parity system is the economic and political domination of the bourgeoisie.

Crushing the revolutionary movement of the masses with the active support of the trade unions was the consequence of this agreement. The leaders of the German trade unions, who forget working-class interests, have taken up the work of restoring capitalism and have not even stopped at supporting bloody repression by the bourgeoisie against the working class.

22. This counterrevolutionary part played by the trade-union bureaucracy, which, thanks to the misery caused by the war, became the leader of many millions of working people, caused a protest movement among the workers. These protests inside the trade-union movement have found expression in the formation of opposition nuclei of Communist groups within the unions, which spread like a network all over Germany

The pessimistic view provoked by the trade-union bureaucracy found expression in the slogan 'smash the trade unions', which is contrary to the interests of the working class and the social revolution. Besides the opposition within the old trade unions, there are a few groups outside of them (Gelsenkirchen Free Workers' Union, General Workers' Union, Syndicalist Union). Each of these organisations is concerned only with its own independent life, instead of conducting any coordinated struggle against the capitalists and their trade-union agents.

To these groups have been added the expelled unions, since the trade-union bureaucracy, terrified by the growth of the opposition within the old trade-union movement and of the Communist nuclei, has started to expel from the central unions entire branches, districts, and locals, as well as separate individuals.

23. In Britain the trade unions immediately after the war began to carry on a stubborn struggle to improve the conditions of labour and consolidate the positions conquered. The great strikes of the coal miners and other trades show the strength and obstinacy of the British proletariat in the struggle. The period after the war has shown to what extent certain leaders in the trade-union movement

in Britain are connected with the bourgeois state. Each strike, each great conflict, has encountered resistance first of all within the organisation itself, as well as in other trade unions. These special features of the British trade-union movement, accompanied by the unquestionable growth of revolutionary ideas – though vaguely understood – are very characteristic. In comparison to the prewar period, the British trade-union movement has undoubtedly made a great step forward.

24. During the war the Shop Stewards and Workers' Committees sprang up, which became comparatively very effective during the years 1917 and 1918. After that time they lost their former influence, though the recognition of the necessity of a revolutionary struggle and revolutionary ideas generally have grown to a considerable degree among the masses of Britain. The weakness of the opposition elements of Britain is due to the fact that they did not coordinate their work among the masses. The unity of all these revolutionary elements could be accomplished by the widening and deepening of the activity of the Shop Stewards and Workers' Committees.

The task under such conditions is not to have the best militants leave the unions in order to create new organisations outside the trade unions, but to see to it that most conscious and active revolutionary elements work organically amid the masses in the factories and the shops, starting from below, and to gradually take the leading position in the trade-union movement. Only such a method – systematic, unremitting, and steady work – can bring real and permanent results in a country with such a developed trade-union movement saturated with old conservative traditions, as is the British trade-union movement.

25. In America, as in no other country, the trade unions and their leading elements play the part of direct agents of capital. For Gompers and his clique, who are at the head of the American Federation of Labor, even the Amsterdam International is considered too revolutionary and they find it impossible to participate in it on account of its 'excessive revolutionism'. The AFL puts all its hopes in the righteousness of the bourgeoisie, and refuses to listen to the feasibility of a revolutionary struggle for a new order. This is the most typical, classical example of the labour leaders' merging with the bourgeoisie and the American millionaires. It is the main reason why these Gompersites talk so much and so loudly about autonomy and independence in the trade-union movement.

The AFL serves as a most reliable tool in the hands of the bourgeoisie for suppressing the revolutionary movement. But it too is drawn into the struggle, for the bourgeoisie is not satisfied with its devotion – the capitalists want to extract from the AFL even greater benefits than they have done so far. If the AFL does not yet enter the struggle itself, then separate detachments of it, local organisations, are getting more and more into conflicts with capital and the state apparatus. If not from the point of view of organisation then from the point of view of ideas, they are more and more abandoning the basic principles upon which the AFL rests.

26. The Industrial Workers of the World (IWW), an independent organisation in America, is too weak to take the place of the old trade unions. The IWW has a purely anarchist prejudice against politics and political action, being divided into supporters and opponents of such a cardinal question as the dictatorship of the proletariat.

In addition to these two organisations there are independent unions, formally independent of the AFL; many of them are independent ideologically as well as in practice from their counterrevolutionary leaders. Therefore, the question of creating revolutionary cells and groups inside the American Federation of Labor and the independent unions is of vital importance. There is no other way by which one can win over the working masses in America than to lead a systematic struggle within the unions.

27. In Italy the circumstances are unique. A great majority of the Italian proletariat accepts the revolutionary struggle and the dictatorship of the proletariat. The leaders of the General Confederation of Labour (CGL) have no faith in revolutionary methods and are nearer in their theory and practice to reformist socialism than to revolutionary socialism. Alongside the General Confederation of Labour exists the Italian Syndicalist Union (USI) and independent unions that, contrary to those of America, are saturated with a deep revolutionary communist spirit. In their practice and in their activity, they have adopted the programme of the Communist International and the International of Revolutionary Trade and Industrial Unions.

28. In the rest of the European countries and in America the labour movement has moved swiftly forward. Inside many old unions, in many countries, important opposition minorities (Czechoslovakia, Poland, etc.) have been formed; in other countries (Bulgaria, Yugoslavia, Norway, etc.) the majority is in favour of the social revolution and the dictatorship of the proletariat. This specific situation of the labour movement in all countries shows the deep significance of the change the working masses have undergone. The lessons of the war and the Russian Revolution were not lost for the large masses. The new revolutionary spirit within the unions is a result of the objective march of events. The task of the leaders of the red unions is to facilitate the process of crystallisation of this revolutionary consciousness, and to organise this growing elemental revolutionary movement for a decisive battle against the bourgeoisie for the proletarian dictatorship.

V Neutrality, Independence, and Socialism

29. Socialism has ceased to be merely a matter of abstract theoretical discussion; it is a practical question of the day. Therefore each workers' organisation must take a definite stand on the subject. The failure to respond to imperative class requirements makes the workers' organisations passive onlookers in the present class struggle. In other words, such an attitude indirectly assists the class enemy. Each union must decide which way to turn – to opportunism or to revolutionary socialism, that is, communism. Herein lies the weakness of neutrality and 'independence'.

30. The aims of the revolutionary unions are the destruction of capitalism and the establishment of a socialist order. The revolutionary proletarian party, the Communist Party, is aiming toward the same goal. Because the aim and the basic methods of struggle are the same, the political and economic organisations of the proletariat cannot exist side by side without finding themselves in the same struggle. Their daily struggle is interwoven. No single campaign can be carried through with any degree of success without mutual aid and ever-increasing contact. Isolated action is foredoomed to failure and defeat.

31. The revolutionary trade unions, therefore, have always been opposed to the idea of neutrality and the independence of the trade unions from the revolutionary party of the proletariat. They knew that such ideas were only a cloak for the purely bourgeois and reformist idea of isolating the economic struggle of the proletariat from its political struggle, with the aim of weakening and demoralising the working masses. Neutrality and independence of trade unions from revolutionary socialism always has been, and still is, the slogan brought forward by the most backward sections of the labour movement of all countries.

During the last few years, as the ties binding the trade-union leaders of all countries to the League of Nations became closer, and as these leaders became increasingly dependent on the bourgeoisie of their respective countries, these leaders championed with increasing emphasis and resolve the idea of independence of the unions from the Communist International. This idea must therefore be decisively and totally rejected.

32. The task of the trade unions is to fight the ideology of neutralism, which weakens and eats away at workers' organisations. As trade unions participate in the social struggle and fight against capitalism and capitalist domination, they lose their prejudices about neutrality and independence with relation to communism.

The present situation imperatively demands that revolutionary unions and the Communist Party act together in fighting for the social revolution and for the dictatorship of the proletariat. Such concerted action is the best practical refutation of the thoroughly worn-out theory of neutrality and independence – a doctrine that has never been carried out in actual practice.

33. Under present conditions, every economic struggle inevitably becomes a political struggle. The struggle itself under such conditions, whatever the numerical strength of the workers involved in a given country, can be truly revolutionary and be carried out with the greatest benefit for the working class as a whole only when the revolutionary trade unions march shoulder to shoulder in the closest cooperation and unity with the Communist Party of the given country. The theory and practice of splitting the struggle of the working class into two independent halves is utterly detrimental, especially at the present moment.

Every engagement in the struggle requires the utmost concentration of forces, which is possible only when all the revolutionary energies of the working class are strained to the utmost, i.e., when all its revolutionary and communist elements are brought into play. Separate revolutionary struggles by the Communist Party and the revolutionary red unions are foredoomed to defeat. That is why unity of action, the organic connection of Communist parties and trade unions, is a necessary requirement for the successful struggle against capitalism.

VI The Amsterdam International

34. The policy of the trade unions of the belligerent countries caused the breakdown of all the international connections that had existed prior to the war, such as the International Secretariat headed by Legien,[1] as well as all the independent international federations (of textile workers, metalworkers, etc.). They broke up – according to their respective locations – into partisans of the Entente and of the Central Powers.

35. The general misery bred by the war, the aggravation of class antagonism, insecurity, uncertainty about tomorrow, growing unemployment, and profound deception caused by the results of the war, acted as a great impelling force in driving the masses into the trade unions. The war brought to the surface

1 The International Secretariat of National Trade Union Centres was formed in 1901 under the leadership of Carl Legien, head of the main German trade-union federation, and was renamed the International Federation of Trade Unions (IFTU) in 1913. Falling apart during World War I, the IFTU was reconstituted in 1919, becoming known as the Amsterdam International.

new layers of workers, aroused them, made them distrust their own individual efforts, and forced the most backward workers to do some hard thinking on the causes and the consequences of the catastrophe that all humanity is now living through. The feeling of international solidarity, so long repressed during the war, awoke with new force in the working masses who had been divided by the war into national units. This new feeling called for rebuilding international connections, the necessity for which is instinctively felt even by the most backward sections of the working class.

36. Hence the efforts of the bankrupt leaders of the trade unions in taking the initiative to rebuild the International and get at the helm of the movement. Having attempted to create an Inter-Allied trade-union International (Leeds 1916),[2] the leaders of the Entente unions began, immediately after the war, to 'restore' international connections by taking part in some of the labour commissions organised for the purpose of working out supplementary articles on labour for the Versailles Treaty. In this way they have sealed, on an international scale, the work of betrayal that they had carried on within their respective bourgeois homelands.

37. The victory of 'democracy' in the international slaughter was signalled by the creation of the International Labour Bureau as a part of the League of Nations, which represents the highest realisation of the idea of peaceful development and class collaboration. This bureau, made up of six labour leaders, six employers, and twelve representatives of bourgeois governments, has for its object not only to study the struggle, but also to steer this struggle along the channels of peaceful development and amicable solution of the conflicts between labour and capital.

38. In Bern (February 1919), and in Amsterdam (July 1919) the trade-union International was officially restored. This International represents the continuation of the nationalistic policy on an international scale. The new International began its work by declaring itself for affiliation to the International Labour Bureau and displaying the devotion of its leaders to world imperialism. Its programme is peaceful development, class collaboration, slow and gradual realisation of socialism, and mortal fear and hatred of the revolutionary movement of the masses.

39. Such international betrayal by those who for many years sold out the workers of their countries wholesale and retail was quite natural and logical,

2 The Leeds Conference was held 5–7 July 1916, attended by representatives from the trade union federations of Belgium, France, Britain, and Italy. During the war a number of inter-allied conferences were held by the trade-union and socialist movements.

but this was in full contradiction with the fundamental interests of the proletariat, which is bleeding to death. We see that simultaneously with the creation of this international bulwark of the bourgeoisie, a movement of protest was growing against this imperialist tendency in all directions and in all countries. This protest, rendered more acute by the growing socialist struggle, did not at first have its own international central organisation. Such a centre was created at the initiative of the All-Russian Central Council of Trade Unions in July 1920, represented by the International Trade Union Council. The birth of this centre for revolutionary trade unionism is the starting point for an implacable war within the bounds of the trade-union movement of the world, carried out under the slogan 'Moscow or Amsterdam'. Cleavage within the old organisations is proceeding at a rapid pace as the economic crisis grows more intense, and as the proletariat loses confidence in the prospects for peaceful development.

40. The very fact of the creation of the Red Trade Union International gives a tremendous impetus to the growth of the number of partisans of the Red International. This fact, and the formation of various groups in the international trade-union movement on one side, and the decomposition of the Amsterdam International on the other, puts before the revolutionary trade unions of all countries the question of the methods to unify their own forces, as well as the methods to be used in attacking international capital and the yellow leaders who are at the head of the Amsterdam Trade Union International.

VII Methods of Struggle

41. The most conscious elements of the revolutionary unions will not be able to defeat the old leaders if they detach themselves from the masses and their daily needs and hopes. The work must be carried out on the battleground of the conflicts by which the masses are deeply stirred. A contemptuous and haughty attitude toward the daily struggle for the material interests of union members will detach the vanguard from the masses, and create a gulf between them and the compact columns of the proletarian army. Therefore, responding ably to the daily struggle and an ability to utilise it from the standpoint of the supreme revolutionary struggle is, in conjunction with the general trade-union struggle for the proletarian dictatorship, the most important question of union tactics.

42. The economic struggle must serve to enlarge our influence. Questions of wages and rates, of securing relief for the war victims, social insurance, unemployment, women's and children's labour, sanitary conditions in indus-

trial establishments, high prices, the housing question, etc., together with taxation, mobilisation, colonial schemes, financial combinations – all these must be utilised as daily material for organisation and militant socialist education. The partisans of the Red Trade Union International must in no case remain outside of the existing labour organisations. On the contrary, our task is to work insistently and systematically within the trade unions, giving the masses of workers a practical example of revolutionary spirit, selflessness, and communism.

It is necessary to conduct systematic and energetic propaganda among the workers in the factories, workshops, and enterprises generally, winning them to the Red International of Trade Unions. This same question – for or against Moscow – must be raised within the reformist unions; for this purpose the followers of the Red International of Trade Unions must make use of all union meetings, congresses, and conferences, counterposing in practical struggle revolutionary socialism to reformism and class collaboration.

43. We shall be able to conquer the masses, and consequently the trade unions, only on condition that we are in the front ranks of the working masses in the struggle for their everyday demands. This standpoint shall in no case be construed as meaning that a call to action under any and all circumstances is advisable. The supporters of the Red Trade Union International must not only be animated by a revolutionary spirit, but must also be irreproachable in discipline and cool-headedness. Assurance of victory is based on intelligent preparation, and on systematic and tenacious action. Rapidness and tenaciousness must go hand-in-hand with a patient study of each situation and its conditions, as well as of the enemy's forces. In class struggles as in war, defence is as important as offence. Both on the attack and on the defensive it is always necessary to have the sympathy of the proletarian masses, and of the social and political forces at hand.

VIII Programme of Action

44. Based on the above-stated principles, the conditions of the international trade-union movement, the economic crisis, the intensification of the class struggle, the growing number of social conflicts and the necessity of preparing the trade unions for the social revolution and the dictatorship of the proletariat – the First International Congress of Trade and Industrial Unions adopts the following programme of action:

45. The basis of trade-union tactics is direct action by the revolutionary masses and their organisations against capital. All conquests by the workers

are in direct proportion to the degree of revolutionary pressure of the masses. By direct action is understood every form of mass movement, such as boycotts, strikes, street demonstrations, seizure of factories, armed resistance, and other revolutionary activities capable of uniting the working class for the overthrow of capitalism. The task of the revolutionary trade unions consists in utilising all forms of struggle so that they serve as education and preparation of the revolutionary masses for future battles for the social revolution and the dictatorship of the proletariat.

46. The last years of the struggle have shown with particular vividness the weakness of strictly craft organisations to meet the situation. The fact that workers in the same enterprise belong to different craft unions weakens their struggle. It is necessary – and this should be the starting point of an implacable struggle – to pass from purely craft unions to industrial organisations. 'All workers employed in the same enterprise should be in the same union' – this is the militant slogan in the field of workers' organisation. The fusion into a single union in a revolutionary way should be put directly before the members of the union in the factories and enterprises, as well as before local and regional bodies and national congresses.

47. Each factory and each shop should become a citadel of the revolution. Old forms of communication between rank-and-file members and the union itself (money collectors, agents, stewards, etc.) are insufficient. It is necessary to strive toward building the union on the basis of factory committees. These committees should be elected by all the workers in the given factory, independently of the union they belong to and the political beliefs they profess. The task imposed upon supporters of the Red International of Labour Unions is to draw all the workers of a given enterprise into the election of their representative body. The attempt to elect factory committees exclusively by comrades of the same party, casting aside the non-party rank-and-file workers, should be categorically condemned. This would be only a nucleus and not a factory committee. The revolutionary party should exercise influence through means of nuclei, committees of action, and through its rank-and-file members, through general assemblies, and the elected factory committee.

48. The first task to be put before the workers in the factory committee is the maintenance of the workers laid off on account of unemployment – at the expense of the bosses of the given branch of industry. It should not be permitted for workers to be thrown out on the street without the employers being in the least concerned with their further existence. The owners must be compelled to pay full wages to the unemployed. This should be put before the unemployed, and especially to the workers engaged in the factories, explaining to them at the same time that the problem of unemployment cannot be solved

within the capitalist system, and that the only way to abolish unemployment is the social revolution and the dictatorship of the proletariat.

49. The closing of factories by companies and shortening working hours are the most effective means through which the bourgeoisie compels the workers to accept lower wages, longer hours, and the abolition of collective bargaining. Lockouts more and more take the form of direct action on the part of the employers against the organised workers. The trade unions must therefore carry on a fight against the closing of factories, and for the right of the workers to investigate the causes of such closures. For this purpose special committees should be organised with regard to the control and monitoring of fuel, raw materials, and orders, for the purpose of verifying the available amount of materials necessary for production, as well as the financial resources in the banks. Control commissions must specifically investigate in the most careful manner the financial correlation existing between the given factory and other factories, for which purpose it is necessary to place before the workers as a practical task to put an end to business secrecy.

50. One of the ways of battling against the mass closure of companies for the purpose of reducing wages and lowering the standard of living, should be occupation of the factories and shops by the workers and continuing production by themselves in spite of the owner.

Due to the lack of goods, it is highly important that production should continue, and that workers not tolerate the premeditated shutdown of factories. In connection with local conditions, the conditions of production, the political situation, and the intensity of the social struggle – the seizure of the enterprises may and should be followed by other methods of action against capital. On taking hold of the enterprise, its management should be given to factory-committee representatives and union delegates specially appointed for that purpose.

51. The economic struggle should proceed under the slogan of 'increase wages, improve working conditions, and defend the fundamental interests of the workers'. The exhaustion of the working class during the war must be compensated for by increasing wages and improving conditions at work. The allegation by capitalists of foreign competition should by no means be taken into consideration. The revolutionary trade unions are bound to approach the question of wages and working conditions not from the point of view of competition between capitalist profiteers of different nations, but solely from that of preserving and defending labour power.

52. The employers are making use of any means in their power to bring about a split in the ranks of the labour movement. They fully made use of women's labour during the war, and continue to use this cheap labour power for the

purpose of cutting men's wages. Instead of fighting the employers, the workers in a number of countries have called for removing women from industry and expelling them from the unions. This policy should be met with determined resistance by the red trade unions. Revolutionary unions must fight for equality of working conditions for men and women and for equal pay for equal work.

53. When the tactics of wage reduction are resorted to by the capitalist class during an economic crisis, the duty of revolutionary trade unions consists in defeating wage reductions in that capitalist industry, in order not to be defeated piecemeal. The workers engaged in the basic industries (mining, railroad, gas enterprises, etc.) should wage their struggle simultaneously, so that the struggle against capital's offensive should touch the very nerve of the economic organism.

It is necessary to have recourse to every means of resistance, from intermittent partial strikes up to a general strike embracing key industries on a national scale. These are powerful measures against the reactionary aims of the world bourgeoisie. The trade unions must attentively follow the world situation, selecting the most favourable opportunity for their economic attack, without forgetting for a single moment that any action on an international scale can be possible only by the creation of true revolutionary class trade unions, having nothing in common with the yellow Amsterdam International.

54. The belief in the sanctity of collective bargaining propagated by the opportunists of all countries must be met with a resolute and determined resistance on the part of the revolutionary trade-union movement. Collective bargaining is nothing more than an armistice. The owner always violates these collective contracts whenever the slightest opportunity presents itself. A religious respect for collective bargaining proves only that bourgeois ideology is deeply rooted in the minds of the leaders of the working class. Revolutionary trade unions, without rejecting collective bargaining, must nevertheless realise its relative value, and must face the question of methods to abolish all these contracts when it proves to be advantageous to the working class.

55. The struggle by workers' organisations against individual and collective employers must be adapted to local and national conditions, and must utilise every experience of working-class struggle. Therefore, every large strike should not only be well prepared, but simultaneously with its declaration, special units should be organised to prevent strikebreakers and to counteract provocative moves on the part of white-guard organisations, encouraged by the bourgeoisie and the government. The Fascists in Italy, Technical Aid in Germany,[3]

3 Emergency Technical Assistance (Technische Nothilfe) was an organisation of strikebreakers

the civic leagues in France and Britain consisting of ex-commissioned and non-commissioned officers – all these formations, with identical aims although different forms of organisation, pursue the policy of disorganising and defeating all working-class actions, with the purpose not only of replacing the strikers by scabs, but destroying their organisations and killing the leaders of the working masses. Under these conditions the organisation of special strike militias and special self-defence detachments is a question of life and death for the workers.

56. These combat organisations should not only resist the attacks of the employers and the strikebreaking organisations, but take the initiative by stopping all freight and goods on their way to and from the factory. In such cases the transport workers should play an especially prominent part. The transportation of freight, which is their duty to stop, can easily be accomplished – by the unanimous support of all the workers of a given locality.

57. All economic struggles by the working class in the next period should centre around the slogan 'control of production'. This control must be effected without waiting for the government or the ruling classes to institute fraudulent control. We must conduct a stubborn war against all attempts on the part of the ruling classes and the reformists to create parity commissions between labour and capital. Control of production must be brought about by direct action; only then will it give definite results. Revolutionary trade unions must resolutely combat the tricks and fraudulent schemes paraded as 'socialisation' by the leaders of the old trade unions and with the cooperation of the ruling classes. All the talk on the part of these gentlemen concerning socialisation have, for their sole object, to sidetrack the workers from revolutionary action and the social revolution.

58. To divert the attention of the workers from their immediate revolutionary task and to awaken in them petty-bourgeois aspirations, the capitalists and reformists are bringing forward the idea of profit sharing, i.e., to return to the workers an insignificant part of the surplus value produced by them. This plan of corrupting the workers should be met with severe and merciless criticism. Not 'profit-sharing', but 'doing away with capitalist profit' – this is the slogan of the revolutionary trade unions.

59. In order to paralyse and eliminate the fighting force of the working class, the bourgeois governments, under the pretext of defending vital interests of the nation, work to militarise separate enterprises and even whole branches of industry. Under the cover of preventing, as far as possible, economic crisis, they

formed by a German government decree of 30 September 1919, with the stated purpose of maintaining essential services.

introduced, in the interests of capital, obligatory arbitration courts and conflict commissions. Still in the interests of capital, some countries introduced withholding taxes on earnings, with the aim of throwing the weight of the war wholly on the shoulders of the working class – the tax collectors being the employers themselves. It is incumbent upon the trade unions to lead fights against these state measures, which exclusively serve the interests of the capitalist class.

60. While conducting the fight for improving working conditions, raising the standard of living of the masses, and establishing workers' control of industry, it must always be kept in mind that it is impossible to solve all these problems within the framework of the capitalist system. For this reason the revolutionary trade unions, while more and more forcing concessions from the ruling classes and compelling them to enact social legislation, should clearly put before the working masses that only the overthrow of capitalism and the establishment of the dictatorship of the proletariat can resolve the social question. For this reason, not a single partial action, not a single particular strike, not a single small conflict should pass, from this point of view, without leaving a deep mark. It is the duty of the revolutionary trade unions to explain these conflicts to the workers, leading the ranks of workers always toward the idea of the necessity and the inevitability of the social revolution and the dictatorship of the proletariat.

Resolution on Workers' Control

1. An analysis of modern economic conditions irrefutably proves that the productive forces of society are in sharp and unsolvable contradiction with prevailing industrial and ownership relations. Prior to the World War this contradiction was evident only to the most advanced proletarian elements. However, the acuteness of the post-war world crisis, affecting equally the victorious, the vanquished, and the neutral countries, brought home this lesson to the large proletarian masses. The endless war, despite the Treaty of Versailles; the general and chronic crisis, despite the absolute necessity of restoring industry – have put society as a whole, and particularly the proletariat of the whole world, face to face with the burning question of its further existence. With the first attempt to solve this question, it becomes absolutely clear that the above-mentioned contradictions have now reached such a degree that the bourgeoisie, having up to the present directed industry as a class, now becomes its disorganiser; i.e., not only does the bourgeoisie not assist any more its development, but on the contrary puts obstacles in its way, and becomes a fetter on production.

The working class is the first to feel very keenly the unbearable burden of this contradiction, because it, more than any other class, is linked to production in great industrial centres, factories, and workshops; and also because the above-stated contradiction leads to wholesale slaughter of the workers on the battlefields, or to mass starvation in periods of unemployment.

This is why the necessity to define the role of the bourgeoisie in the present organisation of industry, and to determine how it fulfils its task – and as a result of this, reorganising the whole system of production by the workers themselves in their own interests – arises first in the minds of the working class. Such a necessity – which really means a prologue to resolving the contradictions of the capitalist system by violent action, i.e., social revolution – poses the question of workers' control over production.

2. This primitive stage of workers' control reveals itself in sporadic attempts of the workers of each enterprise to supervise work, supplies, and the condition of the means of production, to determine whether closing the factory or curtailing production are really based upon necessity and are not a result of the mischievous intention of the owner. But very soon the workers get convinced that passive supervision and control alone are not sufficient to prevent the capitalists from disorganising the work in the factories.

The system of artificially curtailing production or completely closing their factories, adopted by the capitalists of different countries, shows very well the limitations of this form of control. Equally insufficient are the spasmodic

 | DOI:10.1163/9789004712867_032

attempts made by workers of some enterprises to continue production at all costs, even against the will of the factory owner. In such casual attempts – as in Russia after the February Revolution, or not very long ago in Italy, Germany, Britain, and other countries – the basic feature of the new position of the working class on the question of production manifests itself. From the position of a passive and exploited force, which until now was considered as a machine or its appendage, the working class begins to transform the organisation of production, rising to the position of direct inheritor of the bourgeoisie, which now, on account of its class interests, has become the disorganiser of production.

3. To the old type of trade unions, whose activity was limited to the fight for only slight improvements under the existing capitalist system, such a change in the minds of the working masses causes an indisputable blow. The old trade unions, tied together through its bureaucracy with the bourgeois apparatus, and entirely dependent upon it, are powerless to grasp the new problems of production put before the working class, or to find a practical solution for them. This is why, with particular force and rapidity, new organisations are now arising which, still using the weapon of the old trade unions – the strike – for revolutionary purposes, already strive to take over industry. The activity of shop and factory committees is now limited not only to the strike, but is mainly expressed in taking over some functions of the factory owner, especially in the area of supplying the factory with raw materials, fuel, and financial resources, or even the confiscation of factories sabotaged or abandoned by the owners.

This is the reason why in this phase of workers' control the bourgeoisie and its apologists – the leaders of the old trade unions – make desperate attempts to counterpose to revolutionary workers' control the so-called 'industrial democracy', i.e., parity commissions of factory owners and workers, profit-sharing schemes, and other 'democratic' tricks based on the theory of 'equal' rights between labour and capital, on condition of leaving intact the means of production as the private property of the bourgeoisie. This ideal of 'equality' is carefully cultivated by the British trade unions, and received its final expression at the Tenth Congress of trade unions in Germany (1919),[1] and it still dominates the French CGT. In practice it is merely an attempt to fool the working class through the distortion of the meaning of revolutionary workers' control; to turn it aside from immediate revolutionary problems to the entirely outlived bourgeois ideas of the yellow International of trade unions.

1 The Tenth Congress of the General German Trade Union Federation (ADGB) was held from 30 June to 5 July 1919.

4. Of equal significance are the attempts of the yellow leaders of the trade unions to counterpose 'government ownership' to revolutionary workers' control. The bourgeoisie is supporting them, because it cleverly uses the principle of pseudo-socialisation in its own class interests. The fact is willingly obscured that government ownership does not at all mean ownership by the entire population, but only the transition of production from private management of a group of individual representatives of the ruling class to management by this class as a whole. The theory of government control consists in an administration composed of elected representatives either of the government and the workers, or of the owners, the government, and the workers. The representatives of the government were always considered as representing the entire population, and workers' representatives as acting on behalf of a class. Here the falsity of the democratic principle of control on the basis of parity reveals itself as utterly incompatible with revolutionary workers' control, which is based on the negation of the modern state as a weapon of the bourgeoisie, counterposing to it a workers' state that reflects the interests of the toilers.

Workers' control of production is directly counterposed to bourgeois socialisation and bourgeois nationalisation of production. Any attempt at such a reconciliation leads inevitably to maintaining effective control of production in the hands of the bourgeoisie, and will result only in putting the responsibility for this on the working class. On the other hand, such attempts to reconcile the irreconcilable may bring about the disintegration of the new revolutionary nuclei of the trade-union movement in the factories, which is very dangerous on account of the tendency of the union bureaucracy to utilise the fragmentation and lack of coordination of the nuclei's activity, and subordinate them to its influence.

5. No less dangerous is the pseudorevolutionary idea, widely spread among the workers of different countries, that the proletariat can achieve positive results of control even before the overthrow of the capitalist state. The sad experience of workers' control in Italy, betrayed by the opportunist leaders of the proletariat, has emphatically proved the sheer nonsense of this opinion, and revolutionary workers in different countries must avoid the repetition of such experience.

In this connection it is particularly important to keep in view that the application of workers' control in its fullest expression is impossible unless it includes not only technical supervision of production, but also the financial side. Only the full application of financial control reveals to the workers the fundamental basis of the capitalist system. In the process of financial control, the workers learn in practice of the dependence of their factory on the banks and trusts not only nationally but internationally. The disclosure of commercial, industrial, and particularly financial secrets gives the proletariat a true picture of the prime source of the universal sabotage on the part of the bourgeoisie. It reveals the main lever of the system of lockouts, the curtailing of production by establishing short-time work, and other methods artificially bringing about unemployment, cutting wages, disrupting labour organisations, etc.

6. The struggle for financial control leads the working class to an immediate and decisive clash with the bourgeoisie, whose political power is to a certain extent based on financial power. At this stage, control inevitably takes a clear political aspect and requires political leadership. Meanwhile the increasingly frequent cases of seizure of factories, and at the same time the impossibility of managing them without disposing of the financial apparatus, clearly puts before the workers the timely problem of getting hold of the financial system and, through it, of the whole industry. At this stage of workers' control, the contradiction stated in point one resolves itself into the struggle for power between the proletariat and the bourgeoisie, i.e., in the social revolution.

In the process of this decisive struggle – the duration of which is determined by the level of organisation and culture of the bourgeoisie in each country – there is no more question of controlling the factory owner in order to paralyse his 'evil intentions', to fight against his sabotaging activities, or to continue production at all costs, etc. The question now before the proletariat as a class is to take the industry away from the capitalists, to take over in its own hands and under its own responsibility the management of the industrial resources of the country. At this moment workers' control develops into an act of combat by the working class to organise production in factories, shops, mines, and railroads not only in its own interest, or in that of some separate groups of the working class, but for the benefit of the whole proletariat of a given country.

7. The victory of the proletariat is inevitable because the bourgeoisie is incapable of maintaining production in its hands. This brings the proletariat to the difficult task of state reconstruction amid very adverse conditions, primarily because the preliminary stages of workers' control were necessarily linked to the destruction of the capitalist apparatus for running production. To hold power over production in such a situation on the day after the revolution becomes a particularly difficult task. The sabotage of the bourgeoisie and its obsequious flatterers, concealed until now, becomes open and systematic. The factories, shops, government institutions, schools, and universities are left without directing staffs. Not only must the working class physically defend the revolution, but also it must give its best workers to the task of administration. At such a moment the role of mass organisations, including not only the vanguard of the proletariat (the Communist Party) but also the great masses not affiliated to a party, assumes a very important and almost decisive significance.

Nevertheless, the economic organisations of the proletariat can penetrate into the very heart of the working class only through the creation of nuclei in each factory and workshop. This is why the question of the relationship between trade unions and factory committees is now of the utmost importance. Experience has shown that the creation of revolutionary nuclei of production in the form of factory committees is indispensable, especially where the trade unions are either weak or in the hands of opportunist elements. But the work of factory committees must not be localised; otherwise it will easily be paralysed or sidetracked by the bourgeoisie. It must be generalised on a national scale, under the leadership of the vanguard of the working class. This shows that the trade-union machinery must be employed for new purposes: by getting control of the factory committees and turning them into a mighty weapon of control of production by the masses.

8. But the unions can be reorganised in the interests of the social revolution only under two conditions: (1) that their structure changes from craft lines to industrial ones, permitting the unity of all the workers and employees in a given branch of industry around well-defined tasks of production; (2) that in opposition to the yellow and counterrevolutionary trade-union bureaucracy, there is created in each industry a firm and determined revolutionary nucleus to counteract the policy of this bureaucracy, and to keep the organised masses in the factories on the path of the revolutionary struggle for control over production and permanent management of industry.

In their vigorous fight against Amsterdam's attempt to turn the revolutionary aspirations of the proletariat into a sterile control within the limits and interests of the capitalist system, the red unions must pay special attention to the manner in which workers' control is realised: it is an excellent preliminary school for the proletariat striving to take power. This means that before the revolution the slogan of workers' control must be put on the agenda not just for the unity of the workers, not just to make them more revolutionary, but to educate them politically and economically for the future.

The preservation of political power after the social revolution depends very much on the preparation and the ability of the proletariat to conquer and submit to its will the mechanism of production, i.e., whether it will be able to solve not only politically but also economically the basic contradiction mentioned in point one. This task can be achieved by a sufficient preparation, primarily because workers become used to their role of overseeing the boss. The correlation between different branches of industry is seen, and the workers learn to supervise them on a national scale. Thus, after the social revolution, when workers inevitably have to proceed with the nationalisation of the banks, industrial transport, and sources of important raw materials, etc., the proletarian government will have enough workers capable not only to fight for the social revolution, but to build on the heritage of the industrial structure a new socialist economy, new organs of managing production and distribution.

At this stage workers' control assumes the new form of participation of the trade unions in the shaping of new economic organs and management of production, i.e., it transforms itself into one of the organs of economic reconstruction and control of the working class through the soviets and its economic organs.

General Conclusions

1. Workers' control is the indispensable and extremely important school in the work of preparing the large masses for the proletarian revolution.

2. Workers' control must be the order of the day for the workers of every capitalist country, and must be utilised energetically as a weapon of the trade-union movement to disclose financial and commercial secrets.

3. Workers' control must be utilised to transform the trade unions into combat organisations of the working class.

4. Workers' control must be utilised as a means to reconstruct the trade unions on an industrial basis, instead of the outlived guild system, which is harmful for the revolutionary workers' movement.

5. Workers' control is incompatible with bourgeois schemes of 'parity committees', nationalisations, etc. To the dictatorship of the bourgeoisie, it counterposes the dictatorship of the proletariat.

6. When establishing any form of workers' control or occupation of enterprises, great attention must be given to the necessity of attracting the most backward proletarian masses to the discussion of the issues at stake. At the same time, during the process of workers' control, a careful selection of the more capable workers must be made, with the view of preparing them for a leadership role in the organisation of production.

7. For the efficient functioning of workers' control in each locality, it is necessary that the trade unions direct the work of the factory committees, while the trade unions must coordinate the work of the local control committees of the same industry, in such a manner as to avoid any attempt to create 'factory patriotism' on the basis of localised control.

8. For the guidance of the work of the factory committees, the trade unions must from the outset issue special instructions discussing the questions of workers' control, and carrying out a propaganda in the daily press and in factories, not only by explaining the tasks of workers' control, but through reports on

the results of workers' control by enterprise and groups through factory and local assemblies and conferences, etc.

9. With a view of carrying out these aims in trade unions that do not accept the principles of the Red International of Trade Unions, it is necessary to organise strong revolutionary nuclei that will lay special stress on reconstructing the unions on an industrial basis and will maintain the revolutionary character of the struggle for workers' control.

Resolution on Factory Committees

1. For the purpose of carrying out the above-stated tasks (Resolution on Workers' Control) factory committees must be built along definite lines. A question arises whether factory committees should be organised within or outside the trade unions. In Germany and Britain wide labour circles were of the opinion that factory committees must be organised outside the unions, that they should take over the craft unions and entirely replace them. This opinion holds that the form of craft organisation is not adaptable to the needs of the struggle, but should they be reorganised along industrial lines they might, together with the factory committees, become able to cope with the problems.

2. Factory committees cannot take the place of trade unions. Only in the course of the struggle can they go beyond the limits of the individual factory and unite on the basis of separate industries, creating a common machinery for carrying out the struggle.

Hence trade unions have already become central organs of the struggle, although they do not embrace such a great number of workers as factory committees could, representing free organisations accessible to all the workers of a given enterprise. The division of functions of factory committees and trade unions may result from the historical development of the social revolution. Trade unions organise workers for an increase of wages or shortening of working hours on a national scale. Factory committees, being organised for purposes of control of industry, embrace the workers of a given enterprise, and their struggle will only gradually assume a national scale.

Insofar as the rank and file of the trade unions succeed in combating the counterrevolutionary tendencies of their bureaucracy and transform the unions into revolutionary bodies, factory committees will become the nuclei of the trade unions in enterprises.

3. The organisation of factory committees by separate industries and their utilisation for the immediate struggle for working-class interests cannot but influence the modern structure of trade unions. The activities of factory committees shatter the old forms of trade unions built on the craft principle, and hasten their transformation into unions organised by industry.

4. By turning the trade unions and factory committees into a powerful weapon for the social revolution, the revolutionary workers are thus preparing these mass organisations for the great task that they will have to face after the establishment of the dictatorship of the proletariat: the task of becoming the bulwark of the new organisation of economic life on the basis of socialist principles.

 | DOI:10.1163/9789004712867_033

Trade unions reconstructed on the industrial basis and supported by factory committees will familiarise the workers with industrial problems, will prepare the more experienced among them for the management of the enterprise, and effect control over the technical experts. Thus, under the general direction of the workers' government in cooperation with other economic organisations of the workers, trade unions will carry out the fundamental principles of a socialist commonwealth.

The concrete tasks before factory committees are as follows:

(1) To draw the unemployed into the process of production. For this it is necessary: (a) to clearly determine the productive possibilities, taking into account and controlling the available supplies of raw and other materials necessary for production; (b) to shift the available labour force into branches of industry in which a shortage of hands is felt; (c) to secure sufficient aid to the unemployed, paid for by the employers, until they return to work; (d) to establish connections with the distribution organisations in order to get acquainted with the exact needs of the working masses and to conform production to these needs.

(2) To organise the distribution of fuel in order to secure regular work in the enterprise and an adequate standard of living for the workers – i.e., to organise a systematic supply of fuel for the different enterprises as well as workers' households.

(3) To suspend all unproductive work, especially the manufacture of arms, ammunition, and articles of luxury.

(4) To establish control over transport in order to avert strains on transport through unnecessary shipping: (a) prohibiting transport of war materials; (b) prohibiting export of capital; (c) prohibiting an enterprise's export of means of production; (d) prohibiting export of foodstuffs for purposes of speculation. First of all, provision should be made for the supply of food and articles of mass consumption: raw materials, fuel, and materials necessary for production; the conveyance of the working population to the place of work should likewise be provided for.

(5) To establish financial control in order to make possible the valuation of capital and cash on hand in enterprises, of control over banking and other financial operations, and generally of control over banks.

(6) To establish control over the supply and distribution of foodstuffs, by establishing communications between the toiling population of town and of country. Special attention should be paid to the organisation of mutual exchange between town and country of agricultural and factory goods.

(7) To organise control and the fixing of prices on agricultural and factory products that the toiling population is in need of.

(8) To establish control over import and export: (a) in the first place, preference must be given to the import of commodities necessary for the working population and to the maintenance of production; (b) the import of luxury goods should be prohibited; (c) the export abroad of foodstuffs and capital, as well as articles necessary for local production, should likewise be prohibited.

Resolution on the Organisation Question

I General Considerations

1. The present world situation puts before the working class new problems. The worldwide economic crisis involving a disastrous drop in wholesale prices and a market glutted with goods face to face with an actual famine for such goods; the bourgeoisie starting a policy of aggressive warfare against the working class by stubborn efforts to reduce its wages and hurl the workers back to where they stood scores of years ago on one side, and the masses getting more and more embittered on the other side; the inertia of the old trade unions with their worn-out methods – all this compels the revolutionary trade unions to work out new tasks and methods. The decay of capitalism calls for new methods of carrying out the class struggle. The trade unions must adopt a policy of aggressive economic action not only for repelling the capitalist offensive, but also for taking the offensive.

2. The pending social battles and especially those that the working class will have to conduct in the future will impose upon the revolutionary trade unions a tremendous amount of work both in preparing the social revolution and during the revolution itself, as well as after seizing the means of production, transport, and exchange and establishing the dictatorship of the proletariat. The unions will be able to carry out this tremendous work only when they readjust their ranks and day by day prepare the unions in a systematic and organised manner for their future functions as organisers of production, acting at the same time as the basis of proletarian rule.

3. Under such conditions, the question of methods and ways of building up the organisations of labour becomes especially important and significant. The gist of the question amounts to this: creating an organisation at once flexible and mobile, tightly welded with the masses that should, under all conditions of the struggle, both in triumph and defeat, have an indisputable authoritative sway over the wide masses. The entire work of organisation should be steered in such a way that the masses respond whenever the organisation calls upon them for action, and what is even more important, that unsuccessful action does not drive the masses into a listless, apathetic frame of mind and make them turn their backs on the union.

4. Pursuing these aims, the union must concentrate its attention primarily on the work of making its members more class conscious, welded closer together and more disciplined. The work of securing a higher level of class consciousness and closer unity of the membership can be successful only if carried

 DOI:10.1163/9789004712867_034

out in connection with and on the basis of their daily battles under the prevailing conditions. The only kind of organisation that will really be effective is one that closely unites the rank and file with their union, and will train a staff of tireless and self-sacrificing fighters. These fighters will adapt forms of organisation to the needs of the social struggle and the struggle with the enemy. They will also teach the lesson of looking upon their organisation not as an aim in itself, but as a means for realising this aim.

II Unions Organised by Trade and by Industry

5. Trade unions were originally intended simply as organs for the protection of the working class against capitalist exploitation. But as a result of the complicated form of capitalist development and methods of capitalist exploitation, they have had to change their tactics and methods of struggle. The narrow limits of the trade unions that had for their aims mere 'benevolence' become more and more inadequate in the struggle against capital. The exigencies of mutual aid are replaced by a strenuous economic struggle, requiring the reconstruction of the unions from narrow crafts into industrial unions.

6. Notwithstanding the severe acuteness of the class struggle, the working class, in its forms of organisation, is far behind the employing class. The concentration of power, the centralisation of leadership, and uniformity of plans is systematically accomplished by the capitalists in their organisations and by their state machinery in Western Europe and America. The organised expression of the power of the bourgeoisie, regardless of the strong mutual competition that exists, resides in its central organisations formed either by industry or by branches of industry, such as owners of metal works, mines, etc. Employers' organisations, in their offensive against the workers, operate with the entire factory and not with separate groups within each factory. If they do deal with separate groups of workers, it is with the purpose of dividing the workers and playing them off against each other.

7. At the same time, the principle of craft unionism has not been fully abandoned. In Britain, Germany, France, and America, different craft unions can be found within a single industry, very often competing between themselves. This tends to weaken the struggle of the workers, who, instead of coming in as a single solid front, come in separate groups.

The chief problem of organisation consists in passing from the system of craft unionism to industrial unionism. The slogan of 'One union for one industry' should become the slogan of the militant revolutionary unions. All workers of a machine shop, regardless of their occupations or qualifications, beginning with a mechanic and ending with a labourer, must all belong to the union of metalworkers. All workers of a textile factory, beginning with the weaver, the mechanic, the labourer, etc., should all belong to the union of textile workers. By such a system of organisation, the employers would be faced with a strong, united mass of workers of all the workers of the same industry, instead of separate isolated groups.

III Factory Committees

8. The gathering of revolutionary forces in the trade-union movement must proceed under the banner of organisation of factory committees. Factory committees must be elected by all the workers of a given enterprise, independently of their political or religious beliefs. The attempt to create factory committees at meetings of fellow party members, as practised in Germany by the General Workers' Union, is only a caricature and discredits the very idea of such organisations in the eyes of the large working masses. As a matter of fact, under the false name of factory committees, the General Workers' Union established its party fractions. This, of course, is within the right of any organisation, but there is no need to give such high-sounding names to these nuclei.

9. The question of creating factory committees should on no account be delayed until the calling of regular congresses of the unions. The organisation of factory committees must be advocated and applied everywhere, regardless of any preconceived idea. The factory committee organisation, whatever the union it originates from, cannot remain a passive witness to the growing crisis; it must take up and decide the big questions concerning its enterprise. Until the creation of a powerful network of factory committees is assured, later developing into the nucleus of a union, the old connection of the union with the masses remains (representatives, collectors, delegates, etc.).

10. The organisation of factory committees must proceed side by side with the creation of control commissions, whether autonomous or not. It is necessary to teach the workers, by means of specially elected control commissions, to keep careful watch upon what is happening inside and outside the enterprise. The system of permanent or special control commissions must be widely applied. Every activity within the enterprise must be an object of interest for the control commission, beginning with accidents, sanitary conditions, as well as the activity of the government and municipal institutions. It would be desirable to organise the control commissions by trade unions as well as by districts, so as to draw the workers beyond the narrow framework of their enterprise.

11. Revolutionary trade unions should not refuse to make use of the mixed

organisations with limited power created by the bourgeois government in place of real factory committees. The German, Italian, and Austrian bourgeoisie wish to confine the factory committee movement to legal activity. It was a great mistake our comrades made when they refused to participate in the elections of the factory committees, and when they adopted this name for groups of disciples they created (Germany). Revolutionary trade unions should not miss any opportunity to utilise legal institutions for the purpose of undercutting them. The task of revolutionary unions consists in breaking with legal forms in making the factory committees truly revolutionary, and through their everyday, systematic, and obstinate work transform the organisations created by the government into a weapon of revolution. To penetrate such organisations for the sake of bursting them from within – such is the task of the partisans of the Red International of Labour Unions. Boycotts – advocated in some countries even with the best of intentions – cannot be accepted as a line to follow. Such a policy is evidence of underestimating the working masses and overestimating the legal limits of the law.

IV The Conquest of the Old Trade Unions

12. The counterrevolutionary role played at the present time by the trade-union bureaucracy, and the strangling of the revolutionary workers' movement by its intermediaries, awakened in certain sections of the revolutionary proletariat in all countries the thought of leaving the trade unions and creating new purely revolutionary unions – this is the origin of the slogan 'Destroy the unions!' and 'Out of the unions!', which met with a rather favourable reception among those revolutionary elements who were rather despairing and in a pessimistic mood due to the masses' inertia. The policy that revolutionary forces should abandon the trade unions – thanks to which the great masses are abandoned to the influence of the reactionary leadership – plays into the hands of the counterrevolutionary trade-union bureaucracy and must be resolutely and categorically rejected. Not to destroy the trade unions, but to conquer them – i.e., the great mass of workers who are still in the old trade unions – this should be our watchword in the development of the revolutionary struggle.

13. Profiting from the slogan 'Out of the unions!', the trade-union bureaucracy of all countries has begun to expel the leading elements of the revolutionary trade-union movement. This reinforced the pessimistic mood of revolutionaries and gave new life to the slogan 'Out of the unions!'. But it would be a great error on the part of the supporters of the Red International if, being drawn into

this provocation, they were to abandon the trade-union movement and confine themselves in little revolutionary unions.

The workers expelled from the unions should not be dispersed. They must remain organised on the same plane as they were before the exclusion, acting always as a definite, legal part of the union that had expelled them. By no means should they play into the hands of the trade-union bureaucracy and facilitate its struggle against the ever-increasing revolutionary spirit of the masses.

14. Our tactics with regard to the old trade unions should take into consideration that they currently embrace many millions of workers. The task of the revolutionary elements in the trade unions does not consist of detaching from the unions the most conscious workers in order to create small organisations. Their task should be to revolutionise the trade unions, to transform them into a weapon of social revolution, by means of the daily revolutionary struggle. All organisational work should develop along the lines of fighting the treachery and slackness of the trade-union bureaucracy in the struggle for the everyday interests of the workers. To conquer the unions means to conquer the masses, and the masses can be conquered only by systematic and obstinate work, counterposing to the policy of class collaboration that of our strictly revolutionary line of action. The slogan 'Out of the unions!' prevents us from conquering the masses for our cause, and retards the advance of the social revolution.

15. It would be similarly erroneous to consider the organisation of trade unions as an aim in itself. They are but a means to an end. By rejecting the slogan 'Out of the unions!' we must categorically declare ourselves against the fetish of organisation and the watchword 'Unity at any cost and under all circumstances!'. The conquest of the unions does not imply the seizure of the union treasury or its property, but the conquest of its members. The difference is easily forgotten, and the union is often confused with its office, its treasury, and its officials. This 'trade-union apparatus' standpoint should encounter categorical opposition on the part of the revolutionary class-conscious unions. Revolutionary trade unions are against a split. They stand for unity, but they do not fear a split. This should be brought home to every one of us.

V Organisational Tasks in the Principal Countries

16. The practical organisational tasks of the partisans of the Red Labour Union International are different in each country. Though the principles are the same, their practical applications nevertheless change according to the specific features of each country and the form of its labour organisations. The trade-union movement is an organic product of the industrial, social, and economic devel-

opment of a given country. Hence the differences in the structure of the unions, the forms and methods of their struggle. The transformation of pure-and-simple craft organisations into industrial unions is the essential condition for a uniform structure and for unity in methods of struggle. To hasten this process is the most important task of the followers of the Red Labour International.

17. In Italy the union organisations are divided. Nevertheless, the presence of revolutionary elements within the General Confederation of Labour (CGL) does not justify at all the action of the railway transport workers and the Syndicalist Union, who refused to adhere to the general proletarian organisation. The reformist tendencies of the leaders can be counteracted only when all the revolutionary unions combine into one single proletarian organisation. The field is ripe in Italy for the creation of such unity, and for that reason the followers of the Red Labour Union International must in the shortest time possible enter the CGL and fight for and defend their revolutionary position.

18. In Britain, despite a powerful labour movement that is undergoing a radical change, there are attempts at creating new organisations of the IWW or 'One Big Union' type. Such attempts should be absolutely and sharply condemned. The task of the revolutionary workers in Britain is to remain inside those gigantic unions and fight for the acceptance of the principles of the Red Labour Union International. To detach tens of thousands of revolutionary workers and form new isolated organisations would be a crime against the working class of Britain and the whole world. Hence all the organisations that are in accord with the Red Trade Union International must concentrate all their efforts for the purpose of winning over the unions and their local sections, not focusing on the select few, 'the tops', who are not in touch with the masses.

19. In the United States of America, where we have the reactionary American Federation of Labor, some independent unions, the IWW, and other small unions, the principle of staying within the old unions prevails here too. The members of the IWW should join their respective trade unions and spread their propaganda among them to explain the tasks of the working class. The longer they keep themselves aloof from the American Federation of Labor, the greater will be the sufferings of the unorganised workers there and the harder will be the process of advancing their consciousness. The independent unions that favour the Red Labour Union International should coordinate their activities and come to an understanding with those labour councils that officially belong to the American Federation of Labor but agree with our tactics and line of conduct. Coordination and unity of action among the local organisations of the American Federation of Labor and the IWW favouring the Red International should also be established.

In Canada, the labour movement is partially linked to the American Federation of Labor through craft unions that call themselves 'international unions', making very difficult the organisation of the trade-union movement in that country. All unions sympathising with the Red Labour Union International must, in agreement with the Communist groups, work to create a national union federation of Canada, and to free themselves as rapidly as possible from the influence of the American Federation of Labor.

20. In France the revolutionary minority of the General Confederation of Labour (CGT) took the correct stand in condemning the Council of the Rhone Estuary Unions for leaving the confederation. The conquest of the unions in France is proceeding rapidly, and there is no grounds for forming separate organisations. The congress therefore recommends that the small organisation bearing the name 'Confederation of Workers of the World' dissolve its own organisation and join the CGT, and to fight side by side with the revolutionary minority against the pernicious policy of Messrs. Jouhaux, Merrheim, and Company.

21. In Spain, especially in connection with the reaction raging there, it is imperative that the economic organisations form a single unit. The unity that had begun to be realised was blocked by the reformist leaders of the General Union of Workers (UGT). In spite of these reformist leaders, such unity must be put forward as the fighting task of the moment, and carried out over the heads of its opponents. The second task before us in Spain is to form industrial unions on a national scale (metalworkers, textile workers, etc.), which were destroyed on account of mistaken interpretations of federalism. The lack of industrial federations is a very strong obstacle to the struggle of the working class before, during, and especially after the social revolution.

The Communist groups working within the UGT must form a bloc with the National Confederation of Labour (CNT) in Spain for coordinated defensive and offensive action. With regard to the unions that split from the central reformist organisation and accept the standpoint of the Red International of Labour Unions, these must in the shortest possible time affiliate with the National Confederation of Labour.

22. In Germany the situation is more complex and confused. Here the working masses are organised in independent unions. Syndicalists never had any influence. As a result of the treacherous betrayal by the trade-union bureaucracy, after the November 1918 revolution new unions were organised: the Gelsenkirchen Free Workers' Union, the General Workers' Union, the Free Agricultural Workers' Union, the Union of Hand and Brain Workers. All these organisations remain unimportant whether in regard to their membership or their economic and political influence on the events in Germany. The prin-

ciples of these unions are not quite clear due to their slogan of smashing the old trade unions. They bring only confusion into the ranks of the revolutionary workers, and weaken their fighting power against the trade-union bureaucracy.

23. Revolutionary elements in the trade unions have organised within these organisations strong groups and are leading an effective struggle against the trade-union bureaucracy. The bureaucracy answered their action by wholesale expulsion of the leading revolutionary elements and of local groups from the general confederation. The expelled groups of members must not remain isolated. They must unite and establish close connections with the revolutionary fractions, so as not to be inactive in the struggle for the revolutionary conquest of the trade unions. Other organisations sympathising with the Red International of Trade Unions must lead a common campaign under the slogan 'Down with the traitorous trade-union bureaucracy destroying the union!'. They should not pull out of the old centralised unions any new categories of workers.

24. In all other countries the work should go on in accordance with the principles outlined above. In Czechoslovakia and Poland the Red International of Labour Unions is closest to victory. In these two countries there is a powerful Communist movement. The task before those who are against Amsterdam is to wrest the general trade-union centre of their respective countries from the Amsterdam International within the shortest possible time. We can recommend, in general, that within three months, as soon as the resolutions and decisions of the First Congress of the Revolutionary Labour Unions are published, the question of Moscow versus Amsterdam should be voted on by every union in every country.

VI The International Federations of Trades and Industries

25. International trade federations started to appear in the latter part of the nineteenth century. At the beginning of the war there were already approximately thirty international trade federations. The characteristics of these organisations were all the same. They were loosely linked national organisations, coming together with the purpose of adopting unanimous resolutions, knowing beforehand that the elected central organ would not accomplish any work other than gathering statistical data and informative material. Those were not international organisations of struggle; they were organisations for mutual information. There is not a single international activity to the credit of these federations other than the collection of funds during some big strikes, etc.

26. The war destroyed all these federations, and the working class at the cessation of the drawn-out slaughter found it necessary to re-establish the broken links. The same people who for long years during the war tried to prove the impossibility of keeping the international federations intact, and that no proletarian solidarity was possible during the war, have appeared again on the scene. These organisations are characterised by reformism and a lack of class politics. They have based themselves not on a programme of revolutionary action but on social peace and harmony. Their aim is not to wage a united fight against international capital, but simply to inform one another of current events in each country.

27. The Red International from its formation recognised the necessity of having the revolutionary unions remain within the international federations for the purpose of conquering them from within. But as soon as the Amsterdam International began to realise the danger of the changing spirit of the unionised masses, it undertook a series of measures by which recognition of the Amsterdam International becomes a necessary condition for affiliating any union with its separate international trade federation. By this decision, as well as by many others, the Amsterdam International has taken the initiative to split the trade-union movement, expelling from the organisations all those who have pledged their moral solidarity with the International of revolutionary action and class struggle.

28. These decisions force the revolutionary trade unions expelled from their international organisation to unite to fight the Amsterdam International. Having no intention of leaving the international federations and creating new trade federations, and exhausting all possibilities of fighting and working within them, the First Congress of revolutionary labour unions recommends to all unions that advocate the class struggle and the dictatorship of the proletariat to organise international propaganda committees by industry or trade for the purpose of bringing together the dispersed revolutionary elements. These international propaganda committees must conduct propaganda in all countries based on the resolutions adopted by the First Congress of Red Labour Unions, and lead a decisive struggle against class collaboration and the bourgeois illusions of peaceful development.

29. The task of the propaganda committees is not only to make propaganda for the revolutionary class struggle and the dictatorship of the proletariat, but also to expose the intrigues of Amsterdam, which in order to save itself is splitting the ranks of the labour movement. The propaganda committees take the initiative to issue calls for congresses and conferences, to publish the necessary literature, to collect funds, to inform the revolutionary unions of current events in their respective trade, to give early information about strikes and conflicts,

to fight against yellow scabbing tactics – in other words, to apply the principles of the revolutionary class struggle.

30. Each international propaganda committee is connected with the Red Labour International, through its representatives who are on the Central Council of the Red International with a consultative vote. All international propaganda committees perform their duties in close contact with and under the permanent control of the Central Council of the Red International. Conferences and congresses that may be called together by the international propaganda committees should take place only after preliminary consultation with the Central Council of the Red International.

31. Unions expelled from the international federations must not remain dispersed. If they have not yet joined the corresponding international propaganda committee, they should do so at once and place before the international propaganda committee the question of creating an international centre of their trade or industry.

In case of expulsion of a number of unions, the international propaganda committee may, by special decision of the Red International, be transformed into an organisation bureau for the calling of a congress of the revolutionary trade unions involved and creating an international centre to fight against those following the orders of Amsterdam by expelling unions from the international trade federations.

VII Unions Grouping Workers by Nationality

32. The influence of bourgeois ideology upon the proletarian masses is still so strong that in many countries we see trade unions grouping workers by nationality. Thus in Czechoslovakia separate unions exist for Czechoslovak workers only and for German workers only. In Poland, where until recently the unions corresponded to different parties, the amalgamation of the Communist trade unions with those under the influence of the Polish Socialist Party has already taken place. But these unions have still kept their national character. Thus, alongside general trade unions we have Jewish trade unions, with their own special central body. In America we find unions consisting exclusively of Negroes, owing to the old trade unions' refusal to admit black members. This survival of old prejudices should be most energetically and actively combated by the adherents of the Red International of Labour Unions. The fusion of nationality-based trade unions with the other unions of the country must be the concrete watchword in the struggle for unity of the economic organisations of the working class. National prejudices must be defeated once and for all.

VIII Expelled Unions

33. The activity of the Amsterdam International and of national organisations affiliated to it has been marked, for the last few months, by an offensive against the revolutionary unions. Knowing that its last days have arrived, the yellow Amsterdam International proclaims the slogan 'Revolutionists and Communists, out of the unions!'. This offensive on the part of Amsterdam must be met locally with a most decisive and determined resistance under the banner, 'Down with the splitters! Long live the unity of the trade-union movement!'. Under no circumstances should we aid Amsterdam by voluntarily leaving the unions; this would play into the hands of Amsterdam, and would be disadvantageous for the left wing of the workers' movement.

34. The expulsion of groups of individuals and of local sections is usually accompanied by the central organisation forming new units, thus seeking to destroy the unity of the local revolutionary organisation. In order to smash the local revolutionary trade unions, the Amsterdam partisans enter into secret relations with the employers, who in their turn begin an offensive against the workers. As strike funds are in the hands of the central administration of the union, the local revolutionary section is thus left at the mercy of the employers.

35. This monstrous treason must be met with a resolute attack from two quarters. On the one hand, all the forces of the revolutionary unions and the Communist Party must be directed toward the struggle against this treason, disclosing the open as well as secret agreements between the leaders of the trade unions and the enemies of the working class. Without leaving the unions, it is necessary to do everything in one's power to organise as soon as possible the expelled unions according to trade, and to create a national centre of expelled unions. This centre, composed of representatives of local unions, would lead the fight against the destroyers of the labour movement, demanding the readmission of the expelled unions.

IX The Labour Press

36. The creation of a revolutionary trade-union press should become one of the most important organisational tasks of trade unions. The old trade unions possess a widely distributed press with its own traditions. It is necessary to create in each country a leading organ and a series of papers for each industry. The most serious attention should be paid on the part of the partisans of the Red International of Labour Unions to the creation of a press. Following step by step the activities of the leading elements of this or that union, exposing

their inactivity, passiveness, wavering, and hesitation in the everyday struggle, taking up the weaknesses of the Amsterdam leaders, the central organ of this or that industry should be able to bring home to the non-party masses that Amsterdam, besides betraying the interests of the working class in questions of general politics, always takes, in its everyday practical work touching on the vital interests of the working classes, a position that is entirely in contradiction not only with the interests of the working class as a whole, but even with the interests of this or that category of workers.

X Organisation of Women in the Trade Unions

37. The partisans of the Red International of Labour Unions must pay special attention to the organisation of women workers within the revolutionary trade-union movement. No separate organisations for women shall be created. The proletariat is a single whole, and as a class must build its organisations according to industry, disregarding the sex of the toilers.

The women workers, as the most backward category of toilers, are more exploited than the men. The reformist unions, following the course of least resistance, are establishing wages based not on qualification or productivity, but according to the sex of the workers. When any crisis breaks out, the conservative unions take the initiative of laying off the women first. This is a very harmful policy of the old trade unions, against the interests of the working class, and must be met with energetic resistance. The working woman is our fellow worker in exploitation, and our task consists in making her an active militant for the social revolution and the dictatorship of the proletariat. Only those unions that have freed themselves from the old prejudices and have taken upon themselves to defend and safeguard the labour of women merit being members of the Red International of Labour Unions. The aim before them is the same: increasing the army of the social revolution by new and tireless fighters recruited from the exploited and oppressed women workers.

XI Work among the Youth

38. The revolutionary trade unions must pay particular attention to the education of the young members of their union. The old unions, insofar as they dealt with the youth, did so from the standpoint of technical education. Revolutionary trade unions, on the other hand, must concentrate their work on their communist education. There are at present in all countries over a million young

proletarians organised in youth groups and societies. Trade unions must be most attentive to their young members, bearing in mind that it is the new generation that will carry out the social revolution, as well as realising its results.

To conquer the young generation, to educate it, to raise its consciousness about the inevitability of the social revolution and the dictatorship of the proletariat, to make each one of them a conscious militant in the coming great social battles – this is the imperative duty of all the partisans of the Red International of Labour Unions.

XII Conditions of Affiliation to the Red Trade Union International

39. In order for revolutionary trade unions to be able to carry out the above tasks on a national and international scale, the following two conditions are necessary: unity in understanding the goals of the Red Trade Union International, and unity in action in each country. The Red International can realise its goals only through maximum clarity. It is necessary that every union affiliating to the International be informed of its duties and requirements and to what extent they are to be performed.

40. The Red International of Labour Unions has been created to counterpose its clear revolutionary programme to the ambiguous and bourgeois programme of the yellow Amsterdam International. It is therefore clear that membership in the Red International is possible only when certain obligations are fulfilled, without which affiliation becomes purely verbal, as is the case with our opponents.

41. The first condition of affiliation is therefore recognition and fulfilment of the principles of the revolutionary class struggle. This means that only those trade unions can become members of the Red International that carry out the fight against the world capitalist system and all forms of class collaboration – only those who combat, not by words but by deeds, the theory of social peace and the efforts to solve the social question by harmonious cooperation with the ruling classes. The revolutionary class struggle is the basis of the Red International.

42. The revolutionary class struggle must always be conducted with the constant aim in view of overthrowing capitalism and establishing the power of the toilers, i.e., the dictatorship of the proletariat. In order to bring about the social revolution and destroy the class enemy, the working class has to be solidly organised and forge the weapons for this struggle; otherwise it will be defeated during the first days of the revolution. We must oppose the dictatorship of the bourgeoisie by the concentrated power of the working class, which realises

class aims and tasks. The recognition of the dictatorship of the proletariat is the second condition of affiliation to the Red International of Trade Unions.

43. During the first period of the existence of the Red International, in the period of organisation and assembly of forces, there were cases of simultaneous affiliation to both the Red International and the yellow International. An end should be put to such 'double allegiance'. Breaking with the Amsterdam International is for the general trade-union centres a prerequisite for affiliation with the Red International, because such simultaneous affiliation with two mutually antagonistic organisations is inadmissible in theory and extremely detrimental in practice. In the countries where the general trade-union centres belong to the Amsterdam International, separate unions, federations, or national minorities may belong to the Red International and at the same time remain within the old trade-union organisations.

44. The fourth condition for affiliation to the Red International consists in unity of action on the part of all organisations affiliated with it in each country. If, as a transitional measure, we allow the existence of several organisations affiliated with the Red International, then unity of action against the bourgeoisie – both defensive and offensive – is the sine qua non condition. This condition is absolutely essential, as, otherwise, it might happen – as was the case in the March days in Germany – that some organisations belonging to the Red International, carry out an armed fight against the bourgeoisie, while others attack our comrades in the rear.

45. An international organisation is only properly established when its decisions are carried out by affiliated organisations in all countries. The experience of international organisations before, and especially during the war, shows that many organisations do not consider the decisions adopted by international congresses as binding on national organisations. But the Red International cannot adopt that standpoint. It therefore establishes the necessity of international proletarian discipline – i.e., that separate national organisations must submit to the decisions of international congresses and conferences.

Statutes of the Red International of Labour Unions

Preamble

The class struggle has now reached such a degree of development and acuteness that the working class, in order to successfully conduct and complete its struggle for emancipation, must fight against the bourgeoisie as a solid revolutionary class power not only on a national but also on an international scale. Despite severe competition on the world market, the bourgeoisie is closely united in its hatred of the proletarian revolution and solidly linked together against the slightest attempt of the proletariat to free itself from exploitation.

Since exploitation is international, the fight against it must have an international character. All trade-union Internationals that have existed up to the present moment at best were but international statistical bureaus for mutual information. The International Secretariat of Trade Unions before the war was merely an information agency; it did not pursue any militant class aims.[1] The Amsterdam International of trade unions is even less fit to deal with the issues at hand than its predecessor. The first was but an information office; the latter occupies itself with politics of the worst kind, with anti-proletarian, bourgeois politics. It sets forth the idea of class cooperation, social peace, and peaceful transition from capitalism to socialism. In its essence it is an International of action against the struggle for emancipation of the working class.

Against this International of impotence, confusion, subservience to the bourgeoisie – as is the Amsterdam International – we must counterpose an International of revolutionary vigour, of class activity; an International that together with the Communist International will organise the working class for the overthrow of capitalism, the destruction of the bourgeois state, and the establishment of the dictatorship of the proletariat; an International that will seize all the means of production and establish the communist commonwealth.

Such a militant trade-union International can be built only by revolutionary class unions, conscious of the purpose and methods of the defensive and offensive struggle against the class enemy. The task that history has put before revolutionary unions requires the utmost concentration of power, unparalleled intensity, and the greatest self-sacrifice of the conscious vanguard elements of the working class.

1 For the International Secretariat of National Trade Union Centres, see p. 616, n. 1.

 | DOI:10.1163/9789004712867_035

I *Name*

The international congress of revolutionary, class-conscious trade and industrial unions, which unites the revolutionary trade-union organisations of all countries, decides to create a permanent international organisation under the name of the Red International of Labour Unions.

II *Aims and Purpose*

The Red International of Labour Unions has for its aims:

1. To organise the broad working masses in the whole world for the overthrow of capitalism, the emancipation of the toilers from oppression and exploitation, and the establishment of the socialist order.
2. To carry out a wide agitation and propaganda for the principles of the revolutionary class struggle, social revolution, the dictatorship of the proletariat, and revolutionary mass action for the purpose of overthrowing the capitalist system and the bourgeois state.
3. To fight against the corrupting ulcer gnawing at the vitals of the world trade-union movement: class collaboration and social peace, and the absurd hopes for a peaceful transition from capitalism to socialism.
4. To unite the revolutionary class elements of the world trade-union movement and carry out a decisive battle against the International Labour Bureau attached to the League of Nations and against the Amsterdam International Federation of Trade Unions, which by their programme and tactics are but the bulwark of the world bourgeoisie.
5. To coordinate and unify the struggle of the working class in all countries and organise revolutionary actions whenever the situation demands them.
6. To take the initiative of international campaigns about prominent events of the class struggle, to raise funds for those engaged in strikes and other great social conflicts, etc.

III *Membership*

Any revolutionary economic class organisation is eligible for membership in the Red International of Labour Unions if it accepts the following conditions:

1. Endorsement of the principles of the revolutionary class struggle.
2. Application of these principles in its daily struggle with capital and the bourgeois state.
3. Recognition of the need to overthrow capitalism through the social revolution and establish the dictatorship of the proletariat for the transition period.
4. Recognition and submission to international proletarian discipline.

5. Recognition and application of the decisions of the constituent congress of the Red International of Labour Unions.
6. Rupture with the Amsterdam yellow International.
7. United action with all revolutionary organisations and the Communist Party of the country in all defensive and offensive activities against the bourgeoisie.

IV *International Congresses*

The international congress of revolutionary trade and industrial unions is the supreme organ of the Red International of Labour Unions. Congresses take place as often as possible – at least once a year. They determine the general principles, programme, tactics, and statutes; elect the directing organ; and decide the questions connected with the orientation of the Red International of Labour Unions. Extraordinary congresses are called by decision of the Executive Bureau or at the demand of organisations representing no less than one-third of the members of the Red International of Labour Unions.

All trade and industrial unions that accept the programme and follow the directions of the Red International of Labour Unions have the right to send delegates to the congresses.

Representation is distributed as follows:

Every national confederation of trade or industrial unions having less than 10,000 members receives one consultative vote at the congress; national confederations having from 10,000 to 25,000 members send one delegate with decisive vote; from 25,000 to 100,000 members, two delegates with decisive vote; from 100,000 to 250,000, four delegates with decisive vote; from 250,000 to 500,000, six delegates with decisive vote; and for each additional 500,000 members one delegate with a decisive vote is added. International revolutionary trade or industrial federations have the right to two decisive votes each.

Organised minorities in countries have the same representation, but all organisations of a given country affiliated with the Red International of Labour Unions make up a single delegation, within which the votes are divided proportionally to the membership of the respective organisations. Organised minorities and fractions have representation at the congress only in cases when the central labour organisation of that country is not affiliated with the Red International of Labour Unions.

V *Organs of the Red International of Labour Unions*

The Red International of Labour Unions has two organs – the Central Council and the Executive Bureau.

Central Council

The Central Council is composed as follows: Britain, United States, Germany, Italy, Spain, Czechoslovakia, Poland, and France have two representatives each; Russia has four; all other countries having more than 25,000 have one representative with decisive vote; countries having less than 25,000 have one representative with consultative vote. International trade and industrial federations have one representative with consultative vote.

The Central Council directs all the work of the Red International of Labour Unions between congresses; makes all decisions necessitated by circumstances; represents the Red International of Labour Unions before the whole world; acts in its name; gathers in its hands all the materials and documents related to the international labour movement; manages all funds including the International Militant Solidarity Fund; publishes papers and magazines in different languages. In short, it is the organ invested with the power to direct the work between world congresses.

The Central Council meets at least twice a year, dealing mostly with questions of principle and leaving all current work to the Executive Bureau.

Executive Bureau

The Executive Bureau consists of seven members elected by the Central Council, including two members of the country where the headquarters of the Red International of Labour Unions is located.

The Executive Bureau directs all current affairs of the Red International of Labour Unions. It regulates the work of the departments and sections; publishes the official organs of the Red International of Labour Unions; represents the Red International of Labour Unions and the Central Council wherever and whenever necessary; and prepares all questions for the sessions of the Central Council. The Executive Bureau meets at least once a week.

VI *Unity of Action and Unity of Organisation*

Within national trade-union centres, minorities belonging to the Red International of Labour Unions, as well as separate organisations affiliated to it, must coordinate all their actions. In cases where in a given country the central confederation of all unions affiliates with the Red International, no other separate organisations can affiliate with it. Revolutionary organisations supporting the Red International must join the central trade-union confederation of their country.

VII *Financial Resources*

The financial resources of the Red International are composed of regular dues paid by the national organisations affiliated with it and of special contributions. Dues are set as follows: For organisations in which over half of membership fees are paid into the central treasury, dues are at least 1 per cent of the sum paid. For organisations in which one-quarter to one-half of membership fees are paid into the central treasury, a minimum of 2 per cent is assessed. For organisations in which one-quarter to one-tenth of membership fees are paid into the central treasury, a minimum of 3 per cent is assessed. For organisations that receive less than a tenth of membership fees into their central treasury, a minimum of 5 per cent of this income is assessed. Until the necessary fund is created, all financial means will be furnished by the central confederation of the country where the headquarters of the Red International of Labour Unions is located.

VIII *The International Militant Solidarity Fund*

For the purpose of supporting the militant revolutionary struggle of the workers in different countries the congress decides to establish an International Militant Solidarity Fund. This fund is composed of special receipts and collections. Fifty per cent of all the income of the Red International of Labour Unions is turned over directly to the International Militant Solidarity Fund. This fund is to be disbursed by the Executive Bureau, which gives regular accounts about such disbursements to the Central Council.

IX *Connections with International Trade and Industrial Federations*

The Red International of Labour Unions admits to membership not only general trade-union organisations by countries, but also international federations by trade and industry.

The Executive Bureau shall create a special section of trade and industrial federations for the purpose of serving the needs of separate industrial federations and establishing the closest possible connections with them. International trade and industrial federations establish their connection with the Red International of Labour Unions through their special representatives at international congresses.

X *Relations with the Communist International*

To establish close and unbreakable connections between the Red International of Labour Unions and the Third, Communist International, the Central Council:

1. Sends three representatives to the Executive Committee of the Communist International with decisive vote, and vice versa.
2. Organises joint sessions with the Executive Committee of the Communist International for the discussion of the most important issues of the

international labour movement, and for the organisation of common action.

3. Issues, when it is warranted by events, joint appeals with the Communist International.

XI *Relations with the International of Revolutionary Cooperatives*

For the purpose of coordinated action and mutual information, the Central Council of the Red International of Labour Unions sends a representative with consultative vote to the executive body of the International of Revolutionary Cooperatives, as soon as it will definitely constitute itself.[2]

XII *Expulsion from Membership*

Organisations affiliated with the Red International of Labour Unions that by their action have violated the decisions of congresses or do not obey the decisions of the Central Council can be expelled by decision of the Central Council, on condition that the motion of expulsion must be carried by not less than a two-thirds vote.

In case the violation is done by the central bodies of a given organisation, the Central Council of the Red International of Labour Unions must call upon the membership of that organisation to consider, at a special conference or congress, the dispute at issue between their leading body and the Red International of Labour Unions. The question of expulsion is taken up by the Central Council only after the conference or congress of that organisation has reached a decision on the question at issue.

The expelled organisation has the right to appeal the decision of the Central Council at the next international congress, which may confirm or annul the expulsion.

XIII *Internal Structure*

In order to direct the struggle of the proletariat and to inform its members of the situation in different countries, the Red International of Labour Unions must adapt its apparatus to the work it must perform. For this purpose the Central Council develops its apparatus by creating such sections and departments as shall be necessary.

For the normal conduct of affairs and close contact of the Red International of Labour Unions with the workers' organisations of different countries, the Red International of Labour Unions must receive monthly reports from all the

2 For the Cooperative Section of the Communist International, see p. 551, n. 9.

organisations affiliated with it, and members of the Central Council must make periodic trips to the most important countries, especially in connection with the outbreak of big economic conflicts.

XIV *Magazine, Bulletin, and Information*

The Red International of Labour Unions publishes its official organ in four languages (French, German, English, and Russian) and a bulletin in the same languages. Besides those two organs for systematic information and ideological leadership, the Central Council of the Red International shall turn its attention to the system of circular letters and trips to organisations.

XV *Auditing Committee*

The Central Council of the Red International of Labour Unions elects an Auditing Committee of three, which supervises the correct expenditure of funds and gives periodic reports to the congresses on the financial situation.

XVI *Location of the Red International of Labour Unions*

The permanent location of the Red International of Labour Unions is decided by the congress. The time and place of the congress are designated by the Central Council.

Resolution on the Women's Question

The constituent congress of the Red Labour International, agreeing with Comrade Sturm's presentation on women in production and in trade unions, declares:

Wherever capitalism rules or gets a firm foothold, ever-larger masses of women are forced to work for a living. Women are now in ever-greater numbers engaged in all branches of industry and enterprise, which only recently had been closed to women. During the war the work of women assumed tremendous proportions, and in spite of the temporary decline after the war under the influence of the world economic crisis, the social and economic tendencies making for the increase of the work of women have forged ahead. In many branches of industry women predominate, or at least are of very extensive and decisive importance. In some individual trade unions women comprise the majority of the membership, but they take only a small part in the work of trade unions, and in some countries the participation of women in the trade-union movement is hardly perceptible.

The energetic and wide participation of women workers in the revolutionary struggle of the trade unions for the overthrow of capitalism is, however, of the highest importance and of absolute necessity. The joint work of men and women within the union and on behalf of the union is the most successful method, developing their class consciousness by drawing women workers into active participation in that struggle.

It follows from the above-stated facts that:

1. We must pay the greatest attention to gathering and training the women under the banner of the Red Trade Union International. All means of agitation and organisation must be utilised for this purpose.
2. We must insist upon the necessity of having women workers and employees, etc., take an active part in all forms of trade-union life and activity, attracting them to perform all trade-union functions (shop committees, agitation and wage-rate committees, executive committees, etc.).
3. Members of the Red Trade Unions must energetically fight the efforts of the capitalist employers, aided by the governments, to increase their profits and strengthen and maintain their industries by utilising the cheap labour of unorganised women. It is therefore their duty, whenever wages are being fixed in wage-scale agreements and in the relief of the unemployed, to come out for placing women workers on an equal footing with male workers in the same line of work. They must further exert their untiring efforts to improve the working conditions for women engaged

 | DOI:10.1163/9789004712867_036

in industry. They must put up a decisive fight against the weakening of the legislation for the protection of women workers, and take up the fight for having these laws thoroughly improved and made more comprehensive, special attention being given to the protection of pregnant women, women confined after childbirth, and maternity.

4. Members of the Red Trade Unions must put up an insistent, energetic fight against all efforts and attempts on the part of the craft unions affiliated with the Amsterdam International to force women out of industrial employment in favour of men. They should brand and fight all attempts of these organisations, working in concert with the employers, to win small advantages for male workers at the cost of neglecting the interests of women workers.

The constituent congress of the Red Labour International declares that the realisation of the above demands will mean a step forward in solving the problem of drawing the widest masses of women into the revolutionary fight for the overthrow of capitalism.

Resolution on the Unemployment Question

1. The crisis now experienced by the entire capitalist world is not a typical industrial crisis. The World War, the predatory peace terms, the cessation of regular exchanges of goods on the world market, have brought about conditions under which not only were the natural contradictions of the capitalist system clearly brought out in individual countries, but other contradictions embracing the whole world have come to the surface. The stock of finished goods and products of consumption in some countries contrasts with the almost total lack of these products and famine in other countries; the large amounts of raw material rotting in some countries, with the closed factories and workshops owing to lack of these raw materials in other countries. It is impossible to establish the normal utilisation of the means and forces of production in countries under capitalism. The growth of unemployment, which dooms millions of workers to starvation – the same masses who have just returned from the battlefront – can be eliminated only after the overthrow of bourgeois power. For this reason the First International Congress of Red Trade and Industrial Unions sees in the growth of unemployment the symptoms of the approaching total bankruptcy of the capitalist system.

2. This congress points out to the workers of every country that the measures resorted to by the capitalists and the bourgeois governments in connection with unemployment are not aimed at finding a way out of this impasse, but are intended to retain the domination of the bourgeoisie and safeguard its profits. For this purpose they are now resorting to the intentional curtailment of production, which has already shrunk to a great extent, thus further increasing the number of unemployed. In this way they cut wages, weaken the militant energy of labour organisations, and doom the working masses to starvation and hunger.

3. Unemployment menaces every worker. Therefore, the struggle against the conditions brought about by unemployment is a life-and-death question not only for the unemployed but also for those who are still employed.

4. The bourgeoisie is trying by means of unemployment to split the ranks of the working class. It tries to pit the unemployed against their comrades who are still employed, and those who are still working against the unemployed. The most urgent task before revolutionary trade unions is therefore to prevent this misery of pauperisation, fragmentation, and the deterioration of the proletariat's fighting spirit by rallying both the employed and unemployed in a single united front, with a unified aim, uniting them through the agency of special committees. The congress, however, warns against the formation of isolated red unions of the unemployed.

 | DOI:10.1163/9789004712867_037

5. Together with the bourgeoisie, the trade-union bureaucracy tries to sidetrack the attention of the proletariat, not letting it understand the formidable danger that threatens them. Both the bourgeoisie and the union bureaucracy try, by means of various insurance funds and other petty reforms, to arouse in the workers the belief that the existence of the proletariat may be assured even within the framework of the capitalist system. In opposition to this, the revolutionary trade unions forcefully emphasise the standpoint that the question of unemployment in modern capitalist society is not only unsolvable, but cannot be eased for any substantial length of time.

Not in concert with the employers, but fighting against them; not by peaceful capitalist measures, but in open class warfare; not with the help of the bourgeois state, but through its complete destruction and the establishment of the proletarian dictatorship – only thus can the question of unemployment be solved.

6. The Congress of the Red Labour Unions maintains that in face of the present crisis of unemployment, we cannot limit ourselves, regarding relief to the unemployed and starving workers, to those measures that are possible within the conditions of the capitalist order. The workers are hungry; we demand bread for them. They lack clothes and fuel; we insist that they and the workers of the war-devastated countries be supplied with these items from warehouses scattered all over the world, bursting with goods that can find no market. We cannot allow the reduction of wages, even if the prices of articles of prime necessity should begin to drop. The worker who has not yet been thrown out of the shop and the unemployed worker should not consent to accept mere charity, which they are now offered. Their earnings must not be lowered, and the relief of the unemployed must be equal to regular wages.

The war has decreased the supplies needed by humanity, while the needs of the people have grown. We demand that all closed shops and business enterprises be opened and the workers re-employed.

7. The task before the revolutionary minorities in trade unions affiliated with Amsterdam insistently requires all possible energy and determination in favour of these demands for the unemployed. All the efforts on the part of the trade-union bureaucracy to put the unemployed in the position of 'second-class citizens' should be energetically opposed. It is highly important that proletarians still employed should clearly realise that their interests and those of the unemployed are identical. The aim of the minorities belonging to the Amsterdam unions consists in stubborn and energetic defence of these demands. Where, under the pressure of the masses, the trade-union bureaucracy accepts the demands of the unemployed, it is the duty of the revolutionary opposition to

call upon the masses for the immediate realisation of these demands, even over the heads of the leaders.

8. The bourgeoisie seeks to fortify its position at the expense of the lives of millions of workers. It will use the most frenzied resistance to oppose the just demands of the working class. This resistance can be overcome only by the united efforts of the workers of all countries. Mass meetings and demonstrations should be organised by revolutionary unions uniting not only the workers of specific trades or specific countries, but including workers of the entire world.

Insofar as the proletariat becomes victorious, it will be confronted with new tasks, and primarily with the problem of control over production, and then of its management. The workers should be prepared for this. At the same time, they must also be ready for a series of clashes with the bourgeois power, to armed warfare for establishing the proletarian dictatorship, and to the organisation of production on the basis of socialised property.

9. The First International Congress of Red Labour Unions calls upon the working men and women of the whole world: 'Unite! Get ready for the decisive struggle!' The congress says to the unemployed: 'You were the first victims of the struggle – be the vanguard in the offensive. But don't forget, you can win only by closing ranks with the rest of the workers, defending the interests of the entire working class.' Workers at the bench must not hope to escape the lot of the unemployed. The fight of their unemployed brothers must be the fight of all workers, and the red trade unions must resort to all measures directing the fight of the unemployed under the banner of the unions, with that fighting detachment consisting both of the unemployed and of their comrades who are still employed.

Resolution on the Question of War Victims

The question of war victims is a part of the social problem of the present time, which can be solved only by the social revolution and the dictatorship of the proletariat. If the war victims refuse to be satisfied with charity from the hands of their capitalist masters and wish to free themselves from the position that humiliates man's dignity, their duty must be to take part in the struggle of the revolutionary proletariat.

To influence the minds of millions of victims of the war in this direction and free them from the influence of the reformist organisations of the disabled – as well as from the influence of the branch of the disabled of the International Labour Bureau at Geneva – this must be considered as one of the most important objectives of the Red International of Labour Unions.

The congress therefore resolves:

1. To enter into relations with the International Union of War Victims, which agrees with the above point of view, and whose objective is the education of its members in the spirit of the class struggle against capitalism, and against wars brought about by capitalism.[1]
2. To organise departments dealing with questions of war victims in the General Secretariat of the Red International of Trade Unions, as well as in the central union confederations in separate countries affiliated with the Red International.

The trade unions affiliated with the Red International express their willingness to support the victims of the war in their fight for better conditions within the capitalist state, and to call upon those who are not entirely unfit for work in factories to participate in complete solidarity with other workers in the coming struggle for the social revolution and the dictatorship of the proletariat.

1 For the International Union of War Victims, see p. 489, n. 17.

 | DOI:10.1163/9789004712867_038

Resolution on the Labour Movement in the Near and Far Eastern Countries and the Colonies

During recent years a tremendous growth of the trade-union movement is observable in the Near and Far Eastern countries and colonies. The growth of labour organisations is due, on the one hand, to the growth of capitalism in the backward countries of the world, and on the other, to the calamities that fell upon those countries in connection with the catastrophe that humanity now endures.

The countries of the Near and Far East, exploited by world capitalism, along with all colonies in general, are living through an epoch when the revolutionary movement is at its full bloom and develops under two banners. First, under the banner of national emancipation by an oppressed nation from the yoke of world imperialism. Secondly, under the banner of a purely proletarian movement against both foreign and domestic exploiters.

The red trade unions of all countries must pay particular attention to the growth of the revolutionary labour movement in the Eastern countries, fully realising that only the growing labour movement in these countries will be a pledge of their emancipation from the oppression of world imperialism.

The red trade unions must render their fraternal aid to the workers of the colonies exploited by the bourgeoisie of the countries to which they are subjected, and strive to establish close relations with them and lend moral and material support to the revolutionary labour movement.

It must be kept in view that tens of millions of workers struggle in these countries that are awakening to a new communist life, and the revolutionary trade unions will have committed a great error if they fail to notice this fact in the history of humanity.

The might of the European and American bourgeoisie up to now found its main support in the Near and Far Eastern countries and the colonies. The organisation of the exploited masses in these countries, the creation of new revolutionary unions, their unification, the development of their class consciousness to the absolute necessity of the social revolution – all this will be not only an immediate help to the exploited workers, but will also be the best means for struggle against the imperialist bourgeoisie of the corresponding countries.

This is why the congress calls on all revolutionary unions, and particularly the Council of the Red International of Trade Unions, to follow with particular attention and care the movement now spreading in the Near and Far Eastern

 | DOI:10.1163/9789004712867_039

countries, to support the movement and do everything in its power to unite in one fraternal family the organised workers in the advanced capitalist countries as well as in the Near and Far Eastern countries and colonies.

The congress calls upon the workers of Turkey, India, Korea, China, Egypt, and other countries exploited by world capital to enter into the fraternal family of the red trade unions in order to overthrow by their combined efforts the world domination of the bourgeoisie, and on its ruins create an industrial brotherhood of the toiling and oppressed.

Workers of the Near and Far Eastern countries, join the ranks of the Red Trade Unions and fight for the social revolution and the dictatorship of the proletariat!

Appeal against the White Terror

Comrades, the congress notes with deepest indignation the prevailing oppression, enslavement, torture, and brutality to which the vanguard fighters for the emancipation of the workers are being subjected in all capitalist countries.

News reaches us from different parts of the world that hundreds and thousands of our comrades are being thrown into prisons, are subjected to unheard-of brutalities, and are perishing from white-guard bullets. Our international plunderers are not content with the corpses they piled up on the fields of all countries during the world slaughter. They continue now to send to their deaths hundreds of thousands of our best fighters, abandoning their families to certain demise. And all this is committed so that the ruling classes can increase their profits and not be disturbed by the workers in their hideous work. World history has not known a period when an oppressed class fighting for its emancipation has given such a great amount of victims. Even the slaughter of the Paris Communards by the Versailles clique[1] pales in comparison with the brutalities that the ruling classes are committing day in and day out upon the revolutionary workers and their leaders.

In Hungary the brutal regime of Horthy the Hangman is still in full force. He has made up his mind to efface from the heart of the country every trace that would remind it of the soviet regime. Each day brings with it the disclosure of mutilated bodies of our comrades being thrown onto the shores of the Danube.[2]

In Italy the Fascists, who are financed by the kings of industry and the landowners and backed by the government, attack labour organisations, destroy hundreds of workers' clubs, cooperative buildings, massacre or kill workers irrespective of party affiliation, carry out wholesale arrests, and send into exile the workers' leaders whom they did not succeed in shooting from behind a corner. Many of them fell victims to these massacres, and the first among them was Spartaco Lavagnini, the railwayman who was killed in Florence in the offices of the local Communist federation at his secretary's desk; those who succeeded in escaping from the white guards were seized by the police and thrown into prison. Many thousands of workers have met a similar fate, their

1 For the white terror following the fall of the Paris Commune in 1871, see p. 209, n. 5.

2 The Hungarian Soviet government, established in March 1919, was overthrown by troops from Romania and other countries on 1 August. A reign of counterrevolutionary terror ensued; an estimated 5,000 were executed, 75,000 jailed, and 100,000 forced to flee the country.

 | DOI:10.1163/9789004712867_040

only crime being that they belonged to the exploited class. The old fighter, the anarchist Malatesta, seventy years of age, is at present in prison in spite of his years.[3]

In Spain the hired hangmen of reaction are shooting our brother workers and remain unpunished. According to information received not long ago Comrades Arlandis, Evelio Boal, Antoni Feliu, José Domínguez Rodríguez were shot by white guards in the street immediately after they left the prison. Thus the infamy of bourgeois justice has received its final touch from the criminal hands of the white hangmen.[4]

The prisons in Germany cannot take in the thousands of comrades who are sent there by decision of the high courts. Rosa Luxemburg and Karl Liebknecht were treacherously killed. Eugen Leviné was shot down. Sült was killed during an 'attempt to flee'. Max Hoelz was sentenced to life imprisonment. Thousands of other workers have perished in cruel deaths.[5] And this happened in one of the freest republics, in which Social Democrats and trade-union leaders participate. All these atrocities are being done in the interests of capital, to protect the bourgeoisie against the legitimate demands of the working class.

In France, after the attempt made to break up the Communist organisation and crush the youth organisations by means of arresting their leaders and prosecuting them, a new act of class revenge was prepared against the proletariat through the agency of an exceptional law known as the '*lois scélérates*'.

3 Following the defeat of the factory occupations of September 1920, a wave of armed attacks on the workers' movement was carried out by the Fascist bands of Benito Mussolini. Between January and May 1921, 243 labour halls were attacked by fascist squads, with 202 workers killed and over a thousand wounded.

Spartaco Lavagnini, editor of the *L'Azione Comunista*, was murdered by fascist squads in Florence, Italy, on 27 February 1921.

Noted Italian anarchist Errico Malatesta was arrested 17 October 1920 on trumped-up charges concerning an alleged anarchist plot; he was acquitted in late July 1921.

4 For the white terror in Spain, see p. 671, n. 1.

5 Rosa Luxemburg and Karl Liebknecht, the most prominent leaders of the German Communist Party, were murdered by German officers in January 1919.

Eugen Leviné, a leader of the German Communist Party, was the central leader of the Bavarian council republic in 1919. He was arrested, tried, and shot after its overthrow.

Wilhelm Sült was an electrical workers' leader and KPD member. He was arrested on 1 April 1921, and brought to Berlin police headquarters, where he was shot 'trying to escape'.

Max Hoelz led an armed workers' detachment in Central Germany organised in 1920 to fight the Kapp Putsch. Subsequently, Hoelz re-formed his unit, and it functioned during the March 1921 conflict as an independent armed detachment engaging in guerrilla attacks. Captured following the March Action in 1921, Hoelz was convicted and sentenced to life imprisonment. Following an international defence campaign, he was amnestied in 1929.

Those who remember the bloody reprisals of Thiers the Hangman against the defeated Commune will clearly understand what is being prepared by the government of the renegade Briand for the French proletariat.[6]

The reactionary governments of the small states do not lag behind their big brothers. We are informed from Latvia that, beginning in the autumn of 1919 and up to the present time, seven mass arrests of people active in the trade-union movement have taken place in the city of Riga alone, these arrests totalling about 150 or 200 people.[7] Most of them were exiled to Soviet Russia and some of them were shot dead at the border.

On the eve of the international trade-union congress now being held in Moscow, the social democrats started a campaign of provocation in the bourgeois press by giving the names of the trade unions that have decided to adhere to the Red International, as well as the names of their leaders. Wholesale arrests and shootings were the result.

On 9 July, on the Russian border, Comrade Kupermanis, member of the Presidium of the Libau Central Trade Union Bureau, and Comrade Matisons, member of the Riga Central Bureau, were shot dead without trial. Comrade Miglans, member of the Executive Board of the Riga Metalworkers' Union, had also been sentenced to be shot, but he managed to escape from the execution grounds in his underwear and fled across the border.[8]

In Finland no less than 40,000 workers fell victim to the white terror after the civil war, and about 80,000 people were taken to the concentration camps, undergoing there unheard-of tortures and facing certain death.[9] The trade unions were dissolved, and even now the white-guard hangmen go on with their atrocities, as if trying to outdo the feats of the Hungarian hangman Horthy. Trade unions are again being subjected to persecution. Many of their members and responsible workers were thrown into prison for long terms. Among them

6 A number of nationally known Communist and anarchist leaders in France were arrested in May 1920, in the midst of the national railroad strike, charged with having plotted against the security of the state. They were acquitted in May 1921.

The term *lois scélérates* ('villainous laws') dates back to measures enacted by the French parliament in 1893 and 1894 restricting freedom of the press and other democratic rights, directed primarily at acts of individual terrorism committed by anarchists.

7 This is per the English text; the German says '100–150'; the French says 'around 200'; the Russian version does not include figures.

8 On 9 June 1921, ninety-seven labour and political activists were expelled from Latvia. Two Communists, Mozus Kupermanis, a leader of the Trade Union Central Bureau in the Kurzeme region, which includes the city of Libau (Liepāja), and Jēkabs Matisons, an activist in the Trade and Industrial Workers' Union, were killed by Latvian forces.

9 For the white terror in Finland, see p. 418, n. 4.

is Comrade Loukhenko [Louhikko], chief secretary of the Central Federation of Trade Unions in Finland.

In Czechoslovakia, after the general strike in December, thousands of workers fell into the hands of the white guards; hundreds of them were sentenced to long terms of hard labour. Here also democratic court justice is doing its dirty work in the interests of the bourgeois dictatorship.[10]

Men and women workers of the world!

Countless and beyond description are the sacrifices that have already been made by the revolutionary proletariat. These sacrifices were for your sake, for you who are menaced by the same fate. The exploiters' hatred of the working class awakening to a new life is boundless. What is happening today to our comrades languishing in prisons may happen to you tomorrow. Their death may tomorrow lead to your own. If the international gang of capitalists succeeds in crushing and annihilating the combatants who fight for your interests and your emancipation, you will be handed over to the mercy of your tormentors, and will have to go through unheard-of sufferings without any defence.

Workers and comrades!

We call upon you to hasten to the relief of your persecuted brothers upon whom hangs the threatening sword: Unite! Your present unions are insufficient. At the head of them are people who support your class enemies and persecutors. At the head of your trade unions that have affiliated to Amsterdam are still those who betrayed you during the World War. Messrs. Dumoulin, Thomas, Henderson, and Company are sitting at Amsterdam and pretend to represent 30 million workers, but in reality they have given up 30 million workers to the pillage of the white, black, and yellow gangs.

How many workers' lives now perished would have been spared but for the silent submissiveness to the bloody terror on the part of the traitors of the working class as represented by the yellow leaders! They have as yet not lifted a finger to resist the white guards, to organise for this purpose the combat forces of the working class. They have sold themselves to your class enemies. Mr. Thomas is plundering the seven million francs given for his disposal by Vanderbilt and the

10 On 9 December 1920 the government of Czechoslovakia seized the People's House in Prague, headquarters of the Left Socialist (future Communist) Party and its newspaper, *Rudé právo*. A general strike was called in response, observed by one million industrial and agricultural workers, which called for the resignation of the government and issued a series of revolutionary demands. In a number of places workers' councils were set up, as industrial workers seized factories and agricultural workers occupied large estates. The government responded by declaring a state of emergency, and workers were fired upon in several centres. After a week the strike was broken. Following the strike over 3,000 Communists and working-class militants were arrested; they were released later in 1921.

League of Nations. His friends are using all possible means to fight the revolutionists. What do they care about your sufferings, your misery? What do they care that hundreds of thousands of workers will remain without bread; that new hundreds and thousands of them will fall victims to the white terror? They are now partners of the firm that is called 'International Capital'. They are now the servants of the capitalist vampire that will bring new slaughters and new wars. They are responsible for the persecutions to which your brother workers are subjected in all countries.

Workers of the world!

Do not trust these leaders. Break the chains by which Amsterdam has fettered you. Close ranks! Solidarise with your brothers and sisters who fight! Forsake the bloody banners of the betrayers of the working class! Leave en masse the Amsterdam International, which has left you in the lurch at a critical moment and has always defended the interests of your enemies, the capitalists! Consolidate the ranks of your Red Trade Union International!

Down with the hangmen of the working class!
Down with Amsterdam!
Long live the revolutionary class struggle!
Long live the Red International of Trade Unions!

To the Workers of the United Kingdom

The congress of the Red International of Trade and Industrial Unions sends you its cordial and hearty greetings. Especially do we desire to congratulate the one million miners of Great Britain who, during stubborn struggle with the mine owners and the government, have shown such magnificent solidarity over a period of thirteen weeks. The delegates of this congress, now in session in Moscow, have watched the various stages of the struggle with the keenest interest and admiration. We saw how near to final victory the miners were when the full support of the Triple Alliance was definitely promised them, and we shared your regret when their support was withdrawn.[1] We rejoiced when the perfect solidarity and discipline of the miners was in no way weakened in spite of the fact that the Triple Alliance, under threats of your government, refused the promised support. We further hope and believe that at the next attempt – which inevitably must be made under the capitalist system – to increase economic pressure, together with the ruthless exploitation of the master class, we shall witness a true spirit of fraternal solidarity on the industrial field. We hope that the workers will aim directly at the complete overthrow of capitalism and at taking the organisation of industry into their own hands.

We are aware of the struggle of the Ship Joiners and Cabinet Makers, which began last 1 December, and is still being carried on against the wage reductions that the employers are trying to impose.[2] We see that, notwithstanding the prolonged negotiations with regard to labour conditions in the engineering industry, the employers still insist upon wage reductions and that the million and a half workers in the engineering and shipbuilding industry are now confronted with a gigantic struggle, and this at a time when the union's financial resources are already subjected to an exceptional strain.[3] The delegates present at the Moscow International Congress of Trade and Industrial Unions hasten to send their greetings and offer their hearty encouragement to the workers battling for the emancipation of labour. We ourselves are engaged in similar struggles in our respective countries; for the class struggle is worldwide and

---

1 For the British miners' strike, see p. 51, n. 11.
For the Triple Alliance between the British mine, railway, and transport workers' unions, and its actions during the miners' strike, see p. 76, n. 25.

2 The strike of shipyard joiners, led by the Amalgamated Society of Woodworkers, began 1 December 1920 due to a wage reduction by the employers. The strike lasted until August 1921, with thousands of workers in other trades laid off due to the job action.

3 For the engineering and shipbuilding strike, see p. 52, n. 12.

 | DOI:10.1163/9789004712867_041

cannot be otherwise, and it is the duty of all of us to conduct this class struggle in a scientific manner, and in every sectional struggle that takes place to aim at leading the workers more and more definitely toward a proper understanding of their true objective and to develop future struggles for working-class solidarity.

We also urge the absolute necessity of the workers refusing to identify themselves with the schemes and institutions of the ruling class and taking no part therein. We see in all countries that governments are resorting increasingly to violence, imprisoning without trial those who dare to stand out courageously in defence of the workers' cause. In every country, even when they claim to be the most democratic, in old countries as well as in those newly formed as a result of the war and revolutions – everywhere the same methods: imprisonment of leaders and the shooting of the rank and file are constantly resorted to. This limits the use of strike action and makes it imperative for the workers to prepare as a class for the full realisation of the social revolution. Our Russian comrades have set a glorious example for us.

Here, in full view of what they have achieved, we send international fraternal greetings to the workers of Great Britain and Ireland, assuring you of our deep concern for your welfare. Casting aside national and racial prejudices, we extend the hand of good comradeship to all, and to the workers in the engineering and shipbuilding industries in particular. While appealing for organised opposition to the plutocratic employing class, we send our heartiest wishes for complete success.

Long live industrial solidarity!
Long live the social revolution!

To the Spanish Proletariat

With deep emotion and great interest do we watch every phase of your struggle against the exploiters and their protectors – the military and governmental castes. With indescribable horror do we learn of the crimes of the white terror, to which the best of you fall victim.[1] The horrors of the bourgeois power have reached their climax in these bloody acts. By such means the bourgeoisie is trying to decapitate the revolution and strengthen the foundations of the capitalist system, which is shaken under the incessant attack of the organised proletariat. One is filled with admiration in watching your heroic struggle against the ruthless repression, which will become one of the most ignominious pages in the history of the bourgeoisie, and one of the most glorious pages in the history of the proletariat. Comrades, the rulers of today are showing you great honour indeed. Because by putting you in prison, by exiling and murdering you, they clearly show their fear of the great danger that your class consciousness and your will to struggle threatens them with.

If they deal you hard blows, that is simply because your blows strike them hard. And if the weight of reaction daily increases, it is a testament to your intensified revolutionary effort. Be firm, comrades! In spite of the ignominious outrages perpetrated against you, do not give up a single inch of ground in your efforts to overthrow the bourgeois power and the bourgeoisie itself. Remember those who have fallen in the struggle; they are dear to us. But let us not weep – let us avenge them!

In opening its session, the congress of revolutionary trade unions sends you its fraternal greetings and expresses its complete solidarity with you in these days of hard trial that you have so courageously endured. We send you our advice to prepare methodically, to organise systematically, to fortify your militant detachments, so that you may, with a decisive blow, achieve victory over those whose remorseless and cruel yoke oppresses you. Take possession of the means of production – land and factories. Take into your own hands the entire mechanism of social construction, victoriously defending the conquests of the revolution!

Long live the Spanish proletariat!
Long live the world revolution!

---

1 The white terror in Spain reached its peak in 1919, with some 43,000 CNT members jailed, although the violent repression lasted for years. One of the main methods utilised was the *ley de fugas* – extrajudicial murder carried out by the repressive forces under the claim that the suspect was 'attempting to escape'. Hundreds of militants were killed in this manner.

 | DOI:10.1163/9789004712867_042

Greetings to the Russian People

The constituent congress of the Red International of Trade and Industrial Unions, in which several hundred delegates representing revolutionary workers from forty-two countries have participated, nearing the end of its labours, expresses its great admiration for the Russian people, who for four years have been fighting with unexampled bravery, persistence, and self-sacrifice for the triumph of the world revolution.

The congress protests against the continuation of the criminal blockade, which contributes to the further deterioration of economic conditions already critical owing to natural calamities affecting a considerable part of Soviet Russia, thus causing starvation and threatening millions of human beings with death.

The members of the congress bind themselves to fight against imperialism and banditism of the governments of their respective countries. They solemnly declare it to be their bounden duty to advance the class education of the wide proletarian masses for the purpose of uniting them in the Red International of Trade Unions, and direct their actions against the dictatorship of the capitalists and for the dictatorship of the proletariat all over the world.

Sending its warm greetings to the Russian people, to their wonderful Red Army, to their revolutionary peasants and workers, and to those leaders who have taken upon themselves the hard task of defending and organising the revolution, the constituent congress of the Red International of Trade Unions, speaking on behalf of the international proletariat, is conscious of its revolutionary aims and declares that these aims will be attained by its own efforts in cooperation with the Third International.

Long live the unity of the revolutionary forces in the Red International of Trade Unions!

Long live the proletarian revolution of the world!

 | DOI:10.1163/9789004712867_043

APPENDIX 1

Amiens Charter

[*The following programmatic platform of revolutionary syndicalism was adopted by the General Confederation of Labour* (CGT) *of France at its 1906 congress in Amiens.*]

The Amiens Congress affirms article 2 of the CGT's statutes, which says: The CGT includes, independently from every political current, all workers who are aware of the struggle that must be waged to abolish wage labour and the employing class.

The congress views this declaration as a recognition of the class struggle, which brings workers, in the economic framework, into strong opposition to all forms of exploitation and oppression, whether of a material or moral nature, that is employed by the capitalist class against the working class.

The congress applies this theoretical insight through the following points:

In its daily work for specific demands, the trade-union movement strives to coordinate the workers' efforts to improve their well-being by achieving immediate gains, such as reducing working time, increasing wages, and so forth. These efforts, however, are only one side of the trade-union movement's aims. It is preparing for full emancipation through a general strike and an uprising, as its main weapon. It considers that the trade unions, which today are instruments of resistance, will in the future be organisations for production and distribution and the foundations for social reorganisation.

The congress declares that this double task, in the present and the future, flows from the status of wageworkers that weighs on the working class and that compels all workers, whatever their opinion or their political or philosophical tendency, to belong to the essential organisation represented by the trade union.

As a result, the congress assures to all union members the right to take part, outside the union framework, in any form of struggle that corresponds to their philosophic or political conceptions, reserving only the right to ask, in return, that they not introduce within the union the opinions that they profess on the outside.

As for the organisations, the congress declares that, in order to achieve the maximum success, the trade-union movement must carry out action directly against the employers. The confederal organisations, as union bodies, should not concern themselves with parties and sects that, outside and on the side, enjoy full freedom to strive for social transformation.

 | DOI:10.1163/9789004712867_044

APPENDIX 2

June 1920 Conference of Unionists from Britain, Italy, and Russia

[*These are the minutes of the 16 June 1920 conference that laid the groundwork for the Red International of Labour Unions. The meeting was held in the Moscow Union House, premises of the Moscow Council of Trade Unions. The English-language text here is based on the versions published in* The One Big Union Monthly, *December 1920, and in Lozovsky's* The International Council of Trade and Industrial Unions.]

Chairman: G. Zinoviev. Secretary: G. Tsyperovich.

The delegates present were: G. Zinoviev, chairman of the Executive Committee of the Third, Communist International; Great Britain: Robert Williams (Transport Workers' Federation), and A.A. Purcell (Parliamentary Committee of the Trades Union Congress); Italy: D'Aragona and Giuseppe Bianchi (delegated by the Italian General Confederation of Labour); Enrico Dugoni (Italian National Federation of Agricultural Workers), Emilio Colombino (Italian Metalworkers); Russia: A. Lozovsky, M. Tomsky, G. Tsyperovich, V. Schmidt (members of the Presidium of the All-Russian Central Council of Trade Unions), G. Melnichansky (delegated by the Moscow Council of Trade Unions).

Comrade Zinoviev explained the point of view of the Executive Committee of the Communist International on the question of the international unification of the trade unions.

He pointed out the serious danger threatening the revolutionary movement of the world proletariat, owing to the destructive work of the Amsterdam International Federation, which is still gathering round itself millions of workers. The yellow International Federation of Trade Unions is not by any means merely a technical organ of the international movement. Bound up firmly, through the socialist opportunists, Jouhaux, Legien, Appleton, and others, with the League of Nations, first of all through the Washington Labor Bureau, the Amsterdam International Federation is a political weapon in the hands of the Entente, the strongest the Entente has ever possessed.

The task confronting the proletariat is to tear this weapon from the hands of the Entente. But how shall this be done? By the creation of a Communist centre in the heart of the Amsterdam Federation, in order to blow it up from within?

 | DOI:10.1163/9789004712867_045

By the formation of an independent International of red unions as a rival to the yellow Amsterdam Federation? Or by the formation of a trade-union section of the Third, Communist International which, under the direction of the latter shall begin a campaign against the Amsterdam Federation under the banner of communism?

Comrade Zinoviev declared that the Executive Committee of the Communist International, in accordance with the decision of the First Congress, has chosen the latter point of view as the only sound one for the present time. He named several countries, some of which have already agreed to this point of view, and others of which are ready to agree to it in consequence of external circumstances. Thus, for instance, all the trade unions of Soviet Russia have already joined the Third, Communist International in accordance with the resolution of the Third International of the Russian trade unions. The Scandinavian countries, Bulgaria, some of the most powerful German unions and their associations (viz., the Metalworkers' Association, the Railway Employees, the Central Council of the Berlin trade unions), as well as the Triple Alliance of the railwaymen, miners, and transport workers in Great Britain, and the IWW in the United States of North America, etc., are inclined towards this view.

This is why, in the opinion of Comrade Zinoviev, the organisation of the trade-union section of the Third, Communist International would be highly important and practically easy to realise. And at the present time, in order that the Second Congress may deal with an actually accomplished fact, the organisation of this section as an antithesis to the yellow International would not only make clear the attitude the trade unions and syndicates adopt towards the dictatorship of the proletariat, but also give a strong impetus to the growing separation of the working masses of the whole world from the yellow International Federation, which is using its energy in support of the counterrevolutionary Entente.

Comrade Williams, agreeing with the essential thesis developed by Comrade Zinoviev and stressing the growth of sympathy in the ranks of the British trade unions towards the Third International, pointed out that the present conference cannot definitely solve the problem in question, as not all the delegates present are authorised to do so. In addition, it is necessary to carry out a considerable amount of preliminary work in order that the first steps towards uniting the revolutionary trade unions and syndicates should be firmer and more effective. Accordingly, Comrade Williams proposed first to confirm the opinion expressed by Comrade Zinoviev on the position of the international trade-union movement, and to accept his criticisms of the Amsterdam Congress and the yellow International Federation of Legien, Jouhaux, and the others; and secondly, to appoint immediately a provisional committee composed of the delegates present at this conference in order to convoke as soon as possible an international conference of the trade unions standing on the platform of the Third International. This International Conference should be authorised to decide concretely as to what form the Red International of Trade Unions should take.

Comrade Zinoviev read the first clause of the resolution, which was translated into English and Italian, and after that proposed to consider it.

Comrade D'Aragona[1] declared that he must decline to sign this resolution, firstly because he was not authorised by his organisation to do so, and secondly, because he did not agree with some of the expressions used in clauses of the said resolution. Many members of the Italian unions do not belong to the Third International, and are members of the Amsterdam International Federation, and yet they are carrying on a fierce class struggle against the bourgeoisie. Their identification with the yellow International may call forth a protest on the part of the Italian workers.

Comrade Lozovsky pointed out that authority to sign the resolution does not play any essential part in the appointment of a provisional committee for the preparation of an international trade-union conference, which shall decide the question of its relation to the Third International and to the Amsterdam Federation.

Comrade Zinoviev had no objection to make against the softening down of some sharp expressions and proposed to reread the whole resolution.

Comrade D'Aragona agreed to the proposal made by Williams, and asked at the same time that there should be a more precise clearing up of the connection between the red trade unions which will join the (trade-union) section of the Communist International and their national centres. If, for instance, some union joins the Third International, does that mean that that union should automatically leave its national federation because the latter continues to be a member of the Amsterdam Federation?

Comrade Tomsky asked whether the English and the Italian delegations are ready to appoint at once a provisional committee composed of the representatives of the Russian, British, and Italian delegations, with the object of conducting propaganda for organisation work, and also of preparing for the international conference proposed by Williams, and standing in the closest connection to the Communist International?

1 In the version of these minutes published in Lozovsky's *The International Council of Trade and Industrial Unions*, it says here 'Comrade Dugoni'.

All the delegates present gave an affirmative reply to the question put by Comrade Tomsky, and the proposal made by Williams was accepted. Comrade Lozovsky gave his views on the question raised by Comrade D'Aragona.

He pointed out that the admission of a union to the Third International through the section by no means compels it to leave its own national federation, but it is obliged, while remaining a member of its national federation, to prepare the latter to pass to the International of the red trade unions by working constantly in this direction. It is bound as well to aim at splitting all the working masses off from the Amsterdam International Federation of Trade Unions, the answers to which are determined by the character of their relation to the dictatorship of the proletariat.

Comrade Zinoviev, on the question raised by Comrade D'Aragona, pointed out that an analogous position had been observed at Zimmerwald. The delegates taking part in the Zimmerwald conference were not obliged at the time to resign beforehand their membership of the Second International, although even at that time Russia had taken this decisive step, the justice of which has been later on fully confirmed by life itself.

Comrade Lozovsky thought it necessary to make every possible effort to shorten the stage of preliminary organisation work. There is no time for waiting. The trade-union movement has lagged considerably behind the political movement. The isolation of the trade-union organisations from the decisive actions of the political vanguard of the revolutionary working class is keenly felt in many countries. It is necessary, therefore, that all unions holding a determined point of view on the revolutionary class struggle, by their adherence to the Third International should clearly and definitely demonstrate to the working masses the gulf existing between them and the yellow International Federation of Trade Unions. That does not mean, of course, that these unions will not take part in their own international congresses. On the contrary, such participation is obligatory on them.

For that reason Lozovsky proposed to charge the Provisional Committee – which should be appointed immediately – with beginning work for the organisation of an international conference of trade-union federations, syndicates, and trade unions. At the same time he pointed out that according to the information published by the International Department of the Central Council of Russian Trade Unions, not only the Russian unions, but also the trade unions in Spain, Argentina, Brazil, and most of the Polish trade unions have already joined the Third International. The same desire has been expressed by the representative of the Bulgarian *Tesniaki* Communist trade unions, Comrade Nedelkov, now staying in Moscow.

Comrade D'Aragona pointed out that the conference will not elaborate a detailed plan of the new organisation of international revolutionary trade unions, but will establish immediately the following principles: Whether it is necessary or not to begin at once with the organisation of the Red International of Trade Unions in one or another form on the basis of the resolutions passed by the Third International. As far as the Russian trade unions are concerned, this question has been decided in the affirmative. Now it is the turn of the trade unions of the other countries, and first of all, of course, of the Italian and English trade unions. If the delegates at present do not feel sufficiently empowered and able to come to a definite decision on this essential point, this question should be transferred for consideration and decision to the workers of the European countries.

Comrade Williams read the following declaration to the first clause moved by Comrade Zinoviev:

> The present private conference of the revolutionary leaders of the militant trade-union movement of Great Britain, Russia, and Italy, recognising that the existing trade-union International is incapable of directing and controlling the class struggle and crushing the international bourgeoisie through the dictatorship of the proletariat, resolves to convene a more complete and representative conference of revolutionary trade unions for the establishment of a true trade-union International free from any connection whatsoever with the capitalistic League of Nations and with the so-called leaders of the labour movement who have acted the part of social patriots and chauvinists during the World War, and continue to maintain the same policy up till the present time.

The above declaration was accepted by all the members of the conference instead of the clause proposed by Comrade Zinoviev.

Comrade Tomsky proposed, in view of the departure of the English delegation, to charge two members of the Italian delegation and two Russian delegates among those present at the conference with finally working out the declaration.

The proposal received the full approval and consent of Comrades Williams and Purcell, and was accepted.

It was agreed that the revision committee meet on the following day and have for its task the working out of the final form of the declaration and the confirmation of the minutes of the conference. The same committee was charged with the drawing up of the proclamation addressed to the trade unions of all countries in accordance with the resolution proposed by Comrade Zinoviev.

APPENDIX 3

KAPD Resolution on the Trade-Union Question

[*The following resolution was submitted by the Communist Workers' Party of Germany (KAPD) to the Third Comintern Congress and the First RILU Congress, where it was supported by the General Workers' Union (AAU).*[1] *The text here is based on an English translation found in the Comintern archives, RGASPI 490/1/5.*]

1. The trade unions created by the working class during the peaceful period of capitalist development were organisations of workers for the struggle for higher wages upon the labour market, and for the improvement of the conditions of life and labour. It was the aim of the revolutionary Marxians to unite them with the political party of the proletariat, the Social-Democratic Party, in the common fight for socialism.

2. The further development of the trade unions – as well as of the international social democracy – proceeded in accordance with the dialectical law of the evolution of opposites: In the heyday of capitalist society, the form and methods and contents of the trade-union movement could adapt themselves to the capitalist environment, serving the purpose of improving the conditions of the working class within the boundaries of capitalist economy. But about the beginning of the twentieth century, when the turning point of capitalist development had set in, when the crisis of the capitalist epoch had come, with its consequent intensification of the clash of interests between capital and labour, the hour of destiny struck also for the trade unions. International reformism – partly masked behind revolutionary phraseology – was victorious in the political parties as well as in the trade unions. This latter organisation, having monopolised all the means of education, all the material and organisational facilities, relying upon a democratic ideology wherewith capitalist society had poisoned the better-paid workers and even the broad working masses, forced by its general tradition into maintaining the system of capitalist economy, against the objective revolutionary interests of the working class, it dampened the ardour of May Day celebrations and sabotaged the strikes of the masses.

1 These theses were published in the July 1921 issue of the KAPD magazine *Die Proletarier*, under the title 'Thesen über die Gewerkschaftsfrage, über die Betriebsräte und Produktionskontrolle'.

 | DOI:10.1163/9789004712867_046

After the trade unions had put themselves on the side of capital at the beginning of the dialectical development of class conflicts, just then it was demonstrated that the existence of the trade unions was dependent upon the perpetuation of the capitalist economy, which made the further developments quite consistent and inevitable.

3. The same reasons that caused international social democracy, with few exceptions, to hold the masses back from revolution instead of becoming an instrument of revolutionary struggle of the proletariat for the overthrow of capitalism, also caused the trade unions during the war, in the majority of cases, to become a part of the war machine of the bourgeoisie, helping the latter to sweat the workers to the utmost to gain the maximum military efficiency in the interests of the capitalists.

4. By their programmatic and personal connections with the leaders of the Second and Two-and-a-Half Internationals, the trade unions have become the strongest bulwark for the counterrevolutionary democratic policy of these parties. The more the post-bellum necessity in all countries that participated in the war force into the foreground of capitalist state activity the question of very quickly overcoming of the economic crisis caused by the imperialist war, the more did the trade unions – forsaking and casting aside their original purpose – support the policies of the social-patriotic and centrist parties, thus becoming a first-rate political factor.

A second development was going on at the same time. By long-term wage agreements with the employers' associations, by compulsory arbitration, by state participation in the 'regulation' (that is, sabotage) of workers' councils and the right to strike, by state control of the labour market, in short, by a whole well-linked system, the trade unions were made a part of the machinery of the capitalist state whereby, under the mask of industrial democracy, the workers were hoodwinked in every respect and handed over to capitalism. These two processes – the politicisation and governmentisation of the trade unions – are going on in the individual countries of highly developed capitalism, keeping pace with the maturing of the social revolution. In Germany, where the acute fights of the social revolution have already been fought, these processes are fully completed.

The international character of this development manifested itself in the establishment of the International Labour Bureau in Geneva, that traitorous pseudo-democratic association of the yellow Amsterdam League of Nations of the capitalist governments of the world.

Just as the parties of the Second and Two-and-a-Half Internationals have become the main supports of the violence of democratic stages, so the old-time trade unions have now become the mainstays of the dictatorship of capital in the form of legalised industrial democracy.

5. The economic consequences of the war, the complete disorganisation of the world economy, the stupendous high cost of living, the wholesale employment of female and child labour, the deterioration of living conditions – all those circumstances drive the broadest masses of the proletariat on the warpath against capitalism.

On the other hand, the capitalist class in every country strives to overcome the crisis brought about by the imperialist war and to reassert the damaged authority of capital. For the achievement of this end, it must seek to press down the standard of living of the workers even beneath the existing level through a violent increase of exploitation. Herein the capitalist class of all countries makes use of the old trade unions. This is done in various ways: where the crisis has reached its acutest stage – as for instance in Germany – the employers, in league with the trade unions, hoodwink the workers by means of industrial pseudo-democracy; on the other hand, where capitalism is at its strongest – as for instance in England – the employers and the trade unions indulge in sham battles in order to maintain the illusion in the minds of the workers that it is possible to obtain lasting improvement of workers' conditions within the capitalist system of economy.

6. Just as the capitalist state authority is an instrument for the suppression of the open class struggle in general and in the economic field in particular, so the trade unions in the course of their many years' subservience to the capitalist class have become an instrument for the suppression of the open revolutionary class struggle. Just as bourgeois parliamentary democracy is the highest and most up-to-date expression of capitalist state authority in the political field, so in the industrial field is so-called industrial democracy, backed by the trade unions, the highest and most up-to-date form of domination.

In the quest of success in the economic struggle, the broad masses actuated by reformist illusions are carried by the current into the trade unions, where they obtain the first impulse for the revolutionary struggle. The trade unions everywhere have made use of this first wave of fighting for the purpose of attaching the masses to their reformist principles by pretending to lead and secretly sabotaging the first revolutionary steps of the masses. But as the strike situation becomes acute and the workers, driven by necessity, present demands that strike at the roots of capitalist calculation and begin to represent a serious menace to the capitalists as well as to the cash receipts of the trade-union offices and officers, the capitalists and the trade unions join forces to make the continuation of such fights impossible.

7. At the present moment of the decay of capitalism, the working class in all countries – until the final conquest of power – must wage a struggle for

its very existence, varying this struggle according to circumstances, now being on the defensive against the impoverishing tendencies of capitalism and then assuming the offensive against the economic aggression of capitalism. The trade unions are no longer able to lead in this struggle, whether by their structure or by their campaign methods and traditions. The old organisation of trade unions divides the workers into separate craft groups, although the process of capitalist exploitation welds them into one common mass both nationally and internationally. The campaign methods of the old trade unions are – and will in ever-increasing degree continue to be – based upon the observance of legal forms laid down by the capitalists in conjunction with the trade-union bureaucracy. The tradition of the old trade unions is based upon the perpetuation of capitalist economy, not upon its abolition. The forms of organisation, the methods of campaign, and the ideological traditions of the old trade unions have become blended into one historic whole. To keep the workers in these trade unions they must be scared away from communist ideology and from revolutionary mass consciousness; they must be made to believe in the invulnerability of capitalism; they must be prevented from waging successful revolutionary battles; they must be held in the bonds of bourgeois society; they must be prevented at all costs from uniting as an exploited mass, so that they could ever and anon be betrayed to the united forces of capital.

8. In view of the fact that this development of the trade unions in the various countries – in accordance with the respective age of the unions, the historical evolution of working-class ideology, the acuity of the economic crisis – has attained varying degrees of maturity, the Communists are compelled to choose their tactics in every country by careful observations of all these details. Yet with all the variations in tactics, it is the bounden duty of the Communists to participate intensely in the economic struggle of the masses.

This participation must be established upon uniform lines, which can be defined as follows:

(a) The workers as an exploited class must be welded together in absolute solidarity, overcoming all artificial divisions by craft and industry.

(b) To uphold as often as possible the ultimate goal, the overthrow of capitalism.

(c) To prepare the workers for taking possession of the industries and for the establishment of communism under soviets, to fan revolutionary inspiration into the economic struggles for partial aims and partial successes.

(d) To educate the workers in every way to disregard the enslaving laws imposed by the capitalists.

(e) To injure capitalist economy by all available means and actions, and thus to hasten its final crash.

9. Where it has become necessary, for the purpose of maintaining these principles, to create new organisations for combating the old trade unions, or where class-conscious workers have already created such organisations (unions) of their own accord, the Communists must support these unions by propaganda, organisation, and encouragement, joining in the struggle against the old trade unions and backing them to the utmost. It must be the aim of the Communists to imbue these organisations with uniform revolutionary spirit, just as the old unions are held in traditional unity with the forces of counterrevolution. Furthermore, the Communists must exercise the utmost watchfulness that the unions shall not break away from the rest of the workers, but in the industries, at meetings, and in struggles bring the strongest influence to bear upon the widest masses of workers.

It is also the duty of Communists to help these unions in getting rid of syndicalist and pacifist prejudices, to take their stand upon the solid ground of communism, which is the only reliable compass in the turbulence of economic strife.

10. In the period of the decay of capitalism, the economic struggle of the proletariat assumes a political character with greater rapidity than in the period of peaceful capitalist development. Every big economic conflict may place the workers squarely before the question of the revolution. It is therefore the duty of Communists, through all the phases of the economic struggle, to point out to the workers that struggle can be successful only if the workers are victorious in open battle against the capitalist class and begin to build the proletarian dictatorship. Hence it must be the aim of the Communists to permeate the economic organisations of the workers with the communist spirit to the greatest possible extent, to demonstrate themselves as indeed the vanguard of the workers' revolution by the clearness of their watchwords and predictions, and by practical sacrifices, and in this way to win the confidence and the actual following of the widest masses of the workers and their economic organisations.

APPENDIX 4

Women in the French Metallurgy Industry

Louise Heuchel

[*This report was published in the French edition of the congress proceedings, but not in the German, Russian, or English versions. It is not apparent from the French text when it was given. It is also not clear whether it was delivered to the congress plenary, to the commission taking up the question, or to another body.*]

Comrades, I will give a brief overview of the activity of women in the metallurgical industry before and after the war. I don't think the numbers are in question. They were given to me by the secretary of my organisation present here.

Before the war, the female workforce in the metallurgical industry was around 18 per cent. Women were employed especially in bar-turning workshops, small tinsmiths where they soldered tin, cutting, stamping, electricity, etc. Wages varied by occupation. For example, bar-turning mechanics had a daily wage of 5 to 6 francs for ten hours of production, as professionals. In the other categories women, considered as labourers, had a wage not exceeding 3 to 4 francs per day.

The war, which demanded intensive production, was the essential factor in the employment of women workers. If the patriotic impulse brought some women into the factories for the defence of the country, in general the paralysation of all production was the motivation that incorporated women into all branches of industry. Men left the factories for the war; women, who until then had never held a job, manufactured ammunition.

In large metallurgical plants more than 80 per cent of the labour force was female, primarily in large firms manufacturing shells and casings.

We were able to observe the employment of women in the most arduous work, such as the forge and the foundry, even in the complete manufacture of engines of destruction. It was painful for us to note that the woman, who by her social condition should to be the first to revolt against imperialist wars, accepted with indifference the criminal ambitions of militarism by collaborating in the manufacture of munitions.

Women's production was in a way superior to that of men. The exploitation of women's labour was appreciable in every way. Piecework, the ever-increasing cost of living, and her lack of knowledge were the main causes of the higher

 | DOI:10.1163/9789004712867_047

production. An output far higher than the normal production of a worker was demanded of her. Women were unconscious but valuable auxiliaries of the war profiteers of all stripes.

Wages varied between 10 and 15 francs a day, depending on the type of work and the speed of the worker. During the war period there was an average minimum of 60 per cent female labour in all branches of metallurgy.

The armistice put an end to war production, and, as a result, many of the women had to return to their previous occupations. Today specialisation is the only thing that still maintains a female workforce in large mass-production factories, but the average does not exceed 25 per cent.

Currently in France, where the unemployment crisis worsens every day (a result of the inability of the capitalist class to manage production), an average of 50 per cent of the unemployed in metallurgy are women, and women are victims of the crisis in roughly the same proportion as men. We are told that women are tending to disappear from the metallurgical industries.

I say no, Comrade Labonne, we had a higher percentage of 7 per cent of women (at minimum) before the war, and the industry is going through a great crisis. Nevertheless, capitalism will keep exploiting the female workforce because, by her ignorance, she helps to restore capitalism's severely shaken balance. It is you who are responsible for women being your enemy in the factories. You, the men who accepted that a higher production quota was demanded of her along with a lower wage, and had nothing but reproaches for her, without letting her know her duties.

The organisation of women was very difficult due to their lack of knowledge in social matters. Nevertheless, during the struggles in the war factories for the improvement of workers' existence and the ever-increasing cost of living, the woman seemed to shake off her long stupor, and she followed the directives of the trade-union organisations primarily during the events of April 1917, when almost all the metallurgical factories were on strike.[1] We were able to see a certain surge toward the union, but women were guided only by questions of self-interest, and they deserted the organisation again because no special propaganda was made to keep them in the unions.

The strike of May 1920 was very significant for us.[2] Wherever the woman participated in the resistance, it lasted longer.

---

1 In May 1917 thousands of French metalworkers and miners struck in the Paris area, along with 10,000 women garment workers. Demonstrations by the strikers turned into protests against the war.

2 For the May 1920 strikes, see p. 169, n. 10.

The woman is the enemy of the man on social questions. She refuses to participate in any action if there is no immediate interest to her. But this is only because she is uneducated, without any body of ideas. And this is the consequence of the lack of interest that men have shown so far in the emancipation of women. Men did not want to consider that uneducated women were an obstacle to freedom.

Comrades in the delegation said to me, 'There are no women in the unions'. Others said that they were anti-feminists. And still others said that there was no need for us to take up the question of whether the woman in the union had the same rights as a man. To this I answer: She does not have these rights because she does not know them.

I say that in truth we are not doing what it takes to attract and retain women in the unions. So far we have not done any special propaganda, and do not even consider the need for special work to educate women. Up to now we have been considered as negligible beings, incapable of thinking and acting. And I say to the men: if you are thinking of making the revolution without the help of women, you are in error. And if you do not educate them, not only will you not be able to count on their help, but women will also be an obstacle to the formidable task that you have to accomplish.

What I am asking you now is to organise women and make them active, because attracting them to union organising is no longer enough. Women must be educated on economic and social questions. Create women's propaganda groups in the interunion committees or local unions; create a special newspaper, or give them a large place in the already existing press organs, to develop the initiative of each woman worker; create women propagandists (we do not have them and we need them) for our work; create professional courses; consider the formation of factory committees in places where women are predominant, as there are occupations with more than 70 per cent women workers, such as textiles, clothing, laundry, dyeing, shoes, etc.

And I say that this is the preparatory work for the revolution. Because it must not be forgotten that women must be able to educate children, who are the main foundation for the social transformation. In the future, the woman must be the collaborator of the man, and not his enemy.

Chronology

1917

3–11 July	Third Russian Trade Union Conference, held in Petrograd, adopts a resolution calling for revival of the world trade-union movement.
7 November	Bolshevik-led seizure of power by soviets in Russia.

1918

20–27 January	First All-Russian Congress of Trade Unions votes to call an international conference of trade unions to be held the following month. Although such a conference does not take place, this initiative foreshadows RILU's formation.
3 March	Brest-Litovsk Peace Treaty is signed between Soviet Russia and the Central Powers headed by Germany.
30 October	Revolutionary uprisings break out in Vienna and Budapest.
9 November	Revolution in Germany overthrows the Hohenzollern monarchy.
11 November	Armistice ends World War I.
13–16 November	First Pan-American Federation of Labor conference is held in Laredo, Texas, initiated by the American Federation of Labor.
10–18 December	National Confederation of Labour (CNT) of Spain holds congress in Madrid and declares its adherence to the Communist International.

1919

5–9 February	Conference in Bern, Switzerland, of what is to become the Amsterdam International.
21 March	Proclamation of Hungarian Soviet republic.
7 April	Soviet republic is proclaimed in Bavaria, led by pacifists, centrists, and anarchists.
13–27 April	Communists assume leadership of the Bavarian Soviet republic. Counterrevolutionary forces enter Munich 1 May

 | DOI:10.1163/9789004712867_048

and consolidate control three days later. Hundreds of workers are executed, with many more imprisoned.

28 June Treaty of Versailles is signed between the Entente powers and Germany.

21 July One-day strike is scheduled in France by the CGT trade-union federation, with support from the Socialist Party, to protest imperialist intervention in the Russian civil war. The day before the scheduled action, the CGT leadership cancels it, in face of threats from the French government.

28 July–2 August Congress in Amsterdam is held of the relaunched International Federation of Trade Unions (IFTU). The body becomes known as the Amsterdam International.

1 August Hungarian Soviet regime is toppled. A white terror ensues, with thousands executed, imprisoned, and exiled.

22 September National steel strike begins in the US of over 350,000 workers in the largely unorganised steel industry. The strike lasts into January 1920, but is defeated.

29 October–29 November International Labour Organisation, set up by the League of Nations, holds conference in Washington.

1 December Socialist members of Italy's parliament walk out in protest when King Emanuel comes to deliver a speech. The walkout sparks a general strike by Italian workers on 2–3 December, with semi-insurrectional battles in some places.

20–22 December Italian Syndicalist Union (USI) congress in Parma votes to join the Communist International.

1920

13–17 March Kapp Putsch in Germany. A military coup attempts to overthrow the republican government led by the Social-Democratic Party. A massive general strike called by General German Trade Union Federation (ADGB), together with workers' armed resistance, leads to the coup's defeat.

1–28 May French railway strike. Some 1.5 million are involved, as industrial workers throughout France go out in support of it.

15 July Following a series of consultations and meetings in Moscow by Comintern leaders with trade unionists and syndicalists, the International Council of Trade and Industrial Unions is founded. This is the forerunner of the Red International of Labour Unions.

19 July–7 August Comintern Second Congress is held in Moscow. The congress calls for formation of a trade-union section of the Communist International.

30 July–3 August First International Conference of Communist Women is held in Moscow.

31 August–7 September First Congress of the Peoples of the East, organised by the Comintern, is held in Baku.

30 August–30 September Occupation of factories and land seizures occurs throughout Italy. Workers begin to organise production through factory committees and start to create red guards. Leaders of the PSI and CGL refuse to see this revolutionary upsurge as anything more than a simple trade-union struggle, and the movement eventually collapses.

27 September–2 October French General Confederation of Labour (CGT) congress in Orléans is the scene of an intense struggle between the federation's reformist majority leadership and the left-wing Revolutionary Syndicalist Committees (CSR). The latter's resolution calls for affiliation to the Moscow trade-union International.

12–17 October Independent Social-Democratic Party of Germany (USPD) congress in Halle votes to join the Comintern and fuse with KPD to form the United Communist Party of Germany (VKPD), creating a mass German Communist movement. A minority splits off and retains the USPD's old name.

22–27 November Amsterdam International holds congress in London.

9–15 December General strike in Czechoslovakia involves one million industrial and agricultural workers.

16–21 December International syndicalist conference in Berlin. The conference decides to participate in the Moscow congress of red trade unions, but insists on absolute independence from all political parties and stresses the division between political and economic action.

25–30 December French Socialist Party congress in Tours votes to affiliate to the Comintern, giving birth to the French CP. A right-wing minority splits off and retains the old SP name.

1921

15–21 January	Italian SP (PSI) congress in Livorno results in split, as left wing withdraws from party to form Italian CP (PCI).
26 February–3 March	Italian General Confederation of Labour (CGL) congress held in Livorno votes to seek admission to RILU, but with conditions.
2–18 March	Uprising by Soviet soldiers and sailors in Kronstadt fortress guarding Petrograd. The mutiny is forcibly suppressed, as the Soviet Republic fears intervention by hostile imperialist powers.
17 March–1 April	'March Action' in Germany, as CP attempts to turn a defensive proletarian battle into a nationwide general strike and spark a revolutionary uprising. The action fails, leading to a major working-class defeat. The adventurist thrust of the action will be criticised by the Comintern's Third Congress.
31 March	British miners begin a strike to protest the bosses' intention to cut wages. More than a million workers participate. The strike lasts until 27 June.
15 April	Leaders of transport and rail unions in UK refuse to take promised strike action in support of the embattled coal miners. Militant workers label this betrayal as 'Black Friday'.
9–27 May	The Industrial Workers of the World (IWW) holds its Thirteenth Convention in Chicago. The meeting votes to sustain the General Executive Board in removing John Sandgren as editor of *One Big Union Monthly* due to his attacks on the Bolsheviks and Soviet Russia.
26 May–6 June	General strike held in Norway. Called by the Norwegian trade-union federation in solidarity with a strike by seamen against massive wage cuts, the general strike involves 120,000 workers, virtually the entire proletariat of the country.
9–15 June	Communist Women's Movement holds Second International Conference in Moscow.
22 June–12 July	Third Congress of Communist International in Moscow. The congress issues the watchword of 'To the masses!' and adopts a united-front perspective.
3–19 July	First Congress of Red International of Labour Unions is held in Moscow.

9, 14–23 July Second Congress of Communist Youth International meets in Moscow. The congress is attended by 380 delegates from 41 countries.

20–22 July First session of RILU Central Council.

25–30 July French CGT congress in Lille is the scene of a heated struggle between the left and right, with a narrow right-wing majority. Within a year the confederation splits down the middle, as the expelled left wing forms the Unitary CGT (CGTU), which joins RILU in November 1923.

1922

1 January Executive committees of the Communist International and RILU issue a joint appeal, 'For the United Front of the Proletariat'. This call signals the beginning of a campaign waged by the Comintern and Profintern around the world for a united front of workers' organisations to defend the basic interests of the working class against the international capitalist offensive.

Glossary

AAU See General Workers' Union, Germany

Ablett, Noah [1883–1935] South Wales coal miner from age twelve; joined Independent Labour Party 1907, becoming syndicalist; leading figure in Miners' Reform Movement 1911; member of Miners' Federation of Great Britain executive committee 1921–6.

American Federation of Labor [AFL] federation of US craft unions founded 1881; 3.9 million members in 1921; split 1935–6 with formation of Congress of Industrial Organizations; reunited 1955.

Amiens Charter adopted by French CGT in 1906; a programmatic platform of revolutionary syndicalism.

Amsterdam International See International Federation of Trade Unions

Anderson, Z. F. delegate from Latvia to RILU First Congress and Comintern Third Congress 1921; elected to RILU Central Council.

Andreev, Andrej [1895–1971] joined Bolsheviks 1914; a founder of Petrograd Metalworkers' Union 1917; member of All-Russian Central Trade Union Council; attended RILU founding congress 1921; candidate member [1926–30] and full member [1932–52] of CP Political Bureau; deputy chairman of USSR Council of Ministers 1946–53.

Andreytchine, George [1894–1950] Bulgarian socialist; went to US 1913 and joined IWW; organiser of 1916 Mesabi Iron Range strike; arrested 1917 and defendant in Chicago mass IWW trial; became a Communist and fled to Russia 1921; attended RILU founding congress, elected to its Central Council; later held responsibilities in Soviet economy and foreign ministry; supported Trotskyist opposition from 1923; arrested 1927; recanted 1929 and freed; arrested 1935 and sent to labour camp; freed by 1941; worked in Soviet Information Bureau during WWII; in Bulgarian Foreign Ministry after 1945; arrested 1949 on charge of espionage; taken to USSR, tried, and shot.

Appleton, William A. [1859–1940] secretary 1907–38 of British General Federation of Trade Unions, a sub-body of Trades Union Congress [TUC]; elected president of Amsterdam International 1919; resigned November 1920 due to opposition of TUC General Council.

Der Arbeiter-Rat publication created by German workers' councils 1919; became de facto organ of USPD left wing when workers' councils were dissolved under pressure of SPD.

Argentine Regional Workers' Federation [Federación Obrera Regional Argentina, FORA] first national union federation in Argentina; formed 1901 with anarcho-syndicalist character; split into anarchist and syndicalist wings 1915; represented at

RILU founding congress 1921; anarchist wing was initially sympathetic to Comintern and applied for RILU membership, but broke with it by 1922; syndicalist wing included a pro-communist current in which CP members participated.

Arlandis, Hilario [1888–1939] Spanish revolutionary syndicalist; leading militant of CNT from Valencia; delegate to RILU founding congress, where he supported CNT affiliation; after CNT rejected affiliation he helped form pro-RILU CNT-Revolutionary Syndicalist Committees, which in 1930 became Worker-Peasant Bloc [BOC]; edited *La Batalla*; expelled from BOC 1932, after which he joined CP; killed in air attack at conclusion of Spanish Civil War.

Armstrong presumed reference to Sir W.G. Armstrong Whitworth & Co Ltd., a major world armaments manufacturer.

Artem See Sergeyev, Fyodor Andreyevich

L'Atelier [The Workshop] French syndicalist publication 1920–33, published weekly and then monthly by CGT.

Avanti! [Forward!] central daily organ of Italian Socialist Party [PSI]; began publication 1896.

Azimonti, Carlo [1888–1958] Italian trade unionist; became socialist 1904; member of CGL National Council 1912; secretary of CGL and director of *Battaglie Sindicali* from 1921; CGL representative at RILU founding congress 1921; member of reformist Unitary Socialist Party [PSU] after its founding in 1922; forced out of trade-union activity under Fascist rule.

Bakunin, Mikhail [1814–76] Russian anarchist; leader of split with Marxist forces in First International.

Baldesi, Gino [1879–1934] Italian trade unionist; assistant secretary of CGL 1918; a leader of reformist wing of PSI and trade unions 1920–1; left PSI with reformist forces October 1922, becoming member of Unitary Socialist Party [PSU]; vainly sought accommodation between CGL and Fascists; withdrew from political activity 1927.

Ballister See Minor, Robert

Barbusse, Henri [1873–1935] French novelist; wrote about experiences in French army during WWI; founded left-wing veterans' association in France at conclusion of war; joined CP 1923.

Barker, Tom [1887–1970] born in England; lived in New Zealand 1909–14; secretary of New Zealand SP and IWW member; moving to Australia, he edited IWW's *Direct Action*; repeatedly arrested and jailed for anti-war and anti-conscription activities during WWI; deported to Chile 1918; dropped off over border in Argentina; worked on wharves in Buenos Aires and became a leader of Marine Transport Workers' Union; went to Europe as representative of Argentine Regional Workers' Federation [FORA] and its seamen's union; delegate to December 1920 Berlin syndicalist conference and to RILU founding congress 1921;

afterward worked in US for Kuzbas colonisation project until 1926; later settled in London, working for Soviet oil-exporting business; subsequently active in Labour Party left wing.

Bartels, Arthur a leader of German *Unionen*; during WWI member of USPD; editor of its magazine *Ruhrwarte* 1919; joined Gelsenkirchen Free Workers' Union; was its delegate to RILU founding congress, at which he supported syndicalist opposition; joined Gelsenkirchen Hand and Brain Workers' union 1921, which was affiliated to RILU; editor of *freie Bergarbeiter* from November 1921 to 1922.

Batt, Dennis E. [Billings] [b. 1886] tool-and-die maker 1910–19; leader of Communist Party of America 1919; split from CPA and became national secretary of Michigan-based Proletarian Party and editor of its main publication 1920; delegate from Detroit Federation of Labor to RILU congress 1921; expelled from Proletarian Party during first half of 1920s; became labour journalist and supporter of AFL; later editor of *Detroit Labor News*.

Baumeister, Albert [1882–1953] German trade unionist; joined SPD 1910; supporter of Germany's war effort in WWI; after war became member of International Labour Office's Berlin bureau.

Belenky. Probably a reference to **Zakhar Moiseevich Belenky** [1888–1940] Bolshevik from 1905; member of executive committee of Petrograd trade-union council 1917–18; trade-union leader in Urals 1919–20; chairman of Southeast Bureau of All-Union Trade Union Council 1922–7; arrested and shot during Stalin purges.

Belinkis, M. delegate to 1921 RILU founding congress from IWW's Metal and Machinery Workers Industrial Union, credentialed by New York District Council of IWW locals.

Bell, Thomas [1882–1944] Scottish foundry worker; joined Independent Labour Party 1900; a founder and leader of Socialist Labour Party from 1903; leading figure in wartime Shop Stewards' movement; a founder of British CP 1920 and head of its propaganda department to 1925; delegate to Comintern Third Congress and RILU founding congress 1921; remained a leading member of CP until his death.

Bergmann See Meyer, Ludwig

Bernstein, Eduard [1850–1932] German socialist; collaborator of Engels; leading exponent of revisionist current in SPD from 1898; member of USPD during WWI; opponent of Comintern; rejoined SPD 1919; Reichstag deputy 1902–7, 1912–18, 1920–8.

Bianchi, Giuseppe [1888–1921] Italian trade unionist; joined PSI between 1906 and 1908; went to school in Germany, where he worked for Italian agitation organ of German trade unions; expelled from Germany for insulting Kaiser; after living in Switzerland and France, he returned to Italy 1914; editor of *Battaglie sindicali* 1919; attended June 1920 preliminary meeting in Moscow that mapped out RILU formation; elected to CGL executive February 1921; CGL secretary for propaganda and education 1921; CGL representative at RILU founding congress 1921; became ill shortly after leaving Russia and died.

Bidegaray, Marcel [1875–1944] general secretary of French railway union from 1909; member of CGT confederal executive; member of French SP; went with Dissidents in 1921 SP split; supported CGT majority; part of reformist split from SP 1933; died in internment camp during WWII.

Billings See Batt, Dennis E.

Bleimann, Martin [1886–1938] Estonian Communist; general secretary of legal Independent Socialist Workers' Party 1921; delegate to Comintern Third Congress and RILU founding congress; elected to RILU Central Council; later a professor at Communist University in Leningrad; arrested during Stalin purges and executed.

Bloch, Rosa [1880–1922] joined Swiss SP 1912; active in socialist women's movement, president of SP women's committee 1918; CP member following 1921 split; member of Comintern's International Women's Secretariat; delegate to Comintern Third Congress, RILU founding congress, and Second Communist Women's Conference 1921; died July 1922 following botched operation.

Bloor, Ella Reeve [Emmons] [1862–1951] active in US temperance and women's suffrage movement during 1890s; joined socialist movement 1897; prominent in US SP; joined Communist movement 1919; delegate to Second Communist Women's Conference and RILU founding congress 1921; member of CP Central Committee 1932–48.

Boal, Evelio [1884–1921] Spanish unionist; member of CNT central committee from 1918; became provisional CNT secretary general February 1919; murdered in Barcelona by police in extrajudicial execution.

Boisson, Louis [1885–1963] French revolutionary syndicalist; a plasterer, he was a leader of construction workers' union in Marseilles; joined SP before 1910; led small left-wing split from CGT in August 1920 that established Confederation of Workers of the World [CTM]; delegate to RILU founding congress 1921; became part of CGTU April 1922 together with CTM; later an anarchist; imprisoned 1938–9 for advocating military disobedience.

Bolotin, Samuel [b. 1895] machinist; delegate to 1921 RILU founding congress from IWW's Metal and Machinery Workers Industrial Union; credentialed by New York District Council of IWW locals.

Borden See Foster, William Z.

Borghi, Armando [1882–1968] Italian anarchist; frequently imprisoned and exiled; joined Italian Syndicalist Union [USI] 1912; took anti-war position in 1914 and became USI secretary; visited Russia 1920 and met with Lenin; forced into exile from Italy 1923; lived in US 1926–45; remained active in anarchist movement until his death.

Bouwman, Engelbertus 'Bertus' [1882–1955] Dutch docker; joined National Labour Secretariat [NAS] 1905, becoming a central leader; took anti-war position during WWI; broke with anarcho-syndicalists within NAS; joined CP 1920; NAS delegate to December 1920 Berlin syndicalist conference and RILU founding congress 1921; left CP 1927; helped found left-socialist Revolutionary Socialist Party; secretary of NAS 1933–40; member of Social-Democratic Party after 1945, although he largely withdrew from political activity.

Briand, Aristide [1862–1932] French politician; member of SP until he accepted ministerial post 1906; premier of France eleven times, including 1921–2.

British Labour Party formed 1906 by trade-union federation and Independent Labour Party; member of Second International; voted to oppose affiliation of CP 1920; 4.5 million members in 1921.

Brouckère, Louis de [1870–1951] joined Belgian Workers' Party early 1890s; criticised leadership's reformist stance before 1914; adopted social-chauvinist position during WWI and joined government; member of government council 1919–21; leader of party until his death.

Browder, Earl [Joseph Dixon] [1891–1973] joined SP at age fifteen; worked with Foster in Syndicalist League of North America; joined CP 1919; delegate to 1921 RILU congress representing Kansas miners; worked closely with Trade Union Education League; became CP general secretary 1930; repudiated by party 1945 as scapegoat for its wartime line opposing working-class struggles and supporting US war effort; expelled 1946.

Bukharin, Nikolai [1888–1938] joined Bolsheviks 1906; in exile 1911–17; member Bolshevik Central Committee 1917–30; one of central Russian Communist leaders within Comintern from 1919; chairman of Comintern 1926–9; opposed Stalinist forced collectivisation and led Right Opposition in Soviet CP 1928; deprived of leadership posts 1929; executed after Stalin frame-up trial.

Buozzi, Bruno [1881–1944] Italian metalworker; joined PSI 1905; general secretary of metalworkers' union from 1909; member of CGL directing council 1912 and executive commission 1918–21; joined reformist Unitary Socialist Party [PSU] 1922; secretary of CGL from 1925; fled to France 1926 and founded exile leadership of CGL; member of anti-fascist resistance during WWII; arrested and shot by German troops shortly before liberation of Rome.

Burleson, Albert S. [1863–1937] US postmaster general 1913–21; instituted racial segregation in Post Office; prominent enforcer of Espionage

Act, preventing circulation of anti-war and radical material through the mail.

Callam, Albert [1887–1956] German construction worker; member of SPD from 1907; joined Spartacus group 1916, USPD 1917, and KPD 1919; delegate to RILU founding congress 1921; managing director of KPD publishing operations until 1933; emigrated 1934, living in Czechoslovakia, France, and Mexico; worked in East Germany after WWII.

Carm, Adolf S. [c. 1877–1958] Swedish immigrant to US; organiser for Scandinavian Socialist Labour Federation 1906–12; from 1912 assistant secretary and general organiser for what became Workers' International Industrial Union [WIIU]; edited *Industrial Union News* 1920–1; delegate to RILU founding congress.

Carnegie, Andrew [1835–1919] US capitalist magnate; leading figure in steel industry.

Cascaden, Gordon [1884–1948] radical journalist and IWW activist from Windsor, Ontario; edited *Detroit Labor News* and *Auto Workers' News*; wrote for *Federated Press, New York Call*, and *Daily Worker*, as well as local Windsor papers; represented Lumber Workers Industrial Union of Canada at 1921 RILU founding congress and sided with anarcho-syndicalist opposition, but maintained life-long public support for Soviet Union.

CGL See General Confederation of Labour, Italy

CGT See General Confederation of Labour, France

CGTU See Unitary General Confederation of Labour, France

Chin Min [b. 1886] clerk from Seoul; until September 1919 a member of Youth of Korea party; represented Korean Workers' Union at RILU founding congress 1921.

Clemenceau, Georges [1841–1929] prime minister of France 1917–20; a framer of Versailles Treaty.

CNT See National Confederation of Labour, Spain

Colombino, Emilio [1884–1933] Italian trade unionist; member of PSI; reformist; a national leader of metalworkers' union; member of CGL delegation to Second Comintern Congress 1920; attended June 1920 preliminary meeting in Moscow that mapped out RILU formation; later collaborated with fascist unions.

Communist Party of Germany [Kommunistische Partei Deutschlands, KPD] founded December 1918 by Spartacus League and other Communists; fused with USPD majority December 1920 and became briefly known as United CP [VKPD] claiming 350,000 members; 157,000 dues-paying members summer 1921.

Communist Workers' Party of Germany [Kommunistische Arbeiter-Partei Deutschlands, KAPD] formed April 1920 by ultraleft current expelled from CP with over 40,000 members; official sympathising organisation of

Comintern 1920–1; only a few hundred members still active by late 1923.

Confederation of Workers of the World, France [Confédération des travailleurs du monde, CTM] established August 1920 as small left-wing split from CGT; attended RILU founding congress 1921; joined CGTU April 1922.

Cook, Arthur James [1883–1931] South Wales miner; joined Independent Labour Party [ILP] 1905; member of South Wales Miners Federation and its executive committee 1906–18; took anti-war stance during WWI and supported Russian Revolution; founding member of CP July 1920, but resigned early 1921 and rejoined ILP; became member of Executive Committee of Miners Federation of Great Britain 1921; its national secretary from 1924 until his death.

Cosgrove, Pope Pascal [Jack Crosby] [1880–1947] born in Canada; a leader of US SP left wing; elected to CP of America Central Executive Committee 1920; delegate in 1921 to Comintern Third Congress; delegate to RILU First Congress with credentials from Amalgamated Metal Workers, Amalgamated Food Workers, Boot and Shoe Workers, and Amalgamated Clothing Workers minority; treasurer in early 1920s of group organising US workers for Kuzbas colony in USSR; in late 1920s an organiser in Brooklyn for shoe workers, food workers, and dental laboratory workers; sent to China on Comintern mission 1929; a vice president of National Council for Protection of Foreign Born Workers in 1940s.

Creusot presumed reference to Schneider-Creusot, a major French arms manufacturer.

Crosby, Jack See Cosgrove, Pope Pascal

CSR See Revolutionary Syndicalist Committees, France

CTM See Confederation of Workers of the World, France

D'Aragona, Ludovico [1876–1961] Italian trade unionist; joined PSI 1892; a founder of metalworkers' union; spokesperson for CGL union federation from its formation in 1906, and was its general secretary 1918–25; PSI parliamentary deputy 1919–24; headed trade-union delegation to Soviet Russia and was consultative delegate to Comintern Second Congress 1920; attended June 1920 preliminary meeting in Moscow that mapped out RILU formation; opposed founding CP 1921 and remained in PSI; joined reformist Unitary Socialist Party [PSU] 1922; government minister 1946–51.

Dario See Mari, Duilio

Darsono Notosudirdjo, Raden [1893–1976] member of Central Council of Sarekat Islam; founding member of Indonesian CP; its president 1920–5; delegate to Comintern Third Congress and RILU founding congress 1921; member of ECCI 1928–30; lived in Netherlands 1935–50; returned to Indonesia, where he left Communist movement and worked for Ministry of Foreign Affairs.

Dashkevich delegate to RILU founding congress from Ukraine 1921; elected to first RILU Central Council.

Dashnak Party [Dashnaktsutyun] Armenian nationalist party founded 1890; fought oppression by both tsarist Russia and Ottoman Empire; opposed October Revolution and headed Armenian anti-Soviet government 1918–20.

Dautkus, Leopold [b. 1878] member of German *Unionen*; carpenter from Braunschweig in central Germany; represented General Workers' Union [AAU] and KAPD at RILU founding congress 1921.

De Leon, Daniel [1852–1914] central leader of US Socialist Labor Party.

Denikin, Anton Ivanovich [1872–1947] Russian tsarist general; a leader of White Army during civil war; emigrated 1920.

Denisov, I. delegate to RILU founding congress from Ekaterinoslav trade-union council in Ukraine.

De Visser, Louis Leonardus Hendrikus [1878–1945] joined Dutch Social-Democratic Workers' Party 1899; became a leader of National Labour Secretariat [NAS]; belonged to left-wing *Tribune* group after 1909 party split; delegate to Comintern Third Congress and RILU founding congress 1921; remained a leader of CP; imprisoned by Germans 1941; died in British bombing of ship carrying concentration camp survivors.

Díaz Ramírez, Manuel [1888–1962] born in Mexico; lived in US and was active in labour movement 1907–19; founding member Mexican CP 1919 and its general secretary 1921–2; delegate to Comintern Third Congress and RILU founding congress 1921; CP treasurer 1927–8; later withdrew from politics and devoted himself to history of workers' movement in Mexico.

Dimitrov, Georgi [1882–1949] Bulgarian printworker; joined trade-union movement 1900 and SDP 1902; Central Committee member from 1909 of left-wing Tesniaki faction, which became CP; secretary of General Trade Union Federation 1904–23; delegate to 1921 Comintern Third Congress and to RILU founding congress, which elected him to its Central Council; elected to RILU Executive Bureau 1924; secretary of Balkan Communist Federation 1926–7; directed West European Bureau of Comintern 1929–33; arrested in Nazi Germany March 1933 and charged with responsibility for Reichstag fire; acquitted and went to Russia; general secretary of Comintern 1935–43; prime minister of Bulgaria 1946–9.

Disch, Johann Hermann Moritz [1888–1959] a leader of German *Unionen*; joined SPD 1908; secretary of KPD in Bremen 1919; supporter of leftist opposition in party that became KAPD; official in seamen's union, which joined AAU; delegate to RILU founding congress 1921; later lived in Vienna, Prague, Zurich, and Paris; joined Austrian SP 1925; in Nazi concentration camps 1939–45.

Dissidents See French Socialist Party

Dixon, Joseph See Browder, Earl

Djaparidze, Prokofy [1880–1918] Georgian bootmaker; joined Russian social-democratic movement 1898; Bolshevik; chair of executive committee and commissar of internal affairs in Baku Commune 1918; executed following its overthrow.

Domínguez Rodríguez, José [d. 1921] member of CNT; murdered in Barcelona by Spanish repressive forces in extrajudicial assassination.

Donnelly, Ed member of IWW's Agricultural Workers Industrial Union no. 110; delegate to 1921 IWW convention.

Drewnitzky, Viktor [1886–1962] German machinist; joined SPD youth organisation 1904; joined Spartacus League 1917; founding member of KPD 1919; founding member of KAPD, later rejoining KPD; represented General Workers' Union [AAU] at founding RILU congress; delegate to Comintern Third, Fourth, and Fifth congresses; delegate to RILU founding congress 1921; member of RILU secretariat in Moscow 1924–5; held in Nazi concentration camps 1933–45; later headed state shipyard in East Germany.

Dugoni, Enrico [1874–1945] Italian trade unionist; joined PSI mid-1890s; a leader of PSI and CGL; delegate to Kienthal Conference 1916; in PSI right wing after WWI; part of labour/PSI delegation to Soviet Russia 1920; opposed formation of CP in 1921 split; victim of several Fascist attacks; left PSI in split that founded reformist Unitary Socialist Party [PSU]; arrested for anti-fascist activities 1930 and 1932.

Dumoulin, Georges [1877–1963] joined French Workers' Party [POF] 1890s; became CGT asssisant treasurer 1910; opposed 'Sacred Union' and supported Zimmerwald movement during WWI, but rallied to CGT majority 1918; member of 'Dissident' SP after 1920 split; official in International Labour Office 1924–32; CGT secretary for northern region 1936–8; supporter of Vichy regime during WWII; sentenced to death in absentia for his collaboration; hid in a convent 1945–51, after which his sentence was reversed.

Earsman, William [1884–1965] born in Scotland; lathe operator; moved to Australia 1910; member SP 1911; leader of metalworkers' union 1915; influenced by IWW; co-founder of CP 1920; delegate to Comintern Third Congress and RILU founding congress 1921; refused readmission to Australia 1923; moved to England; left CP around 1927; joined British Labour Party 1934.

Emmons See Bloor, Ella Reeve

Engels, Frederick [1820–95] lifelong collaborator of Karl Marx; co-author of Communist Manifesto; a leader of First International 1864–72; political and theoretical leader of revolutionary workers' movement after death of Marx; close adviser of Second International 1889–95.

Farwig, Heinrich [b. 1879] German typesetter; member of SPD; joined USPD 1917 and then Spartacus League; delegate to RILU founding congress 1921; from 1924 an editor of *Die Rote Fahne* and member of KPD's national trade-union department; expelled from KPD as rightist 1929; became functionary in CP (Opposition) [KPO].

FAUD See Free Workers' Union of Germany

Feliu, Antoni [d. 1921] Catalan anarcho-syndicalist; treasurer of CNT; murdered in Barcelona by Spanish repressive forces in extrajudicial assassination.

Fimmen, Eduard 'Edo' [1881–1942] leader of Dutch trade-union federation from 1907; secretary of Amsterdam International 1919–23; forced to resign November 1923 due to his support of united front with Communists and left-wing unionists; leader of International Transport Workers' Federation from 1919 until his death.

Fiurstian elected to RILU Central Council from Armenia.

Flaubert, Gustave [1821–80] French novelist and prime mover of realist school.

Flynn pseudonym of US delegate at RILU congress; a possible reference to Dennis E. Batt; for a discussion of his identity, see page 164, note 2.

Foster, William Z. [Borden] [1881–1961] joined American SP 1901 and IWW 1909; travelled to Europe 1910–11 and was influenced by French syndicalism; returned to US and formed Syndicalist League of North America 1912–14; worked as organiser for AFL unions during WWI; led steel strike of 1919; formed Trade Union Educational League 1920; attended and spoke at RILU founding congress 1921; joined CP 1921; a leader of CP until his death.

Free Agricultural Workers' Association [Freier Landarbeiterverband] German syndicalist union founded 1920; 30,000 members in 1921; attended RILU First Congress.

Free trade unions [Freie Gewerkschaften] See General German Trade Union Federation

Free Unions [Freie Unionen] German syndicalist unions.

Free Workers' Union of Germany [Freie Arbeiter-Union Deutschlands, FAUD] anarcho-syndicalist union; founded 1919; 150,000 members at its peak; rejected dictatorship of proletariat and degenerated into sect; disbanded by Nazis 1933.

French Socialist Party [Section française de l'Internationale ouvrière / French Section of the Workers' International, SFIO] formed 1905 as fusion of French socialist parties; took chauvinist position during WWI; centrists won majority 1918; 180,000 members at time of December 1920 Tours Congress, which voted to join Comintern and change name to CP;

minority ('Dissidents') split off and retained old name; 50,000 members in February 1923.

Gaudeux, Jean [1896–1992] French travelling salesman and revolutionary syndicalist; wounded in WWI; delegate to RILU founding congress; elected to executive of Revolutionary Syndicalist Committees [CSR] July 1921; during late 1920s a member of Socialist-Communist Party and from 1930 the Party for Proletarian Unity [PUP], which joined French SP in mid-1930s; active in resistance to German occupation.

Gaye, Georges [1881–1948] member of French metalworkers' union and SP during WWI; a supporter of Committee for the Third International; became CP member after its founding in 1920; delegate to RILU founding congress 1921; opposed 'Bolshevisation' of CP 1925 and left party.

Gelsenkirchen Free Workers' Union members of anarcho-syndicalist FAUD in Gelsenkirchen who left it November 1920, with 110,000 members; stronghold in Rhineland-Westphalia coal district; 150,000 claimed membership in 1921; KPD members played leading role; joined RILU; in November 1921 fused with two other unions to form Hand and Brain Workers' Union, which affiliated to RILU; dissolved into mainstream unions 1925.

General Confederation of Labour, France [Confédération générale du travail, CGT] founded 1895; initially syndicalist in orientation; leadership followed reformist course from 1914; left wing driven out in 1921; 600,000 members in spring 1921; split became definitive December 1921, with expelled left forming CGTU; CGT membership declined to 250,000 following split.

General Confederation of Labour, Italy [Confederazione generale del lavoro, CGL] formed 1906; allied with Italian Socialist Party [PSI] until late 1922; 2 million members September 1920, 1.1 million 1921; 400,000 members end of 1922; virtually disappeared by end of 1923; expressed sympathy with RILU but remained affiliated to Amsterdam International; suppressed under fascism.

General German Trade Union Federation [Allgemeiner Deutsche Gewerkschaftsbund, ADGB] founded 1919 as reconstitution of earlier Social-Democratic union federation; often referred to as 'free trade unions'; largest union federation in Germany; aligned with SPD; over 7 million members in 1921; dissolved by Nazis 1933.

General Union of Workers, Spain [Unión General de Trabajadores, UGT] union federation formed 1888; close relationship with Spanish SP; over 200,000 members in October 1920; 240,000 members end of 1922.

General Workers' Union, Germany [Allgemeine Arbeiter-Union, AAU] founded February 1920 by ultraleft current that became KAPD; advocated factory committees to replace trade unions; 150,000 members in 1920–

1, declining to 10,000 by end of 1921; maintained existence as sect until banned in 1933.

Gennari, Egidio [1876–1942] Italian Communist; teacher; joined PSI 1897; a leader of its left wing; internationalist during WWI; PSI political secretary 1920; supported Communists in 1921 Livorno split; a vice chairman of Presidium of Comintern Third Congress; favoured fusion with PSI 1922; elected to ECCI 1921; wounded several times by Fascists; forced into emigration 1926; carried out numerous Comintern assignments; died in USSR.

German Seamen's Union [Deutscher Seemansbund, DSB] – formed 1918–19 as part of revolutionary council movement; joined FAUD early 1920; 18–20,000 members in mid-1919; 6,000 in 1921; attended RILU founding congress 1921; separated from FAUD 1922 and joined RILU; merged with German Transport Association 1926.

Ghioldi, Rodolfo [1897–1985] joined Argentine SP 1915; elected vice president of Communist Youth Federation 1917; founding member of CP 1918; delegate to Comintern Third Congress and RILU founding congress 1921; later representative of Comintern's South American Secretariat; general secretary of Argentine CP 1928–34; CP member until his death.

Gieseler, Emil delegate to RILU founding congress from German Seamen's Union.

Girinis, Sergei [Raul Ginsburg] [1882–1961] revolutionary trade-union activist and journalist in Belarus and Lithuania; joined Russian social-democratic movement 1902; leader in Lithuania of Menshevik Internationalist group after 1916; arrested in 1920 and left Lithuania for Soviet Russia in political prisoner exchange; attended RILU founding congress 1921 and was elected to its Central Council representing Lithuania; worked as journalist for *Pravda, Trybuna Radziecka*, and other periodicals; elected to Lithuanian CP Central Committee 1924; died in Moscow.

Gliński See Królikowski, Stefan

Glozman, B. French revolutionary syndicalist, of Russian origin; delegate in 1921 from CGT minority to Comintern Third Congress and RILU founding congress, where he supported Rosmer position; elected to French CP control commission 1922; joined SP 1936.

Godonnèche, Victor [1886–1942] French revolutionary syndicalist; a founding leader of Revolutionary Syndicalist Committees and Committee for the Third International; delegate to December 1920 Berlin syndicalist conference; delegate to RILU founding congress 1921; joined CP after return from Moscow; assistant secretary of CGTU-affiliated printworkers' union; member of *L'Humanité* Administrative Commission 1923–4; part of April 1924 split of revolutionary syndicalists from CP that established *Révolution prolétarienne* in 1925.

'Golos Truda' group Russian anarcho-syndicalist collective named for journal *Golos Truda* (The Voice of Labour) founded in New York 1911; resumed publication in Petrograd 1917 as organ of Petrograd Union of Anarcho-Syndicalist Propaganda; after paper was shut down in 1918, the collective maintained at least semi-legal existence until 1929.

Gompers, Samuel [1850–1924] president of American Federation of Labor 1886–1924 (except for 1895); advocated collaboration with employers, counterposing 'pure-and-simple unionism', based on craft unions, to industrial unionism; supported US entry into WWI; member of labour commission at Versailles conference.

Gorbanov, Petko [b. 1883] engineer; member of Bulgarian Tesniaki from 1911, which became CP; delegate to RILU founding congress 1921.

Gorter, Herman [1864–1927] writer and poet; joined Dutch Social-Democratic Workers' Party [SDAP] 1897; founder of *De Tribune* 1907; a leader of left-wing SDP after 1909 split; internationalist during WWI; supporter of Zimmerwald Left; CP founding member 1918; criticised Comintern policies from ultraleft standpoint; member of German KAPD 1921; left Comintern with it 1921.

Grassmann, Peter [1873–1939] German trade unionist; joined SPD 1893; supported reformist wing; held leadership posts in printers' union from 1894 and German trade-union federation 1919–33; briefly arrested by Nazis 1933.

Grölig, Franz locksmith; delegate from General Workers' Union of Germany [AAU] to RILU founding congress 1921.

Haidt, Ernst delegate from Austria to Comintern Third Congress and RILU founding congress 1921.

Hampel, Adalbert 'Vojtěch' [1872–1944] joined Federation of Czech Communist Anarchists 1910; secretary of Textile Workers' Union in Liberec (Reichenberg); founding member of Czechoslovak CP 1921 and editor of several Communist publications; delegate to 1921 Comintern Third Congress and RILU founding congress, where he served on presiding committee; a leader of Red Sports International; CP senator 1925–9; jailed by Nazis 1943; executed.

Hand and Brain Workers' Union See Union of Hand and Brain Workers

Handlíř, Jaroslav [1888–1942] member of Austro-Hungarian army in WWI, taken prisoner on Russian front; won to Bolshevism after October Revolution; helped found Czechoslovak Communist group in Russia and represented it at Comintern First Congress 1919; returned to Czechoslovakia and became a leader of CP; briefly imprisoned for role in December 1920 strike; delegate to Comintern Third Congress and RILU founding congress 1921; expelled from CP as rightist 1929; joined SDP; died at Auschwitz.

Hardy, George [1884–1966] born in England; emigrated to North America 1906; joined IWW; imprisoned 1917–19; became IWW general secretary May 1920; advocated joining Comintern; attended December 1920 Berlin syndicalist conference, after which he went to Russia and was won to communism; on his return began to organise Communist minority in IWW; after 1922 carried out international missions for RILU; member of Pan-Pacific Trade Union Secretariat 1927–9; active in British CP from 1933.

Harvey, George [1885–1949] British miners' union organiser; early member of Independent Labour Party; became organiser and writer for Socialist Labour Party; founding member of British CP 1920; left CP 1927 but remained sympathiser; Labour councillor 1928–37; continued as a miners' union organiser and local Labour Party elected official.

Hausding, Max delegate from German metalworkers' union from Chemnitz to RILU founding congress 1921; active in KPD opposition [KPO] in Chemnitz in late 1920s.

Haywood, William D. 'Big Bill' [1869–1928] elected secretary-treasurer of Western Federation of Miners 1900; founding member and first chairman of IWW 1905; member of SP National Executive Committee, excluded in 1912 for his syndicalist outlook; became IWW secretary-treasurer 1913; arrested 1917 on frame-up charges of treason and sabotage, convicted and sentenced to twenty years' imprisonment; jumped bail in 1921 and went to Soviet Russia, where he lived until his death; attended and spoke at Comintern Third Congress and RILU founding congress.

Heckert, Fritz [1884–1936] German Communist; construction worker; joined SPD 1902; member of Swiss socialist movement 1908–11; head of construction workers' union in Chemnitz 1912–18; member of Spartacus League during WWI; chaired workers' and soldiers' council in Chemnitz during November 1918 revolution; KPD founding member; Central Committee alternate 1919, full member from 1920; delegate to Comintern Third Congress and elected to ECCI 1921; delegate to RILU founding congress; later a member of its Central Council and Executive Bureau; represented KPD in Moscow 1932–4; died prior to Stalin purges.

Henderson, Arthur [1863–1935] British Labour Party chairman 1908–10 and 1914–17; party secretary 1911–34; elected president of Second International 1920; chief party whip in House of Commons 1914, 1921–3, 1925–7; secretary of state for foreign affairs 1929–31.

Hervé, Gustave [1871–1944] joined French socialist movement 1899; led ultraleft tendency in SP before WWI, calling for insurrection and draft resistance to halt threat of war; became pro-war ultra-nationalist in 1914; expelled from SP 1916; sympathetic to fascism in 1920s; initial supporter of Vichy regime during WWII.

Heuchel, Louise [b. 1892] French laundress and lathe worker during WWI; active in 1919 metalworkers' strike; delegate from CGT minority to Comintern Third Congress and RILU founding congress 1921; member of French CP and its women's commission; elected to CGTU executive committee 1922; in later years worked for International Labour Office.

Hilferding, Rudolf [1877–1941] born in Austria; joined socialist movement as student 1893; based in Germany from 1906; author of *Finance Capital* 1910; opposed SPD support of war credits after 1914; joined USPD 1918; opposed Comintern, remaining in rump USPD 1920; rejoined SPD in 1922 fusion; government minister of finance 1923, 1928–9; forced into exile 1933; arrested by French Vichy regime 1941; tortured and killed by Gestapo.

Hoelz, Max [1889–1933] German Communist; joined USPD during WWI; joined KPD 1919; led workers' armed detachments in Saxony 1920–1 during Kapp Putsch and March Action; expelled from KPD for indiscipline and supported KAPD; jailed in frame-up for murder 1921 and sentenced to life imprisonment; freed after international defence campaign; rejoined KPD; emigrated to USSR 1929; developed criticisms of Stalin regime; targeted by Stalin's secret police; drowned under mysterious circumstances.

Hörsing, Friedrich Otto [1874–1937] joined SPD 1894; executive secretary of German Metalworkers' Association in Upper Silesia 1905; governor in Prussian Saxony 1919–27; led suppression of workers during March Action 1921; expelled from SPD and founded German Social-Republican Party 1932.

Horthy, Miklós [1868–1957] Austro-Hungarian naval commander during WWI; a leader of counterrevolutionary forces that crushed Hungarian Soviet republic 1919 and carried out white terror; regent and dictator of Hungary 1920–44.

Howie, Jack [d. 1953] member of Australian Socialist Labor Party; active in anti-conscription fight during WWI; founding member of CP; president of New South Wales Trades and Labor Council 1919–22; delegate to RILU founding congress credentialed by union councils of New South Wales, Melbourne, and Perth; on his return convinced NSW council to affiliate to RILU; delegate to Comintern Third Congress; elected to Australian Labor Party executive when CP joined ALP 1923, but was removed 1924 when CP was excluded; general secretary of CP into late 1920s; remained member until his death.

Hubacher, Charles [1880–1944] secretary of Swiss Federation of Metalworkers and Watchmakers 1910; founder of weekly *La Nouvelle Inter-*

nationale; founding member of Swiss CP; delegate to Comintern Third Congress and RILU founding congress 1921; after returning from Moscow gave up party work and devoted himself to work as union official.

L'Humanité [Humanity] daily Paris newspaper of French SP and then CP; began publication 1904; 200,000 circulation in 1921.

Ibáñez, Jesús [1889–1948] joined Spanish Socialist Youth 1904, UGT 1905, and Socialist Group 1908; founder and editor of *La Batalla* 1918–19; joined CNT 1919, becoming general secretary of Construction Workers' Union of Asturias; delegate to 1921 Comintern Third Congress and RILU founding congress, where he supported CNT affiliation to RILU; member of Executive Committee of Revolutionary Syndicalist Committees; joined CP, but left it later in 1920s; took part in 1934 Asturias uprising; wounded as combatant in Spanish Civil War; exiled to France and then Mexico.

Independent Social-Democratic Party of Germany [Unabhängige Sozialdemokratische Partei Deutschlands, USPD] formed 1917 by left-wing opponents of SPD majority leadership; 800,000 members end of 1920; majority of party fused with KPD December 1920 and joined Comintern; minority retained name until merging with SPD November 1922; 210,000 members at time of merger.

Industrial Pioneer monthly magazine published by General Executive Board of IWW 1921–6; previously *One Big Union Monthly*.

Industrial Worker newspaper of IWW from 1907; published in Pacific Northwest until 1931, when it moved to Chicago; issued weekly 1921–5.

Industrial Workers of the World [IWW, Australia] established 1907; participated in 1916 miners' strike against conscription; declared illegal during WWI, with principal leaders convicted of 'high treason'; many members joined CP after 1920.

Industrial Workers of the World [IWW, United States] founded 1905 as revolutionary syndicalist union; opposed US participation in WWI; suffered severe repression 1917–18; sent delegates to founding RILU congress 1921 but rejected affiliation to it; many militants joined CP; went into rapid decline in 1920s.

International Council of Trade and Industrial Unions [International Trade Union Council, ITUC] founded 15 July 1920 at meeting of revolutionary unions called on initiative of ECCI and All-Russia Central Trade Union Councils; became RILU in 1921.

International Federation of Metalworkers association founded 1893 by national metalworkers' trade unions; affiliated to Amsterdam International; over 3 million members at end of 1922.

International Federation of Trade Unions [IFTU, Amsterdam International] founded by reformist-led unions at

July 1919 congress in Amsterdam; viewed as continuation of federation founded in 1901 as International Secretariat of National Trade Union Centres (which adopted IFTU name in 1913) and destroyed by WWI; 24 million members in 1921.

International Federation of Transport Workers association founded 1896 by national transport workers' trade unions; affiliated to Amsterdam International; over 2 million members in 25 countries in 1923.

International Labour Organisation [ILO] founded in 1919 as agency of League of Nations concerned with labour conditions, with International Labour Office in Geneva composed of government, labour, and employers' representatives in each country, with goal of world class collaboration; also known as International Labour Bureau; now a United Nations agency; its permanent secretariat is International Labour Office.

Italian Communist Party [Partito Comunista Italiano, PCI] formed January 1921 following split from Italian SP at Livorno Congress; 58,000 members at time of split; 43,000 by end of 1921.

Italian Railroad Workers' Union [Sindacato Ferrovieri Italiani, SFI] founded 1907; led by anarchist-socialist coalition; joined CGL 1925.

Italian Socialist Party [Partito Socialista Italiano, PSI] founded 1892; participated in Zimmerwald movement during WWI; affiliated to Comintern 1919; refused to expel reformist right wing; left wing split off at January 1921 Livorno Congress to form CP [PCI]; 200,000 members before Livorno Congress, dropping to 112,000 by October 1921 and 65,000 a year later; sent representatives to Comintern Third Congress; expelled Turati and right wing 1922; pro-Comintern minority subsequently joined CP.

Italian Syndicalist Union [Unione Sindacale Italiana, USI] Italian anarcho-syndicalist union federation; founded 1912 out of split in CGL; sent representatives to RILU congress 1921, but did not affiliate; contained both anarchist and syndicalist wings; 800,000 members in summer 1920, declining to 150,000 in 1921.

Jackson, John member of IWW's Building Construction Workers' Industrial Union no. 330; delegate to 1921 IWW convention.

Johnsen, Niels [1893–1931] Danish syndicalist; joined Social-Democratic youth group around 1910; leader of antimilitarist organisation 1915; editor of *Solidaritet* 1918; a leader of Union of Oppositional Trade Unions [Fagoppositionens Sammenslutning], representing it at Comintern Third Congress and RILU founding congress 1921; elected to RILU Central Council; joined Danish CP 1922; editor of *Arbejderbladet* 1922–4; left CP 1930 and rejoined social democrats.

Jouhaux, Léon [1879–1954] French unionist; general secretary of CGT 1909–47; originally influenced by anarchism and syndicalism, he became a social patriot during

WWI; member of Governing Body of International Labour Office 1919; vice president of Amsterdam International from 1919, retaining that office when IFTU was re-established in 1945; helped bring about split in CGT against left-wing unionists 1921–2; supporter of Popular Front 1936; in concentration camp during Nazi occupation; in 1947 broke with then-CP-led CGT and went on to found Force Ouvrière union federation.

Jousselin, Louis [1870–1934] French magistrate from tribunal of the Seine; heard case against CGT, ordering its dissolution in January 1921.

Kabanovsky, N. T. delegate to 1921 Comintern Third Congress and RILU founding congress from Azerbaijan central trade-union council; elected to RILU Central Council.

Kakhiani delegate to RILU First Congress from Azerbaijan Council of Trade Unions. Archival records (mandates and delegates' lists) render his name as both N.T. and Mikh. I. This may be a reference to **Mikhail Ivanovich Kakhiani** [1896–1937] – active in student protests and strikes of 1915–17; joined Bolsheviks July 1917; district CP leader in Moscow 1918–20; sent to Baku May 1920; member of Baku Committee of Azerbaijan CP 1920–21; Central Committee member of Georgian CP 1921–30, and was its first secretary 1924–30; arrested and shot during Stalin purges.

KAPD See Communist Workers' Party of Germany

Kapp, Wolfgang [1858–1922] reactionary Prussian politician; led attempted coup March 1920 to overthrow German republic and establish right-wing dictatorship; defeated by general strike and armed workers' resistance.

Kasparson, Alfred Petrovich [August Davydovich Sprogis] [1886–1975] born in Latvia; Bolshevik from 1903; moved to Moscow 1910 and then to Krasnoyarsk 1914; represented Far Eastern Council of Trade Unions at Comintern Third Congress and RILU founding congress 1921; elected to RILU Central Council from Far Eastern Republic; arrested 1938 during Stalin purges, sentenced to eight years in prison; died in Moscow.

Kautsky, Karl [1854–1938] born in Prague; joined Austrian Social Democracy 1874; collaborator of Engels; co-founder and leading editor of *Die Neue Zeit* 1883–1917; prominent Marxist theorist and opponent of revisionism before 1914; centrist apologist for social chauvinism during WWI; joined USPD 1917; opponent of October Revolution and of USPD fusion with CP; supporter of Two-and-a-Half International 1921–3; member of USPD rump that fused with SPD 1922; moved to Vienna 1924; fled Nazis 1938 and died in exile.

Kerensky, Alexander [1881–1970] prime minister of Russian Provisional

Government July–November 1917; overthrown by October Revolution; emigrated 1918.

Kilbom, Karl [1885–1961] joined Swedish socialist movement 1903; secretary of Young Social-Democratic Union 1914–17; internationalist and pacifist during WWI; founding member of Left Social-Democratic Party 1917, which became CP in 1921; delegate in 1921 to Comintern Third Congress and to RILU founding congress, where he was elected to its Central Council; expelled from CP 1929 for 'rightist deviation'; founded dissident Communist party that changed name to Swedish Socialist Party in 1934; rejoined Social-Democratic Party 1938.

Király, Albert [1883–1939] member Hungarian SDP 1900–19 and CP 1919–21; delegate to Comintern Third Congress and RILU founding congress; worked in Moscow for Red Sports International 1921; worked in Peasants' International [Krestintern] 1924–32; arrested and died during Stalin purges.

Kirker, William [1891–1950] Scottish coal miner; active in Bowhill branch of British Socialist Party 1913; local leader of Miners Association from 1917; elected to CP Executive 1921; in early 1920s a leader of left-wing breakaway union, the Fife Reform Miners' Union.

Knight, Joseph R. [1879–1936?] carpenter; born in England; emigrated to Canada 1907; organiser of One Big Union in Ontario and member of Canadian SP; sympathiser of CP; attended Comintern Third Congress and RILU founding congress 1921; joined CP on his return and became Central Committee member.

Knights of Labor first national US labour federation; founded 1869; reached peak membership of 700,000 in 1886; largely disappeared with creation of American Federation of Labor.

Koenen, Wilhelm [1886–1963] German Communist; joined SPD 1904 and USPD 1917; member of USPD Central Committee from 1919; commissar of workers' and soldiers' councils in Halle-Merseburg 1918; helped lead KPD-USPD merger 1920; a vice chairman of Presidium of Comintern Third Congress; active in KPD leadership until exile 1933–45; member of East German CP [SED] Central Committee from 1946; criticised after 1953 workers' rebellion for 'lack of vigilance'.

Kolchak, Aleksandr Vasilievich [1874–1920] tsarist admiral; head of White armies in Siberia and the Whites' 'supreme ruler' of Russia 1918–20; defeated by Red Army; captured and executed.

Der Kommunistische Gewerkschafter [The Communist Trade Unionist] weekly newspaper published by KPD in Berlin 1921–6.

Korolev, E. A. delegate to RILU founding congress from Council of Trade Unions of Abkhazia Soviet Republic 1921.

KPD See Communist Party of Germany

Krause, Joseph [b. 1896] Russian-American IWW member and printer; worked in Chicago printshop on IWW's Russian-language paper; delegate from IWW to RILU founding congress 1921, with credentials from IWW General Executive Board.

Królikowski, Stefan [Gliński] [1881–1937] member Polish Socialist Party [PPS] 1900–6, PPS-Left 1911–18; exiled to Siberia 1915–17; participated in October Revolution in Petrograd; returned to Warsaw and was elected to Polish CP Central Committee 1918; attended Comintern Third Congress and RILU founding congress 1921; worked in Soviet Union from 1929; arrested and shot during Stalin purges.

Krupp German armaments manufacturing dynasty; from 1909 until 1943 it was headed by Gustav Krupp [1870–1950].

Kunte, Adolf [b. 1888] typographer; delegate to Comintern Third Congress and RILU founding congress from Liberec (Reichenberg) in Czechoslovakia 1921; member of Communist Party.

Kupermanis, Mozus [1889?–1921] Communist and deputy chairman of Kurzeme Trade Union Central Bureau Presidium; shot by Latvian government forces on 9 June 1921 during deportation of 97 labour and political activists.

Kurulashvili, Georgy Davidovich [Kurulov] [1893–1937] joined Bolsheviks 1909; held positions in party and metalworkers' union in Samara; secretary of Georgian Council of Trade Unions 1925; secretary of Central Committee of Georgian CP 1927–8, and member of its Presidium 1928–30; deputy chairman Georgian republic 1934; arrested during Stalin purges and shot.

Kurulov, Georgy Davidovich See Kurulashvili, Georgy Davidovich

Labonne, Victor [1877–1954] French revolutionary syndicalist; mechanic from Paris; secretary of metalworkers' union from Seine; member of Revolutionary Syndicalist Committees [CSR]; delegate from CGT minority to Comintern Third Congress and RILU founding congress 1921; supported CGTU affiliation to RILU.

Lansink, Bernardus, Jr. [1884–1945] Dutch anarcho-syndicalist; became a leader of construction workers' union 1909; editor of *Het Bouwvak* from 1914; secretary of National Labour Secretariat [NAS] 1916–23; delegate to December 1920 Berlin conference of syndicalist unions; opposed NAS affiliation to RILU 1921; left NAS to form Dutch Syndicalist Trade Union [NSV] 1924; rejoined NAS 1929.

Lapierre, Jules [1873–1933] joined French socialist movement 1891; from 1903 a local and provincial trade-union leader; assistant general secretary of CGT during WWI; supporter of 'Sacred Union'; after war sought to assert national CGT control over left-wing unions.

Laufenberg, Heinrich [1872–1932] joined SPD 1904; a leader of left wing within SPD in Hamburg; elected chairman of workers' and soldiers' council there January 1919; a leader of National Bolshevism tendency; expelled from KPD 1920; joined KAPD but was expelled from it later that year; co-founder of Communist League; refused all contact with Nazis, unlike his collaborator Wolffheim.

Laukki, Leo [Tiura; Pivio] [1880–1938] joined workers' movement during 1905–6 revolution in tsarist-ruled Finland; moved to US 1907 and became part of Finnish Socialist Federation; became revolutionary syndicalist and joined IWW 1910; arrested 1918 and condemned to twenty years for espionage and conspiracy; member US CP 1921; out on bail, he fled to Soviet Russia; member of Finnish CP Central Committee 1921–5; delegate to Comintern Third Congress and RILU founding congress; elected to ECCI 1921; subsequently university professor in Soviet Union; arrested and shot during Stalin purges.

Lavagnini, Spartaco [1889–1921] Italian trade unionist and Communist in Florence; became active in railway union 1910; joined Italian SP; elected Tuscan regional secretary of railway workers' union 1920; founding member of PCI; murdered by Fascist squads 27 February 1921.

Leder, Zdzisław [1880–1938] leader of Social Democracy of the Kingdom of Poland and Lithuania from 1903; collaborator of Rosa Luxemburg; member of Polish CP from 1918 and Russian CP from 1921; head of German (Central European) section of International Council of Trade Unions in Berlin; delegate to RILU founding congress 1921; worked in RILU 1921–4 and Supreme Council of National Economy of USSR 1924–6; arrested during Stalinist purges; died in labour camp.

Legien, Carl [1861–1920] leading figure in German trade-union movement 1891–1920; joined SPD 1885; chairman of lathe operators' union 1887 and of confederation of prosocialist unions 1890; member of Reichstag from 1893; leading figure in international trade-union movement that became IFTU 1901–14; supported government effort in WWI; called general strike that defeated Kapp Putsch 1920.

Lemoine, Albert [1876–1927] French revolutionary syndicalist and railroad worker; a founder of Syndicalist Defence Committee 1909; joined Revolutionary Communist Federation 1911; delegate from CGT minority to Comintern Third Congress and RILU founding congress 1921; opposed Soviet Russia's actions against Kronstadt rising and Workers' Opposition; delegate to 1922–3 international syndicalist congress in Berlin; a member of CGT-Revolutionary Syndicalist federation formed 1926.

Lemoine, Claudine [1883–1976] assistant secretary of clothing workers' union of the Seine; delegate from

France to RILU founding congress 1921; general secretary of CGTU Federation of Clothing Workers.

Lenin, Vladimir Ilyich [1870–1924] became active in Russian social-democratic movement 1892–3; a founder of *Iskra* 1900; central leader of Bolsheviks from 1903; called for new International 1914; organised Zimmerwald Left to fight for this goal 1915–17; leader of October Revolution; chair of Soviet government 1917–24; founder and leader of Comintern.

Leval, Gaston [1895–1978] French anarchist who fled to Spain at beginning of WWI; member of CNT delegation to RILU founding congress 1921; after returning to Spain he opposed CNT affiliation to RILU; emigrated to Argentina 1923, but returned to Spain 1936 to participate in revolution and civil war; remained an anarchist until his death.

Levi, Paul [1883–1930] joined SPD 1909; collaborator of Rosa Luxemburg; joined Spartacus group during WWI; a founder of KPD 1918; chair of CP 1919–21; led struggle against ultraleftism and for unification with revolutionary majority in USPD; expelled from party as result of his public denunciation of March Action; founded Communist Working Group [KAG], which joined USPD and was part of SPD-USPD fusion in 1922; a leader of SPD left wing until his death.

Leviné, Eugen [1883–1919] born in Russia; participant in 1905 revolution; subsequently settled in Germany and joined SPD; member of Spartacus group and a leader of KPD; central leader of Bavarian council republic in 1919; arrested, tried, and shot after its overthrow.

Lezhava, Shamshe Konstantinovich [1876–1938] became active in social-democratic movement in Georgia 1896; Bolshevik from 1903; participant in 1905 and 1917 revolutions; delegate from Georgia to RILU founding congress 1921; arrested during Stalin purges 1937; shot.

Liebknecht, Karl [1871–1919] joined SPD 1900; first president of Socialist Youth International 1907–10; first member of German Reichstag to vote against war credits December 1914; a founder of Spartacus current; imprisoned for anti-war propaganda 1916; freed by 1918 revolution; a founding leader of KPD December 1918; murdered by rightist officers during Berlin workers' uprising January 1919.

Liebknecht, Wilhelm [1826–1900] participant in 1848 revolution in Germany; collaborator of Marx and Engels; cofounder of German Social Democracy 1869 and, with Bebel, leader of SPD until his death; chief editor of *Vorwärts* 1876–8, 1891–1900.

Lindgren, Edward [b. 1879] member US SP 1908; member of New York SP executive committee 1910–19; founding member of Communist Labor Party 1919; member of its central executive committee; delegate to

Second Comintern Congress 1920; member of Workers Party district executive committee 1919–22.

Lloyd George, David [1863–1945] British Liberal Party leader; prime minister 1916–22.

Loriot, Fernand [1870–1932] teacher; joined French SP 1901; treasurer of teachers' union 1912; a leader of internationalist forces in France during WWI; secretary of Committee for the Third International in France; became part of CP at Tours Congress; jailed 1920–1; elected CP international secretary January 1921; a vice chairman of Presidium of Comintern Third Congress; delegate to RILU founding congress; withdrew from CP leadership 1922; opposed 'Bolshevisation' 1925–6; quit party 1926; later collaborated with Left Opposition led by Trotsky.

Loucheur, Louis [1872–1931] French capitalist and politician; economic adviser at Versailles Treaty negotiations; minister of liberated regions 1921–2.

Louhikko, Emil Konstantin [1888–1961] metal foundry worker; became involved in Finnish labour and social-democratic movement 1910; secretary of Union of Metal Workers 1915; chairman of metal industry in Finnish soviet government 1918; escaped to Soviet Russia after its overthrow; briefly affiliated to CP; went back to Finland and became secretary of Central Trade Union Confederation [SAJ] 1920; arrested October 1920 and sentenced to 12 years in prison; released 1924; confederation secretary until 1926; secretary of new social-democratic Central Organisation of Trade Unions [SAK] 1930–9.

Louzon, Robert [1882–1976] joined French socialist movement 1899; worked on *La Vie ouvrière* from 1909; moved to Tunisia 1913; became part of Tunisian Communist movement 1919; expelled from Tunisia 1922; belonged to tendency in French CP led by Monatte and Rosmer; resigned from party December 1924 after their expulsion; part of *La révolution prolétarienne* group from 1925.

Lozovsky, Solomon Abramovich [1878–1952] joined Russian social-democratic movement 1901; joined Bolsheviks 1904; Bolshevik Conciliator 1908–11, after which he abandoned activity in Russian revolutionary movement; lived in Geneva and Paris 1909–17; active in French revolutionary labour movement, becoming member of French SP and CGT; during WWI was active in Committee for the Resumption of International Relations; returned to Russia 1917 and joined Bolsheviks; publicly opposed early moves by Bolshevik leadership, for which he was expelled; readmitted to party December 1919; became secretary of All-Russian Union of Railway Workers 1918; general secretary of RILU 1921–37; member of CPSU Central Committee 1939–49; deputy minister of foreign affairs 1939–45; acted as party representative in Jewish Antifascist Committee; arrested

1949 when committee was dissolved; tried secretly in 1952 together with 12 other prominent Yiddish writers in USSR; shot in prison.

Lumivuokko, Johan Henrik [1884–1938] chairperson of Finnish woodworkers' union 1912–17; chairman of Trade Union Confederation 1917–18; member of Social-Democratic Party 1914–17; commissar of labour in short-lived Finnish Soviet government 1918; fled to Soviet Russia after its defeat; delegate to 1921 Comintern Third Congress and to RILU founding congress, elected to its Central Council; worked as lecturer and journalist in Soviet Russia; arrested and executed during Stalin purges.

Lunacharsky, Anatoly V. [1875–1933] joined Russian social-democratic movement in early 1890s; became Bolshevik after 1903; broke with Bolsheviks as part of *Vperyod* group after 1905 revolution; rejoined 1917; people's commissar of education 1917–29; then chairman of Academic Committee under Central Executive Committee of USSR.

Lundström, Pâr Jeârj [b. 1885] typesetter from Stockholm; member of Social-Democratic Party 1901–17; founding member of Swedish CP; delegate in 1921 to RILU founding congress from Fackliga Propagandaförbundet [Trade Union Propaganda League].

Luxemburg, Rosa [1871–1919] born in Poland; a founder of Social Democracy of the Kingdom of Poland and Lithuania 1893; later lived in Germany; led SPD left wing in opposition to revisionist right wing and, after 1910, against 'Marxist Centre' led by Kautsky; leader of Spartacus current during WWI; imprisoned 1916–18; founding leader of KPD December 1918; arrested and murdered during workers' uprising in Berlin January 1919.

Maciejewski, Józef [1887–1937?] Polish bricklayer; joined social-democratic movement and construction workers' union in Warsaw 1906; imprisoned by tsarist regime 1908; escaped and went to Germany; returned to Poland 1913; founding member of Polish CP and its Central Committee; chairperson of construction workers' union; delegate to Comintern Third Congress and RILU founding congress 1921; repeatedly arrested in Poland for CP and union activities 1922–4; moved to USSR 1925; edited Polish-language newspaper published in Kiev; later worked in Soviet trade-union movement; arrested during Stalin purges and shot.

MacManus, Arthur [1891–1927] British metalworker; member of Socialist Labour Party from before war; leader of British Shop Stewards' movement during WWI; member Central Committee of British CP from its founding 1920; party chairman 1920–2; member of Comintern ECCI 1922–6; imprisoned in Britain for sedition 1925; died during visit to USSR and buried in Red Square.

Madsen, Alfred [1888–1962] leader and newspaper editor for Norwegian

Labour Party [NLP] from 1914; member of radical wing of party, which took over its leadership in 1918, affiliating to Comintern in 1919; editor in chief of *Ny Tid* 1920; delegate to Comintern Second and Third congresses 1920 and 1921; a secretary in Norwegian Confederation of Trade Unions, he represented it at RILU founding congress 1921; elected to RILU Central Council; member of NLP Central Committee 1920–35; its parliamentary leader 1925–31 and 1940; government minister 1928 and 1935–9.

Maier, Anton [1884–1954] German railroad worker in Württemberg; as USPD member he became part of Communist Party in 1920 fusion; member of state parliament; delegate in 1921 to RILU founding congress, at which he was elected to its Central Council; resigned from KPD November 1922 and joined SPD.

Mainwaring, William [1884–1971] Welsh coal miner and trade unionist; member of South Wales Miners Federation and Miners Federation of Great Britain; became an opponent of Communists in union; later a Labour Party member of Parliament.

majoritaires reformist leadership of French CGT; engaged in fight with left-wing forces of Revolutionary Syndicalist Committees [CSR], whom they would expel by the end of 1921.

Makhno, Nestor [1889–1935] Ukrainian anarchist; began involvement in armed actions agains tsarist regime 1906; imprisoned 1908–17; formed armed partisan band August 1917 that over next four years fought both white and red armies in Ukraine; following defeat of his forces by Red Army, he fled Russia in August 1921; eventually moved to Paris.

Malatesta, Errico [1853–1932] Italian anarchist and follower of Bakunin; began antimonarchist activity in 1860s; sentenced to death three times; spent 12 years in prison and 35 years in exile; lived in London 1900–13, before returning to Italy.

Malzahn, Heinrich [1884–1957] German mechanic; active in metalworkers' union; joined SPD 1906, USPD 1917; member of revolutionary shop stewards during WWI; member Executive of Workers' and Soldiers' Councils November 1918; chairman of Berlin Council of Factory Committees; joined Communist Party in 1920 fusion; opposed 1921 March Action but organised strike in Ruhr; represented VKPD opposition at Comintern Third Congress; delegate to RILU founding congress; expelled from party January 1922, he joined Communist Working Group [KAG]; rejoined KPD 1923–4; rejoined SPD 1930; imprisoned by Nazis 1940; joined East German SED 1946.

Mann, Tom [1856–1941] toolmaker; became active in trade-union movement 1881; joined British Social-Democratic Federation 1884; a leader of London dock strike 1889; first president of Dockers Union after 1889; founding member and secretary of Independent Labour Party from 1894;

lived in Australia 1901–10, coming under syndicalist influence; after returning to Britain tried to establish British syndicalist movement; opposed British war effort in WWI; joined British Socialist Party 1917; secretary of Amalgamated Engineering Union 1919–21; founding member of CP 1920; delegate to Comintern Third Congress 1921; delegate to RILU founding congress, where he was elected to its Central Council; chairman of British RILU bureau 1921–4, and of National Minority Movement 1924–9; remained in CP until his death.

Marchand, René [1888–1950] French journalist and correspondent in St. Petersburg; enlisted in Russian army during WWI; won to Bolshevism, he joined French Communist Group in Moscow; his articles and books on Russian Revolution had impact in France; delegate to Comintern Third Congress and RILU founding congress 1921; returned to France 1926; broke with communism a year later.

Mari, Duilio [Dario] [1889–1926] Italian anarcho-syndicalist; lived in US 1907–19 and joined IWW; leader of Italian Defense Committee in Chicago; deported from US in 1919 during 'Palmer Raids'; joined Italian Syndicalist Union [USI] 1920; one of its two delegates to RILU founding congress 1921; later was part of revolutionary syndicalist faction that opposed affiliation to RILU.

Martínez Anido, Severiano [1862–1938] Spanish military leader; civil governor of Barcelona 1920–4, notorious for carrying out murders of CNT members; minister of the interior 1925–30; minister of public order in fascist-controlled territory during Spanish Civil War 1938.

Marx, Karl [1818–83] co-founder with Engels of modern communist workers' movement; leader of Communist League 1847–52; co-author of Communist Manifesto; editor of *Neue Rheinische Zeitung* in 1848–9 German revolution; central leader of First International 1864–76; published first volume of *Capital* 1867.

Massiano See Repossi, Luigi

Matisons, Jēkabs [d. 1921] Communist and activist from Trade and Industrial Workers' Union in Latvia; shot by Latvian government forces on 9 June 1921 during expulsion of 97 labour and political activists.

Matta, Enea [1888–1974] Italian carpenter, active in factory committee movement in Turin and correspondent for *L'Ordine nuovo*; member of Communist faction of PSI that became Communist Party [PCI]; delegate to Comintern Third Congress from PCI, and to RILU founding congress from CGL minority 1921; forced to emigrate 1922; moved to France and joined CP; fought in resistance to German occupation in WWII.

Maurín, Joaquín [1896–1973] became active in Spanish revolutionary struggle 1911; joined CNT 1920; editor of *Lucha social* 1920–2; delegate to

Comintern Third Congress and RILU founding congress 1921; secretary of CNT executive committee October 1921–June 1922; a founder of CNT-Revolutionary Syndicalist, which was close to CP; left CNT 1923; CP member from 1924 until 1930, when he opposed Comintern's ultraleft turn and was expelled; in 1931 founded Workers' and Peasants' bloc, which fused with Trotskyists to create Workers' Party of Marxist Unification [POUM] 1935; imprisoned in Spain 1936–46; lived in New York City from 1947.

Melcher, Erich [1892–1944] German toolmaker; joined SPD 1910, USPD and Spartacus League 1917; founding member KPD; became full-time trade-union official in metalworkers' union 1919; expelled 1921 for Communist activity; delegate to RILU founding congress 1921; worked in KPD national trade-union department 1922–3; expelled from party 1928 as 'rightist'; a founder of CP Opposition [KPO]; joined Socialist Workers' Party [SAP] 1932; imprisoned by Nazis 1934–44; died in Auschwitz.

Melnichansky, Grigorii N. [1886–1937] joined Russian social-democratic movement 1902; lived in US 1910–17 to escape repression; member of Moscow Military Revolutionary Committee in October 1917; member Soviet Council of Labour and Defence 1918–20; subsequently worked in trade unions and on economic issues; represented Moscow Council of Trade Unions at June 1920 preliminary meeting in Moscow that mapped out RILU formation; arrested during Stalin purges; died in prison.

Mensheviks originally minority ('Mensheviki') of Russian Social-Democratic Labour Party at its 1903 congress; opposed October Revolution; subsequently an opposition force to Soviet government; affiliated to Two-and-a-Half International 1921–3.

Merrheim, Alphonse [1871–1925] French syndicalist; leader of metalworkers' union; led internationalist current in CGT during WWI; participant in 1915 Zimmerwald Conference; supported Zimmerwald movement until 1917, then allied with reformist forces in CGT; forced by illness to withdraw from union activity 1923.

Meyer, Ludwig [Bergmann] [1861?–1942?] member of German *Unionen*; metalworker; member of Spartacus group during WWI; part of split from KPD that formed KAPD 1919; delegate to 1921 Comintern Third Congress from KAPD, and to RILU founding congress from General Workers' Union [AAU]; retired from politics 1922; died in Nazi concentration camp.

Michel See Relenque, Michel

Michelovich, Teviy Moiseevich [1896–1920] Bolshevik in Yekaterinoslav Province; chairman of Berdyansk Revolutionary Committee in Ukraine; executed by Makhno forces 12 December 1920.

Miglans Latvian Communist; member of Executive Board of Riga metalworkers' union; escaped to Soviet Russia 9 June 1921, during government expulsion of labour and political activists.

Mikadze, Archil [1896–1937] member of Georgian Trade Union Council; attended June 1920 preliminary meeting in Moscow that mapped out RILU formation; leader of ITUC bureau in Baku for Turkish-Caucasian-Persian region; following 1921 Georgian people's commissar of labour and later trade; arrested and shot during Stalin purges.

Milkić, Ilija [1882–1968] a founder of salesworkers' union in Belgrade 1901; founding member of Serbian Social-Democratic Party 1903; elected to secretariat of Serbian trade-union federation 1905; lived in France and Switzerland during WWI; attended Kienthal Conference as supporter of Zimmerwald Left 1916; supported October Revolution and moved to Soviet Russia 1919; joined Yugoslav Communist group in Russia; attended first three Comintern congresses; delegate to RILU founding congress 1921; moved to Vienna 1922 to join secretariat of Balkan Federation; returned to Yugoslavia 1926 and ceased political activity.

Minor, Robert [Ballister] [1884–1952] political cartoonist; joined American SP 1907; moved towards anarcho-syndicalism by 1912; went to Soviet Russia 1918 and was won to communism; joined US CP 1920; attended Comintern Third Congress and RILU founding congress 1921; elected to CP Central Committee 1922; editor of *Daily Worker*; remained a leader of CP until his death.

minoritaires See Revolutionary Syndicalist Committees, France

Monatte, Pierre [1881–1960] French revolutionary syndicalist; member of CGT leadership committee 1904; founded *La Vie ouvrière* 1909; worked with Trotsky in internationalist opposition to WWI; won to communism 1919 and became a secretary of Committee for the Third International; imprisoned nine months 1920; supporter of *minoritaires* within CGT, which became CGTU, and advocated affiliation to RILU; joined CP spring 1923; expelled for opposing anti-Trotsky campaign 1924; founder and editor of *La Révolution prolétarienne* 1925–39 and 1945–7; active in resistance to Nazi occupation.

Monmousseau, Gaston [1883–1960] French revolutionary syndicalist; went to work on railroad 1910, becoming left-wing union leader; member of executive committee of Committee for the Resumption of International Relations 1919, which became Committee for the Third International; became editor of *La Vie ouvrière* 1921; leader of *minoritaires* within CGT; general secretary of CGTU 1922–32; attended Second (1922) and subsequent RILU congresses; joined CP 1925; parliamentary deputy 1936–40; active in resistance to Nazi occupation; elected CGT secretary 1945; member of CP Central Committee at his death.

Morgan US capitalist family centred in banking industry; business empire was founded by John Pierpont Morgan [1837–1913].

Moscow daily organ of Comintern Third Congress; published in English, German, and French, 25 May–14 July 1921.

Müller, Hermann [1876–1931] joined SPD 1893; elected to its executive committee 1906; supported chauvinist majority during WWI; German foreign minister 1919–20; chancellor 1920 and 1928–30.

Müller, Richard [1880–1943] joined SPD 1906 and USPD 1917; active in German metalworkers' union; organised Berlin revolutionary stewards; leader of workers' and soldiers' councils during and after November 1918 revolution; became part of Communist Party in 1920 fusion; member of its Central Committee; supported Levi 1921; delegate to RILU founding congress; left KPD 1922; later withdrew from political activity.

Murphy, John T. 'Jack' [1888–1966] metalworker from Sheffield, England; during WWI a member of national council of Shop Stewards' movement, representing it at Second Comintern Congress 1920; joined Socialist Labour Party 1917; founding member of CP 1920; member of Central Committee and its industrial organiser; took part in creating International Trade Union Council, setting up its British Bureau; delegate to Comintern Third Congress and RILU founding congress 1921; forced into background when Comintern's ultraleft course began in 1929; expelled from CP 1932; subsequently active in left wing of Labour Party; later withdrew from politics.

Murray, Dan former chairman of Western Federation of Miners in Butte, Montana; member of IWW's Lumber Workers' Industrial Union no. 120; delegate to 1921 IWW convention.

Mussolini, Benito [1883–1945] former leader of Italian Socialist Party left wing and editor of *Avanti*; took chauvinist, pro-war position and was expelled from PSI 1915; founded Fascist movement 1919; dictator of Italy 1922–43; executed by Resistance forces.

National Confederation of Labour, Spain [Confederación nacional del trabajo, CNT] anarcho-syndicalist federation founded 1911; grew rapidly after WWI, reaching 700,000 members by end of 1920; 28,000 members at end of 1922; affiliated to Comintern 1919 and to RILU 1921–2, formally withdrawing in 1923; joined Berlin-based anarcho-syndicalist International Workers' Association.

National Labour Secretariat [Nationaal Arbeids-Secretariaat, NAS, Netherlands] founded 1893 as main socialist trade union; after social democrats split from it, became left-wing rival to major Dutch union federation; 36,000 members in 1921; attended RILU founding congress 1921; affiliated to RILU 1925–7.

National Trade Union Office [Reichsgewerkschafts-Zentrale] German CP centre created December 1920 to supervise trade-union work.

Nedelkov, Ivan See Shablin, Nikolai

Nin, Andreu [1892–1937] joined Catalan nationalist federation 1911; member Catalan Socialist Federation 1913–19; joined CNT 1919, becoming its general secretary 1921; supported affiliation to Comintern; delegate from Spain to Comintern Third and Fourth congresses 1921, 1922; played leading role at RILU founding congress; lived in Russia 1921–30; RILU deputy secretary under Lozovsky 1922–8; joined Left Opposition 1926; returned to Spain 1930 and helped organise Trotskyist opposition; founding leader of Workers' Party of Marxist Unification [POUM] 1935; kidnapped and murdered by GPU during Spanish Civil War.

Nogin, Viktor [1878–1924] joined Russian social-democratic movement 1898; elected to its Central Committee 1907; Bolshevik conciliator; deputy people's commissar of labour 1918–21; delegate to 1921 founding congress of RILU, at which he was elected to Central Council; head of CP central audit commission 1921–4.

Norwegian Confederation of Trade Unions [Arbeidernes Faglige Landsorganisasjon] formed 1899; closely tied to Norwegian Labour Party; 150,000 members mid-1920; vacillated for several years between Amsterdam and Moscow, but never joined RILU.

Nor-Yono See Darsono Notosudirdjo, Raden

One Big Union [Canada] militant union formed in Western Canada 1919; membership reached 40,000–70,000 by late 1919; 5,000 members 1921; joined Canadian Labour Congress 1956.

One Big Union Monthly published in Chicago by IWW 1919–21; succeeded by *Industrial Pioneer* February 1921.

One Big Union Propaganda League [OBUPL, Australia] formed 1918 by former IWW members after IWW was outlawed, emphasising industrial union organisation methods; some of its ideas were soon coopted by moderate trade-union leaders.

Oudegeest, Jan [1870–1950] leader of Dutch railroad workers' union from 1898; secretary of Amsterdam International 1919–27; chairman Dutch Social-Democratic Workers' Party 1927–34; member of International Labour Office Governing Board 1919–28.

Ozol, Fritz Ivanovich [1876–1939] tailor; joined Russian social-democratic movement 1904 as Menshevik; active in trade-union movement; joined Bolsheviks 1908; in Siberian exile 1914–17; elected member of Presidium of All-Union Central Council of Trade Unions 1918; chairperson of garment workers' union 1921–5; delegate to Comintern Third

Congress and RILU founding congress 1921; member of Russian CP Central Control Commission 1921–2; died in Moscow.

Palmer, A. Mitchell [1872–1936] US attorney general 1919–21; notorious for 'Palmer raids' during Red Scare.

Pan-American Federation of Labor initiated by the US AFL, with first congress held in Laredo, Texas, 13–16 November 1918; second congress held in New York on 7–10 July 1919; third congress held in Mexico City 10–18 January 1921; organisation formally dissolved 1934.

Pavlović, Pavle [1888–1971] joined Serbian SP 1905; union activist; founding member of Yugoslav CP; in emigration 1921–3; supporter of CP minority faction; member of Presidium at RILU founding congress 1921; elected to RILU Central Council; delegate to Third and Fourth Comintern congresses; jailed 1923–4; held legislative and union posts in Yugoslavia 1945–50.

PCI See Italian Communist Party

Perepechko, Ivan [1897–1943] active in printers' union in Ukraine; joined Bolsheviks 1914; secretary and vice chair of Southern Bureau of All-Russian Central Council of Trade Unions 1920–1; delegate to Comintern Third Congress and RILU founding congress 1921; supporter of Workers' Opposition; member of presidium at Tenth Congress of Russian CP; elected candidate member of CP Central Committee 1930; arrested during Stalin purges; died in prison camp.

Pestaña, Ángel [1886–1937] Spanish anarcho-syndicalist; joined CNT 1914–15; appointed editor of *Solidaridad Obrera* 1918–19; represented CNT at Comintern Second Congress 1920; arrested and imprisoned numerous times; an opponent of anarchist armed-action perspective, he was expelled from CNT 1931 over opposition to Spanish Anarchist Federation influence; founded Syndicalist Party; during Spanish Civil War served as general subcommissioner for war in popular front government; readmitted to CNT 1937.

Petermeier, Hans [1899–1938] German Communist from Munich; participated in defence of 1919 Bavarian Soviet republic, for which he was sentenced to imprisonment in absentia; became member of KAPD and functionary of General Workers' Union [AAU], representing them at RILU founding congress 1921; left AAU and KAPD later that year, rejoining KPD; involved in preparations for October 1923 uprising; worked for Comintern in Italy 1924–6, then moved to USSR; arrested and executed during Stalin purges.

Polish Socialist Party [PPS] founded 1892–3; nationalist in orientation; right-wing faction adopted chauvinist position during WWI and supported Pilsudski dictatorship in 1926; left-wing faction split in 1906, joining in creation of CP in 1918.

Pollitt, Harry [1890–1960] joined Independent Labour Party around 1909; leader of Shop Stewards' movement during WWI; founding member of British CP; a leader of Hands Off Russia campaign; delegate to Comintern Third Congress and RILU founding congress 1921; organiser for RILU 1921–3; became CP national organiser 1923; its general secretary 1929–39, 1941–56.

Popov, Dimitri [1878–1924] active in Bulgarian socialist student movement; became leader of Tesniaki Party, which became Bulgarian CP in 1919; delegate to Comintern Third Congress and elected to ECCI 1921; elected as proxy to RILU Central Council; participated in 1923 Bulgaria insurrection, escaping to Vienna.

Le Populaire [The People] Paris daily published 1918–37; reflected views first of united SP right wing, then post-split 'Dissident' party.

Proletarier KAPD newspaper published in Berlin 1920–7.

Proudhon, Pierre-Joseph [1809–65] French revolutionary theorist and anarchist; founder of mutualist philosophy; jailed under Louis Napoléon 1849–52; his views criticised by Marx.

PSI See Italian Socialist Party

Purcell, Albert Arthur [1872–1935] trade-union activist in Britain from 1890; opposed WWI and was spokesperson for Hands Off Russia movement; member of labour delegation to Moscow 1920, involved in discussions over founding new trade-union International; member of CP 1920–2; president of Trades Union Congress 1924–7; president of Amsterdam International 1924–7; Member of Parliament 1923–4, 1925–9.

Radek, Karl [1885–1939] joined revolutionary movement in Austrian Poland before 1905; a leader of left wing of Polish and German workers' movement; internationalist during WWI, collaborator of Lenin and supporter of Zimmerwald Left; joined Bolsheviks 1917; member of Russian CP Central Committee 1917–24; vice commissar for foreign affairs 1918; Soviet emissary to Germany 1918–19; member of ECCI 1920–4 and its Presidium 1921–4; reporter at Comintern Third Congress; with Trotsky, a leader of Left Opposition in Russian CP and Comintern from 1923; expelled and exiled 1927; capitulated 1929; Soviet journalist 1930–6; arrested 1936; convicted in Moscow trial 1937; exiled to labour camp; murdered by prisoner instigated by secret police.

Ramírez See Díaz Ramírez, Manuel

Rathenau, Walter [1867–1922] German capitalist and political leader; organiser of Germany's economy during WWI; became minister of reconstruction May 1921; foreign minister January 1922; advocated collaboration with Entente powers but also negotiated Treaty of Rapallo with Soviet Russia; targeted as Jew by right-wing forces; assassinated 24 June 1922.

Rees, Alf G. [b. 1884] railway unionist from Brisbane; member of Australian Socialist Party; delegate to Comintern Third Congress and RILU founding congress 1921; part of unification of Australian Communist forces shortly afterward.

Reichmann, Franz [1880–1941] carpenter; joined Swiss socialist movement 1904; associate secretary Zurich woodworkers' union 1912–40; editor of *Holzarbeiter-Zeitung* 1912–36; member of CP 1921–3; delegate from his union to RILU founding congress 1921; returned to SP; president of Swiss construction and woodworkers' association 1937–40.

Reinstein, Boris [1866–1947] born in Russia; joined revolutionary movement 1884; emigrated to US and joined Socialist Labor Party [SLP], heading its relations with Second International; sent to represent SLP at Stockholm international conference in 1917, he returned to Russia and joined CP; responsible for international propaganda in People's Commissariat of Foreign Affairs; later worked in Comintern apparatus.

Relenque, Michel [Moïse Kneler] [b. 1886] Russian-born French anarchist and syndicalist; began political activity 1913; in 1919 joined Revolutionary Syndicalist Committees [CSR], becoming part of its 'pure syndicalist' wing; attended RILU founding congress 1921; later accused of being Soviet agent.

Renaudel, Pierre [1871–1935] leader of right wing of French SP; social patriot during WWI; parliamentary deputy 1914–19, 1924–35; opposed SP affiliation to Comintern; led 'neosocialist' split from SP 1933.

Repossi, Luigi [1882–1957] Italian Communist and trade unionist; lathe operator; member of PSI from about 1900; jailed for anti-war activity 1917; leader of Milan metalworkers after WWI; supported PSI left wing; member of PCI executive 1921, in charge of trade-union work; delegate to RILU founding congress from CGL minority; editor of *Il Sindacato Rosso*; parliamentary deputy 1921–6; supported Bordiga current; jailed 1926–8; expelled from CP for opposing condemnation of Trotsky 1928; continued Communist activity; interned during war; joined PSI after fall of Fascism.

Revolutionary Shop Stewards, Germany [Revolutionäre Obleute] loose association of revolutionary workers, with strong base among metalworkers and in Berlin; played prominent role in January 1918 strikes and November 1918 revolution; led by workers' delegates who were also members of USPD; participated in January 1919 Berlin uprising; ceased functioning thereafter; a number of its members became CP members, with some joining anarcho-syndicalist FAUD.

Revolutionary Syndicalist Committees, France [Comités syndicalistes révolutionnaires, CSR] formed 1919 as left-wing minority within CGT, with Pierre Monatte as secretary; 300,000 members; expelled from CGT 1921, after which it formed Unitary CGT [CGTU].

Riehs, Jakob [b. 1882] metalworker; founding member of Austrian CP

November 1918; delegate to Comintern Third Congress and RILU founding congress 1921; worked in Soviet Union during 1920s; expelled from Austrian CP 1929; joined SP after 1945.

Rosmer, Alfred [1877–1964] revolutionary syndicalist; leader in France of internationalist opposition to WWI; represented Committee for the Third International at Comintern Second Congress 1920; as leader of Revolutionary Syndicalist Committees [CSR] participated in preparations for RILU establishment, helped lead International Council of Trade and Industrial Unions; member of ECCI in Moscow 1920–1; delegate to Comintern Third Congress; played leading role at RILU founding congress 1921; divided time between France and Russia until 1924; expelled from CP for opposition to anti-Trotsky campaign 1924; organiser of Left Opposition in France 1929–31; broke with Trotsky 1931 but collaborated with him and Fourth Internationalist movement after 1936.

Die Rote Fahne [The Red Flag] daily newspaper of German CP; began publication 9 November 1918; founded by Karl Liebknecht and Rosa Luxemburg.

Rühle, Otto [1874–1943] joined SPD 1896; German Reichstag deputy 1912–18; second deputy to oppose war credits after Liebknecht; a founder of Spartacus group and KPD; part of October 1919 split that established KAPD; represented it in Moscow summer 1920; expelled late October 1920 and help found General Workers' Union [AAU]; rejoined SPD 1923; helped defend Trotsky against Stalin frame-up.

Rykov, Alexei [1881–1938] joined Russian social-democratic movement 1898; supported Bolsheviks 1903; elected to Bolshevik Central Committee 1917; commissar of interior 1917–18; chair of Supreme Council of National Economy 1918–20; on Presidium at RILU founding congress 1921; deputy chair (1921–4) and chair (1924–30) of Council of People's Commissars; removed from CP Central Committee 1930 as part of Stalin's attack on Right Opposition; people's commissar of communications 1931–7; arrested and executed during Stalin purges.

Sandgren, John [1874–1932] anarcho-syndicalist; born in Sweden; toured US in 1909 on behalf of Swedish Trade Union Confederation to raise money for general strike in Sweden; remained in US and joined IWW; editor of Swedish-language IWW newspaper *Nya Världen* 1919; editor of *One Big Union Monthly* 1919–20, dismissed from post because of attacks on Soviet Russia.

Scheidemann, Philipp [1865–1939] joined German Social Democracy 1883; member SPD executive 1911; co-chair of Reichstag fraction 1913; social chauvinist during WWI; led in suppressing workers' revolution 1918–19; German prime minister February–June 1919; forced by Nazis into emigration 1933.

Schmidt, Vasily Vladimirovich [1886–1938] Bolshevik from 1905; lived as exile in Germany 1907–11; secretary of Petrograd Bolshevik Committee and Central Council of Petrograd Trade Unions 1917; people's commissar of labour 1918–28; delegate to Comintern Third Congress and RILU founding congress 1921; candidate member of Russian CP Central Committee 1918–34; arrested 1937 during Stalin purges; executed.

Schneider French capitalist family based in iron and steel industry; holdings developed into Schneider-Creusot armaments company.

Schoenbeck, Willi [1886–1957] joined SPD 1905; member of Spartacus League; founding member German KPD; head of the Rhineland/South Westphalia party organisation 1920–2; delegate to Comintern Third Congress and RILU founding congress 1921; secretary in KPD trade-union department 1923–4; expelled as rightist 1929; joined CP Opposition [KPO]; rejoined KPD and carried out underground work under Nazi regime; imprisoned 1945; played minor role in unions afterward; died in East Berlin.

Schüppel, Max Willi [b. 1887] German delegate to RILU founding congress from Gelsenkirchen Free Workers' Union 1921.

Second International founded 1889 as international association of workers' parties; collapsed at outbreak of WWI; pro-capitalist right wing reconstituted as Bern International 1919; merged with centrist Two-and-a-Half International 1923 and became Labour and Socialist International.

Sergeyev, Fyodor Andreyevich [Artem] [1883–1921] joined Russian social-democratic movement 1902; Bolshevik; escaped from Siberia to Australia, where he was active in socialist and labour movements 1911–17; leader of Soviet Ukraine 1918–19; chair of mineworkers' union 1920; member of Russian CP Central Committee 1920–1; delegate to Comintern Third Congress and RILU founding congress; killed with several other delegates in train derailment 24 July.

Serrati, Giacinto Menotti [1872–1926] joined Italian socialist movement 1892; leader of Maximalist left wing of PSI; internationalist during WWI; led PSI in affiliation to Comintern 1919; opposed break with reformists and remained head of PSI after PCI formation 1921; led PSI's pro-Comintern current into fusion with PCI 1924.

Sexton, James [1856–1938] general secretary of National Union of Dock Labourers 1893–1922; officer in Transport and General Workers' Union 1922–8; Labour Party Member of Parliament 1918–31.

Shablin, Nikolai [Ivan Nedelkov] [1881–1925] joined socialist movement 1897; member of Bulgarian Tesniaki Party, which became CP in 1919; member of its Central Committee; a signer of 1920 call for formation of Red Trade Union International on behalf of Bulgarian unions; Comintern Second Congress delegate; elected to ECCI 1920; carried out underground work in Bulgaria after 1923; captured by police and murdered.

Shatov, Bill [Vladimir Sergeevich] [1887–1938] Russian-born anarcho-syndicalist; emigrated to US 1907; joined IWW and led its Russian section in New York; returned to Russia after February 1917 Revolution; Red Army commander during civil war, helping lead Tenth Army in defence of Petrograd in 1919; appointed minister of transportation in Far East 1920; exiled to Siberia 1937 during Stalin purges; executed.

Shaumyan, Stepan [1878–1918] Armenian revolutionary; joined Russian social-democratic movement 1900, siding with Bolsheviks in 1903 split; central leader of Baku Commune April–July 1918; executed after its defeat.

Shlyapnikov, Aleksandr G. [1885–1937] joined Russian social-democratic movement 1901; Bolshevik from 1903; during 1917 member of Petrograd Soviet executive committee and chairman of Petrograd metalworkers' union; first commissar of labour after October Revolution; leader of Caspian-Caucasian Front during civil war; leader of Workers' Opposition 1921–2; member of Bolshevik and CP Central Committee 1915–17 and 1921–2; expelled from CP 1933; imprisoned 1935 during Stalin purges; executed.

Shop Stewards, Britain movement originating in Scotland 1915; grew during wartime strike wave; put forward revolutionary demands opposed to official trade-union leadership's no-strike policy; declined after 1918, with many militants joining CP.

Shop Stewards, Germany See Revolutionary Shop Stewards

Simon, Josef [1865–1949] joined German Social Democracy 1885; chairman of Central Association of Shoemakers 1900–33; Reichstag deputy 1912–18 and 1920–33; USPD member 1917–22; rejoined SPD; member of German Economic Council 1920–33; active in underground work under Nazis.

Sirolle, Henri [1886–1962] French railway worker and revolutionary syndicalist; leader of CGT *minoritaires*; member executive committee of Committee for the Third International 1919–20; elected assistant secretary of Federation of Railway Workers 1920; imprisoned May–June 1920 for strike activity; delegate in 1921 to Comintern Third Congress and RILU founding congress, where he presented view of 'pure syndicalists'; quit CGTU 1922 and supported revolutionary syndicalist splitoff; advocated remaining in RILU and forming syndicalist opposition [CGT-SR]; rejoined CGT 1927; active in railway management under Vichy regime.

Skoropadsky, Pavlo [1873–1945] Ukrainian aristocrat and tsarist general of Cossack origin; installed by German occupiers as hetman of Ukraine April–December 1918; fled to Berlin after ouster by Red Army.

Smith, Herbert [1862–1938] coal miner; joined Independent Labour Party 1897; president of Yorkshire Miners' Association 1906–38; vice president (1917–22) and president (1922–9) of Miners' Federation of Great Britain.

Smith, Walter [1885–1927] active in Western Federation of Miners after 1901; joined IWW 1909; editor of *Industrial Worker* 1912–13; member of Lumber Workers Industrial Union no. 120; delegate to 1921 IWW convention.

Social-Democratic Party of Germany [Sozialdemokratische Partei Deutschlands, SPD] founded 1875 from fusion of Marxists and Lassalleans; central party of Second International; majority leadership backed German war effort 1914; left-wing oppositionists formed Spartacus League 1916 and USPD 1917; headed restabilisation of German capitalist rule after November 1918 revolution; USPD rump reunited with it at Hamburg Congress in September 1922; 1.1 million members 1921.

Souchy, Augustin [1892–1984] German anarchist from 1911; a leader of Free Workers' Union of Germany [FAUD]; editor of its organ *Der Syndikalist* 1922–33; in Moscow to attend Comintern Second Congress 1920; while there participated in meetings related to RILU founding; a secretary of anarcho-syndicalist International Workers' Association from 1922; left Germany 1933, living in France, Spain, and Mexico; returned to Germany 1961; worked for International Labour Organisation 1963–6.

SPD See Social-Democratic Party of Germany

Stetter, Johannes [1885–1963] German carpenter; joined SPD 1903; USPD 1917; KPD 1920; full-time party secretary in Stuttgart 1918–23; expelled from KPD during internal conflict 1926; rejoined SPD; helped in reconstruction of West German unions after 1945.

Stinnes, Hugo [1870–1924] German industrialist; built vast economic empire after WWI, starting from coal and steel industry, moving to media, public utilities, banks, and other areas; during 1918 revolution, negotiated concessions to trade unions; later campaigned against eight-hour day and nationalisation; had ties to far right; opposed Versailles Treaty.

Sturm, Hertha [1886–1945?] German Communist; joined SPD 1911 and KPD January 1919; living in Munich, was jailed two months for role in Bavarian workers' republic 1919; delegate to Comintern Third Congress, Second International Communist Women's Conference, and RILU founding congress 1921; member International Women's Secretariat in Berlin 1921–4; removed from leading posts in KPD as 'rightist' 1924; worked with Zetkin in Moscow 1924–8; returned to Germany; again removed from party staff, labelled rightist; worked with left socialists of 'New Beginning' in Germany 1934–5; arrested 1935, she was tortured, and jailed for many years under Nazi regime; believed to have been killed in Allied air strike.

Sült, Wilhelm [1888–1921] chairman of shop stewards among electrical workers in Berlin and member of German CP; organised strike during March Action; arrested by police 1 April 1921 and shot while 'trying to escape'.

Swedish Workers' Central Organisation [Sveriges Arbetares Centralorganisation, SAC] Swedish revolutionary syndicalist federation founded 1910 in split from social-democratic confederation; 35,000 members in 1920; sent delegates to RILU founding congress, where they were associated with German syndicalist opposition; affiliated with anarcho-syndicalist International Workers' Association established in 1922.

Swiss Trade Union Federation [Schweizerischer Gewerkschaftsbund] founded 1880; close ties to Social-Democratic Party; 225,000 members in late 1920;

Der Syndikalist [The Syndicalist] weekly newspaper of German syndicalists published in Berlin; began publication 14 December 1918.

Szántó, Béla [1881–1951] office clerk; member of Hungarian Social-Democratic Party 1904–8; commissar of war in Hungarian soviet government 1919; member of CP Central Committee 1919–20, 1922; delegate to Comintern Third Congress and RILU founding congress 1921; worked for Comintern in Vienna 1921–2; head of Hungarian CP in exile 1926–9; moved to Moscow and worked for many years in Comintern apparatus; after WWII worked for Hungarian government on agrarian questions and as ambassador to Poland.

Tanner, Jack [1889–1965] leader of British Shop Stewards during WWI, which he represented at Comintern Second Congress; delegate to December 1920 Berlin syndicalist conference; joined CP 1921; leader of CP-led National Minority Movement in 1920s; became right-wing opponent of CP in 1940s; continued to hold prominent posts in British trade unions until 1954.

Tellalov, Kirill Bulgarian artist; delegate to RILU First Congress 1921.

Thiers, Adolphe [1797–1877] French journalist, historian, and politician; president of Third Republic 1871–3; presided over suppression of Paris Commune.

Thomas, Albert [1878–1932] joined French SP 1902, becoming leader of its right wing; deputy in parliament from 1910; supported French war effort and became minister for munitions 1916–17; first director of International Labour Organisation 1919–32.

Thomas, James Henry [1874–1949] British railway union president 1905–6 and organising secretary from 1906; Labour Party Member of Parliament 1910; chauvinist position during WWI; elected treasurer of Second International 1920; head of Amsterdam International 1920–4; withdrew rail union's support for British miners' strike, helping lead to its defeat 1921; cabinet minister 1924 and 1929–36; broke with Labour Party 1931.

Thyssen, August [1842–1926] German industrialist; established iron, steel, and coal family empire; succeeded by son Fritz [1873–1951], who helped finance Nazis from 1923.

Tiedt, Karl [1881–1938] joined SPD 1899; seriously wounded in WWI; USPD 1917; came to German CP in 1920 fusion; was chairman of International Federation of War Victims and Disabled from 1919; Reichstag member 1925–8; editor of *Die Ehelosen* from 1925; expelled from KPD 1926 due to magazine's articles on sexual questions.

Tillett, Ben [1860–1943] British trade-union leader; initially influenced by syndicalism, but later moved to right wing of labour movement; leader of British dock workers 1887–1931; chauvinist position during WWI; chairman of Trades Union Congress 1928–9; Member of Parliament 1917–24; 1929–31.

Tiura See Laukki, Leo

Tommasi, Joseph [1886–1926] cabinetmaker, carpenter, and mechanic; joined French SP 1904; union activist; supporter of CGT left wing during WWI; member of CGT administrative committee 1919; supported SP affiliation to Comintern; joined CP 1921 and was elected to its steering committee; delegate from CGT minority to Comintern Third Congress and RILU founding congress 1921, where he supported RILU-Comintern links; forced into exile by French police 1924, becoming CGTU representative to RILU in Soviet Russia; supporter of Left Opposition; lived in Moscow until his death.

Tomsky, Mikhail [1880–1936] joined Russian social-democratic movement 1904; Bolshevik; active in trade-union movement in Reval and St. Petersburg; arrested and exiled 1909–17; president of All-Russian Central Council of Trade Unions 1918–21, 1922–9; general secretary of International Trade Union Council 1920–1; member of Russian CP Central Committee 1919–34; a leader of Right Opposition to Stalin after 1928; charged with terrorist connections during Stalin purges, he committed suicide prior to his arrest.

Trotsky, Leon [1879–1940] joined Russian social-democratic movement 1897; supported Mensheviks 1903, but soon broke with them; internationalist and supporter of Zimmerwald movement during WWI; joined Bolsheviks and elected to Central Committee 1917; people's commissar of foreign affairs 1917–18 and of war 1918–25; a leader of Comintern; leader of Left Opposition in Russian CP and Comintern from 1923; expelled 1927; exiled abroad 1929; called for new International 1933; main target of 1936–8 Stalin frame-up trials; founding leader of Fourth International 1938; murdered by agent of Stalin.

Tsyperovich, Grigorii [1871–1932] joined Russian revolutionary movement 1888; arrested 1894 and sentenced to ten years' exile; participant in trade-union movement in St. Petersburg from 1907; exiled abroad 1911–17; joined CP 1919; took part in establishment of International Trade Union Council 1920; delegate to Comintern Second and Third congress; a leading participant in 1921 RILU founding congress, elected to its Central Council; later worked in Commissariat of Foreign Affairs and in Leningrad administration.

Turati, Filippo [1857–1932] founding member of Italian SP [PSI] 1892; leader of its reformist right wing; founder and editor of *Critica Sociale* 1891–1926; parliamentary deputy 1896–1926; opposed Italy's entry into WWI but supported national defence as war went on; opponent of October Revolution and Comintern; expelled from PSI 1922; formed reformist Unitary Socialist Party [PSU]; emigrated to France 1926.

Turcescu, Nicolae [Nicolae Gorniski; Wilhelm Friedrich König] [1900–1964] founding member of Romanian CP; delegate to Comintern Third Congress and RILU founding congress 1921; left Romania in early 1920s for USSR; arrested and imprisoned during Stalin purges; returned to Romania in 1950s.

Two-and-a-Half International term used by Communists for International Working Union of Socialist Parties, or Vienna Union, an alliance of centrist social-democratic parties formed February 1921; merged with Second International to form Labour and Socialist International 1923.

Umbreit, Paul [1868–1932] journalist and editor for German trade-union federation.

Union of Hand and Brain Workers [Union der Hand- und Kopfarbeiter] Berlin-based syndicalist organisation formed 1919; 13,500 members 1921; represented at RILU founding congress; merged in November 1921 with Gelsenkirchen Free Workers' Union and Agricultural Workers' Association to create organisation of same name, tied politically to KPD.

UGT See General Union of Workers, Spain

Unionen German syndicalist unions.

Unitary General Confederation of Labour [Confédération générale du travail unitaire, CGTU] founded in France 1922 by revolutionary unionists driven out of CGT; affiliated to RILU 1923.

Uruguayan Regional Workers' Federation [Federación Obrera Regional Uruguaya, FORU] founded 1905 with anarchist orientation; represented at RILU founding congress 1921; debate within federation in 1921–3 led to split of supporters of Russian Revolution and Communist movement, who formed Unión Sindical Uruguaya.

USI See Italian Syndicalist Union

USPD See Independent Social-Democratic Party of Germany

Vanderbilt US capitalist family, centred originally in railroads and shipping; business empire was founded by Cornelius Vanderbilt [1794–1877].

Varga, Eugen [Jenő] [1879–1964] economist; joined Hungarian Social Democracy 1906, CP 1919; people's commissar for finance in Hungarian Soviet government 1919; emigrated to Soviet Russia after its fall; worked for ECCI; delegate to Third and subsequent Comintern congresses; prominent Soviet economist until criticised by Stalin 1947; later partially rehabilitated; died in USSR.

Vecchi, Nicola [b. 1883] Italian revolutionary syndicalist, active in union movement from 1909; member of executive committee of Italian Syndicalist Union [USI]; one of two USI delegates to RILU founding congress 1921; supporter of USI affiliation to RILU and collaboration with Italian CP; delegate to RILU Second Congress 1922; abandoned active participation in workers' movement by mid-1920s; emigrated from Italy 1931.

Verdier, Guillaume French revolutionary syndicalist; CGT leader in Decazeville (Aveyron) 1919–21; member Central Committee of Revolutionary Syndicalist Committees; advocated affiliation to Comintern; signed pact with anarchist syndicalists 1921; supported 'pure syndicalist' wing in CGTU; left CP, probably in 1922.

La Vie ouvrière [Workers' Life] French syndicalist weekly published by CGT 1909–14 and from 1919; affiliated to CGTU in 1922–3.

VKPD See Communist Party of Germany

Volan, Elias [1887–1974] became active in Norwegian trade-union movement 1905; member of left-wing opposition movement during WWI; became deputy chairman of Norwegian Confederation of Trade Unions 1920; delegate to RILU founding congress 1921; chairman of construction workers' union 1923–7; served on CP executive after Norwegian Labour Party split in 1923; broke with CP and rejoined NLP 1929; member of Trade Union Confederation secretariat 1931–4, 1938–53.

Walling, William English [1877–1936] American labour reformer and writer; founding member of NAACP 1909; joined SP 1910; resigned 1917 due to its opposition to US entry into WWI; later worked for AFL.

Watkins, Nat coal miner from South Wales; delegate to 1921 Comintern Third Congress and RILU founding congress, at which he was elected to RILU Central Council; became national organiser of Minority Movement 1924; elected to British CP Organisation Bureau 1925; dropped out of party 1929.

Weissmann, Robert [1869–1942] state secretary in Prussia; national commissioner of public order in SPD-led German government; died in New York.

Wells, Hulet M. [1878–1970] became socialist 1905; editor of *Socialist Voice* 1911; chairman of Washington State SP 1913; president of Seattle Central Labor Council 1915–16; convicted of sedition 1918 and imprisoned for two years; delegate to 1921 RILU founding congress from Seattle Central Labor Council; national lecturer for Friends of Soviet Russia; founder of Unemployed Citizens' League of Seattle 1931.

Wille, Artur [b. 1894] mechanic from Berlin; joined Spartacus League during WWI; member of KAPD and General Workers' Union [AAU]; delegate to RILU founding congress 1921.

Williams, George [b. 1885] US anarcho-syndicalist; bookkeeper for IWW Lumber Workers union; secretary of IWW's General Defense Committee 1921; wrote for *Industrial Pioneer*; leader of IWW delegation to RILU founding congress; wrote reports published in *Industrial Solidarity* attacking RILU, later published by IWW as pamphlet.

Williams, Robert [1881–1936] secretary of National Transport Workers' Federation 1912–22; member of British Labour Party Executive 1918–21, 1922–6; part of British labour delegation to Moscow 1920; attended meeting to discuss founding new trade-union International; joined CP 1920; expelled 1921, accused of having betrayed miners' strike.

Wilson, Havelock [1859–1929] president of National Sailors' and Firemen's Union 1887 until his death; supporter of class collaboration and collective bargaining; refused to support British Labour Party and aligned himself with the Liberals.

Wilson, Woodrow [1856–1924] Democratic Party president of US 1913–21; led US into WWI 1917; issued Fourteen Points 1918, which promised liberal non-punitive peace and a League of Nations.

Wirth, Werner trade unionist from Zurich; Swiss delegate to Comintern Third Congress and RILU founding congress 1921; elected to RILU Central Council.

Wissell, Rudolf [1969–1962] joined SPD 1888, becoming part of its right wing; from 1901 full-time German trade-union functionary, focusing on social policy issues; member of Council of People's Deputies (German government) 1918–19; member of ADGB union federation executive committee 1919–24; minister of labour 1928–30; retired from public life under Nazi regime; helped rebuild SPD after WWII.

Wolffheim, Fritz [1888–1942] joined SPD 1909; part of ultraleft current in Hamburg SPD during WWI; joined KPD 1918; leader of National Bolshevism tendency together with Lauffenberg; expelled 1920; joined KAPD but then was expelled August 1920; attempted to continue nationalist-socialist activity but evolved to right; in close contact with left wing of Nazi Party led by Strasser; arrested 1934 during Nazi purge of Strasser current; died in concentration camp.

Workers' International Industrial Union [WIIU] formed 1908 by supporters of DeLeonist Socialist Labor Party following split with IWW; based in Detroit; only a handful of members by 1921; sent delegate to RILU founding congress; disbanded 1925.

Workers' Opposition group within Russian CP formed September 1920; called for trade-union control of industrial production and greater autonomy for CP union fractions; its positions were rejected by Tenth Russian CP Congress in March 1921; later raised criticisms of measures adopted related to introduction of NEP; ceased organised activity following its censure at RCP's Eleventh Congress in March–April 1922.

Wrangel, Pyotr Nikolaevich [1878–1928] Russian tsarist general; commander of White forces in southern Russia 1919–20; emigrated to Yugoslavia 1920; subsequently led White exile army.

Wright, Chester [1883–1964] editor of *New York Call* 1914–16; broke with SP over its opposition to US entry into WWI 1917; became director of AFL information and publicity 1920; English-language secretary of Pan-American Federation of Labor 1919–27; later editor of International Labor News Service.

Yudenich, Nikolai [1862–1933] Russian tsarist general; leader of White forces in northwest during Russian Civil War; emigrated 1920.

Zetkin, Clara [1857–1933] joined German socialist movement 1878; editor of SPD's women's journal *Die Gleichheit* 1891–1917; organised first International Conference of Socialist Women 1907; elected secretary of International Socialist Women's Bureau; organised internationalist conference of socialist women 1915; joined KPD 1919; named general secretary of International Women's Secretariat 1920; founder and editor of *Die Kommunistische Fraueninternationale* 1921–5; opposed ultraleftism in party during March Action 1921 and thereafter; attended RILU founding congress; member ECCI from 1922; attended Comintern's Second through Sixth congresses; headed Communist Women's Movement 1921–6; opposed 'Bolshevisation' campaign 1924–5 and Stalin's ultraleft turn from 1928; remained prominent figure in German CP and Comintern, without recanting, until her death in Moscow.

Zimmerwald reference to movement formed at 1915 conference in Zimmerwald, Switzerland, attended by leftwing and centrist socialist parties and currents, following collapse of Second International in 1914; a second conference was held in Kienthal, Switzerland, in 1916.

Zinoviev, Grigorii [1883–1936] joined Russian social-democratic movement 1901; Bolshevik; elected to Central Committee 1907; internationalist and collaborator of Lenin during WWI; chair of Petrograd Soviet 1917–26; chairperson of Comintern 1919–26; participant in 1920 discussions over founding Red Trade Union International; on death of Lenin, formed troika with Stalin and Lev Kamenev to isolate Trotsky from central leadership 1923–4; broke with Stalin 1925; together with Trotsky and Kamenev, led United Opposition to Stalinist course 1926–7; expelled 1927; recanted and was readmitted 1928; arrested 1934; convicted in Moscow frame-up trial and shot.

Bibliography

Adi, Hakim 2013, *Pan-Africanism and Communism: The Communist International, Africa and the Diaspora 1919–1939*, Trenton, NJ: Africa World Press.

American Federation of Labor 1921, *Report of the Proceedings of the Forty-first Annual Convention of the American Federation of Labor*, Washington, DC: Law Reporter Printing Company.

Andreucci, Franco and Tommaso Detti (eds.) 1975–9, *Il movimento operaio italiano: Dizionario biografico 1853–1943*, 6 volumes, Rome: Editori Riuniti.

Arbeidernes Faglige Landsorganisation 1921, *Beretning 1921*, Oslo: Arbeidernes Aktietrykkeri.

Arshinov, Peter 1974 [1923], *History of the Makhnovist Movement 1918–1921*, Detroit: Black & Red, available at: www.ditext.com/arshinov/makhno.html.

Baev, Jordan and Kostadin Grozev 2014, *An Odyssey Across Two Worlds: George the Bulgarian and Soviet-American Relations during the First Half of the 20th Century*, Sofia. English translation available at: https://www.academia.edu/5891252/Andreytchine_Eng2014

Bauer, Otto 2021, *The Austrian Revolution*, Chicago: Haymarket Books.

Birchall, Ian 2020, 'The Comintern's Encounter with Syndicalism', *Marxist Left Review*, 20 (Winter): 117–40.

Biulleten' pervogo mezhdunarodnogo kongressa revoliutsionnykh, professional'nykh i proizodstvennykh soiuzov, nos. 1–17, also published as a book: *1-yi mezhdunarodnogo kongressa revoliutsionnykh, professional'nykh i proizodstvennykh soiuzov. Stenograficheskii otchet*, Moscow, 1921.

Biulleten' II. Kongress Krasnogo Internatsionala Profsoiuzov v Moskve. 19 noiabria–2 dekabria 1922 goda, Moscow/Petrograd, 1923.

Bock, Hans Manfred, 2017 [1969], *Syndicalisme révolutionnaire et communisme de gauche de 1918 à 1923: Contribution à l'histoire et à la sociologie de la Freie Arbeiter-Union Deutschlands (Syndicalisten), de l'Allgemeine Arbeiter-Union Deutschlands et du Kommunistische Arbeiter-Partei Deutschlands*, available at: aaap.be/Pdf/Anton-Pannekoek/Pannekoek-fr-2017-Bock-Syndikalisme-Et-Communisme-De-Gauche.pdf.

Borkenau, Franz 1962, *World Communism: A History of the Communist International*, Ann Arbor: University of Michigan Press.

Borodin, M.M. 2021, *The Great Betrayal: Black Friday and the 1921 Miners' Lockout*, London: Menmore Press.

Bourrinet, Philippe 2017, *The Dutch and German Communist Left (1900–68)*, Leiden: Brill.

Broué, Pierre 1997, *Histoire de l'Internationale Communiste 1919–1943*, Paris: Fayard.

Broué, Pierre 2005, *The German Revolution 1917–1923*, Leiden: Brill.

Browder, Earl R. 1921, 'The Red Trade Union International: The First World Congress of Revolutionary Unions', *The Toiler*, 15 October, 9–10. Available online at Marxists Internet Archive.

Bulletin, The First International Congress of Revolutionary Trade and Industrial Unions, nos. 1–16, Moscow, 1921.

Bulletin des 1. Kongresses der Roten Gewerkschaftsinternationale, nos. 1–7, Moscow, 1921.

Bulletin du Premier Congrès International des syndicats révolutionnaires, nos. 1–16, Moscow, 1921.

Cachin, Marcel 1998, *Marcel Cachin Carnets 1906–1947*, Volume 3, 1921–1933, edited by Denis Peschanski, Jacques Girault, and Serge Wolikow, Paris: CNRS Éditions.

Cain, Frank 1982, 'The Industrial Workers of the World: Aspects of Its Suppression in Australia 1916–1919', *Labour History*, 42 (May), 54–62.

Cannon, James P. 1973, *The First Ten Years of American Communism*, New York: Pathfinder Press.

Carr, Edward Hallett 1953, *The Bolshevik Revolution 1917–1923*, Volume 3, New York: Macmillan.

Cascaden, Gordon 1922, *Shall Unionism Die? Report on 'Red' Union International Congress*, Windsor: Industrial Union League of Canada.

CGTU 1922, *1er congrès tenu à Saint-Étienne du 25 juin au 1er juillet 1922*, Paris: Confédération Générale du Travail.

Chambelland, Colette 1968, *Syndicalisme révolutionnaire et commuisme: Les Archives de Pierre Monatte*, Paris: Françços Maspero.

Clay, Sir Arthur 1911, *Syndicalism and Labour: Notes upon Some Aspects of Social and Industrial Questions of the Day*, New York: Dutton.

Cliff, Tony 1979, 'The Bolsheviks and World Communism', in *Lenin*, Volume 4, London: Pluto Press.

Cliff, Tony and Donny Gluckstein 1986, *Marxism and the Trade Union Struggle: The General Strike of 1926*, London: Bookmarks.

Commissione Confederale in Russia 1921, *Russia sindacale: Rapporto dell'on. Giuseppe Bianchi al Congresso confederale di Livorno*, Milan: Codara.

Communist International 1924, *Protokoll: Fünfter Kongress der Kommunistischen Internationale*, Hamburg: Carl Hoym Nachf.

Degras, Jane (ed.) 1971, *The Communist International 1919–1943 Documents*, 3 volumes, New York: Frank Cass.

Dobbs, Farrell 1973, *Teamster Power*, New York: Pathfinder Press.

Donato, Gabriele 2012, 'Fra Mosca e Berlino: La collocazione internazionale dell'USI', in *Almanacco di guerra di classe 1912–2012*, Unione sindacale italiana (USI-AIT).

Draper, Theodore 1957, *The Roots of American Communism*, New York: Viking Press.

Draper, Theodore 1986, *American Communism and Soviet Russia*, New York: Vintage Books.

Farrell, Frank 1979, 'Australian Labour and the Profintern', *International Review of Social History*, 24, 1, 34–54.

Favilli, Paolo 2016, *The History of Italian Marxism: From Its Origins to the Great War*, Leiden: Brill.

Fimmen, Edo 1922, *The International Federation of Trade Unions: Development and Aims*, Amsterdam: International Federation of Trade Unions.

Foner, Philip S. 1965, 'The Industrial Workers of the World 1905–1917', in *History of the Labor Movement in the United States*, Volume 4, New York: International Publishers.

Foner, Philip S. 1991, 'The T.U.E.L. to the End of the Gompers Era', in *History of the Labor Movement in the United States*, Volume 9, New York: International Publishers.

Foster, William Z. ca. 1921, *The Russian Revolution*, Chicago: Trade Union Educational League.

Foster, William Z. 1955, *History of the Three Internationals: The World Socialist and Communist Movements from 1848 to the Present*, New York: International Publishers.

Fowkes, Ben 2017, 'The Red International of Labour Unions (RILU): An Exploration of Some of the Issues', in *Global Faultlines*, available at: emarvakfi.org/RedInternationalOfLabourUnions.pdf.

Groppo, Bruno 1982, 'La création du Conseil international des Syndicats (Moscou, juillet 1920)', *Communisme*, 1, 5–45.

Gruber, Helmut (ed.) 1967, *International Communism in the Era of Lenin*, Ithaca, NY: Cornell University Press.

Gruber, Helmut (ed.) 1974, *Soviet Russia Masters the Comintern: International Communism in the Era of Stalin's Ascendancy*, New York: Anchor Books.

Hallas, Duncan 2008, *The Comintern: A History of the Third International*, Chicago: Haymarket Books.

Hansen, Joseph 1977, 'Trotsky's Transitional Program: Its Origins and Significance for Today', in Leon Trotsky, *The Transitional Program for Socialist Revolution*, New York: Pathfinder Press.

Hardy, George, 1956, *Those Stormy Years: Memories of the Fight for Freedom on Five Continents*, London: Lawrence & Wishart.

Haywood, Harry, 1978, *Autobiography of an Afro-American Communist*, Chicago: Liberator Press.

Haywood, William D. 1969, *The Autobiography of Big Bill Haywood*, New York: International Publishers.

Howie, J. 1921, *Reds in Congress: First Congress of the Red International of Labour Unions, Moscow, July 3rd, 1921*, Sydney: Industrial Print.

Industrial Workers of the World (IWW) 1969, *The Founding Convention of the IWW: Proceedings*, New York: Merit Publishers.

International Labour Office 1921, *First Special International Trade Union Congress: London, November 22–27, 1920*, Geneva: ILO.

International Labour Office 1931, *Dix ans d'organisation internationale du travail*, Geneva: ILO.

Isitt, Benjamin 2007, 'Searching for Workers' Solidarity: The One Big Union and the Victoria General Strike of 1919', *Labour/Le Travail*, 60, 9–42.

Ives, Martyn 2016, *Reform, Revolution and Direct Action amongst British Miners: The Struggle for the Charter in 1919*, Leiden: Brill.

Johanningsmeier, Edward P. 1994, *Forging American Communism: The Life of William Z. Foster*, Princeton: Princeton University Press.

Kahan, Vilém 1990, *Bibliography of the Communist International (1919–1979)*, Leiden: Brill.

Klugmann, James 1968, 'Formation and Early Years 1919–1924', in *History of the Communist Party of Great Britain*, Volume 1, London: Lawrence & Wishart.

Kornbluh, Joyce L. (ed.) 1968, *Rebel Voices: An I.W.W. Anthology*, Ann Arbor: The University of Michigan Press.

Lazitch, Branko (ed.) 1986, *Biographical Dictionary of the Comintern*, Stanford: Hoover Institution Press.

Lehning, Arthur 2000, *La Naissance de l'Association internationale des travailleurs de Berlin: Du syndicalisme révolutionnaire à l'anarchosyndicalisme*, Paris: Éditions CNT.

Lenin, V.I. 1921a, 'The Party Crisis', in *Lenin Collected Works*, Volume 32, Moscow: Progress Publishers, p. 53.

Lenin, V.I. 1921b, 'Preliminary Draft Resolution of the Tenth Congress of the R.C.P. on the Syndicalist and Anarchist Deviation in Our Party', in *Lenin Collected Works*, Volume 32, Moscow: Progress Publishers, pp. 245–8.

Lewis, Ben and Lars T. Lih (eds.) 2011, *Martov and Zinoviev: Head to Head in Halle*, London: November Publications.

Lozovsky, Soloman A. 1920, *The International Council of Trade and Industrial Unions*, New York: Union Pub. Association.

Lozovsky, Soloman A. 1978, *Program of Action of the Red International of Labour Unions*, Montreal: Red Flag Publications.

Maitron, Jean and Georges Haupt (eds.) 1971–, *Dictionnaire biographique du mouvement ouvrier international*, 11 volumes, Paris: Éditions Ouvrières.

Marx, Karl 1985, 'Trades' Unions: Their Past, Present and Future', in *Marx and Engels Collected Works (MECW)*, Volume 20, Moscow: Progress Publishers, pp. 91–2.

McArthur, John, David Proudfoot, Allen Hutt, and Ian MacDougall 1981, *Militant Miners: Recollections of John McArthur, Buckhaven, and Letters, 1924–26, of David Proudfoot, Methil, to G. Allen Hunt*, Edinburgh: Polygon Books.

McDermott, Kevin 1988, *The Czech Red Unions, 1918–1929*, Boulder: East European Monographs.

McDermott, Kevin and Jeremy Agnew 1997, *The Comintern: A History of International Communism from Lenin to Stalin*, New York: St. Martin's Press.

Meaker, Gerald H. 1974, *The Revolutionary Left in Spain, 1914–23*, Stanford: Stanford University Press.

Millington, Chris 2015, 'Communist Veterans and Paramilitarism in 1920s France: The Association républicaine des anciens combattants', *Journal of War & Culture Studies*, 8, 4, 300–14.

Milner, Susan 1990, *The Dilemmas of Internationalism: French Syndicalism and the International Labour Movement, 1900–1914*, New York: St. Martin's Press.

Murphy, J.T. 1921, *The 'Reds' in Congress: Preliminary Report of the First World Congress of the Red International of Trade and Industrial Unions*, London: British Bureau, Red International of Trade and Industrial Unions.

Ness, Immanuel and Dario Azzellini (eds.) 2011, *Ours to Master and to Own: Workers' Councils from the Commune to the Present*, Chicago: Haymarket Books.

Pagès, Pelai (ed.) 2019, *Andreu Nin: Cartas desde Moscú (1921–1930)*, Toledo, Spain: Laertes Editorial.

Palmer, Bryan 2007, *James P. Cannon and the Origins of the American Revolutionary Left 1890–1928*, Urbana: University of Illinois Press.

Pearce, Brian 1959, 'Some Past Rank and File Movements', *Labour Review*, 4, 1 (April–May), 13–24, available at: www.marxists.org/history/etol/writers/pearce/1959/04/rankandfile.html.

Peirats, José 1971, *La CNT en la revolución española*, Volume 1, Paris: Ruedo Ibérico.

Pestaña, Angel 1921, 'Report Submitted to the Confederal Committee of the CNT by Delegate Angel Pestaña Regarding His Conduct at the Second Congress of the Third International', available at: theanarchistlibrary.org/library/angel-pestana-report-submitted-to-the-confederal-committee-of-the-cnt.

Ponomarev, Boris Nikolaevich 1984, 'The Socialist Revolution in Russia and the International Working Class, 1917–1923', in *The International Working-Class Movement: Problems of History and Theory*, Volume 4, Moscow: Progress Publishers.

Pringsheim, Klaus H. 1965, 'Trade Unions and the Chinese Communists', *Southwestern Social Science Quarterly*, 46, 2, 111–21.

Produktionskontrolle und Betriebsräte: Referate der Genossen Ziperowitsch und Heckert auf dem ersten Kongreß der Roten Gewerkschafts-Internationale nebst den angenommenen Resolutionen, Berlin, 1921.

Red International of Labour Unions 1921a, *Resolutions and Decisions of the First International Congress of Revolutionary Trade and Industrial Unions*, Chicago: The Voice of Labor.

Red International of Labour Unions 1921b, *Resolutionen, Statuten, Manifeste und Aufrufe des ersten Internationalen Kongresses der Roten Fach-und Industrie-Verbände, 3. Juli bis 19. Juli 1921*, Berlin: Verlag der Roten Gewerkschafts-Internationale.

Red International of Labour Unions 1921c, *Résolutions & Statuts adoptés au 1er Congrès International des Syndicats Révolutionnaires, Moscou, 3–19 Juillet 1921*, Paris: Librairie du Travail.

Red International of Labour Unions 1921d, *1-yi mezhdunarodnogo kongressa revoliutsionnykh, professional'nykh i proizodstvennykh soiuzov. Stenograficheskii otchet*, Moscow, 1921.

Red International of Labour Unions 1922, *Resolutions and Decisions of the 2nd World Congress of the Red International of Labour Unions: Session 19 November to 2 December 1922*, London: Red International of Labour Unions.

Red International of Labour Unions 1923, *II. Kongress Krasnogo Internatsionala Profsoiuzov v Moskve. 19 noiabria–2 dekabria 1922 goda*, Moscow-Petrograd, 1923.

Resis, Albert 1964, *The Profintern: Origins to 1923*, PhD thesis, Columbia University.

Riddell, John (ed.) 1984, *Lenin's Struggle for a Revolutionary International: Documents 1907–1916, The Preparatory Years*, New York: Pathfinder Press.

Riddell, John (ed.) 1986, *The German Revolution and the Debate on Soviet Power: Documents 1918–1919, Preparing the Founding Congress*, New York: Pathfinder Press.

Riddell, John (ed.) 1987, *Founding the Communist International: Proceedings and Documents of the First Congress, March 1919* (*1WC*), New York: Pathfinder Press.

Riddell, John (ed.) 1991, *Workers of the World and Oppressed Peoples, Unite! Proceedings and Documents of the Second Congress, 1920* (*2WC*), 2 volumes, New York: Pathfinder Press.

Riddell, John (ed.) 1993, *To See the Dawn: Baku, 1920 – First Congress of the Peoples of the East*, New York: Pathfinder Press.

Riddell, John (ed.) 2012, *Toward the United Front: Proceedings of the Fourth Congress of the Communist International, 1922* (*4WC*), Leiden: Brill.

Riddell, John (ed.) 2015, *To the Masses: Proceedings of the Third Congress of the Communist International, 1921* (*3WC*), Leiden: Brill.

Rodriguez, Arturo 2009, 'The Communist International in Spain: Origins of the Spanish Communist Party (P.C.E., 1919–1922)', published online at: www.marxist.com/the-communist-international-in-spain-origins-of-the-spanish-communist-party-p-c-e-1919-1922.htm

Rodriguez, Arturo Zoffmann 2018, '"Off to Moscow with No Passports and No Money": The 1921 Spanish Syndicalist Delegation to Russia', *European History Quarterly*, 48, 3, 435–61.

Rosmer, Alfred 1973, *Moscow Under Lenin*, New York: Monthly Review Press.

Rubenstein, Joshua and Vladimir P. Naumov 2001, *Stalin's Secret Pogrom: The Postwar Inquisition of the Jewish Anti-Fascist Committee*, New Haven: Yale University Press.

Rushton, P.J. 1973, 'The Trial of the Sydney Twelve: The Original Charge', *Labour History*, 25 (November), 53–7.

Russian State Archive of Social and Political History (RGASPI), Moscow, fond 534, opis 1, files 4–10. Materials from the RILU First Congress.

Sassenbach, J. 1926, *Twenty-Five Years of International Trade Unionism*, Amsterdam: International Federation of Trade Unions.

Service, Robert 2007, *Comrades! A History of World Communism*, Cambridge, MA: Harvard University Press.

Service, Robert 2012, *Spies and Commissars: The Early Years of the Russian Revolution*, New York: Public Affairs.

Sexton, John (ed.) 2018, *Alliance of Adversaries: The Congress of the Toilers of the Far East*, Leiden: Brill.

Shipman, Charles 1993, *It Had to Be Revolution: Memoirs of an American Radical*, Ithaca, NY: Cornell University Press.

Smith, S.A. 2017, *Red Petrograd*, Chicago: Haymarket Books.

Spriano, Paolo 1967, *Storia del Partito comunista italiano*, 7 volumes, Turin: Einaudi.

Spriano, Paolo 1975, *The Occupation of the Factories: Italy, 1920*, translated by Gwyn A. Williams, London: Pluto Press.

Swain, Geoffrey, 1987, 'Was the Profintern Really Necessary?', *European History Quarterly*, 17, 1 (January), 57–77.

Sworakowski, Witold S. 1965, *The Communist International and Its Front Organizations: A Research Guide and Checklist of Holdings in American and European Libraries*, Stanford: Hoover Institution Press.

Taber, Mike (ed.) 2018, *The Communist Movement at a Crossroads: Plenums of the Communist International's Executive Committee, 1922–1923*, Leiden: Brill.

Taber, Mike (ed.) 2021, *Under the Socialist Banner: Resolutions of the Second International 1889–1912*, Chicago: Haymarket Books.

Taber, Mike and Daria Dyakonova (eds.) 2022, *The Communist Women's Movement, 1920–1922: Proceedings, Resolutions, and Reports*, Leiden: Brill.

Tosstorff, Reiner 2005, 'Moskau oder Amsterdam? Die Rote Gewerkschaftsinternationale 1920 bis 1937', *Utopie kreativ*, 177–8 (July–August), 704–8.

Tosstorff, Reiner 2005, 'The International Trade-Union Movement and the Founding of the International Labour Organization', *International Review of Social History*, 50, 399–433.

Tosstorff, Reiner 2016, *The Red International of Labour Unions (RILU) 1920–1937*, Leiden: Brill. Haymarket paperback edition published in 2017.

Trotsky, Leon 1977, *The Transitional Program for Socialist Revolution*, New York: Pathfinder Press.

Trotsky, Leon 1981, 'Who Is Leading the Comintern Today?' in *The Challenge of the Left Opposition (1928–29)*, New York: Pathfinder Press.

Trotsky, Leon 1996, *The Third International after Lenin*, New York: Pathfinder Press.

Turner, Ian 1969 [1967], *Sydney's Burning*, Sydney: Alpha Books.

Weber, Hermann and Andreas Herbst (eds.) 2004, *Deutsche Kommunisten: Biographisches Handbuch 1918 bis 1945*, Berlin: Dietz Verlag.

Weiss, Holger 2016, 'Between Moscow and the African Atlantic: The Comintern Network of Negro Workers', *Monde(s)*, 10, 2, 89–108.

Weiss, Holger 2021, *A Global Radical Waterfront: The International Propaganda Committee of Transport Workers and the International of Seamen and Harbour Workers, 1921–1937*, Leiden: Brill.

Westergard-Thorpe, Wayne 1979, *Revolutionary Syndicalist Internationalism, 1913–1923: The Origins of the International Working Men's Association*, PhD thesis, University of British Columbia, available at: open.library.ubc.ca/soa/cIRcle/collections/ubctheses/831/items/1.0094837.

Wilkinson, Ellen 1921, 'The Red Trade Union Congress', *The Communist*, 17 September. Available online at Marxists Internet Archive.

Williams, George 1921, *The First Congress of the Red Trade Union International at Moscow, 1921: A Report of the Proceedings*, Chicago: Industrial Workers of the World.

Williams, Gwyn A. 1975, *Proletarian Order: Antonio Gramsci, Factory Councils and the Origins of Communism in Italy 1911–1921*, London: Pluto Press.

Wohl, Robert 1966, *French Communism in the Making, 1914–1924*, Stanford: Stanford University Press.

Wynn, Charters 2022, *The Moderate Bolshevik: Mikhail Tomsky from the Factory to the Kremlin, 1880–1936, Leiden: Brill.*

Young, Evan E. 1921, 'Brief Report on the 1st World Congress of RILU: Moscow – July 3–19, 1921'. Available online at Marxists Internet Archive.

Zagladin, V.V., et al. (eds.) 1984, 'The Socialist Revolution in Russia and the International Working Class (1917–1923)', in *The International Working-Class Movement*, Volume 4, Moscow: Progress Publishers.

Zumoff, Jacob A. 2014, *The Communist International and US Communism 1919–1929*, Leiden: Brill.

Zurbrugg, A.W. 2017, *Anarchist Encounters: Russia in Revolution*, London: Merlin Press.

Publications

Avanti
L'Humanité
Industrial Pioneer
L'Internationale Syndicale Rouge
International Press Correspondence
Die Kommunistische Internationale
Labor Herald
Labour Monthly
Moscow/Moskau/Moscou
One Big Union Magazine
Die Proletarier

The Red Labour Union International
Die Rote Fahne
La Vie syndicale
Workers' Monthly

Index

Printed in the United States
by Baker & Taylor Publisher Services